STATE AND
COMMUNITY
GOVERNMENTS IN THE
FEDERAL SYSTEM

STATE AND COMMUNITY GOVERNMENTS IN THE FEDERAL SYSTEM

Charles Press

Kenneth VerBurg

Michigan State University

John Wiley & Sons,

New York
Chichester
Brisbane
Toronto

Library of Congress Cataloging in Publication Data:

Press, Charles.
  State and community governments in the federal system.

  Includes Index.
    1. State governments. 2. Local Government—United States.
3. Federal government—United States.
I. VerBurg, Kenneth, joint author. II. Title.

JK2408.P72   No.353.9   78-22064
ISBN 0-471-02725-1

Printed in the United States of America

1 2 3 4 5 6 7 8 9 10

PREFACE

Our text treats the states and communities as part of a federal system—a system that we believe has become more centralized since the early 1960s. Yet we feel states and communities continue to play a very important role in shaping American public policy. We suggest that the politics of federalism has thus become vital to the study of state and community governments. Intergovernmental relations—how the national, state, and community governments interact with and influence each other—is the key to an understanding of domestic policy choices. We have found this a rewarding approach, one that has enlivened our teaching, and we assume other teachers have had similar experiences.

We have innovated by introducing policy in the form of case studies—what we call "policy boxes." As teachers we agonized over how to handle topics such as "The Politics of the Environment" or "The Politics of Health, Education and Welfare." They usually are found jammed together in chapters at the end of government texts where they get brief treatment in the last few weeks of the course. The content of these chapters often seems static and artificial. Therefore, we occasionally have ended up by presenting in lecture-discussion a case study in an attempt to make the policy areas more interesting and important to students. It was a short step when writing this text to introduce "policy boxes" in each chapter. We have included two in a chapter to give the instructor a choice and to deal with different aspects of the material. In 28 such policy boxes, we have covered most of the subjects found in the usual collection of "policy chapters" in a way we hope that will interest and involve students and add to their class discussions as they have to ours.

For our colleagues and would-be textbook writers we have a testimonial. The aid and encouragement we received from John Wiley &

Sons is exceptional. Everyone in that firm aided us enthusiastically in so many ways, and we thank them. We especially thank our editor, Wayne Anderson.

We also are grateful to the academics who served as our editorial readers and made helpful suggestions: C. Frederick Stoerker of Kingsborough Community College in Brooklyn; J. Oliver Williams of North Carolina State University at Raleigh; John Harrigan of Hamline University in St. Paul; and Richard J. Sullivan at John Tyler Community College in Virginia. We suspect you know who is responsible for any errors that might remain.

Charles Press
Kenneth VerBurg

CONTENTS

ministration in Action. Methods "to Control" the Bureaucracies.

11. Participation by Elites and other Citizens 413

Major Political Participants—Members of Political Elites. Participation by Non-Elite Citizens. The Costs and Benefits of Political Participation. The Media Help Reduce Information Costs. The Alienated Non-Participants. Social Movements as Political Participation.

12. Political Interest Groups in States and Communities 457

The Lobbying Process in America. Political Interest Groups in the States and Communities. State and Community Governments as Arenas for Lobbying. Lobbying down at the State Capitol and in City Hall. Control of Lobbying Practices.

13. Political Parties in States and Communities 497

The Development of American Parties. How American Parties Are Organized. Who Chooses the Party Candidates? Running the Political Campaign. The Party in Office Governs. How Nationalized Are the State and Community Party Units?

14. Intergovernmental Relations and Community Problems 541

The Local Setting for Intergovernmental Relations. Annexation and Consolidation. Voluntary Cooperation Approaches. Can the States Coordinate the Communities.

The Future of the American Federal System

PHOTO CREDIT LIST

Chapter 1
2: Chuck Harrison/New York State Assembly.
23: Department of Housing and Urban Development, Chicago.
26: Metro Phoenix Chamber of Commerce.

Chapter 2
38: Wyoming Travel Commission.
47: USDA Photo.
58: Bruce Roberts/Photo Researchers.
60: K. Rosenthal/Stock, Boston.
62: Chuck Harrison/New York State Assembly.

Chapter 3
73: Dev O'Neill.
77: H.W. Fechner/Franklin D. Roosevelt Library.
85: John Collier/Detroit Free Press.

Chapter 4
105: Agency of Development and Community Affairs, Montpelier, Vermont.
111: County News.
114: Agency of Development and Community Affairs, Montpelier, Vermont.
133: (top left) ESSA.
(top right) Soil Conservation Service/USDA.
(center) NOAA.
(bottom) NOAA.

Chapter 5
164: (top) Historical Pictures Service.
(bottom) Culver Pictures.

Chapter 6
215: Barbara Martz/Lobsenz-Stevens, Inc., New York State Lottery.

Chapter 7
237: Shien Studios.
248: Chuck Harrison/New York State Assembly.
255: *Des Moines Register and Tribune.*

Chapter 8
283: Ellis Herwig/Stock, Boston.
292: Tim Carlson/Stock, Boston.

Chapter 9
327: Ron Nelson.
343: Teri Leigh.
365: Charles Gatewood.

Chapter 10
371: Ellis Herwig/Stock, Boston.
389: Federal Highway Administration.
393: AFSME Public Affairs Department.

Chapter 11
414: *Chicago Tribune.*
435: (top) Charles Gatewood/Magnum.
(bottom) Alex Webb/Magnum.
447: Ira Rosenberg/*Detroit Free Press.*
453: Gerhard E. Gscheidle/Peter Arnold.

Chapter 12
466: Mark Godfrey/Magnum.
475: AFSME Public Affairs Department.
492: Common Cause.

Chapter 13
498: Milton Rogovin/Photo Researchers.
519: Judy Gurovitz/Photo Researchers.
533: White House Photograph.

Chapter 14
550: HUD.
551: USDA Photo.
579: *The State Journal.*

THE STUDY OF STATE AND COMMUNITY POLITICS

Olga Moore, in her book about Wyoming politics, describes how students "politicked" when she attended the University of Wyoming at Laramie. The whole student body rode a chartered train down to Cheyenne to lobby at the state legislature for a new university library. They marched behind the band through the muddy streets, up to the state capitol and into a joint session of the legislature. "We were greeted with thunderous applause. Handsome Bob Carey was governor and he extended official greetings. He announced that win or lose, the legislature would hold a dance for students in the rotunda. . . . The Glee Clubs never sang so well, the speakers never conjured up more eloquence. 'Come see us! Let us show you the campus we love so much! Eat with us at the Commons, cheer with us on the football field, *sit with us in the library! And come soon before it falls down!*'"[1]

Experiences such as this one are great teachers, especially when they are as much fun as this one seems to have been. From them we learn about the excitement of state and community politics in a way that we could hardly get from a textbook. But a textbook can help considerably in filling out the

[1]Olga Moore, *I'll Meet You In the Lobby*, J.B. Lippincott, N.Y., 1950.

details. We urge you to get a little politically involved when you can, but in the meantime we trust you will also learn some useful things from this text.

The Practice of Politics. At the heart of the subject matter that we will be studying is politics. By "politics" we mean using whatever power resources individuals or groups have to shape policy closer to their own desires. Politics is played within the boundaries set by *government structure*—the "rules of the game." Politicking by diverse individuals gives us *governmental policies*. Thus the practice of politics ties together government structure, the political process, and policy.

The University of Wyoming students had few of the major power resources, such as organization or money. The rules of the game did not even permit them to be voters. But they did have one major political resource to spend—their superabundant energy. They did get their new library building. Other students have also "played politics" for a variety of causes, from bonuses for Vietnam veterans to changes in local rape laws. Butchers, bakers, barbers, and bankers, plus mayors, county commissioners, and Wichita county linemen or their union representatives, have done the same with varied success.

All have played politics to try to get policies somewhat more to their own liking. Sometimes their actions have ennobled the state and community governmental process; sometimes they have disgraced it. The same is true of the policies they have shaped—some have proven to be

Student pages in the New York State Assembly.

wise and farsighted, others have been disastrous. We will provide you with illustrations of both.

Overview.   In this chapter we begin by reviewing the development of the study of state and community politics, and note the two conclusions early students reached—that government structure and the practice of politics are central to the study of state and community policymaking. We note how modern political science stresses examining policy outputs and the uncertainties of democratic policymaking. Then we will examine what we regard as the most important aspect of present day state and community politics—that these governments are parts of the American federal system. Their intergovernmental relations with each other and with the national government have become an important part of our understanding of their politics and policies.

EARLY STUDIES OF STATE AND COMMUNITY POLITICS

We will begin this short review of how the study of state and community governments developed by looking at several "approaches" that we still find important today.

De Tocqueville and Bryce

It is ironic that the first two persons who took a close look at how our state and community governments worked were a French aristocrat and an English lord.

Alexis de Tocqueville was a French government official whose *Democracy in America* was written after a visit in the 1830s. Viscount James Bryce, whose *American Commonwealth* was published in 1888, was a professor of civil law at Oxford University, a political leader in the Liberal party, and later the British ambassador to America. Both books can still be read with profit today.

Why do their observations still make good reading? As with political scientists since Aristotle, both de Tocqueville and Bryce looked at the government structures and the interactions among them, the politicking, and the policies that emerged and asked what makes some particular policies emerge rather than others. These early scholars are also worth rereading because they rooted their answers in the raw materials of politics, the social, economic, and cultural setting of government. Both also emphasized how the federal system was important in understanding state and community government and their politics.

De Tocqueville concluded that the spirit of equality permeated all

American social institutions. Being an aristocrat, he feared that the result would be "a tyranny of the majority." He was afraid that in trying to make or keep all citizens equal, the national government might stamp out all individuality and excellence. But he argued that in America the spirit of "leveling" was restrained because policies in America were administered by locally elected officials, rather than by a national bureaucracy. Local differences and individuality would thus always be protected and preserved.

Bryce, more so than de Tocqueville, studied state and community government structure and legal rules. But he also examined the social and economic composition of the states and their localities, as well as their geography and history and the personalities influential in their policy making. He stressed, particularly, the political significance of the mass immigration of Europeans of different cultures to America, the migration of citizens within the nation, and the effects these had on state and community government and policy processes—for example, the development of the boss system in American cities.

Like the late V.O. Key, Jr., some think the greatest American student of state politics, Bryce argued that government and politics could be understood in terms of the mixture of social, economic, geographic, historical, and even psychological facts. This social setting shaped the politics as well as the governmental structure.

Students have not always agreed with the analyses of de Tocqueville and Bryce, but most agree that a good place to start when looking at government is with its social setting—the state- and community-based influences on policymaking. This will be our starting point in the next chapter.

The "Good Government" Reformers

The professional political scientists entered the scene around 1900.[2] Bryce's conclusions, supported by a municipal reformer, Seth Low, and a political scientist and textbook writer, Frank J. Goodnow, set the pattern for the academic study of state and local government. For the next forty years or so the professors, in effect, were marching side by side with the "good government" reformers. (The professional politicians mockingly called them "goo-goos.") Many political scientists of today feel that as a result of this alliance, the study of state and community governments stumbled and lurched too far in the direction of analyzing all policy differences in terms of legal structure.

[2]The first textbooks in American government appeared about 1900 and their authors emphasized description of government structure and reform. The first collection of materials on state government was a book of readings by P.S. Reinsch, published in 1911. The first textbook was Arthur N. Holcombe, *State Government in the United States*, 1916. For fur-

The professors had stopped diagnosing what was happening in the practice of politics and concentrated on describing government organization. They preferred to preach structural reform. They were convinced that they had all the answers that would lead to the perfecting of government structure and organization. Their preoccupation with structure took them further and further from the social setting that had formed Bryce's original insights. It also led them perhaps to emphasize too much, even for their day, the separation of state and community governments from the national government.

This effort has been described as "the efficiency and economy" movement because its main concern was to make state, city, and other community governments more honest, efficient, and economical. Less reverent critics dismissed their detailed studies of state and community government organization as "manhole counting."[3]

We should not imagine, however, that this "antipolitics" approach to political science was not rooted in what early political scientists observed going on around them. Two very real conditions that inspired the reform political science were the corruption the reformers saw as the result of the urban political machine and the promising beginnings of the scientific management movement.

The Impact of Bosses and Machines. Bryce had described and condemned machine politics as "the heaviest batteries" of "Satan." City governments were corrupt, he concluded, because of "the Spoils System, with the party machinery that keeps it oiled and greased and always working at high pressure." Supporting the machines, he found, were "the ignorant multitude, largely composed of recent immigrants, untrained in self-government . . . paying no direct taxes and therefore feeling no interest in moderate taxation and economical administration." At the same time, he complained, "able citizens [were] absorbed in their private businesses, cultivated citizens [were] unusually sensitive to the vulgarities of practical politics, and both sets [were] unwill-

---

ther particulars, see Roy V. Peel, *State Government Today*, University of New Mexico Press, Albuquerque, 1948, 1–5. At least two earlier studies also exist, one by a Pennsylvania legislator and the other by a governor of Virginia: Benjamin Franklin, *An Historical Review of the Constitution and Government of Pennsylvania, From Its Origin*, London, 1759, reissued by Arno Press, Books for Libraries, and Thomas Jefferson, *Notes on the State of Virginia*, Paris, 1785, reissue, N.Y. Harper and Row, 1964.

[3]Perhaps the most biting criticism of the political science produced by these professionals is Lawrence J.R. Herson, "The Lost World of Municipal Government" *The American Political Science Review*, 51, 1957, 330–345. We have based much of our comment on the excellent essay that reviews this development by Wallace S. Sayre and Nelson W. Polsby, "American Political Science and the Study of Urbanization" in Philip Hauser and Leo F. Schnore, editors, *The Study of Urbanization*, John Wiley and Sons, N.Y., 1965, 115–156.

ing to sacrifice their time and tastes and comfort in the struggle with sordid wire-pullers and noisy demagogues."

Bryce was English and we may, perhaps, forgive him for his failure to note that *not all* state or city machines were led or supported by immigrants. For example, Thomas Platt, a Republican U.S. senator of Yankee origin, fashioned an extremely effective and corrupt organization with the votes of respectable white Anglo-Saxon Protestants living in picturesque upstate New York villages and towns. (At a later point we will examine how he managed this.) Similar "Anglo-Saxon" machines could be found in Michigan, Indiana, Ohio, and other midwestern states and communities. Moreover a spoils system was not and is not an exclusively urban phenomenon. Few governments cling as tenaciously to the patronage system for handing out jobs or contracts as governments in many of those pastoral county courthouses or rural village halls we pass by when we get off the interstate highways.[4]

The Impact of Scientific Management.   American political scientists also thought they saw a beacon of hope—the birth of scientific management in American industry. Frederick Taylor and his associates in the early 1900s invented time and motion studies to analyze various manual tasks, from milking a cow to laying bricks. Using stop watches and, later, movies, they analyzed each motion made by the fastest workers. From their observations they then determined the "one best way" to do the task.

Turning next to the way industries organized their work forces, Taylor and others concluded that industries also could be organized in "one best way." They tried to apply science to organization to discover "principles" of efficiency and economy in order to maximize profits. It was a short step for political scientists and reformers to apply the same procedures to government. In the process they decided that scientific management principles could produce a more economical and efficient government, and also eliminate corruption! Administrative reform seemed to be the cure for city and state bossism!

"Good Government Principles."   The principles that the "good government" reformers developed are as current as today's newspaper. We will meet them many times throughout this work. They are frequently championed by diverse groups and individuals—bureaus of governmental research housed at state universities, organizations supported by business and industry, taxpayer associations, and reform groups such as the League of Women Voters, Ralph Nader's Raiders, and Com-

---

[4]An excellent antidote to some of the mythology about rural government is Roscoe C. Martin, *Grass Roots*, University of Alabama Press, University, 1957.

mon Cause. Organizations of public officials, such as the Council of State Governments, National Municipal League, and the International City Management Association from time to time also recommend these principles. So do politicians such as governors aspiring to make a record of achievement.

What are these "good government principles"? The "good government" reformers argued first that the best-organized government structures were those that eradicated politics from administration and replaced it with nonpartisan, administrative expertise. Second, they concentrated power in the chief executive—governors, mayors, or city managers. The executive would then have the power to keep the bureaucracy on its toes and could be held accountable for successes and failures. Thus, creation of a nonpartisan centralized bureaucracy was considered the key to "good government."

From these two simple principles flowed a variety of reforms. Among them, for example, was the council manager system to replace the old style mayor and council. Reformers assumed that in council manager government, the council would make policy and a professional expert, the city manager, would administer it through a nonpartisan bureaucracy.

The reformers also restructured government so that all agencies fitted into departments according to function, and argued that departments should be organized in a kind of pyramid, or hierarchy, with all agencies reporting up the line through administrative superiors to a single chief executive head. The number of departments, they said, should be small so that the chief executive would not have to supervise more department heads than was possible under the "span of control" principle.

Many governors built their reputations on such reforms. You may also recognize that this is the kind of reorganization that President Jimmy Carter brought to Georgia when he was governor in the 1970s. He cited the experience often in his campaign for president in 1976.

Other parts of the reform package included nonpartisan elections, civil service, modern budgeting practices, and the short ballot. Above all else, however, the reformers yearned for governmental decision making by trained professionals. And as we shall see, that is the direction in which national, state, and community governments—cities, counties, and school districts—are moving today.

The Incompleteness of the Structural Approach. Little doubt can remain that the reform movement caused a radical change in the way community governments operate. The reformers alone did not smash the city machines, but they were an important part of the process.[5] They had less immediate impact on state government structure, although their championing of such changes as the direct primary revolutionized state politics. In large measure as the result of reformist efforts, state and community governments became more honest, efficient, and economical. The reformers also made a substantial contribution to the study of government. They were empiricists, rather than theorists, and they looked at the real world of government structure and attempted to describe it accurately.

All of us have benefited from the reformers' study of organization; we can find one or more reforms or ideas that we strongly approve of, and several that seem at least worth experimenting with. Why then, beginning around World War II, was this approach to the study of state and local government criticized so enthusiastically by political scientists?

Criticisms of the reform movement. Political scientists began to ask if administrative reform sometimes resulted in unintended and not always desirable outcomes. Some political scientists argued that reformers seemed to forget that governments would have to be staffed by human beings, rather than by "neutrally competent" robots. The reformers would have been astonished to discover that the professional administrators who filled those neat little boxes on their organization charts were sometimes self-serving; that the administrators had goals and policy preferences of their own, sometimes even deciding that they knew better than executives, the city council, or legislature what the people should want and get. And perhaps of equal importance, the reformers underestimated the difficulties of keeping administrators accountable to the elected officials.

Most important, the reform approach seemed to deny that politics should have anything to do with making policy—a peculiar set of "blinders" for political scientists to put on. They failed, we think, to emphasize sufficiently that our federal system is maintained by politics among units as well as by legal rules. The structural reformers assumed that all citizens wanted the same things and the only problem was to fashion a government structure that would give them their wants in the most efficient, economical, and honest way. There could be only "one best goal," as there could be only "one best way" to pro-

[5]Students also attribute the decline of city machines to the end of large scale immigration after 1924, the welfare policies of the New Deal, and the spread of civil service reform with national government encouragement, and the criminal prosecution of some of the major "city bosses." See Alexander B. Callow, Jr. (ed.), *The City Boss In America, An Interpretive Reader*, Oxford University Press, N.Y., 1976, 265–330.

vide it. To this extent the structural approach gave an incomplete picture of state and community government policymaking.

Values in conflict.   After World War II younger political scientists began asking questions such as these: How could reform theory deal with disagreements among professionals? For example, professionals in the state park and recreation department, and their counterparts in the state highway department might not agree on what was "the one best goal" in respect to a tract of land. The highway engineers might think it was the best route for a new interstate highway; the park department experts might see its best use as a wildlife refuge. Each, perhaps, could argue that any other site for its project was inefficient and uneconomical. The difficulty lay in reaching agreement on "the one best goal." This was a problem of political choice among competing values rather than an engineering problem of finding out which was a more economic or efficient way to use the tract of land.

Why did "the one best way" of administration not always work out? Why, for example, the critics asked, did the adoption of council manager government in some cities result in high-quality services and clear savings for the taxpayer, while in others it seemed to create continual turmoil, inefficiency and waste, was under constant attack by citizens and the local newspaper, had rapid turnover of managers, and sometimes ended in abandonment of the plan altogether?

These are examples of the trouble that results for reformers when citizens or professionals hold competing definitions of "the common good."[6] We find that in such cases, efficiency, economy, and even sometimes honesty of officials may seem irrelevant in deciding between two goals. The immigrant masses of the big cities that Lord Bryce observed wanted something more from government than efficiency—they desperately wanted (as we might also want in their place) the annual summer picnic for their children, the grocery basket at Christmas, or the patronage job for a prospective son-in-law—things that made their own lives in the ghettos of their day less dreary. When the second or third generation of these immigrants became more wealthy and moved to the suburbs, *they* might want only efficiency and economy and council manager government, but their grandparents embraced the machine if it brought just a little light into their lives.

---

[6]A writer on state politics, James Reichley, has argued that three conflicting kinds of human goals exist in the history of Western culture. The Hebrews stressed creating an ideal social order through religion, the Greeks stressed liberating the spirit of the individual through use of reason and the Romans stressed productivity of material goods. Each has been valued differently, he argues, by different governments. *Detroit Free Press*, August 15, 1976.

When values and goals are in competition or conflict as they often are in respect to important state or community issues, decision makers may decide among them by a flip of the coin, follow their own preference, or decide by politics—a process in which citizens and officials expend power resources to shape policy outcomes more to their liking. Democratic government rests on the principle that many decisions still need to be made through the practice of politics because citizens do not always want the same things from government. This is the element the reform movement tended to forget.

The Muckraking Journalists

Through the whole "good government" reform period, though, there were some people who concentrated on politics and the social and economic factors that fed policy preferences. You, perhaps, will not be astonished to discover this group was America's expose-hungry journalists.

President Theodore Roosevelt, back in 1903, called such journalists "muckrakers." He had in mind the character in *Pilgrim's Progress*, the John Bunyan allegory, who spent his life raking around in rubbish and garbage heaps looking for treasure. The fact that the journalists' feet were always in such muck, the President suggested, colored their outlook. Others, equally critical, have called such journalists "inside dopesters."

The most important of the muckrakers were then on the staff of *McClure's* magazine—Ida Tarbell, who described in articles how John D. Rockefeller cheated and connived to create the Standard Oil "trust"; Ray Stannard Baker, who investigated the corruption in labor unions, as well as the way blacks were treated; and perhaps the most important of them all, Lincoln Steffens, who, in *The Shame of the Cities* and *The Struggle for Self Government*, exposed corruption of community and state governments in all their many varieties.[7]

Such journalists now prefer to be called investigative reporters. America has had many such journalists since the time *McClure's* magazine flourished, including reporters such as Drew Pearson, Frank Kent, and Richard Neuberger, and in our own day, Jack Anderson and Less Whitten. Perhaps we should also include such investigators as Ralph Nader and the Watergate team of Woodward and Bernstein; and even *Rolling Stone* and the more lurid exposes of the *National Enquirer*.

[7]Lincoln Steffens, *The Shame of the Cities* (1904), reissued Sagamore Press, New York 1957, and articles on state governmental corruption in *The Struggle for Self Government* (1906), reissued by Johnson Reprints Corporation, New York, 1968. See also his remarkable and influential *The Autobiography of Lincoln Steffens*, Harcourt, Brace and Co., N.Y. 1931.

The Attack on the Reformers.   Moviegoers who have seen *Chinatown* will recognize the way these crusading and investigative reporters viewed the world and its leaders—inevitably corrupt, especially those who posed as "pillars of society." Lincoln Steffens was among the first to discover that he himself preferred the company of the bosses and the ward heelers to that of many "respectable" community leaders, including reformers. The bosses at least, he suggested, were human. He quoted with enthusiasm Boss Martin Lomasney, who said that the people wanted "not justice but mercy." In modern terms we might say they wanted welfare programs to soften the blows many received in the slums of Boston, rather than a punchcard they should not fold, staple, or mutilate. A number of academics have argued that the political machine served precisely this welfare function.[8]

Steffens also recognized that the bosses were "of the people" they governed. The citizens of the bossed cities wanted governors like themselves—representative in that they, too, were Catholic Irish or Poles or in many rural areas, WASPs. Such notions made many of the crusading journalists skeptical about structural reforms. They doubted that the reform programs were even getting at the basic problems. Instead, they wanted social reform—a basic restructuring of social, economic, and political institutions.[9]

The Attack on "Respectable" Businessmen.   A major strand of the muckraker attack was a strong bias against businessmen. They argued that the so-called respectables, the capitalists who manned private business and industry, inspired much of the corruption of state and community governments. The muckrakers described what they called "invisible government": how public officials closed their eyes to conflicts of interest, how lobbyists bribed or used other illegal influence, how public officials bent the rules for the rich and powerful, and how the political parties were fashioned into machines to further the interests of business.

The Incompleteness of "Crusading Journalism."   If a fault of the "good government" reformers was to disregard the informal social, economic, and political processes and to concentrate too much on the formal structure of government, the fault of the muckrakers was the re-

[8]Robert K. Merton, *Social Theory and Social Structure*, The Free Press, N.Y., 1957, 71–82. See also other selections in Alexander B. Callow, editor, *The City Boss in America, An Interpretive Reader*, Oxford University Press, N.Y., 1976.

[9]The distinction between structural and social reformers at the turn of the century is discussed in Melvin G. Holli, *Reform in Detroit, Hazen S. Pingree and Urban Politics*, Oxford University Press, N.Y., 1969.

verse. Some journalists found it almost second nature to argue that formal government structure was meaningless and of no consequence.

A conspiracy theory.   The muckrakers expected that "the mayor was always a figurehead; that a shadowy 'they' were the ones who made the 'real' decisions." Too often without really proving it, the journalists assumed that behind the formal structure we will always discover an organized conspiracy of economic notables. This view of social processes has been described as "a devil view of history" because everything is assumed to be due to one evil cause.[10]

Some political scientists regard the economic dominance view of politics as having merit under some circumstances, but being too simplistic as an explanation of the whole state and community political process. This is the view we take. Some examples of the questions about state and local government that this view leaves unanswered are the following: If businessmen had so much control, why did they permit policies that they publicly opposed? Why did the business magnates, for example, allow the welfare state services to the poor to grow so rapidly at the state and local levels? What interest did "they" have in the growth of state and local bureaucracies and regulations? Why did "they" permit their critics to publish exposes of business and industry in the mass circulation newspapers, magazines, or books, that the large business corporations and conglomerates own and therefore control?

"Sensationalism!"   Another aspect of muckraker journalism was its attempt to play with readers' emotions. A one-time crusading publisher, William Randolph Hearst, stated he wanted the readers of his newspapers to rise out of their chairs and cry out "Great God!" Muckraking journalism has some serious faults when viewed as social science—mainly those associated with getting and holding readers at any cost, trying to shock the reader—faults which are sometimes described as "yellow journalism." The crusading journalists often painted everything as black or white—heroes versus villains. They played up the colorful and dramatic, and facts that contradicted got lost in purple prose. Often the exceptional was presented as the typical. A picture of the state treasurer with his hand in the till was left in the reader's mind as the typical officeholder. In addition, the crusading reporters

[10] We suggest that "classic" statements of the "conspiracy" view of the political process can be found in C. Wright Mills, *The Power Elite*, Oxford University Press, N.Y., 1956, and Robert and Helen M. Lynd, *Middletown*, Harcourt Brace, N.Y., 1927, and *Middletown in Transition*, Harcourt Brace, N.Y., 1937. For a more recent application to state government see Frank Trippett, *The States, United They Fell*, World Publishing Co., Cleveland, 1967.

sometimes got careless with their facts or slanted their stories outrageously in their eagerness to make headlines. The writing was colorful and full of emotional and suggestive words with a negative, inside dopester's tone: "boodle," "The Ring," "juice," "graft," and "strike bills." The writers projected the glib cynicism of what they often were—disillusioned idealists.

But with all of these faults, the inside dopesters were a welcome relief from the stodginess of many traditional state or local studies conducted prior to World War II as well as some since that time. The inside dopesters were fun to read, and they understood that the exercise of power would always be a part of policymaking.

THE STUDY OF STATE AND COMMUNITY POLITICS TODAY

We hasten to note that some political scientists did excellent studies of state and community governments and politics before World War II that examined government structure and the political process, without being either dull or sensational. They also emphasized a third aspect related to structure and process—policy outcomes. Belle Zeller, one of the first women political scientists, did a critical study of politicking in the New York state legislature. Peter Odegard looked at the politics of the Anti-saloon League, Harold Gosnell gave a dispassionate examination of the Chicago political machine, and the place of blacks in it, and Harold Stone, Don Price, and Kathryn Stone did an excellent series of case studies of council manager government.[11] Such studies, which are still held in high regard, suggested the future direction the discipline might take, but they were the exception rather than the rule for pre-World War II political science.

How Policy Gets Made

We will throughout this text emphasize the relationships between government structure and politics. Our special concern with the policies that result and their effect on the lives citizens live is illustrated in a series of short case studies—two per chapter—what we call "policy boxes." Our first addresses a major problem—uncertainty.

[11]Peter Odegard, Pressure Politics, The Story of the Anti Saloon League, Columbia University Press, N.Y., 1928; Belle Zeller, Pressure Politics in New York, Prentice Hall, N.Y., 1937; Harold F. Gosnell, Negro Politicians: The Rise of Negro Politics in Chicago, University of Chicago Press, Chicago, 1935, and Machine Politics: Chicago Model, University of Chicago Press, Chicago, 1937 and Harold A. Stone, Don K. Price and Kathryn H. Stone, City Manager Government in Nine Cities, Public Administration Service, Chicago, 1940.

The Problem of Uncertainty. We will observe throughout this book that decision makers are continually coping with doubt and uncertainty about the effects of a particular policy. For example, see Policy Box No. 1, "One for the Road," and try your hand at predicting what the effect of a particular regulation will be. State and community decision makers are also attempting to make changes in policy without causing extensive social conflict or convulsions—an added aspect of uncertainty in making policy.

POLICY BOX NO. 1 "One for the Road"

The prohibition movement started in the 1870s, much as the antismoking movement of today began. In general it was middle and upper-middle-class people who became prohibitionists because of alcohol's effects on family life—anyone who has watched what alcoholism can do to a family member or friend can appreciate their concern. Evanston, an upper-class suburb of Chicago, became the headquarters of the WCTU (Women's Christian Temperance Union), which led in the crusade for national prohibition. By 1914 fourteen states, mostly in the rural South and Midwest plus a few in New England, had prohibition. But twenty-six states had adopted some form of prohibitionist legislation, in eighteen states by popular vote.

On January 20, 1919 the nation adopted the Eighteenth Amendment for nationwide prohibition. During the 1920s bootlegging and "speakeasies" flourished, openly flaunting the law until, on December 5, 1933, the Twenty-first Amendment repealed nationwide prohibition. Only North Carolina, Mississippi, Kansas, Oklahoma, and South Carolina had majorities against repeal. Clearly, Americans opted for temperance rather than abstinence. It is also clear that they decided it is up to the states and local communities to set the policies in respect to alcohol. Today some communities exercise their privilege to make the selling of beer, wine, and liquors illegal. Most states have some regulation and a few have many regulations.

Let us look at one of the most common regulations—the purchase of alcohol by young people. As you read, ask yourself whether the policies described are reasonable in respect to goals and to choice of method. Can we reasonably expect them to achieve what they are supposed to achieve? Following the principle of eighteen-year-olds voting, twenty states allow eighteen-year-olds to purchase liquor, twenty-two allow them to purchase wine, and twenty-five allow them to purchase beer. What are the reasons that less than half of the states allow such purchases? One reason, according to the Michigan Office of Substance Abuse Services, was "a dramatic increase in highway crashes involving young people" after 1972 when the Michigan drinking age was lowered. Among eighteen to twenty-year-olds the rate was 27 percent higher than for other age groups.

Also at issue is the fact that some eighteen-year-olds are still high school students and some school administrators strongly favor raising the drinking age. Opponents say that raising the drinking age to nineteen or twenty-one years of age

---

(as is the case in twenty-five states in respect to liquor) would do little to curb abuses because officials cannot enforce the law. Also, opponents argue, it deprives citizens of rights when they are otherwise legally considered adults.

Consider the control pattern in Utah, a state that successfully regulates the sale of alcohol to achieve the goal of lower consumption—a state where the Church of Jesus Christ of Latter-Day Saints (Mormon) supports abstinence. Utah has the lowest consumption rate among the eighteen states where consumption is severely regulated. Its goal is to discourage drinking as much as possible. The state, in 1968, voted down a referendum that would have allowed liquor to be sold in bars and restaurants by the drink. Resort and restaurant owners complained bitterly. Presently liquor can be purchased by the bottle until 10:00 p.m. But patrons at a restaurant must bring their own bottle in a bag and may not take it home since it is against the law to drive with an open bottle in the car. Restaurants may also sell "mini-bottles" but the servers may not pour. The mini-bottles, ironically, are relatively potent since they contain 1.6 to 1.75 oz., while a normal drink is 1 oz. Wherever liquor is sold, sellers must post a sign that says, "The consumption of alcoholic beverages purchased in this establishment may be hazardous to your health and the safety of others." Finally, as in nearly twenty other states, Utah has a monopoly in warehousing alcohol.

Few people now argue that alcoholic consumption should be completely unregulated or that prohibition would work. What then should states do about the obvious problems caused by alcohol abuse?

What do you think? At what age should states or communities permit a person to purchase liquor, wine, or beer? Why? Should states pass and strictly enforce laws against driving even if a person has had only one beer or glass of wine, as is the case in Great Britain and Scandinavia? Are we certain enough of the outcome of drinking while driving to justify such a law? Should states or local governments regulate places that sell spirits with meals? If so, how? Should these establishments be held legally responsible if a patron later has an auto accident? What about liquor stores? (How should they be regulated, if at all?) Are there advantages for a state in having a state-owned spirits monopoly, aside from the revenue produced? What disadvantages are there?

Government policymakers develop strategies to deal with the problems of uncertainty. One method they often use is simple delay; a hope that the problem will go away or that a clear solution will emerge. Another strategy is "incremental" decision making, that is, making small changes in present policy and waiting to see what will happen. Still another is to compromise or only go part of the way; sometimes a compromise includes parts of opposing policies, which is called "splitting the difference." For example, state or local officials attempt to meet some of the demands of ecologists without going so far that industry and labor get up in arms. The result is a slow, sometimes inconsistent, process of gradual and peaceful change.

The Problem of Social Justice.   These techniques for coping with uncertainty in a federal system are often unsettling to reformers and other citizens as well. They raise the question of whether state's rights, social tranquility, or more certainty about policy outcomes should always be preferred to the demands of simple justice. Should busing of school children be discontinued, because it sometimes results in social conflict, at the expense of doing less to achieve equal educational opportunities for black and white?

Government policymakers, in an effort to maintain the peace and achieve more justice—even if it is not the full justice that reformers desire—sometimes think it necessary to reach political compromises on issues where they cannot anticipate all the results, or where they think massive changes will disrupt the peace, or simply because state-based groups object. In principle, massive rebellion, or fear of it, or even the political threats of state or community citizens should not be cause for compromising justice. However, the rule of law depends upon popular support, or at least popular acquiesence, even in dictatorships.

Thus, when knowledge is incomplete and uncertainty is high, the democratic process is likely to move slowly. We will find that state or community policymakers prefer delay, incremental change, and compromise, unless proponents are able to demonstrate a ground-swell of popular support for their reform proposals, or else are able to produce convincing evidence that what they propose will achieve the results intended.

This is what democratic policymaking in a federal system is all about. You will sometimes find it a frustrating business. It is clearly an imperfect system, but we think no better one is possible where so much is uncertain. We believe, and we hope you do too, that in the long run such democratic politicking is mankind's last best hope. Only under such a system of decision making do we think that human rights which we hear so much about today, will exist at all.

Modern students of state and community politics have a major advantage over students of the past—we now have available a great deal of data carefully compiled for our use. We cite here only a few of the major sources that we will refer to throughout this text and you may wish to consult them if you have a special project assignment.[12]

[12]For data on state governmental structure, consult the latest edition of *The Book of the States* published every two years by the Council of State Governments in Lexington, Kentucky. The data from many of our tables come from this handy source. For a discussion of a state's political configurations, see Michael Barone, Grant Ujefusa and Douglas Mat-

Federalism Requires Additional Compromises. Our federal system in-
sures that policymaking does not consist of orders from the national
government that produce automatic compliance in the states and communities. We operate under a system of intergovernmental relations
among the agencies of the national government, the states, and the
community governments. The governments of the states and communities are politically semi-independent, rather than subunits in an administrative hierarchy directed from the top.

Policy then becomes a process into which some bargaining almost always enters. National guidelines will sometimes be evaded or may be
reshaped to suit the interests of citizens at state or community levels.

We can thus expect conflict and controversy occasionally and, perhaps more often, stalemate. But especially we will find that this pattern of intergovernmental relations encourages additional policy compromises beyond those caused by uncertainty about a policy's effect.

The impact of these intergovernmental relations within the American federal system is what we will look at next.

INTERGOVERNMENTAL RELATIONS IN THE FEDERAL SYSTEM

Our states and community governments are embedded in a federal
system. We think this point is so important that we have used it in the
title of our text. In Chapter 3 we explain more fully what we mean by
that sentence, emphasizing, particularly, how national actions have
changed state policymaking. Here we want only to remind you that we
will try not to treat state governments and politics as if they were isolated in a few buildings at the state capital, or local government as if its
mayors, managers, county commissioners, or school superintendents
had no important contacts with state or federal counterparts or with
each other.

---

thews, *The Almanac of American Politics*. This volume is also published every two years
by Gambit, Inc. of Boston. Finally, for social and statistical data about states or communities, consult *The Statistical Abstracts*, published by the U.S. Bureau of the Census. You
can find many of these census data reprinted in the commercially produced almanacs and
encyclopedias.

The basic source for government structure for American city governments is *The Municipal Year Book*, International City Management Association, Chicago, issued annually. A
standard text is Charles Adrian and Charles Press, *Governing Urban America*, McGraw
Hill, N.Y., 5th ed. 1977.

The basic source on county government is *County Year Book*, National Association of
Counties and the International City Management Association, issued annually. See also
Sidney S. Duncombe, *County Government in America*, National Association of Counties,
Washington, D.C., 1978.

Our Changing Federal System

The interactions among national, state and community governments are sometimes chaotic, often without central direction. New York City residents, for example, fought to prevent Britain and France from landing their SST Concorde jets at Kennedy airport because of the noise and pollution the planes were said to create. The national government, meanwhile, viewed the matter as a foreign policy question that should not be decided by the people and government of just one American city.

But the intergovernmental relations are not complete chaos. We believe several emerging trends are creating more coordinated policymaking.

The Emergence of National Goals.

The Emergence of National Goals. The balance of power in our federal system between the states and the national government has been changing—especially since the middle 1960s. At first the national government focused largely on foreign policy while the state and community governments handled domestic matters. Since the Civil War and certainly in the twentieth century, however, a new pattern has emerged. The federal government is now setting national goals in most domestic policy areas: welfare, civil rights, civil liberties, housing, transportation, health, and education. As Lee S. Greene noted as early as 1968, "Nothing of any significance escapes the attention of the national government. It seems impossible to find any exception."[13]

But this does not mean that "the Feds" are administering all the services themselves. Rather, they are "encouraging" the states and their local governments to give up some of their independence and help the national government achieve national goals by administering programs in cooperation with the national government. And the states and community governments are doing so.

This system becomes even more complex because in very few domestic areas is the federal government taking over completely, even in terms of setting goals. Many of the decisions, as well as the administration, remain in state and local hands. Consider, for example, a major expenditure such as that for building streets and highways where we find that most federal funds and goal setting has focused on the interstate highway system. But these interstates are built by the states and the network of streets and sidewalks that you used to get to class today

---

The U.S. Census Bureau also publishes a *Census of Governments* every five years on years ending with the number 2 or 7.

[13]Lee S. Greene, "The Condition of the States" in Lee S. Greene et. al., *The States and the Metropolis*, University of Alabama Press, University, Ala., 1968, p. 21.

were almost surely planned as well as built and maintained by either a state or one or more community governments, or the two of them together.

In some policy areas, such as welfare or management of the economy, federal policymaking is widespread, and only islands of state or community action and control remain. In other policy areas such as fire and police protection, or even education, we find most of the policy is fashioned and administered at the state or community level.

Our first point, therefore, is that national domestic policymaking has increased, but in few important policy areas is it complete. In many areas the federal government leaves important policy decisions in the hands of state and community officials. The policy that emerges is, in part, shaped by the pattern of intergovernmental relations that is developing.

The Expansion of State and Community Government Activities. The second shift in power is that private groups, such as business, industry, religious or social groups, and private individuals also, no longer decide as many things as they once did. Government makes more of these decisions. States and communities are finding new powers and new policy-making functions that were once held by the private sector. The states are the principal regulators of trades and professions— regulation that is becoming more detailed and widespread. States make major health and safety regulations, rules that have ballooned from what they were just twenty years ago. Communities make major decisions with respect to land use, building construction, and education; they regulate a host of activities that once were decided in the private sector, such as racial and sexual discrimination, the number of hospital beds, air pollution, and noise levels.

No longer can a private organization intimidate black citizens without fear of interference from government, as the Ku Klux Klan once did. The federal government, in many of the policy areas listed above, encourages the states or their community units to exercise increased discretion; for example, setting the level of payments of Medicaid, deciding school attendance policy, or setting minimum standards for exhaust emission on cars (as California has done to combat smog).

Thus, along with the increase of federal influence on state policymaking, we find an expansion of state and local activities, and state and local employees and expenditures. Economists have described state and local government of the last decade or so as a major growth industry of the nation, with good reason. Between 1950 and 1972, state and local expenditures jumped 700 percent (from $12.8 billion to $87.2

billion) and the number of employees more than doubled (from 4.3 million to 10.8 million). From 1902 to 1972 state and local expenditures rose almost 1900 percent.

With the increase of government decision making at the community level, more and more of state activity involves trying to coordinate the activities of its cities, counties, townships, villages, school districts, and those other special districts that citizens create. Such coordination is intended to assure that minimum standards are met throughout the state. Thus we note it is becoming an increasingly common practice for one or more state agencies to review plans for all school construction to make sure the local school district installs proper fire safety features, sufficient electrical and plumbing facilities, and can pay for the building.

The Bargaining Activities of State and Local Associations

Because of the shift of power to the national level, states and communities have become more active in intergovernmental cooperative groups that help protect and extend their own interests. The first such organizations were the Council of State Governments and the National Governors Conference, and at the community level the National Conference of Mayors, the American Municipal Association, and the National Association of Counties. In addition, a great variety of functional professional groups have organized, from city police chiefs to state purchasing officials.

These groups have become especially important in intergovernmental relations in the last few decades and have thus added a new dimension to bargaining within the federal system. They lobby in the U.S. Congress, approach federal agency heads, and bring cases to the federal courts. At the same time they strengthen ties among themselves, exchange information, and make a common front with their counterparts. Intergovernmental relations is no longer the atomized process it was in the early years of the twentieth century.

Special Aspects of State Government in Intergovernmental Relations

We will argue that federalism, and particularly the kind of centralizing federalism found in America today, highlights two important aspects of state governments. It helps blur the activities of states as compared to other levels of government. Also it makes state vulnerability to influence by interest groups of special significance in the intergovernmental bargaining because their officials represent different constituencies and interests than do national officials.

State Government is a Less Visible Government.   Most of us never notice how shy and retiring state governments are.[14] Citizens often fail to give the states full credit for all they do.

If you ask what the national government does, you can immediately conjure up a picture of President Jimmy Carter wrestling with the Russians (or our allies) and stressing human rights. We can imagine federal administrators planning changes in food stamp programs and Supreme Court justices fashioning positions on the death penalty.

We can also visualize rather easily what mayors, city managers, school superintendents, or county clerks do with their time. Community officials do such things as check on the fire department, run the schools, keep tabs to assure that the city or county has a full supply of pure water, that "chuck holes" are being repaired, that the garbage collectors are making their weekly rounds, and oversee the other services that affect our everyday lives.

But what do state governments do?   What keeps the governor busy? What is that vast bureaucracy at the state capital up to?

Most citizens see only a few things that the states do, such as running the state university system. Another state activity that we readily identify is the state police force. Whether we are driving in Arkansas or in Rhode Island, the same neatly dressed officers—usually polite to a fault—and their cars with the revolving button lights on the roof, are in evidence. We might also associate drivers' licenses and automobile licenses with state government. If we think a little longer we might remember that the states run some institutions such as mental hospitals and prisons—don't they? Almost everything else that state governments do is also a little blurry to many of us and to the average citizen.

If you are wondering if this is really so, you might be convinced by the consistent results of a survey that the Advisory Commission on Intergovernmental Relations conducts every so often. The responses suggest that citizens believe that the state government gives them the least for their tax dollar. (See Figure 1-1) We think this is in part because citizens are uncertain what those mounting state taxes pay for.

Why states lack visibility.   Two reasons account for this relative invisibility. One reason is that states are in the middle in carrying out many functions in conjunction with other governments. The federal government often gets the publicity at the policy initiation end—sponsoring an expanding number of research and health service grants, for example.

[14]This point was emphasized many years ago by York Willburn in "The States as Components in an Areal Division of Powers," in Arthur Maas, (ed.) *Area and Power, A Theory of Local Government*, The Free Press, Glencoe, Ill., 1959, 75–82.

Figure 1-1

From Which Government Do You Get Your Money's Worth?

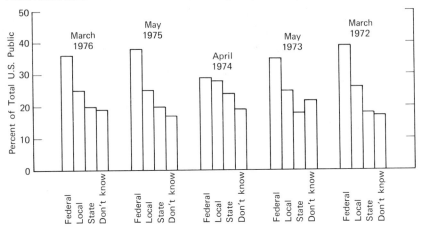

SOURCE: The Advisory Commission on Intergovernmental Relations, *Changing Public Attitudes on Government and Taxes*, S-5, 1976, Washington, D.C.

At the other end, where the citizens live, the county or city health department delivers such services as the well-baby clinic and gets the lion's share of the credit from clients of this beneficial program. State health officials are also involved, but what they do goes largely unnoticed by the citizen.

Second, most of the media do not cover state governments in much depth. An old saying sums up the situation, "News does not depend so much on the occurrence of events, but on the presence of reporters." We will find that at state capitals the news corps is fairly limited because of the economics of media reporting. Continuing coverage of state governments is too expensive for all but the news services and a very few major newspapers or television stations, plus those located in the capital city. Local or federal stories can be more cheaply and conveniently covered in detail.

Therefore we can expect a certain fuzziness when we try to look closely at what state governments do. This is a point we will return to several times.

State Governments Are Vulnerable to Influence. Writing in a "liberal" journal, *The New Republic*, in 1964, Christopher Jencks asked the blunt question, "Why bail out the states?" (He was attacking the idea of federal revenue sharing—giving federal funds with few strings attached to the state governments.) He answered his own question as a number of other liberals have done before and since—Why, indeed? The states, he claimed, are "unfit to govern."

Does the State of Illinois have a role in this project?

Jencks recognized, of course, that exceptions existed. Some state governments, he said, have performed admirably. Yet he concluded, "Even a casual survey of twentieth century American politics suggests that the fifty states have been major pillars of the status quo. Conversely the major force for innovation and progress has been the federal government."[15] What helps explain this condition?

States and their communities are producer-oriented and thus are particularly vulnerable to influence from business and industry. Policy Box 2, "Frost Belt and Sun Belt," discusses some of the reasons why this is so. The federal government, we will argue, has been somewhat more concerned with the interests of consumers, at least up to the point when major firms began migrating to places such as Taiwan or South Africa. We will, of course, find exceptions to this generalization, but it is one that many observers subscribe to. Let us look at why states and their local governments have been so producer-oriented.

States and communities compete for industry. States and their local governments are heavily dependent on industry for the wealth and economic well-being of their citizens. Federal grants have reduced this dependence only slightly. About 80 percent of state and local revenues are raised within state boundaries; a large share of the tax is paid by local industries and their employees. When industry leaves, it takes tax base and increases layoffs. Some of the laid-off workers then col-

[15]Christopher Jencks, "Why Bail Out the States?" *The New Republic*, December 12, 1964, 8–10. Conservatives, of course, do not necessarily agree with defining federal innovation as "progress." For the conservative viewpoint see the essays of Russell Kirk and James J. Kilpatrick, in Robert A. Goldwin, (ed.), *A Nation of States, Essays on the American System*, Rand McNally, Chicago, 1953.

POLICY BOX NO. 2   Frost Belt and Sun Belt

In 1976, our bicentennial year, for the first time in history more Americans lived in the South and the West than in New England and the Midwest. Between 1970 and 1976 the fastest growing state was Arizona with a 27.8 percent increase. In general midwest and northeastern states and communities lost population or had modest gains. Declining populations meant loss of representation and political influence in the U.S. House of Representatives; population gains meant gains in political influence.

Nor were population losses equal across the board. Migrants from the Frost Belt to the Sun Belt states and the West gained a disproportionate number of the better educated, the managerial-scientific classes, and perhaps most important of all, the middle class who were the nation's major taxpaying group. Still entering the Northeast were Puerto Ricans. Blacks from the rural South were slowing down their migration, however. But left behind in the Frost Belt were a disproportionate share of those who were unemployed, or on welfare, or in lower income, lower taxpaying groups.

An additional impact of these population shifts was revealed in a careful study by the *National Journal*, published on June 26, 1976. Jobs were also moving south and west—New York lost jobs, Illinois stayed even, and the Middle-Atlantic states grew only 1.7 percent, but employment increased 17 percent in the South and 25 percent in the Mountain states.

But worse from the standpoint of the older industrialized areas was the *National Journal* finding that federal policies seemed to be helping the Sun Belt grow at the expense of the Northeast and Midwest. For every dollar paid in federal taxes, the five Great Lakes states received 70 cents, the Middle-Atlantic states received 83 cents, the New England states 96 cents, and the Great Plains 94 cents. But the South received $1.14, the Pacific states $1.17, and the Mountain states $1.30. The largest share of these expenditures were for welfare, social security, and highways.

Even more important differences showed up in defense spending—for military bases and in defense contracts. In 1975 the federal government spent $623 per capita in the West, $412 in the South, $309 in the Northeast, and $207 in the Midwest. A 1977 study paid for by 16 Northeast and Midwest states claimed that between 1950 and 1977, federal defense expenditures, if distributed on a "fair share" basis, would have resulted in 686,000 more jobs in their region. Instead they lost 11,500 jobs, while the South added 340,000 and the West 159,000.

Sun Belt representatives responded that not all of the Sun Belt was growing equally in prosperity—those with energy sources such as Texas, Oklahoma, and Louisiana were growing fastest, while other states still had poverty problems. Few disputed the general picture of what was happening to the Northeast and Midwest, however. (Check the *National Journal* special issue for detailed statistics.)

The question is what is to be done about it—or can, or should, anything be done? New England organized the Coalition of Northeast Governors. They suggested that the federal government should pay more of the welfare costs and wanted it to underwrite a Northeast Energy and Development Corporation to finance industrial expansion. The Joint Economic Committee argued that federal spending should be channeled to depressed regions. Midwest governors argued that new government facilities should be located in their states and that military bases should not be shifted to the Sun Belt states.

In 1976 the northern coalition in the Congress, led by Representative Michael J. Harrington of Massachusetts caught the southerners off guard and got the distribution formula of community development block grants changed so that the 90 percent of the increase in funding went to the Northeast and Midwest.

At some points the debate has become acrimonious. At the White House Conference on Balanced National Growth held in February 1978, Governor George Busbee of Georgia suggested that General Sherman's burning of Atlanta in 1864 was the South's "first urban renewal project." Senator Moynihan of New York responded that the fiscal collapse of New York City would be as devastating to the Northeastern states as Sherman's march to the sea was for the South.

What do you think? Should anything be done by the national government to help the older industrialized areas? Why? Can anything practical be done? Are federal policies the major reasons for this population shift? If not, what might be some of the other reasons? Can we expect this population trend to level off in the near future? Will you be living in the Southwest after you graduate?

lect unemployment insurance. If they do not find new jobs, some become welfare clients. Retail business may also drop, thus causing fall-off in sales tax collections.

But states and communities can hardly avoid or lessen the effects of competition by setting up tariff walls against the manufactured products or raw materials of other states. Nor can they keep their citizens, including trained college graduates, or industries from migrating. The basic strategy forced upon them is to keep local conditions attractive for their present industries, and make them so for industries seeking new locations.

Massachusetts has been doing this in respect to the electronics industry. But in 1976, Massachusetts voters considered two constitutional amendments—to change the graduated income tax rates and eliminate lower rates for large users of electricity. Kenneth H. Olsen, president of Digital Equipment Corporation, one of the world's largest computer manufacturers, publicly criticized these proposals. He announced that his firm in the future would expand in other New England states and in the Southwest. Though first quarter profits were up 46 percent over the past year, he said, "We don't want to be too big in an area that is unstable."[16]

[16]Lansing *State Journal*, October 30, 1976.

The Sun Belt lures commerce.

Some states have adopted the tax forgiveness program for new industry, a technique first used by the state of Mississippi. Some offer a direct subsidy. Pennsylvania, in 1976, gave Volkswagen a $40 million, thirty-year loan at 1.75 percent interest for the first twenty years, plus $40 million worth of other inducements to locate its plant at New Stanton.

For the same reason state governments are reluctant to regulate too severely business or industry that can migrate from the state. Thus as we might anticipate, when the United States government set up its unemployment insurance system in the 1930s, only one state, Wisconsin, had a first-rate operating program of unemployment insurance.

Given the facts of interstate competition it is understandable that state and community governments would almost be forced to be more friendly to producer interests than the national government. Even liberal governors, such as those of New York or Connecticut have often been, or liberal mayors, do not relish a decline in the state or local economy. Hawaii will always be concerned about any policy that affects the price of sugar or pineapples. Florida and California will always be interested in whatever affects vegetables and grapefruit. Minnesota will not overlook the 3M Company (Scotch Tape), General Mills, Pillsbury, or Minneapolis Honeywell.

Interest group influence in small republics. James Madison, in the Tenth Essay of *The Federalist Papers*, suggested a second fact that explains state and, also in this case, local vulnerability to influence. A major advantage of a large republic, he argued, is that it would be composed of so many factions and interests, that no one of them could ever completely dominate. But the reverse, he maintained, would be true in a small republic, such as a state, city or county.

Such has proven to be the case in some states and many smaller communities. A single producer interest or a few related ones, or even an important family or other grouping have been able to dominate for long periods of time. Dupont at one time was said to control in a small state such as Delaware, and oil in states as large as Texas and Oklahoma, or companies such as the Pennsylvania Railroad and U.S. Steel in Pennsylvania, or even a religious group such as the Mormons in Utah. Other researchers claim to have found the same pattern in many communities. This kind of political influence seems to have been especially sought by the extractors of natural resources that are rooted to the state—coal in eastern Kentucky or West Virginia, lumber in Oregon and California, or iron ore in Minnesota.

We will argue later in more detail that these patterns of dominance are changing, especially in respect to manufacturing. Industry is becoming more dispersed throughout the nation. Agricultural crops have also become more diversified. North Dakota is using irrigation to switch from grain to alfalfa and beef. The Carters of Georgia planted peanuts instead of cotton. Soybean growers have moved into Arkansas—into areas that were once one-crop economies. Irrigation has brought a citrus industry to Arizona. And people are also migrating. In "down east" Maine, there are now more people "from away," just as Alaska is getting more settlers from the "lower forty-eight."

Even with this changed pattern, however, most industries and most of the crops produced are concentrated somewhat more in some states than in others.

Vulnerability to reform movements.　The side of the coin that can easily be overlooked, we think, is that state and community governments have also been more vulnerable than the national government to reform movements large and small. Social movement activists of today such as environmentalists who want to ban throwaway beer cans or supporters and opponents of gay rights or abolitionists, prohibitionists, and suffragettes in the past achieved state or community victories long before they had similar national influence. For the past five to ten years state and community governments have been influenced by a variety of such cause groups, some of which were organized around a single issue.

In part this influence is greater because of the homogeneity of many states and communities. When the Populist movement of revolt among farmers began in the 1890s it was to be expected that "Raise Less Corn and More Hell," the battle cry of one of its leaders, would sweep Kansas. Almost everyone there was a farmer or depended on farming. "Black Power" today has had the same kind of instant success in some of our major cities.

In addition, state and local governments have been organized on a more democratic basis than has the national government and this, too, makes them more vulnerable to citizen reform groups. More of their officials are elected and elections are generally held more frequently. In every state but Delaware, new constitutions as well as constitutional amendments must be voted on by the people; this is also commonly the case in respect to city charter changes. Moreover, in twenty-three of the states constitutional amendments or legislation, or both, may be "initiated" by the voters; and, again, many communities have the same procedure. Proposition 13 of California, a measure that drastically reduced taxes, became law by this process. In about half that number of states, officials may be forced to face "recall" elections, as is the case in many communities, even cities as large as Cleveland, Ohio where a young mayor in 1978 staved off a recall in a very close election. Almost all states and localities nominate governors and other officials in party primaries, rather than in party conventions.

For all these reasons state and local government officials, rather than national government officials, have been more vulnerable to the special interests, the reformers, and even sometimes to the average voter. This is a fact of some significance in the pattern of intergovernmental bargaining between the national and the state and community governments. State and community governments reflect a different array of interests and constituencies in the bargaining over policy.

A Final Comment

Most state and local government texts give little more than token acknowledgment of the importance of federalism and the impact of intergovernmental relations on state and community policymaking. We hope to do more than that—we hope to keep federalism as our central focus. At times we may become so deeply involved in describing the structure or politics of the state or one of the community governments that we will, for the moment, forget the other levels. If so, we ask for your understanding. Our intention is to emphasize and reemphasize the importance of intergovernmental relations. We think that federalism, in its present form, is the most important fact for you to understand in being able to follow how our state and local governments operate today.

HIGHPOINTS OF CHAPTER 1: THE STUDY OF STATE AND COMMUNITY POLITICS

We began by (1) looking at the development of the study of state and local politics beginning with (a) de Tocqueville and Bryce who rooted their analysis in the social and economic environment of politics; (b) the "good government" reformers who stressed efficiency and economy of governmental organization; (c) the muckraker journalists who stressed the political process; and (d) today's political science, which combines an interest in policy produced with government structure and the political process. We noted that most state and community policymaking occurs in an atmosphere of uncertainty and compromise—especially so in a federal system. We then stressed (2) an aspect of present day study of states and communities; the intergovernmental relations among national, state and community governments. We noted (a) that states and communities are embedded in a federal system with the national government today exercising a great deal of influence on their policymaking; (b) states and communities have grown in size and importance as decisions once made by private groups are made by government; (c) state government activities are relatively invisible to the average citizen; and (d) state and community governments have been more vulnerable to influence than the federal government, whether by interest groups, reformers, or average citizens.

2

STATE-BASED INFLUENCES ON STATE AND COMMUNITY GOVERNMENTS

In this chapter we will look at the social and physical environment of state and community governments—what we call "state-based" influences on the structure and political process of states and their community governments, as well as on the policies they make. In the next chapter we look at an important influence from outside—the actions of the national government that also affect how states and communities operate.

How Distinctive Are the States?

Novelists and other writers have often dwelled on their state's distinctive social, historical, or physical features. Our concern is whether such features help explain differences in state and community government structures, politics, and policies.[1] In addition, we want to know if government decisions do not also contribute to some of the differences we see.

[1]The American Council of Learned Societies, for example, is compiling a *Linguistic Atlas of the United States*. Professor Hans Kurath observes that Midwest shoppers carry home their potatoes in what they call a "bag" but New Englanders use a "burlap" or "gunny," and in the Southwest it is a "tote" or "tow." He narrows down such speech patterns to states and localities. The guest who asks for a squirt of "tonic" in his drink, when he means what the rest of us call "soda water," is from Boston,

For example, Federal Reserve System statistics tell us that the largest number of "rubber checks" are passed in Texas. They average $4 million a day. Nationally, bankers expect 7 out of every 1000 checks written to bounce. In north central Texas, the figure is twice the national average. To what can we attribute that intriguing variation—the "wheeler-dealer" spirit of an oil boom economy, the large open spaces, a heritage of the wild West—or is it the result of something Texas government does or does not do?

Political scientists are just beginning to examine such interesting differences and relate them to state-based influences in the economy, the society, and in government. In this chapter we will look particularly at the policy areas that political scientists have examined, and some of the answers they came up with. In this and later chapters we will note how these same factors are related to state political and government structure.

Overview. We will begin by examining several sets of data that describe how living conditions vary among the states. Many such conditions may be related to the type and quality of government services provided by states and communities, but they also are related to the social and physical environment of a state's government. The kind of politics and government a state has, we will argue, is shaped by such state-based facts. We will then review the important state-based influences under the following main headings beginning with the most important influence found thus far—*economic development*. We next review the impact of *politics and government* and then *geography*—mountains and rivers, climate, and natural resources; *history*—experiences of the past; and *population characteristics*, including, especially, the ethnic, racial, and religious groups that settled the state.

THE LIVES PEOPLE LIVE IN DIFFERENT STATES

Back in the 1920s and early 1930s an iconoclast and political gadfly, H.L. Mencken, edited *The American Mercury*. The major targets of his usually biting prose were what he described as "the Bible Belt" (the Deep South). He set out to show that they, especially, were "the most timorous, sniveling, poltroonish, ignominious mob of serfs and goose-steppers ever gathered under one flag in Christendom since the end of the Middle Ages."

Cape Cod, Nantucket, or the Merrimack Valley into New Hampshire and along the coast of Maine. Hugh McCann, "What You Say Tells Where You're From," *The National Observer*, July 11, 1977, p. 20.

Mencken began a series of articles published in 1931 that he typically called "The Worst American State."[2] But he and his coauthor, Charles Angoff, did not write the articles like the usual sarcastic *Mercury* editorials. Rather, they began with the then current United States Bureau of the Census data. They added to it whatever reliable data they could locate elsewhere. They came up with one hundred six tables in which they compared the forty-eight states and the District of Columbia—presenting these data under four major topics—wealth, education, health and public order. They then ranked the states on the reasonable assumption that it is better to be rich than poor, educated than ignorant, well than sick, alive than murdered.

What H.L. Mencken and Charles Angoff Found

One of the comparisons was dentists per capita. They found one dentist for every 966 people in Oregon, as compared with one for 4850 in South Carolina—a difference of roughly five to one. When they looked at a more serious statistic—the death rate among children in the first year of life, they found the infant death rate in New Mexico was 145.5 per 1000 live births, over twice the national average, and three times that of Washington state at 49.0 per 1000. Even the odds of being murdered had differences that were startling.[3] In 1929 murder occurred about twenty-six times more often in Florida than in Maine, North Dakota, or Vermont.

But we may say, "That was almost half a century ago. We would not find that much variation today." Partly, we would be right. The editors of *Lifestyle* magazine, as closely as possible, recently redid many of Mencken's tables with 1970 data.[4] What do we find?

The Picture Today

In Table 2-1 we compare data for the years 1930 and 1970. We find things have improved in the worst state, with slightly more dentists per

[2]Charles Angoff and H.L. Mencken, "The Worst American State," *The American Mercury* 24, September, October, November, 1931, 1–16, 177–188, and 355–371. Reprinted in part in Charles Press and Oliver Williams, *Democracy in the Fifty States*, Rand McNally, Chicago, 1966.

[3]It can be argued that some of the differences Angoff and Mencken found result from poor reporting procedures used in 1930. We have selected illustrations that were more likely than not to have been reported accurately: deaths, murders, or the lists of dentists supplied by professional dental groups, rather than less reliable data such as "reported robberies."

[4]John Berendt, "The Worst American State, A Statistical Reckoning," *Lifestyle*, December 1972, 6–13.

100,000, nearly half as many homicides, and an infant mortality rate less than one-fourth of what it was in 1930, and lower in 1970 than it was in the best state in 1930. At the other end of the tables, where we find the best state, the improvement is similar for two of the measures: We find that the homicide and infant mortality rates are down in roughly the same ratio as in the worst state. Only the supply of dentists per 100,000 is lower.

Next look at the ratio between worst and best state in 1930 and in 1970. We find that homicide ratios are relatively unchanged. For the other two measures, however, the gap between the best and worst has narrowed. If we compare the median states of 1930 and 1970, we discover changes in the same direction, suggesting that the changes in state living conditions are occurring in more than a few extreme cases. Forty years has shown us some progress.

Other researchers confirm that a long range trend toward modernization has been occurring. For example, Richard Hofferbert and Ira Sharkansky reported that in 1900, Alabama had a per capita income of only 31.49 percent of that of Connecticut;[5] by 1967 it had risen to 56.04 percent. Similar closing of the gap is occurring in respect to urbanization, illiteracy, and percentage of population employed in manufacturing. (See Table 2-2)

The gap between the best and worst states is closing. Yet we still have a way to go toward economic development when a baby has twice the chance of surviving its first year in Nebraska than it does in Alabama. We should also note that the differences among communities within a state may also be great. For example, in most states, the

TABLE 2-1 Comparisons of Worst and Best States, 1930 and 1970.

	Worst State		Best State		Ratio Between Worst and Best	
	1930	1970	1930	1970	1930	1970
Dentists per 100,000	20.0	23.0	115.0	67.0	6–1	3–1
Homicide per 100,000	25.8	15.3	1.0	.5	26–1	30–1
Infant mortality per 100 live births	14.6	3.1	4.8	1.3	3–1	2–1

SOURCES: Charles Angoff and H. L. Mencken, "The Worst American State," *The American Mercury* (September, October, and November 1931).

John Berendt, "The Worst American State, A Statistical Reckoning," *Lifestyle*, December 1972, p. 6–13.

[5]Richard I. Hofferbert and Ira Sharkansky, "The Nationalization of State Politics," in Richard I. Hofferbert and Ira Sharkansky, (eds.), *State and Urban Politics*, Little, Brown and Co., Boston, 1971, 463–474.

TABLE 2-2 Socioeconomic Development in Selected States[a]: 1890–1960.

State	1890	1900	1910	1920	1930	1940	1950	1960
				Percent Urban				
Alabama	10.1	11.9	17.3	21.7	28.1	30.2	43.8	55.0
Arizona	9.4	15.9	31.0	35.2	34.4	34.8	55.5	74.5
California	48.6	52.4	61.8	68.0	73.3	71.0	80.7	86.4
Connecticut	83.5	87.2	89.7	67.8	70.4	67.8	77.6	78.3
Iowa	21.2	25.6	30.6	36.4	39.6	42.7	47.7	53.1
New Jersey	60.7	70.6	75.2	78.4	82.6	81.6	86.6	88.6
Ohio	41.0	48.1	55.9	63.8	67.8	66.8	70.2	73.4
Oklahoma	3.7	7.4	19.3	26.6	34.3	37.6	51.0	62.9
West Virginia	10.7	13.1	18.7	25.2	28.4	28.1	34.6	38.2
				Percent Illiterate				
Alabama	b	24.2	16.4	16.1	12.6	b	6.2	4.2
Arizona		22.1	16.1	15.3	10.1		6.2	3.8
California		3.9	3.1	3.3	2.6		2.2	1.8
Connecticut		4.7	4.8	6.2	4.5		3.1	2.2
Iowa		1.8	1.3	1.1	.8		.9	.7
New Jersey		4.3	4.4	5.1	3.8		2.9	2.2
Ohio		3.1	2.6	2.8	2.3		2.3	1.5
Oklahoma		3.7	4.0	3.8	2.8		2.5	1.9
West Virginia		8.3	6.1	6.4	4.8		3.5	2.7
				Percent Population Employed in Manufacturing				
		(1899)	(1909)	(1923)	(1931)	(1939)	(1947)	(1958)
Alabama	b	2.8	2.5	4.4	3.1	4.0	6.9	7.2
Arizona		2.5	1.5	2.4	1.3	1.2	2.0	3.4
California		5.2	3.2	5.8	3.5	3.9	6.5	8.1
Connecticut		17.5	14.3	18.0	11.9	13.6	20.5	16.1
Iowa		1.9	2.0	3.1	2.4	2.5	5.7	6.1
New Jersey		10.7	8.4	12.9	8.2	10.4	16.4	13.4
Ohio		7.4	6.5	11.5	7.6	8.6	15.3	12.5
Oklahoma		.6	.2	1.1	.9	1.1	2.5	4.1
West Virginia		3.4	2.7	5.4	3.7	3.8	6.6	6.3
				Per Capita Personal Income (1929)				
Alabama	b	$ 88	b	b	$ 324	$282	$ 869	$1,462
Arizona		321			591	497	1,295	2,019
California		365			995	840	1,839	2,722
Connecticut		278			1,029	917	1,900	2,854
Iowa		202			577	501	1,449	2,024
New Jersey		277			931	822	1,790	2,652
Ohio		222			781	665	1,612	2,335
Oklahoma		114			454	373	1,146	1,841
West Virginia		117			462	407	1,098	1,671

SOURCE: Richard I. Hofferbert and Ira Sharkansky, "The Nationalization of State Politics." In Richard I. Hofferbert and Ira Sharkansky (Eds.), *State and Urban Politics*. Boston: Little, Brown, 1971, p. 467.

[a]Selected on the basis of closest approximation of the mean percent urban in 1920 in the United States Census regional groups.

[b]No data available.

chances of survival for a baby in the suburbs are a good deal better than for a baby in the central cities. But do not overlook the significant fact that things appear to have improved dramatically in 40 years as modernization has spread.[6]

In another way the comparison between 1930 and 1970 is less encouraging. Mencken gave an overall ranking to the forty-eight states (see Figure 2-1). Using similar procedures *Lifestyle* ranked the fifty states. Lifestyle's editor found some shift in the ranking of specific states, but overall found surprisingly little change. Seven of ten top states of 1970 were in the top ten category forty years earlier. Many of the same states rank among the bottom ten.

We conclude that America is not yet a mass society in which state differences are irrelevant. State-based factors still appear to have an important influence on the kinds of lives citizens may lead. They tell such things as our odds of being moderately well off, of being mugged, of owning a home of our own, or of our chances of getting health care or even of surviving—they affect both our life styles and life chances.

These state-based conditions, we think, will also have an important influence for some time to come on how state and community governments operate and on what they can accomplish.

EXPLANATIONS FOR THE DIFFERENCES IN LIVING CONDITIONS

Do we know the main causes for these differences among states? The answer has to be "only partly." What we have, at best, is like the first few chapters of a detective novel; one in which, unluckily for us, the last chapters have not yet been delivered. We have suspicions and, perhaps, a few good clues, but we know only a few things for sure.

We look first at a few of the difficulties in explaining differences and then begin examining some of the major explanations.

The Wyoming Highway Death Rate Problem. According to the National Safety Council, Wyoming had the highest auto fatality rate of the fifty states in 1977.[7] Why? Let us try to list some possible reasons.

We remember that the citizens of Wyoming have to drive in some very nasty weather in winter. Even Interstate 80, which cuts across the

---

[6]On a less optimistic note, the gaps in some areas may be widening as industry moved from northern and northeastern states, to the Southwest. See Kirkpatrick Sale, *Power Shift, The Rise of the Southern Rim and Its Challenge to The Eastern Establishment*, Random House, New York, 1975.

[7]The cities with the most auto accidents per capita are (1) Houston, (2) Detroit, and (3) Chicago. The safest cities are Keene, N.H., and Sioux Falls, S.D.

Figure 2-1
Overall Ranking of States

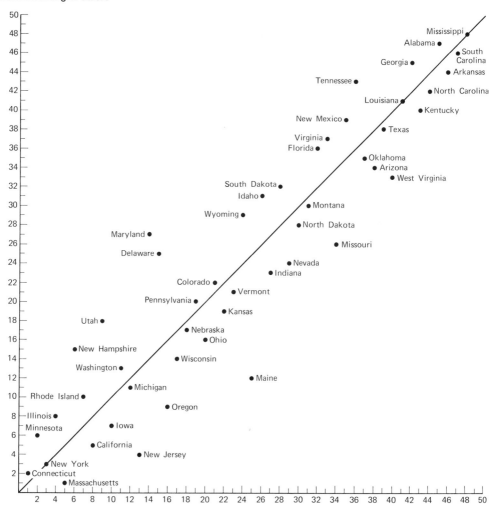

If states had the same ranking in 1930 and 1970 (as did New York, Louisiana and Mississippi) their points would fall on the diagonal line. All points below the diagonal line are of states whose ranking was lower in 1970 than in 1930. The reverse is true for states above the diagonal line.

SOURCE: Charles Angoff and H.L. Mencken, "The Worst American State" *The American Mercury* 24, September, October, November 1931, 1–16, 177–188, and 355–371; and John Berendt, "The Worst American State, A Statistical Reckoning," *Lifestyle*, December 1972, 6–13.

Wyoming Route 220, thirty miles east of Casper.

state, will have days of hazardous driving when it snows. We also remember, if we have ever traveled up to Yellowstone and Grand Teton National Parks, that the geography presents drivers with mountainous roads, including narrow, winding turns with dizzying tilts. Wyoming is not a particularly rich state either, or a very populous one. Perhaps it can only afford to cover its large and sometimes rugged land area with two-lane highways where wider roads might be safer. It is, in fact, one of four states where the surfaced road mileage is less than the nonsurfaced. Yet we find statistically that Wyoming citizens own more cars per capita than those of any other state. Also it is a state that attracts many tourists—perhaps they are involved in many of the accidents. It also has some open cattle range. Some people will also surely argue that part of the cause of the accident rate is Wyoming's tradition of individualism, a wild West prejudice against fencing people in with rules, including such restraints as low speed limits. John Gunther reported in 1946 in *Inside U.S.A.* that Wyoming (along with Louisiana and South Dakota) were the only states not to require driving licenses, and in 1976 the Carter administration reported that Wyoming drivers most frequently exceeded the 55 m.p.h. national speed limit.

What we find from the Wyoming case is that an explanation must include what social scientists call multiple influences, rather than, as in most detective stories, a single cause; and this is true in other policy areas as well. We also find that characteristics can merge or react against one another—a poorer state with a milder climate may have a lower death rate than Wyoming, for example. We also note the obvious—the same factor or factors may not explain differences in other policy areas. What helps explain highway deaths may not help explain miscarriages from chemical environmental pollution. Finally we see that not all of the "hypothesized causes can easily be put into statistical terms—a tradition of individualism, for example. Nevertheless, we have enough hard data to begin analysis of problems such as these.

Political scientists in the 1960s began following the method of comparisons used by Angoff and Mencken, but with two important differences—political scientists were able to use computers and thus handle at the same time a good deal more data; they also applied sophisticated statistical analysis to the data. They could, therefore, relate a given policy output to a wide variety of data and weight the influence of different sets of variables.[8]

Economic Development—A Major Explanation

The researchers found that a set of variables associated with economic development (what we also call modernization), were most clearly related to a variety of state and community policy outputs, such as welfare expenditures or educational levels.

The four factors associated with modernization are (a) rate of urbanization, (b) level of education, (c) level of industrialization, and (d) per capita wealth.

The Angoff-Mencken data pointed in a crude way to the same conclusion. The data suggested, as does more modern research, that if you wished to live in desirable surroundings, you were most likely to find them in 1930 in a state that had gone at least a little distance along the road to modernization and economic development. There you were also likely to find urbanization and high educational standards, as well as wealth and industrialization.

The Impact of Economic Development.   Let us summarize briefly the importance of these state-based economic facts on the government, politics, and government services of a state.

[8]We may be deceived by surface indications, what statisticians call spurious correlations or colinearity among explanatory variables. Statistical techniques can determine whether the observed behavior and a seeming "cause" are both more strongly related to a third variable which is the "real cause."

When a state or community is underdeveloped economically and socially, it was found to affect its political and government development as well. Economic facts are related to development of a democratic political process—the kind of interest groups, power structure, and political participation found in a state or community. Finally, economic development is also related to the quantity and quality of government services provided.

Economic development also influences the role of the states and of their communities in national affairs. Traditionally the more economically developed northeast states have led in innovations and in quality of government, while the less developed states and communities, especially those of the South, have been followers lagging behind. Presidential candidates were frequently recruited from Massachusetts and New York and the governors and mayors of states such as these set the national patterns and trends.

Today the Sun Belt states experience an economic boom, while the Frost Belt areas experience economic decline—government financial crises in Pennsylvania, Massachusetts, New York, and, especially, New York City. Note also that as the South has developed economically, a new democracy has at the same time become increasingly characteristic of its politics and modernization of its government structure. The services that southern states and communities provide have also increased in quantity and quality. Booming states, such as California, are moving into national leadership positions once held exclusively by the Northeast. Georgia has provided us with a president.

Nevertheless we find that while economic development has been most clearly documented by researchers as the state-based fact influencing living conditions, it does not explain all or, in many cases, most variations. The limitations of an "economic determinist" explanation (one that assumes all variations are caused by economic facts) will be noted next.

Evaluating the Economic Development Explanation.   We will find a number of important qualifications that limit the importance of the economic development explanation.

The four elements of modernization do not always occur together or all at the same rate, as was once supposed. Other factors affect the process of urbanization, industrialization, or level of education, and wealth may occur independently of the other three. Economic development is thus not as simple as we once imagined and its several aspects differ in their impact.

We also find that economic facts have a different impact under different conditions and points in time. Norman C. Thomas studied voter divisions over a five-year-period in a series of nonpartisan elections involving a proposed new constitution. He found economic facts had a varying impact. In one election the economic status of voters best explained the result. But the outcome of other elections could be better explained by such factors as rural-urban residence, or identification with an interest group or party preference.[9]

What the Norman Thomas research suggests is that the conflict of the political process itself changes voters' perceptions and causes variation in citizen response. Economic characteristics no longer automatically predict the election result.

Researchers also found economic development varied in impact from policy to policy. In some cases modernization had little effect or even a negative effect on desired policy outputs. For example, the wide open spaces without industry score high when we look at such important things as low levels of air and water pollution, such as New Yorkers find in Vermont, or when we wish to shun the Coney Island type of scenic spots (tourist traps).

Finally we need to recognize that economic development explains only part of the policy outputs—their maximum impact only explains about 40 percent of the variance, leaving 60 percent explainable by other factors. Ira Sharkansky writes "the noneconomic explanations of public policy are often stronger than . . . economic explanations." He notes that while economic variables are highly correlated with welfare, health, and education expenditures, they are considerably less so for highway and natural resource expenditures.

He also notes that many of the correlations between economic development variables and political process and policy outputs are not strong associations. "Numerous states," he writes, "either surpass or fail to meet the political or policy traits that 'tend to correspond' with their social or economic characteristics."[10]

Part of the reason for this finding, no doubt, is because the impact of some of the other state-based influences is difficult to put in quantifiable terms—the impact of historical events for example. The economic development data, however, such as per capita wealth or industrializa-ation, population density, or educational levels attained are readily quantifiable.

Thus we emphasize that economic development is the best predictor

[9]Norman C. Thomas, "The Electorate and State Constitutional Revision: An Analysis of Four Michigan Referenda," *Midwest Journal of Political Science* 12, February, 1968, 115–129.

[10]Ira Sharkansky, *The Maligned States, Policy Accomplishments, Problems and Opportunities*, McGraw-Hill, New York, 1972, 38–39. See also Ira Sharkansky, *Regionalism in American Politics*, Bobbs-Merrill, Indianapolis, 1970, Chapter 5.

of living conditions and government performance that we have found thus far. But economic facts are not so overpowering as to rule out the independent effects of many other variables—including government and politics, a state-based influence on policy, that we will examine next.

State and Community Governments and Policy Variations

Do the political process and the government structure have an impact on the kinds of policies a state has, independent of the state's economy? For a time some political scientists assumed that the findings about economic development made politics, and even democratic government itself, unimportant or irrelevant in explaining policy outcomes. Economic variables were even found to influence the development of such political·variables as party competition. Given these facts, we might well ask, Why study government or politics at all?

We find a number of reasons to challenge what to us is a gloomy conclusion.

The Democratic Threshold Effect.   Several studies suggest that economic development seems to affect policymaking most clearly below a minimum "threshold" of development. Below a certain point of modernization it appears that lack of economic development has an especially important impact on the quantity and quality of health, education, welfare, and other services available. We find this reflected in Mencken's tabulations. The states with higher development move about in the "living condition" rankings. But not so, those with little economic development. The same dozen or so are always trapped at the bottom of almost every table. Citizens of such "preindustrial" societies seem to be in a situation similar to that of the state of nature noted by the political philosopher Thomas Hobbes in *The Leviathan*, "No arts, no letters, no society, and, which is worst of all, continual fear and danger of violent death, and the life of man solitary, poor, nasty, brutish and short."

For the higher ranked states we find that matters other than wealth or economic development begin to have an independent effect of their own. We cannot predict these states' level of services as well from the measures of economic development. Some social scientists have suspected that a threshold is passed when enough wealth is available to encourage creation of a democratic political process.[11] People, in order

[11]The hypothesis is suggested by Seymour Martin Lipset in *Political Man*, Anchor Books, Garden City, 1959, Chapter 2, "Economic Development and Democracy," 27–63.

to politick effectively, have to be living somewhat above the level of a grinding poverty. Once politics becomes important, economic facts become less so, because the economic conditions themselves to some degree can be changed or controlled by the citizens themselves. Poverty loses its dramatic hold on the citizens of the state or community.[12]

The Politics of Redistribution. Political scientists have also found another type of evidence that demonstrates the importance of government and politics in explaining variations among states and communities. Researchers have found that at any particular level of economic development and government expenditure, a state's politics determines which citizens will benefit from the money spent.[13] A democratic politics influences whom the state's money is spent on, the changes in spending levels, and how the money is raised.[14] Democratic politics thus encourages what political scientists call "redistributive policymaking." By redistributive policymaking, we mean taking wealth or any other advantages from those who have them in abundance and redistributing them to the "have nots." The level of "average spending" can remain the same under widely differing systems of distribution.

V.O. Key, Jr., in his study of eleven southern states, first suggested how a democratic politics would encourage the redistribution of government benefits.[15] He found low levels of economic development and a generally stagnant one-party politics in 1949 in the South. With a few exceptions, he found large masses of citizens who benefited very little from government programs and smaller numbers who benefited much more. Key suggested that perhaps a more democratic politics, including a measure of party competition, would distribute what government benefits there were in a different way.[16]

[12]A study of developing nations found just such a lessening of socioeconomic influence after the middle levels of development had been reached. B. Guy Peters, "Public Policy, Socio-Economic Conditions and the Political System: A Note on Their Development Relationship" *Polity* 5, Winter 1972, 277–284.

[13]Brian R. Fry and Richard F. Winters, "The Politics of Redistribution," *American Political Science Review* 64, June, 1970, 508–522.

[14]Yong Hyo Cho and George Frederickson, *Determinants of Public Policy in the American States: A Model for Synthesis*, Sage Professional Paper in Administrative and Policy Studies, Beverly Hills, Volume I, 1972, p. 49.

[15]V.O. Key, Jr., *Southern Politics in State and Nation*, Knopf, N.Y., 1949. We think this is the best book that has ever been written on state politics. We confess also to agreeing with those political scientists who regard it as the best book ever written by an American political scientist.

[16]Key's argument has sometimes been oversimplified as "party competition equals payoffs." Charles O. Jones recently pointed out that Key made a much more politically sophis-

At this point let us look at some of the other state-based influences on policy making. As we have already noted, many of these are difficult to quantify, though in some cases researchers have made ingenious attempts to do so.

We also insert here Policy Box No. 3, "Whither West Virginia." This is a state whose many difficulties appear to stem from a variety of causes. At the same time, it is a state of great per capita mineral wealth. We will give you an opportunity to suggest a way or ways out of its difficulties—an exercise that will, perhaps, help illustrate vividly to you the importance of state-based characteristics for public policy making, and the inability, thus far, to change these patterns from the outside.

Geography, Climate and Natural Resources

It is said that if you see one Nebraskan standing alone, he or she is likely to be squinting at the sky looking for rain. If you see two, they are talking about the weather. Climate, along with other geographic facts, assumes this kind of importance for farmers, some industries, and to some extent for the rest of us. Thus, we will examine briefly the facts of geography, natural resources, topography, and the weather.[17] They are, after all, a kind of given factor, a stage on which the government and politics of states and communities are played out.

The Impact of Geographic Conditions. Geography's impact is often difficult to measure statistically. Yet we can easily see how such geographic facts as rivers and mountains, climate, and natural resources influence policymaking. They may affect (1) the wealth of states and communities, (2) the interest groupings that arise, (3) the ethnic settlement patterns, (4) the political factions that develop, (5) the cost of providing government services, (6) the feelings of isolation from the whole, as experienced by a part of a state or community, and (7) the relevance

---

ticated argument, specifying conditions other than party competition that would affect payoffs and noting that party competition might not in itself be a sufficient condition for such payoffs. See Charles O. Jones, "State and Local Public Policy Analysis: A Review of Progress," in the American Political Science Association, (ed.), *Political Science and State and Local Government*, APSA, Washington D.C., 1972, 33–34.

[17]The best of the regional state studies give an important place to the facts of geography, beginning, of course, with *Southern Politics in State and Nation*, by V.O. Key, Jr., Knopf, N.Y., 1949. The only attempt we are aware of to cover these facts and systematically relate them to politics in a kind of national rundown of the states is found in an excellent brief summary by Edward W. Chester, *Issues and Responses in State Political Experience*, Littlefield, Adams and Co., Totowa, N.J., 1968, Chapter 2, "Sectional Rivalries and Capital Transfers," 12–27.

POLICY BOX NO. 3   Whither West Virginia?

Many things that make a state the way it is are "givens"—its geography, climate, history, or population composition. We can do little about them directly. But the government and the economy responds to our efforts, and through them we can lessen or even guide the impact of some of the "givens." We will be asking you to look at West Virginia to figure out what can be done to improve the lot of its citizens.

We begin with the problems. The people of West Virginia are among the nation's poorest (the state ranks forty-seventh in family income). They are rural, but not farmers, isolated back in the hollows and the hills. The state's educational system and many of its other government services rank toward the bottom. How can we explain these facts in a state with vast mineral wealth—one that ranks fourth in the nation in mineral production, coal and natural gas?

Let us look at how some of the "givens" have shaped the state. Every county is in the Appalachian range—West Virginia is perhaps the most mountainous state in the union. Roads are expensive to build. Flat land for air strips, agriculture, or industry is scarce. The people live in isolated communities with poor communication among them and fierce sectional rivalries. Religious fundamentalists attack the teaching of evolution in the Charleston schools.

West Virginia's history is peppered with violence. The state was torn out of Virginia during the Civil War. We are amused by songs about the blood feuds between the Hatfields and the McCoys, but they really happened—a grim and senseless slaughter that decimated families during the 1880s. Unionization of the coal mines in 1912 brought full-scale civil war with forty killed in one confrontation. The year 1921 brought further battles. Mine disasters have been frequent and spectacularly tragic.

Besides coal mining, the only industry is the processing of chemicals around Charleston, and an infant tourism. The coal mines are absentee owned. Because of mechanization of the mines, the use of strip mining, plus the drop in demand for coal since 1945, unemployment has been high—up to 40 percent in some coal areas. Many small mines and some big ones have closed. Half the state's counties have 15 percent or more of their citizens on relief. West Virginia is among the most heavily unionized states, but twice in the 1960s the union leaders were found guilty of conspiracy with mine owners ("sweetheart contracts").

Only 5 percent of the people are black and many of them are leaving. So are many white natives. It is one of three states with a massive population loss reported in the 1970 census—by age twenty-four years about 70 percent of its youth have migrated. Yet out of fierce loyalty, many return on weekends from as far away as Ohio and Michigan.

Why haven't the state's politics helped to solve these problems? They have been largely one-party Democratic patronage-oriented, and corrupt. In one recent election, thirty-three of fifty-five counties turned in more votes than they had eligible voters. A former governor is in the penitentiary and a recent one was just acquitted of charges. The mine owners have always fared well—strip mining was largely unregulated until the federal government acted. Until 1971 no tax was placed on coal

mined and taken from the state—and this severance tax now brings in only a fraction of what the state sales tax brings.

The federal government's war on poverty was born in John Kennedy's mind when he campaigned for the presidency in West Virginia in 1960. But it, too, has collapsed. West Virginia's national legislators include the majority leader of the U.S. Senate.

Yet great wealth in coal exists side by side with grinding poverty. In 1976 an heir to a fortune, "Jay" Rockefeller became governor. Can he do anything to break out of this economic stagnation?

What do you think? Would you try to attack the communications, education, or the economic problems, or try to clean up the state's politics first? Can you improve the life of the citizens without changing the culture and lifestyle of the people who live back in the hollows? Is this kind of cultural imperialism justified? How would you try to encourage economic development? Would you encourage a rebirth in coal mining during the energy crisis—perhaps by keeping taxes low? How about tourism, or bringing new industry to the state? Or perhaps the answer is through some federal program. What kind of program? How much should the federal government intervene? Or will federal intervention just make the state a large welfare reservation? Or do you think nothing can be done. Should we just allow people to migrate until only those who have jobs remain?

SOURCE: for further reading see Neal R. Peirce, "West Virginia: The Saddest State," in *The Border South States*, Norton, New York, 1975, 151–207; John Fenton, *Politics in the Border States*, Hauser Press, New Orleans, 1957, 82–125; and Theodore H. White, *The Making of the President: 1960*, Pocket Books, New York, 1961, 93–137.

of ecological issues. Let us observe some of these influences within a single state—Tennessee.

Tennessee's political geography.   Tennessee has three "grand divisions" that differ economically, socially, and politically. To the east are the hills and narrow valleys. This is the territory most isolated from the rest of the state in its economy, wealth, and politics. A plantation economy was impossible and so the hill country has few blacks. Its people opposed leaving the Union in 1860 and have been strongly Republican since. It is an area of marginal agriculture, mining, and high rural poverty. The cost of providing some services is high because of the hilliness. Strip mining has resulted in major ecological problems. The western Tennessee division has flat fertile agricultural land of the Mississippi bottoms, big cities, many blacks from slavery days, and a continuing civil rights problem. In the western cities laborers and blacks are becoming increasingly politicized, but the social patterns of the past, not too different from neighboring Mississippi, are also apparent. It is the traditional Democratic stronghold of the state. In the central division is the affluent livestock and tobacco area. It is liberal and affiliated with the Democratic party, but not as much as the western part of the state. Its liberalism, according to one set of observers, has been shaped by a great regional newspaper, *The Nashville Tennessean.* It is the base for potent interest groups of agriculture and industry.

The divisions are repeated in government structure. The state constitution requires that each of these grand divisions have one public service commissioner, no more than two of the five supreme court justices, or three of the nine court of appeals judges.[18] Also party tickets are balanced by division.

Evaluating the Geographic Explanation.   Geographic facts once had a much greater impact on living conditions than they do now. A falloff in the annual rainfall in the early decades of the twentieth century might have resulted in the rise of third parties and the number of protest votes cast in farm states, or so at least some researchers claimed.[19]

[18]William Buchanan and Agnes Bird, *Money As a Campaign Resource: Tennessee Democratic Senatorial Primaries 1948–1964,* Citizens Research Foundation, Princeton, N.J., 1966, 13–14.

[19]A.C. Townley, the founder of the Nonpartisan League of North Dakota was a flax farmer wiped out by the weather, rather than by the banks or grain elevators, a fact occasionally alluded to by those who observed NPL history and NPL attacks on banks and grain elevators. Townley claimed the banks should have extended further credit to him, rather than foreclosing.

The richness of the soil once determined in large measure a state's basic wealth. Swampland inevitably brought disease and misery. And distances were also more important. State capitals and county seats had to be located with travel by horse and buggy or train—a day's ride—in mind. It took days for the news to travel from one end to the other in the "Big Sky" state of Montana. Areas such as Michigan's Upper Peninsula, western Nebraska, northern California, and Martha's Vineyard (an island in Massachusetts) have all had movements to "secede" and form new states. All are less isolated by geography than they once were.

Technology, medical discoveries, scientific farming, air conditioning, and improved transportation and communication methods have all lessened the impact of brute geographic facts on living conditions and on government and politics. But as we have noted, such facts still have influence. We have, as yet, no theory that helps us state this influence with a degree of precision.

Explanations Based on Historical Experiences.

How does past history influence present policymaking in the states? Almost every state has some event, often associated with a particular political leader, that still has an impact on the way its politics are conducted.

The Heritage of Political Leadership.   We can sometimes quite clearly see the historical effect of one person or of a political dynasty on a state's present government and politics. The LaFollettes left behind a Wisconsin that still strives to meet the reformers' standards of good government efficiency. Those outside Nebraska may not remember Senator George Norris, but the impact of his reform activity is easily found in this state's government structure. Nebraska is the only state with a nonpartisan unicameral state legislature and the only one whose electricity is completely provided by public utility districts (PUD's). Even private citizens such as the Mayo Brothers of Rochester, Minnesota, who established the world famous Mayo Medical Clinic, or William and Karl Menninger of Topeka, Kansas, who established the Menninger Foundation, the largest training center for psychiatrists in the world, have had a direct impact on their respective states—in both cases making their states very sensitive to health needs.

The Influence of Events.   We find that dramatic events have also had a lingering influence on today's government and politics. Nevada was settled because of the gold and silver strike at the Comstock Lode in

1859. A "lucky strike" mentality remains. Hopeful prospectors are still digging around where the lode petered out. Others are trying for a quick strike at the Reno and Las Vegas blackjack tables.

In Michigan the sit-down strikes erupted in the General Motors factories in 1937 as the first step in organizing the auto industry. Democratic Governor Frank Murphy refused to call out the state militia against the strikers—then the usual way of ending strikes. The state government and General Motors thus did not break the strike and the first unit of the auto industry became unionized. This event, in part, explains the strong ties of the United Auto Workers (UAW) to the Michigan Democratic party. States such as North Dakota, Wisconsin, and Minnesota, in which third-party protest movements flourished, still reflect an independence in their politics and a liberalism in their policies and a willingness to experiment in governmental structure.

The special influence of the Civil War. The historical event that we believe has had the most lasting and widespread effect on the states and their communities is the Civil War. V.O. Key, Jr., in *Southern Politics*, described the hill country of western North Carolina and Virginia and eastern Kentucky and Tennessee as areas opposed to secession because they contained no plantations or slaves. To this day they remain Republican strongholds. At the same time, we find in southern Illinois, Indiana, and Ohio, the areas in which Copperhead secessionists flourished, a Democratic tendency to offset the Republicanism of the northern parts of these states. Other states have their "Little Dixie" areas—Audrain County in Missouri or southeastern Oklahoma which was settled by Confederate veterans.

Parts of southeastern Minnesota, the areas closest to the rest of the United States, were the first settled and had the heaviest Civil War enlistments and the heaviest casualties. Subsequently these areas also produced the most lopsided majorities for the Minnesota Republican party. And at the state capitol building in Montgomery, Alabama, the Stars and Bars of the Confederacy until recently flew above the American flag. The statue of Jefferson Davis on the capitol lawn is also a reminder of the stirring events of the 1860s. For a century Alabama and the rest of the south voted solidly Democratic.

Evaluating Historical Explanations. The difficulty we experience in using historical events or past political leaders to explain present state politics is that what we argue is often very speculative. It is tempting to explain every event of today by digging up some long forgotten fact of history and make a plausible case for its influence. But it is necessary to do more than make a plausible case. Political scientists have been trying to demonstrate genuine historical influences through the concept of "political culture," looking at the "effects" of political experiences, rather than attempting to trace precisely individual "causes."

What Is a State or Community Political Culture?   The political scientist Lucian Pye defined political culture as "the set of attitudes, beliefs, and sentiments that give order and meaning to a political process." These attitudes derived from past experiences, provide citizens with a set of "*underlying assumptions and rules* that govern individual and group behavior in a political system."[20] They become a guide for proper and acceptable political behavior.

Such a set of attitudes or political cultures, are learned by each succeeding generation by what we call "political socialization." Thus our parents, school teachers, priests, ministers, and rabbis, as well as political leaders, all consciously and unconsciously teach us the assumptions of our state's or community's political culture—a set of attitudes or values that guide us in the practice of politics.

Political culture thus answers several questions for the individual citizen, questions such as: (1) What should government do? (2) How should government be structured? (3) What rules of the game should be observed? and (4) Who should participate?

Daniel Elazar's Political Culture Theory.   Can we discover empirically a distinct political culture within separate states or communities? We know of only one attempt that has been made to tie political culture into present state and community policymaking. Daniel Elazar traced the initial streams of population movement from the East Coast into all of the other states.[21] Where the migrants settled, he argued, they brought a distinctive political culture.

Elazar traces three major population flows: one originating in New England, one from the middle states, and the third from the southern seaboard. Each weaves across the continental United States with some deflection from a simple east-west routing as they reach natural geographic barriers such as Appalachia or the Rockies. For example, he maps a migratory stream from the southern seaboard across to Texas, and then one branch up along eastern Colorado and Wyoming and into western Montana, and the other west into southern California.

The heart of his theory is that each stream carries a different set of political ideas and beliefs—a distinctive political culture. Elazar de-

[20]Lucian Pye, "Political Culture," *International Encyclopedia of the Social Sciences,* The Macmillan Co., N.Y., 1968, volume 12, p. 218.

[21]Daniel J. Elazar, *American Federalism: A View from the States,* Thomas Crowell. N.Y., 1966, Second Edition, 1972.

fines these three political cultures as the moralist, individualist, and traditional.[22] Thus, states or communities may have a homogeneous political culture or they may combine two or three such cultures, depending on the patterns of original settlement. (See Figure 2-2)

The Moralist political culture.　The Moralist political culture, Elazar says, formed its ideas from experiences in the original Puritan settlements of New England. It answers our four questions as follows: (1) *What should government do?*—it should serve the common good. (2) *How should government be structured?*—to maximize democratic participation and to provide a high level of public services to all citizens. (3) *What rules of the game should be observed?*—politics should be conducted on high principle rather than self interest, deceit, or corruption. (4) *Who should participate?*—all citizens have a duty to participate and contribute to the common good. All are responsible for others of the commonwealth.

From the moralists, Elazar claims, have sprung many of the reform movements that have blessed or plagued our state and community politics: ecologists, abolitionists, "good government" reformers who want honesty, efficiency, and economy in government, prohibitionists, consumer advocates, suffragettes, prison reformers, and many others. Most of these crusades came thundering out of the Northeast, he says, but today, he finds, the most moralistic state is Minnesota.

The Individualist political culture.　The Individualists settled the middle colonies (New York, New Jersey, and Delaware) and moved west from there. Their belief system resulted from the experiences of taming and winning the West—a kind of frontier ethic. They argued that individuals should be able to do pretty much as they pleased. Their answers to the four questions would have been: (1) *What should governments do?*—it should do as little as possible beyond supplying only minimum rules to keep competition open; (2) *How should government be structured?*—to keep public officials and services to a minimum and allow citizens to take care of themselves. (3) *What rules of the game should be observed?*—whatever emerge as absolutely necessary in the

[22]Elazar's categories can be viewed as a reworking of familiar historical data. The moralist, or Puritan belief system, has been studied intensively. For a study discussing its influence in western settlements, see Louis B. Wright, *Culture on the Moving Frontier*, Vintage Books, N.Y., 1941. The individualist political culture seems to us as similar to that of the Jacksonians. See for examples, Glyndon G. VanDeusen, *The Jacksonian Era 1828–1848*, Harper & Row, N.Y., 1959, and Lee Benson, *The Concept of Jacksonian Democracy*, Atheneum, N.Y., 1961. An excellent study of the traditionalist culture of the South, but one that discusses other southern thought patterns, is W.J. Cash, *The Mind of the South*, Vintage Books, N.Y., 1941.

Figure 2-2
The Distribution of Political Cultures Within the States.

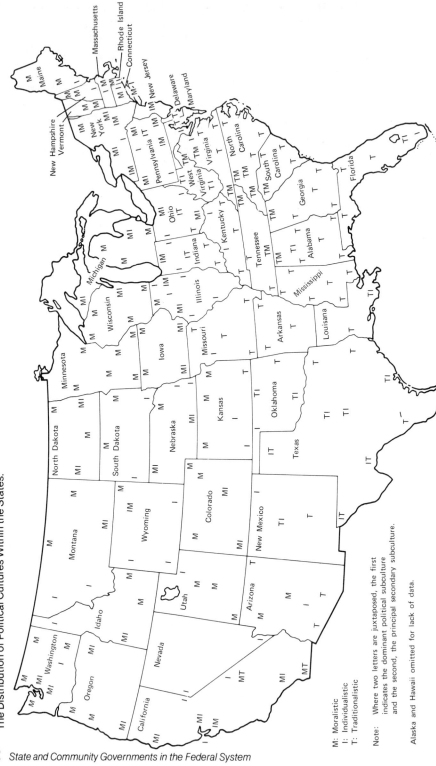

M: Moralistic
I: Individualistic
T: Traditionalistic

Note: Where two letters are juxtaposed, the first indicates the dominant political subculture and the second, the principal secondary subculture.

Alaska and Hawaii omitted for lack of data.

SOURCE: Daniel Elazar, *American Federalism, A View From the States.* (New York: Thomas Y. Crowell, 1972).

rough and tumble of the market place. It is every man for himself (and women had best step aside)—John Wayne style. (4) *Who should participate?*—it was up to individuals to participate as they wished in their own self-interest.

These were the rugged individualists who, beginning in the Jacksonian frontier, tromped over everyone else in order to homestead and later, during "the Gilded Age" of the late 1800s, to build the nation's railroads, exploit its mines and forests and oil wells, and then retire into imitation castles to enjoy their millions. They saw trickery and corruption as an inevitable part of politics. The state that Elazar found, which most purely defines the individualistic ethic today, is that haven of get-rich-quick drifters, and male and female golddiggers—Nevada.

The Traditionalist political culture. The Traditionalists formed their ideas from the experience of the aristocratic plantations of the South. Perhaps you have visited the grounds of Robert E. Lee's home, now a national shrine above Arlington Cemetery across the Potomac from Washington, D.C., and in sight of the Capitol building. There you get the full flavor of a thriving plantation community.

Here is how the traditionalists answer the four questions: (1) *What should government do?*—in a traditionalist society the major feature to be nurtured is the aristocratic family—in the Lee case the FFV (First Families of Virginia). (2) *How should government be structured?*—so the "best" families will rule from the top of the hierarchy. (3) *What are the rules of the game?*—notions of chivalry to women, a code of honor, and embellishing one's proper station in life, were basic rules that were drummed into everyone who shared this lifestyle. *Noblesse oblige* and paternalism were expected from the leaders, and obedience from the lower orders. (4) *Who should participate?*—the male aristocrats should make the decisions, but it was their duty to take care of their women and be responsible for the lower orders of society.

Which state is the most traditional? Mississippi gets the nod from Elazar.

Political Culture and Policy. How then would political culture affect state policy of today? Consider divorce. The Traditionalist, with notions of protecting the family, would oppose easy divorce laws. The federal court case challenging Nevada's "slot machine" divorce laws, we note, originated in the South, in North Carolina. The Individualist would respond differently—something like, "If you have the cash in hand to pay the lawyer, what you do is your own business," as in Nevada with its easy divorce laws. As is often the case, we find that the reasoning of the Moralists would be a bit more tortured. On principle, they would oppose easy divorce. On the other hand, they would also conclude that a person should do what is "morally right" for society and for all concerned. "Thus under certain conditions . . . ,"—it comes out that Moralists can be either for or against divorce—just so they have a good moral reason to rationalize whichever course of action they choose. You can now play this game yourself with such policies as abortion, abolition of slavery, or pot smoking.

Evaluating the Political Culture Explanation.   The Elazar theory of political cultures has some difficulties. One problem is that we sometimes suspect that the reasons people give to others to justify their actions may be a rationalization of self-interest rather than a learned political culture response. Those aristocrat plantation owners at the top of the hierarchy, for example, have always been more imbued with the Traditionalist political culture norms than have the poor blacks and poor whites out picking the cotton in the fields. These poor blacks and whites seem to adapt relatively easily to Individualist, or even Moralist viewpoints. Otherwise how can we explain slave revolts or why a Fugitive Slave Law was necessary or where southern populism came from?

Other criticisms are based on the difficulty of mapping and interpreting population migrations. These emigration streams, of course, zigzag, rather than follow state boundary lines clearly. As Elazar recognizes, states are almost always a mixture of political cultures. This fact creates problems. Illinois and Ohio, for example, have elements of all three cultures in combinations difficult to disentangle at the state level, although they may provide useful insights to community politics.

It also seems to some political scientists that the "Elazar" political cultures are more clear-cut in the homogeneous groups found in a rural or small town setting. Urbanization seems to blur their effect. Alan Grimes reaches this conclusion in a study of what he calls the Puritan ethic.[23] He examines how this set of beliefs related to such issues as women suffrage, prohibition, and such progressive measures as initiative, referendum, and recall. He finds the heartland of such notions in the rural and sparsely populated western states that were originally settled mostly by New Englanders, as in rural Kansas. Urbanism and industrialization, he suggests, distort these political styles even in Kansas.

Finally we suspect there may be many other blurrings. Could Louisiana's "Old South" traditionalism remain unaffected by the onslaught of Huey and Earl Long, whose rough and tumble populist approach to politics was to turn traditional ways on their head and shake them? Yet on Elazar's maps, no individualist or moralist streams or pockets are

[23]Alan P. Grimes, *The Puritan Ethic and Woman Suffrage*, Oxford, N.Y., 1967.

found in northern Louisiana where these two governors were reared. We suggest, therefore, that a certain kind of static quality may cling to socialization theories such as this one. If followed too rigidly, they may lead one to assume that a set of ideas such as Puritanism are a kind of "measles" a society can never get over if caught during its youth. We thus are led, perhaps erroneously, to discount more than we should all of the other experiences that people have that may change a basic outlook of their childhood days.

Testing of the Elazar theory. Let us look at the most thorough attempts to test the theory empirically. Ira Sharkansky has made one of the first such successful analyses.[24]

The strongest correlations found were with political participation. In Moralist states, Sharkansky found, citizens voted and participated in politics and government to a greater degree, in Traditionalist states they participated least, and Individualist states fell in between. Correlations of political culture to favoring a strengthening of the bureaucracy and increasing the level of policy outputs were very weak, but still significant. These relationships were weakened when urbanism and personal income were introduced into the analysis, indicating that these factors caused part of the relationship. Nevertheless political culture still had an independent influence, and especially so in respect to political participation.

Sharkansky concludes his examination with reservations similar to some we have raised. He especially emphasizes the impressionistic nature of some of Elazar's mappings. Nevertheless he notes that political culture does have some independent influence on a state's government, politics and its policies. What remains to be done, he suggests, is to refine the measures of political culture by basing such measures on findings from public opinion surveys.

[24]Sharkansky assumed that the three cultures lay on a scale in respect to three basic attitudes: encouraging political participation, strengthening the bureaucracy, and gaining high levels of service performance. He rated the traditional culture as least favorable to each, and the moralist culture as most favorable, with the individualists in between. He then added together the cultures found in each state in terms of Elazar's map designations so that states could be ranked by their dominant political culture pattern. He correlated this ranking with twenty-three measures that could be related to the above three attitudes. He found statistically significant correlations in the expected direction on fifteen measures. Ira Sharkansky, "The Utility of Elazar's Political Culture: A Research Note, 2 *Polity*, Fall 1969, 66–83. See also Leonard G. Ritt, "Political Cultures and Political Reform: A Research Note" *Publius* 4, Winter 1974, 131–134, Citizens Conference on State Legislatures, *State Legislatures: An Evaluation of Their Effectiveness*, Praeger, N.Y., 1970, and Charles A. Johnson, "Political Culture in American States: Elazar's Formulation Examined," *American Journal of Political Science* 20, August 1976, 491–509.

Population Characteristics: The Basic Social Facts

How does the composition of the population affect state government structure, politics, or policymaking?[25]

We deal briefly in this section with other explanations of differences based on ethnic, religious, and racial heritage, and sex and age composition. Race and ethnicity, of course, are entangled with the historical and cultural aspects, which have already been discussed. For example, why is Minnesota so moralistic? Lutheran Swedes, Daniel Elazar explains, are heavily Puritan in Minnesota (if not in Sweden). Ethnic background, he thus argues, reenforces the Moralist political culture.

Ethnic Influences. In almost every state and community we still find traces of ethnic and religious settlement patterns reflected in present day politics. Notice, for example, the difference in place names between what would seem like two similar states, Washington and Oregon. The New Englanders who settled Oregon gave its cities such nostalgic names as Portland, Salem, Pendleton, Medford, and Newport. Up in Washington, the place names are more often Indian in origin: Seattle, Tacoma, Walla Walla, Spokane, or Yakima; a reflection of the state's early days as a fur-trading outpost of the John Jacob Astor empire. We find the same kind of pattern in the naming of many Arkansas towns after Biblical places—a reflection of the types who settled such cities as Mount Olive, Jericho, Jerusalem, or Palestine.

Some states still play what politicians have called "League of Nations" or "United Nations politics." New York Democrats once put together the ideal ethnic slate of Lefkovitz, Fino, and Gilhooey, which was a not very subtle appeal to the major factions of the Democratic party—Jews, Italians, and Irish.

In many states and communities this impact is being somewhat diluted as sons and daughters leave home to go to college, and then scatter across the nation. But it is far from being washed away. It is especially strong in New England. Duane Lockard based his study of New England politics on these ethnic and religious facts. Robert Dahl cited the path to major offices taken by ethnics in New Haven, Connecticut.[26] Italians still remember with some justifiable pride John Pastore's election as governor of Rhode Island in 1946, the first governor in the na-

[25]A recent study by John Wanat and Virginia Gray found that size of state population is related to more costly services. Virginia Gray and Elihu Bergman, (eds.), *Political Issues in U.S. Population Policy*, D.C., Heath, Lexington, Mass., 1974.

[26]Duane Lockard, *New England State Politics*, Princeton University Press, Princeton, N.J., 1959 and Robert A. Dahl, *Who Governs, Democracy and Power in an American City*, Yale University Press, New Haven 1961, 52–62.

tion of Italian origin. Until then, the Irish had controlled the top office, giving only the lieutenant governorship to Italians. But the Rhode Island Irish were not oblivious to political realities. As the journalist Samuel Lubell wryly noted, "In 1938, the state legislature declared Columbus Day a legal holiday, less in tribute to Columbus' discovery of America than to its discovery that every fifth voter in the state was Italo-American."[27]

The Politics of Race.   How does race influence state policymaking? Ticket balancing also appears to be influenced by race. By 1976 two states, Colorado (George Brown) and California (Mervyn Dymally), had black lieutenant governors, but no state had by 1978 elected a black governor.

We can also show how race has affected distribution of government services—above and beyond the facts of economic wealth. The "blues" singer, Bessie Smith, who had achieved both wealth and fame, died in the 1930s as the result of an auto accident because she was refused admission to a white hospital.

Minority groups, including both ethnic and racial groups, have frequently been at the poor end of the state statistics of health, education, and welfare. This was probably true of turn-of-the-century immigrant groups, and the same is true today. In Alaska, for example, the average life span of Eskimos is under forty years.

Let us return briefly to the figures on deaths per 1000 live births and look at the breakdown by "white" and "other races." We find that Mississippi in 1960 reported a death rate of 26.6/M for whites.[28] This is slightly above the national average of 22.9/M. But what of the "other races" category? The national average was 43.2/M for other races, but Mississippi reports well above that, at 54.3/M. It is clear that a large part of Mississippi's rate of deaths per 1000 live births can be explained by the health care received by the other races among its citizenry. Seemingly, pregnant black women had not been receiving the same health care as pregnant white women in Mississippi.

Which other states in 1960 were also high in "other races" deaths in the first year of life—above 50.0/M? The answer, happily, is "very few." They were Alaska, Arizona, New Mexico, North Carolina, South Dakota and Utah. Again rates for "whites" were close to, and in some

[27]Samuel Lubell, The Future of American Politics, Harper and Brothers, N.Y., 1951, 73–74.

[28]See The American Almanac, The U.S. Book of Statistics and Information, Grosset and Dunlop, N.Y., 1973, Table 82, p. 61. This volume is a selective compilation of figures taken from The Statistical Abstract of the United States with an introduction by Ben Wattenberg, formerly of the U.S. Bureau of the Census.

A candidate who won in a county commission race campaigns in Charlotte, North Carolina.

states, below national averages. What will you find in respect to "other races" in these states?—again, a higher than average concentration of minority groups—Eskimos, Indians, blacks, or Spanish-speaking Americans.

Part of these differences may be explained by the fact that some of these minority groups have lived outside the mainstream of American life; in some cases they live in traditionally rural ways that are most accurately described as premodern or preindustrial. Another explanation for the differences is, of course, the ugly fact of racial or ethnic discrimination.

We should pause here to ask the question, Did the figures change over the 1960–1970 decade? In each case the answer is an emphatic yes! The rates dropped nationally in 1970, and in most of these states we find sharper drops in the death rates of "other races" than in the "white" category. This means that the gap between the death rates in these two categories is closing nationally, and we find that the gap is also closing in most of these seven states. Part of this drop is undoubtedly the result of federal programs that influence policymaking in respect to medical care in all the states—a topic discussed in Chapter 3.[29]

Our point has been that state-based racial and ethnic facts are not irrelevant to the understanding of a state's politics or the way its residents live. We have included here in Policy Box No. 4 "Lo the Poor Native American," a discussion of the position of America's first inhabi-

[29]Experts suggest that infant mortality rates are a good *social indicator* of health and nutrition factors. One policy that can reduce child death rates, that is encouraged with federal grants, is prenatal care—proper nutrition and health care before the child has been born. In a study by Johns Hopkins University of Maryland, infant mortality rates between 1969 and 1973 showed a 26 percent drop among nonwhites, paralleled by a similar increase in use of family planning services. Associated Press report, July 25, 1976.

tants—the Indians. They present a special case of the impact of racial and ethnic factors on the kind of life one leads.

Women in State and Community Politics. Wyoming women were granted the right to vote in 1869 while Wyoming was still a territory. Women were expected to purify politics. In fact, at the turn of the century, women suffrage was vigorously opposed by what was then described as "the liquor interests." The women suffrage and prohibition movements were closely allied, especially in the West.

POLICY BOX NO. 4   Lo, the Poor Native American

Americans who read about the revenue sharing act are sometimes astonished to find that these federal funds are distributed not only to state and community governments exercising general powers, but also to tribal governments of Indian reservations. We have here another example of the special and complex relations between the rest of American citizens and its native Indian population. Let us review a few of the facts.

America has about 800,000 Indians. Their unemployment rate is 40 percent, with about double the national average of high school drop-outs—nearly 60 percent of Indians have less than an eighth-grade education. The conditions of poverty that many Indians live in is reflected in the higher than average tuberculosis and infant mortality rates, as well as a lower life expectancy. The degree of social disorganization and despair is reflected in exceptionally high alcoholism and suicide rates.

Here is their history. The early pioneers drove the Indians always further west—despite the fact that the Northwest Ordinance of 1787 guaranteed the Indians that their land would not be taken without compensation "except in just and lawful wars authorized by Congress." There were no authorized wars. Instead, President Andrew Jackson proposed to resettle all Indians west of the Mississippi River. These laws were passed in 1830 and 1834 and included exclusion also from Missouri, Arkansas, and Louisiana. As settlers pushed westward and appropriated lands that had been deeded to the Indians by treaty, undeclared wars broke out with the last important action at Wounded Knee in South Dakota in 1890.

The next solution of "the Indian problem" was to create "reservations" and make Indians the earliest dependents of a welfare state. Indians today may live on one of 115 principal reservations. There are a total of 277 reservations in all, located in 31 states. But 50 percent of Indians now live off the reservation, in urban society. Most observers conclude that the reservation system helped to destroy Indian culture without preparing the Indians to cope in the white man's society. The Indians on the reservations held land as a tribal community and this land would not be subject to state or local taxes. The Indians also had their own tribal courts; in the 1960s, however, these courts were specifically required to guarantee the accused the same rights protected in federal courts.

What is the legal status of Indians? They were *not* enfranchised by the Fourteenth Amendment in the 1860s and until 1924 Indians born on a reservation could only become citizens of the land of their forefathers by naturalization! Practically speaking, they were denied the right to vote until recently, either through their own indifference, white social pressure or, until the passage of the Voting Rights Act of 1965, by literacy tests. Only in the 1970s have they had an electoral impact, and then only in a few states and communities.

Up until the 1960s the Indians largely accepted discrimination, including laws that prohibited them from buying liquor. They were treated pretty much as dependent children. In Oregon the Klamath tribe was allowed to sell valuable timberland, in part to private industry and the rest to the federal government, with members of the tribe dividing the proceeds. Then came some turnabout with the birth of militancy in the American Indian Movement (AIM), but perhaps more important action was taken by traditional tribal leaders. The Indians went to court and lobbied Congress. In 1970 the government ceded back to the Taos a wilderness area of their traditional lands in New Mexico. In Alaska in 1971, the American Federation of Natives received 62,500 square miles of land plus a settlement of $965 million. In Maine, Indians laid claim in the courts to large sections of the state; this case is still pending. These claims were all based on treaties of the 1800s or before. In other states those treaties had granted Indians perpetual fishing and hunting rights, despite state game laws, or control of access to lakes or streams. Indians are now insisting on these rights. Presently a bill has been introduced in Congress that would settle all land claims and make Indians subject to the same laws, despite treaties, as other citizens.

In earlier days, large parts of reservations were sold to non-Indians for quick cash. Presently such non-Indians, who are generally farmers, are subject to Indian courts. An additional cause of resentment is that these non-Indians, living within reservations, must pay state and local taxes. Another problem is that Indians do not pay state cigarette and liquor taxes; other state and local residents argue that they should, since Indians are eligible for, and do in fact collect, benefits that are paid for by those state taxes.

Two basic problems emerge—Indian poverty and Indian rights as citizens.

What do you think? Should the reservations be disbanded and states treat Indians as they do other state citizens? Should the treaties made in the nineteenth century be honored even if they take precedence over present state laws? Is the problem one that should basically be handled by the federal government, rather than the states, or should the programs channel federal funds through state governments and let the states or communities work out the programs? What kind of solution is fair to the Indians? What should be done to help solve the problems of Indian poverty, lack of education, and unemployment? Should programs be undertaken even at the risk of destroying the traditional Indian language and culture?

SOURCE for further reading: For the problem viewed from an Indian perspective see Dee Brown, *Bury My Heart at Wounded Knee*, Holt, Rinehart and Winston, N.Y. 1970.

Public opinion data do show differences in participation and preferences by men and women voters with voting participation by women below that of men, but rising, and preferences generally for more conservative candidates. Yet women have not voted or acted as a bloc—even on such distinctively "women's issues" as abortion on demand or the adoption of the Equal Rights Amendment (ERA). In the early 1970s pro and con women's groups organized, lobbied, and demonstrated side by side in the state legislatures on these matters.

But more women, though still a relatively small number, are getting elected to office and more to offices in which government and politics is a full-time career. It took fifty-four years after getting the vote to elect the first woman governor in her own right—Ella Grasso of Connecticut in 1974. A second, Dixy Lee Ray, was elected governor of Washington in 1976.[30] In 1976 two women lieutenant governors in 1978, six. Seven

[30]The first women governors succeeded to the office—as a widow—Nellie Tayloe Ross in Wyoming in 1924 or, as a stand-in for a husband ineligibile to run, Lurleen Wallace in Alabama in 1966 (he could not by law succeed himself) and Meriam A. "Ma" Ferguson of Texas in 1924 and 1932. (Her husband had been impeached).

New York State legislator, J. Amatucci.

to ten as secretary of state and six as state treasurers both years. In all, in 1976 there were fifty-one who held statewide elective posts. The number of women legislators in 1978 was six hundred eighty-five, or 10 percent of the total, and only a very few have become state judges or top administrators. North Carolina and California have women chief justices. In 1978 there were five hundred sixty-six women mayors—ninety-five in cities with a population of over 10,000. The number of women city council members was 5365. Women mayors serve in cities as varied as Lincoln, Nebraska; San Antonio, Texas; Raleigh, North Carolina; York, Pennsylvania; San Jose, California; Ames, Iowa; St. Petersburg, Florida; Oklahoma City, and Phoenix. In all these categories of elected office some change is apparent in recent years, but the increase has been a very gradual one. The full impact of women in office-holding positions is still to be felt.

Age and Politics. Do young adults have special influence on state or community government, politics or policymaking? Georgia was the first state to allow eighteen year olds the vote. Governor Ellis Arnall sponsored the idea in 1944, in part because of his competition with ex-governor Eugene Talmadge, who had running battles with the state university. Arnall's public argument was the familiar one—"If you're old enough to fight, you're old enough to vote." His private hope was that university students would support the kinds of candidates he favored—a generally correct surmise. In 1971, the Twenty-sixth Amendment made eighteen the voting age in all states.

Most studies suggest that the major impact of eighteen-year-olds voting has been by those who are college or university students. Look at the county vote data in your own state. You will probably find greater support in student precincts for the more liberal candidates of both parties as compared with the average of the state. This holds true even in years when more conservative candidates carry the state and the campus precincts. It has also been relatively easy to collect signatures on campuses for initiated proposals that were popular with college-age students, such as repeal of abortion and local marijuana laws, ecology issues such as throwaway bottle bills or regulation for licensing atomic energy plants, bonuses for Vietnam veterans, and other such issues. But the larger electorate generally absorbs the votes of young adults without too much impact, except in communities where the concentrations of young people is high—such as in university or college towns where the student vote may be important in local races and issues.

The other age group that may have a special impact on state or community policymaking is its senior citizens. We find this only in the few Sun Belt states—California, Arizona, and, especially, Florida. California, since the 1930s, beginning with the Townsend Movement for Old Age Pensions, has had organized retirement groups active in politics.[31] More recently the effective groups have caught up with the times and adopted names such as The Grey Panthers.

Presently in southern Florida the retirees have become a potent political force, generally favoring more conservative candidates and special government programs and agencies for the aged. In other states their influence has been less clear, in part because the retired are a smaller portion of the total population, and also because political participation declines among older people. Nevertheless a series of issues exists that is of special concern to the older citizens—the condition of nursing homes, the quality and cost of medical care, property taxation exemption for the retired, and special ramps and facilities for the handicapped. In some cases the federal government has stepped in with programs, but a number of these issues are still decided upon and administered by the states or local communities.

A Final Comment

What we have been reviewing in this chapter is a host of "internal" influences that explain important political and government variations— what we can call state-based influences. But as Morton Grodzins noted, "the nation's diversities exist in a larger unity." States are part of a federalized government system. In the next chapter we will look at

[31]For a case study of George McLain, the chairman of the California Institute of Social Welfare, a potent political force in California in the 1940s and early 1950s on behalf of the retired, see Frank Pinner, Paul Jacobs and Philip Selznick, *Old Age and Political Behavior*, University of California Press, Berkeley, 1959.

a major "external" political influence that we have several times already referred to—the influence of the national government on the states. This "outside" influence has the potential for reducing the impact of the state-based influences on living conditions. During the last forty years, especially, state and community officials have not very easily been able to forget that a national government shares the American landscape and its citizens with them. And it is this relationship that we will examine in Chapter 3.

HIGHPOINTS OF CHAPTER 2: STATE-BASED INFLUENCES ON STATE AND COMMUNITY GOVERNMENTS

What have we thus far established as to the differences among states? (1) We found the differences in living conditions among the states to be of great importance. (2) We then examined the highway death rate of Wyoming and concluded that there are a number of different influences and they may vary in their impact by policy area. (3) We next noted the major state-based influence discovered thus far to be in elements of economic development—urbanism, industrialization, education, and wealth. (4) Next we observed some of the limitations of the economic development explanation and how politics and government influence outcomes through the threshold effect and redistribution. We then examined differences explained by geography, climate, and natural resources.

3

STATES AND COMMUNITIES IN A CENTRALIZING FEDERAL SYSTEM

In our day the states of the Union and their citizens seem to be becoming more alike. For example, after his sixtieth birthday John Steinbeck, the Pulitzer-prize winning novelist, set off from his New York apartment on a "side road tour" of America. He drove a pick-up truck camper and was alone, except for his poodle, Charley. In his youth, during the Great Depression, Steinbeck had bummed freights and hitchhiked across the country. From these experiences he wrote such novels as *The Grapes of Wrath, In Dubious Battle,* and *Cannery Row.* Now as he neared retirement he set off again to talk to ordinary Americans to find out if America had changed.

He took a leisurely tour through forty states, mostly around the borders of the nation—from New York City to the tip of Maine, across to Washington state, down to Salinas, California, where he grew up, across the southwest through Texas, up to Virginia, and finally, dog tired, a final stretch back home.

What did he discover? He still found some of the differences that gave his nation its great variety. His novelist's eye struck such seemingly trivial but telling details as the wording of road signs. In the New England states he found terse, tight-lipped instructions "without a word or even a letter wasted." In New York State the signs shouted out commands every few feet—"Do this! Do that!" In Ohio, signs were phrased as polite suggestions—and so on across the country.

But more important, he discovered the differences he had remembered from his youth being washed away by a technology nationwide in its impact—Americans watched the same fare of radio and television and consumed the same products from white bread to rock and roll, all produced with assembly line efficiency, and the states were now closer to each other because of the airplane and modern throughways.

Steinbeck found something else he had not anticipated—a united American citizenry. He wrote:

"This is not patriotic whoop-de-do; it is carefully observed fact. California Chinese, Boston Irish, Wisconsin German, yes and Alabama Negroes now have more in common than they have apart. . . . It is a fact that Americans from all sections and of all racial extractions are more alike than the Welsh are like the English, . . . or the lowland Scot like the highlander. It is an astonishing fact that this has happened in less than two hundred years and most of it in the last fifty. The American identity is an exact and provable thing."[1]

Now two decades later, the pace of change has even perhaps quickened. At the interchanges along the interstates in Georgia, South Dakota, or Oregon we see the same familiar Texaco service stations, the "golden arches" of one of the 3800 MacDonald franchises, or the Holiday Inns. We might even forget we were not home if we did not look at red dirt or wheat fields or giant evergreens. Inside the motels we know we will see on the TV the same Walter Cronkite or Archie and Edith and hear the same ads about "plop-plop, fizz-fizz."

The Nationalization of a People

Technology and industrialization have also encouraged population movements. The moving van is an American institution. The Great Depression, World War II, and the postwar boom accelerated movement—the shift of blacks from the South, migration to the West and Southwest, as well as the continuing movement from farm to city and then to suburb. Each state has become more diversified and somewhat more like every other state.

Actions taken by the national government, beginning with the New Deal programs to combat the Great Depression of 1929 to 1939 have

[1]John Steinbeck, *Travels with Charley, In Search of America.* Bantam Books, N.Y. 1962, p. 208.

also blurred differences. As people have moved across state lines and become more like each other, they in turn have demanded more national action to help solve problems that are now seen as national problems.

The Nationalization of a Governing Process

All of this is to suggest that our federal system has also changed over 200 years. Students who took a course in state and local government fifty years ago during the "Roaring Twenties" studied a different system than the one we look at today. No longer do the states dominate, nor, we think, is it any longer a union in which states and national government share power equally. It is, we suggest, becoming a nationally directed system, but one in which states and communities still hold significant "clout."

We think the state governments are carving out a new role for themselves in the federal system. It is a kind of "crossroads" function in the federal system. They bring local- and state-based viewpoints to the making and implementation of national policy. But they also bring the more general viewpoints of the nation and state to community policy-making and administration.

Overview. Ours is a unique and complex system of government organization—one we will look at closely in this chapter. First we will look at the legal structure of our federal union. Then we will examine the politics of federalism. We argue that power has shifted from the states to the national government, and will trace that development. We will examine how the federal system is operating today, covering such topics as voluntary cooperation and coordination by federal actions. We will end by looking at what role is left to the state—what functions they handle and how they defend themselves against federal domination.

THE LEGAL STRUCTURE OF FEDERALISM

America in 1787 invented modern federalism. Of course, in antiquity scholars found a few federations among the Greek states and even earlier in biblical Israel. In this section we will examine the legal relationship of the states to the national government that the founding fathers established—and note how it has changed. We will also review the legal ties of the possessions to the nation's federation. The other part of the federal picture is the local governments. We will discuss these in the next chapter.

Unitary, Confederal, and Federal Governments

Generally, governments are of two types. Those in which all legal power is concentrated at the center are called *unitary.* Such unitary governments can, of course, set up and abolish local units as they wish, and grant them whatever legal powers they wish. Most governments in the world today are unitary—France, Denmark, Egypt, and Israel.

The second type is one that some political scientists would hardly call a government at all—a *confederation.* The subunits set up a central unit, usually for a temporary emergency, and hold onto the real power; the central body has very little legal power. The League of Nations was, and the United Nations is, a confederation.

The Weakness of Confederations.   We have had two confederations in U.S. history. Both started as leagues of states to fight a war. One was our first "government" under the Continental Congress established by the Articles of Confederation (1776–1789). The other was the Confederate States of America of 1860 to 1865, formed by eleven southern states. Both were handicapped in trying to fight wars in which member states made decisions on supplies, government powers, and even the terms of soldier enlistments. (Washington crossed the Delaware into New Jersey on Christmas Day, 1776 because the enlistments of many state militia serving under him were to expire on January 1, 1777. "His" soldiers would then return home.)[2]

Federalism As a Compromise.   In a *federation,* both states and the central government have significant legal powers—both, for example in America, can directly tax individuals. More important, neither can abolish the other or drop membership.

It is well to remind ourselves that the Founding Fathers did not adopt a federation on grounds of political philosophy, but rather as a political compromise. Some of the delegates to the Constitutional Convention, such as Alexander Hamilton and others, wanted a unitary government that would have abolished the states. Others who called themselves "anti-Federalists" fought bitterly the efforts to change the confedera-

---

[2]Burton J. Hendrick argues that Jefferson Davis as president of the Confederacy was unable to direct the war effort effectively because of the central government's weakness. "It (the Southern Confederacy) was founded on a principle that made impossible the orderly conduct of public affairs." (p. 11) See *Statesmen of the Lost Cause, Jefferson Davis and His Cabinet,* Literary Guild, N.Y., 1939, 409–432.

tion. If a vote had been taken among the delegates, it's very likely that federalism would have gotten some lukewarm first-place votes, but would have been the second choice of most delegates. The compromise for federalism was not an unusual outcome from a gathering of astute politicians.

The American Federation

Legally only the national and state governments have *sovereign power*. By sovereign power, we mean the legal power to govern granted by the basic law. All independent nations have such sovereign power.

The legal powers of both state and national governments are granted in the U.S. Constitution. We find in Article I, Section 8, a list of eighteen "delegated" powers that the national government can exercise. The Constitution also lists some powers that the states may *not* exercise, and some that neither level of government may exercise. Other powers not in conflict with national powers are "reserved for the states."

All other units of government in the American federation, such as the District of Columbia, United States territories or commonwealths associated with it, or the variety of local governments (cities, counties, school districts, towns and townships, and special districts) were set up for the convenience of either the nation (in respect to the territories or commonwealth), or the states (in respect to local governments). In the legal sense, territories or local governments are not sovereign bodies.[3]

Achieving Statehood

A local unit of government in the American system becomes "sovereign" only by becoming a state. Only a few, such as Vermont and Texas, were once ever independent nations and so were already sovereign.

How did other kinds of units become states? First, the citizens must petition Congress to enter—petitioning involves asking permission to elect delegates to prepare a draft constitution. The U.S. Congress must pass an enabling act giving such permission. If the territorial voters in a referendum approve the proposed constitution, the unit then may formally apply for admission. Congress must accept the application by joint resolution and the president must sign it. Then the flag makers figure out where to add another star.

[3]Some readers in Kentucky, Massachusetts, Pennsylvania, and Virginia will note that these states are called commonwealths. In a legal sense they are, nevertheless, states; the only American commonwealth (legally) is Puerto Rico.

Can Special Conditions Be Imposed? Can Congress or the president set special conditions for admission of a state? Yes and no. We say yes, because becoming a state involves some careful politicking, and no because the Supreme Court has ruled that all states are legally equal and no special conditions can be imposed legally.[4] Yet Arizona submitted a constitution in 1912 that President William Howard Taft in a fit of pique vetoed because it allowed for recall of judges. Arizonians dutifully removed the offending clause and once admitted, put the provision back into their constitution.

"Semistate" Status

We Americans always feel uncomfortable at the thought that we have colonies. On the other hand, we have not wanted to grant some of our "possessions," or "territories," or "trusteeships" either statehood or independence.

We granted independence to the Philippine Islands, an area the size of Arizona, and with a population in 1970 of 41 million. They had become "associated" with the United States in 1898 as the result of the Spanish American War. Their official national language was Filipino, although many of the residents today still speak both Spanish and English. In 1934 Congress voted to grant them independence by 1946. In that year they became an independent republic.

Other territories, such as Hawaii and Alaska, have become states—both in 1959. And other units still remain in an in-between condition. We have not quite figured out in which direction these units should go.

Each of those next described, except the "possessions," have residents who are all U.S. citizens. They elect a delegate to the U.S. Congress who can vote in the House Interior and Insular Affairs Committee, but not on the floor. Their residents can be drafted, but, except for Washington D.C. residents, they cannot vote in presidential elections. They have their own constitutions and elect their own legislatures and executives. The "possessions," though, still have executives appointed by the president. Let us review the legal status of a few of these "other units" of the federal system.

The District of Columbia. Washington, D.C., our nation's capital, had a population in 1970 of 756,540, large enough for statehood since its population was greater than any one of the following states: Vermont,

---

[4]Readers in Texas may be aware, though, that Texas has one special privilege; that state may, if it wishes, divide itself into four states—a provision granted it when it left the status of independent nationhood to become a state. So perhaps in this case, all states are equal. But Texas, it seems, is four times more equal than other states.

New Hampshire, North Dakota, South Dakota, Delaware, Montana, Idaho, Wyoming, Nevada, or Alaska. In 1961, through the Twenty-Third Amendment, residents of the District finally gained the right to vote for president and vice-president, as well as gaining three votes in the electoral college. Residents also now may elect their own mayor and council, and levy local taxes. But Congress still may veto any actions of the Washington D.C., city council. In 1978 the U.S. Congress submitted a proposed constitutional amendment to the states to permit the District full voting powers in both houses of Congress.

The Commonwealth of Puerto Rico. Puerto Rico is a Caribbean island with a population greater than that of twenty states. Since 1950 Puerto Ricans have had self-government with many trappings of statehood—an elected governor, senate and house. They have their own court system and their own constitution, flag, anthem, official flower, tree, and bird. But Puerto Rico also is not sovereign. The acts of its government must be consistent with the U.S. Constitution and with the Federal Relations Act of 1950, and only the U.S. Congress can change the terms of the Act. Further consideration of the island's legal status is found in Policy Box No. 5, "What Is a Commonwealth? What Is Puerto Rico?"

U.S. Territories and Possessions. The distinguishing features of these units of government appear to be their small population (under

POLICY BOX NO. 5   What is a Commonwealth? What is Puerto Rico?

We like to forget that our federal system contains units that can be regarded as colonies. Fidel Castro for years has put the "imperialist" tag on the Commonwealth of Puerto Rico; Cuba's representatives to the United Nations periodically urge the U.S. to give Puerto Rico its freedom. On the island itself about 5 percent voted for this course in the last election; more intellectuals favor independence than do other citizens. Separatists attempted to assassinate President Truman, and ever since have initiated sporadic acts of terrorism. They sprayed bullets at U.S representatives seated on the floor of Congress and bombed American buildings in New York, Chicago, and elsewhere. Yet most Americans are only dimly aware of Puerto Rico's legal status.

Puerto Rico is about the size of Connecticut or Delaware. It became a part of the United States as spoils of the Spanish American War. It provided a major military base, and later, protection for the Panama Canal. The people speak Spanish and have the highest per capita income in the Caribbean; yet this income is only half that of the poorest state. About half the population receives food stamps; the unemployment rate in 1978 was 21 percent. About three million people live on the island. Its population density of 900 people per square mile is among the world's highest. (Nearby Cuba has 140 per square mile.) As a result, an additional 1½ million Puerto Ricans have migrated to the mainland—70 percent to New York City and others mainly to the New England states.

Through 1916, Puerto Rico was called a territory. It had its own house of delegates. The president of the United States appointed its governor and the majority of its executive council. Its court cases were handled by the Circuit Court of Boston. Puerto Rico sent a resident commissioner to the U.S. House of Representatives who could speak on issues, but had no vote.

In 1917, during World War I, Congress made Puerto Ricans American citizens. This act increased their powers of local government, but also made them subject to the military draft. As citizens they also could migrate freely to the United States mainland.

During the depression of the 1930s the independence movement gained support. Violence erupted on the island. President Truman, in 1946, appointed the first island native as U.S. governor—a man who had been resident commissioner in Washington. In 1948 the island was permitted to elect its governor for the first time and Luis Munoz Marin was elected. He had been political leader of the legislature for many years and was the son of the island's first resident commissioner.

In 1950 the U.S. granted Puerto Rico commonwealth status with power to draft its own constitution. In 1951 commonwealth status was approved by Puerto Ricans by a vote of three to one, but an unknown number of independence voters abstained since the choice was only between commonwealth or territorial status.

What does commonwealth status mean? It is clear that it is not the same as statehood. For one thing Puerto Ricans pay no income tax, although their commonwealth taxes are probably roughly equivalent to this tax. Yet they receive most of the federal welfare benefits that other U.S. citizens are entitled to, such as food stamps and aid to dependent children, as well as services of almost every federal department from the Conservation Service to the Weather Bureau. The residents are U.S. citizens who cannot vote for president, but send delegates to both national party conventions. If Puerto Rico were to become a state, its population would entitle it to more representatives in the House than twenty other states. In his last days in office in 1976 President Gerald Ford recommended statehood.

What do you think? Is Puerto Rico "ready" for statehood? What standards should we use to decide this? Would it create special problems to allow Puerto Rico to become a state if its citizens so wish? Or should we require it to be a state? Or should we allow it to be independent if it wishes to be? Or have we the right to make it independent, no matter what its citizens desire?

SOURCE: For a balanced presentation of Puerto Rico's problems see Kal Wagenheim, *Puerto Rico, A Profile*, Praeger, N.Y., Second edition, 1975.

100,000), small geographic size, and strategic military value. Most, but not all, are islands in the western Pacific.

The territories are the Virgin Islands (purchased from Denmark in 1917), American Samoa (acquired from Spain in 1899), and Guam (another "spoil" of the Spanish American War). The possessions include the Panama Canal Zone (officially a U.S. government reservation); Wake, Midway, and some other minor islands; some minor Caribbean Islands, and the United Nations Trusteeships in the Caroline, Marianas, and Marshall Islands. In 1978 we made a treaty with the Republic of Panama to cede them full control of the Panama Canal Zone in 2000. In addition we have twenty-five islands southwest of Hawaii that are in dispute. The U.S. claims all twenty-five of them, but Great Britain claims eighteen and New Zealand claims seven. The U.S. offered commonwealth status to all of the Trust Islands, but only Saipan and the thirteen other of the northern Marianas were interested. They voted 78 percent in favor in 1977, but Congress has yet to act.

The Virgin Islands send delegates to national party conventions.

OUR CHANGING FEDERAL SYSTEM

The legal rules originally established a pattern of intergovernmental relations, but that is only the beginning of the story. Throughout our history political considerations have gradually altered the relationships among the federal government and states and communities.

Those who try to understand federalism with only the logic of constitutional law to aid them are likely to become frustrated, baffled, and sometimes outraged. They find constitutional phrases that meant one thing to the U.S. Supreme Court in 1800, another in 1900, and something else in 1978. What has happened is that the judges interpret federal legal relationships according to the problems and mood of their times. As the political scientist Roscoe Martin observed, American government practice can best be understood as a pragmatic response to felt needs.

That we have become one united nation with a common outlook, as John Steinbeck suggested, has changed our present-day notion of what the legal arrangements of federalism are, or should be. And this change, brought about by technology, mass communication, and population mobility, has been reflected in court decisions and day-to-day intergovernmental relations.

As we look next at the changes in our federal system, we will consider only the relations between the "sovereign" units—the states and the nation. We will ask how powers are divided between the two levels.

The Period of Dual Federalism (1788-1900)

Our nation began with a pattern of federal–state relations that has been called *dual federalism*. The constitution "delegated" eighteen powers to the national government, and except for powers denied both levels, "reserved" the rest of the powers for the states. The states and the nation divided most functions. Each level carried out its own functions in its own way without much interference from the other. Morton Grodzins compared this kind of federal system to "a layer cake."[5]

It is difficult to read the U.S. Constitution, we think, without being impressed at how close this is to the kind of system that the Founding Fathers had in mind. The Constitution gave the national government a very few specific functions to carry out—foreign relations (including national defense), setting tariffs, supervising commerce that crossed state lines, settling interstate disputes, coining money, establishing a common standard of weights and measures, establishing a national post office and post roads, determining a national copyright law, and

[5]Morton Grodzins, *The American System, A New View of Government in the United States,* Rand McNally, Chicago, 1966, 8–9.

governing the District of Columbia. The federal government also controlled the admission of new states. Yet the Constitution in the national supremacy clause did specify that if state and national powers came in conflict, the national would prevail.

Each state government then decided the important domestic issues, such as whether a person would be a slave or not, the definition of almost all crimes and the punishment for them, how to provide for the public health, safety, education, welfare, and morals, and almost anything else that concerns us as citizens.

National Actions In the States. In those early days do we we find any involvement of the national government into "local" concerns? We find some, but until the mammoth intervention in respect to slavery, national impacts were isolated. Financing the state militia provides a case. As early as 1808 the national government took over 80 percent of the financing of the state militia, or as it came to be called, the National Guard. This was a military function and an important national one, since the troops were used in Indian wars. Also the Army Engineers helped the states in the building of some roads and canals. The national government sent Lewis and Clark in 1803 to explore the West for the benefit of settlers. And in 1817 in *McCullough* v. *Maryland*, Justice John Marshall and the Supreme Court broadly interpreted the constitutional clause that said the national government could use any means "necessary and proper" to carry out its powers. And in 1837 the rivers and harbors improvement program, generally referred to as pork-barrel legislation, began, although a few years before Andrew Jackson had vetoed a plan to build a national road in Maysville, Kentucky as interference with state functions. In 1862 the Homestead Act provided for settlement of the frontier. So isolation was not complete, but nevertheless we conclude that most national powers were used sparingly and most of the icing of the federal system—the important legal powers— was on the bottom or state layer of the cake.[6]

Why the Relationship Changed. The first significant federal intervention occurred as the result of the Civil War—the abolition of slavery. But the national government was much less successful in attempts to guarantee voting rights to black males or to end racial and religious

[6]Daniel Elazar has argued that these interventions indicate that a pattern of "cooperative federalism" was always characteristic. We argue that the dominant pattern was one of dual federalism. For his argument, see *The American Partnership, Intergovernmental Cooperation in the Nineteenth-Century United States*, University of Chicago Press, Chicago, 1962. For a counterargument by the historian Harry N. Scheiber, see *The Condition of American Federalism: An Historian's View*, U.S. Government Printing Office, Washington, D.C., Committee on Government Operations, October 15, 1966.

discrimination. Other federal actions to help state governments during the 1800s were isolated responses to particular pressures. The Land Grant College Act of 1862 was passed to help educate farmers. Experiment stations for agricultural research followed in 1887. Finally between 1887 and 1889, with considerable hesitation, Congress also created the Interstate Commerce Commission to regulate interstate railroads, passed the Sherman Silver Purchase Act to inflate currency and help end the depression, and passed the Sherman Antitrust Law to control monopoly trusts. All of these were thought to be matters the state "should" handle—all were passed during times of intense agricultural depression and agitation.

The End of Dual Federalism.   When did the period of dual federalism end? Most students find it difficult to state a precise date. It could have been in 1913 when, by constitutional amendment, the federal government received the power to levy an income tax.[7] Others might choose 1932 when President Franklin Roosevelt's New Deal expanded federal activities.

We suggest that the presidency of Theodore Roosevelt, beginning in 1901, is probably as good a date as any. It is not just that national intervention in state affairs increased. It is that Theodore Roosevelt was the first president to argue consistently and without apology that federal intervention would be needed for states to fulfill their goals and thus was fully justified. He set about demonstrating how the national government could help, whether the problems involved regulation of business, settlement of strikes in the coal fields, conservation of natural resources, or race relations. We favor this date because the Roosevelt presidency set the ideological groundwork for the next phase of federal–state relations—the period of cooperative federalism.

The Period of Cooperative Federalism (1901–1963)

Those, like Theodore Roosevelt, who defended what was called cooperative federalism, argued that the federal government should intervene because the states were too weak financially or could not control an activity because it crossed state lines. How could one state control the Standard Oil monopoly that operated in almost every state? How could the states build a nationwide highway system without federal help, as was given in the grant program in 1916? State and federal action must

[7]One writer argues that any federalism that adopts a national income tax should no longer be classed as federal because of the shift of power to the central body that results. Karl Lowenstein, "Reflections of the Value of Constitutions in Our Revolutionary Age," in Harry Eckstein and David Apter, (eds.), *Comparative Politics, A Reader*, Free Press, N.Y. 1963, p. 157.

The Great Depression—
hunger lines such as this
led to federal intervention.

intermingle as in a marble cake. But the inspiration for intervention
was state rather than national goals.

Ideas about cooperative federalism came to full bloom during the
presidency of Franklin Roosevelt. In 1932, at the depths of the Great
Depression, states and their cities needed money for handling welfare
loads and unemployment. Governors saw the national government as
the only real hope in turning the economy around. They welcomed massive public works projects such as those of WPA, the Tennessee Valley
Authority and public housing. Also the national government began with
the aid of the states dealing with the depression-created problems of
big business, big labor, and agriculture. Still largely regarded as
"local" and capable of solution at the state or community level were
most problems involving public safety, health, education, and morals.

And as late as the 1960s, some members of Congress still argued that federal aid to education was probably unconstitutional as well as undesirable.

The Modern Period of Federalism (1964 to the Present)

In 1964 when President Lyndon Johnson announced his program for the "Great Society," he changed the pattern of state-federal relations. All problems came to be viewed, at least in part, as "national." Crime, sewage disposal, library services, education, poverty, pornography, and so on were all national problems. National leaders no longer talked about "cooperating" to achieve state purposes. As James L. Sundquist points out, beginning in the early 1960s federal legislation clearly stated that their purpose was to achieve national goals.[8] The pattern of state–federal relations had shifted—the system became more centralized with the national government exercising more power. The frosting had moved to the top, something like a pineapple upside-down cake.

Permissive Federalism. The political scientist Michael Reagan noted that this change in purpose was encouraged by changes in legal relationships between the national government, states, and communities. By 1964 the Supreme Court no longer believed that the Constitution reserved any functions exclusively for the states. What functions the states still carried out by themselves, Michael Reagan argued, were what the federal government wished and permitted them to—this is why he called the new relationship "permissive federalism."[9] We will argue later that the political strength of states and communities also determines which functions the states will handle and control.

Functional Federalism. Others emphasized the changes in federal-state-local administrative patterns. They note that at all levels of government power has shifted from elected political officials to appointed administrators. Terry Sanford, a former governor of North Carolina, likened the new pattern to a picket fence. The crossbars he called the national, state, and local governments holding the pikes together. And the pikes he described as professional administrators who work at all three levels of government. One pike represents welfare administrators, another highways, and so forth.[10]

[8]James L. Sundquist, "The Problem of Coordination in a Changing Federalism," *Making Federalism Work, A Study of Program Coordination at the Community Level*, The Brookings Institution, Washington, D.C. 1969, 1–31.

[9]Michael D. Reagan, *The New Federalism*, Oxford University Press, N.Y. 1972.

[10]Terry Sanford, *Storm Over the States*, McGraw Hill, N.Y., 1967, 80–81.

Samuel Beer prefers to call this type of decision making "functional federalism."[11] He argues that vertical coalitions of professionals in single policy areas are working for common goals, but he also says they are joined by nongovernment professionals—those employed by private universities, by research agencies, and related business corporations. The political arms, the executives and legislatures, still influenced policymaking, Beer argues, but many of the day-to-day decisions are made by cooperating professionals.

These administrative professionals in federal, state, and community governments, and those in the private sector who work with them, often share the same outlook and goals. We expect that where a common training exists in professional schools, as with forestry or education, this similarity in viewpoint would be especially strong—one writer calls it "guild loyalty." Movement of personnel from one level to another, national conventions, and professional journals, we expect, strengthen these professional loyalties. At times the loyalty to a guild and its values may clearly overshadow the loyalty that professionals may feel to the level of government that employs them.[12]

Administrators at state and local levels also have the financial means to become more independent and, indeed, this is what two researchers found was happening. Those state administrators in agencies that received a sizeable portion of funds from federal grants reported feeling more independent from the governor and state legislature.[13]

We also find conflicts between administrators at state and national levels. State professionals attempt to manipulate federal funding agencies to maximize the funds they get and minimize federal supervision. State professionals also at times have their own pet programs to which they quietly divert federal funds. Or they find some federal regulations poorly conceived and if they can, circumvent or ignore them. Some things, the state or local people just never get around to doing.

As we would expect, we tend to find more friction when a function is handled by administrators from a variety of professional specialities—as is sometimes the case in civil rights. Alfred Light also notes that federal control is less when the state administrator is directly re-

[11]Samuel H. Beer, "The Adoption of General Revenue Sharing: A Case Study in Public Sector Politics," *Public Policy* 24, Spring 1976, 127–195. Beer argues further that a new federalism based on the political power of local governments may be evolving. Revenue sharing, to be discussed in Chapter 5, is indicative of such a reverse flow of power.

[12]For a discussion of guild influence, see Harold Seidman, "Cooperative Federalism," *Politics, Position and Power, The Dynamics of Federal Organization*, Oxford University Press, N.Y., 1970, Chapter 5, "Cooperative Federalism," 136–163.

[13]George C. Hale and Marian Lief Palley, "Perceptions of Federal Involvement in Intergovernmental Decision Making," *Public Administration Review*, forthcoming, 1979.

sponsible to an elected official, such as the state's attorney general or secretary of state.[14]

This suggests that the "picket fence" relationships among administrators at the three levels are not as simple as outsiders sometimes think. We find a degree of give and take with the precise outlines of the relationships still not wholly understood.

The Division of Functions Today

In a few fields of activity that were formerly the responsibility of states, the national government now exercises major control. Since the Great Depression, the national government has made the major decisions about the activities of Big Industry, Big Labor, and Agriculture. The states have supplemented federal programs in each area, enough so that all of the big interest groups do some lobbying at the state capital. But the major regulations are made nationally. The same is becoming true of other fields, especially social welfare, the interstate transportation system, public housing, and air pollution, (probably because control of air purity so clearly requires regulation across state lines).

However, when we look at many other activities we see a different picture. Higher education, regulation of the professions and trades, mental health, and prisons are still largely controlled by state decisions. So, also, are matters of marriage, divorce, and adoption, and almost all criminal prosecutions and civil cases. National grants and rules affect each area, but the basic policies are still largely made at the state level.

We also find that decisions in fields once made almost exclusively by groups in the private sector now are at least partially made by state and community governments. It is the states who regulate nursing homes and set up new facilities of their own. Their universities and community colleges have moved into higher education; and so forth, for a myriad of activities.

Finally we find that some activities are still mainly controlled at the community level with varying degrees of state supervision. These include such important matters as primary and secondary education, law enforcement, fire protection, land use control, recreation and water and sewage regulation.

What it adds up to is that activities important to all of us are still state or community controlled. Here diversity and its costs are seen as acceptable and even desirable. In addition, we sense there are some

[14]Alfred Light, "Agency Perspectives on Intergovernmental Relations: Explaining the Attitudes of State Administrators," mimeo research paper, Texas Tech University.

activities that citizens are reluctant to have nationally controlled—even in the face of serious breakdown and problems. At the top of this list is law enforcement, followed by primary and secondary education. Finally for economic reasons and, perhaps, for less defensible reasons because in some cases racial discrimination is clearly a part, is a desire to keep land use control a community function.

CO-ORDINATING A COMPLEX FEDERAL SYSTEM

The centralizing trend we have described is leading us toward a much more complex government system—one in which governments at all levels cooperate in providing services. Nationalization or centralization is far from complete. We still have a system in which both states and national governments have the legal power to act in many functional areas and states and communities still have the political power to act independently.

More than in the past we face problems of coordination of the activities of federal, state, and community governments. How can we bring about the order that society thinks necessary at a given time? How can we encourage cooperation where needed, and reduce unproductive conflict?

Coordination by Constitutional Clause

The Founding Fathers anticipated some of the problems of coordination. We find three clauses in the U.S. Constitution that are designed to help each state carry out its own laws with some cooperation from other states and, at the same time, to prevent a state from discriminating unreasonably against out-of-state citizens.

The Full Faith and Credit Clause. The Constitution provides that each state must give full faith and credit (recognize as legal) the acts and decisions of the courts of other states in civil matters. Wills, marriage licenses, corporation charters, and a host of other legal documents are covered, but criminal decisions need not be. What is a crime in Connecticut need not necessarily be recognized as a crime in Missouri.

In general this arrangement has worked reasonably well. The difficulties arise over the question of which state may claim the parties of a case as residents as, for example, in divorce and child custody cases. Cases hinge on the question: In which state were the husband and wife residents when their marriage floundered? When the question of residency is settled, the custody of the children can be settled. Sometimes that is not easy, but in most instances the cases are readily solvable.

The Interstate Rendition Clause. A person commits a crime in Montana and is picked up by the police in New Mexico. If Montana wants to prosecute, its governor must formally request the governor of New Mexico to turn the prisoner over to Montana officials. This process of interstate rendition is covered by a constitutional clause.[15]

In most cases, as we would expect, the procedure works without a hitch. But the Supreme Court has interpreted the constitutional clause as not absolutely requiring a state to turn over the accused person. The governor of New Mexico may refuse to do so and give no reason at all.

Cases of refusal are rare. Most modern cases have involved blacks found guilty in a southern state and captured in a northern state. Among the most famous involved the author who wrote a book about his escape from a Georgia Chain Gang. But other cases also crop up. Recently Governor Ray Blanton of Tennessee refused to return to Oklahoma a "Grand Old Opry" performer, Faron Young, who was wanted in connection with a New Year's eve performance he gave in Tulsa. Politics may encourage governors to refuse to return a wanted person because they find their action very popular with a significant segment of their own state's residents and voters.

The Privileges and Immunities Clause. What is unreasonable discrimination against out-of-staters? We find the U.S. Supreme Court justifiably vague. We know that state colleges and universities can legally charge out-of-state residents significantly higher tuition fees. And, out-of-staters usually pay more for hunting and fishing licenses. On the other hand, nonresidents can not be kept out (as California tried to do to "Okies" and "Arkies" during the Great Depression). Nor can states prevent nonresidents from starting a business or owning property.

Undoubtedly some discrimination against out-of-staters exists in almost every state. One method of keeping out competing produce or nursery stock, for example, has been to require extensive inspections. Out-of-staters may be required to pass a license exam—for example, lawyers can not hope to pass easily the bar examination in a neighboring state. If faced with them, we might regard some of these practices as unreasonable. The U.S. Supreme Court appears to be reluctant to intervene in any but extreme cases of discrimination such as those involving significant costs for nonresidents and striking at basic constitutional guarantees.

[15]The process is also sometimes called extradition, though technically this term only applies to such procedures between independent nations.

Voluntary Cooperation Among the States

Part of the reason we have a U.S. Constitution is that New York and New Jersey could not agree on the building of a lighthouse at Sandy Hook. Their representatives discussed this issue at the Annapolis Convention that preceded the Constitutional Convention in Philadelphia. Once in the Union, the reasons for cooperation among the states became, as we would expect, more obvious. The lighthouse was built and the states have voluntarily entered on a number of other cooperative ventures.

The advantages of such cooperation must generally be clear-cut to the participating states; otherwise they would not cooperate. Without undervaluing such cooperation, we can also readily see the limitations involved—as a general rule, states will not cooperate just for the general good. All U.S. citizens were advantaged, for example, when states voluntarily agreed to adopt the same type of traffic signals. But states or their cities that had already invested heavily in one kind of signal were reluctant to scrap investments immediately for the common good. Voluntary cooperation takes time and patience, as well as a clearly recognized benefit.

Let us review some of the common and more successful forms of voluntary cooperation.

Reciprocal or Retaliatory Legislation.   The simplest method of cooperation is one of "I'll respect your law if you respect mine." Thus tourists driving from New York to San Francisco need not buy an auto license in each state—although truckers may be required to. Wisconsin and Minnesota allow each other's residents, under certain conditions, to enroll as state residents in the state university systems. Floridians, on the other hand, must deal with doctors close to retirement age who wish to practice there; they put up stiff accreditation barriers. Illinois and Indiana and several neighboring states have worked out relationships in respect to income taxes for residents of one state who work in another, so that the states can avoid double taxation and reduce tax evasion.

The Uniform Law Movement.   In 1892 a committee of the American Bar Association proposed that all states adopt the same law in respect to certain commercial transactions. They formed an organization called the National Commission for Uniform Laws (now affiliated with the Council of State Governments). Their first success was, as we would expect, in respect to commercial transactions—a law called the Uniform Negotiable Instruments Act. Since then they have had few other laws adopted by all states, but a number of their model laws have been adopted by forty or more states, including, for example, the Uniform Narcotics Drug Act, a traffic code, and a consumer credit code.

The difficulty, as we noted, is that states refuse to adopt such laws when it places them at a disadvantage. In addition, even when the laws are adopted, state supreme courts may and do interpret them in different ways. Finally, individual state legislatures may subsequently amend the laws in different ways.

Nevertheless the impact of the movement has helped achieve a measure of uniformity, especially in the field of business law.

The Copying of Innovations.   States also cooperate, in a sense, by copying useful innovations from each other since such change encourages a degree of uniformity. The earliest studies suggested that a few states became national or regional innovators. Other states looked to them for ideas and so such ideas as budget standards, controlled access highways, or age anti-discrimination laws spread through the nation and brought about a degree of uniformity.

In recent years the role "model states" has become less important, while that of professional associations has grown. Each profession in its journals and at its conventions spreads new ideas.[16]

An additional source of innovative ideas is the federal government. In some cases, such as adoption of civil service, federal pressure has forced states to adopt the innovation. In other cases, such as the adoption of a Congressional Budget Office, the publicity given the national action has led some states to adopt similar procedures.[17]

Agreements and Compacts.   States may join in a formal agreement or compact with other states to achieve a common purpose. The U.S. Congress must also formally approve such compacts, although in some classes of cases it has stated its agreement in advance.

States use the compact most frequently in the development and control of rivers. For example, the Colorado River Compact involves seven states. Its first project was building Hoover Dam. Other compacts have involved flood control, water pollution, dredging for shipping, or recreational development. In 1967 all of the states joined a compact on education for the purpose of advancing educational goals.

The Council of State Governments.   The Council of State Governments, organized in 1925, is an association of states and their officials. It initially served as a clearinghouse of information. The council publishes the *Book of the States* every two years, a journal called *State*

[16]Jack L. Walker, "The Diffusion of Innovations Among the American States," *American Political Science Review* 63, September 1969, 880–899.

[17]Virginia Gray, "Innovation in the States: A Diffusion Study," *American Political Science Review* 67, December 1973, 1174–1185.

Government, and a great many specialized reports, as well as providing technical advice to states on individual problems. The Council is also the umbrella organization for the myriad of organizations of state officials, such as the National Legislative Conference, and Conferences of Chief Justices, Attorneys General, Lieutenant Governors and other officials. The Council is also a lobbying organization before Congress and the U.S. bureaucracy. It is particularly active in arguing for state clearance of federal grants to communities and for the revenue-sharing program.

The National Governors Conference.   In 1976 the National Governors Conference left the Council, unhappy over the Council's lobbying efforts. The Governors Conference helped to establish near the capitol building a Hall of the States building which houses a number of state associations and individual state lobbyists.[18]

Coordination by Federal Action

The federal government has also attempted to coordinate activities in selected policy areas. We can see no pattern of development—all of the methods we will describe, except one, have been used almost from the start of the Union. We will discuss the exception first—the Advisory Commission on Intergovernmental Relations (ACIR).

The Advisory Commission on Intergovernmental Relations.   During the Eisenhower years various groups made great efforts to "reverse" the flow of power from the states to the national government. National

[18]For a description of lobbying activities of state and community officials see Donald H. Haider, *When Governments Come to Washington, Governors, Mayors and Inter-Governmental Lobbying*, Free Press, N.Y., 1974.

The National Governors Conference convenes in Detroit, 1977.

commissions were set up to recommend functions the states could "take back." Though the state officials were heavily represented in these groups, the effort came to little. Only two functions were found to "return to the states": vocational education and design of municipal waste treatment plants. But, to "take them back" would require the states or communities to take over financing. The governors in conference listened glumly and declined with thanks.[19]

But the commissions in 1959 did encourage Congress to establish a permanent body called the Advisory Commission on Intergovernmental Relations. The ACIR has state, local, and national representatives, as well as a paid research staff. It provides an ongoing assessment of the federal system. Its reports have been studies of intergovernmental relations with recommendations in some cases for Congress, and in other cases for state or community governments. The ACIR has had few critics. It has avoided polemical argument and, instead, has concentrated on strengthening states and communities and finding ways in which states and national government can cooperate to achieve common goals.

Federal Assumption of Services.   Very rarely has the federal government completely assumed responsibility for programs that once were under state jurisdiction. Some exceptions are establishing the Federal Reserve System in 1914, the Social Security program in 1935, and the Tennessee Valley Authority in 1935. Each of these takeovers merged what the states had done with some new programs, and several required heavy financial investments. Presently some professionals in the field are urging the federal government to take full responsibility for welfare programs—both in financing and administration. This would include the Medicaid program, of which states now pay half. Few politicians seriously suggest other major transfers. Most federal action is cooperative with states and the communities.

Achieving Uniformity by Constitutional Amendment.   Most amendments to the U.S. Constitution from the Eleventh on restrict state powers. Mostly amendment writers have been concerned with the election process—voting rights for blacks, women, eighteen-year-olds, and residents of the District of Columbia, direct election of United States senators, and elimination of poll taxes. Slavery was abolished by amendment, and of course, the original amendment on prohibition of liquor

[19]See the description in Glenn E. Brooks, *When Governors Convene*, The Johns Hopkins Press, Baltimore, 1961, 100–105.

took away states rights, though the repeal amendment returned the power to act to the states. Only one other amendment markedly added to national powers—the right to levy a graduated income tax.

This drift is what we would expect, since only the Congress can propose amendments. The states can only accept or reject congressional proposals, not make any of their own. Still, many of the provisions included in amendments that limited state powers had already been adopted by a number of states—women suffrage or the abolition of poll taxes, for example. In a sense we might argue that a national majority of states encouraged use of the amendment process to bring lagging states into line and impose a general uniformity.

Uniformity Through Court Action.   The federal courts act as the official referee of the federal system. Some "states righters" complain that at the same time, the judges seem to be wearing the uniforms of the Washington "Nationals."

Whether or not this is fair, it appears to be inevitable if general chaos is to be avoided. There can be little doubt that beginning with Justice Marshall's early decisions, the Supreme Court has become a great force for national uniformity in respect to civil rights (racial discrimination—treatment of criminals), free speech, press, and religion, structure of state governments (one person-one vote), and the content of policies in selected policy areas, such as abortion.

Some critics argue that the court has moved too fast and too far ahead of public opinion, as they say was the case in busing or abortion decisions. In areas such as divorce and child custody "childnapping," we might argue that the Court has, perhaps, dragged its feet too long by allowing diversity that occasionally leads to unnecessary complications, legal costs, and heartbreak in a nationalizing society. But such questions are, of course, a matter of opinion. What is not is that court decisions have encouraged uniform procedures and thus made cooperation and coordination easier among states and community officials.

Uniformity by Federal Grant.   Perhaps the most widely advertised method of achieving uniformity is by the federal government's offering the state government funds for programs—if, the states will but follow certain guidelines. The practice dates back to before the Union was formed, when under the Articles of Confederation, the western lands were divided into townships. These six-mile-square areas were each divided into thirty-six sections, each a square mile. Congress granted these lands to the states, but required them to set aside a section in each township, and later two sections, to support public schools. The federal government also used the land grant procedure for establishing agricultural colleges and, of course, to encourage railroad building by private operators.

About 80 percent of federal grants are detailed in what states and communities are required to do to get the funds. In the last decade the federal government has begun to experiment with grants that allow more discretion and choice at the state and community levels. We will discuss the various types of grant programs in detail in Chapter 6, State and Community Finances.

THE POLITICS OF FEDERALISM

Some may be inclined to believe, given the description of the rise of national power, that the end of the states as effective governing units is inevitable. Some also argue that it is desirable. The British political scientist Harold Laski, in 1939, argued, "American federalism is obsolescent and should be abandoned."[20] Some present-day political scientists agree.

We will argue that the "crossroads function" mediating between national and community policymaking is an important one and one we believe the states are capable of filling.

The Obsolescence of Federalism?

The political scientist Martin Landau concludes that the age of permissive or functional federalism is actually the age of the slow death of federalism. He thinks this is a reasonable development because he feels that federalism should not be regarded as an end in itself. We should not struggle, he suggests, to maintain a "specified balance of power and jurisdiction between state and nation." Rather, federalism should be regarded as "an instrument of social change, a problem-solving device that possesses utility only for a specified set of conditions." He argues that "once upon a time this country embarked on a voyage to nationhood." The federal system was established to become the instrument for creating a unified nation. And now "that nation concealed under federalism (has) finally emerged." The need for a federal division of powers has ended. "It is one of those instruments so designed as

[20]Harold J. Laski, "The Obsolescence of Federalism," *New Republic*, May 3, 1939, 367–369.

to outmode itself by its achievements." It has been a "dramatic success," and, therefore, is now "useless."[21]

Others who still see value in having some form of state system argue that our present state boundaries are anachronistic. In Policy Box No. 6, "Why Not Abolish the States?" we review the suggestions of several geographers to redraw state lines.

Defenders of Federalism

Other political scientists are not so sanguine about the nation's ability to dispense with the states or the federal system. They argue that positive benefits flow from decentralization, especially decentralization in which the subunits have *political* power to resist central direction.

[21]Martin Landau, "*Baker v. Carr* and the Ghost of Federalism," in Glendon Schubert, (ed.) *Reapportionment*, Charles Scribner, N.Y., 1965, 241–248.

POLICY BOX NO. 6: Why Not Abolish the States?

If you look closely at the states, you may come to the same conclusion as that of several geographers—that state boundaries are irrational and inefficient. Some political scientists have reached the same conclusion.

A glance at the map shows some of the problems. Begin by looking at shapes. Geographers think states should be compact. Note how West Virginia snakes out stems to the north and east like a cantaloupe vine. Or why should Florida have all that western coastline that could logically be southern Alabama? Why should that Upper Penninsula be part of Michigan or that pipestem be attached to Idaho?

Should not states be similar in size? Why have differences in area from Rhode Island's 1214 square miles to Alaska's 586,412 square miles?

Look next at the natural barriers within and between states. Since east and west are so different in the Dakotas, should we not have an East and West Dakota, rather than a North and South Dakota? Are not the hill areas of western Virginia, North Carolina, eastern Kentucky, and Tennessee more like West Virginia than they are like the rest of their states?

Geographers say that rivers as boundaries are a hangover from days when the river provided a military barrier. Today they argue that the river valleys should be in one state—as is most of the Missouri River. Both sides of the Missouri are in Montana, then North Dakota, South Dakota, and Missouri. But the river forms a boundary between Nebraska and Iowa and thus, geographers argue, breaks up a natural community between two states. Our biggest river, the Mississippi, forms a boundary

---

along its whole route, except for small portions at each end in Minnesota and Louisiana. If we drew boundaries logically we might use straight lines, such as are found in Utah, Wyoming, Colorado, and other western states.

States, the geographers argue, should be built around a metropolis; some suggest regional centers. The Chicago *Tribune* recognizes that it publishes for "Tribuneland" or "Chicagoland," an area they define as southern Wisconsin, southwest Michigan, and northern Illinois and Indiana. Should not Connecticut and northern New Jersey be part of the same state that holds New York City since so many people living in those states commute daily to the "Big Apple."

Are not the older historical differences unimportant and blurring out? Thirty years ago, the political scientist Roy V. Peel argued that we should move to regional governments, since states are no longer as distinctive in culture as they once were. In redoing the map we might also take into account the relative wealth of the states, or we might try to set up distinctively urban or distinctively rural states. Or perhaps it would be better to have some kind of mix of each. Or should we try to draw the lines so that they would make reasonable administrative districts for various federal programs?

On pages 92 and 93 you will see the maps as two geographers have redrawn state boundaries—one of thirty-eight states, the other of sixteen regions. They have even provided names.

What do you think? Should state boundaries be redrawn? Would there be any political or social costs? Would some groups or individuals gain and some groups or individuals lose? Which groups or individuals? Would it strengthen the states when opposing the national government? What kind of logical system makes the best sense? On what principles would you construct the new states? Do you think the effort would be worth the trouble? Why?

SOURCE: Roy V. Peel, *State Government Today*, University of New Mexico Press, Albuquerque, 1948; Stanley D. Brunn, "Geography and Politics of the United States in the Year 2000," *The Journal of Geography*, April 1973, 42–49 and G. Etzel Pearcy, *A 38 State U.S.A.*, Plycon Press, Fullerton, California, 1973.

Administrative Efficiency.   Vincent Ostrom attacks the assumption of those he calls "centralists"—that an efficient administrative system can be devised in which all direction and decisions come from the center. He argues that state exercise of political power, rather than being dysfunctional, encourages efficiency. It provides feedback that must be heeded because states and community leaders represent more than the administrative field offices of federal agencies. It allows selective innovation; innovation which, if unsuccessful, is contained within a single state and, if successful, can be made national in scope.[22]

[22]Ostrom's full argument is stated in Vincent Ostrom, *The Political Theory of A Compound Republic*, Public Choice Publication, Blacksburg, Virginia, V.P.I & S.U., 1971.

Reducing Value Conflict. Others, sharing Ostrom's view, argue that federalism helps to reduce conflict by allowing local majorities to follow differing policies. For example, we find wide variation among states in their laws on gambling. Nevada has the casino reputation. A few others operate state lotteries and some are relatively straight-laced. If there were a national law, what would we have it be—wide open gambling in the Nevada style, some gambling that would be nationally regulated, or no legal gambling permitted at all? Putting the question this way makes some citizens wonder if the U.S. is ready for a uniform gambling law, or whether the existing variations may not have some benefit.

This question of variations that Americans will tolerate boils down, we think, to how much we believe a national consensus has developed in respect to a specific issue or program. If most American citizens want the same thing, the benefits of diversity among the states are largely imagined. When there are wide variations or even if an intense minority desires difference, conflict such as erupted over the Supreme Court's decisions on busing and abortion will likely result. That conflict seems to take its most severe form over cultural and life-style issues. In some cases conflict to achieve uniformity may be a price worth paying, in others, not. Deciding which is the case is a political question.

The States and Communities as Political Training Grounds. Supporters of federalism argue also that state and community office has often been a training ground, a sorting-out process for selecting national leaders. Partially this has been the case, although not all national officials have had state or community experience similar to that found in the political careers of Jimmy Carter or Walter "Fritz" Mondale who were both statewide elected officials. We have also all observed the benefits that may result because state and, especially, local government offers opportunity for participation by nonprofessionals who want to "play" at politics, but who are not yet sure they want to make a career of it.

Federalism and Freedom. Finally we come to the argument that federalism protects the freedom of citizens—if in no other way than by providing important elective offices that the party out of power may capture and use to criticize the national administration. Some political scientists believe this argument has been overstated.[23] They note that

---

[23]William H. Riker, *Federalism, Origin, Operation, Significance*, Little, Brown and Co., Boston, 1964. See also Franz Neumann, "Federalism and Freedom: A Critique" in Arthur W. Macmahon (ed.) *Federalism: Mature and Emergent*, Doubleday and Co., Garden City, N.Y., 1955, 44–57.

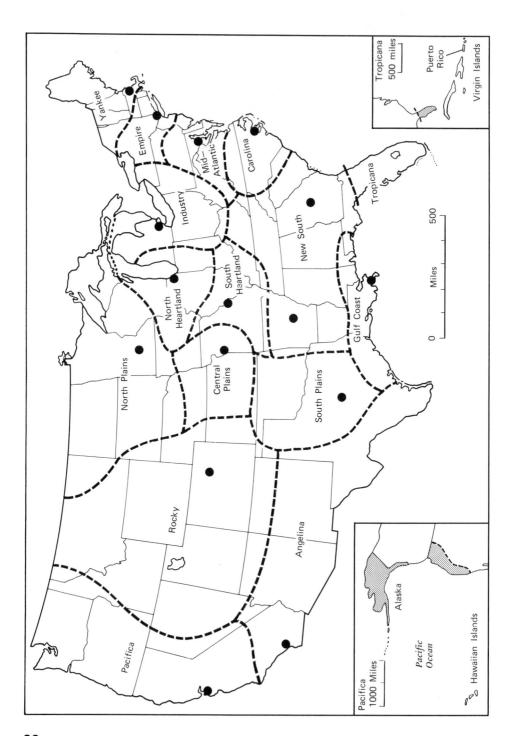

Yankee

Empire

Mid-Atlantic

Carolina

Industry

North Heartland

South Heartland

New South

Gulf Coast

Tropicana

North Plains

Central Plains

South Plains

Rocky

Angelina

Pacifica

500

Miles

0

Tropicana
500 miles

Puerto
Rico

Virgin Islands

Pacifica
1000 Miles

Pacific
Ocean

Alaska

Hawaiian Islands

the freedoms protected may be freedoms that should not be protected, such as the freedom of Mississippi whites to discriminate for many years against local blacks.

Nevertheless we suspect that with many of us it is an article of faith that federalism does protect freedom. This is most clearly apparent when we ask ourselves whether we would favor centralizing all police into a single national force. Some citizens are also disturbed by an increasing tendency of new regulations to be issued from the nation's capital—they are, perhaps, most seriously disturbed by those from administrators or the courts who are not elected. For example, state governments as widely separated as Alaska and Louisiana in 1977 to 1978 legalized the use of Laetrile to fight cancer—a drug that professional medical researchers say is useless and which the federal government has barred from the market. Is this defense of local freedom to be applauded? Perhaps not. Still it is, perhaps, indicative of a feeling of uneasiness—a feeling that from time to time, we should remind officials at all levels that uniform rules should rest on the consent of the governed in a democracy. Even when the governed are wrongheaded, perhaps it is better to persuade them of their errors, rather than try to overwhelm them.

We conclude, not suprisingly for the writers of a state and community government text, that enough reasons still exist to justify the preservation of the federal system.

How Do States Defend Themselves from National Domination?

It is the political realities of American politics that preserve the federal system rather than the legal phrases that describe the division of powers. When a decision about that division is made by national elective officials, states and communities tend to have their greatest influence. When the courts make policy, as they have recently about many matters, state governments tend to have their least influence. Decisions made or implemented by federal administrators permit some state and community influence; it is about divisions in administrative responsibility, in fact, that some of the most important issues are presently being fought out. We look at the weapons states possess that permit them to bring state-based viewpoints to national policymaking—what we have called the crossroads function.

Influence Through National Legislators.   An important rule of American politics is that a senator or representative, once defeated for renomination or election, cannot reasonably hope to run successfully for office anywhere again except back in his or her home state. Career ambitions thus encourage "national" representatives to cultivate the opinion of their district and states.

This fact leads U.S. senators and representatives to intercede with federal officials on behalf of home state individuals and interest groups. Morton Grodzins argued that "the most important and pervasive method of legislative participation in the administrative process is through activities of individual legislators on behalf of local constituents. Workers on Capitol Hill call this their 'case work.' "[24]

State interest groups and national legislators. Such case work may be more than working out a snarl in a Veterans Administration pension. Some home state groups urge national representatives to oppose replacing state regulation with national regulations. Such groups usually feel they have more influence with state or community governments than they would in the national political arena—the extractive industries that mine coal and ore or drill oil have sometimes dominated their states to the point of scandal. But other home state groups with less questionable motives may also feel that a state that depends on the industry's prosperity will give a more sympathetic hearing to their problems.

Allied with the larger interest groups are many smaller industries and professions that are now largely regulated by states, such as lawyers, insurance agents, realtors, accountants, doctors, dentists, and many others. They, too, recognize that they are likely to have more state than national influence. These groups will fight hard to keep control at the state level and often work through their U.S. senators and representatives.

A different kind of group may also favor state power, such as social or religious groups that, through accident, are concentrated within a few states and have more than average influence within them. The Mormon church has such influence in Utah and Idaho. The Catholics are especially strong in states such as Massachusetts and Connecticut, and favored state control of such matters as abortion or sale of birth control devices. Southern whites were, until recently, strong defenders of states rights in order to maintain racial barriers.

State government contacts with national legislators. It is becoming apparent that these "national" officials cultivate more than just the voters or local interest groups. They also develop strong ties to state and community officials. Recent studies reveal regular meetings some-

---

[24]For an extended discussion see Morton Grodzins, "American Political Parties and the American System," *Western Political Quarterly* 13, December 1960, 974–998.

times publicized in newspaper stories between these U.S. senators and representatives, and governors and members of the state bureaucracy or legislature. When a bill is being considered in Washington D.C. the senator's staff, perhaps, will contact state or local officers with specialized knowledge to find out what impact the law may have in the home state.

At the same time state legislators and administrators, now more than in the past, lobby their national representatives. Sometimes such lobbying is at the urging of groups such as the Council of State Governments, the United States Conference of Mayors, or some professional association, such as the National Association of Social Workers. Some of this lobbying by state and community officials, of course, is the result of their own specialized interests in a particular national program.

State Influence on Presidential Elections.   A second major line of defense for state power is the political party system, and especially the rules that exist for nomination and election of presidents. They work out, we discover, so that citizens and party leaders of every state have some influence over who is nominated and elected as president and vice president. Presidential candidates must cultivate state and community political leaders, officials, citizens, and interest groups. Disaffection by state or local party leaders may cost the loss of a state (special effort by local leaders may result in its gain). Mayor Richard Daley of Chicago was thought to have won the 1960 presidential election for John F. Kennedy by winning Illinois for the Democrats.

The electoral college rules magnify the influence of state party officials, the winner in a state gets all its electoral votes. A small number of votes in a large closely contested state, such as Ohio, may be the difference between victory or defeat in the whole election. Presidential candidates, thus, are forced to cultivate state party leaders, state-based interest groups, and state voters.

National influence on state officials.   At the same time, the national party or national officials can do little to influence the choice of state or local political leaders, nor do they have major methods of disciplining them. The national party may refuse to seat dissident state leaders at the national party convention, as happened to some Mississippi Democrats in 1964. They may deny them patronage "plums" or even prosecute state or community officials for income tax evasion or other crimes, as happened to the Huey Long faction of Louisiana under Franklin Delano Roosevelt. But all of these methods of discipline are also likely to hurt the national party and the president, as well. The net gain may be very little, since the disciplined state or local politician keeps getting reelected and may, in fact, gain new popularity by claiming "national interference" in state or local affairs. At the same time congressional votes needed on a president's "must" legislation may fade away. Future support in elections may be lukewarm as it was in some states after the disastrous Republican national convention of 1964, or that of the Democrats in 1972. The president and national party leaders will move carefully before they undertake such disciplining.

The balance of federal political power.　When we describe the situation from the state and community viewpoint, it suggests that all battles are won by the states. This is a false impression, for, as we will discuss later in Chapter 11, our party system is beginning to centralize, thus increasing powers of national officials. Nor are all state and community officials always lined up on one side with the national party leaders on the other. In a few cases that may occur. More frequently, however, some state and local officials are lined up with the president and some parts of the national party against other state or local officials or party leaders. The national party may indeed move to discipline some state leaders at the insistence of leaders from other states.

Over the long haul the national officials, especially if led by the president, are likely to win at least part of what they desire—because their desires are in part a response to what they believe significant segments of voters and some state officials desire. But they are not likely to win all they want and they will pay a cost. The rules permit state officials, party leaders, interest groups and ordinary citizens to slow down, delay and even check for the time being the national elected officials.

State Government Resistance to Federal Administrators.　We find sometimes that state governments will also resist what they regard as unwise or unworkable federal policy. They may succeed in getting Congress or the federal administrative agency to compromise or even to relax all enforcement efforts. This happened when Nebraska, Kentucky, Idaho, and Minnesota refused to provide mandatory training and testing for farmers who used highly toxic chemicals. The national Environmental Protection Agency finally suggested as a compromise that farmers should be required to take some training in the application of such chemicals, but that they did not have to pass a test that would demonstrate that they were qualified to use the materials.[25] Or the state may

[25]"States Ignore Pesticides Control," *State Journal*, Lansing, Michigan, May 18, 1976.

attempt to delay implementation of the federal policy. Minnesota, for example, became the first state to require a state license from the Board of Health before a federal atomic energy facility could be built.

States in the Federal Courts.   As we have suggested, the federal courts have been among the most important agencies in centralizing decision making in our federal system. States have gone to court occasionally and won battles with the federal government—as when twenty-six states and Puerto Rico sued to prevent food stamp cutbacks in 1976. Presently the Pennsylvania legislature has brought suit to appropriate federal grant funds before they go into the budget of administrators—a point we will discuss in Chapter 7 on legislatures. But generally states and communities opposing federal regulations have lost in the courts.

Intergovernmental Relations and Community Governments

Here we briefly sketch in high points of the changing relations between state and national governments and community governments. We will treat the topic of intergovernmental relations more fully in Chapter 14.

The contacts among the units of the American federal system are a mixture of the legal and the political. Both the state and federal governments have legal powers that permit a great deal of intervention in community affairs. Practically, though, the communities still have considerable political power to resist and delay such intervention.

States and Their Community Governments.   The relations between states and their local governments are similar to those between the states and national government. Again we note the crossroads function—in this case, bringing more general viewpoints into formation of policy at the community level. At one time state and local functions were somewhat separate. But increasingly we find attempts by states to guide local activities.

While legally the relationship is unitary we find the political pattern of cooperative federalism. We can see in most states that dual federalism, if it ever existed in pure form, is now dead. Localities no longer travel alone as they wrestle with what once were regarded as purely local problems. States and their local governments now cooperate—services such as water pollution or even crime control are seen, at least in part, as a state problem.

We can also see the shaping of the familiar features of both permissive federalism and functional federalism. States are not content simply to intervene occasionally on a few aspects of a functional area to help localities on the local problems. States are beginning to establish their own broad-scale goals. State agency administrators are beginning to view themselves as responsible for a wide variety of local programs in the area of their functional specialty as, for example, in the push in a number of states for statewide land use planning and control.

How States Attempt to Influence Community Decisions. States, in a few cases, have taken over from community governments full responsibility for specialized services, such as crime lab work, arson investigation, tax assessment of industrial property, or the inspection of hospitals or industry. They also commonly provide grants to local governments—grants with strings attached.

In respect to such services as education, health, welfare, and general property tax assessment, state administrative agencies have strengthened their supervisory role. Direct supervision is accomplished through inspections, requiring reports, establishing training classes for local officials, review of construction or other plans, and conferences. The health department lobbies the legislature to tighten up local septic tank inspections, while the state treasury requires local governments to follow uniform accounting procedures, and the welfare department requires that county welfare workers be hired under state rules and often from a state-prepared register.

In addition, states regularly add to the duties they require local governments to perform. We find that a common complaint of local officials is that the money to carry out the program does not always accompany the requirement, for example, that the state requires local health departments to inspect restaurants, or the counties to pay burial fees for indigent veterans, without providing the funds.

Community resistance to state control. We should not, however, conclude that the cities, school districts, and counties are left powerless. They, too, have political power, especially in respect to state-elected officials. Governors, state senators, state representatives, attorneys general and other officials need local political support—support of party officials, interest groups, and community voters. Communities also use the familiar tactics of slowdown or delay to resist state administrative supervision.

Federal-Community Relations. Beginning in the 1930s the federal government began to deal directly and on a relatively regular basis with community governments. Among the first important programs of this sort were the public housing project grants. Such contacts continued to grow after the war years and sharply increased in the early 1960s, when the federal government embarked on programs designed to help solve the problems found in America's great cities—poverty, racism, crime, and other forms of social disorganization. To a lesser extent, but still in a noticeable way, federal programs also reached many rural communities, especially those with poverty problems. Other grant programs that expanded federal-local contacts included water and air pollution, building of sewage plants or airports, urban mass transportation, and urban expressway construction.

Part of the reason that the federal government so frequently chose to bypass the states during this period is that many federal administrators and politicians regarded state governments as grossly inefficient and also as unsympathetic to the problems of urban areas. This pattern has changed somewhat since, but some suspicion of the states remains at both national and community levels.

State reaction to "Bypass" provisions. The state governments, especially through the National Governors Conference, objected strenuously to direct federal-local relations. They want "pass through" legislation—federal grant programs that contain provisions that: (1) the state authorize community participation in federal grant programs, and (2) the grant monies pass through the state controls. In addition, states prefer to have and sometimes obtain the power to receive federal funds as a block grant that they could then allocate to communities within the state as they thought desirable. Funds in respect to police administration have been handled in this fashion.

The states, through lobby efforts in Washington, have made some headway in becoming federal grant coordinators for community governments, but they have also lost some of these battles.

Recent expanded federal-local contacts. Almost unnoticed by state officials are the number of newer federal grant programs that have increased federal-local contacts. One of these is general revenue sharing, which was passed first in 1972. It arranged for the federal government to send funds to states, cities, counties, and townships. For the first time in the nation's history the federal government has direct contact with every local government in the country that carries out general functions. And some strings are attached. Community governments that accept the funds may not, for example, discriminate in hiring on the basis of race or sex and they must report how the funds were spent. If local communities become dependent on the funds, they may find it difficult not to comply, even if later the federal government adds other requirements.

Other federal programs also are reaching into community governments. CETA, the Comprehensive Employment Training Act, provides community governments with employees who are paid with federal funds. Financially hard-pressed local governments are grateful at the same time that they become more dependent on such aid. Also, the federal government, in attempting to alleviate the recession of 1976, granted funds directly to the high unemployment communities, rather than working through the states.

The impact of the federal courts in communities. All of us have become familiar with the increased concern of the federal courts with community efforts to achieve racial integration of schools through busing. But a great many other types of community concerns, from affirmative action to pornography regulation, crime control, or registration of voters, are being decided in federal courts. It is a rare mayor or county commissioner who today is not sensitive to the actions of this arm of the federal government.

A Final Comment

As we look back over the kind of complex system Americans have created, we can see many successes and we also may occasionally be dismayed. What appears to be among the most complex, conflictual, and frustrating of governing systems may be among the world's strongest. It has flexibility. It allows for orderly change without revolution to meet new social conditions. It is a system that provides an endless course of options. It provides for uniformity where the needs seem clear-cut to many citizens, but at the same time preserves some local "clout" for handling problems. It distributes political power in ways that assure that centralization will not come easily by fiat, but only as the need for it (sometimes with an element of pressure) becomes accepted by a democratically governed people. In this kind of system, as John Bebout once observed, the national government has been the states' best friend—without a national government, states could not otherwise exist as independently as they do.[26]

[26]John E. Bebout, "The States' Best Friend" *National Civic Review* 53, February 1964, 70–73, *passim*.

HIGHPOINTS OF CHAPTER 3: STATES AND COMMUNITIES IN A FEDERAL SYSTEM

In this chapter we looked first at (1) the legal facts of federalism—the legal portion of states, local units, the District of Columbia, the Commonwealth of Puerto Rico, and the other territories and possessions. We then examined (2) how the actual powers exercised by the national governments and the states had gradually shifted from state dominated to a nationally directed system. We then examined (3) how the states voluntarily cooperate and how the federal government, using especially its grants, has brought about national direction. We ended by looking at (4) the role left to the states, and especially emphasized their growing tendency to direct the actions of their own local units.

COMMUNITIES IN THE FEDERAL SYSTEM

Except for the few people who have traveled to the moon, seldom have any of us been any place not in the jurisdiction of several local governments. Although these local governments affect our lives very directly—we may have been born in one of their hospitals, ridden their buses, drunk their water, studied under their teachers, and picnicked in one of their parks —most of us are often confused on how they all fit together. Let us look at these local governments from a national perspective, say that of the president, or the head of a national agency.

The View from The Nation's Capital

What such national officials see is a large number of local units of government—over 80,000—and a great deal of variety, as well. All are units created by the states, but what they do, how they select their officials, what powers they exercise, and what their relationships are to each other varies among states and often within the same state.

Also sometimes befuddling are the names of the local units. In Alaska, for example, boroughs are pretty much the same as counties elsewhere. But in Pennsylvania, New York, and New Jersey, boroughs are urban governments, only a step below a city. These distinctions provide no little problem for national government, especially when the Congress and administrators try to determine which should qualify for a specific federal aid program.

U.S. Bureau of the Census reports provide the best overall source of information about types of local governments and how many there are. (See Table 4-1.)

The long-term trend in the number of local governments has been downward as the result of consolidation of school districts and elimination of townships. But more recently—from 1972 to 1977—we find special districts and new cities have increased, and we find an upturn in the total number again.

Overview In this chapter we will consider this composite picture of community governments. We begin by looking at the development of local governments. We will find that these governments came about as pragmatic responses to new conditions. We will also see in the overall pattern an assumption that two main types of local governments could handle most problems—for rural areas (counties and townships) and for urban areas (cities and villages). These units at first were seen to be basically self-contained—insulated from and unaffected by each other. But the assumption proved to be false as technology diminished the differences in the kinds of problems each had to deal with. Next we will consider the legal framework of today's community governments and their legal relationships to the states. Then we turn to the organizational structures they employ, and why these are used. Finally we will consider the limitations of community governments, and why state and federal governments have become involved in what were once largely thought to be local affairs.

LOCAL GOVERNMENTS ON THEIR OWN—ALMOST

The states have been ambivalent about their community governments—on one hand we find that the states have given the localities a broad range of functional powers—powers to carry on activities that some local citizens wanted their communities to conduct; on the other the states have also insisted that the local units carry out these duties in specific ways—ways local officials complain are too detailed. They ask with some justification—Are we to be treated as adults or as children by the state?

State Ambivalence Over Local Unit Powers

History helps us understand the present pattern of state-local relations. We note that cities, rather than the states, were first on the scene. Some cities, for their time, had extensive service programs

TABLE 4-1 Number of Local Governments—1952, 1972, 1977

Governments	1952	1972	1977	Percent Change 1952– 1977	Percent Change 1972– 1977
Counties	3,052	3,044	3,042	- 3.3	-0.1
Municipalities	16,807	18,517	18,856	12.2	1.8
Townships & Towns	17,202	16,991	16,882	- 2.2	-1.0
School Districts	67,355	15,781	15,260	-77.3	-3.3
Special Districts	12,340	23,885	26,140	111.8	9.4
Total	116,756	78,218	80,120	-31.4	2.4

SOURCE: U.S. Bureau of the Census, *Census of Governments*, 1978.

under way before state governments were organized. At the same time these new states were concerned with other matters—the development of natural resources and encouragement of outlying settlements.

This early relationship had costs for the states—administrators in the cities, not the states, often were the first to develop expertise in police and fire functions, public health, education, water supply, roads, sanitation, or whatever. City officials therefore became leaders and state officials followers in many of these policy areas. Just where, when, and how the states should move into urban program areas was later to become a puzzle to state officials.

Courthouse in Montpelier, Vermont.

Yet the states had the legal power to create local units and to specify which functions they were to handle. During the nineteenth century, state officials exercised such control mainly for partisan political advantage. But in more recent times we find that many persons have concluded that only state governments or, perhaps, the federal government can solve many local problems—especially those of large cities such as New York, but now also of the suburbs and small and middle-sized cities, such as we find in rural Maine and Vermont. Many state officials have come to conclude that they have a responsibility to coordinate their local governments, but they are left with a pattern of state-local relationships that still handicaps this effort.

The Rural-Urban Division of Local Government.   The form of local governments that the states created were pragmatic responses to what state officials saw—(1) a sharp division in the governing needs between rural and urban areas, and (2) the self-evident fact that local governments could manage most local problems by themselves and at the same time could carry out some state responsibilities.

The set of governments established for rural areas were generally counties—in some northern states these were supplemented by townships. The counties were designed so that residents could reach the county seat and return home in a day's buggy ride. The idea was to give counties a uniform organizational structure, the freedom of residents to choose their own officials, and the authority to exercise as state branch offices some basic powers—law enforcement, courts, jails, elections, taxation, and land records. Rural areas did not need much more government than that.

State officials, though, recognized that the urban areas might need to be organized differently and to have some additional powers. (They, in fact, already had them in many cases.) When people in new communities saw the need, they could ask the state legislature for permission to establish a village or city government. More often than not, these cities assumed the county's duties within their limits, as well as exercising other powers. The cities had representatives on the county board of supervisors or commissioners and continued to pay county taxes. But they received few services from the county.[1]

When citizens living on the fringe of a village or city wanted municipal services, they could annex and join the village or city. Then as two or more cities, through annexation, extended their boundaries to each other, the two cities could consolidate and become a single new city.

[1]This is a footnote for a limited audience. Almost everywhere, cities are a part of a county and their residents pay both city and county taxes. But Virginia's cities and a few large cities such as St. Louis and Denver are separate from counties.

The Response to Technology. The apparent division between rural and urban governments began to collapse under twentieth-century conditions. Technology blurred the distinction. Transportation, first light rail interurban lines and later automobiles, enabled people to live in small satellite communities outside the cities. Moreover, new septic systems and well-drilling techniques, as well as the extension of electric and telephone wires, provided basic amenities in the countryside once available only through city governments.

The earlier pattern of relationships between states and community governments, however, persisted long after the point when the conditions that inspired them have all but vanished.

The Politics of State-Local Relations

Local governments exist as legal entities with the permission of the states. They are subject in minute detail to state rules. At the same time, we find that these local governments are able to influence these state rules through the political relationships.

Dillon's Rule. Local governments, unlike the federal government or the states, do not derive their legal authority from their own sovereign status. We find, instead, that the states create the local governments and enable them or limit them by law in respect to the functions they perform. The judicial rule that undergirds this relationship is Dillon's Rule. It states that municipal corporations possess only those powers that (1) have been granted to them specifically, (2) are necessarily or can be fairly implied in the expressed powers given, and (3) are indispensable to the declared objects and purposes of the corporation.[2]

As we might expect, a legal doctrine such as this could provide a highly constraining environment for local officials. At times it has provided just that. We will see later, though, that state officials and state legislatures must apply this doctrine in a political context. It is the political context that gives the localities greater flexibility and independence than Dillon's Rule would seem to allow. In Policy Box No. 7, "The Worst Open Dump in Iowa," we can see some of this political and, indeed, legal independence being displayed.

Local governments, then, have a great stake in the actions of the legislature and state agencies. They respond to this condition in the same way that private interest groups do—they take aggressive action to influence state and national legislative and administrative decisions that

[2]See John F. Dillon, *Commentaries on the Law of Municipal Corporations*, 5th ed., Little, Brown and Company, Boston, 1911.

POLICY BOX NO. 7   The Worst Open Dump in Iowa!

Piled up for three-quarters of a mile on a roadside in Johnson County, Iowa, are rusted car bodies, mangled corn cribs, abandoned refrigerators, worn out mattresses, thousands of beer cans, and debris of every imaginable description. Local folks called it the "Lone Tree Dump" after the nearby town in southeastern Iowa. State officials called it "the worst dump in Iowa right now" (October 1976).

The Lone Tree Dump was more than just an eyesore to the few passersby on the gravel country road. One of the problems was that as the garbage and trash accumulated, some of it, especially during flood season, had gotten into a nearby creek that runs into the Iowa River. In this way the Lone Tree Dump has become one of the major pollution sources for one of Iowa's larger streams.

The Iowa Department of Environmental Quality ordered Johnson County to prevent further dumping and to clean up the mess. The order allowed the county thirty days to do the job. Johnson County officials agreed that it ought to be cleaned up, but they did not think their citizens should have to pay the costs. They estimated cleanup cost to be $1 million. State officials said they had no money for the cleanup.

In addition to their unwillingness to foot the entire cleanup bill, Johnson County officials noted that the county did not even own all the land included in the dumpsite area. Some of it, they said, was owned by the state conservation commission and another portion by the U.S. Army Corps of Engineers. In addition, Johnson County officials noted that the dump was located near the place where Johnson County and three other counties join. They claimed that all of the refuse was not dumped in the Lone Tree Dump by Johnson County residents. Johnson County supervisor Lorada Cilek said, "The county is willing to accept the responsibility if it's our land and we get the money. We're not trying to shirk our responsibilities." In the meantime the Johnson County Board of Supervisors ordered the county attorney to appeal the state order.

Peter Hamlin, director of land quality management for the state, did not agree that the county had been doing everything it could to stop the dumping and to find the cleanup funds. Hamlin said that the county owns thirty-three feet of land from the center of the road and "that's where the dumping has been taking place." The garbage dumped on state land, Hamlin said, "has been pushed there by county road maintenance workers."

Hamlin said that all the county has done was to post a few signs, telling folks that dumping is illegal. At the least, Hamlin suggested, the sheriff should "nab a few of the dumpers and fine them. That would help." Hamlin also suggested that the county could put a large steel box at the site to accommodate the people who do dump there and build a strong fence around the rest of the area to discourage dumping big loads. The sheriff said that he and his men were too busy to patrol the dump. He suggested that the county hire a watchman to stay at the dump.

Peter Hamlin was not encouraged by the immediate outlook. He said the county's appeal of the order will mean that a hearing will be scheduled in Iowa City, and then the county can appeal the order in the courts. And during this process,

affect them. They form organizations, employ lobbying agents, and use public funds to finance them.

Lobbying and Local Government Associations

Local public officials and employees exercise their political power through personal contact with state and national legislators, but also work through statewide and national organizations. These groups provide a variety of informational and educational services to their members, but their main purpose is to lobby higher level governments—legislators and administrators—for favorable actions. Often, they direct local officials to contact state or national legislators on specific issues and bills. Occasionally we will also find these associations in court, participating in a case they consider important to the overall interest of their local unit membership.

The state municipal league usually represents the broad interests of the middle-sized and smaller cities and villages in the state. The larger cities are likely to have somewhat different interests, and so are likely to have their own agent or employee assigned to lobby state government, and often the state municipal league as well. At the national level, both large and small units will be represented by the National League of Cities. And most big-city mayors will be members of the U.S. Conference of Mayors. Some large cities have their own lobbyist in Washington as well.

The pattern for county governments is a bit more complex because the various county officers often have their own separate associations. County commissioners usually operate at the state level under the aegis of a state association of counties. In addition, however, county clerks may have their state association—as do the sheriffs, health boards, probate judges, dog catchers, and others. With so many speaking for county government, messages from counties to the state legislatures sometimes become competitive and garbled. The National Association of Counties is the principal voice of county commissioners in the nation's capital, although many county officer groups have their own lobbying associations as well.

A somewhat comparable situation pertains to the field of education. School board members and school administrators, as well as parent and teacher groups, each have a state and national association. The powerful teacher groups usually seek to improve the economic and working conditions of teachers.

Although these organizations are not part of the formal governing structure, they play an extremely important part in the shaping of intergovernmental relations and the formation of state and national policies. In many instances these associations are initiators of public policies at the state and national levels. For the last two or three years, for example, the National Association of Counties has been printing pictures of dangerous bridges on county roads as a preliminary step to pressing for a federal bridge assistance program.

The Effectiveness of Local Government Lobbying

In some instances local officials can cooperate very effectively in exercising their political clout. State legislators and members of Congress must go back to their districts, account for their actions, and stand for reelection. Few legislators want to go back to the district to explain, for example, why they voted to reduce federal or state aid to local governments—particularly if the reduction may lead to a local tax increase or cut in services. Community officials, especially when they, too, are elected on a partisan ballot, can make it tough for a legislator who does not help the local government at the state capital.

But local government agents also face intense opposition on a large percentage of the issues that concern them. The fight may come from a competing local government organization, a state employee union, or a private interest group, and even come from members of their own organization. A proposal for metropolitan consolidation may be advocated by central cities and opposed by suburban cities. Smaller counties often oppose reforms that are advanced by large counties, even though both pay dues to the same state association. The issues that these local associations are most likely to battle over are state aid, mandated programs, reorganization, annexation, collective bargaining, and wage and hour laws.

When local government interests conflict over an issue, the result is likely to be a stalemate and legislators then are not held responsible in the same way they would be over a matter on which local officials agree.

We recall a recent incident in the Michigan legislature to illustrate this point. The state teachers' association was pressing for the right to strike, a change that the school board association opposed. After considerable haggling in the legislature over the matter, the House Speaker "locked" representatives of the two groups in a nearby motel room to hammer out a compromise. After several weeks of meeting, they failed to agree. The legislature, as a result, made no change in the law.

Thus, although the states have a virtual life and death hold over the local governments, at least legally, the states are not able to use these powers fully to coordinate the affairs of local government. The political environment undercuts the power of the state to coordinate strongly. And so the states remain at least somewhat ambivalent regarding where and when to use their coordinating powers.

Lobbying by the National Association of Counties before the U.S. House Administration Committee on a proposed Universal Voter Registration Act. Giving testimony are an election commission from Monroe County (N.Y.), a Philadelphia city commissioner, a NACO legislative representative, a Los Angeles County registrar-recorder, the Michigan Director of Elections, and the Montgomery County (Md.) elections administrator.

THE TYPES OF LOCAL GOVERNMENT

Local units must obtain an authorization from the state in order to exist as a legal entity. The states have used various methods in granting legal powers to the local units as we will discover as we review in some detail the several types of community governments.

The County

Counties, as we saw earlier, began as state branch offices—each principal state officer had a counterpart in the county. The governor's counterpart, for example, was the county sheriff for law enforcement purposes, while the local agent for the secretary of state was the county clerk. Later, as state-organized departments such as health, welfare, and the like were formed, their county counterparts were also established. The idea was that county agencies would be the working arms of the state agencies, carrying out the state programs at local levels. These arrangements were imbedded in the state constitutions and today much of this pattern remains in the forty-eight states that have counties.[3] Direct election of county officials, rather than appointment by their state counterpart, produced stronger county officers—both politically and administratively—than otherwise would have been the case.[4]

Regional Variations. Counties were an adaptation of what the colonists knew in England, though modified to fit the conditions in the new land. In some states they were large in land area and carried out most local functions. In other states the reverse was true. New England settlers, for example, faced fierce climatic conditions, angry Indians, and difficult traveling conditions. Moreover, New England colonies were small and their economies, based as they were on fishing and shipping as well as agriculture, led to the development of compact communities, each with its own town government. Under these conditions the county did not gain much stature.

[3]Only Connecticut and Rhode Island do not have counties at all. As we noted earlier, Louisiana calls its counties parishes and Alaska calls them boroughs.

[4]County government has variously been called the "headless wonder" and the "dark continent of American government." In part this is because counties have no executive officer to attract attention and because very few books deal with county government on a national basis. The basic ones are Paul W. Wager, (ed.), *County Government Across the Nation*, University of North Carolina Press, Chapel Hill, 1950; Herbert S. Duncombe, *County Government in America*, National Associations of Counties, Washington, D.C., 1978; and John C. Bollens, et al., *American County Government*, Sage Publications, Inc. Beverly Hills, California, 1969.

The southern colonies faced entirely different conditions and developed strong county governments. Large parcels of land were granted to individuals who developed the plantation agricultural economy. The climate was mild and the rivers navigable. Settlement patterns, thus, were widely dispersed. Under such circumstances counties, controlled by a county court of landed gentry, flourished. Even today the county judge (not a judicial officer) is an important figure in county governments of the South.

Two other patterns of county organization developed. Pennsylvania, a state that formed both counties and townships, chose to have county boards of only three directly elected commissioners. Under this system counties became the dominant rural units. New York State influenced by the New England pattern, began by establishing towns. It later switched to a county commission approach similar to that of Pennsylvania. Neither proved satisfactory and so a compromise was reached calling for townships with each township supervisor serving as a county supervisor. Under this arrangement counties and townships shared local powers and duties. The later migrations from New York transplanted this form of county government in several midwestern states. But this method of selecting the county board was later largely undone by the U.S. Supreme Court rulings on one-person, one-vote representation in 1962.

The western states established large counties with small, directly elected, county commissions.

The Town Meeting

As we noted, the conditions peculiar to the settlers in New England led to the formation of town-meeting government. The New England colonial legislatures, and later the state legislatures, gave each town its own government and conveyed legal powers to them through general state laws.

Town formation had a heavy church influence at first—most were formed around church parish lines; some were organized as a result of schisms in the churches. We find that for the most part, the town forms a natural community—an urban settlement surrounded by a rural countryside, with a single town government.

Perhaps most characteristic of the town meeting is the extent to which *direct* democracy has been maintained through the annual meeting. The citizens of each town set aside a day for an annual meeting to elect the town officers, listen to reports from citizen committees and officials, and vote on the annual budget.

As with other governments, the town meeting has undergone change. Some urban towns, for example, now use a form of representative de-

Town meeting day, a citizen questions the elected officials.

mocracy where a hundred citizens or so are elected to act for the others. And town meetings, especially in Maine and Vermont, have hired town managers or have full-time clerks who serve as the chief administrative officers.

The Township

Except for townships in New York, New Jersey, and Pennsylvania, the early township was simply a surveyed area, six miles to a side. They were required by the Northwest Ordinance of 1787, at the urging of Thomas Jefferson, who sought to make of them "pure and elementary republics." Each was to have its own government, similar to the town meeting. In many of the Northwest Territory states, townships have not survived as governmental entities, as the states transferred their powers (road management and tax administration, most commonly) to other governments. In the few states where townships have survived, they are being transformed to perform functions usually provided by cities.[5]

Townships receive their legal powers through general laws of the state legislature. Their governing boards within each state commonly

[5]The U.S. Bureau of the Census identifies Michigan, New Jersey, Pennsylvania, New York, and Wisconsin as being "strong township" states. Illinois permits townships to exist at local option on a county basis. About half the Illinois counties have chosen to maintain them. These are mostly in the northern part of the state where immigrants from New York established the early patterns. The counties in the southern part of the state are modeled after the counties in the South.

are uniform, typically consisting of three officers—supervisor or chair-person, clerk, and treasurer—and two or four trustees, an office with few or no administrative duties. Townships generally continue the practice of holding an annual meeting, but most bear little resemblance to the New England town meeting.

The Chartering for Cities

The states could not readily decide how to grant powers to the cities. The problem was how to give cities legal powers through charters—a set of legal guidelines for a city, similar to a state or federal constitution—without losing state control. Several methods were developed, and some, as we will see, were applied to other local units as well as cities.

Special Act Charters.   Cities and villages are usually created when local residents decide more local powers are needed. Legislatures at first responded to such requests by passing special act charters, a law that applied only to a single city or village. They spelled out in detail its legal powers and government structure. Whenever a new kind of problem developed or local citizens wanted a change in the charter, they had to petition the legislature for an amendment to the charter.

Although several states, mostly in New England and the South, still use this approach, most states and local officials found it cumbersome. It gave legislators, some argued, too much power over their home cities, because without the endorsement of the local area legislator, legislatures would not approve charter amendments. Sometimes, indeed, local legislators proposed charter amendments that city officials did not want—measures designed to get jobs for friends or to undercut political enemies back home. Urban residents also resented the meddling and uncomprehending attitudes of some rural legislators who were determined to discipline cities on such matters as gambling or drinking laws.

By the 1850s Indiana and Ohio outlawed special act charters. Other states sought to limit the abuses by requiring local approval before legislative amendments could take effect.

General Law Charters.   With this approach the legislature passes a law that, in effect, becomes the charter for all cities or villages within a state.

Some states also use a general law charter to convey legal authority to counties and townships. The basic difference, though, is that "the charter" tends to consist of a series of laws passed over many years and together they form a kind of charter. Special districts, like the cities and villages, usually have a single law to which they can turn as their basic enabling statute. School districts have a statutory base similar to that of the counties, except that their laws are usually compiled in a state school code.

General law charters also were not entirely satisfactory for city governments. Any change in the general law affected all, from the largest metropolis to the smallest town. Those that needed a change sometimes found it difficult to convince other cities of its value.

Charters by City Class. The resulting rigidity that became part of the general law charters led the states to classify local units, usually according to population, area, or density. This enabled larger cities to get the kinds of charters they needed without affecting the smaller cities. But it also led to abuses similar to those associated with special act charters. Legislators ingeniously devised criteria to single out a target city—for example, specifying a class of cities with a population between 26,424 and 26,426—generally only one city in the state fit the class.

Optional Form Charters. The optional forms approach provides a kind of catalog of charters from which a city may choose. Each option is a general law, but cities are permitted a range of choices. Thus, the strong mayor form may be Option A, while Option B is the council-manager form. New Jersey offers its cities fourteen different options. Other states that use this approach have a much smaller product line.

Counties may also be permitted options. Utah, for example, permits its counties three options: an elected executive, a council-manager form, or an elected council form. Pennsylvania, New York, Michigan, and Wisconsin also permit their counties alternative forms of organization. The states have not moved faster with optional county forms, largely because state constitutions often specify the basic structure of county governments and require county organization to be uniform throughout a state. Thus, county modernization has come slowly.

Home rule charters. A final approach to charter development purports to avoid the problem of legislative interference. Although the home rule charter approach implies more self-government than is actually conveyed, it does allow a community to propose a charter that the voters then accept or reject. Charters are usually drafted by citizens elected to a charter commission. Charters may be changed from time to time through amendments proposed by the city council, by citizen initiative, or by a new or continuing charter commission. Revisions are then voted on by local residents.

The Iowa legislature in 1851 was the first to grant home rule by law. Home rule purists, however, generally prefer a constitutional provision as the basis for home rule because it presumably makes the legal arrangement less subject to the whims of the legislature. Missouri pioneered constitutional home rule in 1875. The home rule movement, at least for cities and villages, reached its peak in the early 1900s, primarily in the states of the West and Midwest. It had a brief resurgency in the 1950s when two southern states (Georgia and Louisiana) and two border states (Maryland and Tennessee) also adopted home rule provisions. The New England states and those in the South generally, do not employ home rule.

For county governments home rule has been a little longer in coming. A few states, such as California in 1911 and Maryland in 1915, permitted county home rule. But other states, such as Illinois and Pennsylvania, have permitted it only since the early 1970s. Most states however do not provide home rule for counties.

What does home rule provide? Home rule is limited self-government at best. Some states permit home rule only to municipalities that meet specified criteria, such as population or tax base. A more important limitation is that home rule charters do not put city governments beyond the reach of state legislatures. General state laws, such as those to provide freedom of information or open meetings, collective bargaining, or uniform accounting and election procedures, apply to all cities. The fine print of the law usually states "local charter provisions to the contrary notwithstanding."

Local charters are also limited by the law or by constitutions that determine the process for creating charters. States often require the legislature or governor to approve charters before they take effect. Thus, home rule does not imply that a city is free from Dillon's Rule.

Some state constitutions, however, now direct the courts to interpret state laws liberally in favor of the local units. Some students also suggest that home rule should be viewed by the courts as the authority to exercise any power not specifically prohibited by state law—a proposal first made by the political scientist Jefferson Fordham.

What are the benefits of local home rule? To the community itself the main benefit of home rule is that the community decides the form of government and the general pattern of representation—whether to elect at large or by ward, and whether elections are to be partisan or nonpartisan. It also permits the community to determine how many officers to have and which ones to elect or appoint. Local units may design the administrative structure and decide whether the departments are to be headed by elected or appointed administrators, boards, or commissions. As a general rule the localities tend to imitate the neighboring community government, but they also do a bit of experimenting and tinkering on the fine points of organization and structure.

Home rule also offers a community the chance to respond more gradually to changing conditions. As the population of a city grows more diverse, for example, the people may begin to feel that the council-manager form does not meet their needs for political leadership. They may then change the charter to have a full-time mayor or to elect the council from wards. Even when voters do not approve a change, the mere process of considering change can produce a psychological benefit—an attitude that says, "It may not be the best local government but it's our government. It wasn't decided for us by some group of legislators at the Capitol."

The Special Case of Schools

In most states education was treated as a function that required its own special organization—the local school district. It was transportation and ideology that made primary education a special case. States could not deliver educational services on the basis of a day's buggy ride and parents wanted to be familiar with local school conditions.

Because many believed that schools should be "kept free of politics," school districts in most states operate as separate local governments, rather than as a division of a city or county government. Although school districts are subject to a great deal of state regulation, most have locally elected nonpartisan governing boards to oversee the local school systems. They also are free to hire the school superintendent and teachers—teachers who are certified by the state. And although they have their own taxing powers, most need sizeable annual state grants to balance their operating budgets. This fact, together with the unionization of teachers, has drawn the schools foursquare into the tuggings and pullings of state and local politics and, to a lesser degree, federal politics as well.

The most startling structural change in recent years has been the consolidation of many small districts into fewer larger districts. Between 1952 and 1972 we find that the number of school districts dropped from 67,355 to 15,781. The pace has slowed considerably, however—in 1977 school districts numbered 15,260. Professional school administrators and teachers generally urged consolidation because larger districts would provide better facilities and specialized programs, as well as higher salaries. Many states encouraged consolidation by requiring, among other things, every school district to build a high school. Rural districts, faced with these demands, merged with others in similar situations.

Other Contemporary Forms of Local Government

The twentieth-century contribution to the structure of local government has been mainly in reform attempts to bring about coordination among local units.

The Special District. The special district has been the most important mechanism for bridging problems that overlap local boundaries. When local units can not handle a service need alone, generally because it overlaps several units and requires financing from all, they may create a special district unit, with representation of each local unit on its governing board.

Special districts provide a wide variety of functions, from mosquito control and hospitals to sanitary sewer systems and park facilities. They are usually funded by small amounts of local property taxes and revenues they receive for the services they provide. Their number is increasing rapidly. We will consider these in greater detail in Chapter 14 where we focus on the resolution of metropolitan and regional problems.

Structural Changes. Another contemporary approach has been to encourage structural changes in the more common forms of local government. Groups, such as the Committee for Economic Development, as well as federal officials, have proposed an area-wide multipurpose local government, generally for single metropolitan areas. But with few exceptions, such as the Miami-Dade County two-level approach, the plan used in the Minneapolis-St. Paul area, and the city-county consolidations such as that of Nashville-Davidson County scattered around the nation, few major recommendations have been implemented. These, too, will be reviewed in greater detail in Chapter 14.

HOW COMMUNITY GOVERNMENTS ARE ORGANIZED

Alexander Pope dismissed the debate over government form and structure with the couplet:

> For forms of government let fools contest,
> Whate'er is best administered is best.

The difficulty with this apparently simple solution is that over the years people have not always agreed on what is best and often have turned to the form of organization for a solution to their problems. As we discussed in Chapter 1, "good government" reformers saw the political machines as corrupt and graft-ridden evils to be eradicated. But the immigrants, the poor, the widows, orphans, and unemployed saw them as making the difference between starvation and subsistence.

We can catch a sense of what the machines meant to some citizens from the following quotation. The article quotes Ted Dubiel, captain of the thirty-ninth precinct, thirty-second ward in Mayor Richard Daley's Chicago:

"Look here" Dubiel told me, running his finger down the lists he had just pulled from his pocket. "We dispense services. That woman wanted something done about seepage in a depressed alley. He wanted two lids for the garbage cans. They wanted a sign, 'Slow, Children Playing.' She wanted therapy for Sam Nutzio, he's crippled up you know. And this grand old girl, she said the 55 gallon drums we gave her are too heavy. She can't carry them to the street. So I bought her a regular 32 gallon trash can out of my own pocket. And this fella, he told me to get the cheapest lawyer I could find so he could get divorced. I'll do something for him. I have a number of friends who are barristers. I'll tell one of them, 'Do it for 25 bucks, as a favor to me.' "[6]

That the bosses should have asked for little more in return than a vote at the next election seemed a small enough price to the recipients of those city services. But it is the reformers who had the last word in most communities. They put their stamp indelibly on city governments and other local units as well.

Five Elements of "Good Government" Organization.   When we examine what the reformers did to change conditions and tear the city machines apart, we find that they used five structural elements. Organizers of local government produced a great deal of variety in government forms, largely by the way they mixed these five elements into their structural recipes.

The executive power.   How to arrange for policy or political leadership and administrative efficiency is, perhaps, the most important of the five elements and is the key to the name of each form of city government. Is the executive power centered in an elected official, such as the mayor—an official who is likely to give primary emphasis to the political implications of decisions? Or is the government headed by a pro-

[6]James M. Perry, "Dick Daley: Last of the Big Bosses?" *National Observer*, January 1, 1977.

fessional administrator, such as a city manager or a school superintendent—an official who likely will place professional values of efficiency and technical expertise over political considerations? Or does the structure provide for no central executive at all?

Other structural elements. A second element deals with the question of elections—are they to be partisan or nonpartisan? Again we see some trade-offs involved, especially in large cities where life is impersonal. With nonpartisan elections people who have well-known names tend to be elected and members of the weaker party locally, have a better chance of winning. Partisan elections, on the other hand, may mean that power is closely held with the result that access may be difficult for many citizens. But responsibility and accountability may be easier to place.

A third element is representation—will the legislative body be elected from districts (in cities, these are called wards), or by elections-at-large, where voters from the entire city get to vote on every race? Is the council structured to bring together people who represent the various minority, ethnic, and economic groups as ward elections tend to do? Or, will the city choose councillors-at-large, a method that tends to stifle minority voices and accent a majority viewpoint? Some cities, we note, use a combination of at-large and ward elections. Some also nominate candidates by ward and conduct the elections at large.

A fourth element is the term of office—how long are they and will all officers be up for reelection at the same time? The longer the term, the more independent officials will tend to be. And if terms are staggered, citizens will usually find it more difficult to change the majority control and policies than if they can "throw all the rascals out" in one election.

A final element is the size of the legislative body. Two kinds of trade-offs are involved here. One has to do with the kind of work and activities that the legislative body will do. Will the council consist of generalists—people working on committees with broad assignments cutting across several dimensions of public business—as is more likely to be the case with small councils? Or will councillors be specialists—working on narrow assignments over which they tend to exercise virtually complete control. The second tradeoff deals with access. Opportunity for citizen access will tend to be lower with small councils than with large ones.

Basic Organization Plans

For the most part the differences among four basic forms—weak mayor, strong mayor, commission, and council manager—center around the arrangements for policy and administrative leadership. To lesser degrees they rely upon the other four elements.

Weak Mayor-Council Plan. Jacksonian Democrats were the architects of the weak mayor-council for local governments. It reflects two fundamental values: that executives should not be politically and administratively powerful and that citizens should have a strong voice in government affairs through the elective process.

The mayor in this plan, of course, was popularly elected, but so were many other administrative city officers as, for example, the treasurer, clerk, auditor, assessor, and often members of boards and commissions that the plan uses. The plan tended to make administrators and commissions independent of the mayor. As a result the mayors were weak —they did not have much authority over the city's administrative units. In some weak mayor plans, the mayor had authority to appoint board and commission members, but not the power to remove them. Consequently such members were not always responsive to the mayor's wishes.

Under the weak mayor-council plan, councils were often quite large —as many as fifty councillors was not uncommon. Neither was it unusual at one time for a council to be bicameral. Now all city councils except that of Everett, Massachusetts are unicameral. Councillors ran from wards, rather than from the city-at-large, and on a partisan basis. Terms were short—a year or two—and were seldom staggered.

As we study the powers of the council, we can see further how the Jacksonians used policy and administrative leadership considerations to keep the executive administratively weak. Although the mayor often had a veto power over the council legislation, the council had responsibility for developing the city budget, as was characteristic of the period for state governments as well. Mayors thus could provide a check on reckless councils, but not exercise this tool of policy leadership.

The weak mayor-council plan today.   The weak mayor-council form today is used primarily by smaller cities. But they have made substantial modifications in the plan. Councils are much smaller, elections are mostly nonpartisan, and usually a budget is prepared by the mayor. The weak mayor-council plan, with its ineffective system of administrative coordination, is generally viewed as ill-suited to managing the complexities of large modern cities. Chicago, sometimes referred to as the "city that works," has a weak mayor-council form of organization, but Mayor Richard Daley was able to overcome the weaknesses of the system by controlling Democratic party politics—especially through his position as chairman of the Cook County Democratic party.

Figure 4-1
Basic Forms of Local Government Structure.

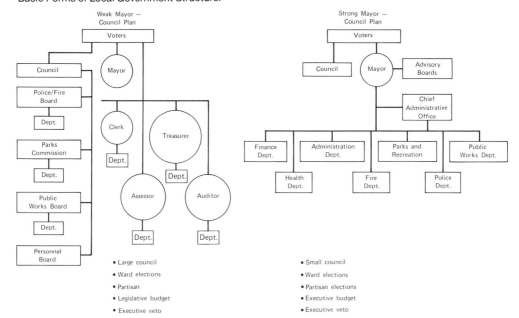

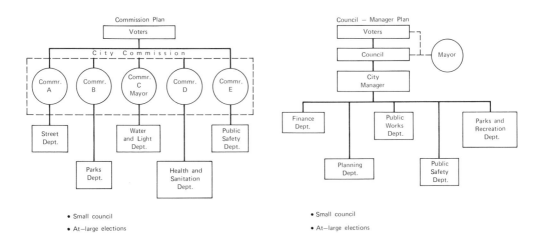

We do not find many other types of local government using this plan today. Counties in some states have some of its features, especially in respect to the number of independent elected officials and the extensive use of administrative boards and commissions. But most counties lack the counterpart of a mayor. Townships also have some features of the weak mayor-council form; a weak executive, several boards and commissions, and legislative budget are a few examples.

Counties and townships in many places today, however, tend to combine executive and legislative functions in their governing boards. They thus violate one of the basic principles of the weak mayor-council plan—the separation of powers.

Strong Mayor-Council Plan. The weak mayor-council plan had some serious shortcomings when used in large, impersonal communities. When things went wrong, it was difficult to know who to blame. The strong mayor-council form, therefore, was the product of a reform movement, a movement that began roughly in the 1880s.

These reforms concentrated primarily on strengthening the mayor's powers by giving the mayor a substantial power over policy development and firm authority over the administrative structure. Citizens continued to elect the mayor, of course, but elected very few, or no other administrative officers. Under the ideal plan the mayor appoints all the department heads and has the authority to fire them as well. The mayor has a veto power, is responsible for developing the budget, and has the responsibility of administering it after the council approves it.

Councils under this plan are small, usually consisting of seven to nine members, and are elected from wards. They serve part time, although we find them serving on a full-time basis in a few large cities. City councillors have no administrative duties. Dissatisfied citizens often complain to city councillors about their problems with city agencies and policies, and these complaints assist the councillors in carrying out their role as critics of the administration.

The CAO modification. A fairly common variation in this plan is the addition of a chief administrative officer (CAO) appointed by, and serving at the pleasure of, the mayor. Though their duties differ from one city to the next, the CAO is responsible for the overall administration of the city government, even to the point, in some places, of appointing the principal department heads—with the mayor's approval, of course. In other places CAOs serve primarily as the chief budget officer. The CAO is to oversee the day-to-day administration of the government and this allows the mayor to perform the cermonial duties of the office and to do the politicking, that is, seeking support for administration policies—politicking with the council and important power centers at the community, state, and national levels.

Because the communities have made many modifications in both kinds of mayor-council forms, it is difficult to classify them with satisfactory consistency. Hence, we cannot determine how many of the approximately 3300 cities with mayor-council governments have strong mayoral forms, and how many do not. What we do find, though, is that the larger the community with a mayor-council plan, the more likely it is to have a strong mayoral form and some type of CAO as well.

Parallels to the strong mayor-council form in other types of local government are generally rare. But we do find them in counties in a few states that permit an elected county executive.

The Commission Plan. Galveston, Texas, in 1900 suffered a disastrous hurricane and the local government had come to a virtual standstill. The Texas legislature suspended the existing government and put in its place a special temporary commission that was to oversee rebuilding the city. Five businessmen were appointed as commissioners. The cleanup and rebuilding effort went so well and so economically that after the crisis the city adopted a new charter, intending to make the plan permanent beginning in 1903.

The central idea of the commission plan is that a small number of people—usually from three to seven—are to be elected from the city at large on a nonpartisan basis. Together they serve as the city council, but individually they are responsible for a major division of the city government, such as the streets and roads department, water and sewer, finance, and so forth. One of these officials also serves as the ceremonial mayor. Usually there are no other elected officials.

Although the plan began accidentally other cities soon adopted it, largely because it offered the short ballot, eliminated partisan politics, and seemingly brought a businesslike approach to city hall.

But as we might anticipate, there was no central administrative coordination, except as the council itself might provide. Commissioners often found it difficult, however, to avoid log-rolling or back-scratching—"You vote from my program and I'll vote for yours." Departments of noncooperating commissioners suffered greatly.

The commission plan today. The number of commission plan adoptions peaked rapidly. By 1917 the number already began to decline. The number has fallen sharply since World War II, but it has not disappeared entirely. The highest use we find is in the Dakotas—half of North Dakota's cities have a commission plan and nine of South Dakota's twenty-three cities use the plan. The largest city in Texas (where the plan began), still using the commission plan is Texas City (population 39,000). We also find a few larger cities, such as Portland, Oregon (population 383,000) and Tulsa, Oklahoma (population 332,000) with the plan. Many of these cities, however, now have a city administrator, thus overcoming what many believe to be the plan's major weakness— the absence of a single executive.

The central feature of the commission plan—the election-at-large of a small, legislative-administrative body—is most common today in county governments. County boards of commissioners in all but eleven of the states have nine members or fewer, and many of these have only three or.five members. A number of the boroughs (smaller urban units) and townships in Pennsylvania also use the plan.

Perhaps the commission plan would have been adopted more widely and remained in use for a longer period of time had not the council-manager plan, which even more closely follows the business model, developed shortly after the commission plan began.

The Council-Manager Plan.   The council-manager plan fit very well with the reformers' criticisms of mayor-council governments—it coincided with the desires of the Short Ballot Organization, it copied very closely the structures of the business corporations (the voters are the "stockholders," the council is the "board of directors," and the manager is the "chief executive"), and it eliminated partisan politics that reformers asserted to be the bane of the cities.

As we consider the five elements of the structural recipes, we see that the council-manager recipe assigned policy and administrative leadership to a professional manager or administrator, whom the council hires and fires. The ideal plan gives the city manager complete responsibility for the city administration. The manager appoints and removes department heads, has responsibilities for budget development and its administration after council approval, and recommends solutions for city problems.

Councils under this form were to be small, consisting of a minimum of five and no more than nine members who were elected for staggered terms from the city-at-large on a nonpartisan basis. Councillors were to have no administrative duties; in fact many city charters prohibit councillors from dealing directly with a department head. Any gripes or complaints about a department are to be channeled through the city manager. The task of the councillors is to act upon proposals of the manager and establish policy for the administration. But because the council is responsible for the manager's length of service, it, too, must share the responsibility when things go wrong.

The plan provides for a mayor whose duties are mostly ceremonial. Ideally, the council should elect one of its own as members rather than to have the mayor directly elected.

Origin and growth of the council-manager plan. Staunton, Virginia, lays claim to being the first city to have hired a city manager. In 1908 the city decided to hire a manager under an ordinance, rather than seek legislative approval for a new form of government. But Sumpter, South Carolina, contested Staunton's claim. Sumpter adopted a "complete" council-manager plan in 1912—a plan that Richard S. Childs developed for Lockport, New York, but one the New York legislature would not allow at the time. Childs was a businessman and president of the Short Ballot Organization. He was later to serve as president and guiding light of the National Municipal League for more than fifty years.

Cities rapidly began to adopt the council-manager plan. More than one hundred fifty cities were using it by 1920. We find that use of the form has increased steadily ever since—especially during the period of suburbanization in the 1950s and 1960s. By 1973 more than 2000 cities in the nation, or about 35 percent, had city managers. We find that more than half of the cities with populations in 1970 of between 25,000 and 500,000 have city managers, although no city over a million uses the plan. About 25 percent of the cities with between a half and one million and about 30 percent of the cities with populations under 25,000 follow the council-manager system.

Modifications in the manager plan. Most cities that use the council-manager plan make modifications in it. In one study researchers found in their sample of 309 council-manager cities that more than 80 percent had either nonpartisan elections or elected their councillors at large, but only 67 percent had both.[7] We also find that some of the larger council-manager cities also have a full-time mayor. Often this is because citizens are divided between a strong mayor and city manager form. During the early 1970s, for example, after a rather stormy period of manager-council fights Grand Rapids, Michigan, voters established a charter commission. The voters rejected a revised council-manager plan and later, probably because manager advocates were angry, voters also rejected a strong mayor-council proposal. In a third election the voters approved a full-time mayor and council-manager form.

[7]Raymond E. Wolfinger and John O. Field, "Political Ethos and the Structure of City Government," *American Political Science Review*, June 1966, 306–326.

The political role of city managers.   Did Richard Childs, who described himself as the "minister" for the council-manager plan, oversell it?[8] Did he promise too much with his praise for "neutral competence"? Perhaps. Norton Long, among others, argued that city managers are not neutral administrators, but are politicians.[9] Until 1952 the managers' code of ethics denied the policy or political role of city managers. Now, however, the profession more readily acknowledges that city managers are often active participants in policymaking and therefore in politics; rather than mere administrators of policies initiated and adopted by others.

Today the problems of cities have shifted from being primarily physical to social in orientation. City managers, once coming largely from engineering and finance backgrounds, were particularly well-suited to an era of growth and expansion when the problems concerned extending streets and utilities and how to pay for them.

Such technical problems remain, of course, but they have been compounded by the human service problems—housing, crime, poverty, and others. Moreover, the standard test of efficiency is not the only test. Representation, citizen participation, equal opportunity, and employee involvement (collective bargaining) requirements have been added to decision processes.

Can the plan and city managers survive and be effective under these changed circumstances? Most observers think they can and will survive. But the effectiveness of city managers, we think, will require that the managers have a broad understanding of the social issues and a recognition of their own limitations and the limitations of their role in exercising political leadership under certain circumstances. When the community is reasonably agreed upon what it wants for the community, manager leadership will dominate. If, however, a community disagrees over what is wanted or needed, the elected official role tends to grow in importance under all circumstances.[10]

Table 4-2 reports opinions of city managers and CAOs in respect to structural arrangements for the mayor and councillors. We find that most do not favor stronger political roles for elected officials, at least

[8]Childs argued that mobilization of support required condensation of the idea to a "catch phrase, even if false in many of its material applications." See Richard J. Stillman, "The City Manager: Professional Helping Hand or Political Hired Hand?" *Public Administration Review*, 37, November/December, 1977, 659–670.

[9]Norton Long, "Politicians for Hire," *Public Administration Review*, 25, June, 1965, p. 119. Also see Karl A. Bosworth, "The City Manager Is a Politician," *Public Administration Review*, 18, Summer 1958, 216–222.

[10]For more on the condition of the council-manager plan, see the "Symposium on the American City Manager," Keith F. Mulrooney, (ed.), in *Public Administration Review*, 31, January/February, 1971, 6–46.

TABLE 4-2 Attitudes of Managers and Chief Administrative Officers Regarding Election and Status of Mayor and City Councillors

Election and Status of Mayor and Councillors	Percent Favor	Percent Neutral	Percent Opposed
Full-time Paid Mayor	5.7	22.4	72.3
Direct Election of Mayor	47.6	29.9	22.5
Councillors Elected by District	17.9	25.6	56.5
Councillors Elected At Large but Residing in District	44.4	32.8	22.8
Mixed Councillors: Some At Large Some by District	24.4	38.3	37.3
Full-time Paid Council	3.7	14.7	81.6
Full-time Staff for Mayor	8.7	20.1	71.3

SOURCE: Adapted from *The Municipal Year Book*, 1975, International City Management Association, Washington, D.C. p. 151. Reproduced by permission of the publisher.

in terms of the arrangements on which they were questioned. Yet they reflect considerable differences from the doctrine that Richard Childs and other advocates of the council-manager plan preached. (Note that the data in Table 4-2 reflect opinions of some 1600 city administrators from cities of all sizes. The detailed data tend to indicate that those from the larger cities were less strongly opposed to some of the deviations from the plan than were those from smaller municipalities.)

Other uses of professional managers. We also find adaptations of the manager plan in a variety of other types of local governments throughout the country. We find this aspect in county government and in a number of townships and towns. Professional managers are especially common in special districts—superintendents in school districts, hospital administrators in hospital districts, airport managers in airport districts, health directors in mental and public health districts, and so on. Because some of these agencies are often less visible to the general public and have a rather narrowly defined mission, these managers are often able to direct both policy and administration. The part-time council or board members in these types of local government seldom seriously challenge the recommendations of the professionals and, unless the community has somehow become aroused about program failures or costs, the councillors rarely challenge successfully.

Variables Influencing the Choice of Government Form

Why do some communities adopt a mayor-council form, while others use a council-manager plan?

Political scientists have theorized that certain community based variables influence such decisions. Among them are the social and economic status of the residents, dominant religious groupings, the region of the country in which the community is located, as well as city size, rate of growth, and other factors.[11]

Most recently, political scientists Thomas Dye and Susan MacManus have tried to identify the relationship of a number of variables to government form, type of election, and constituency through the use of different statistical techniques from those that the others had used. They theorized that cities with high proportions of foreign-born populations would have a mayor-council government with partisan elections and ward representation, and that newer cities would have a council-manager form with nonpartisan election and representation-at-large. On the basis of the known data of about 243 central cities, they used their methods to predict form, election type, and representation. They then compared the predicted results with the actual practices in these cities.

How well were they able to predict?   Dye and MacManus found that a high percentage of foreign born population was the best predictor for the mayor-council plan and a low percentage, the council-manager plan; that the regional variable was best for predicting whether elections are partisan or nonpartisan, and that the foreign-born population was again best to predict ward elections as opposed to at-large elections. But they also noted that certain city variables, such as rate of growth, size, and age are important, as are some population characteristics—mobility, density, race, education, and others.

Importantly, they also found that the procedures could predict more accurately if they controlled for region, that is, if they used their methods to predict within regions, rather than on a nationwide basis. (Compare the percentages of correct predictions in Table 4-3 and 4-4.)

A battle for power   Where does all this leave us? We find that we have only partial answers. What we have found, though, is that the political battles over local community government structures are not fought for esthetic reasons—how the government will appear on an organization chart. Although their beliefs may not be entirely valid, citizens believe that the way local government is structured determines, at

[11]Among these students are James Q. Wilson and Edward C. Banfield, "Public Regardingness as a Value Premise in Voting Behavior," *American Political Science Review*, December, 1964, 876–887; Robert Alford and Harry Scoble, "The Political and Socioeconomic Characteristics of American Cities," *The Municipal Year Book*, 1965, International City Management Association, Chicago, Illinois, 82–97; and Raymond C. Wolfinger and John Osgood Field, "Political Ethos and the Structure of City Government," *American Political Science Review*, June, 1966, 306–326.

TABLE 4-3 Predicting City Government Structure; Percent Predicted Correctly On Ethnicity, Region, and Twelve Independent Variables

	Ethnicity	Region	Twelve Independent Variables Combined[a]
Form: Mayor/Manager	54%	51%	67%
Election: Partisan/Non-partisan	50%	60%	72%
Representation: Ward/At Large	65%	40%	71%

[a]These variables are city size, growth rate, mobility, density, median family income, homeown - ership, median school years completed, white collar employment, percent nonwhite, percent foreign born, region, and age of city.

SOURCE: Adapted from Thomas R. Dye and Susan A. MacManus, "Predicting City Government Structure," *American Journal of Political Science*, May, 1976, 257–271.

TABLE 4-4 Predicting City Government Structure; Percent Predicted Correctly On Eleven Independent Variables Controlled By Region

	Northeast	South	Midwest	West
Form: Mayor/Manager	76%	81%	78%	74%
Election: Partisan/Nonpartisan	79%	80%	68%	89%
Representation: Ward/At Large	71%	70%	81%	82%

SOURCE: Adapted from Thomas R. Dye and Susan A. MacManus, *ibid.*

least partly, who will have how much access to the officials in city hall or the county courthouse and, indeed, who the officials are likely to be and to whom they will be most responsive. What citizens fight over, then, is who will have control (power) over the formal reins of local government institutions. (In Chapter 11 we will consider the informal dimensions of power and influence.)

THE LIMITS OF COMMUNITY GOVERNMENTS

In 1977 the University of Nebraska's Center for Applied Urban Research ranked one hundred major American cities in terms of their attractiveness. They used data on eighty separate community characteristics and concluded that the top four cities were Lincoln, Nebraska (where the study was made); Madison, Wisconsin; Des Moines, Iowa; and Omaha, Nebraska. Detroit, Michigan; Gary, Indiana; and Newark, New Jersey were at the bottom.[12]

Their conclusions were quickly disputed. One urban politics student called the study "racist trash." The ranking, he said, calls most attractive "those cities with the fewest blacks moving in."

[12]Associated Press dispatch, Lansing *State Journal*, July 5, 1977.

Others also objected. The following is part of what one city newspaper editor fired off.

This was a salubrious day for Lincoln, indicating a slackening of the customary breeze from the sand hill country. Lincoln is a fun place for small boys to grow up because there is usually plenty of runny asphalt to chew on in the summer.

A neighboring town of Wahoo has been famous for a century as good duck hunting territory, and Lincoln is not far from the Missouri River, which periodically refreshes the farm land with deposits of silt left by high water and imparts a picturesque appearance to flooded dwellings.

Oh, to be in Lincoln now that July's here with the Platte River running eight feet under the riverbed. When a use is found for cockleburs, Nebraska will be wealthy.[13]

The Problems Local Governments Face

The editor did not seek to mask the displeasure in his satirical reply. But he inadvertently alluded to an important point—that part of what makes a place attractive or unattractive is a function of what nature left.

Nature's Gifts.   Much of what nature left or provides, city hall or the county courthouse can do little about—the amount of sunshine or rain, the rate of flow in the rivers, the mean temperature, the grade of the terrain, and so on. In some other respects, though, how city policies adapt to natural conditions can be enough to make the difference between an attractive and unattractive community. The Buffalo city council, for example, cannot regulate the amount of snow that falls on the city, but they usually can make conditions tolerable by having a well-equipped and well-staffed crew ready when it comes. Galveston, Texas and Miami, Florida cannot stop the hurricanes, but by adopting and enforcing appropriate building codes, providing warning systems and cleanup crews, they can hold losses and misery to a minimum. And city hall cannot change the course of a major river, but it can provide bridges so that getting across is little problem. And with proper drainage facilities, city hall can prevent most basements from flooding, or with zoning, prevent people from building in low-lying flood plain areas.

A part of what local governments do, then, is to develop and enforce public policies that help the community to adjust to what nature provides. In this sense we say that government is adaptive—adaptive to the conditions of nature.

[13]"No. 1?—Says you," *Detroit Free Press*, July 21, 1977.

Social, Economic, and Technological Forces. Local government is adaptive to other forces as well—especially social, economic, and technological change. Let us consider a few examples.

How did the suburbs and central cities adapt to the population migrations of the 1950s and 1960s, a social force that neither could control? Some suburbs adopted zoning ordinances that set minimum lot widths of one hundred feet or more. This did not stop the in-migration, but it did have an effect how many could move in and set the minimum economic status for them.

Central cities adopted policies, too—policies that failed to stop the out-migration. Urban renewal was intended, in part, to provide more space for commercial development and to encourage the development of exclusive city apartment projects. This and other policies did little to stop the outflow and may have added to it. Later on, in recognition of the changing composition of their populations, some cities adopted policies that met present citizen needs, such as day-care centers for working mothers for example, or with a policy that requires city employees to be residents of the city. Central cities also began providing hot lunches and programs for old people who might otherwise have been placed in institutions at high costs to the city.

Technology has also forced adaptive policies. At one time city administrators sprayed entire cities with DDT to kill mosquitoes. Later they found out that DDT also killed the birds and they stopped the spraying programs. Cities and other forms of local governments lengthened airport runways when they found that jet aircraft could not maneuver as the propeller-driven craft could. Later they thickened the runways to accommodate even larger airplanes that technology brought on. In the meantime they tore down their railroad terminals or sold them for restaurants. And they built parking ramps for the automobiles, closed down their bus systems, and tore out their streetcar and interurban lines. In an era of energy shortages, they have begun to restore some of these facilities—adapting to different conditions again.

Great Changes And Adaptive Changes

The sociologist Roland Warren theorizes about the kinds of changes that take place in communities. Some changes—the natural, social, economic, and technological types of changes—take place independent of our own actions. We call them great changes. A second type, those policies that seek to accomodate or adapt to the great changes, are adaptive changes.[14]

[14]Roland Warren, *The Community in America*, 2nd Edition, Rand McNally College Publishing Company, Chicago, Illinois, 1973, p. 362.

Roland Warren notes that the most important changes that take place in community life, the great changes, are not controllable at the community level—changes such as unemployment, wars, baby booms, or aging population. Purposive or adaptive changes, he suggests, "at best alleviate the side effects of the more basic changes."[15] Local governments, then, can do little more than guide the great changes, and then, only at the fringes. But these adaptive actions are nonetheless important. They help us to understand that what people and groups want from their local governments are policies that accommodate or resist the great changes, or those that at least make them tolerable. We will consider this matter next.

What People Want From Local Governments. The great changes do not affect every community in the same way at the same time. Nor do such changes affect all individuals in the same community similarly. Consider airplane technology and the need for longer and heavier runways, for example.

A community that has no airport at all may care little how long runways for jets have to be. The impact will fall largely on those communities that have airports and want jet service. Similarly, the people who never travel by air will not care much, either. But manufacturers who need to ship parts by airfreight, people in sales, and others who travel by air a great deal, as well as hotel operators and the convention bureau manager will all think it is important to have jet service. In fact we might well find these various interests, probably working through the chamber of commerce, lobbying city hall or the airport board for jet service. They are responding to a technological great change, and are seeking an adaptive policy.

As the government quietly begins securing options on land for the runway extensions, another group of people may organize against the program. These are people who suddenly see themselves being affected very directly by this technology—they are people who live in the path of the take-off and landing patterns. Among other things, they are likely to experience sagging property values. We see conflicting claims of the local government based on different ideas of how adaptation to great changes should occur.

Our wants may be conflicting. It is not only the claims of two groups that may conflict. We also find that an individual may make conflicting claims on his or her local government. Suppose, for example, that we want the city to provide an environment of safety—safety from criminals, from fire, from disease, and from reckless drivers. But we also

[15]Ibid. p. 363.

want low taxes. The two wants conflict and we need to specify how safe and how low.

Or we may simply want government to leave us alone. "We just don't want government telling us what we can do with our property." Yet we may want government to do something about our neighbor who keeps two or three junk cars in the back yard. The city cannot meet both of these wants fully.

Most of us would readily agree with the general premise that community governments should provide their citizens with a complement of basic services at an efficient level. We would, no doubt, have much less agreement, however, as to whether that premise means that the community should provide halfway houses for the mentally ill or former prison inmates (especially if they are in "our" neighborhood), tax-free housing to the aged, or a retirement home in Florida, as one Michigan city does.

If our wants from city hall and the county courthouse conflict and are contradictory, we might wonder how the policymakers can settle, or at least temporarily resolve, these claims. One technique will be through incremental policy changes—small and gradual changes, rather than changes that depart dramatically from existing policies. But the ideas regarding the purpose of government in the community will likely set the direction of these changes. This set of ideas or values tends to determine how the community defines the public interest.

Community Goals and Images.   The political scientists Oliver P. Williams and Charles R. Adrian described four different types of communities in terms of how citizens of each see the central purpose of its local government.[16]

Development and Growth.   One type of community saw the central role of government as one to promote economic development and growth. Such a community, of course, would view with favor such conditions as a growing population, expansion of industry, and the building of high office buildings. Its zoning policies, for example, would accommodate the needs of growth. It would have little trouble deciding the public interest in the airport runway extension that we discussed above.

Amenities for living.   A second type of community sees the central role of government as providing and securing the amenities of life.

[16]Oliver P. Williams and Charles R. Adrian, *Four Cities*, University of Pennsylvania Press, Philadelphia, Pennsylvania, 1963.

Most communities, of course, provide certain amenities, even if they might be only city water, sewer service, and tree-lined streets. But the communities that judge the public interest in terms of amenities typically place the greatest emphasis on the home and neighborhood environment, rather than on the working environment. The managers of industry will likely find an unreceptive city council if they propose policies that impose social and environmental costs on the neighborhoods. In a university town having an amenities policy orientation, we might find the conflict focusing on the question: How can we keep student housing from becoming a "student ghetto"?

Keep things as they are. A third policy orientation outlined by Williams and Adrian is preservationist in tone. It is a "caretaker" government, a conserver of community traditions. It is antigrowth, antiplanning, and antizoning. It resists innovation and change. The theme of this policy in such communities is that growth threatens the current lifestyle and so they resist rather than accomodate it. Policy Box No. 8, "Waterford, Virginia, Confronts Great Change," provides an example of this kind of community. Note how it seeks to preserve its "gifts from nature," in the face of social and technological change.

Arbitrate the conflicts. A fourth view is that local government should serve as the arbitrator among the conflicting interests in the community. In such communities people see the process of government as important as the government services produced. As we might expect, in a community that places an emphasis on the need for access by all community interests, policy output becomes less predictable than in the other types of cities. Public policy tends never to reach a kind of permanent settled stage; the conflicting claims are only temporarily settled at a point where costs to one element are tolerable and benefits to another at least minimally acceptable.

Strategies For Redefining The Community Public Interest

The risk in typologies such as this, of course, is that we attempt to explain every policy in terms of a specific community type. What we find in the real world is a mixture. Nevertheless, the typology provides us with a way of identifying central tendencies regarding how communities define their public interest.

We should also note, however, that definitions of community public interest can change with circumstances. Communities with life's amenities or antigrowth orientations, for example, may become more pro-

POLICY BOX NO. 8
Waterford, Virginia, Confronts Great Change

Waterford, Virginia, is a small town of 350 people located about 35 miles northwest of Washington, D.C. Its 85 buildings span more than 200 years of construction. It was first settled in 1733 by Quakers. Today, residents are descendants of the German, Irish, Scots, English, Welsh, Swedish, and Africans who came later.

The Catoctin Creek that flows through the town supplied it with power to operate its grist mill, a mill that was the town's economic base and its reason for being. The old mill still stands today, a museum piece to an age long since passed. Waterford's winding, unplanned roads provide passersby with sparkling views of the surrounding countryside and the Blue Ridge Mountains.

In 1970 Waterford was designated a national historic landmark, not because it was the site of any significant historical event, but because of its "uncompromised integrity of the relationship between built and natural environments." It has no sprawl. The edges of Waterford are clear and distinct.

But Waterford has problems.

- It has been discovered. Washington D.C. is not far away and at least a few residents make the daily commute back and forth. Some of its properties have increased in value more than 100 percent over the last decade. And subdividers have not overlooked Waterford's atmosphere and amenities.
- In 1974 the U.S. Army Corps of Engineers and some water utilities announced plans to build a dam in the Catoctin Creek that would impound water to meet the needs of the D.C. metropolitan area. If the dam is built, part of Waterford will be permanently flooded, including the old grist mill.
- Waterford's water system consists of old antique wells, some of which are contaminated. Townfolk do not like the idea of a modern water system that might include a water tower.
- The town has no sanitary sewer system. And in 1974 thirty homes had defective septic systems and forty had contaminated wells. Loudon County received a grant to build a sewer system, but residents fear that an out-of-town disposal plant will encourage development in the surrounding area. In fact, the proposed plant was designed to serve the needs of as many as 150 more houses than there now are in Waterford. Residents believe, though, that an in-town disposal plant will be visually disruptive.

Waterford has an active citizen foundation dedicated to the restoration and preservation of the town. The foundation has acquired several buildings, restored them, and sold them for other uses. It has also taken a number of steps to purchase open land to maintain the surrounding landscape. At least some of the people believe that to save the town and have the surrounding area built up would be a hollow victory.

What we see in conflict in Waterford are the preservationist values of the residents, the desire of other people to share in the environment, the standards of the county health department for safe drinking water and sanitary disposal of wastes, the desire of developers to build high-quality houses, and the water needs of the District.

The townfolk are suddenly confronting the twentieth century problems, problems that seem irreconcilable. They are wondering what will happen.

What do you think should happen? Whose demands should have priority— the wants of a few hundred people in the countryside or the needs of hundreds of thousands in the urban area? Should the needs of the urban area run roughshod over the wants of small-town folk? Whose interests are the people of Waterford looking out for—their own or some regional or national public interest having to do with saving old small towns? How much say should towns like Waterford have in determining what happens in surrounding areas?

SOURCE: This case is based on Carol Galbreath's article, "Waterford, Virginia; Continuity and Change in an Historic Village," *Small Town*, March 1977.

development if unemployment levels rise or existing industries shut down or move away.

The community orientation, we find, is also important to the political strategies that citizens will employ in advocating or opposing change.

Approaches to Community Change. The images we hold of a community influences how we will adapt to the great changes. We consider here two types of strategies. The *collaborative* strategy will likely be used when a large majority of the community is in agreement about the community image. The *contest* strategy will be employed when the community is divided over its definition of the public interest.[17]

The Collaborative Strategy. If the community holds to one of the first of these images—developmental, amenities, or caretaker—they assume that individual interests are the same as community interests and the only real problem they have is to talk patiently and quietly about differences until the other party understands in terms of the image of the city that both accept.

Because we assume agreement on the "community good," the collaborative approach leads us to rely on technical expertise and scientific fact to point to solutions and carry out policy. If we all agree on the merits of jet service to our community, the urban planner and other experts can explain to us why the runways must run east and west, rath-

[17]Roland Warren, Op. cit., 375–402.

er than some other direction. We may not be pleased about how the adaptive policy affects us individually, but we place the community interest over our individual interests or wants.

This strategy, then, depends upon two levels of consensus. The first concerns the overall goal; the second concerns the decision-making process we use to decide how we adapt. Warren suggests that it is lack of consensus on goals that has made the collaborative strategy less useful. He cites three reasons:

1. People are less likely to believe that the public interest is the same for all. In the absence of agreement on the public interest, one begins to examine whose particular interests are served by a given decision-making structure.
2. A growing number of people see the decision-making structures as serving various segments of the community differently. They attribute it to the "system"; they believe that conditions will not be otherwise, and therefore refuse to play the game by the old rules.
3. The legitimacy of the once-powerful and unquestioned community decision-making structures is being challenged. The challengers would argue that these structures are not impartial arbiters, but self-serving, and as such no longer have the right to determine the policies.

The Contest Strategy.   What we see, then, is a pressure for the reallocation of power. We see demands to deal with matters that seem never to get on the public agenda.[18] These pressures and demands lead to adoption of the contest strategy. It operates on the belief that interests are pluralistic and that policy does not affect all groups and individuals in the same way; that the recognition of these differential effects cannot be talked away by token actions. Controversial matters are to be confronted and faced four-square. A contest, then, one that involves politicking among groups and individuals holding different basic goals, is seen as a legitimate and necessary method of resolving issues.

And so we see that blacks, women, poor, Chicanos, city workers, and neighborhood groups do not ask for representative (or token) participation. Instead they demand to be a part of the bargaining process where the hard compromises are hammered out. They demand a direct role in the process regarding the allocation of costs and benefits. These groups are insisting upon a transfer of power.

These contests over the last fifteen years or so have produced a variety of "norm-violating" actions—actions that go beyond traditional

[18]Peter Bachrach and Morton S. Baratz, "Two Faces of Power," *American Political Science Review*, December 1962, 947–953. The second face of power, they noted, is to keep matters off the community agenda. This view is discussed in more detail in Chapter 11.

politicking and that many saw as not being part of the American way—sit-ins, demonstrations, boycotts, and even, on occasion, violence. But contest strategies have also employed more widely accepted techniques—organizing election campaigns, initiating court cases, and pressuring local, state, and federal legislators and agency administrators. Often the contest strategists have concentrated their efforts at national and state levels. When these are unsuccessful, pressures for change may be placed on individual communities.

A Final Comment

We began this chapter by discussing how the states extended powers to their local governments—in part to exercise powers on behalf of the states themselves, and to meet local needs and wants. The creation of these local governments was based on the twin assumptions that urban areas would be sharply distinguished from rural areas and that urban and rural governments, therefore, would be different in structure and in powers.

By the beginning of the twentieth century technology undercut the validity of these assumptions, and as the distinctions between rural and urban began to fade, so did the differences in powers accorded to the urban and rural types of governments. Thus, although the needs of local government have changed, the states have found that for the most part they are able to make only minor modifications in the way local governments are structured. This is so, even though the states have the legal power to make the neccessary changes. Often the states lack the political power to institute significant change, largely because the local units have developed a political power of their own to resist, guide, and slow down proposed changes.

As we will see in Chapter 6, when we discuss state and local finances, the local governments have become less economically independent than they once were. In the face of economic pressures they are more susceptible to state and federal efforts to coordinate local activities. We will examine the federal and state efforts to coordinate local programs and policies in Chapter 14.

HIGHPOINTS OF CHAPTER 4: COMMUNITIES IN THE FEDERAL SYSTEM

Our first major consideration in this chapter was that the states created local governments on the assumption (1) that two basic sets of local governments were needed—one for rural areas and one for urban areas. We saw (2) that the states established the rural governments to be branch offices of the state itself and (3) that they were reluctant to give to cities the freedom and power to go about the process of governing the urban areas. We discussed (4) how the early conditions established an environment of intergovernmental relations that kept the states' role as coordinator of local government to a minimum. We noted that in recent years, though, the states have become less ambivalent about their responsibility and that they are dealing with local problems more aggressively than they once did.

We next discussed the question (5) of how the localities are governed—we reviewed the major forms of local organization and how they are related to the costs and benefits of community government programs. Finally, we examined what power was used for in the communities. We found (6) that much of what happens in communities is beyond the direct control of local governments and (7) that often they can only make policies that adapt to the "great changes." We saw (8) that local policy bodies face conflicting claims over what these adaptive policies should be, but we also noted (9) how communities tend to develop a general framework of values for defining their public interests. We closed by considering two views of the public interest and how (10) one led to a collaborative approach to community decision making, and the other to a contest strategy.

5

STATE CONSTITUTIONS

Few states have a constitutional heritage equal to Connecticut's—"The Constitution State." We refer to the dramatic incident of the Charter Oak.[1] This is the story.

In 1662 the Connecticut colony received a very liberal charter from King Charles II. The charter did not even provide for a royal governor, but allowed the legislature to choose its own. In 1686 a new king, King James II, decided to revoke that charter and merge Connecticut with other colonies into a "Dominion of New England"—Sir Edmund Andros was appointed governor general. Andros demanded that the old Connecticut charter be returned to the Crown. The news of this reached Connecticut during Christmas 1686— the legislative assembly dallied and delayed. Finally in October, 1687, Andros arrived from Boston with a body of soldiers to confront the assembly then in session. The story at this point gets very interesting.

[1]The tree unfortunately blew down on August 21, 1856. It was carved up into souvenirs. From some of the wood a chair was built that is still used by the lieutenant governor when presiding over the Connecticut State Senate. A monument was put up on the spot in Charter Oak Place in Hartford. Historians do not vouch for all of the details of the story as we have told it. For the source of our account, see George Stimpson, *A Book About American History*, Harper and Brothers, N.Y., 1956.

The "People's Governor," John Treat, made a lengthy speech arguing with Andros against giving back the Charter. The discussion between the two lasted until after dark. Suddenly all the candles went out. When the candles were relit, the charter was gone!!

According to the story, a Captain Joseph Wadsworth hid the charter in the hollow of an old white oak tree nearby. It lay there for over a year. Then, in the peaceful but glorious Revolution of 1688, King James was replaced in England with William and Mary and what seemed at the time a more temperate Royal Government. The document was taken out of "the Charter Oak" and dusted off and restored to its old legal position. In 1776 it was changed only slightly to become Connecticut's first state constitution. It then lasted until 1818—a lifespan of 156 years. Even after the 1818 revision large parts of the original charter remained and may still be found in today's Connecticut constitution.[2]

State constitutions have fallen on harder times since 1688 and 1776. Most have not been held in much reverence. Reformers, as well as academic authorities on the subject, have become critical of their style and content. The documents are described as "horse and buggy" constitutions, suited only to the needs of the nineteenth century. Occasionally we come across some newspaper columnist who holds them up to ridicule and digs clauses out of one of them, such as the requirements that women may only run for library boards or that duelists cannot hold office in the commonwealth, and everyone smiles in agreement—state constitutions are antiques. All the glory that was Connecticut's is forgotten.

A Defense of State Constitutions?   Today state constitutions have few defenders. We plan to be among the few. We think that scholars, newspaper reporters, and others should view our state constitutions with more sympathy and understanding. We should give the statesmen and politicians of the nineteenth century who constructed many of these documents at least the benefit of the doubt. We, perhaps, without permanently damaging our own reputations, can credit the constitution writers with having a little political common sense. We may even wish to pay some honor to their faith in democratic procedures because we will find that these complex documents, even today, advance democratic ways.

[2]The only state constitution that dates back to the Revolutionary War times is that of Massachusetts, about which John Adams coined the phrase "a government of laws and not of men." It was adopted in 1780 and became a model for writers of the federal constitution in 1787.

We can also afford to be generous at this point in history because the picture is changing. As we will see, states are finding ways out of some of their worst constitutional tangles. Some of this is being done by the states themselves. Through amendment or convention, state after state has been rooting out those instruments of legal torture that were embedded in these state constitutions. And the states have received a big assist from the national government—especially the federal courts, that have knocked out many state constitutional clauses as contrary to the federal constitution.

We think state constitutions important because, as we have argued in previous chapters, there still exist state-based differences in interests and viewpoints that justify some differences in policymaking and administration. How reasonably states have faced this responsibility to defend variation is reflected in clauses of the state constitutions.

Overview. We begin by looking at the legal theory of state constitutions and how it benefits the courts. Then we look at the reason that constitutions and city charters are so important—they set rules that distribute long-term costs and benefits. Then we examine how constitutions are cluttered with legislative detail and how this may lead to stalemates. We review recommendations to streamline them. We then discuss how constitutions got so full of detail, rejecting the notion that it was the result of an easy amendment process. Rather, we argue, they result from citizens' attempts to deal with unsettling social change. We then reassess the arguments against longer constitutions when the purpose is to bring unsettling events under a form of democratic control. We finally note that through action of the federal courts and the states themselves, constitutions are being changed.

THE LEGAL THEORY OF STATE CONSTITUTIONS

The colonists very early developed a taste for written documents, such as constitutions. The royal charters spelled out how the colonists would be governed and their rights as British citizens. Scholars tell us that these charters largely inspired the first state constitutions. Two colonies, Connecticut and Rhode Island, they say, in 1776 merely changed the words "the King" wherever they appeared, to "the People" and called the results their first state constitutions.

John Locke's Theory of Constitutions

The theory that guided these first state constitution writers was that of the great English political scientist, John Locke (1632–1714). (Locke, incidently, had a hand in writing one of the colonial charters—"the Fundamental Constitutions of Carolina" of 1691.) Locke argued that a constitution is a legal contract (he called it a social contract) between "the People" and those who govern them. Thus, constitutions should not be written by governors, or run-of-the-mill politicians, or any other public officials. "The People" should select special representatives to write their contract. Through these representatives, "the People" would decide what basic powers to grant to those who would govern them. They would set limits on these powers and spell out the basic rules and structure of government. They would put all this into a written document, and this constitutional contract would be approved by "the People" before it would be regarded as being in effect.

As we would expect, these constitutional clauses, of course, would have a greater *legal status* than ordinary law. The laws that a state legislature or a city council passed would have to be guided by these constitutional clauses or they would be illegal (unconstitutional). In fact, everything that governors, legislators, administrators, judges, or local public officials did while in office would have to be in harmony with these basic rules. These were the conditions that "the People" set down when they agreed to let governments make the day-to-day rules.

Finally, the theory argued that any changes in the constitution, or compact, would have to be made by a different and more difficult process than that used in passing an ordinary law and would have to secure the consent of "the People." This might be by a new constitutional convention or, if amendment was to be used, Locke's theory seemed to imply that a vote of the citizens would be required on the proposed change.[3]

Such was the legal theory. Practice follows it in most of the states, and in communities in respect to home rule charters. But it is not followed in respect to the national constitution, since "the People" have no direct role in the amendment process.

The Difference Between the Federal and State Constitutions

State constitutions differ from the federal constitution in two other important respects. The federal constitution is based on the legal theory that the national government can only pass laws in harmony with con-

[3]Actually John Locke himself believed, it seems, that he had written the perfect charter for the Carolinas. He included no amendment clause, but provided the document "should be and remain the sacred and unalterable force and rule of government of Carolina forever."

stitutional powers specifically granted. These, as we noted in the chapter on federalism, are, for the most part, listed in Article 1, Section 8. The states operate under the reverse legal theory. Their constitutions were written with the assumption that state governments could exercise any power they wished, except those specifically forbidden in their own constitutions or in the federal constitution.

Some writers have argued that more words and amendments are added to state constitutions than to the federal constitution because state constitutions spell out what state governments cannot do. Listing all the "thou shalt nots" adds to the words in state constitutions.[4]

A second important difference is that the federal constitution is the supreme law of the Land. If a state constitutional clause is in conflict with a clause of the federal constitution, the federal clause prevails and the state constitutional clause is "unconstitutional."

Written Constitutions Increase the Political Role of Judges

The "negatives" and other complicated phrases of state constitutions add to the political role of federal and state judges. Someone has to tell us what those detailed constitutional provisions allow. In America we turn to judges to tell us what our written constitutions mean in practice.

A major political impact, then, of a legal theory that requires written state constitutions, is that it makes state and federal judges major policymakers. We will touch on this role in this chapter and review it in greater detail in Chapter 9 on state courts.

STATE CONSTITUTIONS: WHY ARE THEY SO IMPORTANT?

We will argue that state constitutions were once more important than they are today. The changed status reflects the process of change in a federal system that has moved from dual federalism to cooperative, permissive, and functional federalism.

The Changing Importance of State Constitutions

It is difficult to put ourselves in our ancestor's skins and know how important state constitutions were to pioneer Americans. We may call the period before the Civil War the springtime and summer of our fed-

---

[4]See Frank P. Grad, "The State Constitution: Its Function and Form for Our Time" *Virginia Law Review* 54, June 1968, 928–973. We disagree with Grad on this point, but find his article among the most perceptive generally on the subject of state constitutions. We use throughout this chapter both arguments and illustrations from it.

eral system. Citizens then saw, as we noted in Chapter 3, that the law hammered out at the state capitol was often of much more consequence to how their day-to-day lives would be lived, than most of the statutes that trickled out of Washington, D.C.

So what went into those state constitutions was not just irritating legal gobbledygook to these nineteenth century Americans—it spelled out the daily rules of how one lived and made a living.

State governments and their constitutions are less important today. Yet, as we have noted, state governments still exercise an important influence in our day-to-day lives, and so what goes into those documents is still worth paying some attention to.

State Constitutions Are Political Documents

The Virginia Constitutional Convention of 1829–1830 had a star-studded collection of politicians as delegates—it is hard to visualize bringing together such a convention today. It included the governor, ex-governors, and United States Senator John Randolph. Former President James Monroe was presiding officer and when he became ill, Philip Barbour, then speaker of the U.S. House of Representatives took over. Ex-president James Madison chaired the committee on the state executive and U.S. Chief Justice John Marshall chaired the committee on the state judiciary. It should have produced a document that would be a model of statesmanship.

Instead the sessions were full of bitter acrimony, and deadlocks were frequent. Some delegates talked of splitting the state in two between the slaveholding east, that favored property qualifications for voting and the high-country west, that did not. (The split did occur thirty years later during the Civil War when West Virginia became a separate state.)

Chapman Johnson was a leader of the liberals. He attempted to summarize what the political battles were about:

We are engaged, Mr. Chairman, in a contest for power—disguise it as you will—call it a discussion of the rights of man, natural or social—call it an inquiry into political expediency—imagine yourself, if you please, presiding over a school of philosophers, discoursing on the doctrines of political law, for the instruction of mankind, and the improvement of all human institutions—bring the question to the test of principle, or of practical utility—still, Sir, all our metaphysical reasoning and our practical rules, *all our scholastic learning and political wisdom, are but the arms employed in the contest, which involves the great and agitating question—whether the sceptre shall pass away from Judah.*[5]

[5]Quoted in A.E. Dick Howard, "For the Common Benefit: Constitutional History in Virginia as a Casebook for the Modern Constitution-Maker," *Virginia Law Review* 54, June 1968, p. 855. The article describes the history of constitution making in Virginia, 816–902.

Constitutional Burdens and Benefits.   Johnson's language is more biblical than we are used to. (His allusion is found in Genesis 49, verse 10.) We can put his thought into modern words as, "These constitutional debates are not over scholarly theory, but over the question: For whose benefit will the rules be made?" The point can be applied to every constitution and every city charter ever written.

Rules are seldom neutral—all differ in their impact on various groups of people. U.S. Supreme Court Justice Oliver Wendell Holmes (1841–1935) once observed that when governments write any rule, whether a law or constitutional clause, they are taking burdens off the backs of some citizens and placing them on the backs of others. Getting those burdens placed in a way that groups or individuals desire, is what politics is all about. It is also what constitution writing is all about.

Delegate Chapman Johnson was saying that we have many theories to justify how costs and benefits should be distributed. Sometimes we think it only fair and just that some should pay more costs, and others not so, depending on our own system of values or beliefs. But it always comes back to the question of whom the rules will benefit.

In Virginia, during 1829 to 1830, the convention delegates fought out whether the rules of the Constitution would serve the interests of the East and their "peculiar institution" of slavery, at what the settlers on the western frontier saw as at their expense. This was the significant political question under dispute.

The long run importance of constitutional burdens.   Constitutions are especially important politically because their clauses are longer lasting than ordinary laws—they give long-term advantages to some citizens over others—the advantages are in status, power, and wealth. For example, one of the major long-term advantages is that constitutional clauses lay down the rules under which citizens can enter the political contests. Some will find it hard to compete, others easier.[6]

How the Missouri Constitution Allocated Some Costs and Benefits.   Let us analyze a state constitutional clause for its political content. We choose a clause of Missouri's constitution, in effect until 1954. The first part of the clause is one we will find in one fashion or another in probably every other state constitution:

A general diffusion of knowledge and intelligence being essential to the preservation of the rights and liberties of the people, the General Assembly shall establish and maintain free public schools for the gratuitous instruction of all

[6]Robert Dahl, *A Preface to Democratic Theory*, University of Chicago Press, Chicago, p. 137.

persons in the state within ages not in excess of twenty-one years, as prescribed by law.

This constitutional clause states that free grammar, high school, and, perhaps, college instruction may be provided by the state for youngsters up to age twenty-one. We know from a study of history that at one time such clauses were not easily adopted. They were the outgrowth of a massive agitation by such nineteenth century educational reformers as Horace Mann (1796–1859), and of William T. Harris (1835–1909), who opened the first permanent kindergarten in St. Louis in 1873. All argued that education should be free to all.

The redistributive effect.   Politically this clause, when put into effect by the state legislature, redistributed costs and benefits. It meant that the state or community would not deprive the children of poorer citizens of schooling because their parents could not affort to pay. Also it came to mean that girls in Missouri had the same right to be educated as boys. We find that Missouri did not discriminate between children of aliens and those of American citizens; indeed, we see that the state did not charge out-of-state tuition to children of parents who did not live in Missouri or who had just moved there from other states.

We take this unequal sharing of costs pretty much for granted nowadays as only "fair and just." This clause was what political scientists call a "redistributive policy." It took away from some people and gave to others. It redistributed costs and benefits. These may have been costs in terms of money, social status, or political power—without the clause someone would have to exercise power in deciding who went to school and who did not. For example, once this clause was put into effect, boys had to compete with girls over grades and school prizes. Later, perhaps, they may have found the same competition when applying for admission to college or entering the job market, though that took some time in coming. In the distant past such competition was not even possible. Also, richer citizens had to pay for the education of children of the poor. They might argue that this was unjust, and at one time most citizens agreed. Citizens without children, or citizens whose children had grown up and even left the state, found they must pay for the education of other people's children! By listening carefully you will hear this complaint even today.[7]

[7]The modern political scientist, whose research has called our attention to the distributive functions of policymaking, is Theodore J. Lowi. See especially his book, *The End of Liberalism*, W. W. Norton, New York, 1969. He distinguishes between "distributive policy" (a settled and accepted division of resources), "redistributive policy" (a new definition of how resources should be distributed) and "regulatory policy" (enforcing the rules that maintain the present distribution of benefits).

Long-term effects. The point that constitutional clauses have longer term impact than ordinary law, is made even clearer when we look at the sentence that follows the constitutional provision that we quoted above.

> Separate schools shall be provided for white and colored children, except in cases otherwise provided by law.

Since the Supreme Court case of *Brown v. Topeka Board of Education* (1954), we know that sentence is no longer legally enforceable in Missouri or in any other state. Still, as long as it was in the Missouri Constitution (a period of almost a hundred years), people thought that it was not only unwise policy to have racially integrated schools—it was also unconstitutional. If a white principal in Sedalia in 1903 had decided to admit to the all-white school, a dozen or so blacks from the community in which ragtime pianist Scott Joplin then lived, what would have happened? Many unpleasant things. Legally the sheriff would have had to arrest the principal unless, of course, the state legislature had specifically authorized such school integration. Getting such authorization would have been very, very difficult—but getting that sentence changed in the Missouri Constitution in 1903 would have been next to impossible.

State constitutional clauses are important because they distribute political benefits and costs over a long period of time.

WHAT DO STATE CONSTITUTIONS CONTAIN?

To most of us the prospect of curling up in a big easy chair before a roaring fire on a rainy Sunday afternoon, with a copy of our state constitution in our lap, is not inviting. Yet many of us have at least scanned the seven articles that make up our national constitution. Why the difference in our reactions?

Our Cluttered State Constitutions

Length is likely to be one difference between state constitutions and the federal one. You can read through the federal constitution in a half hour or so. Connecticut, Virginia, and Vermont are the only three states whose constitutions number less than 10,000 words, the length of the national constitution. So unless the capital of your home state is Hartford, Richmond, or Montpelier, you will find that its constitution is probably a somewhat bulkier document—perhaps three or four times longer than the national constitution.

State constitutions have had a growth and weight problem. Back in 1914 a political scientist, James Quayle Dealey, examined these documents and found that they averaged 19,000 words.[8] He noted that they averaged 5,000 words in 1800, and charted a steady growth in average length through the nineteenth century. We updated his calculations and today the average is 30,500 words! Thus, state constitutions have had a steady growth rate of about 15 percent every ten years.

Style Deficiencies.   You will also sense, we think, that the national constitution has style—clauses roll out with a fine sweep. Even its old-fashioned phrasing breathes an air of historic dignity. If you dip into your state constitution, you are likely to find your eyes get tired and restless. You begin skipping and you bog down. It is likely to be dull reading because it is full of awkward constructions and convoluted sentences. A great deal of it looks like matters that could be handled in ordinary laws, and the experts tell us this is often the case. No one, we think, would think seriously of amending the federal constitution to ban throw-away cans and bottles, or detail the procedures for getting a dog license—but such clauses have been put in state constitutions.

A minor point is that many of our state constitutions also have an air of sloppiness and shoddy construction. When university researchers looked into Florida's seventy-year-old constitution, as the professors they were, they spotted over 200 misspellings and grammatical errors.[9] It is difficult to be properly respectful in the face of such casualness.

Detail Invites More Detail.   If we (as Louisiana once did) spell out the detail of how to choose the board of commissioners to the Port of New Orleans and determine what they do, it will take a constitutional amendment about half the size of the federal constitution. Moreover every later change or clarification requires more amendments. Rolling stones may gather no moss, but not so with state constitutions. As the clauses get more involved the constitution becomes like a snowball rolling down a hill, picking up whatever rocks, branches, or beer cans are in its way as it rolls along.

Legalese.   State constitutions are also likely to strike you as full of "whereas" language. State constitutions appear to many as booby-trapped with tricky legalisms. They seem to be the kind of documents

[8]James Quayle Dealey, *Growth of American State Constitutions*, Ginn and Co., N.Y., 1915, Chapter III.

[9]For a summary of what else they found, see Manning J. Dauer and William C. Havard, *The Florida Constitution of 1885—A Critique*, Public Administration Service, University of Florida, Gainesville, 1955.

that delight lawyers—not just any kind of lawyer, but the kind of county courthouse lawyer who revels in litigation over whether beauticians may be permitted to give shaves and "shags" to male customers.

The Problems Caused By Clutter.

Detailed legal phrases in themselves may seem harmless, but they can cause unexpected difficulties. Some judges are very literal-minded, and sometimes turn these convoluted phrasings into nightmares for the current government. The Oklahoma Constitution, for example, stated that the corporation commissioner had the power to regulate "all transportation and transmission companies," and then went on to list them, "railroads, express companies and (even) Oklahoma steamship lines"! They overlooked listing airlines, possibly because airplanes had not yet been invented. The Oklahoma Supreme Court in 1947 struck down as unconstitutional the power of the corporation commissioner to regulate commercial airlines because they were not on the constitutional list. In Kentucky, in 1938, the state Supreme Court decided that voting machines were unconstitutional because the constitution said voting should only be by "official secret ballot." In both cases the constitution was changed.

Local governments, as we noted in Chapter 4 in respect to Dillon's Rule, have particularly suffered from restrictive interpretations of state constitutions.

What Do the Reformers Want to Change?

Since the time of Teddy Roosevelt, at the beginning of the twentieth century, state constitutions have received increasing criticism from political scientists and civic reformers. The National Municipal League, in 1921, began circulating drafts of what it called a *Model State Constitution*, a short, streamlined, and businesslike document containing all of the reforms the League recommended. From time to time the League now puts out revised editions for the states to ponder and, hopefully, copy.

What Modernizing State Government Means.
The authorities on state constitutions have found many things to criticize—they echo most of the points we have covered above. To understand why they regard change as so necessary, however, we need to look at their assumptions about what state government should be doing in today's world.[10]

[10]An early, concise, and often-quoted statement of the reformist's prescriptions for state constitutions is found in William B. Munro, "An Ideal State Constitution," *The Annals of*

Reformers want active state goverments. Most of the critics of state constitutions at one time or another argue that the states need modern constitutions. What "good government" reformers mean is that present day technology, industrialization, urbanization, and the movement of population has drastically changed life in present day America. They conclude that a "hands off" or "do nothing" state government, with constitutions full of "thou shalt nots" is obsolete, or "horse and buggy" today. The reformers believe that state government should take vigorous action to try to solve the problems that grow out of modern conditions. *They do not distrust government.* Rather, today's reformers want to see state and national governments able to provide many benefits for citizens, free of constitutional restrictions.

So the reformer's first assumption about state constitutions is that *limitations on a government's power to act are usually bad.* There are too many limitations in state constitutions and they should be rooted out!

Reformers want efficient state governments. The "good government" reformers also argue, as we noted in Chapter 1, that state and local governments must be streamlined to act more effectively and efficiently.

So the reformers' second assumption about state constitution is that *state constitutions should make state government more efficient by centralizing power, and professionalizing.*

It is when state constitutions are measured by these standards that the reformers find them wanting. The legislation in the documents, the sloppy language, and the tricky legalisms all make the constitutions a great deal longer, but also tie the hands of state government—to act at all, much less to act effectively. They also advantage the status quo groups.

What Do the Reformers Recommend That A Constitution Should Contain?

Almost universally, the authorities recommend brevity—cutting down the number of words. As one suggests "The best constitutions are usually brief—but they are not the best because they are brief, but because they best meet the needs of state government." Long-windedness is almost always closely associated with all of the characteristics of state constitutions that reformers have called undesirable.

---

the American Academy of Political and Social Science, 181 September 1935. More recent publications are W. Brooke Graves, editor, *State Constitutional Revision*, Public Administration Service, Chicago, 1960. See especially the thoughtful comments of Harvey Walker and David Fellman. You might also wish to refer to a very useful small pamphlet by Robert Dishman, *State Constitutions: The Shape of the Document*, National Municipal League, N.Y., Revised Edition, 1968.

The experts tend to agree that constitutions should only contain certain core, or basic, features: (1) a description of major state offices and how they are filled, (2) limitations on the powers of state government—especially the civil liberties found in a Bill of Rights, (3) the structure and powers of community governments, and (4) a method for amending the constitution and calling new constitutional conventions. They do not object if citizens want to begin with a preamble that proclaims worthy ideals. But you will find that judges give no legal effect to preambles because preambles are not an official part of the document.

HOW DID STATE CONSTITUTIONS GET SO COMPLICATED?

The question of how state constitutions got so long is important, we think, because it leads us to look at the role states played in creating a more democratic government system for all Americans. It also makes us at least consider whether under certain conditions, extra detail in constitutions may not be desirable.

Are State Constitutions Too Easy To Amend?

The common method by which constitutions are amended has two steps: proposal and ratification.

The federal constitution has been amended twenty-six times in almost 200 years. (The first ten of these amendments, the Bill of Rights of 1791, were practically a part of the original constitution.) Only one state, Massachusetts, has a constitution that even lasted that long. All but a handful of state constitutions have been amended dozens of times —Texas 218 times in 100 years, South Carolina 417 times in 80 years. Even Alaska had 11 amendments to its new constitution in the first 15 years; Hawaii had 38 and in addition, adopted two constitutions in the first 15 years of statehood.

What slows down amendments to the federal constitution? Clearly the proposal process is the roadblock. Out of the thousands of constitutional amendments suggested, all but thirty-two were screened out by Congress. Of those formally proposed, only six have not been ratified, including at time of writing, the proposed Equal Rights Amendment (ERA) and that to give Washington, D.C. full representative status.

Proposal of Amendments. Amendments are proposed in every state by a vote of both houses of the state legislature. We propose changes to the federal constitution in the same way—by a vote in both houses of Congress. Most state provisions of proposal by this method require ma-

CALIFORNIA VOTERS PAMPHLET

PRIMAR

JUN

compiled by
SECRE1

Analyses by
Legisla

AVISO:

Una traducción al español de este follete del votante puede obtenerse si completa y no envía la tarjeta con porte pagado qu encontrará entre las páginas 56 y 57. Escrib su nombre y dirección en la tarjeta en LETR/ DE MOLDE y regrésela antes del 26 de maye de 1978.

---

⑬ **Tax Limitation—Initiative Constitutional Amendment**

Arguments in Favor of Proposition 13

Limits property tax to 1% of market value, requires two-thirds vote of both houses of the legislature to raise any other taxes, limits yearly market value tax raises to 2% per year, and requires all other tax raises to be approved by the people. Why then the amendment? President Carter said "our tax system is a National disgrace".

Our audit figures show loss to local governments at about $5 billion, not $7 billion as claimed by the state finance director.

Assembly leader Paul Priolo said "it's a tough amendment but the state can live with it. It means public officials will have to go to work".

Noted UCLA tax expert Dr. Neil Jacoby writes "This unjust process must be brought to an end". "A 1% limit would still leave property tax revenue *far above* the level required to pay for property-related governmental services, street lighting maintenance, sewers, trash collection and *POLICE* AND *FIRE PROTECTION*".

According to the State Controller's office, state agencies will still collect more than 33 thousand million tax dollars every year after this amendment passes. We think this is more than enough. *The people will save 7 thousand million dollars every year* for themselves.

This amendment will make rent reductions *probable*. Otherwise *rent raises are certain as property taxes go up.* It will help farmers and keep business in California. It will make home and building improvements possible and *create thousands of new jobs.*

The amendment DOES NOT reduce property tax exemptions for senior citizens. DOES NOT remove tax exemptions for churches or charities. DOES NOT prohibit the use of property tax money for schools.

To make California taxes FAIR, EQUAL and WITHIN THE ABILITY OF THE TAXPAYERS TO PAY, vote YES on Proposition 13.

HOWARD JARVIS
Chairman, United Organizations of Taxpayers

PAUL GANN
President, Peoples Advocate

The Legislature will not act to reduce your property taxes. As a Senator and Legislator for 11 years, I, like you, have been totally frustrated with the Legislature's failure to enact a meaningful property tax relief and reform bill.

What Ronald Reagan describes as the "spenders coalition" of spendthrift politicians and powerful special interests are spending millions to defeat Proposition 13.

Your Yes vote will NOT require a reduction of vital services like police or fire, nor any tax increase. Your Yes vote will require a tough Governor take the lead in cutting wasteful, unnecessary government spending 10 to 15%.

More than 15% of all governmental spending is wasted! Wasted on huge pensions for politicians which sometimes approach $80,000 per year! Wasted on limousines for elected officials or taxpayer paid junkets. Now we have the opportunity to trade waste for property tax relief!

If we want to permanently cut property taxes about 67%, we must do it ourselves. Join Democratic Senator Robert "Bob" Wilson and me, a Republican Senator, in voting Yes on Proposition 13.

JOHN V. BRIGGS
State Senator, 35th District

Rebuttal to Arguments in Favor of Proposition 13

PROPOSITION 13:

GIVES nearly two-thirds of the tax relief to BUSINESS, INDUSTRIAL property owners and apartment house LANDLORDS;

TRANSFERS your LOCAL CONTROL over neighborhood and community program funding to state and federal government bureaucracies;

PROVIDES absolutely NO TAX RELIEF for RENTERS;

REDUCES drastically police patrol services and fire protection while INCREASING home insurance COSTS by 50% to 300%;

REQUIRES new taxes to preserve CRITICAL SERVICES. Doubling the sales tax, substantially increasing the income tax or increasing the bank and corporation tax by 500% are the potential alternatives;

SLASHES current local funding for PARKS, BEACHES, MUSEUMS, LIBRARIES and PARAMEDIC PROGRAMS;

PENALIZES our school CHILDREN by CUTTING operating school budgets by nearly $4 billion, further lowering the quality of education;

PLACES a disproportionate and unfair tax burden on anyone purchasing a home after July 1, 1978;

INCREASES your state and federal INCOME TAXES and HANDS the IRS nearly $2 BILLION of your tax dollars.

Check the FACTS. Talk to your local officials; talk to your schools and talk to your business and labor organizations and demand to know what cutbacks in essential services would occur if Proposition 13 passes.

JOIN the LEAGUE OF WOMEN VOTERS
CALIFORNIA TAXPAYERS ASSOCIATION
LOS ANGELES CHAMBER OF COMMERCE
LEAGUE OF CITIES
COUNTY SUPERVISORS ASSOCIATION
CALIFORNIA RETAILERS ASSOCIATION
and countless others who are opposed to this IRRESPONSIBLE MEASURE which CUTS $7 BILLION from critical services.

VOTE NO ON 13!

HOUSTON I. FLOURNOY
Dean, Center for Public Affairs,
University of Southern California
Former State Controller

TOM BRADLEY
Mayor, City of Los Angeles

GARY SIRBU
State Chairman, California Common Cause

Arguments printed on this page are the opinions of the authors and have not been checked for accuracy by any official agency.

58

California Voters Pamphlet description of an initiated constitutional amendment— Proposition 13 (1978). Note that the text is in Spanish as well as English.

---

jorities similar to that of the U.S. Congress, or they make their constitutions more difficult to amend with special procedures.[11]

Proposal by initiative. A second method of proposal is also used in some states and communities—one more democratic than legislative

[11] Almost half the states use the same method as Congress does—proposal by two-thirds (67 percent) in both the senate and house. In another ten states we find it almost as difficult—proposal by 60 percent of both houses. Another half dozen or so of the states also re-

proposing methods. In 1902 Oregon became the first state to use the initiative and seventeen states, most in the Midwest and West, plus the Virgin Islands now use it. States such as Massachusetts, North Dakota, Oregon, Michigan, and California have constitutional amendments proposed this way at almost every state election. The federal constitution cannot be amended by the initiative, a condition discussed in Policy Box Number 7, "A National Initiative for Constitutional Amendment."

---

quire proposal by a majority, but add an additional requirement that makes proposal more difficult—the proposal must pass the legislature twice, in two successive sessions. Finally we have some peculiar cases that make legislative proposal more complicated and even more difficult. Vermont only permits amendments to be proposed once every ten years; the Colorado legislature may not propose amendments to more than six articles at one time; Arkansas, Illinois, Kansas, Kentucky, and Montana all limit the number of amendments that can be proposed at one time. In only nine states is the method of legislative proposal clearly easier than at the national level—proposal by a simple majority (51 percent).

POLICY BOX NO. 9:   A National Initiative for Constitutional Amendments?

In 1977, when President Jimmy Carter was attempting to gain Senate votes for his Panama Canal Treaty, Senator Robert Griffin (R., Michigan) urged Secretary of State Cyrus Vance to suggest an advisory referendum in which all of the citizens could vote their preference. Secretary Vance replied "I would not recommend it." Holding a national popular referendum is not a new idea. In 1938 a constitutional amendment by Louis Ludlow (D., Indiana) proposed that the U.S. could not declare war without a popular vote unless we were attacked first. William Jennings Bryan and pacifist groups had earlier proposed the same. And earlier in the fight over the prohibition amendment, its opponents in Ohio had secured a law that would require ratification of prohibition by a vote of the people in Ohio should such a bill ever be passed. But in 1920 the U.S. Supreme Court declared this procedure unconstitutional. Perhaps earliest of all, Senator Robert LaFollette (R., Wisconsin) proposed allowing citizens to initiate and ratify by vote, amendments to the federal constitution.

We have had a return of progressive and populist sentiment. A number of individuals are proposing for the national level, changes first used in the states such as abolition of the electoral college and election of the executive by popular vote, or a nationwide primary to nominate presidential candidates. In 1977 Senator James Abourezk (D., South Dakota) and Mark Hatfield (R., Oregon) proposed a constitutional amendment that would accomplish what Senator LaFollette had desired some sixty-five years before. Proposal of amendments to the federal constitution would be by petitions containing signatures equal in number to 3 percent of the voters in the last presidential election—on the basis of the 1976 election, that would require 2,446,550 valid signatures. Ratification would be by majority vote of the people. The federal constitution could thus be amended without Congress or the state legislatures being involved, just as is the case in those states having the constitutional initiative.

Senator Abourezk justified his proposal by arguing that "our democracy is based on the notion that the people can govern themselves." He noted that six of the last ten constitutional amendments to the federal constitution "have in some way extended voting rights." This proposal, he claimed, would be "a further step in this evolutionary process."

It is difficult to judge what the effects of any structural change will be, at least in specific detail, although state experience may help in this case. The present method of amending the federal constitution is unlike that of any state because ratification is not by popular vote, but by a vote of three-quarters of the state legislatures or, if Congress specifies it, three-quarters of specially elected state conventions.

Still, the experience of some states that use the initiative process and all of those that use popular votes for ratification, give us some guidelines as to what we might expect. For a beginning it is highly probable that this kind of change would make the federal constitution much easier to amend. For example, one bottleneck has been that Congress has formally proposed very few of the thousands of proposals suggested.

What would be the political effects of easy amendment? To discover what kinds of amendments would be proposed by initiative, we would need to look at which groups might raise the nearly 3 million signatures required and which of these have proposals that the public opinion polls suggest would be adopted. George F. Will, political scientist and newspaper columnist, suggests "any national initiative would be dominated by an intense, unelected minority using direct mail, television commercials, and other techniques of mass persuasion."

What do you think? Do you favor extending the initiative to the federal government? Has its use hurt or helped the states? How would it affect such groups as blacks, women's rights groups, or Indians? Civil liberties groups? Would it increase or decrease the powers of Congress, the President, the Supreme Court or the bureaucracy? Would it help business or labor, liberals or conservatives, Democrats or Republicans? If you oppose the idea, do you think we should also eliminate the initiative from state constitutions—if you favor it, do you think all states should be required to use the initiative? Suggest three amendments you think would be adopted if we had the initiative at the federal level.

The constitutional initiative is carried out as citizens circulate petitions containing the proposed change and, after they collect a required number of voter signatures, the amendment is placed on the ballot. (Twenty-one states allow citizens to propose ordinary laws, as well, by the same process.) The number of signatures needed to propose constitutional amendments varies by state. In North Dakota it is by 20,000 electors. The most common provision, one we find in twelve states, ties it to a percentage of the vote in the last election for governor or some other statewide office. Usually the number of signatures must equal 8 to 10 percent of the number of votes cast. A few states require an absolute percentage of all eligible voters, and some make it a bit more complicated for the petition circulators. For example, Ohio has the kind of requirement you have to read twice to get straight—10 percent of all electors must sign, and the signatures must be so distributed to include 5 percent of the voters for governor in the last election in each of at least one-half of the counties.[12]

Ratification of Proposed Amendments. Amendments are ratified in a more democratic way in the states than at the national level—that is, all states, except Delaware, require a vote of the people for either legislative or initiative proposals. Ratification of amendments to the federal constitution is by approval by at least three-quarters of the state legislatures.[13]

Only a few states make ratification especially difficult. Take the so-called "brewer's amendment" of Minnesota. From 1857 through 1898 Minnesota had one of the easiest constitutions to amend. Then it looked as if a constitutional amendment against the "liquor traffic," that is, statewide prohibition, would pass. The brewers got their own amendment passed first—they designed it to make statewide prohibition more difficult to adopt. It required that a *majority of those participating in the election* must vote yes for the proposed amendment to be adopted. Thus, if 100,000 citizens went to the polls and only 50,000 bothered to vote on the amendment, it would fail even if every one of them voted for it. The change meant that anyone who voted in the election, say, for governor or president, but skipped voting on a proposed amendment, was, in effect, voting "no" on the amendment—an amendment could get more yes than no votes, but must in this example get at least 50,001 "yes" votes to pass.

Tennessee and Illinois had similar provisions with worse results, perhaps because voting participation generally has been lower in those states than in Minnesota. Tennessee could not get an amendment

[12]Given the present-day interest in citizen participation, it is astonishing to find few recent studies of the constitutional initiative exist. Among the best of the older studies are V.O. Key, Jr. and Winston Crouch, *The Initiative and Referendum in California*, University of California Press, Berkeley, 1939; Winston Crouch, "The Constitutional Initiative in Operation" *American Political Science Review*, August 1939, 634–639; Joseph LaPalombara and Charles Hagen, "Direct Legislation: An Appraisal and a Suggestion," *American Political Science Review*, June 1951, 400–421 and Daniel S. McHargue, *Direct Government in Michigan*, State of Michigan Constitutional Convention Preparatory Commission, 1961.

[13]Congress may also choose to have ratification by three-quarters of specially-elected state conventions, as they did for adoption of the original federal constitution, and one other time—for the ratification of the Twenty-first Amendment in 1933, repeal of national prohibition.

passed for eighty-three years. It took a major civic reform campaign to adopt a few needed changes. "Good government" reformers in Illinois got a change with great difficulty. They carefully publicized what they called a "gateway" amendment, one that would allow adoption if three-fifths (60 percent) voting on the amendment approved.

There are two other quirks. Delaware, as we noted, is the only state that does not allow the citizens to vote on constitutional amendments. To be adopted, amendments must pass the legislature twice, by a two-thirds vote each time. The other special case complicates matters even more. Georgia allows counties to adopt amendments to the state constitution that apply only in that county. This has resulted in a constitution of 500,000 words, the longest in the nation.

Is Length Caused By An Easier Amendment Process?   In two respects the answer is yes. We found that those eighteen states that allow proposal by initiative, on the average have longer constitutions than do the rest of the states.[14] But the initiative only seems to help lengthen constitutions when some other motivation is already present—it is not the sole explanation. We find that some states permitting proposal by initiative have among the shortest state constitutions: Arizona (18,500 words), Nevada (17,270 words), and Nebraska (19,975 words). Also we found that those states with unusually restrictive proposal or ratification procedures also had shorter constitutions.

But when we examined the length of those constitutions that have the identical proposal process as the federal government—a two-thirds vote by both houses of the legislature and no initiative, we find the average length to be 24,432—about two and one-half times longer than the federal constitution. In addition such states have constitutions that vary in length from 14,500 in Kansas to 54, 000 in Texas.

Other factors than the legal rules, we conclude, account for most of the length of state constitutions.

Constitution Length and Social Change

A productive way of looking at state constitutions is to consider them a reflection of the conditions found in the society that produced them. Texans in the nineteenth century, for example, found it important to include a clause that made it a crime to have barbed-wire clippers hid-

[14]We found the eleven state constitutions that date from the nineteenth century, and also permit initiative, averaged 32,015 words. The other twenty-two constitutions that also date from the nineteenth century, but that do not allow initiative proposal, averaged 23,735 words—a noticeable difference. But the nine twentieth century constitutions without initiative, average 26,669 words. The seven twentieth century constitutions with initiative average, about the same, 26,462 words.

den in your saddlebags. What the Texas constitution writers were dealing with was a growing and a rapidly changing society, in this case, disappearance of the open range. Like it or not the nation was changing. What those who built the railroads did after the Civil War was often shocking, but they left behind a developing nation—one that in half a century moved from rural to urban and was well on the way to full industrialization.

At the same time the state governments were called upon to make decisions that would control or guide these changes. All of the major social forces of the day thus focused on what these governments did and what was in their constitutions. It was only to be expected that under such conditions constitutions would grow steadily longer as one group or another attempted to stake out a position and stabilize conditions to its own advantage.

The Bryce Hypothesis.   James Bryce in his classic work on the American system, *The American Commonwealth* (1888) observed that extensive amendment of state constitutions was more frequent in newer states with "fluctuating populations" and where there were "quick and sudden changes" in social and economic conditions. He found long constitutions in states with population and wealth growing "with unexempled speed." Also he found long constitutions in the South, where he noted that the abolition of slavery had changed radically the social and economic basis of the whole society.

Citizens and legislators, Bryce argued, put detailed clauses into constitutions to "meet new conditions and check new evils." With life less predictable, the constitution writers attempted to "cement in" the old ways of doing things. They tried to bring what they saw as a runaway situation under some kind of control.

What the Political Battles Were About

Let us take a closer look at the content of those cluttered and detailed constitutions. Perhaps we can understand a little better what moved our forefathers to make all those detailed amendments.

Statements of High Principle.   We will begin with what appear to be harmless clauses—phrases and platitudes that seem to have no legal effect. Vermont's constitution still reminds its citizens of the value of piety, as follows: "Every sect or denomination of Christians ought to observe the Sabbath or Lord's Day, and keep up some sort of religious worship, which to them seem most agreeable to the revealed will of God."

What political battles lay behind including this clause about Sunday worship? We remember that strict observance of the Sabbath at one time was required in Vermont by law. When this policy was changed, this "token" clause was put in the constitution to appease the defeated, and probably disgruntled minority who saw the times changing and did not like the change. At the same time it told everyone else that they now had the right to worship as they wished. So we have what looks like a piece of nonpolicy, embedded in the document and swelling it out. But who are we to criticize the statesmen of Vermont for using this relatively harmless way of bringing about peaceful change? Perhaps this clause made some of the losers of that political battle feel that all was not lost in a wicked world.

We find similar statements being put into today's constitutions—high-sounding phrases about things we value, or feel we should value—racial and sexual equality, ecology, the rights of labor or of the handicapped. Such clauses may have no legal effect, but do recognize the legitimacy of certain ideals of the past that are waning or ideas whose day is not yet come. Their net effect is to make state government appear legitimate in the eyes of selected citizens—particularly those who, for the moment, may be disgruntled by a reform that has come too fast for them, or not fast enough for someone else. We think anything that helps to increase loyalty, voluntarily given, is not unimportant and a little extra clutter in a state constitution or local charter may be a small price to pay if it keeps such people from becoming disenchanted with their government.

Democratizing State and Community Governments.   Seventy-nine Virginians from Culpepper County marched to battle in the War of 1812. On the way they discovered that only four of their number were eligible to vote. From such discussions the struggle to democratize state and community governments began. It led to extensive revisions of state constitutions that spelled out the legal rights of citizens—first to vote, then to hold office, and then to expand the number of offices and issues decided by election.[15]

The bitter battles to expand citizen participation in America were fought in the states over the clauses in their constitutions. Before the Civil War the state constitutions determined completely who would participate at national, state, and community levels, since the federal constitution allowed states to set requirements for national, as well as state, elections with the clause, "Electors in each state shall have the

[15]The actual voting requirements in postcolonial times depended on the availability of free or cheap land. In his study of Massachusetts voting at the time of the Revolutionary War,

qualifications requisite for electors of the most numerous branch of the state legislature." Thus by liberalizing state constitutions, state citizens were also democratizing the national government as well.

Dorr's Rebellion—Rhode Island Resists. Thomas Dorr (1805-1854), lawyer and Harvard University graduate, agitated to amend the voting provisions of the Rhode Island constitution that dated back to the original Royal Charter of 1763. Only those owning $134 in land value could vote—a tidy sum, even in the 1840s.

In 1841 Dorr illegally called "a People's Constitutional Convention." The legislature then called its own state constitutional convention. Both submitted constitutions to the voters, and Dorr's was approved. The legislature's constitution was overwhelmingly rejected.

In 1842 Dorr was elected governor under his constitution, while a man named Samuel King was elected under the rules of the old constitution. The state militia was called out by the incumbent governor and it sided with Samuel King. Dorr fled, and Dorr's Rebellion was over.

The conservatives then called a second constitutional convention and liberalized voting requirements somewhat. Meanwhile Thomas Dorr was caught and put in prison. After a year in confinement he was released in poor health and, as was said in those days, a broken man, but one who was widely regarded as a hero and martyr by the democratic radicals everywhere.[16]

Democratizing state constitutions did not always come easily.

---

the historian Robert Brown concluded that most of the Bay State's white male citizens were then able to meet the land holding requirements—not only because land was cheap on the frontier to the west—but voting officials did not always strictly enforce the law here and in other states. Robert E. Brown, *Middle Class Democracy and the Revolution in Massachusetts, 1691-1780,* Cornell University Press, Ithaca, 1955. For a short run down of voting requirements in 1776, see also Allan Nevins, *The American States During and After the Revolution, 1775-1789,* Macmillan, N. Y., 1924; reissued New York: Augustus M. Kelley, 1969, p. 170. But the historian Merrill Peterson estimates that in New York by 1820, only about 75 percent of white adult males were eligible under property qualifications to vote for house members and only 40 percent met the stiffer requirements to vote for state senators. In Virginia, at the same point, roughly half of white males were eligible; a figure boosted to 66 percent after the changes of the 1829-30 state Constitutional Convention. Merrill D. Peterson, ed., *Democracy, Liberty and Property, The State Constitutional Conventions of the 1820s,* Bobbs-Merrill, N. Y., 1966. Peterson provides excellent short summaries of the politicking of three constitutional conventions: that of Massachusetts of 1820-21, New York of 1821 and Virginia of 1829-30. The bulk of the book is selected excerpts of the convention proceedings.

[16]For a study of Dorr's Rebellion from a modern, "new left" perspective, see Marvin E. Gettleman, *The Dorr Rebellion, a Study in American Radicalism 1833-1849,* Random House, N.Y., 1973.

The battles over woman suffrage were first fought in states and communities.

The extension of voting rights. By the time of the Civil War, universal white manhood suffrage was embedded in almost every state constitution.

Almost every time a new state was admitted, or an older state held a constitutional convention, we find a weakening of property and religious requirements. The six new states that entered the Union between 1816 and 1821—Indiana, Illinois, Mississippi, Alabama, Missouri, and Maine—all had universal white manhood suffrage in their constitutions. But universal white manhood suffrage did not come in one sweep. South Carolina, in fact, did not adopt universal male suffrage until 1868 (under a Reconstruction government).[17]

The enfranchisement of blacks came in 1865, followed by a long, bitter struggle to extend the vote to women (1920), and finally to eighteen year olds (1971). All amended state constitutions by amending the national constitution in a way that would apply to all states.

Democratizing government structure. The Jacksonians of the frontier, who were among the most active in getting voting requirements lowered, also worked to make citizen participation more effective. They began putting clauses into the state constitutions that would bring government closer to the people. We have the Jacksonian reformers of the 1820s to thank for the fact that so many state and community officials are elected including, in one state, the state printer, and in many local governments, such administrative officials as treasurers or drain commissioners.

The Jacksonian reformers also set about making terms short, usually, at most, two years, and introduced such requirements as that governors and treasurers could only serve one term. Also, part of their program was what they called "rotation in office" and what we call the spoils, or patronage, system. The victorious party or faction upon taking office, would throw all the state office holders out and fill the government offices with their own supporters.

The "Special Interests" Added Constitutional Provisions. The Jacksonians brought government "closer to the people." They also made it more vulnerable to less idealistic interest groups as well. State constitutions became especially open to the influence of organized interest groups such as blossomed in America's period of railroad building, rapid industrialization, and massive population shifts just before and

---

[17]Two forces slowed down the movement of wider participation. One was the prejudice against blacks and the other, fear of laboring classes of the urban centers. Fletcher M. Green, *Constitutional Development in the South Atlantic States, 1776–1860*, University of North Carolina Press, Chapel Hill, 1930. See especially Chapter 5 "The Democratic Awakening: 1800–1830, 171–200.

after the Civil War. Lewis A. Froman, Jr. compared an assessment of state interest group strength made by political scientists, to the length of state constitutions. He found that where interest groups were very influential, constitutions were longer and more detailed.[18]

The kinds of clauses that "the big interests" placed in state constitutions usually dealt with special formulas for taxing their property—at less than the usual rate, or provisions against regulating their right to do business or exploit a state's natural resources as they pleased.

The cut-over timber areas of northern Michigan and Wisconsin, the strip mine areas of southern Illinois, the disappearance of the buffalo from Nebraska's Great Plain (decimated by "Buffalo Bill" to feed the railroad workers), and the virtual elimination of fur-bearing animals in the Far West suggest how free these entrepreneurs were of interference by states or communities. The smoke and grime that belches from the United States Steel Corporation mills on the beaches of Lake Michigan and drifts across Interstate 80 at Gary and Hammond, Indiana, reminds us that day is not completely past.

In some of today's state constitutions we find similar provisions in respect to such interest groupings as physicians, lawyers, beauticians, realtors, optometrists, and school teachers. We find provisions for the boards that regulate such professions that assure heavy representation of the interest groups to be regulated. Thus, at one time the California Constitution established a mining board that would have five members "representing the mining industry," the board of commissioners of the Oil and Gas Division were elected by "oil and gas operators in each of five districts," and the State Board of Forestry would have "members chosen to represent the pine and redwood industries, forest land, livestock and agricultural operators and water users."[19]

Special Restrictions on State Legislatures. We find legislative detail in constitutions also because almost every reform movement in American history has blamed the state legislature for many of its troubles. Reformers of every stripe during the nineteenth century tried to take away the power to act from what they considered untrustworthy legislative officials.

Limiting legislative sessions. A simple way to cripple their effectiveness was to limit the length of legislative sessions. Lieutenant Governor

[18]Lewis A. Froman, Jr., "Some Effects of Interest Group Strength in State Politics," *American Political Science Review* 60, December 1966, 952–962.

[19]These examples are quoted by Grant McConnell, *Private Power and American Democracy*, Knopf, N.Y., 1966, p. 186, and taken from *California State Government, a Guide to Organizations and Functions*, California State Department of Finance, Sacramento, 1951.

Richard O. Ristine of Indiana once humorously observed, "Our constitution states that the state legislature can only meet fifty-five days every two years. Some citizens seem to think it should be two days every fifty-five years." He was joking, but it is an attitude that many reformers, faced by corrupt legislatures, once held—and perhaps with good reason.

Today about half of the states have no restriction on the length of state legislative sessions. But of these states, you will find that some set a time limit after which a legislator's *per diem* expenses will no longer be paid. (We suppose the legislators can go on meeting if they wish to.)

Limiting legislative financial powers. Another favorite method was to restrict the legislature's power to tax, to borrow, or to spend. The first of these constitutional restrictions was devised at the time of the Depression of 1837. The midwestern states, after the great success of the Erie Canal in New York during the 1820s, had underwritten extensive canal building. The depression and the beginning of railroad building drove the ambitious projects into bankruptcy. Yet the bonds had to be paid off.

Many states, thereafter, prudently limited in their constitutions, the debts a legislature could incur. North Dakota entered the Union in 1889 with this clause, "Debts shall never in the aggregate exceed the sum of $200,000." Another favorite device was to prevent legislators from raising their own salaries. Official salaries were listed in the constitution. A Kentucky state court recently was persuaded to rule that the original constitution writers meant for subsequent generations to take inflation into account.

Sometimes these financial limitations on legislatures have turned out to be stronger than was planned. The new Alabama Constitution of 1901, for example, "forbade the state to engage in works of internal improvement, lend money or its credit in aid of such improvements, or become interested in or lend money or its credit to any private individual or corporate enterprise."[20] This crippled the fledgling state highway department. Alabamans had to amend the clause seven years later so that the state could legally build and maintain roads and bridges.[18]

Introduction of Legislative Detail. Obviously, if reformers so distrusted legislators, they would also write their own "pet" legislation into constitutions. The Minnesota Constitution at one time described in detail all of the proposed routes of its state highway system, lest some

[20]James D. Thomas, *Government in Alabama*, Bureau of Public Administration, University of Alabama, University, 1969, p. 3.

highway engineer, with ideas gotten, perhaps, at the University, persuade the legislators to bypass a county seat.

The Progressive Reforms of 1890–1914. The Progressives of the 1890s and early 1900s believed state party leaders, legislatures, courts, and usually the governor, were in collusion, bought out by "special privilege."

This was, in fact, especially true of state legislators because they were amateurs in politics—their main occupations were nongovernmental. Wisconsin Governor Robert LaFollette, a leading Progressive, tells how one of his most enthusiastic young legislative supporters, whom he calls "E", voted with his opponents when the railroads threatened to ruin his business by giving his competitors rate advantages. With tears in his eyes, the former supporter, "E", told Governor LaFollette, "I can't beggar my family. I have a wife and babies."[21]

In Policy Box No. 10, "Reformers Then and Now," we discuss in more detail the travails of one of these reformers.

Progressive solutions. The Progressive reformers put into state constitutions and local charters, procedures they devised to smash the interests and the boss system. Among the most important were primary elections in place of party conventions, direct election of judges, the initiative, referendum and recall, civil service, nonpartisan elections, the commission system of local government, and later the council-manager system. They hoped by these methods to return power to the people.

Of course, they also worked hard to stomp out government corruption—the South Dakota Constitution required its legislators of the 1890s to swear they had never received a free railroad pass in exchange for a vote on a bill. The Kentucky Constitution declared that any legislator, judge, or other private officer, who accepted a free pass, would be removed from office automatically.[22]

A favorite Progressive technique was to set up regulatory commissions, such as Minnesota's elective Railroad and Warehouse Commission or the public service commissions of many other states. The Progressives wished to keep these regulatory bodies "out of politics"—by which they meant, free from the influence of "the interests" and political bosses. We thus find in the constitutions, long and carefully detailed descriptions of how these regulatory or administrative agencies

[21]Robert M. LaFollette, *LaFollette's Autobiography*, (1911), reissued in paperback, University of Wisconsin Press, Madison, 1961, 113–114.

[22]James Bryce, Op. cit., Chapter 38, "Development of Constitutions."

POLICY BOX NO. 10:   Reformers Then and Now

Hazen Pingree was one of America's earliest Progressive reformers. His actions were copied by a generation who followed him, beginning with Robert M. LaFollette of Wisconsin. The climax of Pingree's political career centered on gaining passage of an amendment to his state's constitution after he had been repeatedly blocked by the state legislature and state courts.

Detroit in 1889 elected Hazen Pingree, a forty-nine-year-old shoe manufacturer and a successful millionaire, as mayor on a "good government" platform. His platform and first term was conventionally genteel, emphasizing as an issue the need for more street paving. But he ended up being one of Detroit's few four-term mayors and one of its most controversial.

Mayor Pingree first showed a progressive streak over tax policy. He was shocked to find that some major businesses avoided most taxes. His campaign lost him much of his original "good government" support. He lamented, "It takes a lot of pluck to see your old associates pass you by without speaking and not get disheartened and want to give up the fight." Pingree soon was attacking the local gas company and got it to lower its rates. He then established a municipally owned lighting plant, and tried to get the city to buy the local street car company when it refused to lower its fares to 3 cents a ride. He ended in persuading a rival firm to come in and charge lower street car fares. His biographer, Melvin G. Holli, argues that Pingree changed from a reformer, interested only in reforming government structure, to one who desired social reform—a basic change of economic, social, and political institutions in favor of the underprivileged.

Pingree was nominated for governor of Michigan in 1896, partly because local businessmen wanted to get him out of Detroit, and partly because Michigan Republican politicians felt they needed a liberal on the ticket when William McKinley ran against Democrat William Jennings Bryan.

Elected, we find Pingree attacking the railroads. He had found that their land holdings and their railroad stations were assessed by the state at lower rates than other property—industrial, commercial, or citizens' homes.

Pingree's proposals to change the situation by law during his first term were blocked in the state senate by members of his own party, called "the immortal nineteen." He campaigned successfully for reelection on the issue in 1898. He then with great effort forced through a bill setting railroad assessments at the same rate as those for other types of property. But the state supreme court declared his new law "unconstitutional."

Pingree then began to pressure for a constitutional amendment. After the regular session turned him down, Governor Pingree called a special session and then a second special session.

In the glare of publicity shortly before the 1900 election, Governor Pingree finally got his amendment proposed by the state legislature. It was adopted by the voters by an 8-to-1 margin. The "immortal nineteen" took its revenge by having the Pingree amendment take effect after Governor Pingree left office in 1900.

By then Pingree was in poor health and had, in fact, spent much of his private fortune on politics. In addition, some of his trusted aides had been indicted in a government scandal. Others had died or had taken lucrative jobs in private business—one became a banker. Pingree's wife had become so upset by the continued political controversy that surrounded him that she became a recluse in the governor's mansion—refusing to accompany him to political or government functions. At the same time his son became a playboy, and died young.

Pingree's methods were not always what his political opponents considered fair or "nice." He was a populist who flamboyantly took his causes to the people. He attacked his enemies with vigor and made bitter personal enemies. Rumors circulated about his personal habits—particularly his tendency to drown his sorrows at Lansing taverns.

Pingree left office in 1900, traveled to Africa to hunt lions, became ill, and died in 1901 in London, England, at age 60. He had planned to return to run once more for mayor of Detroit to push the reforms he felt were still needed.

What do you think? How does the career of reformers differ between 1900 and the 1970s? Is the career of today's reformers following the same pattern as Pingree's? Is it as risky being a reformer today or does society provide widespread support? Would amendment of state constitutions be as important today, or would today's reformers use other methods to achieve their goals? Finally do you think the costs a reformer like Pingree had to pay were worth the gains he achieved? Does he seem to you to have been motivated more by the desire for "ego trips" than achieving basic reform? What about today's reformers?

SOURCE: The only biography of Hazen Pingree is Melvin G. Holli, *Reform in Detroit, Hazen S. Pingree and Urban Politics*, Oxford University Press, N.Y., 1969, 196–214. See also Robert M. LaFollette, *LaFollette's Autobiography*, University of Wisconsin Press, Madison, reissued 1961; Tom L. Johnson, *My Story*, 1913; Briand Whitlock, *Forty Years of It*, 1914; and Lincoln Steffins, *Autobiography*, Harcourt Brace, N.Y.

should be set up and the precise powers they exercise in regulating "the trusts."

Reform in California.   We can see how the Progressive reformers expanded state constitutions when we look at what happened in California. Governor "Holy" Hiram Johnson (1910–1914) mounted a massive attack against "the interests." Its impact still lingers in the state. Johnson was the son of the Southern Pacific Railroad's chief lobbyist. In a fashion that we suppose Freudian psychologists might itch to speculate about, he devoted himself to smashing Southern Pacific's hold on California politics. He won the governorship in the state's first primary in 1910 and immediately pushed twenty-three detailed constitutional amendments through the legislature! The voters approved all but one proposal, and the California constitution bulged.[23]

The Reformers of Today.   Today we are in another great period of reform and the battle over what should be added to state constitutions and city charters continues. Ecologists, feminists, Nader's Raiders, taxpayer and consumer groups, Common Cause, and others are struggling to add their amendments. Many states are adding constitutional clauses that would have been cheered by the earlier Progressives: clauses restricting state spending, limiting lobbying activities, requiring registration of lobbyists, and reports of their expenditures.

These clauses also add to the bulk of state constitutions—some would argue that much of what the new reformers add is also "legislative detail."

OUR CLUTTERED STATE CONSTITUTIONS: AN ASSESSMENT

The continuing criticism of state constitutions is that the states have filled them with unnecessary detail. We have found this to be true. We have also found reasons in the fact that state constitutions have been intensely political documents. They have dealt with details that citizens saw as specially important. The states also have been governments accessible to voters, reformers, and interest groups.[24]

Making American Government More Democratic

It seems difficult to us to overemphasize the importance of the battles between the early aristocrats and those who wished to democratize American government—between Jacksonian and Progressive reform-

---

[23]Royce D. Delmatier, Clarence F. McIntosh, and Earl G. Waters, *The Rumble of California Politics, 1848–1970*, Chapter 6, "Hiram Johnson and the Progressive Years," John Wiley and Sons, N.Y., 1970, 165–191.

[24]America's first state constitutions are sometimes held up as "models of conciseness and brevity"—falsely we believe. They clearly give evidence of hasty and often sloppy draftsmanship, as well as of incompleteness—much as we would expect of documents prepared in times of revolution and its attendant uncertainty. An excellent study of these early constitutions, citing and evaluating historical interpretations of them, is found in Donald S. Lutz "The Theory of Consent in the Early State Constitutions," a paper delivered at the national meetings of the American Political Science Association, September 1976. Lutz argues that these first constitutions represent a different and more liberal theory of democracy than that which guided writers of the federal constitution.

ers and "the interests." As the result of these battles, for better and for worse, state governments and the national government, as well, are a good deal less oligarchic and aristocratic today than they might have been. But state constitutions are a good deal longer and more involved.

On balance, having constitutions responsive and therefore longer, seems to us to have been a price worth paying. Particularly, we think this is so, because, in an age of permissive federalism, much of the early clutter is being pruned out by federal judges and the continuing efforts of state-based reform groups.

The price of long constitutions would be worth paying again if, in the future, American citizens conclude its government officials or administrators are not as responsive as they wish. Such a condition, it seems to us, would warrant introducing extensive detail, and even restrictions within the state constitution.

Special Cases Require Special Treatment

We think a case also exists for differences among the constitutions of the fifty states, even at the cost of introducing what the experts call "legislative detail." The case for constitutional variety assumes that despite their growing similarity, states still are different in important ways.

At least one of the authorities on state constitutions defends those who wish to introduce more than core materials into state constitutions.[25]

Let us also look at the question of including a particular reform in the document itself. Frank P. Grad argues that this is really a political decision. These are the questions of benefits to be considered: How important is the issue? What special benefits will result? Does the reform require special protection from legislative change? Is the reform a matter in which a settled rule is necessary so that the political battles will die down and action be taken? These are the questions that balance present benefits against future political costs: What are the risks of tying the hands of future citizens when conditions change? Will the clause become obsolete in a relatively short time? Can the matter be handled just as well through legislation? Is special treatment or protection really defensible?

Frank P. Grad notes that even the reformers come to the conclusion that some legislative detail should be in state constitutions. The Model State Constitution, a document generally "sacred" to civic reformers,

[25]Frank P. Grad, Op. cit.

contains clauses that we can reasonably describe as legislative detail. These are a number of "good government" proposals that seem especially important to reformers, such as "local home rule, intergovernment cooperation, modern budget and appropriation procedures, the merit system in public employment, and safeguards for public education (including higher education.)" These seem to reformers to require special protection from meddling by state legislatures. The reformers thus put them into their model constitution.[26]

And this may well be reasonable. As Grad points out, would it not be reasonable to give special constitutional protection to a new civil service system in a state that had a history of one hundred fifty years of spoils politics? Was the Michigan constitutional convention in the early 1960s unwise when it decided to include a detailed description of its new and then controversial Civil Rights Commission in its new constitution, rather than just authorize the legislature to set up such a body? Were states, at an earlier period, that put into constitutions workers compensation clauses or the spelled-out rights of unions to bargain collectively, so mistaken?

A second point Grad makes, is that the states have their own peculiar physical environments and have to deal with the problems that grow out of them. They also have formed their own political traditions. Alaska has a new constitution—one reformers generally admire. In it is a long article detailing how natural resources will be developed. This is a burning issue in the state, as the controversy over the pipeline suggests. Who are we as outsiders to say that in Louisiana, matters dealing with the Port of New Orleans do not require a status above that of ordinary legislation? When New Jersey revised its constitution, reformers felt it necessary to include a provision permitting gambling and games of chance, just as its previous constitution had done, lest the new document be defeated over this issue. Even limitations on debt or balancing of the budget may be so much a part of state political traditions, Grad suggests, that if we attempt to root them out, it will seem wrong to many state citizens.

KEEPING STATE CONSTITUTIONS CURRENT

The outlook in respect to "outmoded provisions" in state constitutions is not as bleak as it once was. We are living through a period of extensive constitutional revision—sometimes the pruning has been done by

[26]Frank P. Grad, Op. cit., p. 949.

state and federal courts, at other times states have written a completely new state constitution, but more frequently, states have revised large sections of these documents.

The Federal Government Changes State Constitutions

Federal court action has eliminated a good deal of what the reformers complain about in state constitutions. The major impacts have dealt with the rights of minorities, criminals, protection for people expressing unpopular opinions, and expansion of state voting requirements. Congress has backed many of these court decisions with legislation such as the Voting Rights Act. A full discussion of how the federal courts affected state constitutional powers in these areas will be found in Chapter 9, The Judges As Legitimizers.

In 1962 the U.S. Supreme Court, in *Baker* v. *Carr*, ruled that both houses of state legislatures must be apportioned on a population basis of one person-one vote. Subsequent cases also applied the principle to community governments.

This decision was a kind of breakthrough for state constitutional revision, as well as encouragement of the federal courts and the Congress to review other aspects of state constitutions. It broke the stalemate in state constitution writing because legislators, fearing reapportionment, had from 1900 on, generally blocked the calling of constitutional conventions.

All this federal activity has meant that when states faced up to a revision of their constitutions, they often found a great deal of deadwood that could be easily cleared away.

Constitutional Revision By States Themselves

Reapportionment was not the only issue that made state legislators reluctant to call constitutional conventions—settled matters can be upset by a wholesale revision of the constitution by a body not under legislative control. Legislators are also concerned with the interests of political allies in other branches of state government, or of clauses affecting organized groups with whom they are sympathetic. In addition a very practical political concern exists over whether a constitutional convention might not produce a crop of budding politicians who might decide to run for legislative seats. State constitutional conventions frequently provide a political platform for the emergence of relative unknowns—George Romney, for example, who went on to be governor of Michigan. Thus, legislators prefer methods of constitutional revision that they can control.

In Table 5-1 we showed the methods used in 1970 to 1971 and 1976 to 1977. Note the great number of proposals by legislatures, and that they are more likely to be adopted than those proposed by initiative or by convention. Also note the general rise in adoptions for all types of proposals.

A New Constitution Through Amendment. Technically a state can adopt what, in effect, is a new constitution simply by adopting a series of amendments to the old one. A series of such amendments may be proposed by the legislature or by a constitutional convention. The advantage the legislature sees in its proposal of amendments is that they keep a close control over the proposal process. Thus, as Table 5-1 indicates, the most common method by which constitutions are revised is not through constitutional convention, but by legislatively proposed amendments.

A disadvantage of legislative proposal is that the legislature has matters other than constitutional revision to look after. Limits on the length of legislative sessions may complicate the matter further. Legislators can ill afford the two, three, or more months of daily deliberations required to make a wholesale revision of the constitution.[27] Finally a number of constitutions limit the number of amendments legislatures may propose at any single election or the number of subjects or articles they may deal with. This makes comprehensive change difficult or impossible unless the legislature submits a proposed amendment that is of the "gateway" type—one that makes amendment an easier process.

A new constitution by revision commission. Legislators, with increasing frequency, are using revision commissions—a method that maintains legislative control without requiring the legislature to work out the detail. The legislature appoints a small body of citizens and "experts" to prepare a revision for them. The body may be instructed to revise the whole document, or to limit its concern to certain articles or subjects.

When finished, the revision commission sends its proposed revision to the legislature. Legislators may revise or even eliminate parts of the proposal before submitting proposed amendments to the voters.

New Jersey successfully used this method in 1947. Its state constitution was rewritten by a commission that often met in private across the Hudson River in a New York City hotel.

---

[27]A Rhode Island constitutional convention met between December 8, 1964 and September 11, 1967, in preparing its proposed revision—a modern record.

TABLE 5-1 State Constitutional Changes By Method of Initiation 1970–1971, 1974–1975

Methods of initiation	Number of States involved		Total Proposals		Percentage Adopted	
	1970–71	1976–77	1970–71	1976–77	1970–71	1976–77
All methods	48	42	403	39.9	55.6	70.2
Legislative proposal	47	42	392	36.9	56.6	74.0
Constitutional initiative	4	8	5	18	20.0	16.7
Constitutional convention	2	1	6	12	16.7	33.3

SOURCE: Adapted from Albert Sturm, "State Constitutions and Constitutional Revision," *Book of the States*, 1970–71, 1972–73, 1974–75.

A phased constitutional revision commission. California devised a variation of the revision commission in the late 1960s. They called it phased constitutional revision. The legislature set up a series of commissions, each with specialists on the constitutional subjects and articles to be reviewed. Each year, over a five- to six-year period, one of these commissions submitted to the legislature changes to a part of the old constitution. Indiana, Ohio, and South Carolina have also used this method.

A constitutional study commission. Another variation is to have a commission, again appointed by the legislature, study whether the document needs revision. Montana used such a study commission in 1970. It recommended a constitutional convention, prepared an enabling act for the convention, drafted a proposed constitution for the convention to consider, and conducted an information campaign for the calling of a constitutional convention. Voters approved calling the convention, and in 1972, also approved the new proposed constitution.

A New Constitution by Constitutional Convention. Only three-quarters of the states authorize the use of constitutional conventions, but the U.S. Supreme Court has ruled that all states may set up such bodies.[28]

[28]The basic bibliographic source on recent constitutional revisions listed state by state, is Albert L. Sturm, *A Bibliography on State Constitutions and Constitutional Revision, 1945–75*, Citizens Conference on State Legislatures, Englewood, Colorado, August, 1975. See also Cynthia E. Browne, *State Constitutional Conventions from Independence to the Completion of the Present Union, 1776–1959, A Bibliography*, Greenwood Press, Westport,

In most states the state legislature can veto the holding of a constitutional convention by inaction. But eight state constitutions have a clause, such as New York's, that requires placing on the ballot at specified times, the question of holding a constitutional convention. New York's provision specified that the question be voted on "at the General Election of 1957, and every twentieth year thereafter." The question of holding a convention may also be put on the ballot by initiative petition, as was done in Massachusetts in 1968 and 1970.

Limited constitutional conventions. Legislatures in the last decade have also called limited constitutional conventions—the conventions may only consider certain topics or revise specific clauses of the old constitution. In some states the question of what a constitutional convention can consider is submitted to the voters by the legislature. In 1968, for example, Tennessee voters agreed to have a constitutional convention consider only one out of five topics that the legislature suggested for review.

Organization of constitutional conventions. Sometimes the constitution describes how constitutional convention delegates will be chosen. Most often we find these details in a special statute prepared at the time by the legislature. It often details the rules the convention will follow, its financing, and whether delegates will be elected on a partisan or nonpartisan basis and composition of delegate districts.

Recent Revisions of State Constitutions

Since 1962 when the *Baker* v. *Carr* decision was made, well over half the states have made some effort at extensive revision.

We find, as expected, a general streamlining of government in most of the proposals—whether accepted or rejected. Present constitutional conventions seem to have been influenced a great deal by the reform ideas of the National Municipal League as found in its proposed *Model State Constitution.*

Let us take a look at what happened to the length of the constitutions extensively revised in the last thirty years or so. In Table 5-2 we listed the twelve states that made complete revisions that were later accepted by the voters. We also compare the size of the old and new documents.

Conn., 1973; Bonnie Canning, *State Constitutional Conventions, Revisions and Amendments, 1959–1976: A Bibliography,* Greenwood Press, Westport, Conn., 1977, and Susan Rice Yarger, *State Constitutional Conventions, 1959–1975, A Bibliography,* Greenwood Press, Westport, Conn., 1976.

TABLE 5-2 Length of Constitutions Before and After Revision

	Date of Revision	Before	After
Connecticut	1965	6,750	7,400
Florida	1968	32,500	21,286
Georgia	1945	32,478	25,000*
Illinois	1970	21,580	13,200
Louisiana	1974	255, 450	26,300
Michigan	1963	15,323	19,203
Missouri	1945	40,000	30,000
Montana	1972	28,000	11,200
New Jersey	1947	6,276	12,500
North Carolina	1970	17,000	12,500
Pennsylvania	1968	24,750	21,500
Virginia	1970	34,250	8,000

*Basic Georgia constitution excluding amendments that apply to only one county. With these included the Georgia constitution is now 500,000 words.

Note that of the successful revisions, we find that nine states shortened their constitutions and three industrialized states lengthened theirs, although in no case was the new one exceptionally long.

Getting Proposed New Constitutions Adopted.   Whether the method of revision proposed is the regular amendment process, proposals of a commission submitted to the voters by the legislature, or a document prepared by a constitutional convention, the universal method of adoption today, except in Delaware, is by a vote of the people. It is in such elections that many recent attempts at revision have floundered.

A crucial decision is whether a new constitution is submitted as a series of amendments that can be voted on separately, or as a complete document on which citizens have either a "yes" or "no" choice. When proposals are voted on separately, generally some of them get adopted—those that have taken the all or none position, as New Mexico, Arkansas, and Maryland did in recent years, have seen all of the work of constitutional conventions go down the drain at once. A few such "all or none" proposals, such as Michigan's in 1963, were accepted—in that case by an extremely narrow margin.

Why Has Adoption of a New Constitution Been So Difficult?   Extensive constitutional revision has been difficult because constitutions are political documents. Cleaning out the cluttered sections has been more than a technical job of putting legal language into good English. As we have seen, at issue are important advantages and disadvantages for specific groups or individuals.

The hard core opponents of change. Researchers generally uncover, as we would expect, a hard core of self-interested opponents—those who would lose by changes. Sometimes these self-serving groups will resort to scare tactics to stir up the suspicions of others. "Why revise the Bible?" was the slogan used in a Missouri campaign.

One such group almost sure to be found in opposition, is that of officeholders who will either be replaced or who view the proposed changes as leading to unpredictable results—frequently officials whose offices were designed for a rural society as sheriffs and justices of the peace, but also state administrators or employees, who might have their jobs changed or eliminated. Also opposed are representatives of established interest groups who hold a privileged position in the constitution.

Generalized opposition to change. Elmer Cornwell and his associates, in a study of seven constitutional conventions, concluded that the basic "gut issue" in the elections was whether a citizen, in general, favored change or felt safer with the status quo.[29]

In favor of change were upper-income citizens, usually highly educated, who favored the proposals made by reformers. These groups believed in the experts and they trusted government. They wanted to see government streamlined and strengthened so it could act more effectively.

Those favoring the status quo were the less successful—the blue collar workers, the less-educated citizens. These citizens were skeptical about the experts and distrusted government in general. They believed that the less government, probably, the better. Those opposed to change did not understand all of the changes proposed nor did they particularly want to. Very possibly, we suspect, they favored limiting what state government could do.

Thus in the Maryland vote, the researchers found suburban Baltimore in favor, but the more rural parts of the state opposed. In New Mexico other researchers found the cities in favor of a proposed new constitution while Spanish-speaking areas were overwhelmingly against.[30]

Special cases of opposition. Researchers also found other reasons in specific campaigns to explain opposition to a new constitution. The proposed new constitution in a few cases became an issue between po-

[29]Elmer E. Cornwell, Jr., Jay S. Goodman and Wayne R. Swanson, *State Constitutional Conventions, the Politics of Revision in Seven States*, Praeger, N.Y., 1975.

[30]Albert L. Sturm, "State Constitutions and Constitutional Revision, 1967–1969," *The Book of the States, 1970–71*, Council of State Governments, Lexington, Kentucky, 1970, 13–14.

litical parties. Some conventions, notably that of New York, were organized on a partisan basis from the start. Voters viewed the changes recommended in New York as being akin to party campaign programs and voted accordingly. In many states, partisanship was purposely muted to avoid such an outcome.

Even when delegates are elected on a nonpartisan basis, partisanship may arise. Jack R. Van Der Slik found that to be the case in the 1970 Illinois convention,—a fact not astonishing in a state in which Richard J. Daley, one of America's last political bosses, was still active.[31]

Another division occasionally found important was "big city" against the rest of the state. In both New York and Illinois, Cornwall and his associates found evidence, both in constitutional convention deliberations and votes against adoption, of an outstate or upstate versus big city division.

The politics of constitutional revision. Conventions that upset too many groups in their revisions, research suggests, face a publicity barrage from a cumulative opposition—groups in opposition that alone may be small, but when banded together can make a great deal of noise in favor of the status quo. They recruit to their position those already inclined to be suspicious of change.

Thus, revising a constitution in convention often becomes a political process of bargaining. Compromise may be necessary to prevent the opposition of such groups as probate judges, county sheriffs, or entrenched interest groups.

Final Comment

We believe state constitutions and, of course, city charters as well, must be viewed as political documents, rather than as exercises in nonpartisan statesmanship. They are the methods by which a generation of citizens attempt to nail down what is important to them and later generations should at least attempt to understand this fact. We suggest that our generation also should introduce changes that will bring state constitutions or home rule city charters closer to needs and desires of present citizens of the states and communities—without making our first concern the length or complexity of the documents we produce.

[31]Jack Van Der Slik, "Patterns of Partisanship in a Nonpartisan Representational Setting. The Illinois Constitutional Convention," *American Journal of Political Science* 18, February 1974, 95–116.

HIGHPOINTS OF CHAPTER 5: STATE CONSTITUTIONS

In this chapter, we began by looking at (1) the legal contract theory of constitution writing, stressing that written constitutions required someone to interpret them and in America that was the federal and state courts. (2) We next asked why constitutions were so important and concluded it was because they set up rules that conferred long-time burdens or benefits on citizens. (3) We then looked at what constitutions contain and found them cluttered with legislative detail that sometimes led to governmental stalemate. Authorities, we found, recommended streamlining and shortening them. (4) We next looked at the problem of why state constitutions got so long and concluded it was not mainly because their amending procedures were easier, but because they were the target of special interests, reformers, and ordinary citizens in a period of instability and change, the nineteenth and early twentieth century. (5) In our assessment of these cluttered constitutions we concluded that under certain conditions, adding to the length of constitutions could be a virtue. Such efforts often represented a reasonable attempt to preserve and extend democratic government and give special protection to what is important in the eyes of present-day citizens. We assumed our generation would do the same without being concerned primarily about length or complexity. (6) We then looked at current trends and found change the modern reformers recommended, coming through the federal and state courts and through constitutional revision. We concluded (7) by looking at the difficulties of constitutional change.

6

STATE-AND LOCAL FINANCE IN A CENTRALIZING FEDERAL SYSTEM

Few of us recall when we first paid a tax, but we can safely wager that it was probably a state sales tax. We did not pay much attention—the tax was only a few pennies. We just took the clerk's word for it, much as we did when we really awakened to the reality of taxes in our lives. That came when we got our first paycheck from MacDonald's or Burger King, or wherever. We looked at the amount of the check with astonishment. The check stub told the story. Not only did "they" withhold for Social Security, but for federal and state income taxes, and perhaps city income taxes as well. It was shocking that "they" would take so much! Students of public finance also have misgivings about American methods of raising tax revenues.

One theme that runs through the study of public finance is that tax experts are critical of the way state and local governments raise taxes. They argue that our state tax systems are regressive and inelastic. By regressive we mean that more taxes are paid by lower-income persons as a proportion of personal income than by higher income taxpayers, and by inelastic we mean that the revenue

How
One
Cartoonist
Views the
Tax Revolt

Reprinted by permission of the Chicago Tribune-New York News Syndicate, Inc.

raised does not expand or rise at a rate equal to or greater than increases in personal income.[1]

We might ask why, then, state officials do not improve the system. Their timidity highlights a second familiar theme—that states complete with each other, as do communities with their counterparts for business and industry. If a state's or a community's taxes are very much higher than those of its neighbors, it risks losing some of its big taxpayers to lower tax states or communities.

This introduces a third theme that we will stress; our federal system is not only becoming politically interdependent, but to deal effectively with state and community problems the federal system is becoming financially interdependent as well. Local governments no longer depend on their own taxes alone, but get a substantial portion of their funds from other governments, just as the states also receive federal funds. These intergovernmental transfers are redistributive among states and communities, thus reducing some of the undesirable features of the state and local taxing systems.

Overview.   Two basic points concern us in this chapter—where the states and localities get their funds, and the program areas they spend them on. We will see that intergovernmental transfers are an important source, a source that has implications for federalism. We will discuss the kinds of taxes these governments levy and evaluate each of them. Then we will discuss the practice of borrowing. Finally we will review how the states and localities allocate or expend these dollars in support of various policy commitments.

[1]Ira Sharkansky, *The Maligned States,* McGraw Hill Book Company, N.Y., 1972, p. 8.

Figure 6-1
1975 State and Local General Function Expenditures

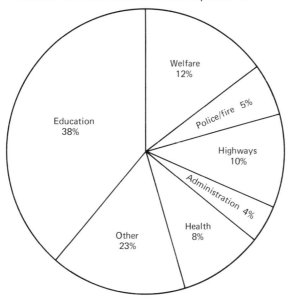

SOURCE: Adapted from *Facts and Figures on Government Finance*, Tax Foundation, Inc., (19th ed.) New York, 1977.

1975 State and Local Revenues

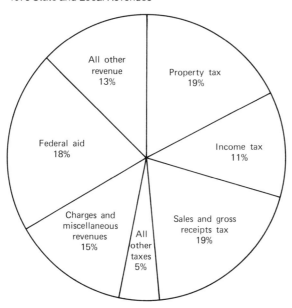

SOURCE: Adapted from Advisory Commission on Intergovernmental Relations, *Significant Features of Fiscal Federalism* (1976 ed.) Washington, D.C., 1976, p. 35.

You may, perhaps, think of finances as a complicated subject. We have tried to make it easier for you by the use of tables and figures. Because our main discussion concerns revenues and expenditures, we present Figure 6-1 here as part of the overview. We hope you will find it useful and can refer to it occasionally as you read along.

THE ROLE OF INTERGOVERNMENTAL TRANSFERS

Intergovernmental transfers of funds generally flow from higher to lower levels, from the nation to the state to the locality. The total amount transferred during 1975 was about $100 billion—the federal government transferred $48 billion from its treasury to the states and local governments, and the states turned $52 billion over to the local governments.

A major effect of such transfers is the redistribution of funds, as poorer jurisdictions receive more than they pay in taxes, while wealthy ones receive less than they pay. Federal funds, more than state funds, are likely to be redistributed according to program needs. Some state transfers are little more than a tax-collection service—the states collect specific taxes and return the total proceeds directly to the local units in which they were collected, and so are not redistributive.

The Federal Transfers by Grants

Federal grants-in-aid, the major form of transfer to state and local governments, go back to the early days of our nation as we noted in the discussion of federalism in Chapter 3. But in the mid-1960s and continuing in the 1970s, federal grant funds rose dramatically, nearly overshadowing previous assistance programs. By 1970 there were more than 500 programs in effect and the trend continues upward. In 1976, for example, federal assistance payments were about 20 percent of total state and local revenues and equal to 38 percent of all state and local tax collections. The network of funding programs and federal requirements became so complicated that even top political officials, such as governors and mayors, had little knowledge of the programs they were approving for federal assistance.

Problems Associated with Federal Grants. The complexity of federal grant programs resulted in serious financial problems for state and community governments. Michael Reagan identifies them for us nicely.[2]

First is the *redistributive* problem. Not all federal grants-in-aid are

---

[2]Michael D. Reagan, *The New Federalism*, Oxford University Press, N.Y., 1972, 86–88.

redistributive. Some tend to make the rich states richer, because poorer states and communities can not afford the matching funds required. Such programs, therefore, do not necessarily put the funds where they are most needed. Especially those grants awarded on a competitive basis give the wealthier communities with the best staffs and best proposals an additional advantage in securing a disproportionately high number of grants. Policy Box No. 11, "Small Town 'Strikes It Rich' in Federal Aid," shows how one small town aggressively sought and got more than its share of federal aid, largely as the result of one person's efforts.

Second is the *allocation* problem. Grants that required local matching funds encouraged states and localities to skew their budgets as they reached out for the federal dollars. Officials would apply for grants even if the programs themselves were not in areas of greatest local need. It is, after all, difficult to reject grants that offer $2 or $3 for each $1 of local expenditure, in favor of programs that must be paid for entirely from state or community funds.

Third is the related problem of *neglect*. Federal assistance programs did nothing to improve the services in unassisted categories, such as fire fighting or fire prevention. We can imagine that the unassisted functions actually suffered as matching funds drained toward the federally assisted activities.

**POLICY BOX NO. 11:   The Small
Town "Strikes It Rich" in Federal Aid**
John Henry Moss was born and raised in King's Mountain, North Carolina. In 1942 he joined the army and went off to war. After the war he became a minor league baseball player, and then a baseball executive in the Detroit Tiger farm system. In 1960 he came back home, and five years later was elected mayor of King's Mountain, a town with 9000 people in the Piedmont area.

Moss has become somewhat of a legend in the area; local mayors think of him as the "man with the golden touch." Why? During Moss' first ten years as mayor King's Mountain received more than $16 million in federal assistance—almost $2000 per person! The mayor specialized in writing proposals for project grants.

Among the projects financed with federal money are a 31,000-square-foot community center, a multi-million-dollar water project that includes a 1500 acre lake, and a new waste-water treatment plant. In addition, the town received more than $4.5 million for downtown business district improvements and other urban renewal. And in October, 1975, King's Mountain received an additional $4 million for 13 projects including daycare centers, urban beautification, and aid for aged and handicapped people.

Why does King's Mountain fare so well? Mostly because Mayor Moss spends ten hours per week reading the *Catalog of Federal Assistance*, a government publication that describes federal grant programs and the pertinent regulations. Moss says, "There is no substitute for taking this book home and going into a corner and just reading."

King's Mountain does not hire high-priced outside consultants. Mayor Moss fills out the applications himself and uses volunteer committees to do some of the leg work. More than 235 citizens serve on fourteen such committees.

Development of the public facilities is having some spin-off effects. More than twenty new industries have located in the area, largely because of the availability of good water supplies. In addition, twenty-five new commercial and retail businesses have been started. Altogether, the potential for new jobs has increased by 2500. Andrew Brown, chairman of the mayor's Youth for Progress committee and a textile worker, said, "When I was growing up, most of the kids would leave town after high school because there was nothing for them to do. It used to be rough around here, but there's been a lot of changes made."

Mayor Moss has not done badly either. He usually runs for reelection without opposition, but in 1975 he had three opponents. Together, they garnered 12 percent of the vote.

Most of us would find it rather difficult to knock this kind of success, ingenuity and hard work, but might we not wonder what this kind of story says about federal grant programs?

What do you think? Should the receipt of federal grants depend on this kind of ingenuity? Should federal grant policies reward a town just because it happens to have a person who is good at filling out government forms? Should a city depend on its own financial resources for many of these projects? Or should the federal government put workers out on the road, like sales people, to call on other small-town mayors and tell them about grant programs they might apply for? And also to help them fill out the forms?

SOURCE: This Policy Box is based on "Midas Touch," *Newsweek*, November 10, 1975, p. 13.

Fourth is the problem of *coordination*. The complexity of the grant programs made meshing programming and spending at the federal, state, or local level a nightmare. Sometimes the grant programs of one federal department worked at cross purposes with those of another department in the same community. Sometimes programs of different agencies from the same federal department were in conflict.

Types of Federal Grants-in-Aid

Each major type of federal grant, we find, has distinctive features that make it useful for certain federal purposes, but also cause some of the problems noted above.

Categorical Grants. About 80 percent of federal grants are categorical grants. Most of these are also open-ended: those in which the federal government agrees to pay a fixed percentage of certain program costs without an annual limit on what can be spent.

Some of the largest categorical grant programs are in public assistance and medical care. For example, states administer "Medicaid" under federal guidelines for people who are "medically needy" or "medically indigent." These laws require states to provide eight basic services, but also allow them to provide, at state option, seventeen additional programs. The federal government reimburses the states at rates that vary with state per capita income. Washington pays at least half the cost, but a greater share in poorer states. For example, the federal government paid about 80 percent of Mississippi's 1973 Medicaid costs.

In spite of this funding arrangement, we find that some high-income states provide broader services than do low-income states and consequently have drawn disproportionately high shares of federal funds. During 1974, for example, California and New York with 18 percent of the national population received 30 percent of the Medicaid funding.

This arrangement, however, does provide the states with flexibility in how they run their programs. We also see some redistributive effects. But we find, too, that Medicaid and other such categoric grant programs have been plagued with administrative and cost problems.

James A. Maxwell and J. Richard Aronson observed that categorical or open-end grants are based on the assumptions that the program services eligible for federal aid can be defined with fair precision, and that policing is not difficult. They note that both these assumptions are seldom correct.[3]

Project Grants. The federal assistance programs of the 1960s that state and local officials criticized most were based on the project-grant approach. To get a project grant, the state or local unit must apply for the funds. Final approval of the funding rests with a federal administrator. Project grants, many argue, are thus subject to a great deal of federal bureaucratic influence and they especially fall prey to most of the criticisms of federal aid that we outlined above.

Project grants, though, are especially designed for experimental programs and demonstration projects. Muskegon, Michigan, for example, received a project grant for a sewage disposal experiment in which waste waters were used to irrigate large tracts of land that before were worthless. The land is now used to grow cattle feed. Project grants can also be used effectively to pioneer in areas of new federal

[3]James A. Maxwell and J. Richard Aronson, *Financing State and Local Governments*, 3rd ed., The Brookings Institution, Washington, D.C. 1977, p. 67.

involvement, or to improve weak programs. Most authorities recommend that project grants should be short-term, and that project results be carefully evaluated.

Block or Formula Grants.   As president in the late 1960s, Richard Nixon proposed to convert major parts of the federal assistance program into special revenue sharing packages. These proposals would have required no matching funds, no local tax effort, and no bureaucrat's approval prior to funding. Congress rejected these proposals.

But the basic idea had strong appeal. Congress later enacted some block (formula) grants as a compromise. They applied to several functions—housing and community development, crime control, employment and training, and mass transportation.

Block grants are made to a general area of activity, such as worker training, and allow state or local governments to allocate the funds as they wish among a list of approved training programs. Thus, we find that with block grants, Congress retains some broad policy control and federal administrators continue to review state and local plans to ensure compliance with federal guidelines. At the same time states and localities have some choice to fit the programs to local needs.

Also important is the fact that the block grant funds are allocated to states and localities as a matter of entitlement by formula. We find they are not competitive in the sense that the best "grantsmanship players" can gain most of the funds. But, because of this characteristic, we may also see federal funds going to some areas that may not be particularly needy.

General Revenue Sharing.   Years before some of the grant-in-aid problems reached a crisis stage, Congressman Melvin Laird of Wisconsin suggested that the federal government should share its revenues with states and communities and replace all grant programs then in effect. A few years later, Walter Heller, a professor and an adviser to Presidents Kennedy and Johnson, and Joseph Pechman, a researcher at the Brookings Institution, outlined a revenue-sharing plan as a supplement to grant programs. They proposed that the federal government share a fixed percentage of its revenues with the states, with no strings attached.

In his first administration, Richard Nixon proposed general revenue sharing. He recommended that an amount of $5 billion be distributed each year.

Congress passed the State and Local Fiscal Assistance Act in 1972. It authorized federal officials to distribute $30.1 billion over a period of five years. A great political fight developed over the formula determining how much individual states and communities would receive. The formula that was worked out used population, tax effort of state and local governments, and personal income, so that poorer states that tax their citizens heavily were rewarded. The money went to the states, who in turn passed along two-thirds of it to the general purpose governments—counties, cities, villages, townships, and Indian reservations.[4]

To the astonishment of many state and local officials, the law contained very few strings. The funds had to be spent in eight "priority areas," which proved to be not very restrictive. Each unit had to follow its normal hearing and budgeting process in respect to the monies, and publish reports in a local newspaper showing "planned use," and later, the "actual use" of the funds. The law also contained antidiscrimination clauses and a labor-backed rule requiring a unit to pay prevailing wage rates when revenue-sharing funds were spent on construction projects.[5]

The 1972 law expired in 1976. Whether it accomplished all of its objectives was almost irrelevant: failure to extend the law, many believed, would have meant fiscal chaos for the state and local governments who had come to rely on these funds.

Congress renewed the act for a three and one-half year period, providing an additional $24.5 billion. It also imposed slightly more rigid conditions, especially in respect to race and sex discrimination, opportunities for citizen participation, and audit procedures.

The Future of Federal Grants.   We have seen that the federal government involves itself deeply and increasingly in state and local financing. It is probable that federal aid in the next ten years will at least stay at the same level and will likely increase. As we noted, the transfers now constitute about 20 percent of the funds of state and local governments.

What is as important as the amount of the funds is how the federal government sets up its grants. As Allen Schick describes it, national leaders in the 1960s blamed all program confusion and failures on inadequacies of the state and local delivery systems and so emphasized categoric and project grants that gave national officials a strong say in how funds were to be spent. Policy leaders of the early 1970s, however,

[4]For an interesting account of the political considerations in the passage of the act, see Richard E. Thompson, *Revenue Sharing: A New Era in Federalism?* Revenue Sharing Advisory Service, Washington, D.C., 1973.

[5]For an early assessment on how well the revenue-sharing program worked, see Committee on Government Operations, U.S. Senate, *Revenue Sharing: A Selection of Recent Research*, U.S. Government Printing Office, Washington, D.C., 1975, 8–19.

saw the problem as too much "intrusion by Washington into the conduct of government by states and localities." They concluded that "meaningful and enduring remedies would not be forthcoming unless the federal government stopped telling local officials how to run their programs and so began experimenting with block grants and revenue sharing that gave local officials stronger control.[6]

Enduring remedies are, perhaps, a bit much to hope for, but it does not seem likely that we will soon return to the grant format of the 1960s. Public interest groups, such as the Council of State Governments, the National Association of Counties, or the American Federation of State, County, and Municipal Employees—organizations that, incidentally, were strengthened by the policies of the 1970s—would strongly resist such a change.

State Intergovernmental Transfers

The states also transfer funds to their local governments—and these have also increased rapidly during recent years: from $19 billion in 1967 to $52 billion in 1975, an increase of almost 300 percent.[7]

Reasons for State Aid.   We might wonder why the states, which often plead poverty to the federal government, should distribute so much of their funds to the local governments. Note how political factors enter the picture.

State Responsibilities.   Some traditionally "local" functions are now seen as responsibilities of state government. Primary and secondary education, for example, is carried out by local districts in all states except Hawaii (it began statehood with education as a completely state-funded program). But state constitutions frequently define education as a state responsibility. School districts commonly may levy only a property tax, and it has not been adequate to meet the rising costs of public education. In order to keep the schools operating, the states have provided state aid. Moreover the property tax does not produce an equal amount of money (on a per student basis) in each of the districts. Some, arguing that the educational opportunities thus differ widely from district to district, filed a spate of lawsuits claiming that the unequal funding was a violation of the Fourteenth Amendment to

[6]Allen Schick, "Conceptual Perspectives on Policy Management Assistance," *Public Administration Review*, Special Issue, December, 1975, p. 719.

[7]Advisory Commission on Intergovernmental Relations, *State Aid to Local Government*, Washington, D.C., 1976.

the Constitution. Several state supreme courts, such as that of California, agreed that the financing method was unconstitutional.[8]

Although the U.S. Supreme Court did not agree, the state court decisions prompted action in several state legislatures. Legislatures did not agree to provide full funding, but many did increase school aid—aid that now accounts for 50 percent or more of all state aid payments to local governments. They also changed the distribution formulas to assure that each district has at least state-set minimum funding per student.

Tax Collection Effectiveness. Government units that cover a larger geographical area are generally more effective and efficient in collecting taxes than are those with a smaller territory. As the federal government is more effective than the states, so the states are more effective than localities.

It is difficult and costly to administer certain taxes in small geographic areas. The states thus collect such taxes and then distribute the funds to the localities where collected or according to a formula. These kinds of state collected, locally shared revenues account for substantial portions of state aid.

Special Interest Influence. Various special interest groups lobby for state taxation and the return of the money to communities, with the funds earmarked for specific services. Better Roads Associations, for example, find it much easier to lobby for higher taxes and favorable allocation at one place—the state legislature—than in fifty or one hundred or more counties of a state.

Program Direction. We find that states also use transfers to stimulate specific local programs. For example, governors and legislators can encourage local units to create regional councils of government, to merge school districts, or give property tax relief to older people or farmers. They may use state aid to encourage local officials to consolidate local courts or transfer health programs from small cities to counties. Under "Dillon's Rule," states (as we discussed in Chapter 4) have the authority to force such changes, but local cooperation is often more easily achieved when financial incentives are offered.

Local Pressures. State aid sometimes reflects the political clout of community governments. To illustrate, consider a governor who wants to give state aid to help solve ghetto problems in a large city. That gov-

---

[8]The case in California had perhaps the greatest initial impact. *Serrano* v. *Priest,* 938254, L.A., California Supreme Court, 29820 (1971).

ernor is often made to recognize that other local units will not stand by quietly and let it happen. Other cities, and perhaps the counties, will fight side by side, not to stop the aid, but to get a share of the funds for themselves as well. To their credit, state executives have been more successful than we might expect in basing the distribution formulas on tax effort or need rather than simply on per capita basis, but political pressures also influence distribution.

Also, more frequently than in the past, localities "gang up" on the legislature to pressure for financial assistance to pay for programs that the state requires communities to provide. County jail improvements to meet state standards or barrier-free public buildings for handicapped persons, are recent examples of state-mandated changes. The localities argue that the states should pay at least part of the costs.

PERSPECTIVES ON STATE AND LOCAL TAXATION

Average citizens, until recently, have underestimated how much state and community governments collect in taxes and from other sources. With a few broad brushstrokes, we will present an overview of the situation.

Trends in State and Local Taxation

In 1975, exclusive of government transfers, states and communities obtained a total of $215 billion—$142 billion from taxes and $73 billion from charges for services, and other miscellaneous, and trust revenues. This compares with $305.4 billion the federal government collected that year (about 59 percent of the combined total). Thus, $4 out of every $10 were collected by the state and local governments. (See Figures 6-2 and 6-3 for a comparison of federal with state and local tax collections and major sources of general tax revenue.) The cities, counties, school districts, and other local units together collected $83.7 billion of the above $215 billion. That was 16 percent of the combined federal, state, and local taxes and charges for 1975.

Also important is the direction of the trend in state and local taxation. State and local taxes have been rising relative to federal taxes. And this is a long-term trend. In 1954, for example, the states and localities collected only 30 percent of the national tax bill; in 1964, 37 percent, and in 1975, 41 percent. And tax collections by the federal government have been dropping in relation to the Gross National Product (the total value of all goods and services produced in the nation during a year), while state and local tax collections as a percent of the GNP have increased. (See Figure 6-4.)

Figure 6-2
Growth in Federal and State/Local Tax and
Other Revenues—Selected Years

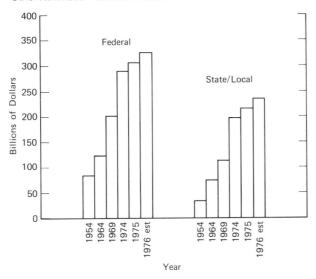

Figure 6-3
Major Sources of State/Local General Tax Revenues—Selected Years

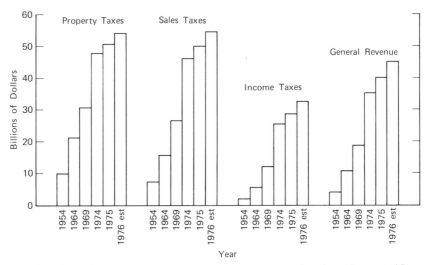

SOURCE: Advisory Commission on Intergovernmental Relations, *Significant Features of Fiscal Federalism* (1976 ed.) Washington, D.C.

Figure 6-4

The Relative Growth in Federal Taxes Lags the State-Local Sector, Selected Years 1948–1975 (Federal, State, and Local Taxes as a Percent of GNP)

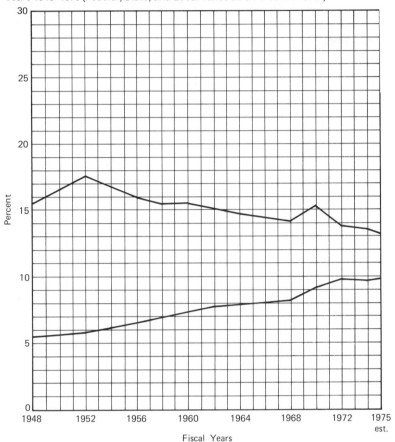

SOURCE: Advisory Commission on Intergovernmental Relations, *Significant Features of Fiscal Federalism*, (1976 ed.) Washington, D.C., p. 30.

Variations in State and Local Tax Burdens

When we ask where state and local taxes are highest, we might get different answers depending on the measure we use. In terms of dollars collected per person, we find that only seventeen states collected more than the 1975 national average of $665.60. These states tend to be clustered in New England, Mideast, Middle Atlantic, and the West. The per capita tax in New York ($1009) exceeded its nearest rival California by almost $120. (See Figure 6-5.)

Figure 6-5
Per Capita State-Local Taxes, 1975

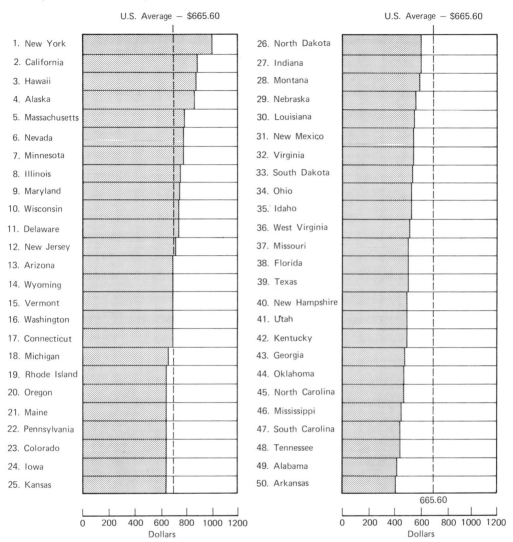

SOURCE: Advisory Commission on Intergovernmental Relations, *Significant Features of Fiscal Federalism, 1975,* Washington, D.C.

Measuring tax levels on a per capita basis, however, can be misleading because the measure is not related to the ability to pay, or state "tax effort." A wealthy and a poor state, for example, can both have a flat 3 percent income tax; the wealthy state will collect much more per capita than the poor state and may be above the national average, but the wealthy state can, nevertheless, be well down the list in terms of tax effort.

As we might expect, some of the states with high per capita taxes also rank high in tax effort—in fact, six of the top ten in per capita volume are also among the top ten on the effort measure. (See Table 6-1.) But we also find some surprises. States with below average per capita collections, such as Maine and New Mexico, rank sixth and ninth in terms of tax effort. Vermont and Arizona, states with per capita revenues at the U.S. average, were also among the top ten on the effort scale. Vermont, in fact, was second in effort, but only fifteenth in per capita receipts. In terms of effort, then, taxes in these states were well above the U.S. average of about 12 percent of personal income.

By contrast, we discover states with rather high per capita tax revenues, but with lower positions in the tax effort listing. Some examples of high per capita rank and low tax effort are: Alaska, New Jersey, Delaware, and Connecticut.

Where have taxes been rising most rapidly in relation to personal income? Taxes grew nearly three times faster than personal income in Delaware and more than twice as fast in Alaska during the 1953 to 1975 period. (See Figure 6-6 for a state-by-state view.) By region, the sharpest increases took place in the Middle Atlantic states and in the Great Lakes and Far West regions.

Evaluating State and Local Taxes. At four-year intervals, the Advisory Commission on Intergovernmental Relations surveys public opinion regarding its tax preferences. Citizens reported that they preferred the sales tax first, income tax second, and property tax a distant third.[9] Experts sometimes use different criteria—matters we consider next.

Equity. Early in our history we measured wealth mostly in terms of the amount of real estate a person owned; we considered it the best test for ability to pay. Today we generally view income as the best "yardstick." We argue that people and corporations with high incomes have a greater ability to pay and should pay more, proportionate to their incomes, than do low-income families and businesses. Economists

[9]Advisory Commission on Intergovernmental Relations, *Significant Features of Fiscal Federalism, 1976,* Washington, D.C., p. 6.

TABLE 6-1 State-Local Tax Revenue as a Percent of Personal Income for Highest Ten and Lowest Ten States and Comparison of Ranks

Highest Ten States				Lowest Ten States			
State	Tax Revenue As A Percent Of Personal Income		State Rank On Per Capita Basis	State	Tax Revenue As A Percent Of Personal Income		State Rank On Per Capita Basis
	Percent	Rank			Percent	Rank	
New York	15.72	1	1	Georgia	10.02	41	43
Vermont	14.65	2	15	New Hampshire	10.01	42	40
California	14.27	3	2	North Carolina	9.98	43	45
Hawaii	14.01	4	3	Texas	9.96	44	39
Minnesota	13.96	5	7	Missouri	9.91	45	37
Maine	13.70	6	21	Arkansas	9.87	46	50
Wisconsin	13.62	7	10	Alabama	9.59	47	49
Arizona	13.48	8	13	Florida	9.52	48	38
New Mexico	13.20	9	30	Ohio	9.51	49	34
Massachusetts	13.12	10	5	Tennessee	9.51	50	47

SOURCE: Adapted from Advisory Commission on Intergovernmental Relations, *Significant Features of Fiscal Federalism*, 1976, Washington, D.C., p. 45.

call this progressive taxation. Taxes that take larger proportions from low-income earners, for example, a flat-rate tax, in which everyone pays $50 whether they earn a million dollars a year or just $51 a year, are regressive.[10]

Administration. Taxes that involve collection costs high in proportion to the revenues collected are considered ineffective. So tax experts and officials ask, Is a large new bureaucracy needed to figure how much each taxpayer must pay? Will the tax encourage bootlegging or other violations that will lead to high enforcement costs? Is the tax easy for citizens to understand and pay?

Elasticity. Some taxes, such as a head tax, produce revenues without regard to the level of economic activity. Tax experts prefer taxes that have elasticity, that is, taxes that produce revenues at a rate equal to or greater than the rate of increase in personal income or gross na-

[10]James A. Maxwell and J. Richard Aronson, Op. cit., p. 108, and Joseph A. Pechman and Benjamin A. Okner in *Who Bears the Tax Burden?* Brookings Institution, Washington, D.C., 1974, maintain that equity in taxation should be judged on the basis of the total system of taxes on which a person pays; not simply on the basis of a single tax. They rightly ask, Are federal, state and local taxes, in combination, progressive or regressive? They argue that the combined tax structure appears to be progressive or naturally proportionate depending on whether the costs of corporate taxes and property improvement are absorbed in profits or passed along to consumers in higher prices.

Figure 6-6
State-Local Tax Burdens Between 1953 and 1975[a]
Tax Revenue Related to Personal Income

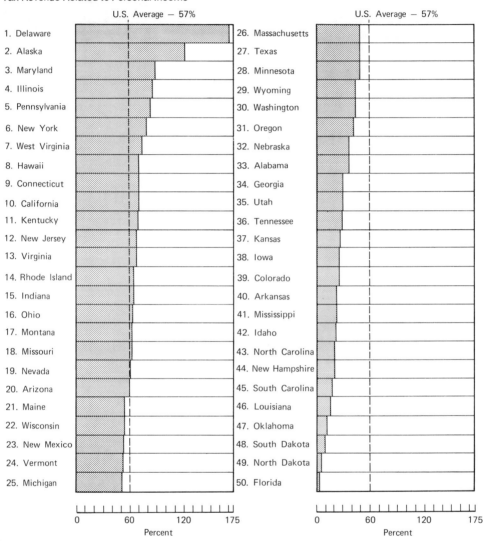

SOURCE: Advisory Commission on Intergovernmental Relations, *Significant Features of Fiscal Federalism, 1976*, Washington, D.C.

[a]Average state-local tax burdens rose from 7.6 percent to 11.9 percent of personal income—an increase of 57 percent.

tional product. A highly elastic tax, such as a graduated income tax, is a tax that generates revenue at a rate faster than the growth of the economy. (Taxes with high elasticity, of course, also fall in revenue production more rapidly than the rate of decline in economic activity.) A tax that produces the same amount, no matter what the level of economic activity, is inelastic. Inelastic or low elasticity taxes require more frequent rate changes during inflationary periods. Politicians usually prefer taxes with high elasticity where tax payments increase automatically.

Competition. Another consideration of tax experts and public officials is the effect a new tax or tax increase will have on the competitive position of the state, relative to other states, or a community with a neighboring community. As we have noted, states, especially, are concerned that their taxes be generally in line with neighboring competitive states, lest they encourage business and industry to locate elsewhere. Communities face somewhat the same problem, but usually to a lesser degree.

Rationale. Each tax must be based on reason in order to receive general public support. A tax on each evergreen shrub we have planted in our front yards, for example, does not seem reasonable by any standard and so would be resisted and paid reluctantly. We find these rationales expressed in catch-phrases, such as "ability to pay," "everyone should pay some taxes," or "sin taxes (on cigarettes, liquor, or gambling) will discourage smoking or whatever." Each of these reflects a basic philosophy about taxation. From time to time we will see these catch-phrases being used in tax reform debates.

In the next section, we will discuss how these considerations relate to the specific taxes states impose.

THE MAJOR STATE AND LOCAL TAXES

Sales Taxes

When the clerk at the local hardware store tells us that our purchases come to $1.90 and "eight cents for the governor," we are inclined to ignore the tribute exacted because it does not seem to amount to very much. Yet that clerk and all the others around the country collected nearly $25 billion during 1975.

Sales taxes constitute the single largest tax source for the states—more than 30 percent of the tax receipts of the states in 1975. If we take into account state excise taxes—hidden sales taxes that are added into the price on items such as gasoline or cigarettes—the total sales tax receipts swell to more than $36 billion, nearly half the states' general tax revenues during 1975!

When did states start levying such taxes? Oregon pioneered modern excise taxes with a gasoline tax in 1919. Within ten years all of the states were using this means to fill state coffers. In 1975 most states taxed gasoline at from seven to nine cents per gallon.

Iowa first taxed cigarettes in 1921. Most other states delayed the tax on cigarettes because it was difficult to enforce. With federal legislation manufacturers and distributors found the tax more difficult to evade and by 1961 all the states, even the tobacco-producing states, had a tax on cigarettes. The rates vary widely—from two and a half cents per package in Virginia to twenty-one cents in Connecticut.

Excise taxes on liquor are handled in two basic ways—thirty-three states use a license system and assess a gallonage tax. The other seventeen have state monopolies on liquor sales and receive their taxes in the form of profits on sales.

Falling property tax collections during the Great Depression brought on the general sales tax. Mississippi in 1932 was the first, but thirteen more states enacted the tax the next year. By 1940 nearly half the states had sales taxes. In 1977 only five states (Alaska, Delaware, Montana, New Hampshire, and Oregon) still had none. Sales tax rates in the states vary from two cents to seven cents on a dollar's purchase.

Evaluating Sales Taxes.   As we saw, sales taxes have rated rather high in public opinion surveys. One of the reasons, we suspect, is that everyone pays it, including visitors in the state—an important fact for states that have a substantial tourist business. Let us review the sales tax in terms of the five criteria we discussed earlier.

Equity.   Because poor people spend larger proportions of their income in consuming the necessities of life than do those who are wealthy, general sales taxes are regressive. In Table 6-2 we see that families with annual incomes of $5000 pay twice the effective rate as do families in the $25,000 income range.

People who criticize the sales tax—liberals, labor union leaders, and some economists—have lobbied to reduce its regressiveness. Eliminating the tax from items such as food, medicine, and clothing, as some states have done, has reduced its regressiveness. Other states by giv-

TABLE 6-2 Estimated Percent of Income Paid in State and Local Sales Taxes by a Family of Four, 1972

Income	Percent of Income
$ 5,000	1.8
7,500	1.6
10,000	1.4
20,000	1.1
25,000	0.9
50,000	0.7

SOURCE: ACIR, *Significant Features*, 1973–74 Edition, p. 53.

ing sales tax credits against the income tax liability achieve a similar result.

Administration. We find that this tax has administrative advantages that its critics often overlook. First, we pay the tax in unnoticeable amounts except when we make large purchases. Second, we, as consumers, always have the tax paid up to date. Third, someone always figures the tax for us—not a little matter when we think of complicated income tax forms. In addition, merchants collect these taxes for the states, although a few states pay them for their services.[11] The main administrative problem is to make sure that the retailers turn all receipts over to the states.

Elasticity. The sales tax is an inelastic tax. While sales taxes produce more revenues in good times, we find that the growth in revenue does not keep pace because, with growth in personal income, greater proportions of incomes are placed in savings, rather than spent for goods and services. But when economic times are bad, revenues do not fall as rapidly as income. People continue to buy. The money they use may come from unemployment compensation, welfare payments, or savings, but they still pay the tax.

Competition. State officials can set tax rates on sales and excise taxes without being too concerned about interstate competition. Substantial rate differences will cause only a minor flow of business to areas of lower taxation, except in a few border towns. But Nebraska, with its population concentration in the east, must be sensitive to the tax rates in Iowa, lest the residents of Omaha spend most of their money in Council Bluffs.

[11]James A. Maxwell and J. Richard Aronson, Op. cit., p. 106.

Thirty states permit cities or counties to levy a sales tax, but local rates are usually one cent or less. States with isolated communities, such as Colorado and Alaska, understandably allow cities to tax up to four and five cents. When local units do levy a sales tax, they usually "piggy back" on a state sales tax and the state makes the collection for the localities.

Rationale. Many excise taxes link users of specific services to paying the tax supporting the service. For example, many states use gasoline taxes for road improvements and maintenance. Such benefit taxes— direct linkups of money to a service (called earmarking)—can produce some problems. It is not easy to use these revenues for other functions. Interest groups, such as Better Roads Associations, jealously guard "their" money; they fight its being spent even for related functions, such as public transportation or the state highway patrol.

A second rationale for some excise taxes is that they may limit the use of certain products, such as liquor or cigarettes. The idea, often expressed with moral overtones, is to tax sin. Legislators thus can create two "goods" with only one "bad"; they can increase appropriations for education or cancer research and discourage the use of liquor (another "good") by increasing the liquor tax (the one "bad"). While one such proposal was being debated in the Michigan legislature, a jokester put up a sign in a bar that legislators frequented—"Have a Shot for a Tot."

Personal Income Taxes

Why does the income tax come in a poor second in popularity to the sales tax? And why is it opposed among low income as well as some high-income populations? Most of the negative opinion, we think, comes from negative experiences many citizens associate with the federal income tax. Citizens have to fill out complicated tax returns. They hear about millionaires and corporations that pay no federal income tax. Tax loopholes, presumably only for the rich, get wide publicity while the president talks of eliminating the credit for interest on mortgages and opposes tax credits for college tuition payments. As we would expect, such experiences lead to misunderstanding of the income tax and mistrust of the bureaucrats and politicians who write the rules.

In spite of such negative attitudes about personal income taxes and progressive tax rates, forty-one states and many municipalities have adopted a personal income or payroll tax.

Wisconsin, in 1911, was the first state in modern times to levy a personal income tax, predating by two years ratification of the Sixteenth

Amendment, which authorized the national personal income tax. By 1930 fourteen states, in addition to the territory of Hawaii, had it, and by 1937, as the states searched frantically for new sources of revenue, the number had increased to twenty-nine. It was not until the 1960s and 1970s. however, that most of the remaining states began to levy personal income taxes. New Jersey adopted it in 1976 in response to a school finance crisis.

Personal income tax receipts totaled $19 billion in 1975, were second most important, and accounted for about 25 percent of total state tax revenues. However, for a few states that have no general state sales tax, such as Wisconsin and Alaska, the income tax has been the major source of tax revenue.

Varied Patterns.   Personal income tax programs among the states are diverse. All but five states have graduated rates of taxation—rates that increase as the level of taxable income increases—but the number of steps and percentages applied vary widely. Mississippi, for example, provides for two rate steps: one at 3 percent applying to the first $5000 of income, and the second at 4 percent for incomes over $5,000. Alaska, by contrast, in 1976 had twenty-four tax steps from $4000 to $400,000 with rates ranging from 3 to 14.5 percent.

They also vary in the way they handle personal exemptions. Almost all use a personal exemption similar to the federal exemption of $750 per dependent, but the range of such exemptions runs from $100 to $4500, with most between $750 and $2000. A half-dozen states instead permit a taxpayer to take a tax credit in place of an exemption. Unlike the federal personal income tax plan, twelve states, mostly in the South, set low exemptions for dependents and thereby "discriminate" against large families.

A handful of states tie their state personal income tax plans directly to the federal income tax. They specify that the state tax will be a percentage (from 15 to 25 percent) of the federal tax bill. This piggy-back approach assures a progressive income tax and provides simplicity for the taxpayers and administrators. However, it complicates things a bit when Congress changes its tax rules and rates.

Evaluating Personal Income Taxes.   We evaluate the personal income tax by the same set of standards that we used for the sales and excise taxes.

Equity.   We generally think of the personal income tax as a progressive tax. As we saw above, however, a few states (mostly in the

Midwest) tax at a flat rate. Also, many of the other states have a small number of steps and a narrow range of rates. Thus, many of the state income taxes, at best, are only moderately progressive.

Administration. States administer their personal income taxes rather economically, the cost being less than 2 percent of what is collected.[12] Costs are low, in part, because evasion of the tax is difficult for most of us.

Two factors account for high levels of compliance. All states, except North Dakota, require employers to withhold the taxes from paychecks, Second, the U.S. Internal Revenue Service cooperates by sharing federal income tax return information with the states. By matching computer tapes they quickly identify discrepancies in federal and state tax returns.

Perhaps one of the most difficult problems of administration involves incomes that are earned in two or more states and incomes earned in a state by nonresidents. As we noted in Chapter 3, reciprocity agreements between states help solve this problem.

Elasticity. The personal income tax can be highly responsive to changes in personal income, but how elastic a system is depends on whether the system has flat or graduated rates. One source estimated that in three states studied, for each 1 percent increase in the gross national product, the personal income tax yield increased by 1.75 percent. As incomes rise, not only is more income taxable, but some of it is taxed at higher rates if the state has a graduated tax.

The income tax is also sensitive to economic downturns as well. Receipts can drop sharply. For this reason industrialized states that specialize in durable goods, such as Pennsylvania does with steel products, do not put all their revenue eggs in the personal income tax basket.

Competition. State officials are concerned about the effects their taxing programs have on jobs in their states. Personal income taxes probably do not affect this a great deal—at least in terms of which state workers move to. At the community level, though, we may find people making residential decisions partly on the basis of which governments have an income tax.

We should note that the concern with competition is always on the minds of state legislators and other officials. It is possibly for this reason that we find that Pennsylvania, Indiana, Illinois, and Michigan all

[12]James A. Maxwell and J. Richard Aronson, Op. cit., p. 113.

have flat-rate personal income taxes. Ohio also competes for jobs with these states. Its income tax is graduated, but its rates are comparatively low.

Rationale. All legislators would rather vote for increases in expenditures than increases in taxes. One rationale of the income tax is that legislators do not need to increase rates very often because it is an elastic tax. These tax revenues increase faster than personal incomes rise, and thus keep pace with inflation.

In flat-rate tax states, though, the problem is a little different; tax rates may have to be raised more often. But legislators can make modest sounding increases *in the rates*, such as 0.1 percent or 0.2 percent on a temporary basis, and can later vote to make the increases permanent.

A second rationale for the personal income tax is that it is the fairest tax. It is progressive, taxing those most able to pay, and does not require a tax from people who have had a bad year.

The Property Tax

At the turn of the century and even into the second decade, the property tax was the most important tax for both state and local governments. The Great Depression virtually marked the end of state dependence on property taxes. In 1927 the states were still receiving more than 25 percent of their revenues from property taxes, but by 1942 this had dropped to less than 7 percent.

After the war most of the states stopped levying a general property tax altogether, but kept taxes on certain types of property, such as that owned by utilities and railroads, or intangible properties (stocks, bonds, mortgages, and bank deposits). This still accounts for about 5 percent of state tax revenues.

The property tax is now essentially a local government tax. It finances a substantial portion of city and county operations, primary and secondary schools, and community colleges in some states, as well as special districts that operate hospitals, recreation programs and facilities, airports, and other programs.

However, even for local governments the property tax is not as important as it once was. In 1927, for example, taxes on property produced about 75 percent of the local government revenue; in 1975 it produced 31 percent, according to the U.S. Bureau of the Census. Yet, the property tax was still the most productive *local tax*. Even in the middle 1970s, it accounted for more than 80 percent of *locally produced tax* revenues.

Evaluation of the Property Tax.   An early authority, Edwin R. A. Seligman, once remarked that the property tax was a good tax, except that it is wrong in theory and does not work in practice. He was partially joking, but let us look at some of the problems with the property tax.

Equity.   The property tax is regressive—Seligman made this point over eighty years ago, and it is generally still accepted today as valid, although recently a few individuals have questioned the assumption.[13]

A number of states have already made changes to make the tax less regressive than it once was. The principal device is called a "circuit breaker." It gives taxpayers either a direct payment or credit against the state income tax when property taxes on a person's home exceed a specified percentage of the family income. The effect is that states are subsidizing high local property taxes. More than half the states have adopted circuit breaker legislation.

One of the problems with the circuit breaker, however, is that taxpayers often do not understand how it works. In 1977 Michigan officials found that many citizens did not realize that their state income taxes were lower because of their high property taxes. (We note that federal income taxes are also lowered by property and some other state and local taxes we pay.) In 1978 we find some states facing citizen initiatives to cut the property tax, even where states have adopted circuit breaker laws.

Administration.   The property tax is difficult and costly to administer. In order to be sure that each property owner pays a fair share of the tax, properties must be assessed fairly among local assessing units because taxing units (schools, airports, community colleges, and others) sometimes overlap several assessing units. If assessment practices are not uniform, some taxpayers will pay more than they should while others pay less, even though properties they own are similar. Because assessing involves an element of judgment, uniformity is difficult to attain.

It is difficult, in part, because the political incentives encourage assessors to set property assessments below true market value. Most of us are pleased when our assessor assesses our property at less than

---

[13]Edwin R. A. Seligman, *Essays in Taxation*, MacMillan and Co., N.Y., 1895. They argue that the important consideration is whether the combined taxes a person pays are regressive, not whether a single tax is regressive. See for example, Henry J. Aaron, *Who Pays the Property Tax? A New View*, Brookings Institution, Washington, D.C., 1975. Aaron suggests that current income may be an inadequate measure of ability to pay because of federal tax loopholes that favor the rich. He argues that "permanent income" should be used. It measures the property tax burden on owners of capital.

we would be willing to sell it for. Where assessors are elected officials, we are likely to reelect them if they keep our assessments low, and vote for their opponents if our assessments are high. Moreover, low assessments also mean that the jurisdiction will pay less of the taxes supporting the community college, for example, and will also receive larger state aid payments based on "need."

What are the remedies for this kind of political chicanery? One is equalization. A state or county agency attempts to correct the discrepancies among assessing units by raising some and lowering others.

Property tax reformers suggest other remedies as well. They maintain that assessing should be done not by elected officials, but by professionally trained people who are appointed and thereby more sheltered from the political pressure. Reformers also argue that many of the community assessment units are too small to be able to hire and pay professionally trained assessors—that assessing should be done by counties or even by states. Both practices are becoming more common.

Elasticity. Property tax revenues generally increase at about the same rate as economic growth, but because of the administrative cycle of the tax, it tends to lag by a year or more behind market values. The property tax is both liked and disliked for this reason.

Local officials like it when property values rise or when building is booming because their revenues increase without their having to increase the tax rate; and when building stops and revenue from other sources drops, the property tax revenues generally hold their own, at least for a time.

But property owners, especially homeowners and farmers, dislike the tax for the same reasons. They have to pay higher taxes because property values, and therefore assessments, have increased, even though to their minds the property they own has not changed at all. Similarly, they are unhappy to have to pay the property tax when the business or farm had a losing year or when the homeowner was out of work. Especially disgruntled are those people on fixed incomes—during inflationary periods their incomes may rise very little, if at all, and at the same time they may see their property taxes "skyrocket" because of rising construction costs and property values.

Competition. States sometimes compete with each other by giving long-term tax exemptions for industries that locate or expand in the state. Some even build plants for new industry for lease over a long period. And because such facilities are publicly owned, they are not taxed. Localities may also use these techniques to entice new industries. But localities also compete with each other within a state. This competition usually takes the form of efforts to keep property taxes low and services to the industries high.

Many exemptions, however, were not made for competitive reasons alone. Legislatures have also used exemptions to grant benefits to certain social and economic groups for a variety of reasons, some of which we may find defensible, and others not. Over the years state constitutions and legislatures have removed many kinds of property from tax rolls—one study found more than eighty-five different kinds of exemptions. Government-owned property is the largest exempt class, followed by property of religious, charitable, and educational institutions. Exemptions also result from effective lobbying for favored treatment by agricultural, industrial, veterans, or other groups. Finally governments also use exemptions as incentives—to encourage industry to install pollution control equipment or developers to build housing for low-income families or senior citizens.

Such exemptions, of course, erode a community's property tax base. More important, the exempt properties are not distributed equally among local units. Typically they are concentrated in central cities where exempt properties may run as high as one-third of the total property values.[14] And people benefitting from the exemptions are not limited to central city residents. Local governments thus demand, often successfully, state aid payments to make up the lost tax revenues.

Rationale.   An early rationale for the property tax, of course, was that property was a good measure of wealth. Today property taxes are levied largely on the theory that the services financed by these taxes largely benefit local property owners. The Tax Foundation takes this view when it counters the arguments that the property tax is regressive and maintains that the benefit-tax ratio favors people of low income.[15] (See Table 6-3.)

In general, this rationale does not fit the experience of many people, and, as a result, the tax is coming under growing attack. Governor Wendell Anderson, for example, successfully ran for governor of Minnesota on a property tax reform in 1970 (he called it "an unfair burden" on senior citizens). In California in 1978 a citizens' group circu-

[14]Debra R. Sanderson Stinson, *Tax Exemptions in Central Cities and Suburbs: A Comparison Across States,* Institution for Social and Policy Studies, Yale University, New Haven, Connecticut, 1975. This is a study of tax-exempt properties in twenty states where data were available. Typically, the records on tax-exempt properties, and especially on the value of them, are not maintained. As a result, the real scope of tax exempt properties is unknown.

[15]*Tax Burdens and Benefits of Government Expenditures by Income Class: 1961 and 1965,* The Tax Foundation, N.Y., 1967.

TABLE 6-3 Tax Benefits and Government Expenditures by Income Class

| Income Class[a] | Percent of Total Income | | Benefits of Government Spending | Ratio of Benefits to Total Tax Burden |
| | Taxes | | | |
	Property	All Taxes		
All families	3.8	30.4	22.9	1.0
$ 2,000– 2,999	6.9	28.1	109.0	3.9
3,000– 3,999	5.2	26.7	65.0	2.4
4,000– 4,999	4.2	29.1	33.7	1.2
5,000– 5,999	4.2	29.4	29.7	1.0
6,000– 7,499	3.8	28.5	25.4	.9
7,500– 9,999	3.5	28.5	22.1	.8
10,000–14,999	3.3	30.6	20.0	.7
15,000 and over	2.4	44.0	16.3	.4

SOURCE: *Tax Burdens and Benefits of Government Expenditures by Income Class, 1961 and 1965*, Tax Foundation, N.Y. 1967.

[a]Money income after personal taxes.

lated an initiatory petition—called the "Jarvis amendment" or Proposition 13—to cut property taxes by 50 percent or more. In other states as well, voters and state legislators are seeking major changes in property tax laws, some proposing to reduce the tax by more than half. If such proposals are adopted state officials face great problems in raising other taxes or cutting costs to offset lost revenues. Even the threat of such proposals causes state officials to scurry to make adjustments in the property tax. (In California, Governor Brown supported a 30 percent cut in property taxes to head off the growing support for the "Jarvis amendment," but California voter's rejected the plan and voted instead for Proposition 13.)

Corporate Taxes

The major local tax that corporations pay is the local property tax. At the state level there are three major types of corporate taxes: the corporate income tax, the corporation franchise tax, and the severance tax.

Forty-five states have a corporate income tax, but altogether this tax produced less than $7 billion in 1975—8.2 percent of total state tax revenue. The amounts, though, vary widely by state. For example, six states (California, Connecticut, Massachusetts, New York, Pennsylvania, and Tennessee) obtained more than 10 percent of their revenues from this source and accounted for more than 33 percent of the total corporation income taxes paid to the states. Most states tax at flat rates.

The corporation franchise tax is a fee, in effect, for the privilege of doing business in the state. This source provided an additional $1 billion to the states in 1975, but, again, the variations among states are substantial. Eight states accounted for nearly 75 percent of these receipts.

Severance taxes are a charge for extracting natural resources that are generally irreplaceable—oil, natural gas, coal, iron ore, and even lake fish and lumber. Only a few states raise substantial amounts from severance taxes—mainly Texas, Louisiana, and Oklahoma, which together raised $1.3 billion of the $1.7 billion produced in 1975.

Evaluation. Let us look at corporate taxes in terms of the criteria we have been using to evaluate other taxes.

Equity. We find that state taxes on corporations are regressive. Not only do most of the states tax corporate incomes at flat rates, but those that have graduated rates use only a few steps and low rate ranges. Corporation franchise taxes and other state taxes on corporations do not usually take profitability into account. Some economists argue that corporate taxes are passed along to consumers in higher prices and thus are in fact regressive, whether the tax rates are graduated or not.

Administration. Some corporation taxes, such as the franchise tax, are relatively easy to administer because it is usually based on the net worth of the company. Administrative problems of the corporate income tax concern allocation of earned income among the states in which the company does business and these problems grow more difficult as corporations, even relatively small ones, become interstate or international in scope. Some tax economists consider this a severe problem and argue that the only way it can be resolved is to have only the federal government levy the tax and distribute the receipts among the states.

Competition. The struggle to keep a good "business climate" keeps taxes on corporations low. Is the concern justified? Most studies find that many factors, such as markets, raw materials, trained labor force and, more recently, supply of energy influence business and industrial location decisions. Still the total tax bill is one factor. As one study pointed out, however, the really important question is the treatment a company receives relative to its competitors. Corporate tax managers watch carefully the locational choices made by the principal firms in their industry. Management is anxious that their tax costs, like other costs, be kept in line with those of their competitors.[16]

Such findings may be reassuring, but when we hear that a specific industry is leaving the state for good, the statements are often not sufficient to quiet business, industry, and others. Politicians will be tempted to make a major political issue of the "business climate." Such complaints, of course, do not focus on taxes alone, but also on the costs of unemployment compensation and workers' compensation, as well as on state policies toward unions and enforcement of environmental standards.[17] Still, taxes provide an easy target in such campaigns.

Thus, even though tax considerations may be marginal, state officials do not like to lose the contests for industrial development and so they look very closely at their competitor states. It is not mere coincidence, for example, that Georgia, West Virginia, Virginia, Tennessee, South Carolina, and North Carolina all have flat-rate corporate income taxes at the rate of 6 percent. Nor is it a happenstance that Connecticut, which competes with New York for business development, has the same corporate income tax rate as New York, even though some other New England states have corporate income tax rates at half that level. Connecticut's locational advantage seems to be such that it can levy what New York does without being overly concerned about the rates in other neighboring states.

Elasticity. Most corporate taxes are not graduated, and thus are not very responsive to changes in economic climate. Franchise taxes are highly inelastic because they are usually not based on economic activity or on profitability.

Rationale. Corporations are legal "persons." The rationale for corporate taxes, then, is that corporations, like other persons, should be taxed. In addition, governors and legislators argue, corporations benefit from the opportunity to do business in their states, and ought to pay for the privilege.

Severance taxes have a different basis. The rationale here is that the companies are using up natural resources that, in effect, belong to

[16]Advisory Commission on Intergovernmental Relations, *State-Local Taxation and Industrial Location*, Report A-30, Washington, D.C., 1967, p. 62.

[17]Strictly speaking, these are more like insurance premiums rather than taxes. Nevertheless they are important business costs influenced by state policies. In 1975, unemployment compensation "taxes" were more than $5 billion; worker compensation "taxes" that year were $1.7 billion.

the people and in time will be depleted. In addition, the development of natural resources often leaves massive scars on the landscape and states levy severance taxes also to pay restoration costs.

Miscellaneous Taxes and Charges

We have discussed the major tax revenue producers for state and local governments. The states also have found other sources that produce rather substantial amounts of revenue. All together, these taxes, fees, and charges account for nearly 20 percent of the total revenue. Motor vehicle license fees, for example, produced nearly $3.7 billion in 1975. Inheritance taxes produced almost $1.5 billion. Taxes on legalized gambling—parimutuel betting and lotteries—produced nearly another $1 billion for the states. In Policy Box No. 12, "Lotteries: Voluntary Taxation or Sucker Betting?" we raise the question of how appropriate gambling is as a means of taxation. Smaller amounts were produced from fees for documents and property transfers, hunting and fishing licenses, operating liquor establishments and amusement centers, and from other permits, examinations, and registrations that the states require.

POLICY BOX NO. 12:   Lotteries:
Voluntary Taxation or Sucker Betting?
A number of the states seemingly have adopted the position, "If you can't beat 'em, join 'em." At least that is what about one-fourth of the states have done with respect to a variety of forms of gambling. With the exception of state-regulated casino gambling in Nevada and Atlantic City, New Jersey, and betting at horse-racing tracks, the states have rigorously opposed and outlawed gambling, even in some states to the point of outlawing church-sponsored bingo. And, of course, the states continue to outlaw all forms of privately-sponsored gambling activities. Few law enforcement officials, however, have ever believed that they have done more than scratch the surface in controlling gambling. One report suggests that gambling is the largest single business in the country—it suggested that more than $75 billion annually is spent on various forms of illegal gambling.

Beginning with New Hampshire in 1964, the states gradually have begun to broaden their involvement and, indeed, sponsorship of legal gambling. An average of one state per year since 1964 has created its own lottery. Several states have expanded their gambling operations. Some now license bingo fund-raising activities by social and religious organizations. Most notable of the expansions is the opening of Atlantic City as the "Las Vegas East" casino gambling center in 1978.

A
Lottery
Winner!

Why do some states have lotteries? For the same reason the thirteen colonies did—to raise money for the state treasuries. Politicians, under pressure to increase expenditures and at the same time to keep taxes down, find the lottery an easy way out. Supporters of lotteries argue that people are going to gamble anyway, so the state, rather than underworld gangsters, should get the profits. Thus state lotteries have become a form of voluntary taxation. Other proponents of state lotteries suggest that if people have the opportunity to gamble legally, the state can undercut the profit of racketeers.

How successful have the state lotteries been? State lotteries, so far, have avoided the scandal that closed the lotteries of a century ago, but the revenues produced for state treasuries remains relatively low—less than 1 percent of the revenues in states that have lotteries. As a form of taxation, lotteries are inefficient—usually about 45 percent goes for winnings, 10 percent for administration, sales, and advertising, and 45 percent to the state coffers. The Michigan lottery, which is one of the most profitable, had a profit of only $100 million in 1976.

As competitors with underworld gambling, lotteries have probably been failures; it is not likely that state lotteries can compete successfully with illicit operations. State lotteries, for example, give poor odds by comparison, and have a low payoff rate; and state lotteries do not offer the players credit as the friendly bookie does—it's cash only with state lotteries. The illicit operations have another advantage—they do not report winnings, nor do they make deductions for income tax purposes. Opponents of state lotteries argue that state involvement has probably made underworld operations more profitable by making gambling more respectable.

Although state lotteries are a voluntary form of taxation, opponents argue that, even so, lotteries are a regressive tax. Through lotteries, they say, the government makes poor people poorer. Proponents say this is not so, that lotteries are only an inexpensive form of entertainment for people of all income classes.

Other opponents suggest that lottery administrators are under increasing pressure from politicians to raise more money for the state treasury. Administrators respond with more advertising, TV shows to announce the big winners, and new games to increase the level of activity. Thus, they draw more people into playing. The ads do not say that most people will lose money in the lottery; nor do they carry a warning that gambling may be addictive and damaging to your financial well being. The state, opponents say, is engaged in false and misleading advertising. The lotteries, they say, are a consumer rip off.

Some suggest that buying lottery tickets is like eating peanuts—at $1 per peanut.

What do you think? Should the states be using the lotteries and other forms of gambling to raise revenues? Are the gains for the treasury worth the risks to society? Should lottery ads carry warnings about the odds and payoff percentages? In order to discourage welfare recipients from playing the lottery, should lottery administrators be prohibited from awarding winnings to people on welfare? Are lotteries a legitimate source of state revenue? Apply the five criteria we used in this chapter to them.

SOURCE: This policy box is based on Neal R. Peirce, "Are State Lotteries Innocent Fun Or A Consumer Swindle?" *Detroit News*, June 12, 1977; J. F. TerHorst, "Is New Jersey's Gamble Worth the Risks?" *Detroit News*, November 19, 1976; and "The Legal Numbers Racket," *Newsweek*, November 3, 1975, p. 31.

An important source of revenue for local governments, a source not customarily seen as a tax, are the fees and charges for specific services. Perhaps the principal charges are for water and sewer services; but there are also fees for parking, refuse collection, court services, electricity (if the city has its own power company), hospital services in a city hospital, tuition in schools, park admission permits, and many others.

These fees fall on users of the service in direct proportion to the extent of use. In some instances these fees are sufficient to pay for the service and turn a profit for the city or county.

Movement Toward a More Diversified Revenue Base

State and local governments have modified their revenue systems substantially since the Great Depression to finance their expanding public services. What can we expect in the future?

We think that the states and localities are moving toward an even more diversified revenue system. In comparison with revenue sources twenty years earlier, 1974 revenue sources were more balanced. The principal revenue generators (sales and property taxes) in 1954 were still the major sources in 1975, but the proportion contributed by them had dropped from 49 percent of the total to 41 percent. (See Figure 6-7.) Producing a larger share of the total revenues were federal aid, income taxes, and miscellaneous charges and revenues. Most observers expect these trends to continue. Thus we should find greater overall stability in state and local revenue systems in the future.

BORROWING AND DEBT IN THE STATES AND LOCALITIES

Historically, the record of state and local debt is "spotty"—people who loan money to states and their localities by buying bonds, notes, or other instruments have not always received payment on time, and in a few instances, not at all. In the 1930s approximately 10 percent of municipal bonds were in default. During the twenty-five years following World War II the record improved considerably, but since 1970 the picture has darkened somewhat.

Improvements in Debt Management

The experiences of the Depression brought changes in borrowing and repayment practices. Some state constitutions or city charters severely limited borrowing powers; many prohibited government officials from issuing general obligation debt (debt secured by taxes) without voter approval. Moreover state legislatures established ceilings on debt—ceilings usually related to the property tax base. States also created commissions to review local bond issues before they could be marketed.

Changes that were long overdue were made in repayment schedules. Most long-term loans of today are made with serial bonds. With these, a certain percentage of the bonds mature each year until the total amount borrowed is repaid. Previously, borrowing governments were required to create a "sinking fund" to which annual payments were to be made. All of the bonds matured at the same time and sufficient money would have been saved to pay the debt. Sinking funds proved too great a temptation for some officials, as they either delayed making sinking fund payments or borrowed from the fund when things got "tight."

Figure 6-7
The State and Local Revenue System, Fiscal
Years 1954 and 1974

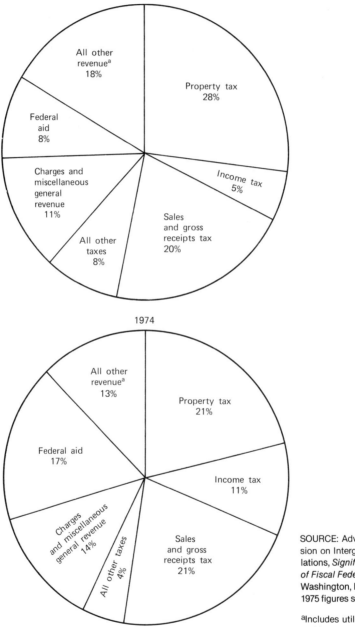

1954

All other revenueª 18%

Property tax 28%

Federal aid 8%

Charges and miscellaneous general revenue 11%

Income tax 5%

All other taxes 8%

Sales and gross receipts tax 20%

1974

All other revenueª 13%

Property tax 21%

Federal aid 17%

Income tax 11%

Charges and miscellaneous general revenue 14%

All other taxes 4%

Sales and gross receipts tax 21%

SOURCE: Advisory Commission on Intergovernmental Relations, *Significant Features of Fiscal Federalism, 1976,* Washington, D.C., p. 20. For 1975 figures see Figure 6-1.

ªIncludes utility, liquor store and insurance trust revenue.

These changes have also resulted in a few problems. Voters have sometimes refused to approve bond issues, even though facilities were badly needed. Voter rejections, in turn, led to issuing *revenue bonds*, which are secured by revenues produced by the facility constructed: often water or sewer systems or parking ramps. Bond buyers see revenue bonds as somewhat risky and so they charge higher interest rates. The higher costs are passed along to consumers of the services.

How Much Do We Owe?

As we can see from Figure 6-8 most of what we owe (about 70 percent of the total) are federal government debts. The states, which traditionally rely less on borrowed money, owe about 9 percent of the debt, while the localities owe about 20 percent. We can see that debt outstanding for all three levels of government has been rising steadily. In terms of the Gross National Product (GNP), however, the extent of the borrowing has remained relatively constant. The GNP is the measure that economists regard as important, in part, because they assume it will continually rise.

The Limits of Borrowing

Borrowing money may create difficulties because it must be repaid with interest. As we know from our personal lives, this is not necessarily bad unless we have borrowed beyond our means to repay.

"Paying as you go" for capital projects, as Nebraska did when it built its state capitol building, or as Virginia did under the Byrd organization (1925–50), appeals to persons with a conservative bent. But it often means a long time before the facilities are built. It also means that many who have paid (through taxes "banked" for them) may not benefit from the facilities. Borrowing—a "pay as you use" policy—tends to place the payment responsibility on those who benefit from the facility.

Local Debt, A Federal Concern. What we saw during New York City's financial crisis in 1976 is that the debt of a single city is not just a local concern. We might have expected that the state would be involved. But when the crisis, and the amount of debt, was greater than New York State could handle, the crisis of New York City became a problem of the federal government. Ultimately, and reluctantly, the federal government provided short-term loans and required the state and city to get their "house in order." As we write, the city continues to face periodic cash shortages. The New York City crisis illustrates an important

Figure 6-8
Total Government Debt Amount and as a Percent of GNP

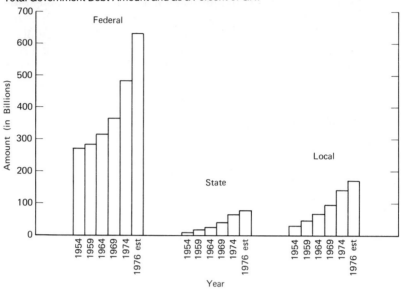

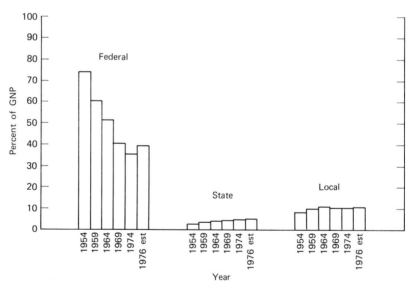

SOURCE: Adapted from Advisory Commission on Intergovernmental Relations, *Significant Features of Fiscal Federalism, 1976*, Washington, D.C., p. 63.

Reprinted by permission of the Chicago Tribune-New York News Syndicate, Inc.

fact we are discovering in other policy areas—that our federal system is financially, as well as politically, interdependent.

Relationship of Interest Costs to Revenues. The aspect of debt that contributes to the current financial crisis is, as we can see from Figure 6-9, that interest payments have been rising more rapidly than state and community revenues. Individual states or localities could experience serious trouble, especially if they had been heavy borrowers and were now faced with an eroding tax base, as is the case for many middle-sized and large cities.

When Should Governments Borrow?

Defenders and critics of New York City offered many explanations for the current financial crisis. A key element was that the city not only borrowed for capital projects, but to finance daily operations as well. A crisis emerged because large banks, such as the Chase Manhattan Bank, refused to renew loans to finance current expenditures. In effect, the bankers said, "This cannot continue. We had better deal with the fundamental problems now." Financial specialists consider such borrowing, quite rightly, we think, as a sign of financial instability.

But bankers generally approve of short-term borrowing in anticipation of taxes or other reliable revenues that will be collected during a

Figure 6-9
Governmental Interest Payments as a Percent of Government Revenue

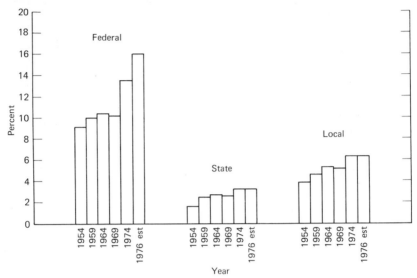

SOURCE: Adapted from Advisory Commission on Intergovernmental Relations, *Significant Features of Fiscal Federalism, 1976*, Washington, D.C., p. 67.

current fiscal year. Financial managers usually refer to this as a cash-flow problem, that is, governments incur expenses before they receive their revenues. For example, school districts must be open for business each autumn, even though they may not receive revenues until they collect property taxes in December. They may solve this cash-flow problem with a short-term loan that they repay when taxes are collected.

STATE AND LOCAL SPENDING PATTERNS

We have seen how state and local revenues have been increasing. Thus it comes as no surprise to find that total spending has been increasing. Let us look at the expenditure side of the picture.

Expenditures in the Federal System

In 1954 total public expenditures were less than $100 billion. By 1976 they had risen to more than $575 billion, an increase of nearly 600 percent. Government spending also increased, relative to the GNP. In 1954 it was 26.5 percent and by 1976 it was 34.2 percent of the GNP.

Not all of the increase, of course, was the result of more or higher quality services. Inflation, as we would expect, also affects government, and it accounts for a substantial portion of the increase. We should also note that the nation's population increased by about 50 million during this period.

The Changing Ratio. We want you to pay special attention to the changing ratio of federal expenditures. In 1929 the federal expenditure was 25 percent, the state and local, 75 percent. The depression, and later the war, changed this. By 1940 the division was fifty-fifty and by 1954 federal expenditures had risen once more to 72 percent of the total. They then dropped steadily until 1970, when they began a slight rise. Federal aid to states and localities, of course, accounts for part of this recent rise. Today the ratio is about 66 percent for federal and 33 percent for state and local.

If we remove federal expenditures for defense and consider only domestic expenditures, the picture changes somewhat. *Domestic* expenditures for all levels have increased more than 900 percent during the period 1954 to 1976, from about $50 billion to more than $450 billion. (Defense expenditures have been declining as a proportion of the total, and in 1975 accounted for about 20 percent of the total.)

State expenditures increased a little more than eight times, while those of the localities rose by five and one-half times. In terms of ratios, the federal proportion of domestic expenditures has steadily risen from 45.5 percent in 1954 to about 60 percent in 1976. The state share has declined somewhat during the period, and in 1976 accounted for about 22 percent. The dramatic drop was with the localities—their share of the expenditures fell from 29 percent to 18.3 percent.

We can get a somewhat closer look at where these changes are taking place by examining Table 6-4. Total expenditures between 1970 and 1975 for social services more than doubled during the five-year period. We think it is significant that in spite of this increase, the state–local proportion remained at 75 percent during the period. It means, we think, that the federal government very strongly influences state-local spending patterns. And it also reflects the continuing importance of states in the delivery of social services.

The federal involvement in school expenditures has remained relatively low. The percentage increase in federal expenditures seems large, but in the 1970 base year federal expenditures for education were very low. In dollar terms, spending for education by the states and localities increased much more rapidly than did federal spending for education.

TABLE 6-4 Total Domestic Expenditures From Own Funds For Social Services, School Expenditures and All Other—1970–1975 in Billions of Dollars

	1970	Percent of Total	1975	Percent of Total	Percent Increase 1970–75	Change in Proportion
Specified Social Services[a]						
Federal	$ 70.4	75.0	$152.8	75.1	117	+ .1
State/Local	23.4	25.0	50.8	24.9	117	− .1
Total	$ 93.8	100.0	$203.6	100.0	117	
School Expenditures[b]						
Federal	$ 6.9	13.3	$ 13.1	15.8	90	+ 2.5
State/Local	$ 45.0	86.7	$ 69.8	84.2	55	− 2.5
Total	$ 51.9	100.0	$ 82.9	100.0	60	
All Other Services						
Federal	$ 32.8	45.5	$ 76.4	61.6	133	+ 16.1
State/Local	39.3	54.5	$ 47.6	38.4	28	− 16.1
Total	$ 72.1	100.0	$124.0	100.0	77	
Total Domestic Expenditures						
Federal	$110.1	50.6	$242.3	59.0	120	+ 8.4
State/Local	107.7	49.4	168.2	41.9	56	− 8.4
Total	$217.8	100.0	$410.5	100.0	83	

SOURCE: Adapted from *Significant Features of Fiscal Federalism, 1976 Edition*. Tables III-X Advisory Commission on Intergovernmental Relations, Washington, D.C. General Revenue Sharing are included as state and local expenditures.

[a]Includes cash benefits and administrative costs under social insurance, public assistance, supplemental security income, veterans and emergency employment programs, health and medical care programs, food stamps, surplus food for needy, child nutrition and welfare, institutional care, economic opportunity and manpower programs.

[b]Includes among other items, expenditures for veterans educational benefits.

It is in the "all other services" category that the federal government's relative participation has increased most dramatically. "All other services" includes community development, criminal justice, highways, agriculture, business—areas where federal grants have grown rapidly.

The Effect of Transfer Payments. Let us return to the longer-term data and consider the picture *after* intergovernmental transfers have been made. In 1954 federal and local governments each accounted for about 40 percent of domestic expenditures after transfers, and the states accounted for 20 percent. By 1971 federal domestic expenditures after transfers amounted to 47 percent and those of the localities amounted to 33 percent. The states' proportion remained the same.

What we discover, then, is that the federal government has moved into a position of dominance in deciding domestic expenditures. Federal officials not only spend the largest proportion, but also influence state and local spending decisions through grant programs. The change we see in these spending patterns illustrates the shift from cooperative federalism to permissive, or functional, federalism. It also highlights the growing financial interdependence of our federal system.

State and Local Government Spending

What accounts for the "lion's share" of state and local expenditures? We find four functions—education, highways, public welfare, and health; and we find it remarkable that these four functions have accounted for more than two-thirds of state and local spending over several decades running up to the present time.

We have developed some graphs to help us better understand the picture. First, we find that the top four functions have accounted for around 70 percent when we look at combined state and local spending in Figure 6-10. And when we separate local from state expenditures we see that the picture of each does not change a great deal—the top four functions account for about three-fourths of state spending (Figure 6-11), and about two-thirds of local spending (Figure 6-12).

Second, when we compare state with local spending, we see that spending for education has dominated at the local level for the entire period. At the state level we note that it has not, but that the proportion spent for education increased steadily over the period. These data, in part, reflect the state responses, first to rising college and university enrollments as the babies of the postwar baby boom reached college age, and then as a response to the financial problems of local school systems. Rising state expenditures are also found for welfare services. They are a response to the growing participation of the federal government in welfare programs.

Third, we also observe that emphases in spending change, to reflect society's concerns and activities. State expenditures for highways dropped, in part, because the interstate system has been nearly completed. Greater spending for public health and welfare, in part, reflects the fact that the average age of our population is gradually becoming higher. We might look forward to further shifts in the overall pattern. The oil shortage and the pressure of the Carter administration to reduce gasoline consumption, for example, could produce a shift in state and local spending from highways to mass transportation.

Figure 6-10

Percents of State and Local General Expenditures by Function, Selected Fiscal Years 1954–1975

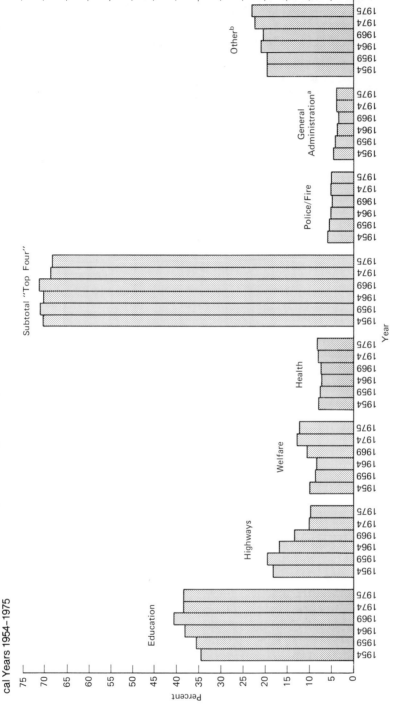

SOURCE: Adapted from *Facts and Figures on Government Finance*, Tax Foundation, Inc. (19th ed.) New York, 1977, p. 137.

[a]Includes general administration.

[b]Includes natural resources, sanitation and sewerage, recreation, housing and urban renewal, interest on general debt, unallocable expenditures, and others.

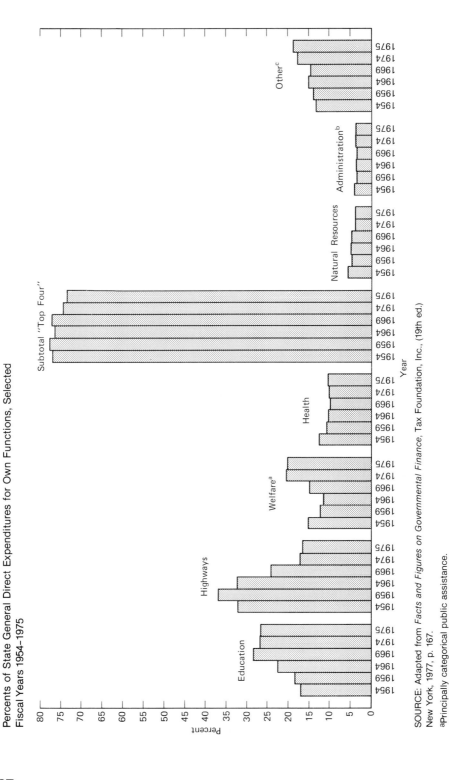

Figure 6-11

Percents of State General Direct Expenditures for Own Functions, Selected Fiscal Years 1954–1975

SOURCE: Adapted from *Facts and Figures on Governmental Finance*, Tax Foundation, Inc., (19th ed.) New York, 1977, p. 167.

[a]Principally categorical public assistance.

[b]Includes financial and general administration.

[c]Principally police, corrections, interest, and social insurance administration.

SOURCE: Adapted from *Facts and Figures on Governmental Finance*, Tax Foundation, Inc. (19th ed.)
New York, 1977, p. 232.

aPrincipally elementary and secondary schools.

bIncludes natural resources, sanitation, recreation, interest on general debt, urban renewal, public
transportation, corrections, local libraries, general public buildings, and other general government.

Figure 6-13
Per Capita State and Local General Expenditures, Selected Fiscal Years
1954-1975

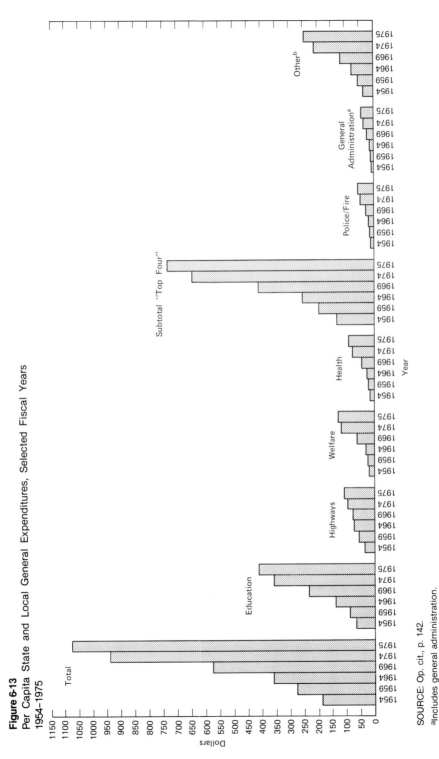

SOURCE: Op. cit., p. 142.

aIncludes general administration.

bIncludes natural resources, sanitation and sewerage, recreation, housing and urban renewal, interest on general debt, unallocable expenditures, and others.

Financial Crises

The pattern of state-local expenditures and the dominance of the four functions in the overall pattern have important implications for dealing with financial crises. During periods of economic downturn, when we find that revenues are going to be insufficient, officials have three alternative ways to deal with the problem.

Governments can borrow, but we have already discussed the problems of borrowing to meet operating expenses. Officials can raise taxes, but legislators and city councillors are usually reluctant to take this step when times are not good. Finally the governments can cut programs and appropriations, but the difficulty with this alternative is that the needs of three of the top four services (education, welfare, and health services) tend to increase during recessions. (Reducing highway expenditures usually does not help much because these revenues are earmarked and can only be used for highways.) In addition, because many of the other services constitute less than one-third of the total, deep cuts would have to be made to make up for the increased demands in the major expenditure areas.

How do governments resolve the dilemma? Usually financial crises are weathered by using all three alternatives. Governments do some borrowing. For example, during periods of high unemployment a state may borrow heavily from the nation's unemployment fund, or the states may borrow from other restricted funds or change accounting methods to give at least some temporary relief. And we see that legislators and city councillors do vote to approve temporary tax increases. We find them adopting "holding the line" budgets; program improvements are deferred, vacant positions remain unfilled, public employees may get little or no salary increases, and they may cut back services—a fire station may be closed or certain school grades may have half days.

In addition, however, state and local governments seek relief from the federal government. Employees may be shifted to federally funded positions or special federal funds may be directed to distressed areas to stimulate local economies or to put people on unusual public-works projects. The involvement of the federal government in state and local financial crises has come to be expected. Federal support does not yet assure the elimination of such crises, but it does shore up the states and localities so that they can work their way out of them. Without this undergirding of the federal system in state and local finance, it is difficult to imagine how the states and communities would overcome such severe economic disruptions.

A Final Comment

As we have seen throughout this chapter, the place of the federal government has been growing steadily in financing the federal system. Not only does Washington contribute an increasing share of state and community revenues, but it assumes an increasing share of the total spending for domestic programs. Only because state and community governments have raised their tax revenues substantially over the years have they been able to hold their own in financing the federal system.

But now, as we write, citizens in California may have taken a major step to limit the capacity of their state and community governments to keep up the pace. Tennessee voters already had limited state spending to a fixed percentage of personal income and New Jersey adopted a similar plan by statute. The Jarvis plan of California (Proposition 13), adopted in 1978 not only severely limited, but rolled back by 57 percent, property taxes on which community governments heavily depended. Citizens and legislators in a number of other states are also readying ballot questions to limit state and local taxation or spending. Journalists referred to the actions as the beginning of a "taxpayers' revolt."

What are the implications for federalism? At this time, of course, we do not know how successful the taxpayers' revolt will be in other states and communities or how citizens of California, New Jersey, or Tennessee will respond when state and local programs are cut. (High school athletics may be eliminated, school bus services may be drastically reduced, health clinics closed, and any number of other service reductions may have to be made.) Some have suggested that the "tax cut" proposals are really only "tax shift." Full effects of the California action were delayed because the state had a $5.5 billion surplus that it immediately shared with local units. In some communities, though, rates for dog licenses, permits and admissions to zoos and art galleries increased dramatically, thus lending some credence to the "tax shift" theory.

What the developing situation seems to portend is that the place of federal government in domestic programs, in the short run at least, will expand much more rapidly than that of state and community governments. That is, the federal system will become even more centralized as a result. State and community governments, therefore, will become even more dependent on federal assistance and more subject to federal guidelines and requirements.

President Carter, after the California election, warned that the state should not look to Washington for lost revenues. It seems probable, though, that such a policy would crumble if a great many states or communities cut taxes or limited spending and pressures for federal aid increased sharply.

Another possible outcome, of course, is that in time the national government itself may be strongly affected by taxpayer resistance. Presently state legislatures are passing resolutions calling for a national constitutional convention to introduce an amendment to limit federal spending.[18] More likely, it seems, that members of Congress will respond, at least for the next election or two, to taxpayer pressures and further reduce federal income taxes and, perhaps, even set national spending limits. As we noted earlier, Congress has greater financial flexibility than the states and could reduce taxes without reducing spending by increasing the national deficit. Should the Congress limit national spending, however, the relative position of the various levels of government would tend to stabilize and the rate of public spending increases would slow down.

Whatever the outcome, it is clear that our travels through a very complicated financial system lead us to conclude that the states and their local governments no longer stand alone. In the revenues they collect we find that the localities depend heavily on states, as the states depend on federal funds. On the expenditure side, we find a steady trend toward more federal involvement in expenditures made by state and local governments, as well as more state involvement in local expenditures.

We should no longer think it unusual that New York State came to the rescue of New York City or the federal government to the rescue of both. All are, in point of fact, a part of what is becoming a more United States.

HIGHPOINTS OF CHAPTER 6: STATE AND LOCAL FINANCE IN A CENTRALIZING FEDERAL SYSTEM

We found (1) that intergovernmental transfers are now an essential part of state and local finance. The federal government (and the states as well) use these payments to redistribute money from the wealthy governments to the poor ones. They also use them to accomplish goals set by federal and state governments.

[18]We note that it is not clear if the Congress would have to call a constitutional convention, even if a sufficient number of state legislatures would adopt such a resolution.

We saw next (2) that the states and localities collect about 40 percent of the total public revenues, but largely through tax systems that are regressive and not highly elastic or responsive to economic activity.

We found (3) that they are gradually building more diversified taxing systems that are more progressive and elastic than they have been.

Because of a number of changes that were made in the administration of state and local debt, we discussed (4) how these governments are able to borrow large sums of money to finance their projects. We noted, though, that excessive local borrowing can lead to fiscal chaos that can only be corrected with the help of the state and federal government.

We noted (5) that spending patterns in the states and localities are dominated by expenditures for education, highways, welfare, and health services. Over time the patterns of expenditure have changed to reflect changes in the general society. But the changes in the future, as they have been in the past, most likely will be moderate rather than massive. Finally we noted (6) that the states and localities can make some adjustments in their revenue and spending patterns to help them weather financial crises. However, most are now reliant on the federal government to help them work through periods of extended ecnomic distress.

STATE
LEGISLATORS
AS CRITICS

7

Legislative bodies attract more than their share of news media critics. Headlines, such as "Legislators Hoot Down Move to Spurn Pay Hike," "Lawmakers Eye Recess: Budget-Axing Week Arrives," and "City Council Guts Mayor's Housing Plan," are a few examples of how the press often presents state and community legislative bodies.

Do legislators get this unfavorable publicity because news reporters and headline writers dislike state legislatures and city councils? Probably not. Other conditions seem to explain the situation better. One reason, we think, is that reporters get a better view of what goes on in the legislature than in the other branches. The floor debate in the statehouse or county board of commissioners is open to public inspection and, in a number of states, so are committee meetings. Thus, much of the fighting and bickering is open to the public view. Contrast this with the courts that bargain out their decisions behind closed doors and the private meetings the governor holds with department heads. Unless there are leaks, we seldom know what went on.

In addition, many of the statements made by legislators are spontaneous and sometimes twisted. Statements, such as "We'll have the tail wagging the dog instead of the dog wagging its head," or "How much will we owe on June 31?" do not create the best impression. On the other hand many public statements of governors are carefully prepared and rehearsed and the opinions of the courts meticulously written and edited before they are released to the press.

The Legislative Purpose

We think that the central task of legislators is to evaluate and criticize policies that, in the main, are proposed, advocated, and later administered by others. This evaluation, we will argue, is a political evaluation—one that seeks a balance acceptable to the variety of interests in a state. We, thus, are concerned with strengthening what we will call a state legislature's political efficiency. Other branches of state government also evaluate policies for their political acceptability, but for the legislatures, it is the main job. That is why their representativeness is so important—why every group, including state agencies and local governments that can afford to, zeroes in on the legislature to make sure its point of view is heard. It is also why the typical approach of legislators to policy problems is compromise among opposing viewpoints and interests.

As you read this chapter you will recognize that this evaluation is tilted towards preserving stability and the *status* quo. The formal rules give special advantage to the forces of delay and those opposing change.

The legislatures also have a responsibility to perform a distinctive "crossroads" role in our centralizing federal system—making certain that local concerns are not forgotten in making or administering national policy, and that state and national concerns are not overlooked in making or administering community policy.

Legislatures have not always been administratively efficient—their procedures are often confusing and messy and this has earned them much criticism from reformers. We believe it important that legislatures be politically efficient, even at some cost to their administrative efficiency.

Overview.   We will be looking at the state legislatures under six headings: the legislative job; the conditions that contribute to amateurism in state legislatures; the people who become state legislators; how state legislatures function politically—their structure, procedures, and staff; how legislatures relate politically to outside groups, such as parties, interest groups, and the state bureaucracies; and the proposals that have been made to improve state legislatures. We will close with a final note on what we, as citizens, want from our state legislatures.

California Assembly rostrum.

WHAT STATE LEGISLATORS DO

Most of us became familiar with the general process of representation and making decisions by majority vote at an early age. But when it comes to defining in detail what we mean by representation, we become a little uncertain. We will take a closer look here at how legislators go about their task of representing us.

Legislative Functions

What do legislators do in their representative capacity? We find three major activities: (1) they make laws, (2) they assist constituents, and (3) they oversee the operations of the governor and the administrative branch.

Law Making. Making laws is a major way legislators indicate what they think is the balance of political forces in a state. During the 1975 to 1976 period legislators in the fifty states introduced 200,571 new bills—mostly bills to change laws already on the books. In addition, they introduced several thousand resolutions—to state opposition or support for national policies, such as the ban on saccharin, or simply to congratulate the state's high school basketball champions.

Our first reaction is that these are a great many bills. But, in terms of an average per legislator per year, we find that the 7,563 legislators introduced only 13.3 bills each, a rather modest number.

Even so, we may all breathe a little easier when we learn that only about 21 percent of all the bills introduced actually become law.

Why so many bills? We find several reasons for the great number of bills. When we have complex social and economic relationships, we can expect the rules and proposed changes in them to be very numerous. Thus, we find more bills are usually introduced in urban states. During 1975–76, for example, the New York legislature had thirty-eight times more bills introduced than the Utah legislature (34,035, as compared to 890), although New York is only seventeen times larger in population than Utah. But only in Massachusetts and New York were more than 10,000 bills introduced.

The rules of legislatures also help inflate the number of bills. Twenty-four state legislatures treat the two years of a biennium as one session—a bill introduced in the first year remains "alive" in the second session year as well. In the other twenty-six states the bills die at the end of each annual session and are often reintroduced in the next.

Finally we find bills introduced for a variety of political reasons, sometimes as a favor to a lobbyist, interest group, or constituent. In states with bill introduction deadlines, we find "skeleton" bills—bills that are virtually meaningless when introduced, but that may be filled out with content after the deadline if the need arises. Still other bills with little hope of passage are introduced to get a headline in the newspapers back home or to put a legislator in the political spotlight.

Where do the ideas for the legislation come from? Legislators are not the main source of laws—they are, rather, sensitive reactors to problems brought to them by others.

Congressional and Supreme Court actions stimulate bill introductions. Frequently states must pass a law to qualify for a federal grant. For example, the states had to set speed limits on expressways at 55 mph to obtain federal highway money. For similar reasons states adopted at least minimum civil service provisions, "affirmative action" programs for minorities and women, and improved budgetary procedures.

The governor, state courts, and state administrative agencies provide many of the ideas and initiatives for bills. Some will be "innovative" legislation—new policy proposals—but most will propose amending existing laws to deal with problems agencies have run into, such as bills to limit the number of canoeists on certain rivers or to change the allowable cereal content in hot dogs.

Economic interest groups—business, labor, and agriculture—are also an important source. Today we also find consumer groups important as they prepare and advocate bills to license automobile mechanics and to require supermarkets to adopt unit pricing practices. In addition, groups such as Common Cause, pressure legislatures to enact "sunshine" laws that require meetings of public officials to be open to the public; and professionals, such as social workers (it could be urban planners, psychologists, physicians, optometrists, podiatrists, chiropractors, and so on), who want a law to license or raise standards for admission to the profession.

Problems back home in the legislative districts also are a source of bills because what happens there is usually of considerable importance to a legislator. Reelection may depend on how local district problems are handled. The problem may be as small a matter as a law to help a small town build a sidewalk along a highway for children as they walk to school. Or it may be a major economic question to permit a local company to mine on state-owned land.

Of course, legislators themselves may come up with ideas for bills, but these are a distinct minority. Even in respect to lawmaking, legislators react more than they innovate.

Constituent Services.   Beside voting on bills, a legislator is expected to provide services to people in the district—a very important function that we sometimes dismiss as errand running.

Constituents may ask for help in dealing with a state agency. Again we note that legislators react to problems brought to them by others. The citizens may not have gotten their welfare check, or they need a state scholarship to continue in school, help in getting a state job—the list of such matters is practically endless.

A constitutent may even ask the legislator to run errands to obtain schedules for civil service or licensing examinations, find out when school aid payments will be made, get informational booklets, send copies of bills, or arrange meetings with other more important legislators; all these come under the category of "servicing the district." Many who want such services are ordinary citizens, but others are leaders of interest groups and local public officials, such as city managers, school superintendents, or county officers.

Often, of course, the legislators may have no more success with state agencies than do the citizens themselves. But citizens hope that if the legislator intercedes, they will get what they want.

Legislative Oversight.   The legislators also keep tabs on how agencies and programs are run, including, especially, state programs supported heavily with federal funds. This surveillance is usually more a product of other activities than a specific activity in itself—legislators "oversee" when they ask departments to handle a citizen request or complaint. Oversight is also an integral part of law making. A department of natural resources, for example, may propose a change in the law regulating tree cutting in state forests. As a committee considers that bill, questions on hunting policies or campground rules may also be discussed. This is oversight—legislators challenging administrators on behalf of citizens to explain why they are doing what they do. We also find legislators carrying out the oversight responsibility on local government affairs, often in response to matters local officials have raised and want the legislature to resolve.

Appropriations committees exercise legislative oversight as they call upon state agency heads and community college and university presidents to defend budget requests. On such occasions administrators try to put their operations in the best light possible. But, for the legislators, every agency detail is "fair game." In our experience in budget hearings, rarely were college presidents able to leave without being questioned about some embarrassing administrative detail. Often the purpose of such questioning was unclear and seemed little more than harassment. But it reminded college presidents that others had a right to ask questions and expect responses, and that any disgruntled student or parent might be the initial source of an embarrassing question.

Review of executive actions. Legislative oversight takes place, too, when legislatures exercise the "legislative veto"—that is, when they confirm or reject candidates the governor wishes to appoint to high-level offices, the proposals of governors to reorganize executive agencies, or administrative rules that agencies develop to spell out detailed procedures for administering a law. Often these reviews are routine. But if the proposals or individuals involved are at all controversial, legislators are certain to surface troublesome points.

Legislative auditors. The growing practice of having state auditors appointed by the legislature, rather than popularly elected, provides legislators with another oversight function. The legislative auditor audits the financial records and reviews performance data of state agencies to determine if the money was spent legally and efficiently. Auditors can almost always find something amiss and their reports provide legislators with further points for questioning and criticizing.

Special investigative committees. Special select committees to investigate an agency problem or a disastrous event are another form of legislative oversight. Such committees determine who may have been at fault and whether changes in laws are needed. They may also hold hearings for political reasons—a major purpose often is to embarrass the governor or to advance a legislator's career. Depending on the question being investigated, the committee may get a great deal of publicity—headlines and television coverage.

The importance of legislative oversight. As we look at what legislators do, we see that this oversight function is most important to us as citizens. As we will note in Chapter 10 on administration it is the legislature, and not the governor, to whom we should look as being primarily responsible for keeping a measure of democratic control of administrative actions. They also are primarily responsible for striking a politically efficient balance between national and community viewpoints. Legislators can view state operations from the outside and bring many points of view to bear on almost any question. This is why we have called this chapter "State Legislators As Critics."

THE LEGISLATIVE WAY OF LIFE

The political fact that characterizes state legislators above all else, is that most have been and still are amateurs. They are people engaged in the legislative process on a part-time, short-term basis. Legislators, for the most part, cannot give their full attention to this job, and do not hold the position as a professional career. In only a half a dozen states or so, do we find that this is not the case.

The amateur status of legislators is the product of a web of circumstances involving legislators' schedules, life style, salaries, and the staff and facilities they have available to them. We will see how these conditions contribute to this amateur standing—a standing that is frustrating to many legislators as well as to advocates of legislative reform.

Legislative Sessions

During the 1800s when legislatures established a reputation for creating all kinds of mischief, the people responded by limiting the length and frequency of legislative sessions—many state constitutions limited regular sessions to sixty or ninety days every two years. The theory was simple—the shorter the session the less damage legislators could do. These limits have lasted well into our own time, although most states have begun to relax these restrictions.

At the time of World War II, for example, only four legislatures (New Jersey, New York, Rhode Island, and South Carolina) held annual sessions. Thirty years later in 1976, thirty-nine state legislatures officially had regular annual sessions. But we find that voters in Texas and New Hampshire recently rejected proposals for annual sessions and Montana voters decided to return to a biennial session.[1]

Limits on the length of regular sessions serve to keep the job of legislator part time. In 1976 only eighteen states had no restrictions on the length of the legislative session. Six others permitted legislators to continue beyond the constitutional time limit, but allowed no pay or expenses after the deadline. The fact that thirty-two states still impose time limits on sessions indicates that most state legislators are still seen as part-time representatives who should get their work done in short order and go back home.

Special Sessions. In most states, if not all, legislatures do, in fact, convene every year. As a practical matter some actions cannot be delayed to the regular biennial sessions. This is especially so because court decisions and federal programs affect so directly the decisions of state governments. To handle these questions special sessions must be called by the governors almost annually.

As we will see in Chapter 8, governors tend to have the upper hand in special sessions because they usually decide when to call a special session and what items will be put on the agenda. More states now permit greater flexibility on special sessions—thirty-five have no limits on length, and a few even permit the legislature to act on additional matters after those placed on the agenda by the governor have been dealt with.

Life-style Demands

Few legislators would agree that the job is part time. Frank Smallwood, a political scientist at Dartmouth University in New Hampshire who served a term in the Vermont state legislature wrote, "To state it as bluntly as possible, anyone who is interested in making a major commitment to politics had best be prepared literally to give up all else if this commitment is to be fulfilled. There's no way—at least I found no way —to pursue the political life on a casual, leisurely, half-time basis."[2]

The formal schedule alone, does not look too formidable. Typically legislatures meet on Monday evenings, the afternoons of the next three days, and briefly on Friday morning. Midweek mornings are usually devoted to committee meetings, except near the end of the session

[1]Herbert L. Wiltsee, "The State Legislatures" in *The Book of the States*, 1976–77, Council of State Governments, Lexington, Ky., p. 32.

[2]Frank Smallwood, *Free and Independent*, The Stephen Green Press, Brattleboro, Vermont, 1976, p. 223.

when floor action is scheduled. But when we also consider the round of meetings at the capital city and "back in the district," we find the legislators' schedules full and often hectic, at least while the legislature is in session.

Convention Atmosphere.   State legislators differ from members of Congress and city and county governing boards in one important respect—state legislators, for the most part, leave their families to carry out the political job. Members of Congress usually move their families to Washington, while the community legislators, of course, have no need to move. But state legislators spend Mondays through Fridays at the state capital and are at home only over the weekends. Many legislators have no offices and can only meet people in the capitol, or hotel lobbies, or bars and restaurants. This has implications for legislative amateurism and for the legislative way of life. State legislators are on a kind of four-day convention each week during the legislative session.

Frank Smallwood spoke of his experience of motel life at Montpelier and his evening routine that ended with a swim or a sauna. Our impression from personal observation and newspaper reports suggests that some other legislators are not able to handle the convention atmosphere quite as well. A number of them experience alcoholic problems and severely disrupted family lives. Some get involved in minor scrapes with the law. The incidence of personal disorganization among legislators also provides some insights into the life-styles imposed by the state legislative role—as one legislator responded in one of our classes to the question by a student as to whether legislative divorce rates were unusually high—"Oh no sir, not at all sir; no higher than among Hollywood movie stars."

Legislative Compensation

Low legislative pay, perhaps more than any other factor, contributes to the amateur standing. Until the early 1960s legislative salaries in most states were "nominal"—token recognition for their public service. (New Hampshire still reflects the extreme with its "honorarium" of $100 per year. Rhode Island legislators do not fare much better at $300 per year.) The general trend though, is for increasing salary and fringe benefits. In 1964–65, median compensation, including salary and expense money, was $4658 for the two-year period. By 1977–78, the median had risen to $19,550. California lawmakers received the highest total biennial compensation—$61,599.

The compensation, of course, determines the amount of time most individuals can spend on public business. In a few states the pay is, perhaps, sufficient to maintain a middle-class standard of living. But if we consider travel costs and extra living expenses at the capital, as well as the cost of campaigning, we see that for legislators in most of the states, the money is little more than a nice side income.

Legislators in most states, then, have to work at other jobs or have other income. For most of them, law making and representing the constituency has to remain a side interest, a serious hobby engaged in by amateurs. There are implications, too, regarding who can take up this hobby of law making—a matter that we will discuss later.

The Politics of Salary Increases.   Legislatures have not been able to shake the poor public image they gained in the nineteenth century—a fact contributing to their low pay. But perhaps as important are the politics of changing compensation levels. Legislatures traditionally have had to take the first steps to raise their pay because compensation has been set in constitutions or by law. Because new compensation rates ordinarily do not take effect until after the next election, legislators often see a yes vote as benefiting only their successors while they "catch the heat." So it is often difficult to obtain the votes for an increase. One way legislators have been able to increase their earnings is by voting for increases in public employee pension benefits, in which they also participate in some states. As we can see from the account in Policy Box 13, "Pensions: A Temptation Legislators Cannot Resist," this practice is leading to some difficult future problems.

In recent years states have established compensation commissions. The governor appoints a board that meets every two years to set or recommend pay for legislators and other elected state officers. In 1976 nineteen states used this approach.

What we find is that states with such commissions, where the legislature meets every year, and where pay is set on an annual basis, tend to pay above the median level. Conversely, states where pay is set in the constitution, where the legislature meets biennially, and where payment rate is by the day, are usually below the median.

Offices and Secretarial Help

Duane Lockard, a one-time member of the Connecticut senate and now a political scientist at Princeton University, told of a letter asking him to do a small chore. The citizen acknowledged that Lockard was probably busy, but suggested that, perhaps, Lockard's "office" could handle it. Lockard's reaction was, "My office! I had no office staff and indeed no office except for a corner in my hallway at home, where unsorted and unfiled letters, brochures, notes, and thousands of bills constantly threatened to bury my children under a paper cascade."[3]

Lockard's experience in the 1950s was by no means unique. Nor is it unusual for many state legislators today.

Legislators traditionally have made do with minimum physical accommodations and little, if any, secretarial assistance. This is yet another reason why so many are amateur lawmakers. Committee chairmen are slightly better off—at least they can take command of the committee rooms and have the committee secretary answer their mail. Regular members of the legislature often have only a desk on the floor of the chamber. We can recall when in the 1960s the Michigan senate leaders announced a major improvement—telephones were to be installed at each legislator's desk. They were quite an advance over the pay telephones then provided in the lobby.

But office facilities have improved. Nineteen states now provide legislators with private offices, and eight others provide shared office space. Some states have built new office buildings and moved state officers, such as those of the supreme court, out of the capitol to make space for legislators. Although many state capitols are old and drafty, capitol office space is in high demand. In Iowa, officials of the three

[3]Duane Lockard, "The Tribulations of a State Senator," in John C. Wahlke and Heinz Eulau, eds., *Legislative Behavior*, Free Press of Glencoe, Illinois, 1959, p. 296.

Figure 7-1

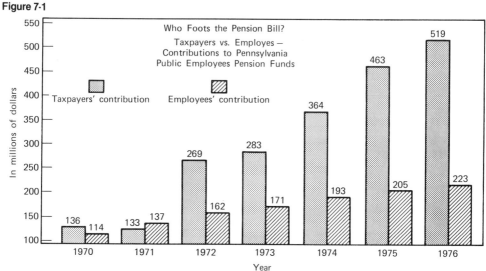

SOURCE: *The Evening News,* Harrisburg, Pa. October 12, 1976 Associated Press dispatch.

POLICY BOX NO. 13 Pensions:
A Temptation Legislators Cannot Resist

Pension systems across the country are in trouble. Many retirement systems cannot afford to pay the benefits they are obligated to pay. The reasons are that retirement benefits are too easy to improve and they are different from most other spending programs. On most spending decisions state legislators must either vote to raise taxes or reduce spending for other programs. But not so with retirement benefits.

When legislators are pressured to improve retirement benefits the temptation is almost irresistible. Voting in favor of pension improvements permits a legislator to please the pressure group without making taxpayers unhappy because taxes do not have to be raised to pay the cost—at least not immediately because the money will not usually have to be paid out for several years, and the bill for the improvements will likely not come due until long after the legislator has left office.

Economists and others say that the proper way to pay for pensions is to pay for them as the employee is working. How much ought to be paid is determined by actuarial studies that project costs on the average working life of employees, what their salaries will be prior to retirement, and how many years employees on the average will live after they retire. In this way pension administrators can determine how much to put aside for investment each pay period.

Public employee groups of all kinds—judges, police, teachers, state workers, and others—pressure the legislators for improved benefits, but when it comes time to pass the revenue measures to pay the costs, many of the interest group lobbyists cannot be found. The legislators face the tax measure for a while and then sidestep it until another year.

The situation in the state of Pennsylvania during the past few years is not unique. Benefits in Pennsylvania for public school and state employees have been rising so rapidly that some estimators predict pension costs will be $1 billion in a few years. The state's personal income tax now brings in about that much each year. (See the chart for a view of how the costs are rising.) In 1974 the legislature presumably passed a pension reform law, but the costs continue to soar by about $226 million a year, and still the unfunded liability for future payments is rising. A cost of living adjustment for people already retired, for example, will cost $500 million over the next twenty years.

Can the problem be controlled? The answer is—Not without some drastic measures. In 1963 Michigan put into its constitution a requirement that all retirement funds, both state and local ones, must be fully paid for as obligations build up. The problem is that pension costs are based on estimates about the future and there is a strong temptation to choose funding decisions on the low side of the estimate, rather than on the middle or high points.

New York City has a pension commission that worked well at first. The legislature followed its advice closely for a few years, but when the commission recommended reforms, the legislature passed watered-down versions of them.

The U.S. Congress passed a law providing stringent regulations on retirement plans provided by corporations a few years ago—they exempted public employee pension plans.

Some observers of the pension crisis say that the real problem is the general public's failure to pay attention to what the legislatures are doing with their money. The problem will not be resolved until the people start paying attention to what is going on.

What do you think? Can the public really protect itself from the "pension rip-off"? Should pension plan improvements be automatically subject to a referendum? Would a law requiring pension costs to be shared equally by employees and the government help? Should a state set up a pension board consisting only of public members with the power to reject all plan improvements and the power to set the rate for funding the costs?

SOURCE: This policy box is based on a series of articles by Tim Pettit in *The Evening News* (Harrisburg, Pennsylvania), October 12, 13, 14, 1976.

branches of government met months in advance of the completion of two state office buildings to decide who would move. A reporter covering the meeting wrote ". . . the system of constitutional checks and balances worked beautifully—the battle was a draw."[4]

Provision of Professional Staff

It is, perhaps, not astonishing that legislators sometimes freely admit having voted for a bill not knowing what was in it. Often state legislators do not even have clerical assistance to paste onto their copies of bills, amendments adopted the previous day. But by 1976, most states at a minimum were providing clerical or secretarial staff to most, if not all, legislative committees, some on a year-round basis.

That legislatures should continue to deprive themselves of adequate supporting staff is a striking commentary on the legislators' view of themselves and their political circumstances—especially when we consider that they have but to vote the necessary funds. Yet we find that dedicated legislators in Maryland and Texas and, no doubt, other states as well, personally pay for staff assistance, and that in Tennessee some local urban governments appropriate funds to provide "their" delegation with staff help.[5]

[4] The *Des Moines Register*, September 30, 1976.

[5] Council of State Governments, *The Book of the States*, 1976–77, p. 40.

New York State legislator, Elizabeth Connely speaks up for her bill in a committee meeting.

WHO BECOMES A STATE LEGISLATOR?

Are short sessions, primitive working conditions, low salary and minimal staff merely a matter of making life less comfortable for the 7500 people who serve in the state legislatures, or is more at stake? We think these factors influence what kinds of citizens become legislators, how long they remain on the job, and affect significantly the ability of the legislatures to carry out their task of being the effective political critics of federal, state, and community government programs and agencies.

Who Gets Elected?

If asked to describe our ideal for the composition of a state legislature, most of us, remembering our democratic training, would say that a state legislature should have a heavy mix of "common people." However valid this democratic view, state legislatures are anything but microcosms of the general population. "The people who become state legislators, as a group, are better educated than the general public, they come from family backgrounds of higher social standing, and they are likely to have lived in their respective legislative districts longer."[6] Moreover legislators, until recently, were overwhelmingly white and

[6]John C. Wahlke, Heinz Eulau, William Buchanan and LeRoy C. Ferguson, *The Legislative System: Explorations in Legislative Behavior*, New York: John Wiley & Sons, 1962. This study of four state legislatures provides an excellent analysis of legislatures and their behavior.

male—the number of women is just beginning to increase. But on certain characteristics legislators do reflect their constituencies—especially on such "birthright" characteristics as race, ethnic group, and religion.

The Occupations of Legislators.

Legislators are unrepresentative in that they have private occupations of higher status than the general population. Although no comprehensive study of the occupational backgrounds of state legislators has been made, we can piece together available information and indicate a general pattern.

From Charles S. Hyneman's study of occupations of legislators between 1925 and 1935 in twenty-five houses (thirteen lower and twelve upper) we get a quick overview. Some 28 percent were lawyers, 21.5 percent were farmers, and 30.9 percent were businessmen.[7] (See Table 7-1.)

In our own analysis of legislators' occupations in eight selected states of today (Table 7-1), we found that the proportion of farmer legislators has fallen, in part, we expect, because farmers today constitute only 4.2 percent of the population.[8] The proportion of lawyers in our modern sample was also lower than that reported by Hyneman, though the number of lawyers is still many times more than their proportion in the general population. The number of legislators with careers in business was higher in the recent sample—37.0 percent—more than half of whom were retail merchants and insurance or real estate agents.[9]

Lawyer-Legislators. Almost half of the signers of the Declaration of Independence were lawyers, and ever since the legal profession has played an important role in American politics (see Table 7-1). But we find significant variations among the states. In Illinois and Pennsylvania we found that almost a third were lawyers. In New York, not

---

[7]Charles S. Hyneman, "Who Makes Our Laws?" in John C. Wahlke and Heinz Eulau, eds., *Legislative Behavior,* Free Press of Glencoe, Illinois, 254–265.

[8]U.S. Bureau of the Census, *Farm Population of the United States: 1975,* Series Census-ERS, No. 47: September, 1976 p. 27, States with high proportions of farmer-legislators are Idaho, Iowa, Montana, South Dakota and North Dakota.

[9]While we find some differences and similarities between our sample and Hyneman's, we should note that recruitment patterns vary among the states. Thus, the results may, in part, reflect the choice of states in the samples. Our choice was limited by the ready availability of information on legislative occupations.

TABLE 7-1 Occupations of Legislators in Selected State Legislatures

	Thirteen Lower Chambers and Twelve Senates During 1925-1935		Eight Legislatures of the 1970s	
	Number	Percent	Number	Percent
Farmers	2,722	21.5	103	7.1
Lawyers	3,555	28.0	343	23.7
Teachers (K–12 Administrators)	—	—	93	6.5
Other Professional	639	5.0	97	6.7
Union Representatives	—	—	18	1.2
Journalism—News Media	369	2.9	21	1.5
Blue Collar & Crafts	205	1.6	48	3.3
Government Employees	—	—	64	4.4
Other White Collar	—	—	38	2.6
Contractors	273	2.2	32	2.2
Manufacturing/Industrial/Management	445	3.5	72	5.0
Insurance/Real Estate	869	6.8	153	10.6
General Sales	525	4.1	101	7.0
Engineers	184	1.5	20	1.4
Banking/Finance	352	2.8	26	1.8
Merchants	1,263	10.0	130	9.0
Not Otherwise Classified	704	5.5	34	2.4[a]
Not Known	584	4.6	52	3.6
Total	12,689	100.0	1,445	100.0

SOURCE: Charles S. Hyneman, Op. cit., p. 255 for the 1925-1935 data. Some of Hyneman's classification titles have been modified. Data for the 8 legislatures were taken from the state manuals for the following states; Illinois (1973-1974), Rhode Island (1975-1976), Oregon (1975-1976), Texas (1970-1971), Michigan (1975-1976), Pennsylvania (1972-1973), Indiana (1975-1976), and Vermont (1973-1974).

[a]This category for the 1970s includes 1.5 percent homemakers, 0.4 percent students, and 0.5 percent retired. Of the Vermont legislators, 27.5 percent indicated they had retired but their career occupations were classified elsewhere when known.

part of our sample, nearly half were lawyers.[10] The proportion of lawyer-legislators in Vermont was the lowest of the eight states at 3.7 percent while the percentages in Michigan and Oregon were around 15 percent.[11]

How can we explain the large numbers of lawyers in most state legislatures? First we note that the nature of the legislative schedules and

[10]We did not include New York in our sample because many of the nonlawyers simply indicated their occupations in their legislative manual biographies as "legislator." This practice, which is becoming more common, reflects the preference of legislators to present themselves as full-time legislators. But it makes analysis of legislators' previous occupations more difficult. South Carolina, Texas and Virginia are also states with a high proportion of lawyer-legislators.

[11]Frank M. Bryan argues that while the correlation between ruralism and farmer-legislator is strong, the same cannot be said for urbanism and lawyer-legislators. His analysis reveals some connection between the two, but the correlations are not so strong as to sug-

the risks that are part of running for office do not fit in with some occupations. But lawyers can accommodate such conditions rather well.

Second, as Malcolm Jewell and Samuel Patterson note, whether in private practice or in legislative service, the lawyers' work does not differ all that much—representing clients is very much like representing a political constituency.[12] "Moreover, service in the state legislature may well enhance the lawyer's career—especially when we consider that the legal profession has a monopoly on certain public offices such as judgeships, prosecutor, or attorney general."[13]

Is the high proportion of lawyer-legislators undesirable? A difficulty, we suggest, is the potential for conflicts of interest. One apparent conflict is the tendency for lawyer-legislator dominance of the judiciary committees that oversee legal and judicial affairs. More important, lawyers also often represent a variety of private clients and a lawyer-legislator or a law partner may, in fact, be "on retainer" by some of the state's important interest groups including those the state regulates, such as utility companies or labor unions.

Shifts in Legislative Composition

The data comparing the 1920s and 1974 suggest a rather high degree of stability in the makeup of state legislatures. Yet legislative makeup also appears to respond to shifts in a state's general population. We already noted the lower proportion today of farmer-legislators. We also see some possible decline in merchant-legislators. Shifts in retailing from individual proprietorships to corporate-owned or franchised outlets managed by employees may explain this change. Teacher-legislators seem to be increasing, perhaps reflecting the growing involvement of teacher unions in politics.

Higher salaries for legislators and longer sessions may also account for some of the shifts in legislative composition. Higher salaries may now make it possible for members of previously unrepresented occupational groups to become legislators. On the other hand, longer legislative sessions may mean that merchants, farmers, and even some lawyers are unable to meet the time demands.

---

gest that urbanism and lawyer–legislators go hand in hand. See his *Yankee Politics in Rural Vermont*, University Press of New England, Hanover, N.H. 1974. See especially 36–42.

[12]Malcolm E. Jewell and Samuel C. Patterson, *The Legislative Process in the United States*, 2nd ed., Random House, N.Y., 1973, p. 76.

[13]Paul L. Hain and James E. Piereson, "Lawyers and Politics Revisited," *American Journal of Political Science* 19, February 1975, 41–45.

How Do People Become Legislators?

This question is easy to answer if we consider only formal qualifications and election rules for legislative candidates. Virtually every adult who is an American citizen, who meets the age and residency requirements of the state can become a candidate for the state legislature.

But the number who actually seek legislative office is very small. What is it that separates those who do from those who do not?

Interest in Politics.   In a study of four states, John Wahlke and his colleagues asked legislators to recall their first interest in politics.[14] They found that some would-be legislators developed political career goals very early in their lives. Some, like people in other careers, planned their moves step by step. Many of these, we think, became active in political parties or found a job, such as legislative assistant, that offered exposure to politics.

Others moved into the legislature almost by accident. They became involved in politics over a neighborhood or school problem, or active in a campus or community action or in local government. Some cut their political teeth in union or business leadership positions. Out of such circumstances they came to see the possibilities for a political career. Soon they found themselves reaching for the next rung on the ladder, a seat on the county commission, or one in the state legislature.

Political scientists refer to this general process as "recruitment"— the selection of people to carry the party banner in a political race.

Recruitment.   Legislative recruiting varies with the political makeup of the state and district. Where two political parties are well organized, local party leaders are likely to recruit legislative candidates. But as Samuel Patterson and G.R. Boynton found in Iowa, party leaders are often assisted by interest group leaders and by community "influentials" who may not be a part of the formal party structure.[15] Party leaders want candidates who appeal to more than the "party faithful," but usually they select party actives. But they may decide chances of winning are better if they turn to a nonparty person, possibly a local hero or respected community leader.[16]

[14]John C. Wahlke, et. al., *The Legislative System*, John Wiley & Sons, N.Y., 1962, p. 70. This section draws upon the research conducted by Wahlke and his colleagues of legislators in California, New Jersey, Ohio, and Tennessee.

[15]Samuel C. Patterson and G. R. Boynton, "Legislative Recruitment in a Civic Culture," *Social Science Quarterly*, 50, 1969, 243–263.

[16]For further reading on recruitment in Oregon, see Lester G. Seligman, et. al., *Patterns of Recruitment: A State Chooses Its Lawmakers*, Rand McNally, Chicago, 1974.

In areas where one party dominates, recruitment patterns differ widely between the majority and minority parties. The majority party nomination "becomes a pawn in the adjustment of claims by party groupings and rewards for the party faithful."[17] Being a party person in this circumstance is a prerequisite. Milton Rakove, describing this kind of "slating" process in Chicago's Democratic party under Mayor Daley, noted two major considerations:

> The primary consideration is, 'Can the candidate win?' The second consideration is, 'If he can win, can he do us any good? If a candidate cannot win, who needs him? If he can win and can't do the party any good, who needs him? If he can win and can do the party harm, who wants him? In other words, the interests of the party and the ability of a candidate for public office to serve the interest of the party come first in building the ticket.'[18]

In safe districts where party structure is not highly organized, as in some rural districts, the party may not be very active in candidate recruitment. But if someone embarrassing to the party organization runs, or if the party wants to purge an incumbent, it may actively recruit a person.

Recruiting by the minority party in "safe" districts is entirely different. The job, we find, is more a problem of finding someone, at times almost anyone, who will permit his or her name to go forward to fill out the ticket—sometimes the party fails to recruit anyone and loses by default. The real contest for the seat, if there is to be any at all, takes place in the primary election of the dominant party.

But political parties are not the only groups that recruit legislative candidates. In districts with weak or fragmented political parties, interest groups such as farmers' organizations, business interests, education groups, labor organizations, and even the officials in community governments may recruit candidates.

We find, too, that self-recruitment or self-selection flourishes under almost all conditions, at least to the extent that people exhibit their desire to enter a race. Even in machine-dominated Chicago, candidates apply for the party endorsement.

Why Legislators Quit—Turnover Rates

High turnover also contributes to amateurism of state legislatures. Although turnover rates in recent years are lower than those of sixty

[17]Malcolm E. Jewell and Samuel C. Patterson, *The Legislative Process in the United States*, New York, Random House, 1973, p. 85.

[18]Milton Rakove, *Don't Make No Waves—Don't Back No Losers*, Indiana University Press, Bloomington, 1975, p. 96.

years ago, experienced legislators are still in short supply in many states.[19]

The 1974 elections produced 1871 new legislators in lower houses—a turnover rate of 34.9 percent. In six states a majority were "first termers," including Alabama with a turnover of 73 percent. Turnover in the state senates was lower—29.4 percent in 1974.

The general working conditions we discussed in part explain the turnover rates. Alan Rosenthal, for example, concludes, "No single factor is believed to matter as much as compensation."[20] We agree.

Reapportionment, Ambition, and Frustration. Reapportionment has also added to legislative turnover. We find that turnover was higher than usual in 1967, the point at which newly reapportioned districts, following the *Baker* v. *Carr* decision, first came into being, and in 1972 and 1974 when further redistricting was necessary following the 1970 census.

Defeat at the polls, seemingly, would further explain the turnover. But, as Malcolm Jewell and Samuel Patterson note, when incumbent legislators seek reelection they are far more likely to win than lose, and election defeats account for a rather small percentage of the retirements.[21]

Legislators are more likely to lose when they try for a new office. We estimate from personal observation that perhaps 15 to 20 percent of legislators at any one time aspire to higher office, and perhaps one-quarter of these actually run. Lower house members can look not only to senate seats, but they, along with senators, can reach for seats in Congress, judicial positions, county offices, or for mayoral positions, and statewide elective posts.[22]

Turnover rates in the lower houses are higher than in the senates because some house members run for the upper house. Because lower house terms are two-year terms in all but four states, representatives must give up their house seats to run for different positions. Senators, by contrast, with four-year terms (in all but twelve states)[23] can seek

[19]Duane Lockard, "The State Legislators," in *State Legislatures in American Politics*, The American Assembly, 1966, p. 103.

[20]Alan Rosenthal, "Turnover in State Legislatures," *American Journal of Political Science* 18, August 1974, 609–616.

[21]Jewell and Patterson, Op. cit., p. 92.

[22]Jewell and Patterson, Op. cit., p. 93.

[23]Illinois employs a combination of two-year and four-year terms. During each ten-year period, a district senate seat has one two-year term and two four-year terms. This system,

Not all legislative time is spent in debate, even in Iowa.

congressional seats, judgeships, and other positions when they, them-selves, are not up for reelection, without risk of losing their senate seats.

Finally, we believe that a part of the turnover results from the frus-trations of the position. Some legislators enter the office with little prior interest or experience in politics; some enter office with overly optimistic expectations about what they will be able to accomplish, and are disappointed. Others undoubtedly leave because they have little patience with the legislative process and may not care much for their colleagues.

HOW LEGISLATURES OPERATE: THE POLITICS OF LAW MAKING

Frank Smallwood, in describing his first legislative involvement as an "academic neophyte state legislator," said, "Little did I realize how much I had to learn as I groped to discover some underlying patterns that would provide a coherent understanding of the new world that lay before me."[24] Ultimately he found several reference points to guide him through the political maze including (1) formal rules of procedure, (2)

therefore, permits two-thirds of the senators to stand for reelection every two years. It also enables reapportioned senate districts to take effect with the first election following reapportionment.

[24]Frank Smallwood, Op. cit., p. 80.

legislative leadership and committees, and (3) informal rules. We will use these as we discuss the politics of law making, and we add an additional one—the legislative staff. As we go along you will recognize that these elements are interwoven. We will also see the tension between administrative and political efficiency—the price for the expression of minority viewpoints is delay.

Formal Rules of Procedure

The route that a legislative proposal follows from initiation to final adoption is a complex one. (See Figure 7-2) The route is beset with pitfalls that may lead to the demise of a bill. To help you gain an overview of the process we have provided a diagram of the steps most state legislatures follow. We note, however, that the legislative process is both a formal set of steps through which a bill most pass and a series of political hurdles. It is the politics, of course, that ultimately determine whether a bill becomes law or does not. But the politics take place within a formal set of rules that limit a free-wheeling political atmosphere and give strength to minority forces and those resisting change. The *status quo* is advantaged but is not always able to win out.

Political Strategies And Legislative Rules. As we look down on the legislature from our seats in the balcony, the floor action often does not appear very orderly or deliberative. Nevertheless, detailed rules govern these actions. These rules establish a behavior pattern and affect the policies produced. Especially during periods when the legislature is in a hurry-up mood, a disgruntled minority or even one legislator can run the "train off the track" through skillful use of the rules. They may delay action on a bill if the presiding officer is not equally skilled. Getting a delay, of course, is not the same as defeating the bill, but it may provide added time for bargaining or rounding up more votes.

As in parlor games and sports, the rules constrain and restrict and also become part of the strategy of the game itself. In legislative politics we find that rules keep the legislative process intact, but also encourage compromise and political bargaining because the rules give power to minorities. In the words of William Keefe and Morris Ogul, "Legislative rules are significant because the methods used to reach decisions often shape the decisions themselves; procedure and policy, in other words, are often interrelated. Never wholly neutral, rules benefit some groups and disadvantage others. They are, commonly, one of the many faces of minority power."[25]

[25]William Keefe and Morris Ogul, *The American Legislative Process*, 2nd ed. Prentice Hall, Englewood Cliffs, N.J. 1968, p. 45.

Figure 7-2
The Formal Law-Making Process

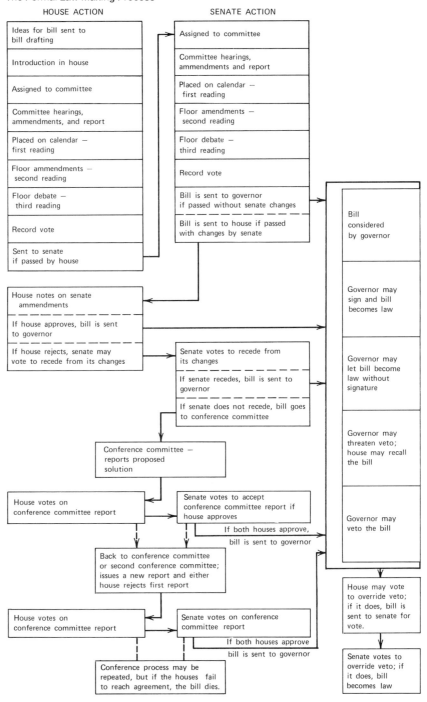

HOUSE ACTION

Ideas for bill sent to bill drafting
Introduction in house
Assigned to committee
Committee hearings, ammendments, and report
Placed on calendar — first reading
Floor ammendments — second reading
Floor debate — third reading
Record vote
Sent to senate if passed by house

House notes on senate ammendments
If house approves, bill is sent to governor
If house rejects, senate may vote to recede from its changes

SENATE ACTION

Assigned to committee
Committee hearings, ammendments and report
Placed on calendar — first reading
Floor amendments — second reading
Floor debate — third reading
Record vote
Bill is sent to governor if passed without senate changes
Bill is sent to house if passed with changes by senate

Senate votes to recede from its changes
If senate recedes, bill is sent to governor
If senate does not recede, bill goes to conference committee

Conference committee — reports proposed solution

House votes on conference committee report

Senate votes to accept conference committee report if house approves

If both houses approve, bill is sent to governor

Back to conference committee or second conference committee; issues a new report and either house rejects first report

House votes on conference committee report

Senate votes on conference committee report

If both houses approve bill is sent to governor

Conference process may be repeated, but if the houses fail to reach agreement, the bill dies.

Bill considered by governor
Governor may sign and bill becomes law
Governor may let bill become law without signature
Governor may threaten veto; house may recall the bill
Governor may veto the bill

House may vote to override veto; if it does, bill is sent to senate for vote.
Senate votes to override veto; if it does, bill becomes law

Types of legislative rules. Each legislative body at the beginning of each session adopts rules of its own, rules designed to make the process of law making more orderly and systematic.

We also find three kinds of rules spelled out in state constitutions— rules that (1) set minimum conditions, quorum, and voting requirements, under which legislators can legislate; (2) govern the speed with which a legislative body may act; and (3) regulate the form and scope of the legislation.

Legislative rules are important because of their political effects. We will find that the rules force the majority to consider the views of the minority, and often to compromise—if the majority hopes to get any action at all. It is this process that strengthens local viewpoints and interests in policymaking for the federal system.

Minimum Conditions: Quorum and Vote Requirements. The political effect of constitutional clauses, such as quorum rules, the requirement of extraordinary majorities, or a roll-call vote if a member demands it is to give an advantage to the minority bloc on any issue. A rather small group of the total body can delay or even keep the legislature from taking official action. The minority can use these rules to bargain for concessions from the majority, or even to kill the bill.

The usual quorum requirement is a majority of the elected membership, but Tennessee, for example, requires two-thirds on the hope that the legislature will discipline its wayward members. Its effect, though, is to make it easier for a small group to block action.

Constitutions also may specify the minimum number of votes needed to pass a bill—typically a majority of the membership or number elected. This means in a body of one hundred, fifty-one must vote in favor, even if only fifty-two are on the floor at the time. Again a few votes among those present may become crucial for passage.

Recording of roll-call voting is widely viewed as being essential to the public's right to know how individual legislators voted. In virtually all states, legislators no longer have the luxury of voting on the final passage of a bill by voice vote or by a show of hands. In states that do not require a record vote, a small number of the members (as few as one in Vermont and New York), can insist on a recorded vote.[26] Under

[26]Before the days of electronic voting devices the demand for a roll-call vote, especially during the hurry-up days at the end of the session, would seldom win the demander any friends. Not only did legislators prefer the anonymity of a voice vote, but they begrudged the time used by the clerk to intone one hundred or more names. A threat to call a roll call could be used by the minority to gain concessions. Virtually all lower houses now use electronic vote recording devices. But twenty-nine of the senates, perhaps because of their smaller size, still use voice roll calls.

such rules we find that the demand for roll-call vote becomes part of the legislative strategy. The first bill Frank Smallwood tried to shepherd through the Vermont senate would have changed the hours during which alcoholic beverages could be sold on Sunday. Opponents insisted on a roll call and Smallwood lost support from some senators who favored the bill, but who did not wish to do "so on the record."

Speed of Passage Rules. The apparent purpose of constitutional clauses that limit the speed with which a bill can be passed is to encourage careful consideration and to prevent hasty adoption of legislative measures. In practice, however, such rules give the minority opportunity to mount its opposition.

The three-reading rule. One such rule requires that bills be read aloud at least three times on separate days (two times in the Dakotas and a handful of other states). As a practical matter, the bills are seldom read aloud—in many states time would not allow for even one full reading—the clerk reads only the title of the bill. In virtually every instance as the clerk begins to read, someone will move that the "bill be considered read" and the presiding officer mechanically states, "Without objection, it shall be so ordered" and, as he or she utters the last syllable, the gavel falls.

Multiple readings, if only by title, indicate the status of bills and prevent quick passage before opposition can form. The first reading announces that the bill has been introduced and that the committee has reported the bill to the floor. A bill on second reading is ready for its first floor action—possible floor amendments. The third reading precedes the final debate and vote on final adoption or rejection.

Layover rule. Another slow-down rule requires that a bill passed in one house must lay over in the second house for a specified number of days—typically five. The rule gives legislators and members of the public time to politick—to marshall forces to support or oppose a bill. The legislatures generally can waive this rule only by extraordinary majorities—another opportunity for the minority to wrest concessions from the majority.

Effective date rule. A third delaying rule sets the effective date of a new law. Normally laws go into effect thirty to ninety days after the legislature has adjourned. But with extraordinary majorities, a law can have "immediate effect." In states where legislative sessions last all year immediate effect may be almost as important as passing the bill. For example, a tax bill passed in June, if given immediate effect, can produce a full year of collections. But the same bill without immediate effect would probably not take effect until April 1 of the next year, and would thus produce only three months' revenues. On legislation where immediate effect is critical, the minority can trade compromises on the measure itself for votes on immediate effect.

Scope and Form Rules.   We find several rules intended to make the legislative process understandable to legislators and legislature watchers. Scope and form rules deal with subject matter of bills and amendments. Four of these rules are: (1) a bill may deal with only one subject that must be stated in the title of the bill; (2) an amendment to a bill may not change the original purpose of a bill; (3) a bill that amends an existing law must contain the sections of the law to be amended with the existing words lined out and the new ones inserted in bold face type; and (4) a law may not be amended by reference in a second law.

These rules are intended to prevent legislative sleight-of-hand. They make it more difficult for legislators to pull the wool over the eyes of their colleagues and they provide legislators, as well as the press, interest groups, and the public, an opportunity to know what is going on.

But these rules can also provide some procedural problems. A change to increase one form of tax and decrease another may be more difficult to enact.

Legislative Leadership and Committees

In spite of the rhetoric that the new legislator may have uttered in the campaign, new legislators follow rather than lead. Moreover we find that the newcomers are somewhat receptive to this role, at least for a time. We gain, from our readings and conversations with new legislators, consistent impressions that during their early months in the legislature they are both intrigued and baffled by the goings on. They seem to have a "now that I'm here, what do I do, how do I start?" kind of feeling.

Ultimately, of course, the newcomers must move out on their own. They have to figure out "who makes things happen and how? Who has the power? How do they use it?"

The Speaker of the House.   New legislators undoubtedly will seek to figure out the power of the formal leaders. In the lower house, the leader that certainly bears scrutiny is the speaker of the house, elected by the majority party legislators. The speaker usually enjoys the informal power gained from support of the house majority and, through rules and custom, wields considerable formal power as well. The speaker usually decides who gets which committee assignments. The speaker also decides which committee gets which bills, presides over the sessions with the power to recognize legislators or "not hear" points of order, administers the house budget, develops the policy on out-of-state travel, and often appoints and fires a large number of legislative employees. Challenges to the exercise of these powers are rare.

How a speaker wins the office may affect a speaker's real powers. If a popular and logical choice for the job, he or she will generally be able to make full use of the formal powers. But if gaining the job required a bitter political fight, he or she may have had to bargain away some powers. For example, in 1959 Democrats held a narrow majority in the Illinois legislature. The Chicago Democrats wanted Joseph D. LaCour of Chicago as speaker; the downstate Democrats' choice was Paul Powell of Vienna. The Republican governor then urged Republicans to give their support to Powell. Powell won, but he had to appoint some Republicans to chair committees.[27]

Gubernatorial "assistance". Whichever party controls the governorship may also be important to the speaker's power. When the same political party or faction controls both the governorship and the lower house, the speaker may be expected to play second fiddle to the governor—a source of potential friction.

For example, Governor Edmund "Pat" Brown of California cleared the path for Jesse Unruh to become speaker by appointing the incumbent speaker to the Appeals Court. But Brown later thought Unruh was ungrateful and stated openly, "If I could have done it all over again, I would never have made him speaker. I would have fought him all the way along the line, because that is what he appreciates more than affection." Unruh, however, felt (perhaps correctly) that he could have won the speakership on his own.[28]

Speakers use their powers. The spotlight is really on the speaker when the governor is of the opposing party. The speaker then becomes a chief spokesman for the opposition party, gaining power and statewide attention in the news media, enough so that the speaker may even

[27]For an excellent account of this fight for the speakership in Illinois, see Thomas B. Littlewood, "Bipartisan Coalition in Illinois," in William K. Hall, ed., *Illinois Government and Politics*, Kendall Hunt Publishing Company, Dubuque, Iowa, 1975; 41–68.

[28]Lou Cannon, *Ronnie and Jesse, A Political Odyssey*, Doubleday and Company, Garden City, New York, 1969, p. 112.

be mentioned as a possible candidate for governor. The ultimate test of such leadership, of course, is the speaker's ability to deliver his or her party's votes.

Speakers can use their formal powers for their own political purpose in many ways. The bargains a speaker can make are almost endless—by the careful use of discretionary powers he or she can strongly influence individual legislative careers. Appointments to important standing and special committees, assistance in advancing or "sandbagging" a newcomer's first bill, giving or denying the opportunity for press coverage, and helping with problems or adding to them—all are devices available to the speaker to get votes when needed to support his or her program. Jesse Unruh maintained a trust fund of money received from "personal friends." He used this money to assist legislators who were loyal to him in their campaigns for reelection.[29]

Senate Leaders. The speakership has no precise counterpart in state senates. We find that senates are small and are more likely to be managed by standing-committee chairpersons, rather than through the leadership of a single individual. Second, many state constitutions make the lieutenant governor the senate president—a person whom senators may consider an outsider because he or she was not chosen by the members. A few state constitutions permit the lieutenant governor, as senate president, to refer bills to committees and even to designate committee assignments. But most give lieutenant governors few formal powers. Customarily, they are not even allowed to debate bills on the floor, and in most states are not even allowed to vote except to break a tie. The powers of lieutenant governors are also limited by custom. Any misdeeds or controversial rulings are quickly challenged.

President pro tempore. The chief position filled by the senators themselves is the president pro tempore, but this is more often a position of honor than power. The usual duty is to preside in the absence of the lieutenant governor. Seven states, though, permit the president pro tempore to parcel out committee assignments. Only in two of these states however do they also refer bills to committees.

The senate majority leader. Each party caucus elects majority and minority leaders. The majority leader, as much as any other senate officer, exercises powers approaching those of the house speaker. But because of customary reliance on committees in many senates, the majority leader is also likely to share a great deal of the power with

[29]Lou Cannon, Ibid, p. 114.

others. One Michigan legislator explained the difference between the speaker and senate majority leader—"The thirty-eight-member senate has thirty-eight prima donnas," he said, "while the one hundred ten member house has one hundred nine sheep."[30]

Legislative leadership in the senate thus depends on the majority leader's skills as an experienced strategist. Leaders will also find a bit of courage helpful. We recall observing an electrifying session when Republican Governor George Romney of Michigan sought to push an income tax measure through a very reluctant Republican-controlled senate. The job fell to Republican Frank Beadle, senate majority leader. At the Monday evening session in which he decided it was time that the bill should be on "the agenda," he moved that when the evening session adjourned (by rule it had to end at midnight), the senate would reconvene at 12:01 a.m. Although his assistant majority leader in protest led a bloc of conservative senators—"real Republicans," he called them—off the floor to caucus and elect a new majority leader, Beadle managed to hold together a coalition of moderate Republicans and Democrats during the night. By the time we left for home with the rising sun shining in the rearview mirror, the shaky state senate coalition had hammered out and passed a state income tax measure.

Committees and Their Chairpersons. Legislatures, because of the large number of subject areas they deal with, must provide a system for dividing the workload and developing specialization. Standing committees become essential.

The committee system also presents a dilemma. Specialization means that small groups of legislators become relatively expert in narrow interest areas, and somewhat uninformed in other areas. The expertise and specialization creates power centers—power centers that may not be very representative of the entire body or of the interests of the state.

With this dilemma as a backdrop we consider the leadership role of committees and their chairpersons in the legislative process.

The problem of specialization. Committees use their specialized knowledge in two basic ways: (1) to conduct the oversight function of the corresponding administrative agency—the committee on natural resources over the department of natural resources, for example, and (2) to screen and prepare for passage bills that they or other legislators have introduced. This may involve "refereeing" affected special interest groups, conducting special studies, and holding public hearings.

[30]The Detroit Free Press, September 17, 1976.

The number of standing committees. How much specialization—that is, how many committees—should a legislative body have? Legislators, it is thought, generally prefer to have many committees—it affords more of them the opportunity to be chairperson or vice chairperson. But the larger the number of committees, the smaller, and perhaps less representative, is the group that handles the interest area and the more narrow their focus. Yet, with a few large committees, the number of small subcommittees markedly increases. Thus, the result is the same—a few legislators handle the interest area.

We find that legislatures have gradually been reducing the number of standing committees. During 1972, for example, the Arkansas legislature dropped from fifty-one committees to twenty. Nationwide, in 1977 the average number of committees per house of representatives was 17.8 and the average per senate, 14.2, considerably fewer than ten years earlier. Yet we still find some states with exceptionally high numbers of committees—North Carolina had 77 committees in 1977.

The problem of committee power. The development of power centers is an unavoidable by-product of committee specialization. Committees and their chairpersons become the managers of this power, sometimes killing bills they do not like, holding up bills wanted by others in exchange for favors elsewhere, or virtually dictating to executive departments certain policies and practices under threats of budget cutbacks or other measures.

For the most part, though, committees and their chairpersons are less important than they once were, or as they are in the U.S. Congress.[31] To limit committee power some legislatures rotate committee assignments from session to session so that individual legislators do not develop the expertise and personal relationships on which much of the power rests. Other legislatures require all committees to report every bill submitted to them, rather than to allow committees to kill bills by inaction. Such rules limit power somewhat, but committees can still report bills with a "do not pass" recommendation, or amend bills so that they are unacceptable to the full body. Legislative bodies also have rules that permit them to "discharge" (remove) a bill from committee. But successful votes on this kind of motion are rare. A "yes" vote may create bitterness and open the way for later retaliation unless the speaker—another major power center, as we noted—endorses the action.

The nature of most state legislatures also serves to curb committee power. The high rates of turnover, for example, means that legislators often do not become sufficiently knowledgeable to exercise great power in the committee's interest area. In addition, the part-time schedule means that legislators are often not around to wield their power, especially in respect to administrative agencies; and finally, because state legislatures tend not to follow the rule of seniority to the extent that Congress traditionally has. Gilbert Steiner and Samuel Gove, on the basis of their study of the Illinois legislature, argue that the power of committee chairpersons in the state houses has often been overstated. Committees, they say, do not "kill bills"; rather, sponsors "let them die." Steiner and Gove suggest that committees often get the credit for killing bills when the bills actually die because the sponsors of bills decide not to push for action on them.[32]

The need for power.   Although committee chairpersons at times may be rightly criticized for excessive power, there is a danger in having people with too little power as well. Without committee power, we might find others, perhaps even smaller numbers of legislators, wielding great amounts of power. We might find legislators unable to reach the compromises necessary to get laws passed.

Committee chairpersons must exercise political power because skills and influence are essential in committee rooms, as well as in house or senate chambers. They become major strategists for major committee bills. They influence scheduling to give priority to some committee bills while others languish.

Conference committees.   What happens in conference committees is especially important politically. After a bill has been passed in the second house, the house of origin may not accept amendments made by the second. If the second house refuses to withdraw its amendments, members from each house are chosen by the speaker and senate majority leader to work out the differences. Usually these are standing committee members. The conference committee version is then submitted to each house. If unacceptable to one of the houses, the committee may reconvene or a new conference committee may be set up.

Although all bills are potentially subject to conference committee deliberations, this type of committee is used most frequently for appropriations bills. Budget bills usually are passed during the end-of-session logjam, a time when legislators have little stomach for extended fights. The conference committee often cuts the final deals on "who gets how much."

[31]William Keefe and Morris Ogul, Op cit., p. 71.

[32]Gilbert Y. Steiner and Samuel R. Gove, "The Influence of Standing Committees in the Illinois Legislature," in Irwin W. Gertzog, ed., *Readings in State and Local Government*, Prentice Hall, Englewood Cliffs, N.J., 1970, 164–183.

Informal Rules

The third point of reference for Frank Smallwood in the Vermont legislature was the informal rules—social norms that guide the behavior of the members. Legislators, like other groups of people who are thrown into a social situation in which they need to work together—develop standards of acceptable behavior. Those who fail to follow the group norms become outcasts. In the legislative setting, mavericks are tolerated and given their due, but little more.

John Wahlke and his colleagues in their study of four states identified a number of important "rules of the game."[33] We will discuss three of them.

Legislators insist on honesty and integrity from each other. Once a legislator gives his or her word, the promise must be kept. If they promise their vote on a bill, they are expected to deliver it—"make your word your bond."

Second, legislators are expected to respect each other's rights and obligations. In the words of one legislator, "Don't meddle in others' business—if a bill doesn't affect you, vote for it." Legislators are also expected to respect other legislators' reasons for voting as they did.

Third, avoid personal attacks. Opposition and criticism should be directed against the issue at hand, not against the person sponsoring it. At times, in spite of opening invocations such as "Dear Lord, help us to do what is right for the citizens of our state and *help us to do it today*," tempers get frayed. After midnight, as one especially grueling session was winding down, one legislator suggested to the chair that his antagonist should be named "the state animal." The antagonist replied that he would rather be the state animal than what his opponent was, "the state bird—a turkey."[34]

The political significance of the norms. The social norms help create a sense of teamwork and tolerance. They fit the general mood of political compromise, and demand such things as that members take their jobs seriously, defend and protect the body and its members from outside criticism, refrain from using every parliamentary maneuver, even when they may be technically permissible, maintain confidences, and avoid "stealing" other legislators' bills.

Obviously the individual legislator cannot abide by all the norms at all times. Some norms contradict others. Some digression from the norms is anticipated and expected, but it is the habitual behavior, not an occasional lapse, that leads to being made an outcast.

[33]John C. Wahlke, *et. al.*, Op. cit., p. 143.

[34]*Detroit Free Press*, July 10, 1977.

Legislative Staff Agencies

During the period when we were in college we thought very little about the legislature as a place where we might make a career. For those who attended college near a state capitol, some part-time work at the state legislature seemed a good way to pick up needed funds. The legislators met only briefly each year, and while they were away one could "hit the books." Legislative employees, then, were mainly clerks and secretaries—a few patronage appointees handled mail, the bill room, and other chores. Of course, there were the full-time secretary of the senate and the clerk of the house—they were political appointees as well. Such were the legislative employment opportunities during the 1940s and 1950s in Michigan, Minnesota, Missouri, and perhaps in some other states even today.

Increased Legislative Staff.   The size of permanent legislative staffs in many states has been climbing steadily and dramatically during the last decade. One writer estimated legislative employees to number 20,000 in 1975.[35] "Housekeeping" costs have skyrocketed—460 percent in ten years![36] But even so legislative spending on itself and staff is about one-fourth of one percent of state government general expenditures.[37]

It is not yet fashionable to speak of the "legislative bureaucracy," but we suspect it soon will be. Also, the appellation the "Fourth House" (the Third House consists of the lobbyists), now given to the congressional staff, we think will also soon be applied to state legislative staffs. The staff personnel are becoming an important new participant in the politics of law making.

Why Have Legislative Staffs Increased?   Some observers attribute the increase of staff to the reapportionment of legislatures in the mid-1960s that sent "younger, broader-based, and probably more competitive, reform-minded leadership to legislatures."[38] At the same time the volume and complexity of state law making has increased. A more fundamental explanation, we think, is that some legislators have concluded that the legislature has become "the stepchild of state government" without the resources to compete with executive and judicial

---

[35]Albert J. Abrams, "The Legislative Administrator," *Public Administration Review*, 35, September–October 1975, p. 497.

[36]*The Council of State Governments, 1976–77*, Op. cit., p. 38.

[37]Ibid., p. 38.

[38]Albert T. Abrams, Op. cit., p. 497.

agencies. The key to such independence, they argue, is information developed by people loyal to the legislature, rather than experts from the governor's office, the federal or local governments, or lobbyists. Moreover the idea of independence includes a desire of legislators to develop their own alternatives, initiatives, and innovations—to become policy initiators, rather than just reactors to the suggestion of others.[39]

Legislators also want to become independent in a partisan political sense. James Heaphey and Alan Balutis note that at least four state legislatures—New York, California, Illinois, and Wisconsin—enlarged their legislative staffs during the 1960s following changes in party control of the legislature and a growth of "sharp antagonism" between the governor and the legislature.[40]

Staff Functions. Legislative staffers perform some routine political chores—write letters, help with constituent services, and arrange meetings and schedules. Though routine these are nevertheless important because they may determine who gains access to the legislators. Other responsibilities are also political, but require more professional expertise. We will review four such professional staff roles.

Bill drafting. In the legislative rush those drafting a bill can make some foolish mistakes. A Kansas law once required trains approaching each other on the same track to stop on a siding and forbade either from proceeding until the other had passed. Legislative service bureaus or legislative council staff are supposed to prevent such errors. They not only review all bills written by legislators themselves before they are formally introduced, but assist, if requested, in putting legislators' ideas into bill form.

Bill analysis. A summary analysis of bills being introduced gives legislators a quick indication of how a bill may affect them and their constituents. It answers, What problem does the bill address? What will the bill do? Who (which interest group) sponsored the bill? Which groups will be affected by it? Who favors it and who does not? The political importance of such a summary is obvious. It is equally apparent why legislators want such summaries prepared by their own staff— people who are sensitive to the legislators' political problems and ambitions.

[39]James J. Heaphey and Alan P. Balutis, *Legislative Staffing, A Comparative Perspective,* Sage Publications, New York, 1975, p. 26.

[40]Ibid., p. 29.

Policy analysis and research. Policy analysis tends to be long term since its goal is to generate policy proposals on various subjects, such as energy, taxation, or environment. A legislator may then be able to take the initiative on important issues and suggest alternatives to the governor's proposals.

Fiscal analysis and review. Legislators place a high value on developing their own fiscal information. They want experts able to evaluate the governor's budgetary proposals and provide budget and tax committees with specialized advice. The staff focuses on spending proposals and checks out revenue projections of the governor or develops independent projections.

The Political Risks of the Legislative Staff. Legislative staffing in most states is in its infancy and in only a few states has reached adolescence. The legislative environment has both its rewards and risks for staff. A former staffer of the New York Assembly states, "Nowhere, except perhaps among those who directly serve a governor, can one find the sustained, high-level participation in public policymaking routinely available for staff people in many state legislatures."[41] As staff, you feel the exhilaration of a short "idea-to-action" time; your ideas appear in newspapers; you hear a legislator deliver a speech you wrote; you feel exposed to and involved in the world of "hard ball" politics.

But staff may find disappointments and risks as well. They may find that the proposal they spent days on has lost by a scant margin, has been changed radically to fit minority objections, or has never been voted on all because "the timing was bad." As a partisan staffer you may have trouble catching on with another if "your legislator" retires. You may even get caught in the political crossfire between two legislators, or the governor and the legislature, and wish you had chosen a safer niche.

The Politics of Law Making

Formal rules, leadership and standing committees, informal rules and social norms and professional staff—all provide the opportunity for the legislative politicking. The effect of most is to strengthen the hand

[41]Albert B. Roberts, "American State Legislatures: The Staff Environment," *Public Administration Review*, 35, September–October 1975, p. 501. See the issue of PAR for a more complete review of legislative staffing.

POLICY BOX NO. 14
Wetlands Regulation in Michigan

In 1972 Michigan adopted an Inland Lakes and Streams Act that was regarded by ecology interest groups as the most important environmental legislation the state had passed. It gave the Department of Natural Resources tighter controls over the use of streams by sports enthusiasts and industry. Its passage led almost immediately to introduction of a general land use bill that would regulate development through the whole state.

In 1974 two Democratic representatives began work on a bill to regulate uses of wetlands, the marshy areas used by birds and animals for breeding grounds and a place where many wild plants grow. The legislators had the help of an interest group called the Environmental Action Council that directed them to the Environmental Law Society, which, in turn, provided them with the rough draft of a bill. The legislators also got a copy of Minnesota's wetlands bill, adopted that year, and consulted with Wisconsin legislators over their proposed shorelands bill.

In March 1975 they introduced a "skeleton" wetlands bill that was assigned to the House Committee of Conservation, Environment, and Recreation, which one of the sponsors headed. The bill was then assigned to a staff assistant to fill out the details. He consulted with Department of Natural Resources personnel and others, including local government representatives. The bill, as presented by the staff member, gave the DNR power to define wetlands and make an inventory of them, but left the regulation of wetlands to counties and townships and, in a few cases, cities.

At this point the committee members met with representatives of farm groups. The bill was rewritten with the cooperation of both the Farm Bureau and the DNR. The DNR would no longer define wetlands—instead, six criteria suggested by experts would be used and, if any of the six were present, the area would be called a wetland.

It was now March 1976 and the whole committee met to "feel out the bill." It was discovered that as written, 80 percent of Michigan would be considered "wetland." Three new criteria were devised and it was stipulated that all must be met. In addition, wetlands already farmed would be exempted, and a special provision would permit certain forest operations on wetlands.

In April 1976 the statewide land use bill was killed in committee—a setback to environmental groups. In May, at the next conservation committee meeting, the committee staff member was instructed to narrow down the wetlands bill further— backers now hoped just to get a bill passed and argued that it could be strengthened later. The new bill exempted all wetlands not contiguous to a lake, river, or stream, added protection for oil drilling interests, permitted farmers to build docks, roads, and dikes on wetlands being farmed, but kept the state inventory provision and the requirement that wetlands could not be drained or filled or used for major real estate development.

The bill was delayed for lack of a committee quorum and, finally, in June 1976 was reported out to the floor. The Michigan Student Environmental Association immediately opposed it because it contained no assurance that wetlands in agricultural use would not be later developed, and it provided no funds for local governments to enforce the bill. It passed the House and went to the Senate.

There the bill was bottled up in committee by its chairperson, a Democratic senator from an iron mining district of the Upper Peninsula. Some legislators believed that the bill would receive no more attention until the House passed a Senate bill permitting the sale of some public lands to private interests—which the House did. The wetlands bill was then reviewed by an iron mining company spokesman who approved it, if the dumping of iron ore wastes was permitted on wetlands. This was added to the bill, but the bill was never given a public hearing and never emerged from the Senate committee that session.

In April 1977 the bill was again introduced in the House. Some of the new committee members were unsympathetic—one, who was a partner in a muck farm raising onions and celery, wanted a provision that would specifically allow the expansion of vegetable farms to muckland. As the bill was now written, the wetlands must be a swamp, bog, or marsh, must be contiguous to a lake, river, or stream, and must support a common list of marshland plants. Meanwhile the chairperson of the House committee had breakfast with the chairperson of the Senate committee, unsuccessfully trying to lobby him into permitting passage of a wetlands bill. The Republican governor announced that since the bill had been introduced two years before, "more than 10,000 acres of irreplaceable wetlands have been lost." He urged action—but to this point no further action has occurred.

What do you think? Are the legislators too sensitive to interest groups? Why are they so concerned about what the interest group representatives think? Did you classify the DNR, ecology, and local government groups as interests, as well as the farm and iron mining groups? Why weren't real estate and land development or industrial groups represented in this process? Should the legislature have speeded up the process? How? Does this case study suggest that minorities have too much power to delay or prevent action?

of minority elements and those resisting innovation—to force those who want change to consider many points of view—to strike bargains for something acceptable to many—to compromise. Some, such as T. V. Smith, political scientist and Illinois legislator, have glorified this process as "the legislative way of life." You will probably be frustrated and sometimes angry with it, but we hope you will never become so discouraged with it not to recognize its merits.

The legislative process is not neat and orderly. At times it is downright messy. But we should not expect much different, for the legislative arena is one in which competing groups display their differences, a place where expression of varying opinions that have any degree of support at all is encouraged. It is a place where "perfect" answers are seldom sought or reached. Rather legislators seek a politically efficient answer—one that accomodates many interests. In Policy Box No. 14 "Wetlands Regulation in Michigan" we review a situation that has thus far resulted in stalemate.

LEGISLATURES IN A FEDERAL SYSTEM

Pressures state legislators feel—those of administrative agencies, news media, interest groups, political parties, local government interests, and the governor's offices—will be discussed in other chapters. Here we will consider the relationship of state legislatures to the national government because of the traditional legislative role as critic of policies suggested and administered by others. How well do they perform that role in respect to national programs that are proposed by the federal government and administered by the states?

The Decline of State Legislatures in a Centralizing Federal System

One frustrated state legislator says, "Federal officials too often act as though governors are synonymous with state government. They give too little thought to the policymaking role accorded to the fifty state legislatures."[42]

As a result of their "misdeeds" in the 1800s, the role of state legislatures in the federal system has diminished, just as has their influence in state government. Legislatures gave up their right to select U.S. senators in 1913 with the adoption of the Seventeenth Amendment, and they lost more power and influence with the flowering of Franklin Roosevelt's New Deal. Congress, rather than state legislatures, became the focal point for new and innovative legislation. With the development of the federal grant programs in the 1950s and 1960s, state, local, and national functions became more intertwined. But national contacts were with mayors and governors and with state and community administrative agencies. State legislatures were involved only marginally, if at all.

Effect of grants on legislative status. The heavy volume of grants-in-aid put state legislatures in a "double bind." They found it virtually impossible to reject federal grants—although the legislature of Indiana

---

[42]Jerome H. Sohns, "A Strong Voice for the States." *State Legislatures*, National Conference of State Legislatures, March/April, 1976, p. 24.

did so for a time—and yet had to vote the matching funds and office space for the bureaucracies burgeoning around them. At the same time the legislatures could not influence the content of federal programs riding the wave into the state.

Daniel Elazar has argued that federal grants tend to reinforce general tendencies. Thus, governors became stronger and legislatures weaker. And "in those states where power is widely diffused among the separate executive departments, federal aid has tended to add to the diffusion, by giving the individual departments new sources of funds outside of the normal channels of state control, funds that can even be used to obtain more money and power from the legislature."[43]

There are several reasons why legislatures were not able to change the direction of the power flow. They met only for brief periods each year; their members, who were part time, were paid at rates that did not permit them to spend more time; and, for the most part, they had no staff to assist them.

Can the Legislatures be Bypassed?

What we find, then, is that legislatures have been bypassed in the growing linkage of federal and state programming. Not only have the U.S. Congress and federal agencies ignored legislatures, but governors themselves have challenged the legislative role in respect to federal grants. Pennsylvania Governor Milton Shapp, for example, argued that the Congress appropriates federal funds and earmarks them for specific purposes and that state legislatures cannot reject subsequent national conditions once it has accepted the federal grant program.[44]

As we write, the issue of whether state legislatures can decide whether a state spends federal aid is being fought in the Pennsylvania Supreme Court.

What the Legislators Want. Legislators, such as Martin Sabo, Speaker of the Minnesota House of Representatives, and in 1977, president of the National Council of State Legislatures (NCSL), argue that it is essential that the legislatures take firm control of federal funds, or face large increases in state budgets and state bureaucratic power.

[43]Daniel J. Elazar, *American Federalism, A View from the States*, 2nd ed., Thomas Y. Crowell Company, 1972, p. 87.

[44]Richard Hickman, *News and Views*, American Society for Public Administration, 27, May–June 1977. The case involved is *Shapp* v. *Sloan and the Pennsylvania General Assembly.*

"The state legislatures are ready," he suggests, "to assume their rightful role in determining how the states spend all of their funds, including those they receive from the federal government."

Legislatures, we think, face an uphill battle. Irwin Feller notes that because of the close cooperative relationships between federal, state, and community agencies, supporting the legislative demands "will be perceived at the federal level as a form of subsidizing a third player in what has been a two-player game."[45] Legislators may also anticipate opposition from state agencies and from local governments.

Growing Support for the Legislatures

Yet state legislatures have made some progress in their demands. In 1969 the U.S. Bureau of the Budget permitted state legislatures to qualify for federal grants-in-aid "on their merits." Some have received federal funds to improve their internal operations and the 1972 General Revenue Sharing Act included the provision at the request of the National Conference of State Legislatures that these funds be appropriated through the normal state and local budgetary processes. A few governors, though, have ignored this requirement, at least for a time. Also the Advisory Commission on Intergovernmental Relations in 1977 proposed "model" legislation that would require all federal funds to be deposited in the state general fund and be expended each year only as the legislature directs in appropriations acts.

Governors, mayors, and state and local administrators generally oppose such legislation. "If we have to wait on the legislature," they say, "the state and its cities and counties will lose millions of dollars in federal grants that require a quick response." The legislators say that for such emergencies they will delegate responsibility to their interim budget committees.

Can The Legislatures Make A Difference?

If the state legislatures become involved in the appropriations of federal funds, what effect will they have? Will they be less eager than governors and administrators to receive federal funds? Will they turn down grants because federal "strings" are too demanding? We think not. Nor do we think that many state legislatures will refuse to meet the

[45]Irwin Feller, "Issues in the Design of Federal Programs to Improve the Policy Management Capabilities of State Legislatures," *Public Administration Review*, Special Issue, December, 1975, 780–785.

federal requirements of federal grants—such as antidiscrimination policies, merit employment, affirmative action, and fair labor standards.

But legislative control over federal funds will affect relationships between governors and administrators, local governments, and the legislatures. Importantly, administrators will have to seek legislative approval. State administrators will have to explain programs, indicate why they are directing program services to one part of the state instead of others, and await a legislative decision. Community administrators will come under new scrutiny in respect to program effectiveness and intergovernmental relations at the community level. Legislators and their staff would surely become more knowledgeable in the process. And their inquiries about certain policies or practices could no longer be blithely put off with responses such as, "Federal 'regs' require us to do it this way," or "Federal 'regs' don't permit that. Sorry Senator."

An important impact of state legislative control over federal funds, it seems, would be to make bureaucrats at state and community levels answerable to state legislatures on matters involving vast amounts of funds that have been largely in control of their agencies. As a result state legislatures will be better able to fulfill their role as evaluators of proposals suggested and administered by others, and the complementary role of making sure local concerns are not forgotten at the national level or national and state concerns in the communities.

IMPROVING STATE LEGISLATURES

State legislatures began early in our nation's history as institutions of hope and relief from oppressive executives. But after a hundred years it was said of them, "Now is the time when men work quietly in the fields and women weep softly in the kitchens; the legislature is in session, and no man's property is safe."[46] In response to legislative rascality, our forefathers put the legislatures into constitutional locks and chains. For the most part, the legislatures languished under these constraints. We will consider briefly the efforts to loosen the shackles and make legislatures responsible units in state governing systems once more. The proposals for reform take two major directions. One seeks to improve the political efficiency of legislatures—making them more representative and enabling more points of view to be expressed. The

[46]Quoted by Neal R. Peirce in "Overruling the Rule-Makers," *County News*, National Association of Counties, Washington, D.C., September 30, 1976.

second seeks to increase administrative efficiency in the legislatures, sometimes, perhaps, at the expense of political efficiency.

Reapportionment

Some critics argue that minorities have too much power in preventing change. Many felt this to be the case between 1920 and 1960 when urban citizens were substantially underrepresented in state legislatures. The stance of one rural legislator summed up what many considered the point of years of rural overrepresentation: "I believe in collecting taxes where the money is—in the cities—and spending it where it is needed—in the country."[47]

The question of legislative reapportionment was battled in legislatures and in the courts without much success until the U.S. Supreme Court in 1962 ruled that the failure of the Tennessee legislature to reapportion itself in more than sixty years violated the U.S. Constitution, to say nothing of the state constitution. In a number of subsequent cases the court ruled that state senates, too, as well as city councils and other local governments, had to meet one-person, one-vote, standards. When the legal dust had settled, the state legislatures were well on the road to becoming reformed institutions. The suburbs gained most because they had become the areas of underrepresentation. The big cities, now declining in population, had long argued for reapportionment, but never really had "their day" in the state legislatures.

The changes in policy outputs by reapportioned state legislatures at first were not as dramatic as some had anticipated,[48] but reapportionment was nevertheless a highly important change. It increased the political efficiency of legislatures as the reform enabled more points of view to be expressed and, importantly, gave the legislatures a sense of legitimacy that they had lost. The policy outputs resulting from the broader expression of opinion began to emerge in the 1970s.

[47]Gene Graham, *One Man, One Vote*, Little, Brown and Co. Boston, 1972, p. 11. The case that turned the tide was *Baker* v. *Carr*, 369 U.S. 186 (1962). *Reynolds* v. *Sims* 377 U.S. 533 (1964) applied the rule to both houses of state legislatures and *Avery* v. *Midland County* (Texas) 390 U.S. 474 (1968) required county boards to be redistricted along one-person, one-vote standards.

[48]See Brett W. Hawkins, "Consequences of Reapportionment in Georgia," in Richard I. Hofferbert and Ira Sharkansky, eds., *State and Urban Politics*, Little Brown and Co., Boston, 1971, 273–298; Thomas R. Dye. "Malapportionment and Public Policy in the States," *Journal of Politics*, 27 (August 1965) 586–601; Hofferbert, "The Relation Between Public Policy and Some Structural and Environmental Variables in the American States," *American Political Science Review* 60 (March 1966) 73–82; and Herbert Jacob, "The Consequences of Malapportionment: A Note of Caution," *Social Forces*, 43, December, 1964, 256–261.

Gerrymandering—A Continuing Problem. Gerrymandering is the practice of drawing political boundaries to strengthen the voting power of one group and weakening or diluting the voting power of other groups. Although the U.S. Supreme Court required state and local legislative districts to be apportioned on the one-person, one-vote principle, it has not addressed the question of gerrymandering except as the practice applies to racial minorities.

Gerrymandering can be a particularly insidious practice for legislators because both majority and minority incumbents can benefit from it—legislators can minimize risks in the next election for incumbents of both parties. The objective of the majority party, of course, is to add to its advantages by drawing legislative boundaries in particular ways, but minority members who cannot contract the districting anyway can be bought off by leaving their districts untouched.

Because gerrymandering is also a powerful technique reducing the representativeness of legislative bodies, we find some pressure to take the responsibility for apportionment from the legislatures and place it in the hands of a somewhat less-interested body. Common Cause, for example, in 1978 sponsored a constitutional amendment in Florida to create a reapportionment commission. The commission would not be permitted to take into account partisan considerations in its decisions.[49]

Unicameralism

The idea of having a one-house—unicameral—legislature—gained renewed attention following the court decision that required state senate districts to be based on population. In 1934, under the leadership of former U.S. Senator George W. Norris, Nebraska adopted a one-house, nonpartisan legislature. Not since 1836, when Vermont abandoned its one-house system, had there been a unicameral legislature. Nebraska still is the only unicameral legislature. We still find an occasional trumpet sounding the praises of this approach, but the interest aroused is only mild at best.[50]

Supporters of unicameral legislatures argue that it produces a small legislature that can be both efficient and economical, and that it is one that citizens can understand. The two-house system, they say, is complicated and its actions are clouded by the buckpassing of interhouse politics and executive "whipsawing" of one house against the other.

[49]David S. Broder, "Florida Attacks Districting," *Detroit News*, February 23, 1978.

[50]See Jesse Unruh, "Unicameralism—The Wave of the Future," in Donald G. Herzberg and Alan Rosenthal, eds., *Strengthening the States: Essays on Legislative Reform*, Doubleday and Company, Garden City, N.Y. 1972, 87–94.

The two-house state legislature, we think, continues to have a place, even in the post-*Reynolds* v. *Sims* era. The two-house legislature may not be as financially efficient as a one-house system, but we judge it to be more politically efficient—achieving a balance acceptable to the variety of state interests. The difference in constituencies—senate districts being larger and more diverse than house districts—as well as difference in length of term, we think, contribute to this political efficiency.

Changing Legislative Rules and Practices

Two national groups, Common Cause and Legis 50 (formerly called the Citizen's Conference on State Legislatures), have been the principal advocates of reform of procedures in state legislatures.

Common Cause is concerned with "the scandalous capacity of money to buy politcal outcomes." It hopes to bring about reform by exposing government and political processes to public inspection. Hence it lobbies for sunshine laws, stricter regulation of lobbyists, public official codes of ethics, public reporting of campaign financing, and public disclosure of candidates' and officials' financial statements. The Common Cause strategy depends on tracing the financial transactions that they believe may lubricate legislative graft and corruption. Common Cause seeks to make legislatures more politically efficient in expression of views and opinions and less dependent on well-financed interest groups.

Legis 50 concentrates its efforts on the internal workings of the legislatures, legislative salaries, staff, and office space. On the basis of five criteria it evaluated and ranked all the state legislatures—it said California's was the best, Alabama's the worst.[51]

The Legis 50 recommendations, we think, will produce legislatures that are more administratively efficient, but the legislative reformers sometimes fail to consider that they may thereby become less efficient politically than they are at present. In our view, the legislative process is not intended to find the one "correct" answer to every problem. Its mission is to develop the "best possible" political response at the time given the particular mixture of interests and viewpoints current in its state. That response must be one that is politically acceptable to citizens. As such it is likely to be a compromise between what experts propose and various segments of society will accept.

[51]See Citizens Conference on State Legislatures (now Legis 50), *The Sometimes Governments*, Bantam Books, N.Y., 1971.

What We Want From the State Legislatures: A Final Comment

At a time when bureaucratic domination is more than a distant threat on the horizon, when interest groups are powerful, when the national bureaucracy occasionally mounts ambitious programs of reform, when local communities sometimes want to "go it alone" without regard for neighboring communities, we look more closely at state legislatures as fulfilling a needed crossroads role in the federal system. If legislators can regain a more honorable place in the government system, they will do so because they are prepared to evaluate politically the actions of the other more "efficient branches" of government—the executive and the bureaucracy at all levels, as well as proposals from the private sector.

If the legislatures can function in this representative capacity and can avoid, unlike their predecessors of a hundred years ago, the use of power for self-aggrandizement, they can carve out a useful role in government. Failure to exercise self-restraint most certainly will result in the renewal of old limitations and structures.

HIGHPOINTS OF CHAPTER 7: LEGISLATURES AS STATE CRITICS.

In this chapter we have argued that the main task of state legislatures is to evaluate and criticize policies that, for the most part, are proposed, advanced, and administered by others. This evaluation, we have noted, is a political evaluation, seeking a political balance that is acceptable to the varied interests within a state. We have seen (1) that legislatures carry out this function through the law-making process, by overseeing the activities of the executive agencies, and by providing services to constituents and interest group representatives.

We noted (2) that legislators in most states, unlike members of Congress and similar to legislators in local government, are amateurs, a status marked by part-time work, low pay, inadequate staff and facilities. We discussed (3) how people with occupations in law and business still tend to dominate the state legislator ranks; but as legislative schedules lengthen and salaries rise, other occupational groups are appearing in greater numbers. We found (4) that state legislators are politically ambitious, which is one of the conditions along with low salaries leading to high turnover rates.

We next considered (5) how state legislatures operate by a complex network of written and unwritten rules, rules that enable minority coalitions and those opposing change to bargain with a power beyond their numbers. But we also saw (6) that a great deal of the power of these bodies rests with the elected leadership positions.

We discussed (7) the growing use of professional staff in the state legislatures, a fact that (8) legislators now cite in support of their contending for a greater role in policy initiation and a more meaningful place in the state–federal decision process. Finally, we noted that (9) the state legislatures have been the object of several reform movements—one seeking to make them more efficient politically by making them more open to public scrutiny; another proposing changes to make legislatures more efficient administratively.

8

GOVERNORS AS STATE LEADERS

At 7:45 A.M. selected state troopers meet Governor "Smith" and his wife at the door of their home and usher them into a shiny black Cadillac. They head to the state capitol, a trip the governor and troopers have made nearly every morning for the last four years. This trip, though, is rather special. It is the last one. This is inauguration day.

Although the governor leaves office by his own choice, it is a rather sad day. He may go on to other successes, perhaps to a job in Washington, a judgeship, or to a position in a prestigious law or business firm, but this is an ending of something very special.

The last few months have been busy. He had to approve and veto a few bills, write notes of thanks to officials he has come to know very well, order a round of gifts for his staff, and make telephone calls to help his assistants find new jobs. He had also to make a number of decisions on the budget for the next fiscal year, a budget that his successor would present to the legislature. Finally, mementos and personal documents had to be sorted, packed in boxes and labelled for shipping—some to the homestead and the rest to the state university library.

As Governor Smith rides to the capitol he wonders if he has overlooked anything. He has been very aware of the "drift toward decentralization"—the period that began immediately after the election when loyalties began to shift from himself to the governor-elect.[1] He has already noted a decline of his power. He knows that in a short while most of the remaining "perks" will be gone. That he will be called "governor" for the rest of his life, is little consolation.

For "Jones," the incoming governor, the situation is quite different. It is a beginning, a time of excitement! Winning the primary and general election were exhilarating, but now it all begins for real. Ever since November, people have been calling him "governor," too, although it is still unofficial until he takes the oath of office.

The last few weeks for Governor Jones have been busy ones too. Assembling a staff was more difficult than he had thought it would be. Some, of course, carried right on from the campaign, but now other talents are needed. Campaign promises have to be worked into a program and already the incoming staff and Governor Jones find the view different from the one they had during the heat of the campaign. What needs to be done about policy areas that he has not had time to consider up to now—rumor, and gossip of new and old staff, as well as speculation stories in the media provide plenty of suggestions. These have only made matters more confusing.[2]

Many questions, however, have been worked out, at least in broad strokes. Inauguration day is a time of celebration. The bright sunshine on the cold, crisp January day looks like a lucky sign.[3]

Standing on the platform in front of the capitol with Governor-elect, Jones and his wife are others for whom it is also inauguration day (sometimes for these executive officers just "one more oath-taking" of many)—the attorney general, secretary of state, lieutenant governor, supreme court judges, and others. The chief justice of the state supreme court administers the oath on Governor Jones' family Bible.

As the ceremonies proceed, a few photographers, professional and amateur, jockey for the best angle. When they are finished, the new governor will deliver a speech of hope and promise. If it is now cold and

[1]James B. Holdeman, "The Modern Governor," Limits of Effectiveness in the Office of Governor, Institute of Government and Public Affairs, University of Illinois, 1963, p. 51.

[2]For an excellent view of the transition from candidate to governor, see Norton Long, "When the Voting Is Over," Midwest Journal of Political Science, 6, 2, May 1962, 183–200. This article is also included in Thad Beyle and J. Oliver Williams, The American Governor in Behavioral Perspective, Harper and Row, New York, 1972, 76–86.

[3]Nearly all states elect their governors in November and install them on January 1, or shortly thereafter.

Massachusetts' Governor Dukakis takes the oath of office in 1975.

snowing, you can bet that the speech will be short. Thereafter follows a round of luncheons, parties and ballroom dances—at least for the new regime.

Governor Smith listens politely, congratulates each of the new officials and then, with his wife, quietly slips out the side door of the capitol—the reality of his new status is almost overwhelming. The state police drivers are not waiting. The ex-governor and his wife smile gamely as they wonder if they should walk or call a cab.[4]

Is the experience of Governors Smith and Jones typical? Yes and no. No doubt, most governors leave the office with mixed feelings. They take pride in successes and are bemused by some proposals the legis-

---

[4]Robert W. Scott, former governor of North Carolina (1969–73) told about just such a transportation problem at the meetings of the Community Development Society of America in Wilmington in 1974.

lature turned down. Most would sense deeply, we suspect, the change in status, but not all would have transportation problems, of course. New York's former governor for fifteen years, multimillionaire Nelson Aldrich Rockefeller (1959–73), would have had his chauffeur and staff standing by in any case. Governor Lester Maddox, Georgia's restaurateur (1967–71), who passed out axe handles in defiance of integration orders, sometimes bicycled home from work, occasionally part of the way facing backwards and sitting on the handlebars. Perhaps he did so the day he left office.

The Challenge of Becoming Governor

Being governor is a memorable experience. For most, (as many as 55 percent according to one study), the governorship will be the peak of their political career and the last political office they hold. A few, such as New York Governors Theodore Roosevelt (1899–1901) and Franklin Roosevelt (1929–33) or Jimmy Carter of Georgia (1971–75), have gone on to become president. Some have become presidential candidates, but lost the election, as was the case with Alfred Landon of Kansas (1933–37) and Adlai Stevenson of Illinois (1948–52). But, like other people, some discover they cannot live on their retirement incomes and take a big step down. Ex-governor Orval Faubus (Arkansas, 1955–67) in 1977 took a job as a bank teller to supplement his income. A very few also end in tragedy. William Marland at age thirty-four was West Virginia's youngest governor (1953–57). He became an alcoholic and ended up as a Chicago cabbie and skidrow bum.

Governors as Political Leaders.   As most of us would, newly elected governors face the office as one in which they want to leave some mark of which they can later be proud. A sense of challenge is probably the key feeling. Control of the office is power—power to do something or perhaps nothing. The challenge is one of articulating what seem to be the emerging needs of the state's citizens—defining what the governor perceives to be the public interest. Often this places the governor at loggerheads with the legislature.

Even with two months to prepare for the transition and as some states now provide, funds for their personal staff, the feeling of challenge persists. A bit of apprehension may also creep in. As Norton Long notes, in most organizations a new recruit "is taught by his superiors and his equals. [But] the political executive is taught by his inferiors and those doubtfully loyal to him."[5]

5Norton E. Long, Op. cit., p. 73.

Overview.   In this chapter, we want to look with you at several aspects of the office of governor in the states. We will look first at the question, Who gets to be governor? We will review how political experience helps them and whether personal considerations, such as wealth, occupation, race, or sex make a difference. Then we will consider the development of the office of governor. Later we will examine the various arenas in which governors exercise leadership. In our final comment we will discuss the question, Does it matter who is governor?

WHO GETS TO BE GOVERNOR?

Ask yourself who in your state you might consider as candidates for governor. You will be impressed, we think, by the fact that the pool of eligibles is really quite small. No matter if your state has 302,000 people (as Alaska did in 1970) or nearly 20 million (as California did that year), the number of likely candidates stays about the same. The possible candidates will certainly not be more than a half-dozen for each major party—and usually less if an incumbent is up for reelection.

We notice that most potential candidates already are in politics. Furthermore, we see that those whom the press and party leaders mention frequently are people who do not deny an interest in the job. Once in a while a candidate who the leaders do not regard as having much of a chance catches on; as for example, Governor Dixy Lee Ray (1976–) did in the state of Washington.

We consider such things as education, occupation, and maybe race and sex. Most likely, no one will even ask whether so and so has a prison record. It is assumed that they do not. A person who is suspected of having an uncontrolled alcohol problem is usually disqualified. Harold Hughes (1963–69), who admitted to once having been an alcoholic, however, became governor of Iowa. Moreover he campaigned in favor of permitting the sale of liquor by the glass. As a populist, he argued that if the "rich people can drink in their country clubs, the working people should be able to get a drink in the corner tavern."

In this section, we will examine some of these major screening devices: (1) how political experience figures in, (2) social economic factors, and (3) personal characteristics.

Political Experience is Necessary

Most candidates for governor have served in public office prior to becoming governor. In one study, Joseph A. Schlesinger found that less than 10 percent of 995 governors between 1870 and 1950 moved directly from private life into the governor's suites.[6] (We remember how Ronald Reagan went from movie star to governor of California (1966–74), but he was an exception.) We find the same pattern among modern day governors. Of the fifty governors in 1974, forty-five held previous government office; of those in 1976, forty-eight previously held office. A large majority of the people who will become governor in the next decade or two are now holding some public office.

Why does our political system require an apprenticeship in public office in order to become governor?

Name Recognition.   Political experience works for would-be governors much the same as it does in nongovernment organizations. At college, for example, as a freshman you have virtually no chance of being elected student council president, even when rules allow it. We know it is not wholly a question of whether you are able. The problem is that you simply are not well known.

Office holding provides opportunity for building name recognition. Name recognition is the lifeblood of a political career. And office holders rarely pass up an opportunity for additional exposure. "To an elected politician," says Myra MacPherson, "there is no such thing as indecent exposure. People who hold public office are as dependent on the voter as a heart attack victim is on an oxygen tent. Obscurity is a dirty word and almost all exposure is decidedly decent."[7]

Opportunity for recognition building is usually not available to the political novice. Hence, the novice begins further back and has to find some way to break into the news. Even political careerists have to do things to separate themselves from the crowd of other politicians. In 1974 candidate David Boren (Oklahoma, 1975–) carried a broom around the state to symbolize the "house cleaning" he would do. Governor Cliff Finch of Mississippi (1976–) carried a lunch bucket around during the campaign and took blue collar jobs—bulldozer operator, grocery clerk, and so forth to demonstrate his identity with "the common people."

Expectations of Others.   Office-holding experience often can create expectations that a particular legislative leader will run for governor. And the press corps, through speculation stories, can also generate such expectations.

[6]Joseph A. Schlesinger in his book *How They Became Governor* provides a detailed analysis of gubernatorial career paths. Michigan State University, East Lansing, Michigan, 1957.

[7]Quoted from *Newsweek*, June 10, 1974. Myra MacPherson is author of *The Power Lovers: An Intimate Look at Politicians and Their Marriages*, G.P. Putnam's Sons, p. 446.

Politicians, especially those who have political ambitions or who have progressed a step or two on the ladder, do not need much encouragement to think about the possibility of becoming governor in the future. A person who wishes to, can easily stop the talk simply by saying, "I am not interested." Once the denials are issued, speculation stories usually disappear. Thus, the frequent mention of a name usually continues with the approval of the candidate. In the final analysis, most candidates are not drafted—they volunteer. The political novice who wants to be a candidate for governor, faces the reverse problem—being taken seriously as a candidate.

Access to Political Tools.   Experience in office also allows access to the tools of politics. Moreover officeholders are able to sharpen their skills in the use of them.

Successful politicians learn how to handle delicate issues and respond to voter questions. They learn how to relate to complex statewide constituencies, to develop skills in recruiting and using campaign staffs, to raise campaign money, and to spend it effectively.

Office holding does not assure the development of such knowledge and skills. Nor is political experience the only way of gaining them. The subtleties are such, though, that the novice is at a marked disadvantage. By practicing in private a person can learn the basketball jump shot or how to judge a fly ball in the outfield. But playing well under pressure requires game experience, even for natural athletes. Most successful candidates develop their "political sense" under game conditions.

Predictability.   Office experience also provides a basis for predictability. It helps those in and around the political scene to judge, but not always correctly, about the way the experienced politician will handle the duties of governor. Predicting behavior of the novice, or maverick, such as Governor James Longley (1974–78) who won in Maine as an independent in 1974, is much more difficult. What will he propose? How will he treat the party faithful? Who will have access to him? Novices represent a great risk to those for whom such matters are of critical importance, such as legislators, lobbyists, administrators, political party leaders, and local government officials.

Which Office Experiences Are Best?

The 1300 people who have been governor in the last one hundred years have gotten there by a variety of avenues. As Joseph A. Schlesinger notes, "There is probably no public office, with the exception of the presidency, that has not at some time been held by a future state governor."[8] Success, however, is not due completely to "blind luck"; Schlesinger's analysis in Table 8-1 shows where some of the better stepping-stones are.

Legislative Experience. More than half the governors between 1870 and 1950, we find, had experience in the legislature. Twenty percent of the governors went directly from the legislature to the executive suite. This should not startle us if we recall that legislators constitute the largest pool of political talent at the state level—more than 7500 at any one time or roughly 100–150 per state.

We note, though, that the percentage of governors with legislative experience declined steadily from the 1870s to the 1940s—from 65 percent to 41 percent. Also, we see that the pattern was not the same across the nation. The six New England states, for example, have drawn frequently upon the legislature for their governors (Table 8-2).

In 1976, however, 70 percent of the governors had legislative experience. The downward trend was reversed—perhaps because reapportionment has produced a more representative legislature.

TABLE 8-1 Pattern of Office Experience of All Elected Governors in the United States, 1870–1950 (n = 995).

Office Types	% With This as Experience	% With This as End Office	% With This as First Office	% With This as Only Office
State legislature	52.4	20.1	31.4	13.1
Law enforcement	32.1	16.3	20.1	8.5
Administrative	29.3	13.7	16.8	5.8
Local elective	19.8	7.4	11.8	3.5
Statewide elective	18.9	15.8	2.1	2.1
Federal elective	13.9	11.2	2.6	2.5
No office	8.8	8.8	8.9	8.8
Other	—	6.7[a]	6.3[b]	—

SOURCE: Adapted from Joseph A. Schlesinger, *How They Became Governor*, Governmental Research Bureau, Michigan State University, East Lansing, Michigan, 1957, p. 11.

[a]Includes 27 Presidential Electors, 12 members of Constitutional Conventions, 10 Governors' Councilors, and 16 for whom no information was available and one Confederate official. "End office" refers to the last office held before becoming governor.

[b]Includes 19 Presidential Electors, 26 members of Constitutional Conventions, 2 Confederate Officials, and 16 for whom no information was available.

[8]Joseph A. Schlesinger, Op. cit., p. 9.

[9]The data we are reporting for 1950 to 1976 comes from recent editions of the National Governors Conference, *Governors of the American States, Commonwealths, Territories*. While the data are reliable as far as they go, the brief biographical sketches may not be

Law Enforcement. States that elect governors without legislative experience occasionally recruit them from the law enforcement field. Schlesinger notes that in frontier communities where maintaining law and order was important, state and local law officers (judges, state attorneys general, federal attorneys, and local prosecutors) often caught the public eye, sometimes as the result of dramatic incidents.

In recent years candidates in urban states have also made their political way to the governorship by fighting organized crime and graft and corruption in politics. Thomas Dewey, governor of New York (1943–55) almost parlayed his crime-fighting fame into becoming president. James R. Thompson, (1976–) U.S. Attorney for Northern Illinois, who successfully prosecuted former Illinois Governor Otto W. Kerner (1961–68) and indicted some other 350 government officials, provides a recent example of a governor coming from the law enforcement ranks. Of the nation's governors in 1976, 20 percent reported some experience in this field; in 1974, 32 percent was reported.

Statewide Elective Office. Most people who have moved from statewide office to the governorship were lieutenant governors. But other statewide elective offices such as secretary of state, attorney general, treasurer, and auditor have made the move occasionally.

Lieutenant governors have an advantage because they automatically become governor if the office becomes vacant. The rate of turnover is fairly high because governors frequently accept presidential appointments—President Carter, for example, appointed Governor Patrick Lucey (Wisconsin, 1971–77) ambassador to Mexico, and Cecil Andrus (Idaho, 1971–77) to Secretary of the Department of Interior, or many resign to become U.S. senators as Wendell Anderson (Minnesota, 1971–77) did. During the 1950 to 1976 period, fifty-five lieutenant governors, (about twenty percent of all governors during this period) moved into vacated offices.[10]

Lieutenant governors have another advantage in that they may be seen as "heirs apparent" to the governorship. They generally do not exercise much power, but frequently they fill in for the governors and have opportunities to display some "gubernatorial qualities."

Other Patterns. Schlesinger identified a few other categories of career paths of governors, none as important as those already men-

---

complete in every case. Therefore, in each instance we give, you might mentally wish to insert "at least. . . ."

[10]Samuel R. Solomon, *The Governors of the States, 1900–1974*, The Council of State Governments, Lexington, Kentucky, 1974. During this period nine legislative leaders in states having no lieutenant governor also became governor in this way.

TABLE 8-2 The Major Forms of Political Office Experience—Distribution by States: 1870–1950

Percent of Governors with Office Experience	Office Types			
	State Legislative	Law Enforcement	Administrative	Local Elective
80–89	Vt.	Mont.		
70–79	Me., Mass., Miss., N.H., R.I.			N. Mex.
60–69	Ala., Conn., Fla., Ga., Ia., Ill., Neb., N.J., S.C., N.C.			
50–59	Ark., Del., Ida., Kan., Md., Ore., S.D., Tenn., Utah, Va., Wyo.	Ark., Ky., N.C., Tenn., Tex., W.Va.	N.H.	S.D., Wyo.
40–49	Ariz., Cal., Ill., Ind., Minn., Mont. N.M., N.Y., W.Va.	Ala., Fla., Ga., Mo., N.Y., Ohio, Pa., S.C.	La., Mich., N.J., N.M., Utah, Vt., Wis., W.Va.	Mass., Wash., N.Y., Utah
30–39	Colo., Ky., La., N.D., Tex., Wis.	Colo., Md., Mich., N.J., Okla., S.D., Vt., Wis.	Cal., Ill., Kans. Me., Md. Wyo., Minn., Neb., Nev., N.Y., S.C.	Idaho, Me., Mich., Neb., N.C., W. Va., Wis.
20–29	Mo., Nev., Wash.	Ariz., Cal., Ind., Ia., Kans., La., Me., Mass., Minn., Miss., N.M., N.D., Va.	Ariz., Ark., Del., Ida., N.C., Ore., R.I., Ind., Miss., Mo., Mont., Okla., Pa., Va.	Cal., Colo., Conn., Fla., Minn., N.H., Ore.
10–19	Ohio, Okla.	Conn., Neb., Nev., N.H., Ore., R.I., Wash., Wyo.	Ala., Colo., Conn., N.D., S.D., Tex., Ga., Ia., Ky. Ohio, Tenn., Wash., Mass.	Ala., Del., Ill., Ind., Kans., Md., Miss., Mo., Mont., N.D., S.C., Tenn., Vt.
0–9	Pa.	Del., Ida., Utah	Fla.	Ariz., Ark, Ga., Ia., Ky., La., Nev., N.J., Ohio, Okla., Pa., R.I., Tex., Va.

SOURCE: Joseph A. Schlesinger, Op. cit., p. 14.

tioned. In only three western states with small populations—Wyoming, Utah, and New Mexico—were administrative positions important.

Member of Congress. The U.S. House of Representatives produced 112 governors from 1870 to 1950. Of the 1976 governors, six had been members of Congress. We might wonder why anyone would leave the Congress to run for governor—governors usually have shorter tenure than members of Congress, have lower pay, and a more diverse constituency. The desire to be head of a government, instead of one of 435 members of the House of Representatives, may account for some of these moves.

Local government experience. Table 8-1 shows that very few governors came directly from positions in local government. As a general rule local elective office, such as city council member or school board member, may be a place to start, but you are not likely to be able to jump into the governor's chair from there.

Governor Jerry Brown (1974–) of California, even with his name (his father had been governor only eight years earlier), had to move from membership on a community college board to secretary of state before he could make it to the governor's chair. Jimmy Carter "paid his dues" as a member of Sumter County School Board before going to the state senate and from there became governor of Georgia (1971–75). Sixteen of the 1976 governors had had some local government experience, but only one, Governor James Rhodes (Ohio, 1963–71, 1975–), had been mayor of a major city (Columbus, 1944–53).

Social and Economic Background

Seeking the governorship is different from virtually every other office but that of U.S. senator and the Presidency. People who run for governor are trying to make the big jump. Campaigning is no longer part-time. It is not a matter that can be managed personally with a few bumper stickers and billboards, nor is it a matter of depending on a few friends. In most states a candidate must deal with a complex constituency that can be reached only through public media and with the help of many strangers.

Can anyone make this jump? In this section we want to see how wealth, social and economic status, as well as race and sex affect the chances of those who seek a "major league" contract.

Wealth. How rich must you be in order to be a candidate for governor? You probably do not have to be a millionaire to make a good race, although several, past and present, have been. As a practical matter, though, you do not have much of a chance if you are poor. If you have to worry about whether you will be able to meet next month's mortgage payment on the house, or the household expenses, you are probably out of your league in running for governor.

Nevertheless some do try it. We recall when Paul Bagwell, a professor of speech at Michigan State University, ran against incumbent Governor G. Mennen Williams (1948–60). Because he became a candidate, he had to leave his university job and, therefore, had no in-

Governor Jerry Brown of California on the "campaign trail."

come—let alone money to finance a campaign. The Republican party, in effect, had to take up a collection to underwrite his living expenses during the campaign. Bagwell lost.

Personal wealth in gubernatorial campaigns, as well as for other offices, however, probably will not be as important in the future as it has been in the past. In the aftermath of "Watergate," legislatures are beginning to tighten up on campaign practices and financing. They are not doing it voluntarily, though. Common Cause and other groups have been pressuring, especially in states with the initiative, to make the changes.

Can importance of wealth be reduced?   Some of the reforms proposed are: partial public funding of gubernatorial campaigns, including primaries, limits on the amount of individual campaign contributions, and limits on campaign spending.

Wealthy candidates have the money to carry them through the lean and lonely times before the primary election. It is then that money is hard to raise and party support may be lacking. Governor Hugh Carey's oilman brother helped him to overcome the failure to get the endorsement of party leaders in the New York 1976 primary.

And even with public campaign funding, candidates must raise money in order to qualify for state dollars.

Money also provides "staying power" to come back for another try, should you lose the first time around. John D. Rockefeller IV came to West Virginia in 1964 to be an antipoverty worker. He ran against Governor Arch A. Moore, Jr. in the 1972 election and lost. But in 1976, "Jay" Rockefeller was able to win the primary election by spending nearly $1 million of his own money.

Public funding of campaigns, thus will not likely eliminate the advantage of personal wealth, but it may broaden the opportunity for those who do not have great wealth.

Occupation and Education. If you were to choose a career that would help you most in realizing your hopes for becoming governor, you would probably go to law school or seek a career in business. Of the 1976 governors, twenty-eight were lawyers. Business was the next highest occupational category listed.[11] Significantly, all but a few of the others had professional occupations—physician, dentist, engineer, and educator.

In terms of *education*, at least on the basis of what the governors of 1976 report about themselves, we would advise you to finish college. All indicated that they had attended college—forty-five had graduated.

Ethnic Origins, Race, and Sex. We find that ethnic groups are not sufficiently large in most states to require absolutely that a candidate be of a certain ethnic background.[12] Still it does no harm to be of the dominant group—and especially in close contests, having the proper "old world" parentage may be an advantage. A Scandinavian origin in Minnesota will be helpful, as will an Italian name in Rhode Island. Spanish or Japanese surnames probably are not helpful in most states, but for Raul H. Castro (Arizona), Jerry Apodaca (New Mexico), and George Ariyoshi (Hawaii), during the 1974 elections such parentage probably helped.

Blacks and governorships. No black has ever been a state governor. However, the prospect for blacks in the future is improving based on what we learned about career patterns. As we have seen earlier most governors have moved through a series of "chairs" before becoming

[11]National Conference of Governors, Op. cit.

[12]Ethnic origin probably is a more important factor in gaining the party nomination for governor in states, than it is in the general election. This would be especially true when there are several candidates of different origins seeking the party banner. With this kind of division in the electorate, the largest ethnic group could be more influential.

governor. A number of the most politically desirable chairs have been occupied by blacks—for example, Lieutenant Governors Mervyn Dymally of California and George Brown of Colorado, and Richard Austin, Michigan's Secretary of State, as well as a number of black legislators, mayors, and members of congress.

Women and governorships. For almost all of our nation's history, parents had dreamed of their sons, but not their daughters, "growing up to be president or governor." It now looks like parents can have this dream for their daughters as well. Only five women have ever been state governor; two of them served in 1977—Ella Grasso (Connecticut, 1975–) and Dixy Lee Ray (Washington, 1977–). In Policy Box No. 15, "Her Honor, The Governor," we briefly review the problems these women faced during their first years in office.

More can be expected, we think, because women also occupy positions from which governors have come. Some who won in 1974 and 1975 elections were lieutenant governors Mary Ann Krupsak of New York, Thelma Stovall of Kentucky, and Evelyn Gamby of Mississippi. Women, like blacks, still face many more hurdles than white males in gubernatorial politics, but the hurdles are no longer in the "impossible" category. By 1978 six women were lieutenant governors.

Personal Qualities. In an earlier time when newspapers and radio were the principal means of reaching the public, candidates depended largely on what the writers and broadcasters said about them. Today candidates can make a direct personal appeal and television makes personality a highly important ingredient of any campaign. It produces a demand for candidates who can handle the medium effectively and appear well to viewers.

Personal appearance. Although personal appearance consists of a combination of factors, voters appear to favor an appropriate middle ground, at least for most male candidates. Hair and dress style are fashionable without being avant-garde. Men are tall without being awkward. Body weight is usually well proportioned. The smile is easy and toothy.

This, of course, sounds like a charm school prescription. It is not very flattering to an educated populace to suggest that such personal appearance factors should be so important in determining who will occupy the executive suites in the fifty states. After all, we have very little control over our biological makeup and whether we have a well-proportioned nose does not say anything about the kind of person we are.

Yet if you would like to test for yourself the extent to which present governors conform to the general stereotype, we suggest that you leaf through the pictures of the governors presented in *Governors of the American States, Commonwealths, Territories* (published biennially by the National Governors Conference of Lexington, Kentucky).

Personality traits. Would-be governors usually project an image of being energetic. Illinois Governor Dan Walker (1975–76) lived up to his name by walking more than 1000 miles during his first campaign for governor. Governor George Romney of Michigan (1963–69) played three golf balls over six holes because he did not have time to play a full round of 18. He also jogged around his neighborhood in East Lansing every morning. Governor Dixy Lee Ray, a former zoology professor, prides herself on the kinds of vehicles she has driven or piloted, for example, an oil supertanker, sports cars, a hot air balloon, and so forth.

Another necessary personal quality we often look for is the ability to instill confidence in others. This calls for a kind of self-discipline; leaders must be able to control their emotions. They should be able to show anger without "blowing up," be sympathetic and sensitive without appearing to "fall apart," and articulate and decisive without giving the impression of being "rash and hasty."

Character or Image Building. Governors must still be people. And, although the governors represent a "club" in which membership is limited and difficult to obtain, we are not likely to get all the desired qualities in a single person.

We need to remember that most of the considerations (experience, social and economic background, and personal qualities) are also symbolic with broad appeal to the politically conscious sectors of society. Note how little we have stressed stands on issues. Such stands are not irrelevant, but we think them secondary to what the electorate regards as projections of "basic character" and what public relations firms call "image building."

Placed in the hands of a professional public relations firm, these symbols we have described can be skillfully manipulated to construct a political image that probably says more about us—what kind of electorate we are and what kinds of symbols we respond to—than it does about the candidate it represents. At the same time we should not become so cynical as to forget that governors, like the rest of us, also may be projecting what are genuine traits. In Chapter 13 on political parties, we discuss such image building in political campaigns.

POLICY BOX NO. 15:   Her Honor, The Governor

On November 29, 1976 Nellie Tayloe Ross celebrated her one-hundredth birthday and also, no doubt, became the oldest living ex-governor. She was the first woman governor. She served as governor of Wyoming between 1924 and 1926, and from 1933 to 1953 as director of the U.S. Mint—"It was," she said, "the best thing I could do for the women's cause at the time."

But Mrs. Ross was the wife of a Wyoming governor, as was Lurleen Wallace of Alabama, elected in 1966 because her husband, George Wallace, the effective governor, could not succeed himself. Miriam Amanda "Ma" Ferguson became governor of Texas on a "Two Governors for the Price of One" ticket in 1924 and again in 1932, because her husband was declared ineligible, having previously been impeached. She stayed in the background while her husband, "Farmer Jim" ran the state as governor.

At last, in the fall of 1974, Ella Grasso was elected governor of Connecticut without the shadow of a governor husband lurking in the background. In 1976 Dixy Lee Ray was elected governor of the state of Washington. How did the fact that they were women affect their political availability and the way that they governed? Judge for yourself.

Ella Grasso was born in Windsor Locks, Connecticut, the daughter of Italian, Roman Catholic immigrants—her father was a baker and saloon keeper, and her mother worked in a General Electric plant. She won a scholarship to Mount Holyoke and ended up with a masters degree in sociology and economics in 1940— *magna cum laude*. She is married to a doctor and has two children. She joined the League of Women Voters and in 1953 won a seat in the General Assembly. She established close political ties to John Bailey, leader of the Connecticut Democratic organization. Mrs. Grasso served as floor leader in the house and then held the office of secretary of state for twelve years. In 1968 she won a seat in the U.S. Congress that she held until elected governor with 60 percent of the vote in 1974 at age fifty-five. In her campaign she pledged to hold the line against an income tax. Because of the recession she felt she was forced to cut back spending by continuing a wage freeze on state employees and laying off 500 workers. Unions, who had supported her, turned against her. She pushed through a reorganization plan that replaced one hundred agencies with twenty-two new ones. In 1978 prominent leaders were threatening to run candidates against her. But she was reelected.

Dixy Lee Ray was single and sixty-two when elected governor. She was born in Tacoma, Washington, a protestant, graduated from fashionable Mills College and went on to get a Ph.D. in marine biology at Stanford. She taught zoology at the University of Washington and was director of the Pacific Science Center—she showed an interest in ecology concerns before it was fashionable to do so. In August 1972 President Nixon appointed her to the Atomic Energy Commission. Later she became its chairperson. In 1975 she moved to the State Department and then resigned to run for governor as an "antipolitics, shake-up-the-government" candidate. She won with 53 percent of the vote and immediately got into hot water with ecologists and fellow Democrats for backing atomic energy plants in Washington and more oil tankers in the Tacoma harbor. Republicans objected loudly as she methodically replaced every appointee of the previous governor with Democrats. She advocated a progressive state income tax and economy in government.

What we see is one woman who came to the governorship by a slow climb up the political ladder; another who jumped in practically as an independent. Perhaps because expectations were unrealistic, both governors disappointed some of their supporters and got in trouble with the press. Will we have a good many more women governors?

What do you think? Do you think these women, who were the first to achieve the office on their own efforts, faced unusual pressures? Which of their career patterns do you think will be more typical of successful women candidates for governor in the future? How much are these women's careers like those of other male governors of their state? Do women face any special prejudices or handicaps in seeking the governorship?

THE LEGAL FRAMEWORK FOR GUBERNATORIAL LEADERSHIP

An Indiana humorist once observed, "We have had the same governor in Indiana for fifty years. He just changes his name and looks every four years." The implication, of course, is that the person who occupies the executive suite makes no difference. As we will argue later in this chapter, we do not subscribe to this view. We believe that it does matter who the governor is in part because one of the main functions of the office is to provide political leadership. Leadership is a personal quality and some people develop it well, others do not. However, we also find some things about the office that either help or hinder what personal abilities the occupant may have. The most important are the governor's legal powers. We will follow the advice of Leslie Lipson, an Englishman who studied the office of governor in the 1930s. He said, "If you want to understand what the governor has become, study what he was."[13]

Colonial Governors.   The king of England appointed most colonial governors, and so they tended to place their loyalties with the king rather than with the political forces in the colonies. The colonists in turn developed a deep suspicion and mistrust of strong governors. Much of this feeling was directed against the English Crown, but as representatives of the king, the colonial governors became handy local targets.

[13]Leslie Lipson, *From Figurehead to Leader,* University of Chicago Press, Chicago, Illinois, 1939, p. 9.

Colonial governors had a substantial amount of legal power, and they appointed the top administrative and judicial officers. The most important of these appointees formed the upper house of the colonial legislatures. Governors could convene and dissolve the legislatures; they could refuse to sign bills with which they did not agree, and the colonial legislatures had no further legal recourse. The colonists, though, learned to bargain with the governors over policy matters because the governors depended on local taxes for their revenue. But through it all the colonists developed a great dislike and mistrust for strong governors.

Early State Governors. In forming new state governments we might have expected the colonists to do away with an executive altogether. What saved the governor's office, primarily, was the general ineptness of the Continental Congress, the generally ineffective national government that had no executive officer. The colonists agreed on the need for an executive officer, but were determined to keep the executive under close control of legislative assemblies.

In Virginia, for example, the legislature elected the governor annually and no individual was permitted to serve more than three years in a row. The governor could not convene or dissolve the legislature, recommend bills, or veto legislation. In addition, his administrative actions were subject to the approval of an eight-member council of legislators and citizens.

New York and Massachusetts tried a different approach. In both states, the people elected the governors. New York even set a three-year term. Massachusetts gave its governor a limited veto power, but the legislatures retained control over the appointing power and a few states, including Massachusetts, surrounded the governor with an advisory council. Thus, the early state constitutions kept their governors in close check.

Governors and Jacksonian Democracy. The 1820s were years of "discontent, born in depression, shaken by bursts of violence and threats of rebellion."[14] The ideas of Hamilton (that society should be governed by an aristocracy) and Jefferson (that the country should remain rural) had begun to run their course. In 1828 a new American hero, Andrew Jackson, was elected president and a new political "truth" emerged that changed ideas about the value and worth of the common man.

As we noted in earlier chapters, the Jacksonians argued that government should involve as many common people as possible. In practice,

[14]Arthur M. Schlesinger, Jr., *The Age of Jackson*, New American Library, 1957, p. 15.

this meant more elective positions and a turnover in appointive ones. They kept terms of office short, expanded the electorate, and encouraged wider use of the spoils system—the winners turn the losers out of administrative office and appoint their own supporters.

The impact of these ideas on the office of governor was mixed. More governors were directly elected, rather than being chosen by legislatures. Some states even gave their governors the veto power as a check on legislatures and made it more difficult for legislatures to impeach their governors.

On the other hand, the ideas weakened the governor's office by dividing the executive powers among many elected state officials and boards.

Lipson assessed the effect this way, "The new maxim of democracy seemed to be 'Divide your government and it cannot rule you.' In actual fact, the result was to cripple the executive. The chief executive was unable to harm the people, but it was also unable to serve them."[15]

The Age of Protest After the Civil War. In the late 1800s, executive power became even more diffuse. As urban centers grew and industry was organized, farmers' protest movements demanded more governmental protection from and regulation of "the interests." Each new regulation led to the creation of a new board or commission responsible to the legislatures. The net effect was to weaken the gubernatorial power. Both the governors and the legislatures came out of the 1800s considerably weaker than they once were. The power of growing industry and the seemingly prevailing attitude of public officials—"take what you can when you can"—led citizens to place little trust in government.

The Twentieth Century—Expanded Legal Powers for Governors

During the last fifteen years or so before the turn of the century, a new type of progressive reformer began to gain influence—they focused their efforts on strengthening executive officers, both governors and mayors. They wanted to clean up what they saw as a political mess.

With corporate business organizations as the model, and economy and efficiency as the goal, the twentieth century ushered in an era of reforms in state government, and as we noted in Chapter 4, in community governments as well. Many of the reforms, such as those advocated by the Short Ballot Organization and the Scientific Management Movement, strengthened the office of governor.

[15]Leslie Lipson, Op. cit., 23–24.

Governor's Legal Powers in Perspective.   The governor's legal powers should be viewed in perspective to the total social and political milieu in which each individual governor uses them. The other power centers within a state with whom the governor must deal and even compete determine how much the governor may need extensive legal powers.

In large urban states, such as Ohio, private interest groups, such as big labor and big business, have great power resources. The governors must have them, too, if they are merely to hold their own. We can imagine governors of a less urban state, such as Arkansas, as being able to hold their own without as strong legal powers.

Administrative Powers.   The new reformers hoped to create an administrative hierarchy controlled at the top by the governor. Every agency would be placed in a department of agencies having related functions. The total number of departments would be of manageable size—say 20 or so rather than the 100 or more independent agencies then existing.

Most students argue that a marked strengthening of the governor's administrative control has resulted. But the changes are not as great as the reformers hoped. Reorganization may have reduced the influence and meddling of the legislature in day-to-day administration, but it did not eliminate it.[16] Ironically, some governors who have greatest influence over administrative departments owe their influence to control of patronage. We discuss the limits of reorganization further in Chapter 10 on administration.

Appointment and Removal Powers.   In order to achieve their goals, the Short Ballot Organization wanted fewer positions elective and more appointive and responsible to the governor. The organization began a process that still continues. But in only two states, Maine and New Jersey, is the governor the only statewide elected official. Most states also elect the lieutenant governor, secretary of state, attorney general, and state treasurer. Except for the office of state auditor and a few other positions in a few states, legislatures no longer make appointments. State senates, though, continue to exercise their consent powers for high-level appointments. Usually, senate approval is routine.

However, even governors who have broad appointing powers, cannot gain immediate control over all state boards and commissions.

---

[16]Deil S. Wright in "Executive Leadership in State Administration," Beyle and Williams, Op. cit., p. 277, reported on a survey of state administrators in which they indicated that legislatures (44 percent) exercised greater control over agency affairs than the governor (32 percent). Twenty-two percent indicated "each about the same." Thus, reorganization may have reduced legislative influence, but not eliminated it.

Terms of appointees usually are overlapping, and we find that governors must often serve a second term before they can secure a favorable majority on a specific board or commission.

Most governors have the authority to remove persons from positions that they have the authority to fill. But legal and political constraints limit this power, too. Removal proceedings may produce messy publicity. Even permitting the unwanted person to resign can have undesirable consequences.

Office Tenure. Tenure in office is affected by two factors—the length of the term, and the number of times governors may succeed themselves in office.

The length of term has been steadily increasing. Although a few states continued to have one-year terms almost until 1920, the more typical pattern from 1850 on was a two-year term. By 1975 all but four states had extended the term to four years. Most of these extensions took place since 1960.

Twenty-one states still permit their governors to serve only two consecutive terms; six, mostly Deep South and Border states, do not allow the governor back-to- back terms, while the other twenty-three states have no limits on office tenure. Generally the potential for reelection adds to a governor's power since mayors, administrators, and legislators may defy a "lame duck" governor but less frequently one eligible for reelection.

Law Making Powers. As we saw in the preceding chapter, governors have to persuade legislators to enact their programs. The formal powers of the governor in the legislative process, become critical to the overall effectiveness of the governor. In the nineteenth century governors either lacked some of these powers or failed to use them to their own advantage. Of particular note are the governor's power to recommend, to veto, to call legislatures into session, and to develop the executive budget. We deal with each of these later in this chapter.

EXERCISING GUBERNATORIAL LEADERSHIP

The job of governor, we think, is little else if it is not the responsibility to lead and to give direction to the policies of the state. Most citizens want one thing above all else from their governor—leadership! They expect the governor to point the way out of state problems. It is natural that they should. It is what the term governor itself means.

This leadership responsibility means that governors must marshall support in government and outside it in favor of their solutions to the problems and needs of society. National leaders and community officials as well as leaders in the private sector look to them to harness the political, economic, and social resources of the state to bring about a sense of purpose in government policies and actions. Governors, more than any other state official, encourage faith and trust in state government and its legitimacy when they succeed in their task. Conversely, when governors fail, they cause disappointment and cynicism about state government and its capabilities.

Governors Set Goals

Governors can do very little aside from their ability to lead and give direction. They cannot pass laws by themselves, run the department of health or any other, personally know about all the details of a state budget, or create a healthy economy. They have neither enough time nor the technical skills and knowledge to manage all these tasks. They can only intervene from time to time to emphasize the direction in which they feel the state should be moving. In Policy Box No. 16 "Governor Faubus Fights School Integration," we review a case of gubernatorial leadership at a critical time in our nation's history. In this case we see that governors do not always seek change; sometimes they prefer the status quo.

Once having won the office, many governors begin to plan actions that will further their political careers.[17] They know they must build a record of achievement and problem solving. And they must do so quickly as the office of governor is transitory and the tenure rather short.[18]

Building a record by having made important differences in at least one or two areas may provide the basis for reelection or a future public office. Many look forward to the possibility of a presidential appointment or a seat in the U.S. Senate. And, of course, it is not uncommon for the politically ambitious to think about becoming vice-president or president.[19]

[17]At various times ambitious people are both honored and criticized for this personal characteristic. It is well worth remembering, as Schlesinger pointed out, that these ambitions are critical in helping governors maintain their influence and power in the administration and legislature. A person who "may go someplace in politics" may take friends along or keep enemies from rising. See Schlesinger in Beyle and Williams, Op. cit., p. 148.

[18]During the 1960s slightly more than 33 percent served five or more years as governor. Now that most of the states permit at least two four-year terms, the average may rise.

[19]During the 1950s, 1960s, and the 1972 national election, governors did not fare very well in the presidential sweepstakes. Adlai Stevenson of Illinois (1949–53) was the Democratic party nominee in 1952 and 1956. Spiro Agnew of Maryland (1967–69) was the Republican

Conrad © 1975 Los Angeles Times

'Psssssst, Jerry . . . back to your mantra!'

A cartoonist's comment on a governor's presidential ambitions.

However high they may set their goals, achievement depends on their ability to set the "tone" of the administration—a tone that responds to what the governor sees as the needs of the day. Al Smith of New York (1923–29), who said the only "college" he knew was the Fulton Fish Market in New York City where he learned about life, is remembered for having insisted that government show concern and do something about the conditions facing the disadvantaged. Governor "Jerry" Brown of California (1974–) set a more modern goal for government by insisting that it "can't do everything and shouldn't try." In earlier times, governors promised to "attract new industry and create

party nominee for vice-president. George Wallace of Alabama ran as the nominee of the American party in 1968. A number of governors, such as Ronald Reagan and Nelson Rockefeller, also sought the nomination. Most of the nominees though were either U.S. senators or former senators. Perhaps the 1976 experience, when governors or former governors were in the thick of the primary combat for the nomination and when one of them won not only his party's nomination, but the election as well, will stimulate the presidential ambitions of governors in the coming years. Governors' chances for presidential or vice presidential nominations are not necessarily enhanced by long tenure in office. Nearly 80 percent of the "lucky" governors over a 120-year period had less than four years experience. The reverse is true for the "Washington" nominees. Long tenure seems to help senators and representatives win the nomination.

POLICY BOX NO. 16: Governor Faubus Fights School Integration

It was the summer of 1957. The place? Little Rock, Arkansas. The U.S. Supreme Court had ruled in *Brown* v. *Topeka Board of Education* in 1954 that separate schools for whites and blacks were inherently unequal. Public schools, the court said, must be integrated "with all deliberate speed."

The time for integrating Little Rock Central High School had arrived. The superintendent and school board had carefully selected nine black students to be the first to attend the all white school, but they had little reason to expect that it would actually happen. After all, federal court orders had been defied just the previous year; once when Autherine Lucy sought admission to the University of Alabama, and again in Mansfield High School in Texas. Perhaps the federal government would again decide not to meddle in what had always been a state function.

Would violence erupt in Little Rock? Most thought perhaps not, but Mayor Woodrow W. Mann took no chances. He had ordered special training for his 175 police officers. Two FBI investigations turned up little evidence to suggest that violence would occur. But as we know now, and as the world knew then, violence flared on September 21—at six o'clock in the morning, two hours before the nine black students were to attend their first classes at Central High.

Why did it happen? Could it have been avoided? Let us look at the actions of the two main actors in this episode and their possible motivations.

Orval Faubus, then in his third year as governor, had been elected as a moderate on race relations. On August 20 he called U.S. Attorney General Herbert Brownell and asked what the federal government would do if violence broke out. Brownell replied that local police would handle the matter. But on September 6, the night before the blacks were to register, Faubus ordered the state National Guard to surround the high school and went on state TV to announce his action. On September 20, the day before classes were to begin, Governor Faubus, under court order, removed the guard detail. But by daybreak of September 21, "husky young rowdies" were surrounding the high school. Some local citizens charged that Faubus' close friend, Jimmy "the Flash" Karam had rounded up the young whites.

When one of the state's leading citizens, Winthrop Rockefeller (later governor, himself) pleaded with Faubus to support the integration, Faubus responded, "I'm sorry, but I'm already committed. I'm going to run for a third term and if I don't do this, Jim Johnson and Bruce Bennett will tear me to shreds."

Did President Eisenhower mislead Governor Faubus into thinking that the federal government would again let court orders be defied? Eisenhower had said earlier, "It makes no difference what I think about the Brown decision. I . . . must do my very best to see that it is carried out." Many though, believed that "the amiable peace loving warrior who had led the West's great crusade in Europe" was loathe to use federal troops to enforce the law. And in a meeting with Faubus on September 14 in a Rhode Island vacation retreat, the president did not say what he would do if Faubus should prevent the blacks from enrolling in Central High. But on September 21, the president ordered out crack paratroopers of the 101st Airborne Division. They

jobs"; to "stand in the school house door to prevent blacks from entering"; to "give the working man a better chance"; or to "modernize state government." For others the goal may simply be to bring a sense of stability to state government after a period of rapid change. Whatever their aspirations, they must make them a consideration in the state policy process. That is where leadership counts. We will look at such gubernatorial leadership in several areas.

Leadership in Public Opinion

Governors are heads of state in somewhat the same way the president is head of the nation. The governor is the symbol of all state government. As such, governors command a great deal of attention from the politically conscious individuals in the state and its communities as well as from the media. Television and radio newscasts and newspapers are readily available to assist in getting their messages across to the public.

Relating to News Media. Governors typically spend a great deal of time and effort in working with the reporters who cover their activities. Not only do many governors hold daily news conferences, but they provide time for "in-depth" interviews, sit for photographs, respond to reporters' telephone questions, and appear on radio or television panel interview shows. In the meantime staffers write press releases by the score and distribute advance copies of the governor's speeches.

Governors carefully cultivate relations with the capitol press corps. They sometimes entertain reporters and their spouses as a group;

make special efforts to know reporters on a first-name basis; and take care to avoid giving one individual too many (if any) "scoops" and by-passing the capitol corps.[20]

The governor's press secretary.   The job of managing press relations belongs to the governor's press secretary, one of the most important positions on the governor's staff. Press secretaries often become the alter ego of the governor. Governor G. Mennen Williams (Michigan, 1948–60) wrote in his "Notes" after leaving office, "My press secretary was my eye and my ears as well as my voice. He was also no small part of my brain . . . , he developed my ideas as I would have liked to do if I had had the time."[21]

Relating to the Public.   Speaking to groups may not reach many people at one time, but over several years, many people get to see the governor "live" in this way. Moreover such events are reported in the news media. Invitations to speak are numerous and care must be used in refusing invitations.

Governors involve themselves in honoring various occupations and groups by declaring special weeks or days—such as Iowa Garden Clubs Week, or Kentucky Horsebreeder's Week. Usually the statements they send are made at the request of the groups—sometimes the groups themselves prepare the statements for the governor. Governors, however, must be cautious that they do not lend their names to a group that may somehow be politically embarrassing.

The kind of problem that can arise is illustrated by Rudy Perpich, who became Governor of Minnesota in 1977. An opera group, trying to raise funds, asked to auction off a dinner in the governor's mansion. The governor agreed. The winner of the auction was one of Minneapolis' best known "madams" who announced that prostitution for too long had been regarded as unrespectable. Gamely and gracefully, Governor Perpich and his wife went through with their part of the agreement and, with flash bulbs popping, greeted their guest.[22]

Governors tape messages in support of the United Way, fund drives for crippled children, and other charities. They greet touring school

---

[20]William K. Hall, *Illinois Government and Politics*, Kendall/Hunt Publishing Co., Dubuque, Iowa, 1975.

[21]G. Mennen Williams, *A Governor's Notes*, Institute of Public Affairs, University of Michigan, Ann Arbor, Michigan, 1961, pp. 16 and 60.

[22]It is said that reporters asked the madam if meeting such famous persons made her nervous. "No," she replied, "I have already met most of them." Perpich's graceful handling of the situation turned what could have been a minus into a plus.

children and send out hundreds of seasonal greeting cards and congratulatory messages.

Answering the mail that reaches the executive office is another public opinion forming technique. Governors receive letters about all kinds of things: a request for a job for a disabled brother-in-law, a citizen complaint about misuse of a state car, the ineptness of a local office holder, or an appeal for a release from prison.

Governors and their staffs spend a great deal of time on shaping public opinion. Coleman Ransone suggested that it may be as much as half their day's schedule. A study of how Governor Richard Olgilvie of Illinois (1969–73) spent a month in 1971 indicated a lower figure of 27 percent of a day's activities, but still it was more than was given to any other.[23]

Why Public Opinion Is Important.   Why do governors spend so much time on public opinion formation, or public relations? Is it a matter of their continual running for office while they are supposed to be running the affairs of state government? Not really. In these public relations activities the governors are doing three basic things.

First, they are being governor "of all the people." They are permitting themselves to be seen as "head of government." Because much of this activity is nonpartisan it serves to break down the partisan political images created during the campaign and helps to build a public sense of trust and confidence.

Second, the governors are plugging their approach to government, educating the public as to why their approach to community mental health is needed. They are explaining why decaying central cities must have special aid, why taxes must be raised or how a tax increase will be damaging to the state's economy, or why state expenditures have to be cut. So, in effect, the public relations work is educational (or propagandist, depending on your point of view).

Third, the governors are keeping the channels of communication open for feedback from citizens. Not only are the news people important in getting the governor's views published throughout the state, but they are important in terms of the information they can give the governor.

Is it important that the public be convinced or, at least, informed? Can governors not simply make their proposals to the legislature and work quietly in the statehouse twisting arms to gain votes for their policies? Certainly they have to do that, but public opinion is the fuel that

---

[23]Richard D. Michaelson, "An Analysis of the Chief Executive: How a Governor Uses His Time," in William Hall, Op. cit., p. 113.

powers the governor's policymaking clout. Because the office is important, governors get a great deal of space in which to explain their position; and if they have worked their nonpartisan appearances well, they also build a great reservoir of trust and credibility. When it comes to getting support for proposals in the legislature, a governor who has the support of public opinion is tough to beat on the important issues.

Leadership in the Legislature

A governor's record of achievement is made or broken in the state legislature. Governors may set policy goals, make promises, and build hopes for solving problems, but if they cannot persuade the legislature to adopt them, the goals will go unmet and the promises unfilled. Governors, fortunately, have a number of tools they can use to help achieve their purposes in the legislature.

Power to Recommend. State governments are not much given to ceremony, but each year in January when the governors present their State of the State message to the legislature, they do engage in a bit of pomp and circumstance. No bands, mind you, but legislators wear carnations or corsages and a delegation of legislators escorts the governor from the executive office to the podium in the lower chamber. (On these occasions, we suspect, the state fire marshall is sent out of town because the number of people in the house chamber well exceeds the rated capacity.)

After the speech, the governor's friends say that the speech was "Great! Creative! Imaginative!" The opponents invariably say, "It's about what we expected" or, "We didn't hear anything new." The details of the governor's recommendations come later in the form of special messages and the introduction of bills introduced by the governor's allies.

What about the power to recommend; is it worth anything? Most political scientists think it is worth a great deal.

The process of recommendation is much the same for the governor as for anyone presenting a proposal. Governors (really their staffs, department heads, or friends) define the problem, study possible solutions, and choose one. They bolster the solution with facts and figures. The legislators who typically do not have similar resources of expertise and facts, often have difficulty challenging the force of well-developed proposals or coming up with reasonable alternatives.

Importance of recommending. What have governors done with their power to recommend? First, they have told the legislature what items the governor wants on the agenda. Second, with a good sense of timing and public relations, the governor sets the schedule for the legislators. Third, the governor may put the legislature in a defensive position. If the legislators do not act they have to explain why. Later in this chapter we will turn to one of the governor's most important areas of recommendation, the state budget.

Lobbying the Legislature.   Governors, unlike quarterbacks who hand the ball off to a running back and watch him go off into the line, exercise a great amount of follow through on their proposals. The executive office staff heavily lobbies the legislature for support of the governor's proposals.

The election of legislative leadership and committee chairmanships may be the first matter that the governor tries to influence because it is important that the governor and the leadership be able to cooperate easily and that they have similar views. Influencing leadership selection must be done very delicately by the governor, but in the end he or she must accept the people chosen and try to work with them. When the legislative majority is controlled by an opposing party or faction, governors, of course, may have little or no voice in who gets the leadership positions.

Typically governors try to develop friendly relations with the members of both parties. Such friendship is built on a composite of many small things. For example, the governor may invite sponsors to the "front office" for a bill-signing ceremony. (This may result in a picture in the local paper.) Friendliness may be a matter of publicly complimenting a legislator, meeting with legislators about local problems, checking with legislators about nominations for positions, or appointing to state commissions and other jobs people whom a legislator recommends. Governors have a number of perquisites that they can share, and they share them purposively.

But executive lobbying involves more than "passing out the perks." It is a matter of hour-to-hour communicating with legislators on the governor's bills. The governor's staff do most of this. They speak for the governor, state his or her views on proposed amendments, negotiate the difficult problems, offer the assistance of the departments when required and, very infrequently, may threaten an incumbent of their party with primary opposition if the legislator "doesn't come around."

Do governors engage in such matters personally? Sometimes, governors attend party caucuses, but rarely do governors appear in the legislative chambers, except by invitation. We recall, however, when Governor G. Mennen Williams (Michigan 1948–60) sat on the davenport at the rear of the state senate chamber one evening, when the senate was voting on a personal income tax, to meet with legislators "at their convenience." Governor Nelson Rockefeller of New York was also known as an "arm twister."[24] We discuss the governor's leadership of his party in the legislature in Chapter 13.

Calling Special Sessions.   The formal rules regarding the calling of special sessions offer governors another tool for working their way with legislatures. If during the regular session, the legislature fails to complete its work, the governor may decide to call a special session. Often the governor may specify the matters that may be considered in the special session. It is true that the legislators do not have to pass the measures put on the agenda by the governor, but if they fail to do so they run the risk of being called back again. Part-time legislators may not like leaving their farms or businesses, summer resorts, or deer-hunting camps to spend ten or fifteen days at the state capitol in a special session. Hence the threat of a special session is often adequate incentive for legislators to resolve their differences with the governor. Full-time legislatures can counter the special-session-calling powers by keeping the legislature officially in session the year around.

We note, however, that calling special sessions also involves risks for the governors. The governor may look weak, if the legislature refuses to approve the governor's proposals. In addition, the legislature may also decide to take up other matters after handling the governor's items. The governor may object to these additional matters.

The Veto.   Governor Otto Kerner (Illinois 1961–68) called the veto the "most direct and important of his legislative powers."[25] Without doubt it is a formidable weapon. Only the governor of North Carolina must make do without it. Its basic use, of course, is to prevent something from being enacted; but through skillful use, it can produce positive results. Governors and their staff often use the threat of veto to get change in a bill before it is passed.

Use of veto power, we find, varies widely. For example, during 1971 to 1972, of almost 55,000 measures adopted in all states, governors vetoed 3.9 percent, or about 2200. However, four states accounted for only 20 percent of the measures passed, but 61 percent of the vetoes, or 1320. In contrast, twenty-three states passed 42 percent of the measures and had only 12.2 percent of the vetoes. The four states (California, Connecticut, Illinois, and New York) had an average veto rate of 12

[24]Eugene J. Gleason and Joseph Zimmerman, "The Strong Governorship: Status and Problems—New York," *Public Administration Review*, January/February 1976, p. 93.

[25]The *Office of Governor*, Institute of Government and Public Affairs, University of Illinois, 1963, p. 86.

percent compared with about 1 percent for the twenty-three states. What explains these wide variations?

What we find is that low or high use does not indicate much by itself. For example, Governor G. Mennen Williams (Michigan 1948–60) did not use the veto very often. Yet it was an effective tool for him. He observed that "even the most conservative Republican knew it was pointless to introduce a right-to-work law while I was governor."[26]

The most common vote requirement for override is a two-thirds vote by each house. A few others set the figure at three-fifths or a majority, Alaska has a three-quarter vote requirement.

The number of overrides is very small—less than 2 percent of vetoes were overridden in the 1971 to 1972 biennium in all fifty states.[27]

Because so few vetoes are overridden governors can often use the veto effectively as a threat, without its registering on a governor's score sheet. And, of course, all threats are not necessarily public. Often governors use veiled threats rather than definitive promises to veto. Definitive and public threats may result in a game of "chicken" where legislatures pass the bill, get themselves off the hook, and put the governor on one.

We would probably not consider high veto rates to be an indication of cooperation between a legislature and the governor. Yet precisely that kind of relationship exists in New York and California. Many of the vetoes are applied to local or private acts—acts affecting only one community or an individual with a claim against the state. Such bills are passed more or less as a favor to the sponsor with the understanding the governor will veto them. Until 1976, the New York legislature had not overridden a veto in more than 100 years. In this respect, at least, the high veto score does not indicate executive-legislative conflict.

Item veto. The veto power is modeled after the president's power, but the states have added a few "wrinkles" so that some governors' veto power is stronger than that of the president. One of these is the item veto. It permits a governor to strike out portions of appropriations bills without killing the entire bill, unlike the president who must make "all or nothing" decisions. Governors in only seven states do not have an item veto, and of these, four are New England states.

[26]G. Mennen Williams, Op. cit., p. 8.

[27]*Book of the States, 1974–75*, Op. cit. The most thorough analysis of vetoes and overrides that we know of was done by Frank W. Prescott in "The Executive Veto in American States," *Western Political Quarterly*, 3 (March 1950) 98–112. Should you need to know about these matters for a specific state, we suggest you write the Legislative Service Bureau at the state capital.

The item veto in Wisconsin goes a bit further. Wisconsin governors have used their power to strike out parts of sentences or even individual words. Governor Patrick Lucey (1971–77), for example, struck out the word "not" in the phrase "not less than 50 percent" in a bill having to do with funds to promote tourism. In doing so, he changed a 50 percent "floor" on state participation in cooperative advertising to a 50 percent "ceiling." On another occasion Governor Lucey crossed out the "2" from a $25 million highway bonding bill thus reducing the authorization to $5 million. But in this case the state attorney general later ruled this an improper use of the item veto.[28]

Expenditure reduction. Governors of eight states have the authority to reduce appropriations.[29] The power to reduce expenditure items, of course, may not be very helpful to a governor who thinks legislative appropriations are too low. But for a governor, such as Michael Dukakis (Massachusetts 1974–78) who thought welfare spending was too high, or Governor Jerry Brown (California 1974–) who thinks overall state spending is excessive, this power makes them the virtual gatekeeper of state funds.

Executive amendment. Four governors have an executive amendment veto power (Alabama, Massachusetts, New Jersey, and Virginia), that permits a governor to return a bill to the legislature with suggestions for change. The legislature can then act on the suggestions, but may make no further changes. The governors' suggestions in most of these states are regularly adopted. The same kind of procedure can be used by governors in other states on an informal basis.[30]

Leadership Over State Finances

The executive budget—one of the principal reforms of the twentieth century that strengthened the executive officers—gave governors a strong leadership role over state finances and, therefore, over state programs. The executive budget did the same for executives in city and county governments. Spending choices are policy choices.

The executive budget, of course, does not mean that governors have complete control over state revenue and spending plans. Technically it

[28]Wisconsin Legislative Reference Bureau, *The Use of the Partial Veto in Wisconsin*, Informational Bulletin, 75-IB-6, 1975, p. 4.

[29]The eight states are: Alaska, California, Hawaii, Massachusetts, Missouri, New Jersey, Pennsylvania and Tennessee. *Book of the States, 1974–75*, 80–81.

[30]Coleman B. Ransone, Jr., *The Office of the Governor in the United States*, University of Alabama Press, University, Alabama, 1956, 182–184.

means that the governor only recommends to the legislature a comprehensive revenue and spending plan. The legislators must then act upon those recommendations, and while it can make changes in the proposed budget, it is significant that they tend not to stray very far from the budget recommendations. If they appropriate funds far in excess of a governor's plan, legislators may have to raise taxes to pay for them. If they try to appropriate much less than a governor recommends, the various interest groups lobby the legislators for at least what the governor recommended. Moreover as we have seen, most governors can enforce their budget recommendations with the use of their veto powers. In recent years a few states have created legislative fiscal agencies as part of the legislative staff. These agencies develop their own revenue forecasts and set general overall spending limits. They interview agency heads just as the governor's budget examiners do. The budget figures recommended by the legislative budget office are then compared to those in the governor's budget at the time of budget hearings. Whether this procedure will develop into a legislative budget-making process and this change the balance of power between governor and legislature has yet to be determined.

In the next few pages, we will review the general framework of budgeting in the states. In the chapter on administrators, we will discuss budgeting again and we will consider it as a means of controlling the administrators.

The Budget Cycle. In small organizations, such as a small city or village, the budget cycle may be very informal, and may require only a few weeks in planning. The larger the organization and the more complex its financial structure, the longer the time period needed to plan the budget.

We find that most states begin the budget cycle in August when the budget bureau decides on the budget request forms and the instructions that will be used. If the state printer can meet the deadlines, the agencies will receive the forms and instructions about the middle of September. Agency heads will have about forty-five days to decide what new programs or program expansions they should request and to calculate how much programs will cost. Typically, they must predict the effect of inflation, how much to spend on salaries, and how many students, welfare clients, prisoners, and so on, they will have to serve in the coming fiscal year. They translate this information into budget requests and forward the forms to the budget bureau, where budget examiners study them.

Sometime during November the budget examiners will meet with the agency heads to question them about specific items. Then the budget bureau develops tentative recommendations. Almost without exception their figures are lower than the agency requests. Meanwhile other specialists are putting some final touches on state revenue estimates. The budget director presents the two reports to the governor for review and final decisions.

The governor's imprint on the budget. As a general rule, these documents are too voluminous and executive time too limited for governors to do much more than examine a summary of the budget they will propose. They, of course, will give special attention to new program proposals that they have asked their staffs to develop, as well as to those areas that are politically sensitive, or that have special problems. Certainly the governors will also want to be well informed about agencies in line for more than the average increase.

The governor's budget then is largely the product of the agencies and administrators' programs funded by state government—budget requests that are adjusted by the governor's budget staff. Moreover there are many items that determine budget levels that the governor can do little about—welfare caseload, number of public school children, unemployment, number of state prisoners, and in some states, even the size of the pay increase for state employees—and, therefore, is unable to control costs of government. We might wonder how a governor can affect the budget under such circumstances. Governors make their personal imprint on the state budget largely with marginal changes—those decisions that give some programs a greater than average increase, and others less, as well as those proposals that the governor rejects altogether. A second major way for the governor to set a budgetary tone is through tax decisions—tax increase, no tax increase, or tax decrease.

The legislature's responsibility. After the governor has reviewed and approved the budget, it is time for the state printer to get ready for another rush job, because soon after the legislature reconvenes in January, its members get copies of the governor's proposed budget.

The legislature breaks the governor's budget down into several appropriations bills—they are introduced and referred to the finance committee. Usually the two houses divide the work—the senate appropriations committee gets certain bills, and the house ways and means committee gets the others.

Because the governor's recommendations are usually lower than what the agency head requested, legislators face demands for increases. Agency heads appointed by the governor face a dilemma. They must be loyal to the governor, but at the same time they want additional funds for their departments. But not all administrators face this problem. People not responsible to the governor—college and university presidents, school superintendents, public employee union representatives, the big city mayors, and others—unabashedly tell the legislative committees why they must have more.

The committees hear them out, listen to the suggestions of committee staff, and with the guidance of the committee chairpersons, work out the amounts that most of the members can agree to. The bills must then be approved by the full house or senate where lobbyists pressure for floor amendments if they did not get their way in the committee. The bills are sent over to the other house, where the process is repeated, often with less intensity. What we find, however, is that the sum of all the bills generally exceeds revenue estimates. This means that cuts have to be made. And, because the two houses seldom agree with the amounts approved by the other, the bills go to conference committee where the deals on the state's budget are made. Often legislative leaders let the pressure build until the last few days of the session—"if the members want to go home, they have to vote the appropriations measures."

Further gubernatorial control. At this point the budget process is nearly completed. All that is needed is the governor's signature on the bills. However, the governor may also veto them or veto certain items.

The governors in many states also have an opportunity to change the budget if revenues collected turn out to be lower than estimated. In this case some governors may make spending cutbacks or, by executive order subject to legislative approval, reduce appropriations. In addition, if appropriations prove less than adequate, agencies, with gubernatorial support, may request a supplemental appropriation later on during the fiscal year.

Lobbying the Budget Makers. The groups and interests, both in the government and outside, who compete for benefits, soon learn where, when, and how to apply pressure to increase or decrease expenditures. They know the schedule followed in budget preparation. At times the pressure points are within the bureaucracy and agencies, at other times it is important to "get the ear of the governor." On other occasions, "sensitizing" the right legislators is important. But because the governor initiates the process and has some important tools to get his or her recommendations adopted, the governor provides the key leadership over state finances.

Leadership in the Executive Branch

The executive branch should be considered "home" for the governor. But as we have noted, governors face problems in controlling the executive branch. State constitutions vest governors with the *chief* executive power, implying that there may be executive powers granted to others. Indeed there are! We begin by focusing on those who are near the center of executive power and then briefly discuss those at the outer edges of it.

The Governor's Staff. The job of governor could prove lonely and discouraging if governors were not surrounded by a small cadre of loyal, dedicated, and mostly anonymous men and women who are the "governor's staff." Some staff members may have gone through the campaign with the governor, but the usual requirements for political appointment—size of political contributions, party loyalty, and place of residence—are not the most important considerations for recruiting staff.

The key requirements are a willingness to work long hours, put the needs of the governor above your own, work with little or no personal credit from outside the governor's office, take the blame and absorb the shock when mistakes are made, and accept a policy decision once it is made.

You had better be satisfied with less than a well-furnished plush office, too. Unless your state has a new capitol, the chances are your office will be a glassed cubicle, a room under a stairwell, or worse yet, a large closet. It is not that the staff is not respected. It is just that when most capitols were built, governors' staffs consisted of a secretary and, perhaps, one assistant. And so, modern day staff has to make do.

Who are the staff people? Mostly, executive staffers are people who like to be at the center of things. At least one will be an experienced political operative. This person is likely to be the head of the staff, the executive secretary.

Several lawyers are also likely to be recruited. One of them will be the governor's legal counselor, to advise the governor on laws that have been enacted, as well as on requests for pardon and interstate rendition. (See Chapter 3) The academic types will include junior professors who want to get an inside view or graduate students in between degrees—Hamilton Jordan of Jimmy Carter's Georgia staff, for example. Not least among the group are journalists, one of whom will be the press secretary. Most of the staff are not covered by the state merit system. The exception is the state troopers who protect the governor's life and chauffeur him or her around the state.

What the staff people do. The staff functions as extension of the governor. In medium- and large-size states, the less experienced staff members will have responsibility for one or more policy areas or state agencies. They keep track of the agency's problems, what new programs it is working on, and new legislation it might be proposing. They must be alert to problems on the horizon that may be damaging to the governor, as well as matters that may go to the governor's credit. They organize information about the agency for the governor's speeches. Others on the staff will serve as liaison with the legislature and special boards and commissions. Still others will work on special problems, such as equal employment opportunity programs. They also check out citizens' complaints and write letters over their own signature (if they cannot help), or over the governor's (if the answer is "yes.").

The staff is very interested in the career of the "boss." Their own careers may take spectacular jumps. Even if the governor only continues in office, their career prospects are not dim. The governor may appoint them to head up a department, or to some other prestigious office in state government. Short of that, the many contacts that the governor has around the state will be used to assure beneficial career placement for years of loyal service.

Management and Budget Department.   A step or two away from the governor's staff, in terms of responsiveness to the executive leadership, is the department of management and budget. This department typically directs the staff functions of state government—those services that affect primarily the government agencies, such as central purchasing, personnel, building management, and construction. But its most important responsibility is to develop and administer the state budget. Although this agency may be staffed by permanent or merit employees, the people in it typically see themselves as being loyal to the governor's office, if not to the current occupant.

The director of the department or, in some states, the director of the budget, is usually the governor's appointee. Because, as we have seen, the governor's role is central to the budget process, few other positions in state government have the potential for making a success or shambles of a governor's administration. Not only does this agency control the information about critical state finances, but it usually screens program proposals from other departments. Governors depend on the budget-making skills to translate the leadership "tone" into policies. Governors must be able to view this department as an extension of their own personal staff.

Other Departments.   More distant from the governor's influence are other agencies. Welfare, mental health services, or those handling economic development will be fairly responsive. Those that are headed by an elected official or by a board or commission (even if the members are appointed by the governor), or funded by earmarked funds will be less sensitive to the governor's wishes.

Elected State Officials.   We find it symbolic that we see the picture of an elected official such as the secretary of state on the wall in some departments where in other departments we find the governor's picture. It serves as a silent reminder to employees of who is in charge in such offices.

The four or five officers that many states elect are likely to be responsive to the governor's leadership only if the governor has a firm grasp on public opinion or the reins of the political party, and if the officers belong to the governor's party or faction. These state officials may even be deadly political opponents of the governor.

Lieutenant governors.   Forty-one states have popularly elected lieutenant governors. Utah's secretary of state is also the lieutenant governor. The other states do not provide for the office. In twenty-two states during 1978, the governor and lieutenant governor could have been members of different political parties. Gradually, the states are moving to elect these officers jointly, as is done with the president and vice president.

Typically lieutenant governors have few constitutional duties. In some states they function as president of the state senate and serve as governor when the governor is absent. In either capacity lieutenant governors can be a problem for governors, should they be of differing parties.

In 1963, for example, Governor George Romney was on a three-week vacation and upon his return to Michigan found the newspapers full of reports by Lieutenant Governor T. John Lesinski on the accomplishments of his acting governorship. Everyone, except possibly Governor Romney, found the stories quite amusing. He, in fact, promised publicly not to leave the state again while Lesinski was lieutenant governor.

Attorneys general.   The attorneys general serve as the state's lawyers, as well as its chief crime fighters. They can be important contenders with the governor for space in the news media and public attention and, as we noted earlier, perhaps for the executive suite itself. Beyond that, the ruling of the attorney general on the fine points of the law can prove troublesome and embarrassing to a governor. In 1974 Governor Richard Ogilvie (Illinois, 1969–73) attempted to overcome this problem by appointing lawyers who would be responsible to him, rather than to the attorney general. The attorney general, who controlled some 200 patronage positions, ruled the action unconstitutional and the governor had to back down.

Secretaries of state.   These officers probably spell less political trouble for the governor than the attorney general and lieutenant governor. But secretaries of state usually have their names printed on drivers' licenses and other documents and as a result are widely recognized in the state. Often they also control many patronage appointments in branch offices that issue driver licenses and auto license plates. Both of these facts can be used to further political ambitions.

These officers can make things difficult for ballot petitioners, and in some states determine (within limits) whose name will appear on presidential primary ballots. Most of their duties, though, are routine and detailed in the law, so their powers in the sensitive area of elections are limited.

Leadership In The Party

People in politics, governors among them, generally have sufficient opposition from the opposite party (or faction in one-party states) and do not seek any more from within their own party. Thus, while governors may not seek to dominate the party, most will make an effort to nurture the good will of party leaders. The enthusiasm and vigor of a governor in party matters depends mostly on how parties figure in the winning and the losing of state elections. As we will see in Chapter 13, candidates who win the nomination and even the office with little or no party support may be difficult for the party to control.

We look at the governor as the head of the state political party largely because the governor is the top elected official in the state. But there are other possible party leaders. One is a U.S. senator. Although away in Washington a good part of the time, the senators often have more than a passing interest in the state party organization. An example is Senator Hugh Scott of Pennsylvania, who in 1962 outmaneuvered the conservative wing of his party to secure the nomination of William Scranton as governor. While he had to threaten to run for governor himself in that fight, he won and kept his party liberal enough to ensure his own reelection in 1964 and 1970.

Other possible leaders of a state political party are people who have not even held state office. Richard Daley, mayor of Chicago, for example, dominated Illinois Democrats for two decades.

Party leadership is earned and having a reputation for winning elections helps. As a "boy wonder with a bow tie," G. Mennen Williams eventually gained control of the Michigan Democratic party by winning the governorship six times and bringing others into state office with him.

Governors earn their leadership posts in the state party by tending to party chores. Taking care of patronage matters is important in some states. Attending fund raisers, helping others in their campaigns for election, and honoring the county chairpersons by notifying them when they will be in the county are some of the ways party leadership is earned. The ease or difficulty with which leadership is attained depends to a large degree on how strong the other party leaders are. It is said that Republican governors in Illinois got along better with Mayor Daley than did most Democratic governors. Perhaps it was so because the Republicans did not threaten Daley's control over the Democratic party.

Is Party Leadership Important?   How important is party leadership to a governor? On balance, it is probably not the most important area of leadership, although it does depend on a governor's goals and standing with the general public. If governors want to wield power in national conventions they must have control of the party's delegates. If they plan to remain governor for several terms it is helpful to control the party sufficiently to cut down primary opposition and to get party support in the legislature on important questions. Having control of the party can be important in legislative battles. In 1977 Governor William Milliken (Michigan, 1969–) lost a battle over legislative-executive powers regarding administrative rule procedures when some of his Republican legislators voted to override his veto. Had Milliken had stronger control over his party, especially at the county level, these legislators may not have dared to challenge the governor on what was a sensitive point.

Leadership In Inter-governmental Relations

We find at least four levels on which governors deal with other governments—local governments in the state, other states, the national government, and with governments of other countries. Strictly speaking, the last of these is the constitutional domain of the national government. But governors often lead state international trade missions and become involved with foreign governments. More recently, governors have been busy "selling" their states to foreign manufacturing concerns, who are considering where to locate plants.

Relations with the National Government.   When Governor Hugh Carey (New York, 1974–), a fourteen-year veteran as a member in the U.S. House of Representatives, ran for governor he said he wanted his governorship "to help shape national policy." Governors, individually, however are not very influential in national policymaking. As Governor Carey soon learned, there are too many matters within the state that demand attention and there is little time left to help Washington.

However, governors have several avenues for dealing with the federal government. One of these, as we discussed, is through presidential politics. A recent outstanding example was the role Governor George Wallace (Alabama, 1963-67, 1971-79) played in the 1968 and 1972 presidential elections. His ability to articulate popular feelings against "big government" and win presidential primaries in northern states not only influenced the policies of the Democratic party, but the Republican party as well. President Nixon, for example, used some of the Wallace rhetoric ("pointy-headed bureaucrats") in arguing support for his revenue-sharing proposal.[31] Jimmy Carter also picked up the Wallace themes in more refined and polished language during the 1976 presidential election.

The National Governors' Conference provides a second vehicle for governors to use to influence policies of the federal government. Governor Woodrow Wilson, (New Jersey, 1911-13 and later, president) at the founding of the Conference in 1908, stated that they were creating an ". . . instrument, not of legislation, but of opinion, exercising the authority of influence, not of law."[32] The Conference, acts through policy statements voted on by its members.

The National Governors' Conference has influenced federal policy decisions, as Wilson predicted it would. Many of their issues revolve around the question of state power. During World War II, for example, President Roosevelt nationalized the employment security program. After the war, pressure from the conference helped return parts of what became a federal-state cooperative program to the states.[33]

On the question of how the federal government should relate to the cities—directly, or indirectly through state capitals—the Conference has been consistent. The governors do not like to have the federal government deal directly with their cities. This question was important in adoption of the general revenue sharing proposal in 1972.

Governors also meet in regional conferences, such as the Southern Governors' Conference or the Midwest Governors' Conference. These meetings focus more on interstate problems within the region, rather than on relationships with Washington.

Governors, of course, are not limited to working through such organizations to exercise influence and leadership in Washington. They can and often do work directly through their congressional delegation in Washington, not only to lobby them for changes in law and policy, but to get them to intercede on problems that a state has with a federal bureaucracy. Some of the governors locate a part of their staff in the

[31]Richard E. Thompson, *Revenue Sharing: A New Era in Federalism?* Revenue Sharing Advisory Service, Washington, 1973, p. 39.

[32]Glen Brooks, *When Governors Convene*, John Hopkins Press, Baltimore, 1961, p. xii.

[33]Glen Brooks, Op. cit., p. 63.

state's Washington office to look after the state's interests in the nation's capital.[34]

A Final Comment

When all is said and done, when we have examined all the fine points of the legal arrangements of the governors' offices, when we have analyzed the politics that apply in each state, does it matter who is governor? Does it make a difference? Or, are politics and policy outcomes, as Thomas Dye and some others suggest, mostly determined by the level of economic development in the state? Can a governor make a difference?

In Chapter 2 we suggested that the environment of politics—geography, wealth, and population—sets boundaries on what is possible. But individuals, through politics, process these raw materials into state policy.

Governors, we think, are an integral part of the political system in each of the states, and who is governor does make a difference. In large part, the difference results from the "tone" of leadership that the governors establish, rather than their just pet ideas or policies. (Remember the Policy Box on Governor Faubus? Would a different person in the situation have made a difference in the outcome of the Little Rock episode?) Governors, by their actions and words, encourage some ideas to arise and be pushed into policy status, while they let others disappear or prevent them from surfacing. To a substantial degree, of course, the tone determines what kind of people governors will surround themselves with, which in turn influences which ideas will get consideration and which ones will not.

We illustrate with Ohio's experience with several governors over a period of time. During the period 1950 to 1976, Ohio's tax effort dropped from forty-first in the nation to forty-seventh. It was also forty-eighth among the states in education, forty-third in health and hospitals, thirty-eighth in public welfare, and forty-sixth in mental health. Frank J. Lausche was governor of Ohio from 1944 to 1956 and held the state to a strict frugal and conservative "pay-as-you-go" philosophy during the entire period. Michael DiSalle (1959–63) advocated tax increases to make some modest improvement in the state's education, mental health, and welfare programs, but was defeated by James Rhodes (1963–71, 1975–) who promised "no new taxes."

Governor Rhodes kept his promise not to raise taxes, at least while he was governor. Instead he pushed a $2 billion bonding program that,

[34]Deil S. Wright, "Governors, Grants, and the Intergovernmental System" in Thad Beyle and J. Oliver Williams, editors, Op. cit., p. 191.

of course, would eventually have to be repaid. Moreover money would be needed to finance the operating costs of the facilities once they were built. But that would be well beyond his term as governor and his successors could deal with that problem.

In 1971 not only did Governor John Gilligan (1971–1975) promise to raise taxes in Ohio, he made the need for raising taxes a major plank in his campaign platform. His first budget was nearly 50 percent higher than Rhodes' last budget.

In the case of Ohio, considering its wealth, the state could not long tolerate its low spending level in education and the social services—Rhodes' bonding program was evidence of this. But we would argue that Rhodes, with his policy of no new taxes, made a difference in how the state was to finance its needs. Had he remained in office, it seems likely to us that when tax increases were unavoidable, he would have pursued a different tax policy than Governor Gilligan, who led and won the fight for a progressive income tax.[35] Our conclusion is that who is governor does matter.

HIGHPOINTS OF CHAPTER 8: GOVERNORS AS STATE LEADERS

In this chapter we examined three main considerations. In the first— Who gets to be governor?—we found (1) that they are people who are politically ambitious, (2) experienced in politics, and (3) that they gain this experience most often in the legislature. We also found (4) that personal characteristics, such as education, personal wealth, attractiveness, and nongovernment occupations are likely to make a difference in one's chances of being governor.

In our discussion of the development of governors as state leaders, we found (5) that governors during the nineteenth century were weak and largely uninfluential, and (6) that through various reforms, the governors of the twentieth century were gradually able to gain power and direction over their state governments. Governors, we found in our third area of discussion, (7) exercise their leadership powers in several arenas: the legislature, in public opinion, over state financial policy, in the executive branch, and in the political party, as well as in national and regional governors' organizations.

We closed by noting (8) that governors can be influential in state policymaking, and to the extent they are, it makes a difference who the governor is.

[35]As it turned out, Rhodes defeated Gilligan in the 1974 election and won reelection in 1978. And so Rhodes gets to oversee the spending of taxes that Gilligan's program now raises.

9

STATE AND COMMUNITY JUDGES AS LEGITIMIZERS

The primary role of judges is to "legitimize" the way laws are applied to individuals. The judges govern the process by which individuals are legally deprived of liberty (and sometimes life itself) and property, as well as to resolve the many disputes that arise between individuals in a complex society. They tell us whether the actions and decisions of the legislature and executive departments at state and community levels are consistent with the national and state constitutions and thus legal. They also tell us which law takes precedence in the event of a conflict between two of them.

Because of their role as legitimizers and resolvers of disputes ideally these judicial officials and the courts maintain a high degree of freedom from outside partisan political influences. They seek to inspire trust and confidence in their impartiality symbolically by wearing black robes, and often by following detailed rituals in handling cases, a personal demeanor that demands their being uninvolved in partisan politics. It is essential that most of us as citizens believe the judges and courts to be worthy of our trust and confidence for if we do not there can be no rule by law—only force and special privilege remain.

Alexander Hamilton observed in the *Federalist Papers* that

judges would not make policy. He assumed they would have "neither the force nor will, but merely judgment." In a legal and technical sense, of course, Hamilton was right. But in a practical sense, he was "dead wrong." As we will see in this chapter, state and federal judges are major policymakers—on some matters *the* major policymakers—in the American system of government.

Judges, of course, are policymakers of a special sort. Judges are less subject to overt and direct political pressures than are other state and community officials. But, because they make so many final decisions on what are political issues, there are pressures. The public, special interest groups, other public officials, and their colleagues in the legal profession exert their pressures on the judges, and often with great effectiveness. In this chapter we will examine the political environment of judicial administration and the political behavior of judges.

Overview. We begin by examining the organization of the fifty-state court systems noting the tendency to diversity. We next look at the way United States Supreme Court decisions have brought the courts together, enforcing the same body of law in many functional areas. We then look at the politics of the judiciary, noting the political pressures both from without and within the judicial system that judges face. Finally we look at the limitations on judicial policymaking, noting the effect of institutional constraints, as well as the influence of public opinion.

THE ORGANIZATION OF THE STATE COURT SYSTEMS

The nation's court systems are a paradox. We find endless diversity on the surface—a diversity we might expect in a federal system. The diversity is in the organization. In all we see 17,000 state and local courts—the states vary widely in the way they organize their courts, define the court jurisdictions, and choose the judges to operate them.

But below all this diversity we see a growing unity in our courts. The unity we find comes about through that important aspect of intergovernmental relations—the application of U.S. Supreme Court interpretations to state and community constitutions, charters and laws. Not only the judges of the federal circuit and district courts, but the judges of the state and local courts as well, are bound to apply the principles of these national court decisions to cases they decide. As the state and local judges consider the state constitutional provisions, state laws, and local ordinances within the constraints of national

court rulings, they are creating a unified judicial system with many important aspects of diversity. We meet again the familiar pattern of change from dual federalism to a centralizing federal system.

STRUCTURE AND JURISDICTION OF STATE AND LOCAL COURTS

We can classify the state and community courts into two categories according to their principal functions—those courts that have original jurisdiction, and those whose main task is to review appeals from decisions of other courts.

Original Jurisdiction. As a general rule the states have three main kinds of courts of original jurisdiction. At the first level we find those that handle minor cases—local courts of limited jurisdiction, such as the justice of the peace courts or municipal courts. In the states that have reorganized their court systems, we find such minor courts have somewhat broader jurisdiction but still have limits on the kinds of cases they may handle.

At the second level are general trial courts that try most of the major state cases. These courts are the "workhorses" of the state court systems where people accused of felonies or major crimes are first tried, and where the civil suits—disputes between citizens or a citizen and the state or local government—are decided in the first instance.

The third type with original jurisdiction are the courts of special jurisdiction. They are family, probate or surrogate courts that handle divorce problems, child custody cases, the settlement of wills and estates, and crimes committed by juveniles.

The Appeals Courts.   All states have an appeals court system as well. The court of last resort in each state is usually called the state supreme court—its main responsibility is to review cases brought to it on appeal. But we find that these courts are also the top management center for the entire state court system. In a growing number of states, an intermediate appeals court also exists, through which most appeals must be channeled before being considered by the state's highest court.

The Minor Courts

States have used many names for their minor courts and even within a single state we find variations. The names do not always tell us the standing of the court. Typically the lower level courts are municipal and justice of the peace courts. Along with them we might also add small claims courts, common plea courts (although Ohio and Pennsylvania use this term to designate their general trial courts), magistrate courts, police courts, and county courts. The term "district court" may designate a lower or minor court in some states, but it refers to a general trial court in a number of other states.

The Jurisdiction of the Minor Courts.   Limitations on jurisdiction and penalties distinguish these courts from the others. As a general rule we find that the courts at the lowest level in the community—the city, village, or rural township—deal with minor state crimes (misdemeanor offenses) and sometimes with low level felonies and violations of municipal ordinances.

Legislatures also define a minor court's limits by the sentence that such courts may impose—typically criminal cases for which the maximum sentence is a year or less. These courts, however, also become in-

TABLE 9-1. Chart of Kentucky's Reorganized Court Compared to New York's Court System

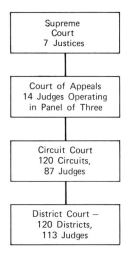

NOTE: Before reorganization, Kentucky had 594 courts—1 supreme court, 120 major trial courts, and 493 courts of limited and special jurisdiction.

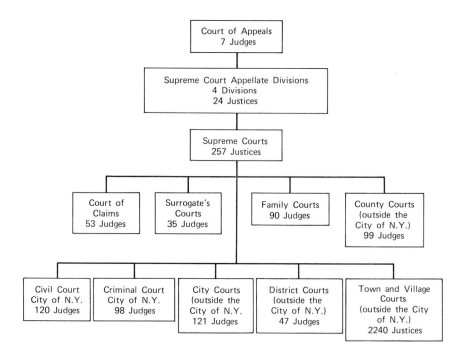

volved in major criminal cases through arraignment proceedings in which they determine that a crime was committed and that the evidence against the person charged is sufficient to "bind the person over for trial" in the general trial court. The judge conducting the hearing, in most instances, also sets the bail.

The minor courts also have jurisdiction in minor civil disputes—cases such as in problems of bill collection or landlord-tenant fights over how much of a damage deposit should be returned. Again the minor courts may consider only cases where the dollar amount in dispute is relatively small. The limits may be as low as $500, as they are in Colorado, to as high as $20,000, as they are in Maine. (Minor courts with high limits are most likely to be part of a reorganized state system where the judge must be a lawyer.)

The Quality of Minor Courts. Courts of limited jurisdiction may also be known as "inferior courts." H. Ted Rubin states that they can well be so-called because (1) The judge is not always required to be a lawyer, may receive an inferior salary and may work in poor physical surroundings. (2) In addition, these courts may not make a verbatim record of the proceedings, and (3) appeals from minor court decisions are typically heard in a general trial court, not in a state's appellate court system.[1]

That we can accurately describe so many minor courts in this way is of some significance. These courts process perhaps as much as 90 percent of the criminal cases of the nation.[2]

Moreover the decisions of these minor court judges do not involve only middle class Americans pleading guilty to speeding tickets. This is where "justice" is doled out to the poor—the drunk and disorderly, vagrants, prostitutes, petty gamblers, and disturbers of the peace—people often unable to defend themselves very well.

Municipal Courts. In the big cities the minor court is most frequently called the municipal court. Rubin, a former judge, describes a scene in the Cleveland Municipal Court:

The Criminal Division of the Cleveland Municipal Court is located in the Police Building at 21st and Payne. The courtroom is well worn, crowded, and noisy. Row on row of benches are peopled with defendants out on bail, witnesses,

[1] H. Ted Rubin, *The Courts: Fulcrum of the Justice System*, Goodyear Publishing Co., Pacific Palisades, California, 1976, p. 47.

[2] President's Commission on Law Enforcement and Administration of Justice, *Task Force Report: The Courts*, U.S. Government Printing Office, Washington, D.C., p. 29.

friends and relatives of defendants, attorneys, social service personnel, and others. . . . The arraignments, hearings, and conferences which occur at the bench are largely inaudible beyond the second or third row of the spectator gallery. Witnesses generally testify from standing positions off to the side of the judge. There is little dignity to the setting. Jailed defendants are brought in and out from a door behind the judge and off to his right. People leaving the courtroom go out a door in the front of the room and off to the judge's left, where outside noise enters the courtroom as the door opens and closes.[3]

What we see in the municipal courts, at least in some big cities, is a continuing stream of people appearing before a judge who dispenses "justice" in "production-line style."

Justice of the Peace Courts.   The counterpart of municipal courts in outlying areas of many states is the justice of the peace (JP). When travel was difficult and slow, the need for the speedy judicial service required a localized judicial system. The JP system met that need and was common to most states.

Justices of the peace, in the Jacksonian tradition, were usually elected from districts or from townships in the Midwest. Usually, they were people with no legal training except the general orientation given by the state association of JPs. Symbolically, one Harlan, Kentucky, local magistrate said his knowledge of the law was vague "but I've got a whole lot of common sense." Their pay came mostly from fees paid by the defendant—the people brought in by constables and local police. These hapless citizens thus were the ones who paid the fee when guilt was determined. If found innocent of the charges, no fee would be paid to the JP. (This practice led some lawyers, only somewhat facetiously, to say that JP meant "judgment for the plaintiff.") Some JPs were able to gather up a rather nice annual income by working out arrangements with area police to be readily available to process traffic tickets. More often than not, the JPs held "court" on their front porch or living room, or in their gasoline station or barber shop. Some even ran ads, such as that of a Boyd County, Kentucky, JP, whose ad read, "Bring all problems to us! We can help in lots of ways. Weddings a specialty and collections a cinch."

This picture of the justice court is fading from the American landscape. States are gradually phasing out or modifying the JP system. Now most JPs must have a minimum level of training or, in some states, they must be lawyers. Many receive salaries instead of fees. And when individual JPs do not meet professional standards, they usually have

[3]H. Ted Rubin, Op cit., p. 54.

severely limited jurisdiction. For example, California now prohibits JPs who are not also lawyers from handling any case that may involve a jail sentence.[4]

Why the JP system survives. The JPs have survived because frequently their judges had close ties with state politicians and the state JP associations have been well organized and able to marshall their forces to counter threats to make them extinct. Moreover finding an alternative that quickly and inexpensively resolves minor cases at a local level has not always been easy. Even where they have been replaced, some features of JP systems remain. For example, states with minor courts headed by lawyer-judges permit them to appoint magistrates (usually nonlawyers) to process traffic tickets and accept guilty pleas for minor offenses.

Small Claims Court. In some states minor civil disputes are also handled, both in big cities and rural areas, by small claims courts. A lawyer-judge usually presides, but often under conditions where litigants present their own cases and waive their rights of appeal. Such proceedings are informal and no transcript is made. These judges often try to reconcile the parties rather than determine right and wrong. Judge Laurence H. Wayne of Houston's small claims court said that he tries to get the disputants to leave the courtroom "arm-in-arm." He was successful in the case of a dispute over which dog owner should pay a veterinarian's fee after a German shepherd bit a chihuahua. Judge Wayne held for the chihuahua.[5] Such courts resolve a great many disputes at a low cost to the disputants—at least a low dollar cost. Emotional costs may be something else. Some small claims court judges announce their decisions by letter to avoid emotional outbursts of losing parties.

The simplicity and low cost of the small claims court do not always favor the average citizen. Retailers, landlords, utilities, and finance companies have learned to use these courts to their own advantage. Citizen defendants may be intimidated by the thought of having to appear in court on their own and so pay the claim. Or they may not show up at all, and a judgment against the defendant is made.

Reform of minor courts. Court reformers seek to eliminate nonlawyer JP courts where they still exist in the hope that the lawyer-judges of small claims courts will be influenced by professional ethics and the

[4]Ralph N. Kleps, "Contingency Planning for State Court Systems," *Judicature*, August/September 1975, 62–66. The case involved was *Gordon v. Justice Court.*

[5]*Newsweek*, January 4, 1974.

desire for a higher level judgeship and, as a result, provide a high degree of judicial fairness even in minor cases. The nonlawyer justice of the peace, the reformers argue, has little to lose if he or she penalizes violators of community standards, even if not done according to the fine points of proper judicial procedure, since JPs have gone as far as they will go in the court system.

General Trial Courts

The cornerstone of the state judicial systems is the general trial court. Most of the Great Lakes states call this court the circuit court, as do a number of states in the South. The Great Plains and Mountain states usually label them district courts, while the New England and the Far West states call them superior courts. New York's designation of them as supreme courts is confusing, at least for non-New Yorkers.

Jurisdiction. The general trial courts are courts of general jurisdiction; they deal with almost any type of case involving state law or its constitution, whether criminal or civil. On the criminal side almost all of the work concerns felonies, those crimes that the legislatures have defined as serious or major crimes. The civil matters they handle are those in which the sum of money involved is high, usually well over $500, and other types of cases that state legislatures see as important, such as divorces. The trial courts deal with misdemeanor cases or minor civil matters only if the losing party appeals a lower court decision.

The states usually organize their general trial courts on a county basis. In heavily populated areas a county general trial court may have as many as twenty or more judges. Where population is scattered the state sometimes sets up a multi-county court district that may have one or two judges who "ride circuit" and hold court in the various county seats. (Abraham Lincoln rode such a circuit as a lawyer following the circuit judge through a group of Illinois counties.)

Professionalization. In all states the general trial courts are highly professionalized. The judges are always lawyers, often with earlier political careers as legislators or county prosecutors. These judges may not maintain a private law practice, although they do serve occasionally as lecturers in law schools.

Lawyers compete to get these jobs, not only because they are prestigious, but because they also pay well. In 1978 the salaries for such judgeships ranged from a high of $49,116 in California to a low of about $25,000 in several other states. As a general rule state legislatures determine minimum salaries which are paid by the state. But often the county may pay an additional amount. This payment as well as the county's responsibility for facilities and staff tend to foster a local perspective, even though the judges are part of the state's judicial system.

Significance of General Trial Courts. As the cornerstone of a state's judicial system these courts, to a very large degree, determine its quality. Why? These judges conduct trials of the most important cases and the facts established then usually form the basis for the final decision. Their decisions, of course, may be appealed, but most decisions are not appealed or accepted for review. And even when they are, appeals courts are not likely to overturn the trial judge unless they find a clear and obvious judicial error.

Trial court judges also decide criminal penalties up to life imprisonment and, in some states, a sentence of death. At the other extreme they have the power to dismiss serious charges (sometimes for what citizens may consider a minor infraction of the accused person's rights), or to decide not to impose a prison sentence or impose only a light one for a serious crime. Most of these judgments are never appealed.

Special Courts

Special courts also are courts of limited jurisdiction, but the jurisdiction is decided by subject matter or clientele. The idea is that the people involved in some cases are so distinctive, or the subject matter so technical, that judicial specialists should handle such cases.

Some of the more common specialized courts are juvenile courts and probate courts. One of the newest types is a housing court such as that recently established in Massachusetts. The family court that deals with divorce and child custody is another type of special court.

Special Court Procedure. Procedures in special courts tend to be more informal than those in general trial courts. Judges often conduct juvenile proceedings more as a conference than as a trial. Similarly, judges of probate or surrogate courts who process wills, oversee estate administration, and rule on requests to commit people to state institutions, follow procedures that seem as much administrative as judicial.

As U.S. Supreme Court decisions come into full play, however, special court actions will become more adversarial. For example, a court rule requiring court-appointed attorneys at public expense in child custody or neglect cases if the parents cannot afford their own lawyer may cause the proceedings to become more combative than when parents have no lawyer to represent them.

Another consequence of court-appointed attorneys will be the eventual elimination of the nonlawyer judges. In a case argued before the

Tennessee Supreme Court in 1976, the state attorney general defended the use of lay judges saying that "... in the simple findings of fact ... no great constitutional or legal issues are likely to arise." But the attorney for two Coffee County teenagers charged with truancy maintained that "lay judges are not trained to rule on the complex issues affecting the liberty of juvenile defendants."[6] Both Kentucky and Tennessee grant automatic appeal to a higher court if the juvenile defendant requests it. Those unfamiliar with this juvenile court system, however, may not be aware of this possibility.

Special Court Administrators. Special courts sometimes operate rather large administrative divisions. Courts dealing with divorce, for example, may employ a staff to handle alimony payments and to chase down those who "skip town."

Juvenile courts also may have large administrative divisions to operate a community detention center as well as "halfway houses" and foster homes that care for children under the court's jurisdiction. But states vary somewhat in how they handle youths under the supervision of the juvenile court. Some observers suggest that the courts should not have custodial responsibility. They say this function should be assigned to a state level youth services agency, as Florida has done. In 1977, though, a majority of states continued to leave the responsibility for custodial care with local juvenile courts.

When administrative divisions are attached to special courts, we note a subtle difference in goals as compared with the regular trial courts. While it is necessary at times for a special court judge to determine guilt or innocence, they more often focus on a resolution of problems much as administrators do. Judge Paul Garrity of the Hampden County housing court, which has an administrative staff to oversee both civil and criminal housing matters under the court's jurisdiction, once outlined two alternatives to a landlord. The court could follow through on the criminal charge, or as an alternative, Judge Garrity suggested, he could assess a fine of $25 if the landlord would correct the problem. The landlord chose the latter. Not only was the housing matter resolved, but the court was saved the work of processing the eighteen forms required in the criminal charge procedures.[7]

Special Courts and Attentive Publics. Because these special courts deal only with limited types of cases, professional people and other citizens with a stake in such cases are likely to develop special links

[6]Nashville *Tennessean*, October 9, 1976.

[7]See John M. Greaney, "Hampden County Housing Court: A Product of Citizen Initiative," *Judicature*, January 1975, 277–280, and "County Housing Court Deals with Full Range of

with, and interests in, these courts. Lawyers who specialize in wills and estates, for example, have a direct interest in how the probate court operates, who the judges are, and their own relationship to the judges. Through their powers to appoint estate administrators, for example, these judges may be an important source of business for the lawyers.

Similarly, state and private agency social workers who handle child abuse or adoption cases may also develop special links to surrogate court judges. Much of their casework must be processed through these courts. Who the judges are becomes important to social work agencies.

This kind of special interest comes under the heading of "court watching," a technique for special interests and citizen groups to evaluate and influence court actions. Court watching, such as that conducted by the Indianapolis Federation of Women's Clubs, has been increasing, but is not new in the sense that people have often tried to organize structures in ways that would help assure favorable judicial outcomes. Many other groups—landlords, merchants, employers, labor unions, or medical societies—at one time or other have tried to get special courts or quasi-judicial agencies established so that they could be more influential in the decisions.

State Appeals Courts

Twenty-seven states have an intermediate court of appeals, which rests in the hierarchy between the general trial courts and the state's court of last resort. We find intermediate appeals courts mostly in the heavily populated states and many of these are recent additions.

These states, as well as the other twenty-three, also have a court of last resort, called the state supreme court in all but five states. West Virginians call theirs the supreme court of appeals. In Maine and Massachusetts, it is the supreme judicial court. Only New York and Maryland have names that may confuse us; they call their court of last resort the court of appeals.

The Appeals Function. Charles Joiner, former law school dean and federal district judge, said that appellate review has two purposes: (1) "... to prevent miscarriages of justice ..." and (2) to teach "... judges, lawyers, and all citizens something about the law."[8]

Housing Problems in Big City, Suburban and Rural Housing," *Journal of Housing*, August/September 1975, 402–405.

[8]"The Function of the Appellate System," in William F. Swindler, ed., *Justice in the States, Addresses and Papers of the National Conference on the Judiciary*, West Publishing Co., St. Paul, Minnesota, 1971, p. 102.

The work of the appeals court judges, thus, differs substantially from that of trial judges. Appeals judges, for example, almost always deal with abstract legal issues. They work with the briefs of the opposing attorneys and hear only limited oral arguments. Rarely do appeals court judges even see the accused. But occasionally a person argues his or her own case as did Marx Cooper, a convicted bank robber. While in prison, he had become an expert on double jeopardy law. He argued and won his own appeal before the Michigan Supreme Court in 1975,[9] as the lawyers say, in propria persona.

Organizational Patterns. Not all states organize their intermediate courts to maximize the educative function of the highest state courts. There are several patterns.

Some states have an intermediate appeals court that operates as a central court. It usually consists of six judges or fewer, holds court in a single location, and serves to relieve workload pressures on the supreme court. When, in 1976, Iowa created a court of appeals with five judges, it used this approach. At the time the court was created, the Iowa Supreme Court had a backlog of 1100 cases—more than a two-year supply of work.[10]

Iowa's approach gives litigants greater opportunity for appeals court reviews, but it has some drawbacks. When an appeals court sits en banc (all together), its decision on a specific case becomes instructive and binding for the whole state, on that case and on others like it. It functions much like the supreme court itself, and supreme court justices may feel that the intermediate court is taking over too much authority.

A second method meets this objection; intermediate courts of appeal are divided into districts. Under this approach cases are reviewed by small panels of judges. This broadens the opportunity for appeals. And while the decisions of these panels have statewide application, they do not have the same standing as the supreme court decisions. Thus, they interfere less with the function of the highest state courts.[11] Large states such as Illinois and Pennsylvania use this approach.

Texas and Alabama use a third approach—they set up different appeals courts for civil and criminal matters. Texas' organization provides an additional twist. The appeals court for civil matters is intermediate; that is, decisions are subject to review by the state supreme

[9]Detroit Free Press, October 31, 1976.

[10]Des Moines Register, September 29, 1976.

[11]H. Ted Rubin, Op. cit., p. 127. We are indebted to Professor Rubin for his classification of the organizational patterns of appeals courts.

court. But decisions made by the court of criminal appeals are final and cannot be appealed to the state supreme court.

Original Jurisdiction. Almost every state assigns supreme courts, and even the intermediate courts of appeal, a few matters in which they have original jurisdiction. For example, in a number of states, citizens can go directly to the intermediate appeals court to get a review of the reapportionment of state legislative or county commissioner districts. Some appeals courts also take direct judicial custody of disputes arising from decisions made by state administrative hearing boards, such as those deciding utility rate setting or workers' compensation claims.

STATE COURTS IN A FEDERAL SYSTEM: THE TREND TO UNITY

Over time we have seen trends both toward and away from uniformity in law. In our day we see the diversity of a federal system being reduced. The United States Supreme Court has been bringing unity to the system of state and federal courts, not by changing their organizational structure, but by unifying the law they apply.

Development of The Common Law

Historically nations considered the resolution of private disputes so important that kings themselves did the judging. It was as a wise judge that Solomon, the third king of ancient Israel, gained his reputation.[12] The law was centralized then in one man.

Our national judicial heritage has its roots in judgments and decrees made by the early kings of England. In time these kings had to appoint magistrates to act for them and a professional judiciary gradually developed. At first such magistrates only acted in the king's name and were expected to apply his prior rulings. But those judges were also linked to the citizens who came to their courts. Community ties were strengthened as the king's magistrates tried to figure out what citizens in their courts would accept as just.

Through their rulings the judges fashioned what became *the common law*, which was based on the general beliefs and customs regarding right and wrong. Thus, the politics of the judiciary from early times involved concern for what the public would think about judicial rulings. But such practices, based as they were on individual and community values, provided too much diversity.

[12]See, for example, the account in I Kings 3:16–28 in the *Holy Bible*.

The body of common law became more consistent as magistrates studied each other's decisions. By applying judgments of prior cases, the judges created a body of "judge-made" law. Judge-made law would tend to remain relatively unchanged over time, but it was not static. Judges introduced new precedents when they found the earlier decisions inappropriate to new conditions and experiences, such as those that followed the Great Crusades and the spread of commerce among European nations.

Statutory Law

The law in our own time differs because it is based on law written by "the people" in constitutions, or by their representatives, the legislators. The common law, for the most part, has been codified in laws passed by state legislatures.[13]

As law took on a statutory, written form, the legislature, rather than the court—at least in theory—was to bring law into line with citizen beliefs and customs. We say "at least in theory" because courts continue to produce "judge-made" law in the form of new interpretations of constitutions or statutes. Even law enforcement officials, whose acts revolve around the courts, help in the process of changing the law. Those legislated laws that lag behind the values, beliefs, and customs of the citizenry, are not likely to be enforced very rigidly. Arresting and prosecuting users of marijuana in many university and college towns, for example, has almost become the exception. Why? Because the police and prosecutors believe that community values and customs no longer support such actions, even though the laws remain on the statute books.

Judicial Lawmaking

State supreme court judges, of course, cannot openly initiate policy changes as can legislators or governors. Judges can only create new policy when someone brings a case to them. The decisions they render and the opinions they give explain their rationale or line of reasoning. Each court decision that redirects policy, then, is based on the particular facts and specific circumstances of a real case involving real people. Their reasoned opinions, in effect, become instructions to lower courts about what to do in similar future cases. The United States Su-

---

[13]Only in the state of Louisiana, whose tradition is French, rather than English, and whose law is based on the Napoleonic Code, has any substantial part of the common law prevailed into the second half of the twentieth century.

preme Court, we note, expresses such policy changes for the nation. State supreme courts do so only for their respective states.

The Politics of Judicial Appeals. Because national and state level courts receive many more requests for appeal than they can possibly handle, they can select those they wish to rule on; and they often select cases that have the greatest potential for guiding lower courts. Moreover attorneys are attuned to the leanings of these top state and national courts. Lawyers who decide whether to appeal cases to the top courts learn to read the signals and appeal cases involving the issues that the courts seem willing to consider in their favor.

Some of this sensitivity to the leanings of the courts is evident from the data on who files for appeal to the U.S. Supreme Court. For example, during the period that Earl Warren, former governor of California, served as Chief Justice of the U.S. Supreme Court (1953–69), the court gained a reputation for being willing to rule favorably for civil liberties groups and criminal defendants. Under such circumstances prosecutors regarded many appeals to the national court as futile.

But as Nathan Lewin, a Washington, D.C., lawyer, observed, under the Burger Court (1969–), the situation was almost reversed. During the court term ending July 1975, only 25 percent of the appeals accepted were from defendants, while 75 percent were accepted from prosecutors.[14]

Civil liberties groups, too, experienced a somewhat less favorable reception at the U.S. Supreme Court in the middle 1970s and often were reluctant to carry forward adverse local court rulings for fear that the highest court would accept the adverse position and apply it on a national basis. Letting the matter rest with the lower court decision would make it applicable only to the specific case and its effect would be limited. Thus, although the courts are not able to initiate cases involving policy issues of concern to them, the restriction does not handcuff the high level courts.

The Federalization of State Laws

Although a case may begin as a state case and be tried and reviewed in state courts, it may yet become a federal case. But such review is not automatic. Defendants can obtain federal court review of a state decision only if they can persuade a federal judge that their federal constitutional protections may have been violated. The principal avenue that

[14]Nathan Lewin, "Avoiding the Supreme Court," *The New York Times Magazine*, October 17, 1976.

state cases travel to become federal cases is the Fourteenth Amendment to the U.S. Constitution. The pertinent clause states that no ". . . state shall deprive any person of life, liberty, or property, without due process of law; nor deny to any person within its jurisdiction the equal protection of the laws." Through these "due process" and "equal protection" clauses, the U.S. Supreme Court has extended much of the federal Bill of Rights to the states. Its overall effect has been to make one federal court out of one national and fifty state court systems, thereby producing a growing unity.

Extending the Bill of Rights. At the outset, the Bill of Rights limited only the national government. Chief Justice Marshall, for example, writing for the court in 1833, confidently stated that "the Fifth Amendment must be understood as *restraining the power of the general government, not as applicable to the states.*"[15] Nearly one hundred years later, the U.S. Supreme Court used the Fourteenth Amendment to apply such rights to the states.

In a 1925 decision, the Supreme Court refused to overturn the New York decisions against Benjamin Gitlow for advocating the overthrow of the government by violent means.[16] But in this case, the court first stated that the First Amendment—liberty of free speech—was a liberty to be protected against state intrusion—that they would take as their definition of liberty in the Fourteenth Amendment the freedom of speech clause of the First Amendment. Later on, case by case over the years, the Court extended the principle to freedom of the press[17] and religion, and other protections.[18]

Treatment of the accused. Ultimately the U.S. Bill of Rights was extended to the way persons accused of committing a crime were to be handled by the state or community police and courts. As a result the Court federalized the way states and localities may treat persons accused of violating their laws.

We find one of the early extensions of the U.S. Bill of Rights to those in trouble with the law, related to the assistance of legal counsel, a right guaranteed by the Sixth Amendment. This right had been seen as pertaining mainly to accused persons who could afford an attorney. Others faced the ordeal of prosecution without legal counsel unless

[15]*Barron v. Mayor and City Council of Baltimore*, 7 Peters 243 (1833).

[16]*Gitlow v. New York* 268 U.S. 652 (1925).

[17]*Near v. Minnesota* 283 U.S. 697 (1931).

[18]*Zorach v. Clauson* 343 U.S. 306 (1952).

they were involved in a serious offense, and bar associations then voluntarily provided legal assistance.

In the "Scottsboro Case" (1932), the U.S. Supreme Court held that legal counsel had to be provided without cost if the defendant in capital cases (those that could involve the death penalty) could not afford to hire a lawyer.[19]

More recently the court extended the right of free legal counsel in felony cases[20] for accused juveniles[21] and for criminal misdemeanors where the accused's freedom is placed in jeopardy.[22] These cases, together with *Mapp v. Ohio*[23] that prohibits the use of illegally seized evidence, and *Miranda v. Arizona*[24] that requires police to inform a suspect of his constitutional rights (including the right to remain silent) as the questioning turns from being investigatory to accusatory, have had a significant impact on the way local police officers do their work and on the local prosecution of criminal cases. The rules have led to increased costs of trying accused persons, because in many instances county governments, which bear most of the cost of criminal cases, have had to pay for both the prosecution and the defense.

These rules have had two other effects. One is the increased use of plea bargaining, where charges are reduced in exchange for a guilty plea to avoid the costs of a trial. A second effect has been the almost meticulous protection of the rights of accused persons on the part of police and prosecutors and by trials and appeals judges, because faulty procedures can mean dismissal of the case "on a technicality," regardless of the evidence in hand.

Some police and prosecutors have argued that such procedures have "handcuffed" them in solving crimes. William Hamilton of the Institute of Law and Social Research, however, reported that in a survey of ninety jurisdictions across the nation, 50 percent of the criminal cases were dropped before reaching the courtroom—about the same ratio as forty years earlier.[25]

The death penalty.   In 1972, the U.S. Supreme Court ruled on the question of the death penalty. By a five to four vote, the court said that as

[19]*Powell v. Alabama* 287 U.S. 4S (1932).

[20]*Gideon v. Wainwright* 373 U.S. 335 (1963).

[21]In re *Gault* 378 U.S. 1 (1967).

[22]*Argensinger v. Hamlin* 407 U.S. 25 (1972).

[23]*Mapp v. Ohio* 367 U.S. 343 (1961).

[24]*Miranda v. Arizona*, 384 U.S. 436 (1966).

[25]*Detroit News*, "Prosecuting Crooks Harder Than Catching Them, Officials Agree," January 22, 1978.

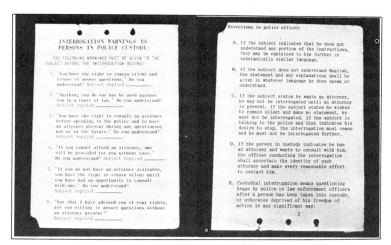

U.S. Supreme Court decisions reach down to the police officer on the beat.

the states were then applying the death penalty, it was a cruel and unusual punishment. The primary difficulty was that the states imposing the death penalty were not doing so uniformly—some people convicted of a given crime received the death sentence, while others convicted of the same crime under similar circumstances received a comparatively light sentence.

Since that time several of the states with death penalties reenacted their death sentence laws mandating the death penalty for murder under specified conditions and required two trials, one to determine guilt and the other, the penalty. In 1976, the Court upheld those laws that assured uniform application in accordance with due process provisions. After a period of more than ten years, during which time there were no executions, the Supreme Court refused to interfere with Utah's planned execution of Gary Gilmore for murders that he had committed. In 1977 he was executed by a firing squad.

The Impact of Nationalization.   Is it significant that the Supreme Court has federalized the Bill of Rights? Yes! It changed how the federal court system relates to state courts and, indeed, to all the other institutions of state government. It forces state court systems to consider the protections of the U.S. Constitution directly, even if it means overturning state constitutional and statutory provisions. To the extent that state courts fail to take the U.S. Constitution into account, they become less and less the final word, even on matters that would otherwise remain state questions.

The federalization of the Bill of Rights, and especially its broadened application under the Warren Court, also changed the way citizens relate to the courts. Many minorities, impatient for full rights and freedoms, found courts more willing to change discriminatory laws and practices than were state legislatures. The young, blacks, Chicanos, and women and other groups sought and received an unusual number of remedies through the courts. The open receptivity of the courts to such a newly broadened range of questions has had a predictable effect—problems once handled (or ignored) in legislative or administrative arenas are brought almost directly to the courts for resolution.

We also note that many other interest groups, such as environmentalists or consumer advocates, have often found that a court case can accomplish on a national basis in a few years what decades and thousands of dollars in lobbying might accomplish in the state legislatures or the Congress.

But Diversity Remains

The unity, though, is not all pervasive. One reason is that while the federal constitution and laws are the same for all courts, most issues, by far, involve state law and are brought into state courts. Because state laws and judicial precedents within each state still differ, important diversity remains as, for example, in divorce and insurance laws. And, as we noted, many decisions are not appealed beyond the original trial court and those decisions remain unchallenged.

We find also that state courts do not always apply U.S. Supreme Court decisions as well as the federal courts might wish. Students have found instances in which they claim state courts disregarded or misapplied federal guidelines: cases about controversial matters, such as prohibiting prayer in the public schools; desegregation and busing cases; cases involving obscenity and pornography; as well as those guaranteeing criminal rights.[26] Unless such matters are litigated in the federal courts—and often they are not—the local or state judge's ruling prevails.

Judges' Personal Biases. We also find another reason why diversity will continue in our state and local judicial systems. It is because judges are more likely to reflect personal biases in their decisions than are legislators or governors. Legislators and governors are forced to compromise their views in order to get elected in the first place and to get anything done while in office. Judges face less pressure to compromise.

[26]For a recent example, see Neil T. Romans, "The Role of State Supreme Courts in Judicial Policymaking: Escobedo, Miranda and the Use of Judicial Impact Analysis," *Western Political Quarterly*, 27, March 1974, 38–59.

For example, Stuart Nagel compared judicial decisions of state judges to a series of social background characteristics of judges, such as race, ethnicity of the judge's name, political party, and religion. He found judges' decisions related to what we would predict to be their biases. Democrats, Catholics, and members of ethnic minorities, he found, were more likely to rule for the criminal than for the state. Republicans, Protestants, and Anglo Saxons were more likely to rule the other way. Ethnic Catholic Democrats also tended to favor the first party in bureaucracy versus corporation disputes, employee versus corporation in injury cases, debters versus creditors and wives in divorce cases.

A Litigious Society

In 1835 Alexis de Tocqueville observed that, "There is hardly a political question in the United States which does not sooner or later turn into a judicial one." Perhaps with the federalization of our laws the only difference now is that the political questions become judicial ones sooner, rather than later.

In recent decades, we have become a highly litigious society. No one takes "no" for an answer anymore. If we have a problem, our first inclination is to file a court suit, rather than seek a change in the law. And, because a legislature passes a law, this is no longer a sufficient reason for accepting it as policy. Whether a person be a job aspirant, a welfare claimant, a professional athlete tied to a team by the "reserve clause" or a teacher who has been denied tenure, the courts beckon enticingly. For that reason Roger C. Cramton, dean of the Cornell Law School, calls the conflict resolution industry "the boom industry of the day."[27]

THE POLITICS OF THE JUDICIARY

Citizens see judges almost entirely in their professional capacity, dressed in their black robes, presiding over courtrooms, scolding a disrespectful lawyer, or agonizing over the future of a young defendant being led away to the state penitentiary. We see judges as "legitimizers" of the law—impartial referees who decide what the law really is, but rarely do we see their political side. Even less frequently does the public see judges as members of a professional bureaucracy.

[27]Roger C. Cramton, "Judicial Law Making and Administration," *Public Administration Review*, September/October 1976, p. 551.

We will next pull the curtain aside somewhat and examine the political aspects of the judiciary. The notion of a political and bureaucratic judiciary conflicts with the common ideas that judges should be independent and able to decide a case free of outside political pressures and influences; but, of course, courts cannot be above the external or internal battling and bargaining, and judges have never been free of outside influences.

Why Courts are Political

Why are the courts and judges unavoidably political? Because state courts are important—important not only to groups inside the judicial system, but outside it as well. The politics, then, center around a continuing battle for control and influence in the courts.

Internal participants in this battle are the judges themselves. Upper level judges do not always agree with each other or with the judges of the lower courts over how the courts should be managed and operated. Also taking part in the internal contests are relative newcomers to court systems—the growing bureaucracy of nonjudicial employees who help judges manage and operate court systems.

Special interest groups to whom the courts are important also seek control and influence in the courts. Among these are industrial and financial groups, labor unions, lawyers, physicians, teachers, state officials, and others—all who can be favorably or adversely affected by court actions. State and local legislators believe that because they pay a judge's salary, they should "carry some weight" with the courts. The governor, as the head of state government and the chief of the party, believes he or she should have some special standing on court operations and on some decisions they make.

Such "influentials," of course, do not have an interest in every court decision—but only in those that are important to them. For example, a state manufacturers' association may not care much whether a court upholds a state law that requires motorcyclists to wear crash helmets. But they will be very interested and will want consideration on workers' compensation decisions. One of the important avenues to influence is the procedure used to select judges.

How State Judges Get Their Jobs

Those who select people to be judges, of course, influence policy outcomes of the courts, if for no other reason than because personal biases figure so heavily in court decisions. Thus, the question of how judges should be selected is not a minor or a purely technical matter.

Methods of Selection.   Americans do not have a uniform method of selecting judges. During the colonial period and the early years of our nation governors, and later state legislatures, made the selections. They tended to recruit legislators or people active in politics. But judges who made rulings contrary to the wishes of the governor or legislature ran the risk of not being reappointed and thus were not regarded by many as sufficiently independent.

With the rise of Jacksonian democracy more and more states began to elect judges on a partisan ballot. In reality this meant that urban and rural party bosses were making the selections, because they controlled the parties and nominating conventions. Judges thus became captives of the bosses.

This fact led lawyers in New York City to form the first bar association in 1870,[28] and also to promote nonpartisan elections and direct primaries. Today, states continue to use both partisan and nonpartisan elections.

Control techniques over judicial elections.   Politicians have found ways to short-circuit election methods. One way was documented by James Herndon, who studied over four hundred elected state supreme court justices. He found that 56 percent of them first gained office through appointment by the governor to a judicial vacancy. They would then run as "incumbents" and have an advantage in the election. When judges who planned to retire belonged to the same party as the governor it was common for them to retire six months or so before their term ended to permit the governor to fill the vacancy with another party member.[29] Some states have counteracted this tactic by declaring interim judges ineligible for election.

As a way to strengthen their influence lawyers' groups began making their own evaluations of candidates and publicizing the results to guide the voters. Gradually the position of the legal societies evolved into the invention of a new method of selection, one generally favored by reform groups, called the merit system or the "Missouri Plan," because Missouri was the first state (in 1940) to give it prominence.

What is the Missouri Plan?   The Missouri Plan consists of a three-step process for selecting judges: (1) a judicial selection commission screens and nominates three candidates for each judicial vacancy; (2) the gov-

---

[28]Richard A. Watson and Randal G. Downing, *The Politics of the Bench and the Bar; Judicial Selection Under the Missouri Non-Partisan Court Plan*, John Wiley Sons, Inc., New York, 1969, p. 7.

[29]James Herndon, "Appointment as a Means of Initial Accession to Elective State Courts of Last Resort," *North Dakota Law Review*, 38, 1962, 60–73.

ernor chooses one of these, and (3) after the judge has served a one-year trial period, the voters decide whether to elect the person to a full term.

Interestingly, Missouri uses the plan only to select judges for the state supreme court, three intermediate appeals courts, and for the general trial courts in Jackson County (Kansas City) and St. Louis. Missouri voters choose the rest of the state's judges on a partisan ballot.

The commission for state court nominations in Missouri has seven members; the supreme court chief justice, three lay members chosen by the governor, and three practicing attorneys. Thus, a majority are lawyers.

Effects of the Missouri Plan. Richard Watson and Randal Downing compared the results of the merit plan of Missouri to the previous partisan election outcomes.[30] They found that under the plan, elections tended to be less interesting to voters, that "plan" judges were more likely than elected judges to be older, to have had lower court judicial experience, and to have attended a state law school.

Not surprisingly, Watson and Downing also found that the Missouri lawyers strongly believed that the plan resulted in "better" judges—after all, the plan gave lawyers, as a group, more influence over who became judge than would an elective or other appointive system. Significantly, Watson and Downing conclude:

> . . . the Plan has not eliminated "politics" . . . that is the maneuvering of individuals and groups to influence who will be chosen as judges. Rather it has changed the nature of that politics to include not only partisan forces but also those relating to the interests of the organized bar, the judiciary, and the court's "attentive publics." Nor has the Plan even eliminated partisan politics in judicial selection. . . . What one can say is that the Plan has altered partisan factors in judicial selection so that ward committeemen and other local leaders and persons active in electoral politics are no longer the major figures in selecting as they were under the elective system. . . . Instead, it is now the governor who looms large in such decisions, and local and state political figures are only influential insofar as their political careers are tied to his.[31]

The State Patterns of Selection. Despite the efforts of lawyers, the Missouri Plan has not spread rapidly to other states. In fact, not until Alaska gained statehood in 1959 did the second state adopt it; by 1977

[30]Watson and Downing, Op cit., p. 343. For examples of how advocates of various election plans idealize their preferred systems, see Elmo B. Hunter, "There's a Better Way to Select Our Judges," and John J. Kennelly, "Don't Destroy the People's Right to Choose their Judges." Both articles are reprinted in Robert L. Morlan, *Capitol, Courthouse, and City Hall*, Houghton Mifflin Co., Boston, 5th edition, 1977, 129–134.

[31]Watson and Downing, Op cit., p. 352.

eleven states and Guam were using the plan to select some of their judges. (See Table 9-2.)

The states remain divided nearly equally among the four basic methods of judicial selection. The method employed, we find, tends to follow regional alignments. The states of the South choose their judges by a partisan election, while the New England states appoint their judges (although not all in the same way). States of the Rocky Mountain region and Midwest favor the Missouri Plan, or nonpartisan election.

Table 9-2 does not reflect all the nuances of each selection system in each state. Few states use a "pure" approach, and in most one approach is used for certain courts and another in other courts. In addition states invent their own hybrid systems. Iowa, for example, used the Missouri Plan to appoint five judges to the newly created intermediate appeals court. A nominating commission, however, presented a list of fifteen names—some state legislators (mostly Democrats, we suspect) thought that the law they had just passed required the Republican governor to get five lists of three names each. Governor Robert

TABLE 9-2. Judicial Selection Methods in Use for Appellate and Major Trial Courts

Merit Plan	Nonpartisan Elections	Appointment	Partisan Elections
Alaska	Florida	California[b, c]	Alabama
Arizona[a]	Idaho	Connecticut[d]	Arkansas
Colorado	Kentucky	Delaware[b]	Georgia[e]
Indiana[a]	Michigan[f]	Hawaii[b]	Illinois[c]
Iowa	Minnesota	Maine[b]	Louisiana
Kansas	Montana	Maryland[b, c]	Mississippi
Missouri[g]	Nevada	Massachusetts[b]	New Mexico
Nebraska	North Dakota	New Hampshire[b]	New York
Oklahoma[h]	Ohio	New Jersey[b]	North Carolina
Utah	Oregon	Rhode Island[d]	Pennsylvania[c]
Wyoming	South Dakota	South Carolina[d]	Tennessee[i]
Guam	Washington	Vermont[b, c]	Texas
	Wisconsin	Virginia[d]	West Virginia
		Puerto Rico[b]	

SOURCE: State Court Systems, Revised 1976, Council of State Governments, Lexington, Kentucky.

[a]Some counties use nonpartisan elections for MTC judges.

[b]By governor, in Cal. with consent of judicial appointments commission for appeals courts, MTC judges by nonpartisan elections; senate consent required in Del., Ha., N.J., Vt., and P.R., Executive council consent required in Me., Mass., and N.H.

[c]Retention plebiscite used for subsequent terms. In Vt., retention vote is by legislature.

[d]By legislature; in Conn. from governor's nominations. In R.I. applies only to S.C. In other states appointment is by governor with senate consent.

[e]County judges by governor with senate consent.

[f]S.C. justices nominated by party, but can obtain candidate status for subsequent terms by self-declaration.

[g]Some counties choose MTC judges by partisan election.

[h]Applies to S.C. and criminal appeals court only, others chosen by nonpartisan election.

[i]Intermediate appeals court on merit plan.

Ray (1969-) appointed Republicans to all five new positions.[32] Pennsylvania and Illinois, to illustrate further, both use partisan elections, but permit incumbent judges to run for subsequent terms on a yes or no plebiscite basis. Many practicing attorneys, no doubt, would favor such a modification in election states because of the questionable way judicial campaigns are often financed, that is, largely by contributions from "working" lawyers.

Tenure, Discipline, and Removal.   Federal judges are appointed for life. Not so for state judges, except for Rhode Island. In New Jersey, reappointment after an initial seven-year term is for life, and in New Hampshire and Massachusetts, judges may serve to age seventy. All judges in the major state courts serve at least four-year terms, and most, longer terms. The state supreme court judges, those most likely to be influential policymakers, serve terms of from six to fifteen years—one state gives them lifetime appointments; others appointment to age 70.

How then can states or citizens rid the courts of judges they consider unfit? The most frequent method, it seems, is to wait for their mandatory retirement or death. But there are other methods.

Elections as one means of removal.   The most common method and the one that results most often in removals is the election process, at least for thirty-seven states. Leaving the job of removing unfit judges to the voters, however, often falls short of the need—less than 10 percent of incumbents are defeated. Most incumbents, especially in nonpartisan elections, have no opposition; and when they do, they are difficult to defeat. In states using the Missouri Plan, of course, judges are not even opposed by other candidates, and as the saying goes, "It's very hard to defeat somebody with nobody." Even in the other states, running against an incumbent is risky for lawyers. As one judicial combatant remarked after such a race, "Well, our man squeaked through—but if the old judge had won, a lot of us could just as well have started building a new law practice in some other state."[33]

Recall and impeachment.   Even more hazardous, especially for criticizing lawyers, is the attempt to remove a judge by recall. Getting signatures on such a petition is difficult and expensive. Rarely has this method been used, even in the few states that permit it. In Policy Box No. 17, "Judicial Expression and Public Opinion," we review the epi-

[32]The *Des Moines Register*, September 25, 1976.

[33]Murray T. Bloom, "Unseating Unfit Judges" in *Capitol, Courthouse, and City Hall*, Robert L. Morlan, Houghton Mifflin Co., Boston, 136–138.

sode of a judge in Madison, Wisconsin, who was recalled—the first in the nation in more than thirty-five years.

Judges may also be removed by impeachment in most states, although the state statutes vary. Tennessee law, for example, names misfeasance or malfeasance in office as impeachable offenses, while Oklahoma specifies "willful neglect of duty, corruption in office, habitual drunkenness, incompetency, or any offense involving moral turpitude."[34] In some states the governor, with the consent of the legislature, may remove judges from office.

The fine language of what offenses constitute grounds for impeachment matters little, as do the statutes that permit governors and legislatures to remove judges. Most legislatures and governors are loathe to undertake the task, and, indeed, few ever do. Usually only in outrageous cases do we find even threats of impeachment, although such threats are occasionally followed by the resignation of the offending judge.

Judicial tenure commissions. If elections and legislative procedures do not rid the courts of unfit judges, how can they be removed? An approach gradually gaining acceptance employs judicial tenure commissions or judicial qualification commissions. This practice is supported by many judges because it lets the courts handle their own problems without "interference" from the other branches. In addition, such commissions can choose from a range of remedies to discipline an errant judge—they are not limited simply to removal.

The state judicial qualifications commissions are patterned after that established by California in 1960. The commissions usually consist of judges, members of the state bar, and lay persons. They investigate complaints from lawyers and local public bodies and, after a formal hearing, either impose penalties or recommend actions to the state supreme court. Penalties range from removal to temporary suspension or censure.

This system appears to work reasonably well, we think—better, perhaps, than removal by impeachment or election. It can be an effective and humane way of dealing with the very delicate problem of judges who have become either physically or mentally disabled and who refuse to retire from the bench. But California Supreme Court Justice Marshall McComb refused to resign at the age of 82, in spite of a recommendation of the Commission on Judicial Performance that he be removed. He was not forced to resign, however, even though he had been accused of falling asleep during oral arguments in the court and

[34]State Court Systems, Revised 1976, Op. cit.

POLICY BOX NO. 17   Judicial
Expression and Public Opinion

In November 1976 three black youths, fourteen and fifteen years old, sexually assaulted a sixteen-year-old white girl in a Madison (Wisconsin) High School. It was the middle of the day and a band class was practicing nearby. The event stirred public concern about a wave of recent sexual assaults in downtown Madison.

The three youths were readily apprehended and prosecuted. One of the youths turned state's witness in the case and was not charged. The judge sent the fourteen-year-old boy to spend a year in a Milwaukee group home for his part in the case. The third boy, who, testimony revealed, was a friend of the victim and attended the same church as she did, was released to the custody of his parents. Meryl Manhardt, assistant prosecutor in the case, argued that this boy, of all of them, should have been sent to a group home.

It was at this point that Dane County Judge Archie Simonson made some remarks that led to a recall petition against him. It was in response to Ms. Manhardt's pleadings for the judge to be responsive to the community desires, to let people in Madison know that sexual assaults would not be tolerated, that the judge lit a fuse that was to result in an explosion about him. Judge Simonson said,

And then you are saying that I should be responsive to the community in what their needs and wishes are. Well, how responsive should I be? Should I adopt a double standard? This community is well known to be sexually permissive; look at the newspapers; look at the sex clubs, the advertisements of sex, the availability of it through your escort services, the prostitutes, they are being picked up daily. Even in open court we have . . . women appearing without bras . . . and they think it is smart as they sit here on the witness stand with their dresses up over the cheeks of their butts and we have the same type of thing in the schools. Sex is really wide open and we are supposed to take an impressionable person fifteen or sixteen years of age who can respond to something like that and punish that person severely because they react to it normally.

Assistant prosecutor Manhardt interceded, "Your Honor, with all due respect, I find your remarks about women's clothing particularly sexist." "You bet it is," replied the judge.

Shortly thereafter, recall petitions were circulated. Signatures totaled more than 35,000, nearly twice the number needed to order an election. The petition campaign reportedly was led by the Madison chapter of the National Organization for Women, the Women's International League for Peace and Freedom, and the Madison Rape Crisis Committee. Their stated concern was that the judge made sexist remarks and that he seemingly imposed a penalty too light for the crime.

Governor Patrick Lucey said that an apology from the judge was in order, but that recall was not. Judge Simonson did not apologize.

Early in the recall campaign both city newspapers supported the petition, but later one backed off—reportedly because of the racial implications in the case.

The editor noted that there was a chance the judge might win the recall vote and wondered what message that would convey to the nation.

Some Madison conservatives, too, were upset with the judge's light sentencing of the youths. They argued that the courts should "crack down on crime."

Some liberals in the city viewed the question in a civil-liberties context. They maintained that the judge was entitled to freedom of speech, especially as a judge. They felt that Simonson was an inept judge, but did not believe he should be recalled. He should be removed, they said, in April 1978—when his term expired. One person from this group said, "This is what a witchhunt is like. This is what is was like with McCarthy in the 1950s."

Judge Simonson, himself, argued that the whole judicial system was at stake in the election. "A judge," he said, "has to be absolutely free to make decisions. He shouldn't have to reflect public opinion."

In September 1977 Judge Simonson became the first judge to be recalled in the nation in more than thirty-five years. In his place, the voters put Moria Krueger, a lawyer who had been specializing in juvenile law. After the election she revealed that her older sister had been the victim of a rapist ten years earlier. She said she did not stress feminist issues during the campaign and hoped that men would not fear her when she became judge.

After the votes were counted, Judge Simonson said that he did not campaign against the others in the election, only against the idea that he should be recalled for what he said.

What do you think? Should Judge Simonson have been recalled? Did the community handle the problem appropriately? Should the governor or the supreme court of Wisconsin have interceded in the case? Should Simonson have apologized? Will the case strengthen or weaken the court system in Wisconsin and other states? Should Wisconsin change its judicial selection and removal laws? How much freedom should we give the judges?

SOURCE: This case is based on several newspaper reports: "Effort to Recall 'Sexist' Judge Touches Off Bitter Debate," *Detroit News*, September 6, 1977; "New Judge Knows the Tragedy of Rape," UPI dispatch in the *Detroit News*, September 18, 1977; and "She's the Winner in the War Over Judge's Words," New York Times Services dispatch in the *Detroit Free Press*, September 11, 1977.

faulted for engaging "in sets of physical exercises . . . during conferences and keeping count in whispered cadence while doing so."[35] For a legislature or executive to take action in such cases might well be seen as being politically motivated. And, perhaps more often than not, it would result in a "stand and fight" position by the justice, and produce a great outpouring of public sympathy for the "defenseless" judge.

[35]*Los Angeles Times* dispatch printed in the *Des Moines Register*, January 8, 1977.

The Judicial Bureaucracy—Who Will Manage?

Nearly all the states historically have had their courts operate through highly decentralized structures, so much so that the state court systems could barely be called a system. The route that appeals would follow was established, of course, as were major rules of judicial procedure. Beyond this, though, the general trial courts, special courts, and minor courts have been outposts of fierce judicial independence—judges, especially elected ones, have strongly resisted "top-down" interference.

Decentralized organization leaves local courts vulnerable to a variety of local influences. Few judges, of course, would tolerate open pressuring of their courts. Still, judges are people and do live in the community. Many have to stand for reelection. Often their salaries are paid, in part, by the county, and local governments also make the appropriations for court staff, court furnishings, equipment, and other perquisites. All these can subtly, and sometimes not so subtly, become a medium of barter. Judges who consider themselves adequately provided for in these respects would find it difficult to rule against the county or against community values in a court battle.[36] Southern judges found it especially difficult to take tough stands for racial integration, and some of those who did paid some costs in local popularity.

The vulnerability of judges is not the only criticism we find of a decentralized system. The legal and judicial profession argues for uniform quality and access to judicial services throughout a state. When dockets are overloaded and cases, especially civil cases, delayed up to five years, the administration of justice suffers. Chief Justice Warren Burger noted, "Delay itself, with the loss of witnesses and the clouding of memories, diminishes the ability of the courts to do justice. It is too serious to be longer ignored."[37] Increased use of the courts, of course, has caused part of this problem. But so also has the increased tendency of judges to administer some of the decisions they make. W. Arthur Garrity, Jr., a federal district judge, for example, practically became the superintendent of schools during Boston's 1976

---

[36]Some current court practices permit judges to show displeasure, even if the county is not involved in a case. Occasionally a judge, unhappy with the treatment received from a county board of commissioners, will reduce the revenues generated by the courts for the county general fund. By charging traffic violators only a fine and no court costs or fees, the judge can direct how the revenues can be used. County boards typically respond to such judicial action because it interrupts their revenue projections.

[37]Warren Burger in a Foreword to "Symposium on Judicial Administration," *Public Administration Review*, March/April 1971, p. 112.

desegregation crisis, deciding such matters as whether the school system should buy tennis balls.[38] In circuit and family courts, supervision of child support payments and administration of other aspects of a case may extend over a ten- or fifteen-year period.

Unification of State and Local Courts.   Court reformers have sought to remedy these conditions through court reorganization, improvement of administrative techniques, and development of administrative support staff. The states have generally followed the system introduced in 1947 in New Jersey by Arthur T. Vanderbilt, state supreme court chief justice; its features are found in the plan of the National Advisory Commission on Criminal Justice Standards and Goals.

This plan places all courts in a single state judicial system, administered by a court administrator responsible to the chief justice of the state supreme court. The plan suggests that all jurisdiction over criminal matters, except for traffic violations, should be placed in general trial courts. The advisory commission further suggested that the rules of the supreme court governing court conduct should apply to both minor and major prosecutions.[39]

Gradually the states are changing to this form of court organization. Six states, including Louisiana, Kentucky, and Alabama, did so during 1974–75 and by the end of 1977 all had court administrators. These administrators collect data and administer state supreme court coordinating rules. Some trial courts also have court administrators with such duties as scheduling cases, managing court employees, and selecting potential jury members.

The Politics of Court Reorganization.   Judges in the trial courts and lower level benches are likely to have mixed reactions to court unification. H. Ted Rubin states that general trial judges as a group are "still too isolated from the crosscurrents of change, still too concerned with managing the cases assigned to them without a strong investment in improving the overall system, too involved in their status and the preservation of their narrow turf. . . ."[40]

[38]*Newsweek*, January 10, 1977.

[39]National Advisory Commission on Criminal Justice Standards and Goals, *Courts*, published with the assistance of a grant from the Law Enforcement Assistance Administration, Washington, D.C., 1973, p. 164.

[40]H. Ted Rubin, Op. cit., p. 216.

These judges appreciate moral and legal support when the supreme court uses its inherent powers to order county boards to pay the costs of a court-negotiated contract with its court employees. But they are also likely to label as "bureaucratic timidity" a court administrator's order to a local judge that he or she must follow a county's normal purchasing procedure to buy courtroom furnishings.

Judges in courts with dockets that are hopelessly backlogged sometimes receive favorably those judges whom the court administrator has temporarily assigned to help out, although they may also regard such assignments as an implied criticism. Judges who are temporarily reassigned may have negative reactions—assignments elsewhere can also be a form of punishment for lazy or uncooperative judges. Similarly judges receiving data from central computer files may consider this technology a solid advance, but when they have to provide data for the file and if the data make them look "bad," they might wonder why the "administrators at the capital" do not let them go on with the business of running their courtrooms. Some judges are not happy having professional administrators introduced into their courts, since the judges, in one way or another, will then have to share the responsibilities for running the courts. Rubin has pointed out that some systems, such as those of Colorado and New Jersey, have, perhaps, become too dependent on central state administrations. He suggests that the trial court judges should have a greater voice in the operation and management of state courts, and that ways need to be found to allow for comment from bottom to top, as well as from the top down.[41]

Conflicts With Other State Officials

The courts are established by state constitutions as the third branch of the government—coordinate and equal with the legislative and executive branches. What happens when these constitutional powers come into conflict? Differences as to what coordinate and equal means in daily operations can cause some first-rate battles. Such conflict often surfaces over court financing.

Conflicts Over Court Budgets. Is equality of the courts maintained when the governor's budget department cuts the court's requests for staff appropriations? What about a legislature that tells the court that it will get so much state funding and no more? What should the governor and the legislature do when the courts ignore budget limits? These

[41]H. Ted Rubin, Op. cit., p. 211.

are not mere speculations. Constitutional confrontations like these do take place.

Former Governor Patrick Lucey of Wisconsin, for example, budgeted less for the state supreme court than the court requested. Harold Wilkie, chief justice of the Wisconsin Supreme Court, responded that, "the court has inherent power to appoint the number of personnel it deems necessary to perform its constitutional functions." He announced that the court was going to begin an educational program for judges and, to do this, more personnel would be hired.[42]

Both the Michigan and Pennsylvania supreme courts have made rulings following this line of argument. In the Michigan case the court ruled that a general trial court judge could *mandamus* (require) the county board to appropriate sufficient funds for as many probation officers as the judge considered necessary.[43] If the county board failed to appropriate the necessary funds, the judge said he would jail the commissioners. The Pennsylvania court ordered the Philadelphia city fathers to restore reductions that they had made in the Common Pleas Court budget. The opinion in effect said that if the court is to be in reality "a co-equal independent branch of our government," the cuts must be restored.[44] Both opinions relied on what is called the "inherent powers" doctrine.

Dissenting opinions (the written view of one or more judges who did not agree with the court majority) in each of the cases point up the contrasts between an aggressive and moderate approach to the conflict. In the Michigan case a minority opinion held that the test should be the ability of the court to operate at all, not "whether it can operate more conveniently or expeditiously." In the Pennsylvania case a dissenting opinion stated that if the case was to be decided on grounds that stressed the coequality of all three branches, it had better be prepared to extend to the executive branch the same power to write its own budget. If the court was not ready to do this, the dissenting judge argued, the court was, in effect, nominating the judiciary for *prima inter pares* status, first among equals. Many state and community legislators would likely argue that the courts have already given themselves such status.

All three instances of constitutional crisis were eventually resolved, but only because one branch was willing to take less than the full ex-

[42]Wisconsin Legislative Reference Bureau, *The Powers of the Wisconsin Supreme Court*, Research Bulletin 76-RB-1, January 1976.

[43]*Wayne Circuit Judges v. Wayne County* 383 Mich 10 (1969).

[44]*Commonwealth ex rel. Carroll v. Tate* 442 Pennsylvania 45 (1971).

tension of its rights. In such instances, one branch has to "blink" first. Although the courts backed down a bit in two of the three cases, they made their point.

LIMITATIONS ON JUDICIAL POLICYMAKING

State and local courts, as legitimizers of the law, have made strong efforts to assert their independence from the other branches of government, as well as to free themselves from political influence of the states and communities. Although they have made significant progress in this respect, we find, nevertheless, some important links that limit and influence judicial power to make policy.

Institutional Limitations

Both state constitutions and state laws provide institutional linkages between the courts and society. We discuss here the office of prosecutor, jury systems, corrections administration, and upper level judges—those linkages that tend to limit the powers of local judges.

The Politics of Prosecution.   Prosecutors as political officials serve as interpreters of community values about crime and perform a critical role in deciding which cases the courts will act on. They thus stand between the courts and local and state police agencies. At the state level the chief prosecutor is the attorney general and at the local level it is the district attorney or county prosecutor. In most states these officials are elected. Their main concern is the prosecution of violators of state law and, as such, these officials determine which criminal cases the courts will be asked to decide. Prosecution of city ordinance violators is left to the city attorney, often an official appointed by the city council.

Prosecution is essentially a political function, not only because most prosecutors are elected officials, but because most have further political ambitions. The office of county prosecutor is an important stepping stone to higher office—a judgeship, a legislative or congressional seat, or even the governorship. Prosecutors are often before the TV cameras as they discuss a violent crime that has shocked the community, when they discuss the details of a nighttime raid on an organized drug or gambling ring, or when they react to a court verdict.

The function is also political because prosecutors make important choices regarding the enforcement of criminal laws. Most crimes of violence, such as murder, rape, and armed robbery, will be prosecuted whenever possible. But whether special attention will be directed toward street prostitution, or organized prostitution in convention hotels, is a political choice; it could be bad for the convention business. Does the prosecutor crack down on pornography and gambling at the city club, or on the numbers rackets in the backrooms of the working class bars, or on shoplifting, fraudulent consumer practices, or "welfare cheats?" These, too, are political choices.

Police agencies also make some of these choices, but they are often heavily influenced by the prosecutor's willingness to prosecute certain kinds of crimes. If the prosecutor, in effect, says, "Don't bother this office with these minor crimes, we're after bigger fish," the police agencies probably will redirect their efforts. In addition prosecutors in some large counties have used federal grants to finance their own task forces to investigate and "crack down" on certain types of crimes.

Prosecutors also exercise a great deal of control over individual cases and may, in fact, screen out many of them before they ever reach a judge for a decision. Much of this is done by managing the plea-bargaining process. The prosecutor may threaten a suspect with a first-degree murder charge if the case has to go to trial, but will allow a second-degree charge if the defendant pleads guilty. Although courts usually insist on supervising plea bargaining, which charges will be made in the first instance is the prosecutor's decision, not the judge's. Plea bargaining, of course, is not necessarily politically motivated, but it does afford the prosecutor the opportunity to build an impressive record of convictions, while at the same time lowering the risk of too many acquittals.

The Jury System. In only a few ways do citizens ever participate directly in governmental decision making. The citizen jury is among the most important. It is defended because it serves to interpret community values to the courts, and thus limits and influences the policymaking of state and local judges. Citizen juries, because they consist of laymen in a world of legal jargon and technicalities, may as a result be only marginally influential on the professional judicial system.

The trial jury. The right of trial by a jury of one's peers, in spite of its traditional importance, has been subject to a variety of attacks from lawyers and judges and sociologists. The juror selection process, for instance, has been characterized as cumbersome, expensive, and time consuming. Typically, potential jurors are selected randomly from registered voter lists, property lists, or some other such list of residents. Upon call they appear for questioning by the lawyers conducting the trial. Some may be excused by law, others by the judge upon special request because of the citizens' occupations or because they have formed an opinion about the case. The defense attorney and prosecutor also may excuse a certain number of potential jurors for no stated reason—lawyers and defendants, for example, may want a maximum number of poor people on a jury considering embezzlement charges against a bank teller. The lawyers may ask that others be excused for a specific reason. Several days of costly court time may be taken to select the jury.

We find other problems in jury selection practices as well. Both the rules and strategies of juror selection produce disparate effects in the makeup of juries—that is, they tend not to be a broad cross section of people in the community. In fact they often have not been, to the point where in some southern courts blacks were systematically excluded.

Those excused by statute tend to be members of politically powerful groups. Those whom judges excuse may often be the better educated who "cannot be absent from their jobs."[45] One way in which the courts have tried to deal with this problem in recent years is by the "one day-one trial" approach. A potential juror need be available for selection only one day and, if not chosen, is excused. Those chosen serve for only one trial. Former procedures required a potential juror to be available for as long as a month—an imposition that most of us would consider substantial, even for an important civic responsibility.

The lawyers' tactics, of course, are seldom intended to produce a fair and impartial jury. In fact the usual strategy, as we noted, is to select a group who would most likely favor his or her side of the case. In recent years some lawyers have even hired specialists to research opinion in the community to determine which types of people are most likely to be favorably disposed to the defendant.[46]

On the other hand, adjustments have been made to reduce the possibility of "hung" juries, that is, those unable to make a decision regarding either guilt or innocence, thus raising the likelihood of a new trial. The U.S. Supreme Court in 1972 ruled that verdicts need not be unanimous in state criminal cases.[47] A few states now allow verdicts by majority vote, rather than requiring them to be unanimous. We also find

[45]There are other subtleties in juror selection. How biased, for example, is a jury on a capital case when jurors who oppose the death penalty are excluded? See George L. Jurow, "New Data on the Effect of a 'Death Qualified' Jury on the Guilt Determination Process," *Harvard Law Review*, 84, 1971, 567–611.

[46]For another technique see Arthur Lapham, "The Jury Card Index System of Obtaining Data on Prospective Jurors," *Texas Bar Journal*, 24, 1961.

[47]*Apodaca v. Oregon*, 406 US 404 and *Johnson v. Louisiana*, 406 U.S. 356.

the states permitting six-person juries for certain types of cases, instead of the traditional twelve, as a further way to cut time and dollar costs.

An additional criticism of the jury system concerns the process by which a jury actually comes to a decision. In cases where the jurors may have been sequestered for weeks, they undoubtedly are eager to pick up with their lives again and will want to decide quickly. They go to the jury room with no transcript of a long and involved trial. How do they decide? What pressures do they impose on the one or two who hold out? What do they do when they tell the judge they can reach no decision and the judge sends them back, in effect ordering them to reach a verdict? Critics ask if this is the way modern jurisprudence should be administered.[48]

Though the trial jury is required only to weigh the evidence and determine the facts—the judges' responsibility is to determine the legal dimensions—we find that juries, in effect, also legislate or establish policy themselves. In a 1977 Michigan murder trial, for example, a jury decided that the woman who admitted killing her husband by setting fire to his bed should be acquitted on the ground of temporary insanity. That a long history of physical abuse existed also was thought to have affected the jury decision. In a 1978 civil trial a jury awarded a judgment of $128 million—$125 million was for punitive reasons—against the Ford Motor Company to a young man who had been burned and disfigured as a result of an auto accident in which the gas tank burst. The judge lowered the judgment. In other cases juries have awarded large judgments against insurance and manufacturing companies, as well as municipalities. In so doing these juries are forcing the law to keep pace with the ever-changing values of the community and society. And though judges overturn jury decisions from time to time, such actions are not taken lightly as we see from Policy Box No. 18, "How Sacred A Jury Decision?"

The grand jury. The grand, or large, jury, often consisting of twenty or more citizens, traditionally has served to determine whether a prosecutor has sufficient evidence to bring a suspect to trial. This use of the grand jury has also proven to be costly and cumbersome and has thus fallen into disuse in many states. This function has been turned over to a lower level court through arraignment proceedings in which the pros-

[48]See Jerome Frank, "Something's Wrong With Our Jury System," in Robert L. Morlan, ed., *Capitol, Courthouse, and City Hall*, Houghton-Mifflin, Boston, 1972, 138–143.

POLICY BOX NO. 18   How Sacred a Jury Decision?

During 1970 Madison College in Harrisonburg, Virginia, was the site of a protest against the Vietnam War. About forty students conducted a sit-in. That a small college, one hundred miles from Washington, D.C., should have a Vietnam War sit-in is not particularly noteworthy. Many colleges and universities were the site of protests and demonstrations. That the protestors at Madison College also were demonstrating their dislike for alleged violations of student civil rights by the college administration, and supporting the cause of some professors whom the college refused to reappoint, did not distinguish this demonstration in any important way either. In fact as far as student demonstrations of the time went, it was probably a rather "run-of-the-mill" event.

In this case the college administrators called in the police to remove the demonstrators from the buidling. A number of demonstrators were arrested, charged with trespassing, convicted, and fined $100 each. Most paid the fines, but seven people asked for a trial in the county circuit court—a trial before the judge without a jury. The judge overruled the request and insisted that they be tried before a jury. The seven defendants were found guilty and the jury recommended a fine of $500 for four of them. For two of the remaining three, Jay G. Rainey and Stephen B. Roschelle (both students at the time), the jury recommended penalties of a $500 fine and six months in jail. The penalty recommended for James W. McClung (one of the professors whom the college refused to reappoint) was a $1000 fine and nine months in jail. All three appealed to a federal court on the grounds that their freedom of speech had been violated. A federal judge agreed, but when the prosecution appealed, the Fourth U.S. Circuit Court of Appeals reversed the federal judge's decision and upheld the original jury findings and recommendations.

By the time the decisions in the cases became final, seven years after the demonstration, the three men were nearly thirty years of age, had families, and were settled in good middle-class jobs: one in employee relations for a manufacturing concern, another as a computer programmer, and the third in the Library of Congress as a public information specialist. But, in September, 1977, Rockingham County Circuit Judge Joshua Robinson ordered the three men off to jail to "do their time." According to one newspaper report, "Suitcases in hand, neatly dressed, they did so."

On his way to jail, Rainey was quoted as saying, "it's a hell of a reason to send three people to jail who've built up their lives in the past seven years." He did not mention that "draft evaders" who left the country in protest of the war were granted amnesty. But certainly the fact had to be in the back of his mind. The county prosecutor said that the usual reasons for sending people to jail—punishment, retribution, or rehabilitation—did not apply in this case. Rather, as Judge Robinson suggested, the reason he sent the men to jail was because he refused to overturn a jury's decision. He had to do it, he said, to uphold the integrity of the judicial process. Jack DePoy, county prosecutor at the time the case originated, said that changing a jury's decision, "undercuts one of the basic principles of our system."

DePoy added, "It's hard to say they should not have exercised their right to protest. They could have served their time instead of appeal. To appeal, they paid their money and took their chances. They knew what they were doing."

What do you think? Did sending the men off to jail preserve the integrity of the state judicial system? Should the judge have made them pay the fine and suspended the jail term? When the appeals process goes beyond a certain time, should the changed circumstances affect the result? Should a new jury reconsider the case or sentence? Is it worthwhile to try to prove a point in court? Should the trial jury system be maintained at all?

SOURCE: This policy box is based on an account published in the *Detroit News*, September 21, 1977.

ecutor establishes the fact that a crime indeed has been committed, and that the evidence is sufficient to bind the accused over for trial.

The citizen grand jury has not faded from the scene entirely, however. It is now used primarily for investigative purposes—to investigate corruption in public offices, or to uncover the intricacies of organized crime and criminal conspiracies. In this capacity they operate in secrecy and can compel witnesses to testify regarding their knowledge. By granting immunity to key witnesses, grand juries are frequently able to gather evidence that often could not otherwise be uncovered. In these proceedings prosecutors draw out the evidence for the jurors to hear and they decide whether charges should be filed.

Corrections Administration. We find that the administration of corrections also serves to limit the judges in their policymaking. Once a person has been convicted of a crime and sentenced to a term in the state prison or to parole, the convict effectively leaves the jurisdiction of the judge and is assigned to the state corrections department.

A trial court judge may make special efforts to assure that a particularly dangerous criminal will serve a lengthy sentence, by sentencing him or her to "life plus five years," for example; but it is the corrections department and the parole board, and not the judge, who determine how long the person will actually be behind bars. States have rules regarding when a prison inmate may become eligible for release and under what conditions, but corrections officials may not always decide to release on the basis of how much "correcting" has been done. Overcrowding of the state prison and inadequate funding, as well as the socioeconomic standing of the convict, may often influence their decisions.

Judges face similar limitations when they release persons convicted of a crime, by reason of insanity, to the state's mental health department. On occasion such persons may undergo a period of psychiatric treatment, and be declared no longer mentally ill and released rather quickly from the custody of the mental health department.

Upper Level Judges.   Finally we note that higher level judges often limit the policymaking initiatives of lower level judges. This comes about largely through the appeals process, but it may also come about through judicial rules and administrative procedures.

At least in theory every decision is subject to review by a higher court. It is the losing lawyer or client, of course, who decides whether an effort will be made to recoup the loss and, in so doing, provide a policy check on the judges. Most judges, we suspect, always have in the back of their minds the possiblity of an appeal and such possibility, together with professional pride, serves to constrain them from wandering too far from established policy. A reversed judge may wax philosophical and say, "I'd rather be right than be upheld," but his or her chagrin is nevertheless evident.

Judicial Policy and Public Opinion

Does public opinion also influence judicial policymaking? The answer, we think, is a clear yes, but we hasten to emphasize that this does not mean judicial policy is controlled by public opinion. As we have indicated, judges as legitimizers of the law seek to walk a tightrope between professional points of view and the political sensitivities that most of them have honed as they worked their way to their place on the bench.

Customs and Beliefs of the Public.   Customs, beliefs, and social conditions were the starting point for observing how judges reach decisions. We see it still important today. State and community judges dealing with pornography, for example, could rule that freedom of speech means exactly that, and that all laws seeking to prohibit pornographic materials are unconstitutional. But judges have not so ruled, because a significant portion of society thinks that some limits should be placed on materials that appeal solely to prurient interests.

Or take the matter of crime. Judges watch TV and see a string of crime fighters from "Baretta" to "Kojak," giving criminals "their just desserts," which may mean "shooting them dead." Judges are also aware of the public—they read the newspapers and the letters to the editors—and can easily find evidence that at least some of the public

Putting pressure on the judges.

want to "take criminals out of circulation for a long time." "put back the death penalty," and other bumper-sticker solutions to crime.

It is difficult, of course, to determine what the true state of public opinion is—pollsters still report a general mood, changed since 1968 or 1970, favoring "surer punishment of criminals." While citizens become used to the fact that they cannot walk after dark in many cities and suburbs without fear of being "mugged," they are not reconciled to that fact. We would, therefore, probably be correct in assuming that most persons now favor more strictness in the handling of crime—certainly more than they did ten years ago.

The other side of the public's feelings, though, is that most do not desire a police state. They are not happy about "third-degree" methods, roughing up suspects, bullying of citizens by police, or about having criminals "railroaded" through the courts to jail. As the sons and daughters of middle- and upper-class citizens were jailed in the late 1960s for drug convictions and participating in demonstrations against the Vietnam war, they and their parents gained some first- hand knowledge about inhumane conditions sometimes associated with our criminal justice system.

The political balance that the supreme court judges are striving for is between the rights of the law-abiding (that is, protecting the security of the community and the innocent), against protecting, in full, the rights of the accused. They have to consider the social setting. Guilt of the accused is often established by police methods that may involve invasion of privacy, particularly in a day of sophisticated electronics. But social costs resulting from what may be too great a concern for the rights of the accused may also be high—higher than society is or should be willing to pay.

As Andrew Hacker states, "Certainly crime tests the limits of liberalism."[49] Complete safety does not seem appropriate to most of us if we achieve it in an exchange for our liberties or the liberties of others. Nevertheless we cannot ignore the fact that the victims of preventable crime are also being deprived of their safety and also of their liberties. Therein lies the American dilemma over criminal behavior. It is also a dilemma faced with some regularity by judges of a state's supreme court and its intermediate court of appeals, and it is also a concern of judges of general trial courts who conduct most of the trials and do most of the sentencing.

Pressures From Politically Aroused Legislators. We also find judges taking into account how public opinion may affect changes in law. Judges may temper their rulings on certain policy questions because of concern for the legislative actions that aroused public opinion may set in motion. We have seen the legislatures respond to public concern over crime, for example, by passing laws that limit judges' authority to make sentencing decisions. Some, such as the Maine legislature in 1975, established a "flat time" sentencing policy—the law specifies for each crime the minimum and maximum sentence that may be imposed. Many judges, of course, would argue that each person's sentence should be decided on an individual basis rather than on a "blanket" basis by law.

Similarly, higher level judges have sometimes sided with county commissioners in their disputes with local judges, at least in part to ward off threats from legislators to pass laws that would more closely circumscribe judicial behavior.

Such concerns for public opinion and possible changes in law and state constitutions, of course, seldom find their way into the legal opin-

[49]Andrew Hacker, "Getting Used to Mugging," *New York Review of Books*, April 19, 1973, 9–14.

ions that the judges render, but judges exercise caution so as not to goad the public into taking drastic actions that will limit even more the authority of the courts to judge individual disputes on their merits and the law.

A Final Comment

We have stressed two themes throughout this chapter. The first is the struggle by state and community judges to give legitimacy to the laws of the state. The state courts publicly emphasize their professionalism and dignified decorum as if judging were a technical procedure free of political concerns. Yet, in actuality state and community judges are engaged in the most delicate of political maneuvering—often an attempt to reconcile opposites. They are trying to adjust the law of our constitutions to present realities. They are trying to balance the requirements of order with the imperatives of liberty. They try to balance the need for economic production with the need to control such production for other community benefits, such as the environment or the ability of employees to earn living wages.

The second theme supplements the first. In the period since 1925, and especially so since 1960, the state and community courts have been federalized. Intergovernmental relations is a major aspect of judicial decision making. The courts remain organizationally independent and diverse, but in large measure are functioning units of a national system of justice. Not every question in dispute, particularly not civil disputes between private parties, has become a part of that evolving national system of justice. But enough has become so to provide the undergirding of a national legal framework for our whole society. In a society that in large measure has become national in scope, the law must conform in some ways to broad national standards if it is to be regarded as legitimate by all of the citizens. The nationalized legal system, in which the state courts play a major role, has made us in this and other respects, one society before the law.

HIGHPOINTS OF CHAPTER 9: STATE AND COMMUNITY JUDGES AS LEGITIMIZERS

In this chapter we began (1) by emphasizing how the federal system encouraged diversity in the organization of state courts. We discerned an underlying pattern or organization similar to that of the national courts, but emphasized how much any state could diverge from it. We next (2) looked at how federal court decisions since 1925 have brought a degree of unity to that system by using the Fourteenth Amendment to apply many of the guarantees of the Bill of Rights to the states. We then (3) examined the political environment of the judiciary, noting how states recruit judges and how the courts seek to assert their independence from the other branches of government—in part by unifying the courts and centralizing court management and administration under the control of the state supreme court. Finally (4) we considered some of the limitations on judicial policymaking. We noted that prosecutors, citizen juries, and correction departments, and judges themselves, influence and limit judicial decisions, as well as the matters that reach the judicial agenda. We also discussed how public opinion influences judicial policymaking.

ADMINIS-
TRATORS AS
STATE AND
COMMUNITY
MANAGERS

10

Early in 1977 a Republican congressman, Robert Michel of Illinois, arguing that bureaucracy and government regulation are growing too fast, quoted William Alton Carter III, "a small businessman and peanut farmer from Plains, Georgia," on the subject of state administrators. "The major complaint I have," "Billy" Carter said, "is that 90 percent of the folks they send here to inspect us don't know anything. We have some kids right out of college who don't know a damned thing. Now they're after me to put a couch in the women's washroom in case someone gets sick. Hell I don't have room to put in any couches. So I told 'em to go to hell, and I haven't done it yet." Representative Michel, who noted that Billy Carter had a brother currently employed by the U.S. government, hoped that this gem of wisdom would come to that brother's attention.[1]

Billy Carter was disturbed, as were many people in business and other citizens as well, because in the last twenty years government has taken responsibility for many decisions formerly made by private individuals and organizations. Government regulations now touch

[1]Marjorie Hunter, "Look Who's a Hero Now in Congress," (New York *Times* Service) Detroit *Free Press*, May 19, 1977, p. 12B.

everything from the length of bread loaves to the qualifications of garage mechanics.

Like many students, politicians, and citizens, we, too, are not wholly comfortable with "big government." Yet it seems unlikely that Americans will substantially reduce the extent of regulation through large scale bureaucracy either at state or community levels. Thus we propose to examine the political role bureaucracies play in policy making and how students and reformers suggest they be kept under control of elected officials.

Overview.   In this chapter we begin by looking at the way state and community services were administered before World War II when state jobs were passed out as patronage by political parties and officials. We will next look at how the state public service was professionalized with two reforms—the merit system and administrative reorganization. Then we will consider how the modern state civil service participates in making policy, and will stress two important facts that encourage such participation—professionalization and public employee unionization. We will end by examining a series of techniques suggested by officials, students of administration, and private groups in an attempt to strengthen the control of elected officials and the public over state administrators.

PATRONAGE POLITICS—AS ONCE PRACTICED IN STATES AND COMMUNITIES

State and local administration, until about 1940, was largely a patronage operation—employees got their jobs through political connections and "paid" for their jobs with "kickbacks" from their salaries.

How the Patronage System Worked

By 1950 less than half the states had comprehensive civil service systems—systems under which employees are hired according to stated professional criteria. Oklahoma, studied by H.O. Waldby was typical of a patronage state.

The Key Criterion: Political Loyalty.   The governor of Oklahoma and his party decided who would work for the state. As a new governor took office, he "threw the rascals out"—firing most of the employees of the previous administration and then spent the first months of his administration throwing new rascals in—handing out state jobs to his own supporters.

State employees were expected to be party workers in political campaigns. In 1932, for example, a rather colorful governor, William "Alfalfa Bill" Murray, hero of the "overall-clad men and ginghamed women," was fighting for voter support of three constitutional amendments. To help out in the final days of the campaign, he gave *all* state employees a two and a half day holiday with orders to work to get out the vote.

A prospective employee first had to secure endorsement from his or her state senator or representative or both. Many legislators only gave such endorsements to persons who had supported their own election with contributions of time or money, or who were backed by someone who had. Applicants also usually had to get their county Democratic committee endorsement. These endorsements were then turned over to the governor's patronage advisor, who kept a record of each legislator's votes and, on that basis, decided how many patronage jobs each legislator "deserved." For instance, Waldby reports, "In 1949 Representative Lonnie Brown of McAlester had occasionally been critical of the administration, while Senator M.O. Counts, also of McAlester, was known as a strong administration man. Senator Counts got to name forty-two employees at the McAlester state prison while Representative Brown sponsored only five."

The Limits of Patronage. But not all state jobs could be filled by patronage methods. Some jobs were too unattractive—Waldby cites such jobs as aides in the state's then poorly run mental institutions. Some jobs required a measure of skill. He notes that the state police was an island of professionalism in Oklahoma's patronage system. Local units, too had difficulty in filling some lower paying jobs that required a bit of skill—Pennsylvania county politicians often had difficulty finding trained bulldozer operators with the "right" political connections.[2]

Although not all patronage employees were incompetents, the situation was pretty much as described by Abe Martin—the sage of Indiana. "Every once in a while," Martin wrote, "we miss a nuisance and find out he's got a political job."

Administrative Structure in a Patronage System

Students describe the state and community administrative structures that resulted as "chaotic." The legislative body often created hodgepodge agencies with independent status. Many were headed by commissions or boards that were sometimes appointed by the legislative body or someone other than the governor or mayor. The terms of office were long and overlapped the terms of governors or mayors and often laws prevented the executive from removing appointees. And at the urging of interest groups, the requirements for agency heads were so narrowly defined that only someone recommended by the interest group would qualify.

Was there then no overall meshing together, or coordination? Occasionally a forceful governor or mayor appeared who wielded his patronage skillfully and ruthlessly and so managed to make legislators and administrators work together. We discover, too, that state or community political machines developed effective control from time to time. But the programs such machines sponsored, while sometimes nicely coordinated, were not always programs that reformers and other "good citizens" might desire.

So state and community governments limped along, generally handling tasks that did not require a professionalized bureaucracy. Sometimes administration was mired in corruption and scandal. Usually it operated inefficiently. But we also find that some outstanding people appeared who viewed their duties with a sense of mission.

Some Outstanding Public Servants. A young Massachusetts lawyer was elected state legislator in 1827. In 1835 he became speaker of the House, and in 1837 was appointed secretary to the newly created state board of education. This looked like an ordinary attempt to get "on the government gravy train"—but it was not. Over the next twelve years Horace Mann not only revolutionized the Massachusetts school system,

---

[2]H.O. Waldby, *The Patronage System in Oklahoma*, The Transcript Co., Norman, 1950 and Frank J. Sorauf, "Patronage and Party," *The Midwest Journal of Political Science* 3, May 1959, 11–26.

but laid the groundwork for public school administration nationally. He collected statistics, raised public interest in education, badgered legislators, secured better teachers at higher salaries, established teacher training institutes and crusaded for better constructed and equipped schools. He ended his career as president of Antioch College, where he crusaded for coeducation. All of this reform and first-rate administration occurred in a patronage system—by a man who was a political appointee.

From 1902 to 1921, Edwin Fremont Ladd provides another example. Ladd served as food commissioner of North Dakota and became known nationally for his fights against adulterated food products. He detailed his findings in carefully prepared reports, for he was a trained chemist. He, too, became a college president of the North Dakota Agricultural College (now North Dakota State University), and served as a U.S. senator from 1921 until his death.

What distinguishes both these men, and many others—men and women—is the fact that they swam against the current of their day. They struggled to improve conditions in areas as widely separated as prison reform, conservation of resources, mental health care, or road construction. They were often bitterly opposed by other state or community employees and by superiors and were condemned as "radicals." Most were fighting and struggling types who overcame the hurdles of handling public services through patronage politics.

How Much Patronage is Left Today?

The dominance of patronage politics is largely a thing of the past in most states and communities, but a good deal still remains. Kentucky, for example, adopted a comprehensive merit system law in 1960 that reduced patronage appointments by 12,000. Still, by 1968, according to the estimate of Malcolm Jewell and Everett Cunningham, 4000 out of 20,000 state employees (20 percent) were not covered by the merit system.[3]

Why Patronage Persists. Patronage "islands" remain in every state and many communities for several reasons. One is that officeholders have been a major source of campaign funds. To illustrate, an Indiana state legislator in 1976 called for strict federal enforcement of laws against "2% Clubs." These clubs required some state and local employees to contribute 2 percent of their annual salaries to the dominant

[3]Malcolm E. Jewell and Everett W. Cunningham, *Kentucky Politics*, University of Kentucky Press, Lexington, Ky., 1968, p. 43.

political party. As a news item stated, "Both major political parties have used such a system in Indiana for decades."[4]

Second, patronage jobs are also one of the most effective ways to build a political organization. John M. Bailey, one-time Democratic National Party Chairman, built such an organization in Connecticut during the 1950s. Bailey's biographer, Joseph I. Lieberman, argued that the skillful handing out of government jobs is as crucial to the politicians' art as "the offer of stock options or fringe benefits or high recompense is to the business executive seeking able and loyal co-workers."[5]

Governors and mayors still find the handing out of government jobs useful in their efforts to dominate their political party and its legislators.[6]

Patronage still exists, also, because it is difficult to follow civil service procedures for some jobs—especially those that involve part-time or temporary help. Thus, even in most of the "pure civil service states," we find patronage considerations in hiring seasonal workers for the highway or parks departments, and appointing lawyers in probate cases.

In the modern industrial society, however, a system of patronage practices to handle most public services is too costly. To fire the whole top hierarchy of a department, as Allen B. "Happy" Chandler and other governors of Kentucky once did, would cripple its program, get a "bad" reputation with professionals in the field, and endanger federal grant funds as well.

PROFESSIONALIZATION OF THE STATE PUBLIC SERVICE

The turn-of-the-century reformers were repelled by the patronage system and considered it a wasteful, corrupt, and spendthrift way to run a government. In its place they proposed to hire a corps of civil servants who would honestly, efficiently, and economically carry out the policy directions of the governor and legislature. The efforts of reformers at the state and community levels had two major thrusts, the merit system and administrative reorganization.

[4]"Roush Expects '2% Club' Ban Enforcement," Indianapolis Star, October 5, 1976.

[5]Joseph I. Lieberman, The Power Broker, A Biography of John M. Bailey, Modern Political Boss, Houghton Mifflin, Boston, 1966, p. 341.

[6]Daniel P. Moynihan and James Q. Wilson, "Patronage in New York State 1955–1959," The American Political Science Review 58, June 1964, 386–301.

The Merit System

In 1883 Congress passed the Pendleton Act, which put a part of the federal bureaucracy under what reformers called "the merit system," and what we also call today civil service.[7] The reformers wanted government to choose most employees on the basis of merit—as determined by some measurement of technical skills and professional competence.

The top positions—department or agency heads—would still be filled by political appointment, as would members of the executive's staff because these jobs are regarded as "policymaking" positions to be filled by persons sharing the governor's or mayor's political views.

But the rest of the bureaucracy would be professionalized—in the apt phrase of Herbert Kaufman, they would typify to the ideal of "neutral competence."[8] The employees would be "neutral" toward partisan politics—to ensure neutrality, rules prohibited employees from participating in partisan politics, except for voting in elections. The employees would be "competent" because they had met special skills and training standards.

Important Elements of Merit Systems.   Though merit systems differ in practice, the following conditions are fundamental.

1. Employees demonstrate their fitness for the job and promotions by passing a test, by previous work experience, or by completion of some type of training.
2. Once past probation, employees can only be dismissed if shown to be grossly inefficient or guilty of criminal activity or a moral lapse.
3. Positions across agencies and departments are classified according to duties and responsibilities. Pay is based on the classification level with separate steps ranked according to length of service.

The Merits and Demerits of Civil Service.   When we compare the merit system to the chaos and political and personal favoritism that are common in a patronage politics system, we can see that civil service

[7]For sponsoring this "reformist" legislation, the Ohio Democratic party denied George Hunt Pendleton renomination to the U.S. Senate in 1885. President Grover Cleveland, sympathetic to civil service, took care of Pendleton—he appointed him minister to Germany—a major political patronage plum.

[8]Herbert Kaufman, "Administrative Decentralization and Political Power," *Public Administration Review* 29, January–February, 1969, 3–15. He names the two other themes we deal with—"the representativeness of patronage practices" and "executive leadership."

brought some reasonable guarantee that pay would be commensurate to responsibilities, promotion based on work performance, and that dismissal would be based on reasons related to work performance. For these reasons alone, we find civil service hard to fault. It clearly contributed to the job satisfaction that state and community employees have a right to expect and to their own self-respect.

Why then do some of its critics call it the "so-called" merit system or the "silly service?"

Supervision is more difficult. Supervisors often find it almost impossible to fire an inefficient employee or even one who has acted improperly. Supervisors find that the required hearings turn out to be very trying—time wasting, filled with personal bitterness—an emotional drain. If found guilty the civil servant may file an appeal—some cases end in the courts. And, of course, the supervisor risks losing the case. If so, the agency is saddled with a now thoroughly alienated employee. Supervisors with one or two such experiences sometimes find it easier to transfer the offending employee or "wall off" the employee by creating some new, but unimportant, tasks for him or her.

Fortunately most state and community civil servants have enough competence and self-respect to do their jobs reasonably well. But a small number, who are less dedicated or skilled, can make a supervisor's job a headache.

Racial and sexual bias. Civil service systems also have not been able to deal very effectively with problems of race and sex discrimination. Most states now have offices of affirmative action or equal employment opportunity agencies. These have some influence in overcoming problems of discrimination, but are also under attack as fostering reverse discrimination. Most such agencies have not been able to root out the subtle ways in which discriminatory practices are perpetrated.

How do we measure merit? In many states merit personnel systems are under attack because the civil service commission is really unable to do what they say they will do—select the best applicant on the basis of skills and experience. One reason is that they are swamped with applicants. Illinois, for example, receives about 120,000 applications each year.

The system tends to break down in selecting candidates for higher level professional positions. Often the central personnel agencies do not have a "register" of qualified people, or the registers are so old that the people on them are no longer interested. Civil service then lets agency heads recruit their own candidates and appoint them on a "provisional basis." Later on when civil service develops a new register for the position, the provisional appointee needs only to pass the test rather than score at the top to keep the job. This may be the only way to work a system that is overloaded, but it bypasses the principle of competitive examination and means that agency heads often select the employee without independent screening.

A further problem is that skills and experience are difficult to evaluate; and even if there are objective standards, testing for them may be impossible and achieving their uniform application is virtually impossible. Whether an applicant gets the job often depends on whether he or she puts down the right "buzzwords," that is, the kind of things the evaluators are looking for. This condition may handicap the timid and those who take too seriously the warning about "false information" on application forms—some threaten loss of job, or even a fine and jail for violations.

What Critics Suggest. Some students and politicians recommend significant changes in the civil service system. They argue that we should turn away from trying to create neutrally competent automatons— what Meg Greenfield of *Newsweek* describes as "the great holy grail of American political reform . . . an idealized, unattainable—and frankly weird state in which there is no discretion, no judgment, no flesh and blood, no better and worse—in short, no human politics." She and others who share her views argue for being less concerned with political bias and more with actual efficiency. They recommend giving supervisors greater responsibility for judging employee performance and more leeway in hiring, firing, and making promotions—if the goal is to create "a genuine merit system."[9]

The Spread of Merit Employment. The civil service system spread very gradually in the national government and much more gradually in the states and communities. New York and Massachusetts set up partial civil service in 1885 and 1886. Then, twenty years later, in 1905, Governor Robert LaFollette set up perhaps the first thorough state civil service system as part of his "progressive idea for Wisconsin." By 1934, however, only seventeen states and the larger cities had some kind of civil service commission.

The impact of intergovernmental relations. Then the dam broke. The Hatch Act of 1939, passed by the national government, required that state employees handling federal funds be free of partisan involvement. In 1947 the Supreme Court upheld the act.[10] Other national ac-

[9]Meg Greenfield, "What Is Merit?" *Newsweek*, March 13, 1978, p. 100.

tions followed, including in 1970 the Inter-governmental Personnel Act that provided grants to improve state and local civil service systems.

Today we find that all states and many local governments have civil service commissions, but states and communities vary in the percent of state employees covered. About half a dozen states still try to limit the system to employees who handle federal grants. As long as the grants were in a few major areas, the states were able to limit civil service sharply. But with federal assistance increasing in both amount and scope, "playing checkers" with the civil service positions becomes more difficult.

We see again how the states and communities can resist federal intrusions, if not permanently, then for extended periods. As we would expect, though, civil service coverage in the states and communities is being steadily extended as government services become more specialized and require more training and as federal grants touch almost every service function.

Administrative Reorganization

In 1909 The Peoples' Power League of Oregon, a "radical reform" group, proposed to concentrate executive power in the hands of the governor; checked only by an independent auditor. Progressives around the country, such as Governor Charles E. Hughes of New York, immediately endorsed the idea. It took another eight years before a state adopted the plan.

The Illinois Reorganization Program.   The first state to reorganize its government for "executive leadership" was Illinois in 1917. A rather remarkable new Republican governor, Frank O. Lowden, wanted government reorganized, his biographer says, in order to "harness more effectively the new economic and social forces born of the industrial age."[11]

What Lowden accomplished provides a blueprint for administrative reorganization. He followed all of tenets of what is now called "traditional public administration,"—and also almost all of the ideas good government reformers had been talking about.

1. He proposed that agencies be sorted out and grouped by function into departments so that all the natural resources agencies, for example, would be in one department.

[10]*Oklahoma v. U.S. Civil Service Commission* 330 U.S. 127, 1947.

[11]William T. Hutchinson, *Lowden of Illinois, The Life of Governor Frank O. Lowden,* University of Chicago Press, Chicago, 1975, 2 volumes. See especially 293–326 of Vol. I.

2. Departments would be organized into a hierarchy with single lines of authority flowing to a point occupied by the department head.
3. Lowden insisted that the overall number of departments remain small, so their heads might meet together easily as a cabinet to the governor. (He called for nine departments and located the directors in offices near the capitol so he could meet with them regularly.)
4. Lowden insisted departments be headed by a single individual, rather than by commissions. "Individuals, not bodies of men, do things," he said.
5. Lowden wanted these department heads to be appointed by the governor, not by civil service or the legislature and to serve at his or her pleasure alone.
6. Lowden created staff agencies to service all of the administrative "line" departments, as the civil service commission and the legal department under the attorney general then were doing. Later other staff departments, such as central purchasing, motor pools, computer services, printing, and building management, would be devised and placed into a separate department of administration.
7. Most important in Governor Lowden's view, was centralizing money management in a department of finance. The finance department director would help the governor prepare an executive budget. Through the budget Lowden hoped he would be able to "manage" the state administrative branch. Never again, he hoped, would legislative sessions end, as the previous one had, with forty-nine appropriations bills passed at the pressure of agency heads without anyone trying to weigh one agency's needs in respect to another's.
8. Lowden created an auditor independent of the governor who would determine whether departments had spent state funds legally. Some states originally designated an elective official to conduct the post–audit. More recently a number have made this officer an appointee of the legislature.

How much did Frank Lowden miss? Very little we think. Most later additions to reorganization were reforms we already discussed in Chapter 8—to "beef up" the governor's staff legal powers and term.

The Politics of Administrative Reorganization. Administrative reorganization has not always come easily. As we would expect, decentralized agencies independent of the mayor, governor, or even a department head have had their dogged, last ditch defenders. The state of Mississippi's Legislative Fact Finding Committee, according to York

Willbern, reported the following as the "typical" response of agency heads to proposals for administrative reorganization: "I think this is one of the very best things that has ever been done in the state of Mississippi. . . . However, my department is of a type, character and kind that cannot be consolidated with any other agency, as its duties and functions are unique . . . transfer of any duties of this department would work a hardship and prevent citizens from receiving benefits to which they are entitled."[12]

Forces for independence and autonomy. An important force for separatism, one Lowden recognized as too difficult to attack, are the elected department heads. These officials, as we noted, are still relatively common in state and community government. Their status is often embedded in the state constitution. They are used to running "their own shop" free of outside direction. To have themselves or their departments report to the governor or mayor, or to be appointed rather than elected, would seem like a demotion.

Reorganization is also opposed by clientele groups or those regulated by the agency if they have established good relations with the agency. Agency independence means having a sign on the door that says, "Chief Executive, Department Heads, and Legislators—keep out!"

Reformers, ironically, also want independence for some agencies. When a new function is begun—civil service agencies a generation ago, or environmental, consumer protection, or civil rights agencies today—the reformers fear that old line department heads or the governor or mayor may soft-pedal or downgrade the new program. It is better, the reformers argue, to put the new function in a separate independent agency where administrators support the goals of the new program. (And who are we to say that they are wholly wrong?)

Sometimes the public wants to keeps a function "free from politics." Thus, after a series of scandals, Alabama set up its prison system out of the administrative hierarchy with an independent board of corrections and institutions to replace the appointed department head. Our state university systems and state and community education agencies are also often given this independent status with the idea of keeping them "free from political meddling" by governors and legislators.

We find that professionalism also encourages the desire for agency independence. "What do governors, mayors, or legislators know about child abuse?", the professional social workers may reason. "Why

[12]This section is based upon the perceptive comments of York Willbern, "Administration in State Governments," in the American Assembly, *The Forty-Eight States, Their Tasks as Policy Makers and Administrators*, Columbia University, Graduate School of Business, New York, 1955, 115–119.

should politics have anything to do with scientific harvesting of the deer herd," the professional in Natural Resources may argue. Independence and separation from the governor's administrative hierarchy lessens the possibility of such "political interference."

The forces work together in Missouri. In the 1930s a constitutional amendment set up a Missouri Department of Conservation under a commission; funding was from the proceeds of hunting and fishing licenses. But the system needed more money. In 1973 a campaign for the new monies and expanded conservation programs began. It was led by the conservation department's "respected staff of trained professionals." Missouri has what conservationists in other states described as "one of the purest conservation departments in the nation." The conservation department published a "Design for Conservation." A constitutional amendment was proposed to levy a special sales tax of one-eighth of 1 percent added to the 3 percent sales tax and was earmarked for conservation. The Conservation Federation of Missouri, a coalition of most of the state's hunting and conservation clubs joined the campaign. "The Federation flooded the state with appeals and news releases, recruited an army of volunteers to talk up the proposal everywhere they went, and enlisted the support of such groups as the Audubon Society and garden clubs."[13] In 1975 the amendment was placed on the ballot and adopted. It doubled funding for the Missouri Conservation Department, and made it more independent than before of legislative or gubernatorial control.

The Spread of Administrative Reorganization. By 1919 Massachusetts, Nebraska, and Idaho, as well, adopted the Illinois model; in 1921 California, Ohio, and Washington followed suit. Cities and counties also adopted features of the plan. In 1949 we find another spurt of such reorganization inspired by the federal government's Hoover Commission reports on federal organization—thirty-three state study commissions were appointed by governors and called "Little Hoover" commissions. Today all states and most communities have adopted some of the features of the reform model for centralizing their governmental bureaucracies. Georgia under Jimmy Carter consolidated three hundred departments and boards into twenty-two departments. The most sweeping recent changes have been in such varied states as Louisiana, Missouri, Idaho, and Kentucky.[14]

[13]James A.O. Crowe, "In the Open" column, "It's Time to Rescue the Michigan Department of Natural Resources from Politicians," Detroit *News*, December 12, 1976, p. 14F.

[14]For a good recent survey from which some of these data are taken, see Neal R. Peirce, "State/Local Report, Structural Reform of Bureaucracy Grows Rapidly," *National*

National Government Influences On Administrative Reorganization?
Federal laws or grant programs do not directly encourage administrative centralization, although some states and communities have used federal planning grant funds for this purpose. Generally federal grants specify that funds must be handled by only one state agency or department, and this has encouraged some centralization.

But we discover also that the links between state or community and national agencies encourage agency independence. In this case it is not so much that the agency becomes organizationally independent—rather, federal grants requirements have encouraged agency heads to pay less attention than they once did to the concerns of governors or mayors, department heads or legislators. Their standard answer to any criticism or questioning is, "That's what is required by the federal grant." To combat this tendency the Pennsylvania state legislature in 1976, as we noted in Chapter 7, included all federal grant monies in its appropriation bills—thus indicating that it had the power to decide whether and how the money would be spent. The courts have been asked to rule on the matter.

How Successful is Administrative Reorganization?   Dale Bumpers, when governor of Arkansas (1971–1975), said his state's bureaucracy was "like a 700 pound marshmallow. You can kick it, scream at it, cuss it, but it is very reluctant to move."

Even as governors and mayors are implementing new reorganization plans, the important question is whether reorganization accomplishes all that Governor Lowden in 1917 optimistically hoped it would. It has certainly increased the executive's power. Executives have been able to exert greater influence than before through the hierarchy and especially, as Lowden anticipated, through the budget powers. Yet most students would say that reorganization by itself has achieved only partial success. Why have bureaucracies become so difficult to control?

STATE AND COMMUNITY ADMINISTRATION IN ACTION

At some point between the onset of the Great Depression and the end of World War II, the federal bureaucracy became "a politically critical mass." The bureaucracy's political resources made it capable of resisting direction by presidents, even when the chain of command had been perfected. Federal administrators could and did begin to exert an independent influence on America's public policy.

Journal, April 4, 1975, 502–508. Also see the most recent edition of *The Book of the States, Op. cit.*, for a brief summary of such actions during the prior two years.

The same process is happening in the states and communities. State and local employees have been increasing rapidly over the past decade. (Figure 10-1). Most states and many communities, we suspect, have reached or will soon reach the point where their bureaucracy also is "a politically critical mass." No longer can we delude ourselves with visions of neutrally competent servants loyally struggling to carry out the demands of their executive superiors. Now we see a body of administrators and public employees who have become a branch coequal to the legislative body, courts, and executive.

How did the reformers go wrong?

The Human Factors of Administration

Modern students of organization reject the simple notion that members of organizations are like pieces on a chess board that can be moved about any way that the head of the organization pleases. They find administrators have their own purposes and goals, and that these sometimes differ very much from the goals of governors, mayors or legislators.

Figure 10-1
The Growth of Bureaucracy

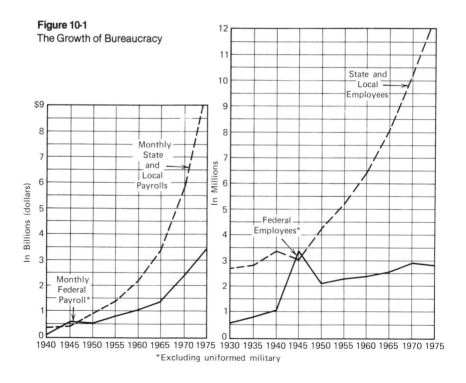

*Excluding uniformed military

James Q. Wilson put it this way—"the behavior of persons who lead or speak for an organization can best be understood in terms of their efforts *to maintain and enhance the organization and their position in it.*"[15] State and community administrators, we suggest, are concerned with more than meekly carrying out the orders of the governor or mayor or city managers—they are at least as concerned with building up their own agencies and with advancing their own careers. They are neither "conservative" or "liberal"—self-preservation comes first; a motivation evidenced in the 1978 "tax revolt" elections.

Two aspects of administration are related to the expression of greater independence by administrators than was true in the past—professionalism and increasing job satisfaction of employees. Typically, higher managerial levels are more concerned with professional values, and lower levels with improving job conditions. Both aspects make it more difficult for executives or legislators to control administrators.

The Impact of Professionalism

Professional administration has resulted in many notable triumphs. Look around your own state or community. Professionals have designed and built modern highway systems and city parkways that combine beauty with utility. "Snake pit" mental institutions have been turned into centers of more humane treatment. Wildlife preserves, local parks, and points of natural beauty and historical interest have been preserved for future generations. State and community libraries have amassed impressive and well-cataloged collections of valuable materials as well as books for the more casual reader.

How do we explain such desirable results? Many students attribute them to "professionalism." *The Encyclopedia of Social Science* describes professionalism as a standard of behavior that emphasizes service to a client, to the community, and to other professionals.[16] The legitimate interests of clients are placed ahead of the professional's personal comfort. Professional goals will not be sacrificed to political pressure or for personal gain. Professionalism is thus a service orientation, one often drilled into professionals during their training. To sacrifice professional norms is seen by the trained professional as a kind of personal disgrace.

[15]James Q. Wilson, *Political Organization*, Basic Books, New York, 1973. See especially 3–91.

[16]C.F. Taeusch, "Professional Ethics," *Encyclopedia of the Social Sciences*, Macmillan, New York, 1934, 12, 472–476.

Having been imbued with the values of professionalism, the state administrator not surprisingly attempts to influence state policymaking. Should the mental health professional stand by idly when the state legislature or the governor's office is debating how to implement a mental health program? Should the city fire chief not resist a proposed budget cut that reduces fire inspections to a level regarded as risky? Should corrections officials have no say in how prisons are designed and run?

The answer that professional administrators give is "certainly not," an answer we would no doubt share in their position. This answer sometimes, of course, brings them into direct conflict with the directives of elective officials.

The Political Resources of Professional Administrators. Professional administrators have resources that enable them to influence state or community policy and resist direction from elected officials.

Tenure. Time is almost always on the side of the administrators. Civil service guarantees administrators long tenure, except for those few administrators at the very top who are chosen by the governor or policy board. Some of them may, in fact, have civil service status and, if removed as top administrators, are able to return to the ranks as second or third level administrators, sometimes at a higher rate of pay. Elected officials, by contrast, serve set terms. We know that it is relatively common for administrators to "wait out" a hostile governor or mayor or powerful legislator, who the administrators know will leave their positions in from five to ten years—administrators have government careers in top positions, spanning fifteen or more years and total government careers of up to forty years.

Delay tactics, of course, will not always guarantee that administrators get their way. But to get their way, a governor or mayor and their staffs may have to invest more time and effort than they planned. They are likely to seek a compromise with their administrators, rather than carry on half a dozen battles with resisting professionals. The delay strategy also holds some risks for administrators—conditions and priorities change, financial and political resources drift away, and new technical and professional values take over. But with their longer tenure, time is on the side of the professionals.

Full-time specialization. Unlike most legislators and even some governors or mayors, administrators not only put in a full eight-hour day on their jobs, but concentrate all their efforts on a relatively narrow range of problems. The director of the state police or the community police chief do not become active or inactive according to the public mood—they are working on it steadily, day-by-day, and year-by-year. Even if mental health or the environment become major government concerns, taking up a great deal of the time of elected officials, this fact does not distract the police professionals from their main responsibility—what should be done about controlling crime.

Financial independence.   Sometimes top professional administrators, especially in state government, but in community government as well, almost get to be their own bosses—they gain control of the spending power of their agencies.

If gasoline tax receipts are earmarked, for instance, for highway programs, it is the professional administrator who figures out ways in which every penny will be spent. Legislators or even mayors and governors may object that money is being spent on "frills," such as new, expensive barriers on the freeways. If questioned, the professional administrators will coldly reply that the earmarked money is dedicated to improving streets and highways, and that this is a justifiable way to achieve that goal.

The pattern of intergovernmental relations also encourages independence by state and community administrators. The provisions of federal grants commonly allow such administrators much discretion on how to spend the funds dedicated to the program—including those contributed by the state. One study of state agency heads, who received at least 25 percent of their funds from federal sources, reported that they were considerably less responsive to state political controls, were more likely to lobby in the state legislature for more funds than the governor recommended, and felt they were, in fact, less subject to supervision by governor or legislature than other agency directors.[17]

Of course, administrative professionals do not have absolute control. But, the resistance of the professionals, especially when combined with interest group power, can be formidable and sometimes insurmountable. To win such battles elected politicians often have to draw upon all of the political resources they can command—compromise or indifference may be more prudent.

Administering the laws.   Art Buchwald, the political satirist, once wrote a column about what happens when a law to repair potholes gets into the hands of Plotkin, a $20,000 a year bureaucrat—"The guy who really runs this country." Plotkin examines the language of the law and

---

[17]George E. Hale and Marian Lief Pelley, "Perceptions of Federal Involvement to Intergovernmental Decisionmaking," Conference of the Midwest Political Science Association. April, 21–23, 1977.

finds it vague, asking, "What kind of pothole does the law cover? How much money should be spent to fill each pothole anyway?" and other questions, ending with "and finally, what constitutes a pothole in the first place?" The story winds on with Plotkin setting up a commission to study the law. Then after a time, he hires a panel of experts to study the report of the commission. Then a new building is required as the agency expands its professional work force and two more years pass. Finally everyone else forgets about the pothole program.[18]

Hopefully all administration does not follow this route. But the story also is not entirely fanciful. Administrators, through detailed rules they develop—rules not always subject to legislative veto—have some leeway in deciding what the law means. This administrative discretion provides opportunity for administrative policymaking. We will return to the topic of rulemaking later in this chapter.

Once the guidelines have been set by the top professional administrators, lower level administrators apply the rules to specific cases. Here, too, administrators exercise discretion. These administrative decisions are only a minor kind of policymaking. But the cumulative effect of such minor decisions can make a major change in how an intended policy works out. Assume that administrators in the unemployment compensation office approve certain types of claims for benefits without challenging them or school administrators do not enforce state immunization laws. Almost imperceptibly, a major change in policy may come about.

Influencing legislation. Do state administrators also influence legislative policymaking? A study of state policymaking by Deil Wright reports that state administrators, when asked that question, estimated that the agency concerned with carrying out a program is the source of about 70 percent of the legislation that affects it.[19]

Expertise as influence on law making. Most governors and mayors and a good many legislators, even experienced ones, do not know precisely what any particular government program is all about. But administrators do, down to the minutest detail. They are experts—they know what the biggest mistakes can be in their field and sometimes know how to avoid them. The head of the state or community elections agency knows all about paper ballot problems and about every type of voting machine now on the market. The election director can give ten

[18]Art Buchwald, "President's Power Pivots on Pleasing Plotkin, the Plodder" Detroit *Free Press*, August 22, 1976.

[19]Deil Wright, unpublished report.

reasons why a particular reform proposal may or may not work. Inevitably governors, mayors, and legislators have to depend upon this professional expertise.

This kind of influence is greatest, of course, where the public believes that expertise seems to work—for example in contagious disease control. We find professional administrative influence less in controversial areas, such as welfare, where the experts do not seem to have solid solutions.[20] We include at this point a brief case study of one of the most criticized programs—Policy Box No. 19,'' The States and Nation Administer Medicaid.''

Client group relations help influence law making. Professional administrators also often have the support of an effectively organized clientele group. (Recall how ecology groups supported the professionals of the Missouri Department of Conservation.) Even large private industries will help lobby administrative programs, especially when their goals and those of the professionals are not in conflict; the state tourist agency will be supported by the motel and resort owners in its ''professional'' efforts. We were once participants in a meeting in which the state department of education called top union and auto industry lobbyists to ask their help in getting a bill passed to create a new community college. We do not know how much these usually antagonistic groups helped, but the bill passed.

Limitations of Professionalism. Professionalism has its drawbacks as well as its benefits so far as the average citizen is concerned.

The single-mindedness of professionals. Difficulties arise when professional administrators are thought by the general public to be too dedicated to the values of their clients or profession at the expense of other values. Parole officers are accused of emphasizing the rehabilitation of prisoners over the safety of ordinary citizens. We sometimes criticize highly trained police officers because in their desire to catch those whom they ''know'' are guilty, they may abridge their civil liberties—through use of some very fancy and very professional electronic equipment. Or environmentalists may accuse the state agricultural professionals of being so concerned with eliminating crop pests that they allow the use of pesticides that may be dangerous to general health.

[20]Fred W. Grupp, Jr. and Alan R. Richards, ''Variations in Elite Perceptions of American States as Referents for Public Policy Making,'' *American Political Science Review* 69, September 1975, 850–858.

Sometimes two sets of professional values conflict. The state parks professionals set up recreational sites in woodland areas while the state foresters post "keep out" signs. One set of professionals is concerned with providing citizens with hiking trails, the other with preserving unspoiled timberland and wildlife from forest fires. Whenever professionals pursue their own values too single-mindedly they run the danger of destroying values equally important to other professionals and to the general citizens they claim to serve.

Professional faddism. Professionals are also subject to faddism. This, in part, results from the intense competition among professionals to achieve major improvements—innovative "breakthroughs." Let us look at the field of state and community mental health so graphically portrayed in the novel and movie, *One Flew Over the Coo-Coo's Nest.* Treatment in the past thirty years has consisted of isolation, work therapy, psychiatry, electric shock treatment, frontal lobotomy operations, and drugs. Today some of the favored treatments include removal of the patient from an institutional environment into halfway houses in the community and use of behavior modification techniques. These

A professional solution to Chicago's transportation problems—The Congress Street expressway underpasses the U.S. Post Office and joins the Kennedy and Dan Ryan expressways.

POLICY BOX NO. 19
The States and Nation Administer Medicaid

Medicaid is a program designed to provide health care for those too poor to pay for it. Congress enacted this program in 1965 in hopes that it would help many of the poor get off welfare rolls. Unlike Medicare, which is a program for senior citizens wholly run and paid for by the national government, Medicaid is a joint federal-state program.

Basic medical services are provided by all states and additional services may be offered. The federal government in both cases pays between 50 percent and 80 percent of the costs, depending upon state wealth. In general the wealthy states provide the supplementary services and the poorer states do not.

Medicaid was an open-ended grant from the start—the federal government pays a percentage of the costs, but cannot control what the amount spent will be—the feds set no dollar cutoff point. The program allows considerable state input—the states decide who is eligible to receive aid, what supplemental aid will be given, and carry out all of the administration of the program, including investigation for fraud.

Both the states and the federal government face skyrocketing costs. In 1965 Medicaid was 33 percent of the state welfare costs; four years later it was 40 percent and has continued to rise. From 1968 to 1970, total Medicaid costs rose 57 percent with only a 19 percent increase in patients.

To get federal funding, supporters perhaps knowingly underestimated the federal cost. But now, even they must be astonished. The estimated federal cost was $200 million a year. Actual first-year costs were $950 million. By the second year the cost was $3 billion. By 1970 it was $10 billion and by 1977, $31.5 billion. Estimates for 1981 are for $52 billion in federal expenditure.

Controversy rages over the reasons. Groups blame each other. The doctors say all the paper work involved and delay in getting paid drives up the costs. Taxpayer groups predictably argue the program is too ambitious—people who do not need help and, indeed, should be ineligible, are "freeloading," welfare clients are receiving better aid than persons of the lower or middle class who work; and politicians, fraudulent doctors, and other medical personnel are "ripping off" the government by performing unnecessary operations and prescribing unnecessary drugs to people who in many cases are not eligible in the first place.

Cases of such fraud are not hard to find. A U.S. senator, to prove a point, dressed poorly and showed up at a clinic in New York City complaining of a fictitious ailment. He rather easily qualified for extensive medical treatments.

Here are some of the abuses found in many states—doctors who have "offices" in their cars and see over one hundred patients a day; medical clinics that run their own pharmacies; hospitals that charge higher rates to medicaid patients; laboratories that do expensive and unnecessary tests and split fees with those who prescribe them; pharmacies that charge for name brand drugs and provide the cheaper generic type; and nursing homes that charge for special care not provided and not needed by many of their residents.

And, of course, inflation is blamed for spiraling costs—general inflation and that brought about by the tremendous demand for medical services caused by the program. Between 1965 and 1971 non-Medicaid health costs rose 50 percent faster than the cost of living. Finally, critics charge that much of the state administration is slipshod. Doctors, though found guilty of fraud, do not have their licenses revoked by state medical boards. Few states investigate payments very closely for fraud. Too many ineligibles are permitted aid.

What do you think? Is this a problem that should be solved by private charities, by finding jobs for people, or by giving aid as welfare payments and allowing the clients to find their own medical care? Or should health care be completely provided by a government program—what critics call socialized medicine? Why has administration of the program been so difficult and full of problems? Is this a state-federal cooperative program that would be improved if it were exclusively state or exclusively federal? Can the program be improved with better and stronger federal controls or should the states be given complete charge? Why haven't the professional values of state and federal administrators prevented the chaos or are those professional values part of the problem?

"experiments" can be expensive in time and money, and sometimes have had tragic costs for clients.

Of course the other side of such faddism is that in the long run we find that professionalism encourages a self-criticism that is somewhat self-corrective. Professional administrators in the field of mental health have bitterly criticized each of the above treatments—articles in their professional journals weigh carefully their benefits and defects. Treatments once heralded as major breakthroughs are now largely abandoned or seen as "barbarous."

Self-aggrandizement of professionals. Not often noted is that single-minded dedication to professional values may entail personal sacrifice by others—especially by less professionalized workers. A professional is likely to regard a job in terms of its opportunities to make a reputation and thereby to advance. Salary, thus, is secondary, at least for the moment. But the less professionalized employees, those who are in relatively dead-end jobs, such as secretaries, bookkeepers, clerks, and guards may be asked by professionals to share their dedication without really sharing in the long-term rewards. Check, for example, the salaries and responsibilities of a few of the executive secretaries you may know. Are they, in fact, being exploited by their professional bosses? Some observers have thought so, and so too, as we shall presently see, have some of these nonprofessionals.

Inbreeding among professionals. Sometimes the relationship is almost incestuous among the administrative regulators and those supposed to be regulated. Instead of checks and balances we find accredited school teachers, often trained at the same state university, in the department of education, in the state association, and on the legislative committees dealing with educational matters. National and community administrators are also likely to be professional educators. Other professions can sometimes duplicate this pattern. Outsiders are apt to suspect that a measure of nonprofessional control or surveillance from mayors or governors might be necessary.

Administrative Policymaking in a Democracy. We have left until last a major objection to policymaking by professional administrators—that professionals sometimes openly oppose the programs advanced by elected officials.

Though professional administrators in state or community agencies influence and even, on occasion, make policy, the key point is that the public, through its representatives, must have the right to review and power to reverse such policy. The theory of democracy holds that the majority and their elected representatives, when they follow accepted procedures, have "the right to be wrong." That faith assumes that the majority will, in the long run, adopt policies that will be beneficial for society. Professionals at times become very impatient with this assumption.

Yet it can be easily demonstrated that policymaking and administration by state or community professionals is not foolproof. Areas of doubt exist about their proposals and their actions. Voters and their representatives need not apologize for holding values contrary to many current professional values. The general public may not desire more and more interstate highways. Legislators, even if misguided, have the right to question whether some of those declared criminally insane should be released from state institutions. Judges may question some of the actions of professionalized police forces.

What we personally are left with is the bias that just as "wars are too important to leave to the generals," so schools are too important to leave to professional educators, health to leave to the medical profession, and peaceful development of atomic energy to leave to administrators, even those scientifically trained. As we will note presently, a growing number of citizens and reformers share this view—as diverse as Common Cause and the followers of the conservative economist Milton Friedman.[21]

[21]For discussion of the problems associated with professionalism in administration see Nicholas Henry, *Public Administration and Public Affairs*, Prentice Hall, New York, 1975, 95–96.

State and Community Administrators Seek Control Over Work Conditions

In 1976 the state of Massachusetts had the first statewide walkout of public employees in its history. Drawbridges left open caused traffic snarls in the state's metropolitan areas, some state employment offices stopped issuing checks, the state laboratory stopped performing blood tests for those applying for marriage licenses, lifeguards left state beaches, and the welfare office in Springfield had only twelve of two hundred fifty case workers reporting to work. The state police had to keep order in state prisons because few guards reported to work; treatment at one of Boston's two sewage facilities stopped; parents of the Paul Dever School for the Mentally Retarded at Taunton were asked by the school superintendent to take their children home or volunteer to work at the school; and all of this was attended by sporadic violence between picketers and other state employees.

The strike, illegal under Massachusetts' law, lasted three days. A court order that threatened the unions with $200,000-a-day fines, finally brought it to an end. At issue was a union demand of increased wages. State officials said that the state could not afford the demands in view of a financial crisis that had led to layoffs and a "hold-the-line" policy on pay and hiring.

With state employees back on the job, negotiations continued under the supervision of a court-appointed mediator. But the larger issue had pretty well been spotlighted for the rest of the nation to see—state and

AFSCME Massachusetts members march to the state capital in Boston protesting delays in getting negotiated pay increases.

also community public employee unions are here to stay. We will not be turning the clock back in the states to patronage politics or the reformers' model of a civil service system—unionization will not go away. What kind of system it will produce in American public employment is still to be seen.[22]

The Extent of Public Employee Unionization. By 1972 the Census Bureau estimated that 23.2 percent of the private sector was unionized, but 50.4 percent of the state and local public work force were union members. As we would anticipate, organization came first in the lower paid echelons: 76.5 percent of fire protection employees, 69.5 percent of teachers, 50.1 percent of sanitation workers, 46.2 percent of highway workers, 45.1 percent of welfare workers, and 41.7 percent of hospital workers. Unionization was greatest in the northeast (65.8 percent of all public employees) and weakest in the south (37.7 percent). It was lowest in smaller units of government and in rural areas.[23]

The Goals of Unionization. The playwright, George Bernard Shaw, once described trade unionism as "the capitalism of the working class." And in a way he was right. Union members like capitalists act for self-interest although both may sometimes provide as by-products, some desirable social benefits.

The goals of unionization center, of course, on improvement of conditions associated with the job—salaries, fringe benefits, pensions, and hours. Like the civil service system, unionization rests on a number of procedures.

1. The union favors procedures that discourage competition or conflict among employees. For this reason we expect unions to favor seniority and job experience, rather than "merit" as the basis of raises or promotions. Unions are suspicious of time and motion studies or other means to stimulate productivity of individual workers, because such studies may pit one worker against another. We are also not astonished to find that unions insist that work duties be precisely defined—specified working hours with the tasks carefully outlined in detail, and they want employees to have a grievance procedure. Also, in order to minimize conflict among employees, the union wants mandatory union membership or at

[22]Neal R. Peirce, "Showdown Year With the Public Employee Unions," *State Legislatures*, August–September 1975, 10–11.

[23]Neal R. Peirce, "Employment Report/Public Employee Unions Show Rise in Membership Militancy," *National Journal*, 7 August 30, 1975, 1239–1249.

least an "agency shop" in which all employees, whether union members or not, must pay a similar fee for the union services.

2. Unions prefer to organize by skill group across the whole of state or community government, rather than by department. Thus if all secretaries belong to one union, the whole of a government will be affected by a strike, whereas if each department is organized separately, the state or community may pit one departmental union against another.

3. The union insists on negotiating contracts for a specified period. As we would expect, this means that after each contract period of from one to three years, the union will make additional demands on behalf of the workers. We assume most workers judge their unions and union leaders by how much improvement they can make in the worker's job conditions. This leads union leaders to a constant search for more "benefits."

4. The union wants power to bring the employer to the bargaining table and encourage concessions. The ultimate weapon is the strike or walkout. Also used occasionally in public disputes is mediation by an outsider, or binding arbitration by a third party, whose decision both union and management agree in advance to accept.[24]

The Political "Clout" of Public Employee Unions.   Back in 1972 Congress was about to debate the revenue-sharing bill in the House. A crucial vote was being taken in the house Rules Committee to determine whether the bill would be sent to the floor with "a closed rule," a rule that would permit debate, but no amendments on the house floor. Such a procedure prevents upsetting the compromises that had been hammered out in committee.

Congressman Spark Matsunaga (Democrat–Hawaii) was opposed to closed rules on principle, and was not very enthusiastic about the revenue-sharing bill itself. As the vote was taken in the Rules Committee, he left for the men's room. The vote went seven to seven. Governor Burns of Hawaii was put through to Matsunaga by long distance telephone. Also brought in to discuss the situation with him was Jerry Wurf, the head of AFSCME, a principal public employee union. The union leader explained to the congressman what all those funds distributed by the federal government to the states and communities would mean to pub-

---

[24]The unions also, of course, want state workers to have the same benefits federal workers have. The unions would like to reverse a 1976 U.S. Supreme Court ruling, (*National League of Cities* v. *Usery*) that, on a five to four decision, said that Congress, using the Commerce power, had acted unconstitutionally when it extended overtime and minimum wage provisions (The Fair Labor Standards Act) to state and local government workers.

lic employees in Hawaii (particularly since AFSCME was the state's largest union). "After some time, he (Matsunaga) was coaxed back into the Committee Room where he cast the decisive vote in *favor* of the closed rule."[25] Could General Motors have twisted arms more adroitly than these two lobbyists from the public sector?

What we are suggesting is that public employee unions are now as involved in policymaking as is any private industry whose future is affected by government decisions. In 1974 government employee groups in California contributed $1.7 million in campaign funds, the largest single contributor of the election. Add to this treasury the manpower and votes controlled by union members and their relatives and friends, and you have some suggestion of their potential influence.

Other instances of the unions' political strength are not difficult to find. In Illinois in 1975 the legislature followed the suggestion of the state public employees' union and gave every state employee an across-the-board raise of $100 a month. Governor Daniel Walker vetoed the bill. The legislature overrode the veto. Or another instance—in a study of lobbying in Massachusetts, North Carolina, Oregon, and Utah—"education" was rated by legislators and lobbyists alike in three of the states as first or second of the ten most powerful organizations. In Massachusetts it was ranked third by legislators and fourth by other lobbyists. Education unions have increased their effectiveness by encouraging their members to run for the legislature and have worked in many states to defeat candidates "unfriendly" to education.[26]

In 1978 public employee unions actively campaigned against proposals to limit state and community spending and taxing powers. In some states AFSCME was supporting moderate tax cut proposals to head off the more extreme measures.

Can we expect unions to make even more attempts to influence policymaking in the future? Probably. Presently unions are attempting to gain an amendment to the Hatch Act of 1939 that would permit federal workers or those handling federal funds in the states or communities to participate in partisan political activities if they wish.

What Unionization Has Accomplished for Public Employees. Senator Daniel Moynihan (D-N.Y.) argues, "Anyone living off the public sector lives well. State college professors go abroad for the summer and state troopers fly to their fishing vacations, while small farms close down, grocers die off, and filling station attendants live week to week."

[25]Richard E. Thompson, *A New Era in Federalism?*, Revenue Sharing Advisory Service, Washington, D.C., 1973, p. 103.

[26]Harmon Zeigler and Michael Baer, *Lobbying: Interaction and Influence in American State Legislatures*, Wadsworth Publishing Co., Belmont, California, 1969, 32–33.

An ACIR study reported that between 1955 and 1973 the average pay of state and local government workers went up 28 percent faster than in private industry. Union leaders such as Jerry Wurf argue that the rise is only "catch up," since public employees at state and local levels were so long underpaid. Whichever is the case, we can probably conclude that unionization has markedly improved working conditions in respect to salaries and fringe benefits.

While these are benefits that the workers enjoy, they also have a beneficial side effect for us citizens as well. Public service, we find, is no longer viewed as a dead-end kind of employment for those unemployable in the private economy. Even at the lower echelons' public employment offers a decent career in terms of wages and benefits.

The Criticisms of Public Employee Unionization. The negative aspects of unionization are in what citizens regard as overprotection for the public employee. (We, of course, cannot expect citizens and state and community employees to have the same definition of "overprotection.") The points at issue are things such as the $25,000 per year average in total salary and benefits that Seattle in 1975 was paying its police and firefighters; the generosity of some public employee pension systems has been criticized, particularly after it was found that generous pensions in part contributed to the New York City fiscal crisis of 1975.

Conflict with professional values. Also, as we would expect, professionally trained administrators argue that unionization sometimes conflicts with professional values. To many professionals, the closing or slow down of the operation of the Paul Dever school for the Mentally Retarded was inexcusable. The professional will damn with equal impartiality an executive or legislature who would let such things come to pass, or a union that would encourage such practices for just the private benefit of employees. In such instances the professional argues, the client's interests are sacrificed to those of the administrator—a practice that cuts the heart out of professionalism. The professional will also resist the notion that promotion should be automatic according to seniority, rather than by performance, or that workers should develop a punch-clock mentality about the services they offer.

Union influence over policymaking. Unionization also has policy implications. Let's look at the settlement of the Massachusetts strike.

The final settlement recognized the right of employees to negotiate working conditions as well as salary. The state, in return, would be allowed to set productivity and performance standards for all state employees, a power most citizens assumed they already had. But state salaries would depend, not on the governor and legislature, but on the results of state tax collections—whether the state had a surplus and how much. Jerry Wurf, the national leader of AFSCME, the public employees union, had commissioned a fact-finding study by economists that had suggested that an adequate surplus was probable in Massachusetts. In effect the legislature no longer has the independent power to spend a surplus as it wishes—the bargain provides it must go into employee salaries.

Perhaps most important of all, unionization adds an important new element in the policymaking process. That process has been dominated by legislators, governors and mayors, and more recently professional administrators. Add to that list, the leaders of state and community public employee unions.

METHODS TO "CONTROL" THE BUREAUCRATS

Whenever a government unit experiences rapid changes in the internal balance of power, we find that attempts are made to return to the more familiar and predictable ways of doing things. This is what happened when administrators became a major factor in policymaking in states or communities. It is not that executives and legislators suddenly became powerless—it is that a new group had emerged to be considered in fashioning policy. As administrators very rapidly became more important and independent, students and politicians, as well as citizens groups, have proposed a series of reforms that they believe will redress the balance of powers. The sheer number of proposed reforms suggests how important elected officials, as well as many students of administration and assorted reformers, consider the issue today.

Executive Influence in the Bureaucracy

One may gain the impression that administrators and union leaders now dominate, or are in danger of dominating, state and community policy making. That is an exaggeration. Executives still have major ways of influencing the actions of bureaucrats. Aside from the patronage that still remains or the appointment or removal of major agency heads; the governor or mayor can subtly or not so subtly harass administrators. The executive staff can make continuous investigations and demand extensive reports. The executive may even propose a reorganization of the agency. Among the most important powers is the executive's ability to direct media attention to how an agency is doing its job. In extreme cases the executive, rather than defending an agency that runs into criticism, may publicly join the criticism and suggest that the agency head resign or that agency functions be drastically curtailed or changed.

Administrators prefer anonymity to open warfare with the mayor or governor. And, in fact, we generally find that the pattern is one of mutual respect and cooperation. Governors or mayors seek to make a record and will often welcome proposals for improvements from administrators—the inauguration of improvements in the park system, or a new program for rubbish and garbage pickup.

We have left for last what is possibly the most important of today's executive controls over the bureaucracy—the chief executive's budget-making powers. Administrators are aware that legislative bodies cut budgets—seldom do they raise items much above levels that the governor or mayor recommends. If the administrative agency has made an enemy of the chief executive, his or her displeasure will be reflected in budget recommendations—the executive can strike at the financial underpinnings of the agency if only to deny further expansion of its activities. Thus, governors and mayors, particularly, have been in the forefront of experimenting with new budget techniques to strengthen their controls over administrators.

Control Through Budget Procedures

The first state to adopt an executive budget—governors put together a revenue and spending plan and submit it to the legislature for approval—was Ohio in 1913. Most early budgets were line items, that is they listed such things as postage, $565; office supplies, $980; printing, $1,200; and so on. When an administrator expended all of the funds for one of the line items, the legislature or budget controller would either grant permission to shift funds from one line to another or give the administrator more funds. As we can see, this approach kept administrators under the careful and watchful eyes of the "budget watchers."

Performance Budgeting. In 1947 the Hoover Commission report on U.S. government reorganization suggested that students begin to consider whether budget line items might not be related to specific performance goals. Each budget request would be tied to a particular "function", "activity," and "project." Legislators and executives would thus get a better idea why the money was requested and how it was being spent.

Instead of putting together all postage expenses, the budget agency would instead list the expenses of each activity. If, for example, the Conservation Department published a monthly magazine on the state's natural beauties, the budget would lump together all costs—postage, printing, preparing copy, photographs, and whatever. The budget item would then appear as "X amount of dollars" to produce the monthly magazine, *Natural Resources*. The postage costs allocated to the project would be indicated along with the other costs of the magazine. This was called performance budgeting.

How performance budgeting worked out. Bureaucrats liked performance budgeting because it generally released them from legislative control over minor details. Legislators at first welcomed the idea because it promised them control over activities and information about what things cost.

The difficulty was that tangible activities, such as the magazine mentioned above or a construction project, were easier to define than some other activities. Services involving personal interactions, information processing, or administrative control were extremely difficult to measure. Nor could the costs of each activity always be precisely calculated.[27] In addition, crude performance measures left out quality control.

Here is an example that highlights some of these problems. Let us assume that the governor's staff calculates the cost of handling complaints by the civil rights commission and decides they are too high. The pressure begins to build for closing a maximum number of cases so it will "look good" on the performance budget statements. But taking a case to court entails a long drawn out and costly process. If an examiner can persuade the person who has presented the complaint to withdraw it or to settle for whatever the other party offers, the case can be closed relatively quickly and at low cost. Then the agency "looks good." The only problem is that budget procedures are encouraging agency personnel to scuttle the very goals for which the agency was created and is supposed to be functioning—getting illegal discrimination practices stopped.

Performance budgeting had a number of spinoffs that attempted to solve some of these problems.

Program-Planning-Budgeting (PPB). The PPB method was developed at the RAND Corporation, a "think-tank" in California, and introduced into government by Robert S. McNamara, then head of the Defense Department. He planned to use PPB to win the Vietnam War.

In 1965 President Lyndon Johnson directed that PPB be used throughout the federal government. It rapidly spread to a number of states—namely California, Wisconsin, Hawaii, Pennsylvania, and

---

[27]Bertram M. Gross, "The New Systems Budgeting," *Public Administration Review*, March/April, 1969, 113–137.

Michigan. But by 1970, PPB was abandoned quietly by neglect in the federal government, and the same began happening in the states.

The PPB idea.   PPB carried performance budgeting to its logical and presumably rational extreme. The process begins by setting broad state or community objectives, usually about ten.   They are then subdivided into "categories," "subcategories," and "elements." Each administrative unit then states its goals in relation to these categories and ranks them in importance, spells out alternative methods for achieving them, and analyzes the cost-benefit ratio for each alternative. This process encouraged agencies to prepare long range plans to meet all of the objectives. The plans were usually for a five-year period and forecast the costs that achieving goals would entail.

Evaluation of PPB.   PPB resulted in some important reassessment of agency activities. Perhaps the major impact of PPB was that for a year or two, it threw bureaucrats off balance and thus strengthened the hand of the executive and his or her budget officers. PPB also seems to have encouraged legislatures to develop their own budget staffs and in time led them to create legislative fiscal agencies. But critics soon pointed out that bureaucrats learned to "work the system" to their advantage and give the governor and his or her aides what they wanted to hear and what would make the agency look good.

In essence PPB was made to order for the professional bureaucrat because spending plans were based on a web of stated and unstated assumptions. Once a governor or legislators accepted some of the underlying assumptions about goals, they were "trapped." PPB advocates presumed that budgeting could be made completely rational. They ignored the politics of resource allocation.

Other criticisms of PPB emphasized the tremendous amount of paper work and complicated calculations that were required. State agencies wrestling with the forms took hours away from assigned tasks while they pondered what their goals " really were."

Aaron Wildavsky is more direct in his criticism. He says, "PPB does not work because it cannot work. Failure is built into its very nature because it demands abilities to perform cognitive operations which are beyond present human (or machine) capacities. Even a modified version—in which all activities are placed in programs that contribute to common objectives, but in which objectives are not ranked in order or priority—is far beyond anyone's capacity."[28]

[28]Aaron Wildavsky, *Budgeting: A Comparative Theory of Budgeting Processes,* Little Brown and Company, Boston, 1976, p. 364.

Zero-Based Budgeting. This procedure was invented by a management consultant, Peter A. Pyhrr, and first attempted in 1970 in two divisions of Texas Instruments, Inc. New Mexico was the first state to try it, but it became popular because a young governor, Jimmy Carter, newly elected in Georgia in 1971, tried it out there.

How zero-based budgeting works. Under this scheme, each manager describes a "decision package" for each activity the agency performs. The administrator works out for each decision package the cost estimates and measures of performance, but also must indicate the consequences of not performing the activity at all, as well as alternative methods for doing it. The manager then must show what would happen if the activity received 85 percent of last years' appropriation, then 90 percent and so on, carrying through to say a 15 percent increase. At each expenditure level the administrator explains what would happen to the activity. The governor or mayor uses these decision packages from many departments to make up his or her own priority list and the recommended funds for each.This is then submitted to the legislative body as the budget. In effect the executive is saying to the agencies, "Let's start from zero. As long as you can make a convincing case for your expenditures, we will support the activity. If you cannot make any arguments that convince us, we cut off the activity at zero."

Georgia began with 10,000 decision packages, which swamped their budget bureau. It ended up with about 2000 decision packages, and the governor became a convert of the method. Jimmy Carter described it as "the only way I know that you can control a bureaucracy."

Evaluation of zero-based budgeting. Zero-based budgeting has been described as the "tightwad" side of PPB. It stresses that the state citizens must get their money's worth. The critics of zero-based budgeting make the same arguments they made against PPB. They especially question whether a large bureaucracy can go through the paperwork and trauma of the zero-based budgeting process each year and note that ZBB pays little attention to the politics of administration—ways administrators can use the system to their own advantage while scuttling its general goals.[29]

[29]For critical evaluations of zero-based budgeting see Donald Axelrod, "Post Burkhead: The State of the Art or Science of Budgeting," *Public Administration Review*, November/December, 1973. See also John D. LaFaver, "Zero Based Budgeting in New Mexico," *State Government* 47:2, Spring 1974. For more supportive views see Peter A. Phyrr, *Zero Based Budgeting: A Practical Management Tool for Evaluating Expenses.* John Wiley and Sons, Inc., New York, 1973, and Phyrr, "The Zero-Based Approach to Government Budgeting," *Public Administration Review*, January/February, 1977, 1–8.

Management Control Techniques

Management techniques attempt to increase accountability—in effect, the superior is asking those at lower levels, "What is it you people are doing down there?"

Management by Objectives (MBO). This method applies to specific activities and their short-range goals. The governor or mayor or city manager, the department heads, in fact, supervisors at all levels can use it at the same time.

How MBO works. Assume we have a state prison system. The director tells his top staff that prison guards should be encouraged to have less hostile attitudes toward inmates. Together they decide that a training program for guards is needed. The state training director gets together with the heads of each prison and they decide how to meet the objective. They agree on the number of training sessions that will be needed and the probable cost in time and money. They then set a specific goal for completion of the training program, being sure it is a goal that seems reasonable to the prison directors—for example, guards will go to four sessions of training, each lasting two hours. One third of the guards will take the training each month. In three months all guards will have had the training. They also agree that they will evaluate the success of the program on the basis of the number of inmate complaints about mistreatment from the guards. The head of the department and the heads of the prison have, in effect, made a contract about achieving the agreed on goal.

This process of agreements is then extended throughout the prison system. Presumably the head of each prison sits down with his aides and works out the specific timetable and other details for the training program, and so on down the line until we run out of supervisors and workers.

What MBO requires next is that the supervisors "check up" on how the training project is going. On a specific date known in advance, in this case probably at the end of a month, the state director meets with the heads of the prisons to find out whether the first month's goal has been met. If not, he or she asks, "Why not?" Unrealistic goals or those having unexpected difficulties of course may be changed and a new contract made.

And so the process grinds along. One difficulty is that we may discover that the system becomes clogged as administrators rush to MBO meetings with their supervisor. The system also does not eliminate the politics of administration. A lax supervisor may, of course, "gut" the system by accepting weak excuses from favored workers. On the other hand we suspect that MBO does occasionally result in some tightening of organization slackness—at least in its early applications.

A Senior Executive Service. Earlier we noted that civil service systems are criticized because top policy positions below the department head level are usually filled by persons protected by civil service, and thus potentially independent of the governor or mayor. A number of states and communities have begun an overhaul of their civil service systems and procedures to strengthen the management powers of the governor or mayor and their department heads.

In 1977, Oregon set up a senior executive service of five hundred top echelon persons. California earlier set up such a service of around six hundred persons. The service members are still be under civil service protection, but they can be appointed to or removed from their managerial positions or transferred at the pleasure of the governor or the department heads. Their salaries fall within a generous range, but are negotiable in terms of performance, rather than based strictly on a position classification. Special fringe benefits are added to make the positions attractive, and bonuses and promotions are given for outstanding performance.

Other Civil Service Reforms Students of management have suggested changes such as—elimination of veterans' preference points for those who have made the transition to civilian life as has been done in Wisconsin, easier methods of dismissal, abandonment of questionable entrance and promotion examinations, end of the requirement that the applicant must be chosen from the top three taking an examination to only requiring a qualifying score, and demotion within the service for poor achievers.

The assumptions behind these proposals were summed up earlier by Meg Greenfield in her criticisms of civil servants as automatons. A city official puts it this way: "it is smarter to accept the risks of the 5 percent graft of a patronage system (as opposed to) 55 percent inefficiency of the civil service." The goal is to give managers more administrative power and make it clear that they then have the responsibility to make the system productive.

Evaluation Research. Evaluation research was popularized by one of the more unsettling pieces of research done in recent years, known as the Coleman Report, published in 1966 as a report of the Office of Education.[30] James Coleman tried to relate the achievement scores of stu-

[30]See Christopher Jencks, et al., *Inequality: A Reassessment of the Effect of Family and Schooling in America*, Basic Books, New York, 1972, and Daniel P. Moynihan and

dents on national tests to their access to educational resources. He looked at student scores for those who attended integrated, as compared with segregated schools, as well as those advantaged or disadvantaged by social and economic factors associated with the teaching or home situation. His dismal conclusion was that many factors that educators had long assumed were related to student achievement could not be shown to have an effect—factors such as smaller classes, expensive audio visual equipment, pleasant classrooms, laboratory facilities, racial integration, progressive or nonprogressive educational techniques, and so on. What did seem to affect learning most was the attitudes the student absorbed from home—the degree to which other members of the family supported and encouraged the student to learn.

A dispute continues on the validity of these findings. But the Coleman report itself encouraged more evaluation research. "Can one," it is asked, "analyze administrative performance to explain why certain results occurred?" Or in reverse, "can we examine a program to see how well it has achieved its goals?" Academics have answered with a cautious "yes" to both questions. The outcome has been a growing literature, numerous consulting firms, and establishment of evaluation teams within government and private agencies. Some evaluation research projects are inspired by legislators or governors; some are required by federal grants; and some are begun by administrative supervisors themselves.

How evaluation research has worked out.   The problems of evaluation research are several. One is the practical difficulty that adequate evaluation often requires the use of sophisticated techniques, sometimes involving extensive computer analysis. A conceptual problem is that of devising measurable performance indicators. By what measure, for example, does one evaluate a food stamp program? Or do we need several indicators? More complex are the questions of whether we will discover that there is a trade-off among our goals—a certain level of food stamp cheaters that must be tolerated if we expect to reach all of the persons who are qualified for the program, or a need to drop some persons from the program to give sufficient aid to others who we believe need it more. Finally the politics of administration may skew results. Will administrators initiate evaluation that may lead to undesirable conclusions? Will they cooperate with outside evaluators whose results they cannot control? Will the political investments in a given program permit acceptance of the findings at all?

We think that with all its difficulties evaluation research is one of

Frederick Mosteller, eds., *On Equality of Educational Opportunity*, Random House, New York, 1972.

the more promising procedures proposed to get at what state and community administrators are doing and how effective they are and, to be sure, how their performance might be improved and controlled by elected executives and legislators.

Legislative Oversight

Perhaps the most frustrated of the participants in policymaking are state and local legislators. With or without justification they sometimes suspect that the laws they pass are being willfully misinterpreted by administrators. The more paranoiac legislators may argue that the governor or mayor and the executive agencies are in league to bypass them. And sometimes they are correct. Legislators have developed a number of procedures to "reassert" their power.

The Legislative Budget. Perhaps the most important innovation has been the re-entry of legislatures into a budget process, which has for the last 75 years pretty much been dominated by governors and mayors. The various modifications of performance budgeting encouraged state legislatures in a few larger states to hire budget staff. (To date few city councils have followed this lead.)

This is how legislative budgeting works. The legislative audit office, which in the past only checked to be sure that expenditures made were legal, is expanded into a general fiscal agency. It is given duties of general budget preparation and analysis. Thus we find that not only the governor, but the legislative finance committees as well, have a trained full-time staff of experts holding hearings and preparing budget documents. We end up with both a legislative and an executive budget for the finance committees of the legislature to consider.

We cannot yet judge accurately what will be the effect of this innovation on budgeting or on the balance of power between the executive and legislature. Whether legislative budgeting will lead to tighter control of approporiations, reinstitution of detailed line-item budgets, or the legislature setting policy priorities, as some of its supporters believe, is still an open question.

Legislative Review of Administrative Rule Making. In 1947 Michigan became the first state to set up a committee in the legislature to review administrative rules. The legislature had thirty days to review and block them. If the legislature took no action, the rules went into effect. In 1969 the Michigan legislature set up a joint committee with members from both houses to handle this function. Both the attorney general's office and the legislative service bureau first were required to comment on each administrative rule. But, in fact, the Michigan legislature rejected few administrative rules. The most recent change in the Michigan legislature is to prohibit the rules from taking effect until the legislature approves them. This provision was passed over the governor's veto. In only four states the legislatures, by resolution passed in both houses and not subject to a governor's veto, may overturn any administrative rule they wish to. In other states legislators can only suggest change. If the legislators agree that a regulation is contrary to law they can ask the agency head to retract it. This is a process of political bargaining. If the legislators fail to get a change they must usually pass a new law—a complicated and difficult process.

A major problem with legislative review is that most review committees have been poorly financed and poorly staffed. Connecticut, for example, in 1976 only budgeted $10,000 to such a committee, a revealing indication of its importance. In states without such review committees or with weak committees, an administrative rule will get full floor consideration only if a particular legislator objects forcefully and repeatedly.

Florida's strong review procedures. In a few states the review committees are well-financed and have trained staffs. What do such committees find? In Florida, in the first year of operation, the staff turned up technical errors in 79 percent of the administrative rules. In 6 percent of the rules the staff argued that the agency had exceeded its legislative authority. More shocking we suspect to legislators, was that the staff found regulations and rules that had the exact wording of bills that had been considered by the Florida legislature and failed to pass.

With the growth of legislative budgeting, we can probably expect a growing importance given to legislative review committees. Legislators in most states now require administrative rules to be published and made available to all legislators and citizens, such as is done by the federal government.[31]

Sunset Laws. This procedure is not, strictly speaking, a reform first pushed by legislators. It was proposed by Common Cause and adopted first in Colorado in 1976, but was only applied to the state's forty-one regulatory licensing boards. By 1978, twenty-three other states had sunset laws and all states and some communities had bills in their legislatures to set up such a procedure.[32]

[31]See William Pound, "Legislative Review of Administrative Rule Making," *State Legislatures*, November–December, 1975, p. 23.

[32]Neal R. Peirce and Jerry Hagstrom, "Is It time for the Sun to Set On Some State Sunset Proposals," *The National Journal*, June 18, 1977, 937–939.

How sunset laws work. State regulation and licensing agencies are reviewed by the Colorado legislature once every seven years. Unless the legislature specifically extends the agency's life within a year of consideration, the agency is automatically disbanded. The review is of expenditures, organization, procedures followed, and of the basic statutory authority for the agency. The agency is given the opportunity to present its case in legislative hearings and is required to present a full-scale written performance report related to expenditures. Agencies whose activites are in the same field all come up for review in the same time period.

Evaluation of Colorado's sunset law. Colorado reported some benefits. Regulatory agencies began to seek out citizen complaints about the businesses or professions they regulated. A number of agencies asked the legislature to pass bills reorganizing their activities. Legislators were less inclined to establish new regulatory agencies and wrote automatic cut-off dates into several new programs.

The most important consequence of sunset legislation in Colorado and elsewhere, most observers argue, is that it would encourage legislators to take more seriously than they have in the past their legislative oversight responsibilities. We should not expect legislatures to eliminate a great many agencies. Colorado eliminated two small agencies, merged two others, and transferred another to a different department. It also revised the enacting statutes for two boards.

Sunset laws also have their critics. Some state sunset laws have been criticized even by backers of the concept, such as Common Cause, as being too ambitious—attempting to review all agencies at once, rather than concentrating on a few as Colorado did. The idea must be implemented gradually, backers claim.

Perhaps the basic criticism, though, is based on an evaluation of Colorado's experience. The Colorado auditor's office prepared extensive evaluation reports of each agency and discovered that some legislators did not read them. Legislative hearings sometimes were erratic and in two cases were postponed for a year—critics said because of the pressure of lobbyists. Few of the general public attended any of the hearings.[33]

---

[33]Irving S. Shapiro, chairman of the Board of E.I. dePont de Nemours & Co., in a speech to the Atlanta, Georgia, Rotary Club on May 23, 1977, suggested going one step further. "Why not zero-based regulation." He asks that regulatory agencies not only be asked to justify their existence, as under the sunset law of Colorado, but also apply the zero-base budget principle to every regulation past or proposed—"to make certain that all of these very expensive environmental and health regulations are still needed in their original dimensions."

Control by Attrition

The conservative Nobel prize winning economist, Milton Friedman, has popularized the notion that the only way for citizens to control bureaucracy is to reduce the resources available to bureaucrats. Florida, for example, in 1976 considered a proposal that would freeze the number of civil servants and relate increases to the state population that the bureaucrats serve. Tennessee and later Michigan voters adopted a proposal for which Friedman himself campaigned. It limits state spending to a fixed percent of the total income of the state. Most far reaching of such proposals in its impact was California's initiated amendment, "Proposition 13," adopted in 1978. It sharply limits community property taxes and requires a two-thirds vote in the legislature to pass a new tax to recover funds lost.

How Much Control is Desirable.   We briefly raise the point here as to whether the need for control has been overemphasized. Should, in fact, the bureaucrats be granted a measure of participation in policymaking? In Policy Box No. 20, "How Much Freedom of Speech for Bureaucrats?" this issue is raised as a conflict between what some administrators regard as professional values and the directives of their administrative superior, an appointee of the duly elected governor.

A Final Comment

This chapter on administration, we suspect, has been somewhat mixed—reflecting, perhaps, our own ambivalence to "big government." Government bureaucracy on a large scale has come to mean more in all our lives. Many of us now or in the future will make our living as state or community administrators. At the same time all of us also at one time or another can echo the sentiments of Governor Jerry Brown of California (1974–) when he said "All government bothers my conscience."

We suspect that some state regulation goes too far in fitting our activities to someone else's plan, attempting to regulate the trivial or extend reasonable regulation to areas that as yet are free from regulation,—areas, some feel, that should be free of regulation in a democracy. Perhaps we even sympathize, in part, with John Barnum, operator of the Little Red Barn Theater and Adult Book Store of Grand Rapids. He was ordered to build a ramp to his stage to accommodate "handicapped exotic dancers." Unless he did so he would not receive a license to present live entertainment. He sued for $75,000 and claimed harassment by community administrators.

POLICY BOX NO. 20   How Much
Freedom of Speech for Bureaucrats?

The state of Tennessee, like most other states, licenses nursing homes to care for elderly people. Many of the people in nursing homes are people on Medicaid; and often they are people who have been in the hospital and released for aftercare to a state-licensed nursing home. The state sets a specified daily rate that it will pay and the nursing homes agree to accept the patients, provide the care, and meet state standards in doing so. To insure compliance with state rules the states have teams that inspect the nursing homes and evaluate the care they provide.

Robert Martin was head of the Tennessee Health Department's section on inspecting quality. Sallie Garris was the section head for the Independent Professional Review Program. On March 17, 1976, the two of them inspected the Monterey Nursing Inn in northwest Nashville. They thought the conditions were sufficiently bad to warrant decertification of the nursing home. A hearing was held in early August, at which time the attorney for the nursing home asked for a more specific list of deficiencies. On September 2 the attorneys for the health department presented the details. Martin thought the state lawyers had done a good job. Nevertheless the health department offered to give the nursing home more time.

Both Martin and Garris bitterly opposed the offer. On September 17 Martin visited the nursing home, but was again dissatisfied with the progress. Thereafter he prepared a stinging memo to his boss, Dr. Michael Bruner, assistant commissioner of the health department. In part, his memo read, "They (the nursing home) responded with cosmetic treatment of their problem that mocked quality improvement. . . . The stench of stale urine today is only slightly less than it was six months ago. . . . The sight of the new paint was blurred by the smell of old urine, the sight of untended bedsores, an open uncovered running sore on a patient who was standing barefoot on the dirty floor."

"After considerable thought," the memo continued, "I believe our present dilemma results from a laxity on the part of the Department of Public Health from the commissioner's office on down. . . . I want you to know that a large segment of the nursing home industry is delighted with our dilemma."

Dr. Bruner, a few days before, according to the newspaper reports had said of Martin's and Garris' opposition to the department's decision to grant more time, "We encourage differences of opinion in our division. I selected both of these people, and I think they have done a good job." Thereupon, Martin released his memorandum to the *Nashville Tennessean*.

After the memo appeared in the newspaper Martin was told to take some annual leave. He refused and was suspended for ten days. Garris was transferred to a "new" job in preventive medicine. Instead of reporting to the new job, she called in sick for the next three days.

Richard Sadler of the state nursing homes association, criticizing federal rules, said in a news release, "The rules, regulations, and survey procedures . . . are written by federal employees who have very seldom, if ever, been inside a nursing home." The release added that the state inspection teams had been "abrasive, arrogant, and demeaning."

Shortly thereafter both Garris and Martin were fired by the health department. Officially Garris was fired for refusing to accept a new assignment. Martin was discharged because he would not give a written statement of conformance to departmental policy.

The *Tennessean* editorialized that state officials were trying to minimize the incident. This was clear, the editor said from a deputy commissioner's statement that read, "I am glad to report that the differences over standards were minimal. If we could have discussed these differences a week earlier, these dismissals might have been avoided."

What do you think? Were the differences over standards minimal? Should Martin and Garris have been fired? How should the case have been handled? (Bear in mind that closing the home would have meant moving the patients elsewhere.) Should a state department have a rule forbidding employees to release documents of this kind to the newspaper? Should administrators be allowed to attack the policies of their department head? The governor? The state legislature?

SOURCE: This policy box is based on newspaper accounts by the *Nashville Tennessean* during late September and early October 1976.

What we have tried to present in this chapter is the idea that at least during our lives, state and local governments managed by large-scale bureaucracies are here to stay and we had best find ways of domesticating them to our democratic ways. Our twin goals are to make bureaucrats act more effectively and to be sure the bureaucrats behave in ways that are responsive to elected officials and average citizens.

We have attempted to present some of the ferment of present times as the states and communities, well on their way to eliminating most of the abuses of old style patronage politics, face up to a new fact that needs to be harmonized with democratic values—a massive, professionalized bureaucracy.

HIGHPOINTS OF CHAPTER 10: ADMINISTRATORS AS STATE AND COMMUNITY MANAGERS

In this chapter we began (1) by looking at how state services and state jobs were handled under a system of patronage politics. We then (2) looked at two reforms that became widespread in the states around World War II—civil service and administrative reorganization. The

impact of these was to create a modern day professionalized state civil service. Next we argued (3) that state civil servants are inevitably drawn into the policymaking arena and that two present day trends encourage administrative policymaking—professionalization of employees and public employee unions. Finally (4) we looked at a series of recent proposals for "controlling" the bureaucracy—new budget procedures, management techniques, strengthening of legislative oversight, and control by cutting off resources.

PARTICIPATION BY ELITES AND OTHER CITIZENS

In the 1950s when the first modern public opinion polls were completed, researchers found some amazing (to them) and also, perhaps, disheartening facts about the citizens of our democracy.[1] Contrary to what they had assumed were the requirements of a going democratic system, they found that a sizeable number of citizens (1) only occasionally discussed issues during an election campaign, (2) had little or no motivation to participate, (3) were poorly informed about the candidates and issues, (4) did not seem to vote on the basis of principle, and (5) that some voters did not seem to be very rational decision makers, sometimes making decisions on what to the researchers seemed irrelevant bases—for example, whether the candidate was short or tall.

The researchers did not conclude that democracy was impossible; rather they decided that democratic theory, as they

[1]Bernard Berelson, Paul F. Lazarsfeld, and William N. McPhee, *Voting, A Study of Opinion Formation in a Presidential Campaign*, University of Chicago Press, Chicago, 1954. Chapter 14, "Democratic Practice and Democratic Theory," 305–323. Their findings were arrived at intuitively by Walter Lippman in books written fifty years ago: *Public Opinion*, Macmillan, New York, 1922, and *The Phantom Public*, Harcourt, Brace & Co., New York, 1925.

had understood it from civics texts and newspaper editorials, was unrealistic.

Other researchers came to similar conclusions from a different perspective. Their studies of decision making in states and communities led them to conclude that a relatively small number of citizens exercised a great deal of political power and a large number exercised very little power at all.

Overview.   We begin by looking at the most politically active and influential citizens—those whom we call political elites. We then consider participation and nonparticipation behaviors of average citizens—those who only participate occasionally and some who rarely participate. We then look at three theories that help us understand, in part, these patterns of participation. We conclude that our state and community governments are probably even more open to citizen influence today than in the past, in large measure because of actions by the national government in our more centralizing federal system.

MAJOR POLITICAL PARTICIPANTS—MEMBERS OF POLITICAL ELITES

Political power, wealth, and status have never been equally distributed in any society, in part because individuals differ in knowledge, talent, and energy.[2] In addition, some individuals inherit a larger than average share of wealth and social status. The social basis for elites appears always to be present.

Such differences develop because organization makes necessary an unequal distribution of political power. When we organize human activity to achieve any goal, we necessarily need leaders who will give the human enterprise a sense of direction. The need to concentrate government decision making in the hands of a few, many argue, is especially great in complex, urban, industrialized societies such as are most of our states and communities—places of high technological development and large-scale organization.

Thus are created three elites that are based on their members having a great share of the political power, wealth, or social status—their membership often overlaps but is usually not identical.

Political Elites and Democratic Decision Making

Government decisions in states and communities are made formally by a small group of officials who by law have been given the power to decide. Thus forming a government automatically creates part of a political elite. But also part of the political elite are those who have major influence on those officials—the private citizens who control major social and economic resources and who are willing to spend them on government and politics. We define as "the political elite" those who legally decide and those who control these major resources and use them to influence government decisions.[3]

Note that control of major resources does not require being the possessor of great wealth. As significant is a person's official position in an important social institution—being head of a labor union, a church,

---

[2] The novelist George Orwell succinctly summed up the human condition in his allegory, *Animal Farm,* when he wrote "All are equal, but some are more equal than others."

[3] We should not assume that members of the political elite are necessarily "self-serving." One of the earliest studies to document the fact that members of elites were sometimes more liberal and more dedicated to democratic values than other citizens was Samuel A. Stouffer, *Communism, Conformity and Civil Liberties: A Cross Section of A Nation Speaks its Mind,* Doubleday and Co., Garden City, N.J., 1955.

or even a social movement, as well as being manager of a great industrial organization.[4]

The Influence of Average Citizens.   Does the fact that a political elite exists mean that "they" make all the decisions and that the participation of the rest of the citizens is insignificant—little more than window dressing? Some political scientists argue this is indeed the case and that most citizens prefer it that way.[5] In the discussion that follows we argue that this is not the case at least not all of the time—that the process of government decision making is a good deal more complex and subtle than this viewpoint suggests.

We suggest how ordinary citizens also influence the decisions of the political elite. Often this influence is minimal. But at other times the elite has been overwhelmed—new groups have become part of the state or community elite, and policies and the elite itself have radically changed. In the last ten years, for example, some community political elites have significantly altered their decisions in respect to blacks, Mexican Americans, women, and homosexuals.

The "Most Powerful" in Illinois.   Players of parlor games, students of social science, and many others try to figure out who the "most powerful" are. Recently the Associated Press published a list of the "10 most powerful people in Illinois." As we will note presently, their research method has some shortcomings, but it is still one method of isolating the political elite. The AP assembled its list by asking a panel of thirty- six leaders from "business, labor, government, education, and other fields" to nominate the most powerful. This is the *reputational technique* used by Floyd Hunter in his study of Atlanta and by others in many community studies since.[6] It assumes that we can isolate a "political elite" by asking a panel of knowledgable experts to nominate the

[4]For an extended discussion of elitism in American Society see Thomas R. Dye and L. Harmon Zeigler, *The Irony of Democracy, An Uncommon Introduction to American Politics*, Wadsworth Publishing Co., Belmont, Calif. 1970.

[5]Joseph LaPalombara, *Politics Within Nations*, Prentice-Hall, Englewood Cliffs, N.J., 1974. p. 53.

[6]The concepts of power, influence, force, and authority all relate to this general topic of power. We do not distinguish among them here as we use power and influence interchangeably as meaning the ability to achieve one's ends in whole or in part and to limit others in achieving theirs. For a more analytical distinction of these terms see Peter Bachrach and Morton S. Baratz, *Power and Poverty, Theory and Practice*, Oxford University Press, New York, 1970, 19–38.

most powerful and then can use a cutoff figure to isolate the top elite. In this case the AP limited the elite to the top ten influential citizens.

Whom would we expect to find to have a reputation for having the greatest political power in Illinois? We find three active politicians—Governor James R. Thompson; mayor of Chicago, Michael A. Bilandic; and the political leader of "downstate Illinois," Alan J. Dixon, Secretary of State. We find three from the business world—A. Robert Abboud, chairman of First Chicago Corp (a bank), Roger E. Anderson, chairman of Continental National Bank, and Thomas Ayers, chairman of Commonwealth Edison, a public utility. Two were nominated from the media—Clayton Kirkpatrick, editor of the Chicago *Tribune*, and Marshall Field, publisher of the Chicago *Sun-Times*. Two others are harder to classify. One is Richard Ogilvie, a former Republican governor (1968–72) and now a Chicago lawyer; the other is Phyllis Schlafly of Alton, head of the national campaign against ratification of the Equal Rights Amendment (ERA).

We note several facts: (1) Politics and government are represented, but more than half of those on the list make their living in private business; (2) only one person, Marshall Field, reached his position through inherited wealth; (3) being head of an important organization, rather than having personal wealth, accounts for political power—Thompson and Bilandic, both having little personal wealth, would not have been on the list a year or so earlier as Daniel Walker was then governor and Richard Daley was Chicago's mayor; (4) business was represented by heads of the state's two largest banks and a utility, rather than by major manufacturers; (5) eight of the ten persons were from Chicago, the state's major metropolitan center; (6) nine of the ten were men; no blacks, no one under thirty-five, and no union leader was on the list; and finally (7) the ten most powerful surely disagree among themselves on a number of important political issues and decisions.[7]

We find few power structure studies of states; most have been of communities.

The Study of Influentials. Students differ over whether states and communities, are controlled by a tight knit power elite or whether the influentials are more loosely organized—that is pluralist.

[7]"10 Most Powerful People in Illinois," Chicago Tribune, July 17, 1977, 23–24.

[8]For summaries of research of both types, see Willis D. Hawley and James H. Svara, *The Study of Community Power; a Bibliographic Review*, American Bibliographic Center, Clio Press, Inc., Santa Barbara, Calif. 1972, and Terry N. Clark, *Community Power and Policy Outputs: A Review of Urban Research*, Sage Publications, Beverly Hills, Calif. 1973.

Power elite studies. The study by Robert and Helen Lynd of the power structure in Muncie, Indiana (Middletown, they called it), pioneered the research. The Lynds lived in the community over an extended period, observed carefully and talked to many persons and then concluded that the power elite of Muncie consisted of a small group of businessmen who were dominated by the "X" family who owned the glass jar and cap company. The formal government was merely a "front" while behind the scenes this informal elite controlled.[9] The Lynds argued that not only a political elite existed but that they acted together as a tightly knit group in almost total control—what we will call a power elite."

Floyd Hunter began studying the power structure of Atlanta in 1950. He used what is called the reputational method by establishing a panel of "knowledgeables" (journalists, civic leaders, and so on), and asked them who ran things in Atlanta. The panel developed a list of forty people, twenty-seven of whom Hunter then interviewed. With this "reputational approach," Hunter concluded that a business-dominated power elite controlled most aspects of Atlanta, largely in ways that most citizens were not aware of.[10]

Other researchers using the reputational method found that many towns seemed to have a similar power elite, usually persons such as bankers, newspaper publishers, main street merchants, industrialists, and others who met for lunch almost daily at the "city club." They argued that these business-dominated power elites made the real decisions, whereas politicans and officials were figureheads.

Criticisms of the power elite findings. Critics of these studies observed that some of the issues that a power elite was reported to oppose were nevertheless approved by voters or by the city council. In other instances, critics pointed to issues that the business-dominated power elite sponsored but that were rejected by citizens or politicians. They thus first questioned the degree to which these power elites were "all-powerful."

These critics also argued that the political elite was not shown to be a tightly organized group. The principal weaknesses of the power elite studies, they maintained, were in the researchers' faulty assumptions:

Abstracts of the earlier periodical literature are found in Charles Press, *Main Street Politics*, Institute for Community Development, Michigan State University, East Lansing, 1962.

[9]Robert S. and Helen M. Lynd, *Middletown*, 1929, and *Middletown in Transition*, 1937. Both are published by Harcourt Brace and Co., New York.

[10]Floyd Hunter, *Community Power Structure*, University of North Carolina Press, Chapel Hill, 1953.

(1) the researchers, by asking questions such as "Who runs things around here?" assumed already that a power elite must exist—ignoring the possibility that businessmen at the top of the economic pyramid may not, in fact, work together in making the decisions; (2) the researchers did not define power for their experts—thus different "experts" could use varying definitions; (3) the researchers, it was claimed, also assumed that the political elite is stable and does not change with changing social and economic conditions; and (4) finally, they assumed that, because others, even so-called experts, think an elite has power, it *actually* does.[11]

These observations led to a new line of research which asked: Who has power over what decisions?

Pluralist Studies.   Robert Dahl's study in New Haven, Connecticut was one of the first major "decisional" studies. Its researchers asked knowledgeable experts to identify who was involved in making a specific decision. Through interviews they attempted to reconstruct the steps in a decision process and to determine the extent of each participant's influence. Dahl studied three areas of decisions and concluded that except for the mayor and his aides, individual influentials participated only in specific policy areas, such as education, political nominations, and urban renewal.[12] Dahl believed that the system of decision making was "pluralist" with competing centers of power both within the political elite and outside it. Edward Banfield, in a study of seven issues in Chicago, reached a similar conclusion.[13]

These and other studies emphasized the diversity of opinion within the political elite, the "slack" in the system caused even by members of the political elite failing to influence decisions as much as they might have, and the importance of political officials and politicians in the decision process.

Criticism of the pluralist findings.   Peter Bachrach and Morton Baratz pointed out that the decisional approach overlooks the fact that a power elite may exercise so much power that it can limit official government decisions to relatively trivial issues. By studying only decisions, they argue, scholars consider only one face of power. Bachrach

[11]A good summary of such criticisms can be found in Nelson W. Polsby, "How to Study Community Power: The Pluralist Alternative," *Journal of Politics*, 22 August 1960, 474–484.

[12]Robert A. Dahl, *Who Governs? Democracy and Power in An American City.* Yale University Press, New Haven, Conn. 1961.

[13]Edward C. Banfield, *Political Influence*, The Free Press, Glencoe, Ill. 1961.

and Baratz assert that there is a second face—nondecisions—the items that did not get on the agenda and alternatives that were not even suggested or openly considered by the community. They argue that researchers need to ask *why* some issues did not emerge. Researchers need to examine the energies that are expended by economic dominants in shaping or reinforcing social and political values— what Bachrach and Baratz call mobilization of bias—in such a way that certain questions and issues are never raised.[14] For example, until recently, issues such as racial integration and discrimination in hiring women or minorities were never on the community agenda for discussion and debate. Suppression of issues can thus be an important aspect of power elite's control.

Does Anyone Make Community Decisions? One further model of how community decisions are made has been presented—that political elites are so loosely knit as to be almost totally splintered. In this case nobody controls—there is no "they" who makes sure some things will happen and others will not. Norton Long suggests that community-wide organization is in fact often weak or nonexistent. "Much of what occurs," he says, "seems to just happen with accidental trends becoming cumulations over time and producing results intended by nobody."[15] Individuals are each involved in their own career games. They follow goals to get ahead in the journalist's game or the lawyer's or downtown merchant's games. The social result of their acts may be accidental— as, for example, the abandonment of central cities by many middle class citizens and industries that individually decided to move to the suburbs. It is hard to imagine a power elite planning this move—in fact, many of the economic dominants of communities fought bitterly to stem this change to preserve central business district property values.

We probably do not feel comfortable leaving it there. Is what happens in a community wholly the result of one accident piled upon another? Most of us will likely say no, if only because we wish it were otherwise. Yet it does appear that some decisions such as the "great" changes we discussed in Chapter 4 are undirected—almost as if communities drift into them.[16]

[14]Bachrach and Baratz, Op cit.

[15]Norton E. Long, "The Local Community as an Ecology of Games," *The Polity*, Rand McNally, Chicago, Ill. 1962.

[16]Terry Clark theorizes that centralization of power, whether a business-dominated power elite or formal structures such as government officials or a boss system, seems to produce "public goods"—policies that affect the whole community—while decentralization of power encourages "separable goods"—those that can be allotted to specific groups or in-

An Assessment of Community Studies

Perhaps the most persuasive finding that emerges from the community elite studies is that a wide variety of decision making has existed.[17] In some communities and states at different times political elites, either dominated by economic leaders or by political bosses, have exercised tight control approaching that found in modern totalitarian nations.[18] The political elite are almost totally unresponsive to the desires of nonelite citizens. In other communities, researchers have reported a pluralism verging on anarchy as the nonelite have penetrated deeply into the decision process.[19] This penetration has been the case especially when a social movement has literally overwhelmed a state or a community's political elite. Such movements may radically restructure the decision process, as did the tax revolt movement of 1978 in California and other states and many communities.

But neither a tightly controlled elite model nor one of pluralism approaching anarchy seems to describe very well the decision pattern of most states and communities today. To us it seems that two forces now characterize decision making in most states and communities: (1) the traditional influence of private economic groups with the acceptance by nonelite citizens of many of these decisions, and (2) a growing pluralism brought about by the increasing role of government, the increasing importance of intergovernmental relations, and the emergence of new groups that are becoming part of the changing state and community political elites.

---

dividuals. Terry N. Clark, Op cit. p. 61. Richard W. Smith reaches a similar conclusion in "Community Power and Decision Making: A Replication and Extension of Hawley." *American Sociological Review*, 41, August 1976, 691–705.

[17]See especially a study of four communities, each with different patterns of influence, as described in Robert E. Agger, Daniel Goldrich and Bert E. Swanson, *The Rulers and the Ruled*, John Wiley & Sons, N.Y., 1964.

[18]Many political scientists believe the closest an American State has come to a dictatorship was Louisiana between 1928 and 1935 under Governor and then Senator Huey Long. For a recent favorable biography see T. Harry Williams, *Huey Long*, Knopf, New York, 1969. See also Allan P. Sindler, *Huey Long's Louisiana*, Johns Hopkins Press, Baltimore, 1956, and Hartnet Kane, *Louisiana Hayride*, William Morrow, New York, 1941. A novel based loosely on a Huey Long-type politician is Robert Penn Warren, *All the King's Men*, Harcourt Brace, New York, 1946. It was also made into an outstanding movie of the same title, starring Broderick Crawford.

[19]For a view that masses, indeed, influence too much the decision making of modern societies, see William Kornhauser, *The Politics of Mass Society*, The Free Press of Glencoe, Glencoe, Illinois, 1959. For the classic statement of the theory that a military-industrial complex controls all of American society, see C. Wright Mills, *The Power Elite*, Oxford University Press, New York, 1956.

Business and Industry Influence. Earlier we noted why states and communities are especially sensitive to the needs of business—because their economies have so heavily depended on business prosperity. Most older community studies document this influence, arguing either that the business community almost completely dominates local decision making, or is strongly influential because of the nonparticipation of average citizens or, perhaps, because citizens tacitly approve of the decisions made. This influence by business and industry clearly is still important in states and communities.

Forces for Change in Political Elites. It also seems that power in communities (and states as well) is now less centralized then it once was. By this we mean that the political elite is made up of more conflicting elements, that its membership has changed over time and continues to change, that citizens have more freedom to criticize actions of its members, and that these actions are, at best, only loosely coordinated.

Erosion of the bases for former elites. We begin with a point mentioned several times before—the growing national diversification of industry and agriculture, the movement of population within communities and among states, and the growth of a national mass communication system. All of these erode the bases of older elites. In the South, for example, the traditional elite that once held relatively tight control in many states and communities is increasingly challenged by other forces in a rapidly changing economy and society. A political elite remains, but its membership as elsewhere is drawn from a wider spectrum of the state or community and now often includes leaders of labor unions, racial, ethnic, and religious group leaders, and many more from the professional class than was formerly the case.

The impact of citizen participation. We should not overlook the possibility that voters also occasionally have a marked influence on who will make government decisions and the content of such decisions. When public opinion supports ideas such as the ecology or consumer movement, it has a way of influencing policy decisions despite the opposition of major business and industrial groups. Robert S. Erikson goes further and, by comparing public opinion poll data of a generation or so ago with subsequent state legislative decisions, argues that the public and the political decision makers were, in fact, in agreement on the issues researched.[20]

[20]Citizen opinions, revealed in Gallup Poll data of the 1930s, were matched with subsequent policy decisions. Erikson found state legislators responsive to public opinion on (1) capital punishment, (2) the proposed child labor amendment, and (3) whether women

Protest movements. The method of protest used so effectively by anti-war groups, civil rights organizations, and environmentalists in the 1960s also has diffused community power by influencing the political elite and adding new members to it. Civil rights groups learned that protest could be a powerful tool, and other groups have used these methods—for example, against private developers of shopping centers and subdivisions. Such protests may concern proposed street widenings, intersection modifications, or school building closings. Protests may be only a passing strategy for the internal relocation of power. The tactic, however, has some inherent problems.[21]

Rulings by the courts. We see diffusion of power in the way individuals use the courts. Even if members of the political elite can "arrange things" in city hall or at the state capitol, they may nevertheless find their goals obstructed by a single individual who files a federal or state court suit. One such example concerned a proposal for the city of Detroit to build and lease a new stadium to their professional football team—the Detroit Lions. To sell the bonds the city had to assure bond buyers that if stadium revenues were insufficient, it would levy a tax to pay the bonds and interest. A promise to levy a tax did not require a referendum, but the city was obligated to issue a public notice. An individual filed suit, saying that the notice was misleading. The state supreme court agreed. The project was scuttled and later a nearby city, Pontiac, built the stadium for the "Detroit" Lions.

Professional administrators and the media. Civil service or merit employment provisions and the growing use of professionals in city hall and county government also tends to relocate power, sometimes in support of the local political elite and sometimes against them. City-paid community development workers, for example, may lead neighborhood groups to oppose neighborhood "improvement" projects; or professional administrators may "leak" stories to newspapers, or in other ways inform the public of misdeeds in city hall or county courthouse. Investigative reporting styles encourage the uncovering of such news." Thus power and control of issues has flowed outward as battles are extended beyond the decision centers controlled by the political elite.

---

should be allowed to serve on trial juries. Robert S. Erikson, "The Relationship between Public Opinion and State Policy: A New Look Based on Some Forgotten Data," *American Journal of Political Science*, 20 February 1976, 25–36.

[21]See Michael Lipsky, "Protest As a Political Resource," *American Political Science Review*, 62, December 1968, 1144–1158. For a review of three cases involving protestors against developers, see Bernard J. Frieden "Environmental Politics," *Urban Land*, Urban Land Institute, March 1977.

The state and national governments.   Permissive federalism, we have argued, produces a flow of power outward to federal and state levels of government. The penetration of federal and state dollars into even the smallest of communities means that federal and state governments are going to have more of a say in what the community agenda is to be and which policy outcomes are to be preferred in areas such as smokestack emissions, municipal accounting and budgeting procedures, the minimum height for police officers, and provision for the handicapped.

We should note, too, that these state and federal policies also tend to shift around power within the communities. Block grants and general revenue sharing, in spite of their public hearing requirements, tend to add to city hall power. The city council and mayor can build the fire station that was turned down in a referendum by using community development funds. We also find, however, that such requirements as environmental impact statements give forces opposing city hall time to marshall their forces.

Today's Splintered Political Elites

What we suggest, then, is that a political elite exists today in the sense that some members of a state or community have a great deal more influence on political decisions than other citizens. But this elite is drawn from many more segments of states and communities than in the past and is not of one opinion on very many subjects. It often behaves more like a gathering of interest group representatives seeking specific gains for the collectivity that each spokesperson represents, rather than as a cohesive ruling class. Given such divisions, the political elite can be more easily penetrated by average citizens.

A second point is one we have made before—power is shifting from the private sector to the public sector. Decisions that once were made without government concern are now influenced or made by government officials. Government officials, who are part of the political elite, are thus no longer the figureheads they may once have been.

Finally, we find power more closely tied to functional areas, especially with the growing influence of professional administrators. Specialists in areas such as education, conservation, or the building of streets and highways have an influence on specific decisions that the political elite has difficulty countering.

Thus we argue that power and influence as well as the potential for the exercise of power rests in many quarters. But many average citizens, we will find, choose not to use what power they have. Many have neither the interest nor the inclination to become excited about or involved in issues that affect them only marginally and they are sometimes inactive even when the issue affects them directly. To the extent that the potential power of average citizens is directed in other ways, members of the political elite who are interested are able to wield power far in excess of their numbers and resources.

PARTICIPATION BY NON-ELITE CITIZENS

Given the existence of a political elite, we can ask: How much participation by average citizens does the functioning of democratic government require? The answer given throughout our history by reformers is that the opportunity to participate must be as great as possible. But as we will see, getting those average citizens actually to participate has not been as easy as the Jacksonians, the Progressives of the early 1900s, or some modern day reformers have hoped. The philosopher and English reformer, Graham Wallis, suggested that most citizens turn to politics with an "indifferent and half attentive mind," and that fairly sums up what recent studies have found.[22]

The Extent of Citizen Participation

The data suggest that about 33 percent to perhaps 40 percent of all citizens may be classified as habitual nonparticipants, since they seldom vote or make other efforts to influence officials. (See Table 11-1)

At the other extreme of the non-elite is a group of politically active citizens who compose perhaps 5 percent of the population—Gabriel Almond aptly called them "attentive publics." He defined them as "an informed and interested stratum before whom elite discussion and controversy take place." Attentive publics come and go with changes of issues and political events.[23]

Between the nonparticipants and the attentive publics are participants whom we will call "average citizens." These are the citizens who vote with some regularity but not in every election and may occasionally contact officials, attend public meetings, listen to political speeches, and discuss public issues.

Attentive publics are most likely to influence policymaking through the interest group process—a topic discussed in the next chapter. Here

[22]Graham Wallis, *Human Nature and Politics,* Appleton Century Crofts, New York, 1908, reissued Bison edition, University of Nebraska Press, Lincoln, 1962, p. 115 and Arthur T. Hadley, *The Empty Voting Booth,* Prentice Hall, Englewood Cliffs, N.J., 1978.

[23]Gabriel Almond, *The American People and Foreign Policy,* Frederick A. Praeger, New York, 1960, p. 139.

we focus on the influence of the other segments that are not part of the political elite, especially those we have called average citizens.[24]

The Citizen Electorate

Voting is often used as a shorthand measure for other forms of political participation—partly because voting is the most basic and widespread form of democratic participation and partly because researchers have found that voting roughly parallels other forms of participation such as writing legislators, attending political meetings, and so on. Voting is also the most thoroughly researched kind of participation.[25] We review some of the findings about voting patterns.

Variation By Level of Government.   Voter participation in presidential elections averages about 55 percent, but ranges among states from 45 percent to 70 percent. Vóting in races for governor runs around 45 percent, while in local elections for mayor it drops to roughly 25 percent. Specific elections, of course, will deviate from these figures. The participation in elections for governor or senator drops when the election is in a non-presidential year.

Variation by State and Region.   We find higher voting participation in the relatively rural states of the North and West, states that Daniel Elazar described as "moralistic." Toward the bottom are the southern states, described by Elazar as "traditional." The larger industrialized urban states of the North are at the center of the distribution. The regional pattern, though, is a weak one and includes a number of striking exceptions among the states.

Variation By Closeness of the Race.   Researchers have found that participation rises when the voter can assume that his vote will make some difference in the outcome. Citizens are rational enough to save

---

[24]Anne Hopkins makes this division—"eligibles" (those whose age and citizenship make them eligible), "participants" (voters), "attentive publics" (feel strongly about issues), and "actives" (amateurs who are involved in political activites short of running for office). Anne H. Hopkins, "Opinion Publics and Support of Public Policy," *American Journal of Political Science*, February 1974, 167–177.

[25]Some recent studies show "modes" of participation with some overlap of categories. Thus Milbrath suggests voting may be regarded as a patriotic act of loyalty to the system. He suggests other modes that have different purposes such as communicating to officials, protesting, working in parties and campaigns, and political activity in communities. Nie and Verba define four modes of participation: voting, campaign activity, citizen-initiated contacts of officials, and cooperative activity through organizations and protests. Most studies, however, have treated participation as a general activity with voting as its cen-

the effort when it becomes apparent that they have no effective choice. The states with highest participation levels tend to have two-party competiton, at least for major offices; those with low participation for long periods traditionally have been one-party states. Again, we can find some exceptions.

Participation and Political Ties. As one might expect, those who hold public office or are active in politics or who have friends or relatives involved are more likely to vote. For example, an early study of voting in Chicago demonstrated that a voter participation campaign increased voter turnout—except in the Irish precincts—where Irish politicians, who then ran the Chicago machine, it seems had already gotten all the potential Irish voters to the polls.[26]

Variation by Status. Finally, the voter studies reveal most clearly that participation is related to educational level, and secondarily, to position in society. (Table 11-2). We use social status as a shorthand measure for how distant a citizen is from the center of social actions—in general, researchers find all measures of higher social status are related to higher political participation. Thus those with the most schooling vote more and those with the least are most likely to be nonparticipants; the wealthy vote in proportionately greater numbers than those having less wealth; the employed more than the unemployed, those at the poverty level are least likely to vote or participate in any way; whites have voted more than blacks; men more than women; the middle-aged more than the young or old; long-term residents in a community more than newcomers; property owners more than renters; Protestants more than Catholics; those with Anglo-Saxon background more than those of other ethnic groups. Again we can expect to find exceptions in particular elections; for example we would anticipate a higher than average turnout of blacks if a black were in a close contest for governor.

The data also suggest that changes in turnout occur along with status changes within society—women have participated in increasing numbers as their status has risen. The same is true of many ethnic, religious, and racial groups.

---

tral feature and this is the tradition we will follow. See Norman H. Nie and Sidney Verba, "Political Participation," in Fred I. Greenstein and Nelson Polsby, editors, *The Handbook of Political Science* Vol. 4, Addison Wesley, Reading, Mass., 1975, 1–74. See also Lester W. Milbrath and M. L. Goel, *Political Participation, How and Why Do People Get Involved in Politics*, Rand McNally, Chicago, 2nd edition, 1977.

[26]Charles E. Merriam and Harold Gosnell, *Non Voting: Causes and Methods of Control*, University of Chicago Press, Chicago, 1924, p. 41.

TABLE 11-1 Participation of Eligible Voters

	1976					1974			
	Percentage Registered of Eligible (18 and over)	Percentage Voting of Eligible				Percentage Registered of Eligible (18 and over)	Percentage Voting of Eligible		
		President	U.S. Senator	Governor	Representative		U.S. Senator	Governor	Representative
Alabama	74.6	47.3	—	—	39.3	74.9	21.8	25.0	23.4
Alaska	89.7	53.6	—	—	51.1	82.2	43.7	46.6	45.0
Arizona	63.0	47.8	47.6	—	46.9	61.8	38.1	38.3	37.7
Arkansas	67.9	51.1	—	48.4	22.4	70.4	38.2	38.5	29.8
California	65.3	51.4	48.8	—	48.7	68.4	41.8	43.1	39.9
Colorado	76.1	61.0	—	—	57.6	71.4	48.2	48.2	45.5
Connecticut	75.5	62.5	61.6	—	61.0	73.5	50.5	51.9	59.2
Delaware	74.7	58.5	55.8	57.1	53.3	71.4	—	—	41.1
District of Columbia	52.1	32.9	—	—	31.1[b]	51.8	—	—	20.2[b]
Florida	64.8	49.8	45.2	—	32.9	62.4	30.8	31.5	18.1
Georgia	68.2	43.5	—	—	37.1	64.8	26.9	29.0	25.3
Hawaii	60.5	48.5	50.3	—	49.0	60.1	43.0	43.8	45.2
Idaho	91.7	60.7	—	—	60.3	84.8	49.1	50.1	47.4
Illinois	81.0	61.1	—	60.1	56.6	77.2	38.3	—	37.3
Indiana	82.7	61.0	59.6	60.0	57.8	81.5	49.0	—	48.4
Iowa	70.0	63.6	—	—	61.8	50.6	45.6	50.0	46.1
Kansas	69.1	59.3	—	—	56.3	71.4	50.2	49.0	49.1
Kentucky	72.2	49.1	—	—	41.7	64.2	32.7	32.6[a]	29.7
Louisiana	73.7	50.4	—	—	40.0	70.3	17.8	17.5[a]	22.4
Maine	93.9	65.2	65.6	—	63.8	90.3	—	52.0	49.5
Maryland	68.1	50.1	47.7	—	46.0	62.5	31.5	34.1	31.4
Massachusetts	69.8	61.0	59.7	—	56.2	71.7	—	45.4	41.9
Michigan	83.0	58.3	55.7	—	54.8	79.3	—	43.6	41.7
Minnesota	94.3	71.7	70.1	—	66.0	73.0	—	47.6	46.3
Mississippi	—	49.8	35.9	—	41.3	77.0	—	47.4[a]	20.3

Missouri	60.5	58.4	57.8	57.2	56.9	65.7	37.0	36.6
Montana	87.8	63.5	61.2	62.0	62.0	77.2	—	51.5
Nebraska	77.9	56.3	—	55.4	55.7	73.5	—	42.4
Nevada	59.2	47.6	—	47.6	47.2	62.0	43.3	43.1
New Hampshire	83.3	59.2	59.8	45.8	56.6	76.5	—	39.8
New Jersey	73.1	58.5	—	53.8	54.5	68.7	—	41.1
New Mexico	68.4	54.2	—	53.6	52.0	69.0	—	44.1
New York	63.5	50.6	—	49.0	46.4	65.7	40.7	38.5
North Carolina	66.4	43.6	43.3	—	40.9	62.7	27.7	26.9
North Dakota	—	68.8	68.8	65.5	67.1	—	55.5	55.0
Ohio	62.9	55.1	—	52.6	51.5	61.0	41.0	40.4
Oklahoma	72.3	56.4	—	—	55.1	71.4	42.3	27.1
Oregon	85.9	62.3	—	—	56.1	72.0	48.5	47.6
Pennsylvania	68.1	54.7	—	53.9	52.5	66.3	41.8	40.6
Rhode Island	84.1	63.4	61.6	61.6	60.0	74.4	—	46.5
South Carolina	57.6	41.5	—	—	40.6	54.5	27.8	28.1
South Dakota	90.8	64.2	—	—	62.9	86.6	60.8	59.4
Tennessee	64.6	49.9	—	48.4	42.3	68.0	—	31.5
Texas	74.3	47.9	—	45.6	43.1	66.4	—	18.4
Utah	89.9	69.0	69.0	69.0	69.5	83.1	56.8	55.7
Vermont	86.9	57.5	56.9	57.8	56.6	84.4	45.3	44.6
Virginia	59.9	48.1	—	44.2	41.5	61.6	—	27.4
Washington	81.4	61.4	58.8	58.8	56.2	79.8	41.7	40.6
West Virginia	84.6	58.6	58.5	44.3	51.8	82.8	—	33.5
Wisconsin	79.9	65.5	—	60.3	61.1	—	32.3	38.7
Wyoming	72.9	58.6	—	58.3	57.1	75.8	—	51.8
United States	70.5	54.4	—	—	—	—	—	36.1

SOURCE: Statistical Abstract of the United States, 1975, 1976, 1977, 97th annual edition, U.S. Department of Commerce, Bureau of the Census, 1977.

aElection in 1975

bDelegate

Opportunities for Citizen Participation

Many issues and decisions are never brought to the attention of average citizens even at election time. The members of the political elite compromise the issue among themselves. A bargain is struck that satisfies the interests represented in the political elite, and it becomes state or community policy. Lest we become paranoid, we should note that this is the way all government systems work; we, as average citizens, delegate decision-making power to the political decision makers and in effect to those who exercise major influence with them—that is, to the political elite with occasional inputs by attentive publics.

Political elites are seldom so powerful in our states and communities as steadfastly to defy expressions of opinion by average citizens. The

TABLE 11-2 Participation in National Elections, by Population Characteristics: 1972 and 1974

	1972		1974	
Characteristic	Persons Reporting They Voted Percent	Percent Reporting Not Voting[a]	Persons Reporting They Voted Percent	Percent Reporting Not Voting[a]
Total	63.0	37.0	44.7	55.3
Male	64.1	35.9	46.2	53.8
Female	62.0	38.0	43.4	56.6
White	64.5	35.5	46.3	53.7
Negro	52.1	47.9	33.8	66.2
18–20 years old	48.3	51.7	20.8	79.2
21–24 years old	50.7	49.3	26.4	73.6
25–34 years old	59.7	40.3	37.0	63.0
35–44 years old	66.3	33.7	49.1	50.9
45–64 years old	70.8	29.2	56.9	43.1
65 years and over	63.5	36.5	51.4	48.6
Residence:				
Metropolitan	64.3	35.7	44.7	55.3
Nonmetropolitan	59.4	40.6	44.7	55.3
North and West	66.4	33.6	48.8	51.2
South	55.4	44.6	36.0	64.0
Sch'l yr. completed:				
8 or less	47.4	52.6	34.4	65.6
9–11	52.0	48.0	35.9	64.1
12	65.4	34.6	44.7	55.3
More than 12	78.8	21.2	54.9	45.1
Employed	66.0	34.0	46.8	53.2
Unemployed	49.9	50.1	28.8	71.2
Not in labor force	59.3	40.7	43.0	57.0

SOURCE: U.S. Bureau of the Census, *Current Population Reports*, series P–20, Nos. 192, 253, and 293. Reprinted in *Statistical Abstract of the United States 1976*, U.S. Department of Commerce, Bureau of the Census, 1977.

[a]Includes do not know and not reported.

problem is often less one of the nonresponsiveness of political elites than the failure of citizens to express preferences.

The potential for influence of the other 95 percent of the citizenry rises when an election campaign such circumstances as the following bring the issue to the attention of average citizens.

A Calamity or Major Inconvenience Occurs.   The assassination of Dr. Martin Luther King dramatized for blacks how much was wrong in past decisions and resulted in rioting and further political participation by average black citizens. But something less than a catastrophe also can stimulate citizen participation. Many white parents viewed the busing decisions by local school boards and courts negatively, and in some communities intense politicking by amateur political participants was the result.

A Problem is Publicized.   A series of newspaper stories that focuses on a government action, whether it be the salary set for the new city manager, administration of the state's Medicaid program, or the condition of county farm to market roads—any of these will bring political elite decisions to the average citizen's attention. The publicity suggests that something may be wrong with the decisions the political elite has been reaching. Pressure may or may not develop for a review of such decisions.

Members of the Political Elite Publicly Disagree.   The political scientist E. E. Schattschneider was among the first to emphasize that a widening of conflict beyond the political elite would not only involve more of the average citizens who were amateur participants, but might also change the outcome of the decision.[27] For example, when a community political elite decides to build a new city hall, they cannot afford to have dissension within the political elite. If members of the political elite widen the conflict by attacking each other publicly, the decision may be changed. As more average citizens became involved and begin to express doubts about the project, the project might even be abandoned.

The Effects of Legal Rules on Citizen Participation

In the past it could be argued that states and communities discriminated against certain groups to the point where it was legally impossi-

[27]E. E. Schattschneider, *The Semi-Sovereign People*, Holt, Rinehart and Winston, New York, 1960.

ble for them to participate. Until 1920 this was the case in respect to voting by women in most states. The most notorious more recent cases of legal discrimination, perhaps, involved blacks and other minorities, such as Indians or Spanish-speaking citizens.

In the 1890s the newly formed Populist party challenged the Democrats in the South, and genuine electoral competition emerged. The Negro held the potential balance of power between Populists and old-line Democrats. Recognizing this, the old-line Democrats took many of their Negro sharecropper tenants to the polls and instructed them to vote for conservative Democrats. This action killed the Populist party in the South and resulted in a rash of laws by former Populists designed to reduce or eliminate Negro voting.

Alabama and Louisiana used the grandfather clause (you could not register to vote if your grandfather had not voted prior to 1860). Virginia adopted the poll tax and literacy requirements. Some states required explanation of complicated constitutional clauses, others used a "general knowledge" question (how many bubbles in a bar of soap?). Blacks as well as many whites were effectively excluded from voting. (Table 11-3).

How Voting Requirements Have Been Reduced.   Despite the sorry history in respect to blacks, the story of citizen participation in America has been one of the steady elimination of legal barriers. State and community governments, as well as the federal courts, have formally abolished one legal restriction on voting after another—restrictions based on property ownership, race, religious creed, and sex. The voting age has been lowered to eighteen for state and national elections. And potentially discriminatory requirements such as the literacy test, poll tax, or unusual residence or registration requirements have been sharply cut back or eliminated. Federal rules also require ballots to be printed in Spanish as well as English, for example, where a substantial number of Spanish-speaking citizens reside.

When states removed the legal barriers to voting, startling rises in participation sometimes occurred. In Mississippi, after the passage of

TABLE 11-3 Blacks Registered to Vote

State	No. of Voters/Year		No. of Voters/Year	
Alabama[a]	78,311	(1900)	1,081	(1903)
Louisiana	130,344	(1898)	5,230	(1900)
Virginia	147,000	(1900)	21,000	(1902)

SOURCE: Jack Bass and Walter DeVries, *The Transformation of Southern Politics*, Basic Books, New York, 1976, 82 and 342.

[a]In fourteen Black Belt counties.

the national Voting Rights Act of 1965 the number of blacks otherwise eligible who registered to vote increased from 6.7 percent in 1965, to 55.8 percent in 1967. In six other southern states the rise was less dramatic, though of considerable political importance: from 30 percent to 46 percent of the blacks registered.[28]

Eliminating administrative discrimination. The federal, state, and community governments are also enforcing the voting laws more fairly. The most striking example of enforcement requirements is again an outgrowth of intergovernmental relations—the national Voting Rights Act. It provided for federal registrars in counties where more than 50 percent of the potential voters did not vote and where some form of literacy, understanding, or good character requirement was in effect. The threat of federal intervention seems to have sharply reduced discriminatory practices that were common just a generation ago.

Opening the System for the Average Citizen. State and community governments, especially, offer a wide variety of access points to the average citizen besides the right to vote in primaries and general elections. The separation of powers multiplies the access points. One may write the governor or mayor, call a state representative or councillor and, except in Nebraska, a member of a state upper house as well, or approach administrators. The voter often chooses directly other officials besides mayor and councillors. Administrative agencies usually must hold public hearings before they can announce certain decisions.

In addition, several features of state and community governments encourage the widening of conflicts and divisions among government decision makers who are part of the political elite. Among the most important are the clear separation of the executive, legislative, and judicial branches and regularly scheduled elections. Judges review past decisions; councils challenge the actions of mayors and managers; candidates appear who attack the decisions made by incumbents or by members of their political faction or party. And a media relatively uncontrolled by government reports these conflicts.

A number of states and communities, by enacting "sunshine" laws, recently have expanded the list of open meetings that members of the press as well as average citizens may attend. The courts are available as another access point. Finally many officials themselves have followed the practice of seeking out citizens. Jimmy Carter, while governor of Georgia, every so often took a week in which he moved from city to city

[28]Jack Bass and Walter DeVries, *The Transformation of Southern Politics, Social Change and Political Consequence Since 1945*, Basic Books, New York, 1976.

throughout Georgia and invited local citizens to phone in questions to him at the local radio station. Other governors or mayors have set aside regularly scheduled periods for ordinary citizens to visit them. City complaint departments or the creation of ombudsman offices may also serve this function. A novel method of increasing such participation is the setting up of neighborhood organizations. We discuss this movement in Policy Box No. 21, "Grassroots Participation in a Great City."

Reducing Legal Barriers Is Not Enough.   It would be comforting if we could assume that once all unreasonable legal barriers were removed, voting and other forms of participation would be uniformly high across states and among citizens in every community. This is not, in fact, likely to be the case. We would find that a sizeable number of citizens still would not vote. How, for example, can we account for 45 percent turnouts in most state races today and lower turnouts at the community level?

We next consider three major theories other than legal barriers that attempt to explain variations in participation among average citizens as well as nonparticipation—(1) a cost and benefit theory, (2) a citizen alienation theory, and (3) social movement participation.

THE COSTS AND BENEFITS OF POLITICAL PARTICIPATION

A moment's reflection will suggest that political participation is not free. Political participation costs, if not in dollars, then in time and effort. All of us have limited amounts of time, energy, and wealth to spend.

We also know that to participate intelligently we need information— what types of positions candidates hold, for instance, and how their actions may benefit us. Such information also is not free for most of us.

As we will suggest, states and communities have been more successful in reducing participation costs than information costs.

Costs are Lower For High Status Citizens

If you drop in to a small town in your state around 10:00 a.m., you will very likely find the Main Street merchants and some local officials gathered at a cafe for morning coffee. The discussions include community gossip as well as local politics. At the same hour you would find many of the housewives and the retired at home, blue collar workers in factories or on road crews and the unemployed walking or driving around looking for work or at home working in the basement or yard.

Neighborhood protests against drug dealers.

The point we are making is that in a small town it takes little effort for local business people to keep up with community politics or to participate in community decisions. They, like other higher status persons, gain political advantages from the positions they hold in society because they are involved at the center rather than the edges of their social system. They can understand without too much effort the benefits

These are some of the people that missed the main street merchants' coffee break.

POLICY BOX NO. 21   Grassroots Participation in a Great City

Thomas Jefferson assumed that democracy could only flourish in a rural environment where neighbors met as equals and discussed common problems. The New England town meeting, a form he encouraged through that part of the Northwest Ordinance of 1787 that divided the midwest into townships, was his ideal. Jefferson believed that in such a government the costs of participation and information would be as low as possible.

But it has not worked out that way. Elected representatives largely controlled the townships and even some New England town meetings although they continued the annual town meeting for elections and sometimes to set the annual budget. Often, it was argued, these, too, were controlled by a local elite, either because few others attended or because a clique would crowd into the town hall early to keep others outside. The form also proved inefficient and unable to cope with the problems of a technological society. The townships could no longer be trusted to handle welfare problems or construct roads. Many could not afford modern fire-fighting equipment or safe water supply.

Some states abolished townships outright. Others merely stripped them of important functions. Still others kept the township names, but allowed these units to evolve into representative governments similar to cities.

But at about the time of World War II, a University of Chicago professor, Saul Alinsky, began applying the techniques of small group organization to sections of Chicago. The earliest, and among the more successful of his organizations, was in the stockyards area where ethnic groups organized the "Back of the Yards Movement" to preserve their neighborhoods. These organizations are similar in some ways to the old style political machines and seem to have flourished in cities with a machine history.

These neighborhood organizations spread to many other large cities—Model Cities had such an underpinning—in some areas taking root and in others, withering after a short period. One place block clubs flourished, oddly enough, was New York City. Over 10,000 of New York's 33,000 blocks are organized. Typically the block club includes residents on both sides of a street of one city block. The clubs have monthly meetings and sponsor many social activities—a weekly volley ball game, block party, and one even held a hayride. But they also engage in political activities. One picketed a massage parlor and drove it out of the neighborhood. Another bombarded pimps with water-filled balloons thrown from roofs. Another put up a sign telling clients of prostitutes that they were taking down license numbers and calling up wives. Many have street patrols and "creep numbers" that residents call when they see suspicious characters. The New York City Police Department has so far trained 32,000 block workers in observing and reporting crime. The block clubs have formed ambulance corps, food co-ops, and credit unions, planted thousands of trees and gardens, lobbied for street signs, garbage can inspection and pickup, pothole repairs, and have pressured owners to fix up buildings and clean up vacant lots. During the "blackout of 1977" block members patrolled their neighborhoods to prevent looting. Baltimore, Boston, and Washington, D.C., have some block clubs and enthusiasts say the movement will spread to other urban centers.

What do you think? Will this movement for block or neighborhood organizations spread or will it die off as the rural township did? Do you think such participation is a healthy sign that should be encouraged? Do you think it encourages other political participation? Would the spread of block clubs by law solve the problems of citizen participation? Why or why not? Can all neighborhoods, rich and poor, rural and urban, be organized? Why did such organizations suddenly spring up in New York City? Should block clubs be given government functions and the power to tax? Would you want your home neighborhood organized on a block club basis?

SOURCE: The basic source is Saul Alinsky, *Reveille for Radicals* University of Chicago Press, Chicago, 1946. See also Alan A. Altshuler *Community Control* Bobbs-Merrill, Indianapolis, 1970, Joseph F. Zimmerman *The Federated City, Community Control in Large Cities* St. Martin's Press, New York, 1972, and Mario Fantini and Marilyn Gittell, *Decentralization: Achieving Reform* Praeger, New York, 1973.

they are likely to get from any policy decision. Information costs are lower for them as compared with housewives, the unemployed, or blue collar workers.

Lower status persons, because of their occupations, generally experience higher costs in time, energy, and even money to reach decision centers and participate.

Thus for the better educated, higher status groups, participation and information costs are less, and the benefits are clearer.

A cost and benefit calculus turns out to be a good rough indicator of variations and participation differences among average citizens. Any factor that raises the costs—for example, the use of voting machines or rain on election day—inevitably lowers participation somewhat. And the drop off in participation consistently is greater among lower status citizens.

Participation Costs

All participation costs can not be eliminated, of course. But in the last decade states and communities have made progress so that, for the most part, we can probably view most of the participation costs that remain as the reasonable burdens of democratic citizenship.[29]

[29]For a compilation of fifteen electoral requirements of the fifty states that add to or reduce costs for the voter see Robert H. Blank "State Electoral Structure," *Journal of Politics*, 35, 1973, 989–994.

The cost that still weighs heaviest on many average citizens is voter registration—an administrative procedure intended to eliminate election fraud.

Registration as a Political Cost. Registration requires some forethought and often a special visit to a city or county clerk's office. Failure to register is one of the reasons most frequently given to pollsters for failure to vote (see Table 11-4).

We do not have a national registration system—the individual states and communities administer their own registration laws. North Dakota is the only state without such a law, although rural parts of other states do without registration.

By registering, the potential voters identify themselves, give their addresses and sign a form. Many states require registration every four years except for persons who vote during that period. Some states require registration every two years and thus add to voting costs because

TABLE 11-4 Participation in Congressional Elections, by Mobility Status and Length of Residence: 1974[a]

Length and Characteristics of Residence	Persons Reporting They Voted Percent	Persons Reporting They Did Not Vote Because They Were Not Registered Percent	Other Reason Percent
Total	44.7	37.8	17.5
Less than 1 year[a]	22.4	62.5	10.1
Previous address, same county	25.5	57.8	19.7
Different county, same State	21.0	63.8	15.2
Different State	14.9	74.8	10.3
Abroad	6.8	88.8	4.4
1–2 years[b]	35.9	48.2	15.9
Previous address, same county	37.1	45.7	17.2
Different county, same State	35.8	49.7	19.5
Different State	33.1	54.3	12.6
Abroad	13.2	81.8	5.0
3–5 years[b]	46.5	34.5	19.0
Previous address, same county	46.1	34.1	19.8
Different county, same State	50.9	31.4	17.7
Different State	47.6	34.1	18.3
Abroad	17.7	75.1	7.2
6 years or more	58.2	22.2	19.6
Length not reported	2.9	95.3	1.8

SOURCE: Adapted from *Statistical Abstract of the United States*, U.S. Department of Commerce, Bureau of the Census, Washington, D. C., 1977.

[a]As of November. Covers civilian noninstitutional population, 18 years old and over.

[b]Includes not reported, not shown separately.

many citizens, particularly those who vote only occasionally, will be unsure whether they voted two years before and will tend to avoid the embarrassment of being denied a ballot. Election officials, though, argue that the two-year registration law helps clear the roll of voters who have died or moved from the district.

Proposals to reduce registration costs. Minnesota lowers registration costs by allowing voters to register at the polls on election day, a plan favored by President Carter. Opponents argue that this opens elections to widespread fraud, and in 1978 Ohio voters rejected this proposal. Many states and communities set up registration booths at certain times in shopping centers or college dormitories or deputize political party workers to go door-to-door to get new registrants.

Among the other experiments to reduce registration costs are the computerized registration system of South Carolina, the postcard registration system first advocated by President Jimmy Carter and used in Maryland and New Jersey, and Michigan's registration when renewing driver's licenses.

Information Costs

Voting intelligently in terms of our own preferences requires paying what we consider reasonable costs to dig out information ourselves or finding someone we trust who has studied the issue and candidates and who will give us cues. Let us first examine efforts to reduce information costs for average citizens.

The Short Ballot Reduces Information Costs. Woodrow Wilson as governor of New Jersey and Theodore Roosevelt as governor of New York both supported the organization of a Short Ballot Movement in the early 1900s. They reasoned that the information costs that voters face in a long ballot were often too great and, as a consequence, many voters skipped voting for minor offices or voted blindly. So, the reformers argued, a major method of reducing information costs was to make the task of voting a reasonable one. Voters should only be asked to vote for major policymaking officials.

It also can be argued that eliminating primary elections or votes on charter or constitutional amendments would reduce information costs and voter burdens. But it seems unlikely that such suggestions will be readily adopted.

Additional experiments in reducing information costs have involved making the ballot itself more informative by allowing candidates to add slogans or other descriptive material. We review such efforts in Policy Box No. 22, "California's Experiment in Reducing Voter Costs."

POLICY BOX NO. 22 California's Experiment in Reducing Voter Costs

At the height of his career as senator from Nebraska, George Norris was faced in the primary by a political unknown who happened to be a grocer and who also happened to have the name of George Norris. California, in 1932, attempted to solve that kind of problem by allowing candidates with similar names to identify themselves on the ballot—thus reducing the information costs for voters. In 1945 the state legislature limited nonofficeholders to three words, but allowed incumbents to use all the words they wished. A 1963 study by the Assembly Elections Committee and a 1974 study by political scientists Gary C. Byrne and J. Kristian Pueschel confirmed what politicians knew—well-phrased designations help bring victory. In 1973, because of uneasiness about changes in districts caused by reapportionment, the legislature extended the law to all elections and eliminated the requirement that it only be used where names were similar. Local election officials decided what types of wording were acceptable for minor races and the secretary of state office for statewide races.

The political scientists who studied races for Republican and Democratic county central committee positions found that the following designations were advantageous—"professor," "incumbent," engineer," and "lawyer." These designations neither hurt nor helped much— "scientist," "businessman," "teacher," "skilled labor," and "political officeholder." These designations hurt—"stock-broker," "Doctor," "Dentist," "Life Insurance Salesman," "Housewife," "salesman," and "Real Estate Broker." Worst of all was no designation. In terms of ethnicity of candidates' names they found Scandinavian helpful, English, Irish, and Greek having little effect, and Spanish, Jewish, East European, and Italian having a negative effect. They also found that candidates with nicknames had a clear advantage.

Candidates word these designations carefully. Campaign strategists often carefully pretest them with public opinion surveys.

How have candidates used the designation? An Orange County supervisor running for the state senate listed himself as "Orange County Legislator." A college professor running for Congress became a "National Affairs Analyst." A butcher called himself a "Meat Purveyor" and a candidate for the assembly who first used "Telephone Line Repairman" changed it to "Communications Specialist."

Candidates with little hope of winning may publicize causes as in "Gay Feminist Activist" or "Socialist Workers' Spokesperson." Issues present a more difficult problem. A San Bernardino school board candidate, against sex education, used "Mandatory Sexology Opponent." Los Angeles had a city council candidate who used "Graft Corruption Fighter."

Some designations are challenged in court and such cases may even delay the printing of ballots. A congressman who moved to a new district tried "Former California Congressman" and lost in court. Even a Beverly Hills woman who wanted to use "Jewish Mother" lost out.

Some critics concede that the designations do reduce information costs for the voters in some cases, but they have also, it is claimed, been used to confuse and even deceive. They suggest instead slogans rather than candidate identification, such as Oregon permits on the ballot, or two hundred-word candidate statements, such as are mailed with sample ballots in California for some local races. Others argue that at least these designations give voters some information—particularly in nonpartisan races where ethnicity or name familiarity becomes crucial.

What do you think? Should the ballot itself give information about the candidates? Do you think a three-word limit is unrealistic? Should incumbents have a special advantage in number of words? Who should decide whether the designation is misleading or false? Do you think the examples given of successfully challenged designations were decided reasonably?

SOURCE: Bruce C. Bollinger, "Ballot Labels Raise Eyebrows" *The California Journal* Sacramento, Calif., 1977, and Gary C. Byrne and J. Kristian Pueschel, "But Who Should I Vote for For County Coroner?" *Journal of Politics* 1974, 778–784.

The Media Help Reduce Information Costs

Some democratic theorists and reformers have been disappointed with the role of the media in reducing information costs for average citizens. Two criticisms are common—that coverage, especially of state and local news, is "spotty," and that media coverage is biased in favor of the views of publishers and owners or of reporters.[30]

How Well Do the Media Cover Politics?   William Gormley studied coverage of state government activities by forty-four jointly owned newspaper and television stations. He found that the newspaper coverage was far greater—they covered a larger number of stories, devoted a higher percentage of their state and local stories to state government, and placed state government stories more prominently than did the television stations.

Gormley, yet, did not believe newspaper coverage itself to be adequate. Of one hundred thirteen daily papers in Texas for example, he reports only thirteen had full-time reporters in Austin, the capital. In Il-

[30]This section dealing with the media is based on a study of newspaper and television coverage of state news by William T. Gormley, Jr., "Mass Media Coverage of State Government," paper delivered at the annual convention of the Midwest Political Science Association, Chicago, Illinois, April 22, 1977.

linois, there were only eight full-time state reporters, excluding those of the Springfield papers. He notes another study that concludes that the wire service bureaus at state capitals are "disgracefully understaffed."[31]

What Types of Information Do the Media Report?   The media are interested in "conflicts between two easily identifiable sides—Republicans versus Democrats, haves versus have nots, wets versus drys." Many of these issues, William Gormley argues, are likely to be "intriguing but ephemeral controversies," rather than more basic, but complex issues. If two state legislators get divorces and marry each other's former spouses, it is "big news." A less dramatic issue, such as how tax assessments are made, is likely to get little attention. In fact, however, media coverage has probably always been of this sort—emphasizing human interest and conflict in order to catch the attention of average citizens.[32]

Given these facts, it is not astonishing to find that government officials attempt to create news events that will be covered.

The manufacturing of government news.   A good deal of state and community news reports what the historian Daniel Boorstin called "pseudo events." The mayor cuts a ribbon to open a new bridge to traffic. Many state fairs have a "governor's day," and pictures appear in the newspapers showing the governor on hand to meet citizens or award a prize to some farmer's son. At the Wisconsin State Fair the state legislature also has a booth. Sometimes such pseudo news events are more issue oriented, as when the governor symbolically visits a state prison and eats a meal with inmates or a mayor visits the site of a slum apartment building a day or so after it has been gutted by fire. Many ceremonies and speeches are this kind of event, "arranged" to call attention to individuals or state or community activities.

Although pseudo events sometimes suggest publicity-hungry candidates or officials, they also often serve a useful social purpose—they

[31]Hoyt Purvis and Rick Gentry, "News Media Coverage of Texas Government," Public Affairs Comment, Lyndon B. Johnson School of Public Affairs, Austin, Texas, 1976, p. 3. Paul Simon, "Improving Statehouse Coverage," *Columbia Journalism Review* September/October, 1973 p. 51, and Thomas Littlewood, "What's Wrong With Statehouse Coverage," *Columbia Journalism Review* March/April, 1972, p. 40 (for wire service coverage). All are cited by Gormley, Op. cit.

[32]An analysis of early political prints of the 1770s concluded that the artists reached a mass market using scandals of royalty, rather than more basic political issues. See Charles Press, "The Georgian Print and Democratic Institutions," *Comparative Studies in Society and History*, 19 April 1977, 216–238.

may reduce information costs a little for the average citizen in respect to some state programs.

Public officials make news coverage easier.   Daniel Walker, while governor of Illinois (1972–1976), flew about the state for short scheduled press conferences in its major cities. Sometimes he sent a cabinet member in his place. Capital reporters were not happy about the practice—they did not care to be scooped by a TV reporter in Peoria. Another technique used is a weekly news conference on videotape to which reporters around the state can phone in questions. Separate videotapes are then mailed to participating stations. New York state provides a studio for radio or TV interviews with legislators—about a quarter of those produced are requested by local stations. Most are sent by the state assembly's radio-TV office and are conducted by their staff.[33]

Public Hearings.   Another widely used method of manufacturing government news is the public hearing. A legislative committee or administrative agency listens as private citizens express their points of view. This sometimes results in new information. More commonly the information is already available. However, the hearing does focus public attention on the issue in a dramatic way—citizens hear other citizens tell how their relatives or they themselves were treated in a state mental hospital, for example. Information costs are thus reduced.

Study commission reports.   Governors or mayors also appoint citizen study commissions to call attention to state or community problems, such as a mounting venereal disease rate, the loss of industry, or whatever. The executive's staff carefully balances the study commission membership among various interest groups, tilting it somewhat toward the governor or mayor's views. The people selected usually have high prestige or specialized knowledge—both have news value. The commission report may reveal little that is new, but the high status of the committee members assures that the press and other citizens will give at least some attention to the issue and the commission's recommendations.

The Role of Television Coverage.   Study after study reveals that most American citizens get most of their news from TV; an estimated 27 percent read no newspaper. As we would expect, the less educated and those from the lower income groups depend more on TV.

[33]Gormley, Op. cit., p. 20.

The economic limits of TV coverage. Television coverage of state news especially, but also of community events, is hampered by the costs of television production. Sending film crews plus reporters out to location is expensive. The TV news thus tends to come from the same easily covered sources and often uses manufactured news, such as staged announcements at press conferences.

Even when a group of stations line up a "stringer" to cover capital stories for them, the problem of transmitting the video tapes throughout the state while the news is still hot is difficult. Tapes for the 6 o'clock news have to be received by around 4 p.m. at the local station, which means they must leave the capital somewhere in the early afternoon. Grounded planes or rush hour traffic can kill the story.

The result of all these constraints is that most TV stations out-state will cover no more state news than they think is absolutely necessary. Gormley found that almost two out of three state stories as compared to less than half of other stories were reported without visual films accompanying them.

The Role of Newspapers. Most studies of newspaper influence conclude, as did that of Bernard Cohen, that the press "may not be successful much of the time in telling people what to think, but it is stunningly successful in telling its readers what to think about."[34] Newspapers tell citizens which public issues should be considered important. Thus by providing a tremendous cutting of information costs for the average citizen who has little time to follow all the actions of the political elite, they also exert their major influence on political decision making.

The best source for news of state and community government is still the newspaper published in the capital city. Many are exceptionally thorough, and their complete coverage becomes a matter of pride to their editors. The editor of the Sacramento *Bee*, for example, explains they have to cover the "nuts and bolts" of state government because many of their readers are legislators and state employees. A small city capital will have a newspaper that is likely to be more thorough than will a metropolitan city, whose paper has many other news stories to cover.

A number of newspapers, of course, cover community news in depth.

[34]Bernard Cohen, *The Press and Foreign Policy*, Princeton University Press, Princeton, New Jersey, 1963. p. 13. For empirical evidence that confirms the statement see also Maxwell McCombs and Donald Shaw, "The Agenda-Setting Function of Mass Media," *Public Opinion Quarterly*, Summer, 1971, 176–187. McCombs and Shaw find that a sample of North Carolina residents rate issues roughly the same in importance as do the mass media to which they were exposed during the election of 1968.

And, they are especially influential when local elections are non-partisan.[35]

The special case of the Union Leader. The Manchester (New Hampshire) *Union Leader* is notorious for its coverage of state government and politics. Few community newspapers cover city hall in as much depth as it does state politics.

The paper's publisher, William Loeb, a dedicated conservative, has mounted biting editorial attacks against politicians whom he dislikes. His paper's stinging editorials, preaching economy, have been credited with influencing the legislature to a "low-tax, low-spending" policy. Politicians appear to believe the newspaper's opinions influence voters because the news and editorials are written in a personalized, easy-to-read style.[36]

A study of the *Union Leader* by Eric Veblen concluded that the paper is widely read for two reasons. First, it dominates newspaper circulation in New Hampshire. It is the only daily newspaper that covers the whole state, and its circulation is well above the next largest paper. Yet as Veblen notes, nineteen other states have newspapers with circulation dominance within their states, but do not have the statewide influence the *Union Leader* does.

Second, the *Leader* is vigorous in political advocacy. The *Leader* cares! As Veblen notes, newspapers in other states rarely employ "the constant conscious and blatant use of news coverage as a vehicle for political advocacy to the extent that it is by the *Leader*."[37]

What the special case of the *Union Leader* suggests is that other newspapers could develop an attentive public of some magnitude for the activities of state government and politics. But seldom does this occur as many are content to pick out a few news wire stories for publication in the back pages.

Government Efforts to Reduce Information Costs

Some states, such as North Dakota and Oregon, attempt to reduce information costs by publishing voter information pamphlets. These per-

[35]For an older, but well researched study of an influential newspaper, see Reo M. Christenson, "The Power of the Press: The Case of the Toledo Blade," *Midwest Journal of Political Science,* 3 August 1959, 227–240.

[36]Eric Veblen, *The Manchester Union Leader in New Hampshire Elections,* The University Press of New England, Hanover, 1975, and Eric Veblen and Robert E. Craig, "William Loeb and the Manchester Union Leader: a 1976 View," paper delivered at the September 1976 meeting of the American Political Science Association.

[37]Veblen, Op. cit., p 178–179.

mit candidates and parties to buy limited advertising at a nominal rate in a pamphlet that the state sends to every voter just before the election. California published such a pamphlet, without advertising, in which the secretary of state's office described the content of each proposition on the ballot. Oregon also publishes a document on campaign expenditures, which is distributed to citizens after the election. Governments commonly use the legal advertisement, presumably to inform voters about special elections or other matters. Such boiler plate in small boldface type is usually published with the want ads. We suggest that it is often little more than a handout of public funds to publishers of "the official county newspaper." Very few citizens pay much attention to the ad, since most of us do not enjoy wading through legalisms set in small type.

Reducing Information Costs by Providing Cues

A number of sources provide cues to average citizens. Higher status citizens may receive cues from civic associations such as The League of Women Voters or research organizations such as those sponsored by universities, foundations or business and industry.[38]

Other citizens will receive cues from social movements, to be discussed later in this chapter, or from interest group leaders or the political parties. These are discussed in Chapters 12 and 13. All of us at one time or another have made use of cues, but we note again that those with higher social status are more likely to receive and correctly interpret the cues.

THE ALIENATED NONPARTICIPANTS

Social scientists have long been interested in those citizens said to be "alienated." Such persons, it is argued, seldom participate in government or politics because they regard the political system as completely unresponsive. The alienated appear to be beyond calculating costs or benefits. Their frustrations have driven them to responses unrelated to the particular situation in which they find themselves. They feel a permanent sense of psychological hopelessness and of powerlessness.

The response of the alienated is usually apathy and nonparticipation. When they do participate, they most frequently take violent anti-

[38]For an interesting study of one such influential group, the Pennsylvania Economy League, see Edward F. Cooke, "Research: An Instrument of Political Power" *Political Science Quarterly*, 76 March 1961, 69–87.

The Detroit riots, 1967.

social action unrelated to possible benefits to themselves. They momentarily strike out at tormenters in vandalism, crime, or other forms of violence and then, after a time, lapse back into apathy.

The Alienated and the Political Cynics.   We should not confuse the alienated with political cynics. Trust in government since Vietnam and Watergate has dropped among all citizens. Political cynics can be found throughout the population as well as at the extremes. But public opinion surveys indicate that political cynics participate at about the same rates as the less cynical in the population. The cynical do not blindly see all politicians as enemies—they have just become more skeptical about government and politics.[39]

Which Citizens Are Alienated?   Some debate is going on among social scientists as to how many citizens are alienated and which groups should be so designated. Most estimate them to be about 10 percent of the citizens, well below the estimated 33 percent of all nonparticipants.

In general, researchers agree that the alienated are concentrated heavily in the poverty groups, the uneducated, and among those who are the most vulnerable victims of racism. Some blacks in big city ghettos act in the classic pattern of alienation and frustration. On the one hand are extreme political apathy and such traditional forms of escap-

[39] Arthur H. Miller, "Political Issues and Trust in Government," *American Political Science Review*, 68 September 1974, 951–972, and Jack Citrin, "The Political Relevance of Trust in Government" *American Political Science Review*, 68 September 1974, 973–988.

ism as drugs and gambling; on the other are sporadic outbreaks of rage: indiscriminate vandalism, sometimes senseless crime against persons, as in the rampage of looting and mugging in the New York City blackout in 1977.

Blacks make up 11 percent to 12 percent of the national population, and hold 0.6 percent of political offices—in 1977 there were 4311 black elected officials, as compared with 4979 in 1976. For every 100,000 blacks, we find nineteen black elected officials; the same number for nonblacks is 282. In 1979 we find there were no black governors, one black lieutenant governor (2 percent), no black United States senator, and 4 percent of the U.S. House of Representatives were black. A growing number of northern cities have black mayors, but the state presently with the greatest number of elected black officeholders is Mississippi, followed by Illinois, Louisiana, and Michigan. About 60 percent of black elected officials are in the South.[42]

The other significant segment of alienated citizens are the very poor uneducated whites.[40] Many of these are rural and concentrated in the mountains of Appalachia. Others live in the nation's large cities and small towns.[41]

What Can Reduce Alienation?   The answer to this question is that we are not sure. Perhaps alienation is reduced among blacks by the knowledge that the number of blacks holding political office is growing.

Michael A. Baer and Dean Jaros studied direct participation by citizens of the fifty states. They found that improving socioeconomic conditions had an effect on reducing disaffection—in other words, the way to reduce alienation is to provide jobs. Baer and Jaros, while recognizing the importance of jobs, also concluded that participation is valu-

---

[40]Harry M. Caudill, *Night Comes to the Cumberlands, A Biography of a Depressed Area,* Little, Brown and Co., Boston, 1962.

[41]See, for example, a study of voting in school referenda by John E. Horton and Wayne E. Thompson "Powerlessness and Political Negativism: A Study of a Defeated Referendum," *American Journal of Sociology,* 47 March 1962, 485–493, and by the same authors, "Political Alienation as a Force in Political Action," *Social Forces,* 38 March 1960, 190–195.

[42]Black office holding is surveyed in Pauline C. Terrelonge Stone, "The Political and Social Correlates of Intra-Group Racial Identification in Black Political Leadership," Ph.D. dissertation, Michigan State University, 1975. See also *The National Roster of Black Elected Officials,* Joint Center for Political Studies, Washington, D.C., 1977 edition and *Statistical Abstract of the United States 1976.* Department of Commerce, Bureau of the Census, Washington, D.C., 1977, Table 746.

able in itself because it gives a feeling of belonging and of being of some value to society.[43]

No democracy can exist with a significant segment of its population alienated and, as Norton Long, a student of urban politics, suggests, walled off on reservations, to rot in the heart of central cities or at the bend of the creek up in the hollow.[44]

SOCIAL MOVEMENTS AS A FORM OF POLITICAL PARTICIPATION

Perhaps more than any other force, such movements have shaped and continue to shape the way state and many community governments operate and the way they conduct their politics. They have also had a major impact by increasing participation in government by average citizens.

One need only run down a partial list of such groups to note how important social movements have been and are today: the Jacksonians, ecologists, consumer advocates, the progressive reformers at the turn of the century, prohibitionists, antibusing groups, women suffragettes, gays and antigays, abolitionists, anticommunists, and John Birchers and other radical right groups. We also include civil rights marchers, the early labor movement, the Gray Panthers of the senior citizens, communists and other radical left groups, Right to Lifers, the old age pension movement, the Know Nothings, the Ku Klux Klan, the farmer protest movements, the student movement, and the anti-Vietnam movement.[45]

It is apparent that social movements are not concentrated at one end of the political spectrum as "liberal" or "conservative." They agree politically only in rejecting the status quo of the dominant political elite. Nor can we unequivocally classify all social movements as "good" or "bad." All of us will find some movements we largely approve of and others that we disapprove of very much.

The Life of Social Movements. How do such movements begin? We do not know. Clearly more is involved than individuals or groups not receiving as many of society's benefits as others do. Injustices continue

[43]Michael A. Baer and Dean Jaros, "Participation as Instrument of Expression: Some Evidence from the States," *American Journal of Political Science*, 18, May 1974, 365–383.

[44]Norton E. Long, *The Unwalled City*, Basic Books, New York, 1972.

[45]Among the perceptive analyses of social movements is Neil J. Smelser, *Collective Behavior*, The Free Press, New York, 1962.

for years and then suddenly become intolerable—a social explosion occurs and a social movement is born. For this to happen, as the sociologist Max Weber put it very well, "hurts long accepted suddenly become moralized." Discriminations that were accepted with little comment suddenly become unjust and intolerable.

What then makes individuals suddenly view as grossly unjust the status quo they long accepted? What appears to be common among many movements, although not all, is a sense of betrayal—betrayal at the hands of friends within the political elite. Suddenly individuals begin to act selflessly for others like themselves, just as students did during the riots of the late 1960s. They attack mercilessly the decision makers of the political elite.

A social movement is born and for a few years greatly influences policy. Then, just as mysteriously, it subsides.

Recent social movements. Howard Jarvis was a life-long Republican and self-styled "Jack Morman" who in his thirties had sold a string of weekly newspapers in Utah and moved to California to go into a small manufacturing business. In 1962 at age 59 he retired and began to indulge in politics as a hobby—running for office and getting involved in various conservative campaigns. He lost in the 1977 mayorality primary in Los Angeles. But in 1978, at age 75, his day finally came. He fashioned a constitutional amendment to sharply reduce California local taxes and began an anti-Big Government campaign to get it adopted by the initiative method as Proposition 13.[46]

This time he hit pay dirt. A receptive public welcomed his efforts. Inflation nationally was edging up into double digits. Since 1967 the dollar had declined 47.6 percent, leaving the average family little better off than a decade before. Middle class citizens found themselves carried along by inflation into higher and higher state and national income tax brackets. Meanwhile property in California skyrocketed in value because of a housing shortage. State and local taxes in California within a decade rose from 25 percent to 30 percent of economic output.

The element of betrayal was also present. Governor Jerry Brown had won office as a candidate 3½ years before and had campaigned to cut back on government. But the state had built up a $5 billion tax surplus, and its budgets and employees had continued to grow. In addition, Governor Brown opposed Proposition 13 from the very beginning. In fact, almost all of the political elite was opposed to the Jarvis proposal—most state legislators, most party leaders, city officials, public employ-

[46]*Newsweek*, "The Big Tax Revolt," June 19, 1978, 20–30.

ees, the large public employee labor unions, the school teachers, even the big banks and corporations who it was claimed would profit most from cutting property taxes, and most economists including a group from one of the state's major universities who predicted widespread unemployment if Proposition 13 were adopted. Public facilities such as local swimming pools and fire stations had signs that they would close if the proposition were adopted. Then an event occurred that dramatized the issue, and "radicalized" the public. A week before the election the Los Angeles assessor released his new assessment notices. Big black headlines throughout the state announced that taxes for some Los Angeles homeowners would triple. The news put Proposition 13 over the top with 65 percent of the vote.

As with all social movements, the fever rapidly spread. A lagging anti–tax drive in Colorado got 250 new recruits the next day, and initiative petition campaigns in other states such as Michigan, Idaho and Utah got the needed shot in the arm. National magazines such as *Time* and *Newsweek* ran cover stories. Tax cut movements were found to be occurring in most of the states. Jarvis was within the week invited to speak in Michigan, Nebraska, Connecticut, Oklahoma, Massachusetts, and Georgia, and local tax-cut advocates began to get local publicity. Politicians got on the bandwagon—even those whom tax-cut advocates had singled out as "big spenders." Governor Jerry Brown reversed his stand and noted how he had originally campaigned for less government and would live with Proposition 13. He was described as "acting like a charter member of the Proposition 13 fan club." President Jimmy Carter praised lowering government spending and indicated he had campaigned to increase government efficiency. Tax cut measures were introduced in Congress. The Gallup poll reported 57 percent of the nation's citizens favored tax-cut measures similar to the Jarvis proposal for their own states. The tax revolt as a movement was off and running.

Social movements in communities show the same patterns. Note the actions in respect to gay activists in Miami's Dade County. The singer, Anita Bryant, and her husband, both deeply religious, had endorsed and made a financial contribution to a business associate in her successful candidacy for Dade County commissioner. Then the Bryants found that the candidate they had supported was sponsoring a bill to expand the rights of homosexuals. Their shock has all the aspects of a betrayal. The Bryants entered the campaign to defeat the bill with all the religious fervor common to social movements and the Gay Rights groups responded in kind. Miami rejected the Gay Rights Regulation by a two to one majority and the gay and antigay movements spread to other communities.

Sometimes the issue involving social movements can become concentrated on a specific event, for example, the construction of a nuclear plant at Seabrook, New Hampshire in 1978—organized by the group known as the "Clamshell Alliance." In the past, bitter community battles have been fought over issues such as local prohibition, unionization of a major plant and, of course, civil rights.[47]

The Psychology of a Social Movement

Social movements are (1) more loosely organized than an interest group, and (2) citizens who participate in movements do not seem to weigh individual costs and benefits. When movements either become more formally organized or when citizens act only because of what they get out of participating, the movement begins to wither and die, though some of the spirit of the social movement may live on for a while in one or more organized groups.

Social Movements as Loose-Knit Organization. The social movement starts with spontaneous actions by groups and individuals at different places. They catch the fever from each other. As students at Oregon State hear that students "trashed" the administration building at Harvard or the University of Pennsylvania, they, too, may be inspired to do something similar.

Movement participants seem to want to parade their identification with the movement to everyone in the "straight" world. Often they adopt special symbols and uniforms or other special kinds of dress such as the Nazis did, grow long hair or cut it short and, perhaps most important, develop their own language with terms that outsiders do not understand immediately ("consciousness raising," "Fanonizing," "boozing"). Nonmovement citizens are apt to dismiss all this as the "freakishness" of "crazies."

In the beginning new leaders spring up and attempts are made to coordinate the activities of the movement into one big organization. This seldom works—at least not while the movement is growing. Sometimes, as with the civil rights movement, competing organizations spring up. At other times one dominant group gradually emerges as did the American Federation of Labor after the early strikes and riots of the labor movement. Sometimes the movement just falls apart, as did the student movement that shrunk first to SDS (Students for a Democratic Society) and then melted away into the Weathermen and other minor factions.

[47]An attempt to put this type of event into an analytic framework is found in an excellent short study by James Coleman, *Community Conflict*, Free Press, Glencoe, Ill., 1957. It builds on the journalistic and researched reports of many specific community conflicts.

California State Highway Patrol at San Francisco State College during the 1960s Vietnam War protests.

Selflessness and Movement Participation.   Outsiders are apt to regard movement participants as mentally deranged. The reason that movement participants seem irrational is that they refuse to abide by a cost-benefit calculus that characterizes the niceties of *normal* civilized behavior.[48] Indeed movement members often act in clearly illegal ways. Women suffragists chained themselves to state capitol fences or screamed at and physically attacked governors and mayors. Carrie Nation, the Kansas prohibitionist whose specialty was throwing liquor bottles at those large polished mirrors found in frontier saloons, announced, "When God tells me to smash, I smash!" Police often arrested her, but this did not stop her. Anti-Vietnam protesters poured red paint on draft records.

The movement participants voluntarily assume major costs and risks. Some movement participants, such as the three freedom riders who went to Mississippi in the 1960s, lost their lives. Others have lost jobs, been ridiculed, or have seen their businesses or careers des-

[48]One theory that emphasizes psychological aspects is that of Eric Hoffer, *The True Believer*, Harper, New York, 1951. He argues that those caught up in movements feel that their lives have already been "spoiled" and they want to lose identity in a social movement.

troyed. We do not know what inspires this kind of selfless behavior, except perhaps the knowledge that one can depend upon many other movement participants who also will act, and the feeling seems to be "if we all act together, we shall overcome, some day."

Movement Decline.   Some success and the beginnings of organization seem to signal the beginning of the end for a movement. Organization leaders begin to worry about their own political careers and the future of the organization they have created. Leaders compete with each other and even attack each other, and in the process kill the impulse of selfless behavior that inspired the movement. Organizations begin to state goals and so uncover differences among participants. And many participants cannot adjust to the discipline that organizations require. Sometimes some original movement leaders are expelled as unorthodox as, of course, has happened many times with the Communist and other radical movements or to Malcolm X and the Black Muslims as well as in such reactionary groups as the American Nazi party.

Once people in the movement began to ask, "What's in it for me?" the movement is dying or dead.[49]

What Do Movements Accomplish?   The major impact of social movements is that they increase citizen involvement in government. In doing so they often also change the ideas held and the actual composition of state and community political elites. This involvement subsides, but the status quo never quite returns to what it was. Movements are also a method of recruiting new leaders. Typically movement leaders spring into prominence out of nowhere. Some fade away again rapidly, but many go on to hold leadership positions in the decades that follow. The latter include people previously unknown, such as Dr. Martin Luther King, Gloria Steinem, George Wallace, Ralph Nader, and Walter Reuther. Hundreds more such leaders can be found in states and communities.

Many movements have left behind monuments in the form of laws or constitutional clauses. Sometimes what was put into law fell far short of movement aspirations; sometimes the movement disappeared without much legal change being accomplished at all. But most movements that have appealed to a wide variety of a state's or community's citizens have left some traces in its government and politics.

[49]Anthony Downs stated a theory of "a systematic issue attention cycle" in respect to the types of issues brought forward by social movements and applied it to ecology. See Anthony Downs, "Up and Down with Ecology—the 'Issue-Attention Cycle,'" *The Public Interest, 28* Summer 1972, 38–50.

A Final Comment

We have suggested that out of necessity most decisions within a state or community are made by a small minority of its citizens—its political elite. This political elite has political power and influence through ownership, or more frequently, through control of the positions they hold in major economic, social, or political institutions. Sometimes such political elites have almost completely controlled states or communities without much influence in decision making by average citizens. At other times citizens have overwhelmed the whole elite decision-making structure and refashioned it for control by an elite with a different composition.

Some reformers seem to hope that the average citizen will someday govern, and that the political elite will disappear. This seems to us a hopeless populist dream—average citizens have matters other than government or politics with which they wish to fill their lives. They desire government by elected representatives because the alternative is impractical and, except for very small communities, impossible. Informing and activating the mass of average citizens on issues, except on an occasional basis, seems to us a visionary enterprise. But these occasional inputs of opinion by average citizens appear to us to be of crucial importance. No political elite is so wise or unselfish that it can afford to dispense with feedback from those who live with its decisions. It is for this reason that the opportunity to participate when one wishes must be maximized if we are to reach our full potential as a democratic nation.

HIGHLIGHTS OF CHAPTER 11: PARTICIPATION BY ELITES AND OTHER CITIZENS

In this chapter we argued (1) that a democratic society is made up of a political elite that makes decisions and citizens who are largely part time or nonparticipants. We reviewed community elite studies and concluded that the political elites of American states and communities are undergoing change with political decision makers becoming more influential in their decision making. Then (2) we examined explanations of nonelite participation in state and community politics. One explanation was the costs and benefits of participating and gaining information. We concluded that participation costs, except for registration, have been markedly reduced. We argued that information costs would be reduced by government action, the mass media and leaders of interest groups, and social movements and political parties who provide cues to citizens. We argued (3) that some citizens are so lacking in benefits that they become totally alienated. Finally we noted (4) how citizens of the states and communities have exercised a great deal of influence through voluntary participation in social movements. Our conclusion was that (5) we should expect only occasional impact on elite decision making by average citizens but that impact was of crucial importance.

12

POLITICAL INTEREST GROUPS IN STATES AND COMMUNITIES

Private organizations that get involved in state and community politics are in bad repute. Political scientists once called them "pressure groups," a term that suggests Jay Fiske arm twisting and bribing his way through the New York legislature to get special benefits for the Erie Railroad. Or it suggests the local streetcar company buying up city councilmen in smoke-filled back rooms. Mark Twain, reflecting on this period of our history, said in a London speech, "I think I can say, and say with pride, that we have some legislatures that bring higher prices than any in the world."[1]

A more recent and sympathetic treatment of private and public organizations in politics by David Truman called them "interest groups," a term that has a more neutral sound. We will follow that tradition.[2]

[1] For a book stressing that this old style kind of lobbying has not disappeared see Frank Trippett, *The States: United They Fell*, The World Publishing Co., Cleveland, 1967. His is, perhaps, the most thoroughgoing journalistic expose of the corruption of state legislatures by "the interests." But see also Robert Allen (ed.), *Our Sovereign State*, The Vanguard Press, New York, 1949, a series of essays by reporters, and Robert Allen (ed.), *Our Fair City*, The Vanguard Press, New York, 1947.

[2] David Truman, *The Governmental Process* Knopf, New York, 1953. Bertram Gross, the author of the other significant study of the period, preferred the

By political interest group we mean an organized group, government or private, that attempts to influence government decision making. Note that among the more active interest groups today at the state and even federal level are employees of community governments—school teachers, fire fighters, judges, county commissioners, and the lobbyists representing America's large cities such as New York, Chicago, Philadelphia, and Los Angeles. Not all lobbying is done by private individuals or corporations.

The Interest Group On Trial

Where in government is interest group influence greatest? Those who have studied the question think that organized groups are much more influential in state and community government policymaking than in that of the national government. They also suggest that the lobbying methods used at the state level are more apt to be questionable and border on the unethical and corrupt than lobbying methods used with members of congress or national administrators.[3]

Does interest group politicking deserve the reputation it seems to have at the state or community level? Journalistic "exposes" suggest that we have not entirely left behind the scandalous aspects of interest group lobbying. In 1976 the Anchorage *News* won a Pulitzer Prize for its series on Teamster Union influence in Alaska.

Lobbying at state capitals and in the communities still has its exotic moments. A U.S. District Court in 1976 was told how the ready-mix cement lobby (road building) in Illinois passed over "$5000 in payoff money in a speeding car on a lonely highway . . . (and of) crisp $100 bills pressed into legislative palms in a men's room of the state house." And in Chicago in 1978, *Sun-Times* reporters purchased a bar and detailed how they bribed community officials to get special treatment. In 1977 it was reported that General Motors had picked up a $1600 din-

---

term "private organizations." See Bertram Gross, *The Legislative Struggle, A Study in Social Combat*, McGraw Hill, New York, 1953.

[3]A study by John Kingdon revealed that three times as many state legislators as congressmen stated that lobbyists were effective. John W. Kingdon, *Candidates for Office: Beliefs and Strategies*, Random House, New York, 1966, 71–72. Lester Milbrath reports that congressional lobbyists state they feel lobbying at the state level is "definitiely on a lower plane," "cruder," "more obvious," "more freewheeling," "more open to corruption," than nationally; Lester Milbrath *The Washington Lobbyists*, Rand McNally, Chicago, 1963, "Federal and State Lobbying Contrasted" 301–304. A most damning indictment of interest group influence in the states is found in Grant McConnell, *Private Power and American Democracy*, Knopf, New York, 1966, Chapter 6, "The State," 166–195.

ner tab for Rhode Island state legislators—at a time when the legislature was debating a car warranty bill opposed by GM.[4]

Bribery, researchers report, is less common today and when practiced is generally more subtle than stuffing smoking pipes with "green tobacco" ($500 bills) and passing them out as favors to legislators or city councillors. Less common also are the kinds of pressure tactics and wholesale corruption that flourished at the turn of the century when the boss system was strong at both state and local levels.

Interest group penetration. A different kind of criticism of interest group influence is mead. Theodore J. Lowi in *The End of Liberalism* criticizes the American political system for fostering what he calls "interest group liberalism"—the abandonment of policymaking by public officials in favor of public policymaking by private organizations. Lowi argues that without doing anything illegal, interest groups have penetrated deeply into government decision making. At the community level realtors sit on planning boards or are appointed to zoning boards of appeal—at the state level, beauticians constitute the board of cosmetology. This type of interest group penetration is, after all, of more political significance than an occasional incident of corruption in the flamboyant style of old-time lobbying.

Overview. We begin by looking at some of the findings about political interest groups in America—who organizes these groups, which groups lobby and why, and what resources are important. Then we will examine at the pattern of interest group lobbying in the states and communities—what kinds of groups lobby, and which are the most important. Then we will look at how state and local government structure encourages lobbying, and what kind of persons become professional lobbyists and the techniques they use today. Finally we will look at the efforts of reformers to control lobbying.

THE LOBBYING PROCESS IN AMERICA

We begin "mapping" political interest groups active in the states and communities by looking at the lobbying process, rather than simply reviewing long lists of "typical" political interest groups. We want to consider some general guidelines that political scientists have devel-

[4]Chicago *Sun-Times*, May 27, 1976, "Illinois Statehouse Bribe Scandal Widens," and *Detroit News* (December 4, 1977), "Lobbyist Calls $1600 Meal a Social Affair!"

oped about interest group activity. These, we think, will tell you whom you should be looking for at your own state capital or at community council and board meeting.

Who Organizes?

Alexis de Tocqueville in the 1830s described America as "a nation of joiners." We certainly like to think of ourselves that way. In fact, however, only a very small portion of our citizens participate in organizations—that is, exclusive of their churches or, of course, job-oriented groups, such as unions. One study revealed that almost two-thirds of all citizens belonged to no voluntary organization (churches excluded) and less than 15 percent belonged to more than one. With churches included, two-thirds of our citizens belong to at least one formal organization while one third are nonparticipants.

A further point is that middle and upper class citizens join more organizations of all types (except unions and churches), and are more active in the organizations when they do join. Among the groups who are more likely to be nonjoiners, as we would anticipate from the data presented in Chapter 11 on citizen participation, are those with lower incomes, renters, manual laborers, those with less than an eighth grade education, farmers, women, and those over sixty and under twenty-five years of age.[5]

Group participation is, of course, a first step to getting represented in interest group politics. If this is so the political scientist E. E. Schattschneider correctly concluded, we think, that "the pressure system has an upper middle class bias."[6] Such citizens are most likely to be represented by a lobbying group either at the state or community level.

What Are the Patterns of Organization?

Is our society too organized? Probably not. Besides a sizeable number of Americans who remain unorganized, those that are organized often belong to competing groups.

[5]A study still valid in its findings is Charles R. Wright and Herbert Hyman, "Voluntary Memberships of American Adults: Evidence from National Sample Surveys," *American Sociological Review*, 23, June 1958, 284–293, reprinted in Robert Salisbury, *Interest Group Politics in America*, Harper & Row, New York, 1970, 71–88. See also Lester Milbrath and M. L. Goel, *Political Participation*, Rand McNally, Chicago, 2nd ed., 1977, and Robert Lane, *Political Life, Why People Get Involved in Politics*, The Free Press, Glencoe, Ill, 1959, 74–79.

[6]E. E. Schattschneider, *The Semi-Sovereign People, A Realist's View of Democracy in America*, Holt, Rinehart and Winston, New York, 1960, p. 32.

Numerous Competing Groups. We have, for example, competing interest groups in each major segment of economic activity (farmers, factory workers, manufacturers, business people, and the professions). In Great Britain, by comparison, each economic segment has a peak organization to which most of the potential members belong. Ninety percent of all British farmers belong to the National Farmers Union. In the United States only 30 percent of farmers are members of any farm organization—and they are split among the American Farm Bureau Federation, the National Farmers Union, the National Grange, the National Farmers Organization, and many specialized product organizations. The Federation of British Industries (organized in 1916) now represents some 85 percent of all manufacturing concerns; the National Association of Manufacturers in the United States represents an estimated 20 percent to 25 percent.[7]

Those groups that are active in American politics, we see, generally represent only a small segment of their potential clientele.

The Impact of Federalism. Our federal system encourages further splintering of private organizations. Farmers in Oregon and Ohio each have their own state Grange. Churches have their Indiana and Iowa synods, labor unions their Idaho and New Jersey state affiliates, professions have their Nebraska and Ohio state bars and Oklahoma medical associations. Even industry is sometimes federalized. American Telephone and Telegraph has a Wisconsin Telephone and Mountain Bell in Colorado, so that each can deal with its own state rate-setting commissions.

We should also observe that the organizations of government officials are also state based—the Arkansas Education Association, the League of Ohio Cities, and the state-based unions of state and community employees.

Each of these state-based organizations turns very naturally to state government to see what it may do for them, and often is affiliated with a national organization that lobbies in Congress.

Which Organizations Are Likely to Lobby?

Lobbying is a secondary activity for most organized groups. We belong to organizations to spread a religion, to bargain for wage hikes, to sell real estate, to hold stock shows, or do any number of other things. They exist for reasons other than to influence officials.

[7]Samuel H. Beer, "Group Representation in Britain and the United States," *The Annals of the American Academy of Political and Social Science, 319,* September 1958, 130–140.

Some of these organizations, however, do lobby because they think government can help them achieve their primary purpose or prevent adverse action. Religious groups, for example, may be greatly concerned about what a city council does about "X"-rated bookstores, but pay little attention to the discussion of plans for a new sports arena.

The Importance of Producer Groups.   Some groups seem to be drawn to lobbying more frequently than others. Those most likely to see major payoffs coming in from lobbying state and community governments are the producer groups.

Citizens organize and spend money, time, and other resources on political decisions most frequently when the decisions affect how those citizens make their living. Producers who manufacture a product or sell a service organize—consumers those who purchase a product or service, are less likely to.[8]

This pattern is not accidental. Note how organization and lobbying rewards producers a great deal, while consumers individually receive very little by lobbying. Let us assume that we manufacture a headache remedy with a "trade" name. We advertise that it has the ingredient most often recommended by physicians for minor aches and pains— which is true. That ingredient is aspirin. Some people think this may be misleading advertising and for fifteen years or more have been trying to get government agencies to stop it. Every consumer has some stake in preventing misleading advertising (assuming hypothetically that this is the case in respect to our remedy). But are those consumers likely to spend equal resources on ferreting out misleading advertising as are producers in fighting such a charge? Compare the individual payoffs to producers and consumers.

Consider other examples. Will taxpayers in a school bond issue election be actively organized against a millage increase that may add $20 a year to their taxes, as school teachers whose annual raises depend on the outcome of the election? Do New York City consumers who receive electricity from Commonwealth Edison have the same stake in a $1.25 raise in average monthly utility bills as does the corporation?

We can see why producers find it profitable to organize and why consumers find it so difficult. The payoffs can be large for producers and minor for any individual consumer.

When Do Groups Lobby Most Actively?

We have what are in effect two types of interest group influence—penetration into the decision-making process through formal representa-

[8]This discussion is based on Anthony Downs, *An Economic Theory of Democracy*, Harper & Row, New York, 1957, "The Returns From Information and Their Diminution," 353–356.

tion on state or community boards or commissions and the more visable activity that we call lobbying. We begin with the discussion of lobbying.

Watchdog Lobbying.   We, of course, expect some "watchdog" lobbying of a mildly active type by those who presently hold some important economic advantage. Some of the major interest groups who have a fairly certain future at the state or community level can afford to keep a lobbyist at the state capital or even to visit community governments occasionally to be sure there will be no surprises in new legislation. They do not seek change so much as preserving the status quo. They want to assess what any proposed change will mean to them and be sure they are consulted before it is adopted.

Uncertainty Encourages Lobbying.   Intensive lobbying comes from a different kind of organization—from those whose economic future is uncertain or is changing. When railroads were expanding they found it profitable to lobby the states intensely. In our day their place is more likely to be taken by other groups whose economic future is less settled—for example, school teachers, civil rights groups, public utilities, certain lawyer groups, or insurance companies. The key condition that motivates intense lobbying is that of *uncertainty*—an inability to predict what will happen to one's economic future.

Upsetting conditions.   What are some of these circumstances? Sheriffs lobby when a bill proposes their jobs be made appointive. School teachers lobby because the level of state aid is always in doubt.[9] (We include here Policy Box No. 23, "School Teachers as an Interest Group.") Changes in technology or the organization of industry, especially, may trigger lobbying as it threatens to outmode some form of enterprise—one-way streets, jitneys versus full-sized taxis, or diesel versus steam-powered locomotives. The invention of a new idea, such as "no fault" car insurance, required the insurance industry to step up its lobbying activity. Established groups will try to protect past ways of doing business—even to return to the good old days. Those who may benefit by a new process or change will try to sweep aside old regulations that stand in their way. Often such disputes lead to state or community governments—to the legislature or council, governor or mayor, the administrators or the courts.

Harmon Ziegler and Michael Baer found that marked changes in population movement in or out of a state were consistently associated

---

[9]The arguments are those of David Truman, adapted to our purposes. See "The Equilibrium of Institutionalized Groups," *The Governmental Process, Political Interests and Public Opinion,* Knopf, New York, 1953.

POLICY BOX NO. 23   School Administrators and Teachers in Political Conflict

Education was supposed to be free from political interference. That was one of the reasons many states created special districts to govern schools, earmarked revenues for educational purposes, and why states established state boards of education with independence from governors and state legislatures. It was also one of the reasons that states passed teacher tenure laws, to give teachers the freedom to teach their subject matter without fear of political reprisals. Parents, teachers, school administrators, and boards of education led the way in providing these various forms of insulation from politics.

But when we examine the school systems in the states and communities today we find they are a political battleground. And the school children are caught between warring groups. Schools were never free from political involvement, but the intensity with which politics over schools is fought in the 1970s is, perhaps, unprecedented.

An emotional and, perhaps, the most important aspect of the political warfare is the battling that the teachers themselves have waged over unionization. Traditionally teachers saw themselves as "professionals," dedicated to teaching. They relied on persuasion, rather than threats or force, to convince the community to provide adequate support for their children's education. Teachers and school administrators banded together in state education associations, and they worked hand-in-hand to secure adoption of laws to help teachers do a better job.

And then in the middle 1960s states began revising laws to permit public employees, including teachers, to organize for collective bargaining. State education associations, gingerly at first and then more stridently, took on the task of converting local teacher associations into unions. Already so organized was the American Federation of Teachers, affiliated from the start with the A.F.L. At first the continued membership of school administrators in such associations was allowed, but later, either by force or on their own volition, most administrators withdrew. By the 1970s education associations became full-fledged union organizations. In 1976 the National Education Association, the largest teacher organization, had 1.8 million members.

What do teachers' unions fight for? The most apparent item is teacher salaries. And, no doubt, collective bargaining and legislative lobbying at state and community levels has brought teacher salaries from low income levels to middle-class ranges. More recently, with falling school enrollments, job security has taken on new importance in the bargaining. Teachers have been holding out for smaller classes. Smaller classes obviously mean that fewer teachers will be let go and, according to the teachers, will improve the quality of education.

The teachers also want a voice in how cutbacks (layoffs of teachers) are to be made. Most state tenure laws void a hearing process when schools make cutbacks for financial reasons. Union officials, such as Dr. Curtis Plott of the Illinois Education Association, argue that administrators and school boards would make the first cuts from among the highest paid and usually older teachers and those whom the "superintendent wanted to fire"— were it not for the tenure laws. School teacher unions want the cutbacks made on the basis of seniority alone. Administrators say they should have the authority to make cuts on the basis of educational needs.

But the teacher unions are not limiting their activity to union-management bargaining sessions. They also seek to amass political power. Their basic strategy is to mobilize their membership to support, with volunteer help and money, candidates who are favorable to education. They work for candidates at all levels. In 1972 the National Education Association's Political Action Committee raised only $27,000 for one hundred forty-one congressional races. But by 1976 the committee had $730,000 to spend on three hundred thirty races. Teachers' unions have especially encouraged their membership to run for the state legislature or, in some cases, have been able to "purge" at elections "unsympathetic" school board members.

One issue that most teacher groups want to win is that of the right to strike. Without the legal right to strike they believe their hand at the bargaining table is weak. Few unions want to experience what the Crestwood Education Association (in a suburban Detroit school district) went through in 1974. The Crestwood teachers went on strike and the board fired all of them and hired new teachers in their places. The Michigan Supreme Court upheld the action.

Critics of teacher unions fear their growing strength. They ask, "If the teachers can tip the balance in the political races, is it possible that they could dominate public policy on education? And is it possible that their influence will be wielded from narrow special interest perspective, without regard to broader public interest considerations?"

What do you think? Should teachers be given the right to strike? Should laws be passed now to discourage the growing strength of teacher and other public employee groups? What changes if any would you suggest? Are teachers any more likely to dominate public policy in education than the state or community chamber of commerce is in public policy over issues in business?

SOURCE: This policy box is based on Meg O'Conner, "Teachers Fight To Hold Onto Tenure," *Chicago Tribune*, August 29, 1976, and Robert W. Merry, "Where Teacher Power Is A Big Political Force," *The National Observer*, October 23, 1976.

with strong interest group activity.[10] We may also assume that the impact of the civil rights movement on the hierarchical society found in some southern states during the 1960s encouraged feverish organization and politicking. So, too, did the movement of industry out of New York and Massachusetts and into Alabama or New Mexico, or even

[10]Harmon Ziegler and Michael Baer, *Lobbying: Interaction and Influence in American State Legislatures*, Wadsworth Publishing Co., Belmont, Calif. 1969, p. 36. We noted in Chapter 5 that James Bryce in *The American Commonwealth* (1888) used such a theory to explain the length of state constitutions.

Changing conditions
reach the family farm.

movement of "downtown" or outside department stores into suburban
shopping centers—a change that may stir local merchants into opposing such malls before city councils as "ecologically undesirable."

Changes and threatened changes are full of uncertainty and unpredictability. The only certainty is that the changes will affect groups in
the society unequally. Conditions such as these lead to active lobbying.

What Resources Help a Group When It Lobbies?

Interest groups do not start out in the political arena equally. They differ in four ways that significantly affect their ability to get what they
want from government: money, members, organizational cohesion, and
legitimacy.

Money and Members.   The major resources that groups have to use to
gain political influence are either *money* or *membership*, or preferably
both.

Money is a valuable resource because with it an interest group can buy almost any other political resource—technical expertise in whatever area is needed, advertising campaigns to change voters' minds, publicity—the list is almost endless.

Members are important because every public official knows that membership can potentially be translated into votes. Each member is connected to family and friends and thereby may influence additional votes.

Few are the community councillors, state legislators, or administrators who will not at least give a careful hearing to groups who possess large financial resources, large memberships, or both.

Organizational Cohesion. Small interest groups sometimes have a special advantage because their membership is likely to be more alike in viewpoint and their representatives can act with little fear of division in the ranks.

The retail druggists and "fair trade." Local druggists at one time got almost every state to adopt "fair trade" laws that said that certain items could not be sold below the list price—the price set by the manufacturer. The laws prohibited the "loss leader" price-cutting practice used effectively by nationwide discount and chain stores such as Walgreens, Rexall, or K-Mart.

Joseph Palamountain analyzed this local druggist lobbying campaign and concluded that druggists succeeded in large part because they were so unified. Independently owned drug stores differ very little from one another in size, business receipts, and in the way each proprietor runs the business. Such corner drug store owners shared pretty much the same problems and agreed on what needed to be done to solve their problems. They willingly supported the lobbying campaign with funds and their own time. Their national leadership encouraged local druggists to form committees in each state legislative district, which then met with local state legislators and with each local U.S. congressman. They told them why they needed a fair trade law. Such united lobbying paid off handsomely in the states as well as in Congress.

The problems of cohesion in large organizations. Maintaining organizational cohesion is sometimes difficult for large-scale organizations. Not all the members support their campaigns fully. Community level members may not share the commitment to the state or national level

---

[1]Joseph C. Palamountain, "Retail Druggists and the Fair Trade Laws," in Robert Salisbury (ed), *Interest Groups in America*, Harper & Row, New York, 1970, 295–311.

goals. Associations made up of many separate units, as for example the state association of realtors, occasionally are split on the question of "blockbusting"—using racial or ethnic changes in a neighborhood to encourage panic selling. Or, the importance of a labor endorsement is less when the Teamsters' Union endorses one candidate for mayor or governor, and the CIO backs another. State chambers of commerce or similar business associations also sometimes find themselves divided by the competing interests of their members. Among the more bitter fights between industrial groups at the state level, each with its own set of labor allies, was that between the Pennsylvania Railroad and the Pennsylvania truckers' lobby. At issue were the weight limits permitted trucks on Pennsylvania roads. At one point even the Chesapeake and Ohio Railroad representatives became critical of the Pennsylvania Railroad's lobbying tactics.[12] A business "umbrella organization" can be torn apart by all-out warfare.

What Others Think of A Group. Political scientists speak of a group's legitimacy in the eyes of citizens and public officials as an important resource. V.O. Key, Jr. observed that:

The status of a group supposedly bears importantly on its political effectiveness. The group may be accepted, respected, feared, heeded, or it may be regarded as ridiculous, inconsequential, irresponsible, suspect, even contemptible. The spokesman for one group may be heard with respect; those of another may even have little opportunity to state its case.[13]

Government officials see some groups as having high status and, therefore, a legitimate claim to participate in policymaking that concerns them. Few, for example, would argue that the views of the state medical society are not highly significant when the state health department is considering a change in the state tuberculosis care program, or similarly that the county medical association should not be consulted frequently by the city or county health department.

Officials even seek out those groups that are viewed as having a legitimate stake in a policy area for information—even when those officials are not wholly sympathetic to the organization. Few state leg-

[12]For a description of this battle royale, see Robert Bendiner, "The Engineering of Consent—A Case Study," *The Reporter*, August 11, 1955, 14–23. When peace came, a new organization, the Council of Eastern Rail and Common Carriers, was formed. It was organized around "piggyback" operations—the transport truck trailers on railroad flatcars.

[13]V. O. Key, Jr., *Politics, Parties & Pressure Groups*, Thomas Y. Crowell Co., 5th edition, New York, 1964, p. 131.

islators would consider revising a regulation in respect to barbering without hearing the opinion of someone officially representing the barbers.[14]

The Pennsylvania Economy League.   Some groups have earned a special legitimacy. The Pennsylvania Economy League provides an unusual example of how the factual information this organization provided public officials over the years became translated into political power. The League is an industry-sponsored organization. Its goal is to keep taxes low and business conditions favorable. Over the past forty-five years, however, it has earned an enviable reputation for the quality of its research. Even labor unions and Democratic party governors occasionally seek the League's advice. Trained professionals prepare reports that are provided free of charge to state and local government agencies. The research is of high quality and objective. Edward Cooke reports that the only question concerning the League's objectivity may be "in the areas of taxation, appropriations and personnel."[15] They tend to favor low spending programs. He concludes that the League's influence on Pennsylvania policymaking has been pervasive because of the prestige and legitimacy it has in the eyes of state administrators and legislators. Pennsylvania officials accept their findings and recommendations as impartial and legitimate information and advice, often without dispute. Such civic study groups have built the same kind of legitimacy in many communities—the Cleveland Citizens League, the New Detroit Committee, and various taxpayers' leagues.

Anticipated reactions.   Some groups are viewed as so crucial to the economic health of a state or community that their legitimacy is never questioned. Legislators and other officials may even anticipate the organization's wants—officials have what political scientists call "anticipatory reactions." This is frequently the case when an industry dominates the economy the way agriculture does the Dakotas or luxury hotels and other tourist attractions do in Miami. Legislators and administrators may even be ahead of the industry in planning ways to attack a problem that is developing. This also tends to happen to important manufacturing industries that experience severe problems. Officials may, in fact, seek out the lobbyist with proposals to help.

[14]For a discussion of how information is translated into power see Anthony Downs, *An Economic Theory of Democracy*, Harper & Row, New York, 1957, Chapter 11, "The Process of Becoming Informed," 207–219.

[15]Edward F. Cooke, "Research: An Instrument of Political Power," *The Political Science Quarterly, 76*, March 1961, 69–87.

The continuing advantages of legitimacy. Organizations that have benefits accruing from their legitimacy or status have a distinct advantage over other organizations, even after their status begins to slip. They already have a stake in preserving the policy *status quo*—some may have already penetrated deeply into government agencies. Inertia and uncertainty about the effect of policy change make it easier for the lobbyists of groups viewed as legitimate to defend their position than it is for lobbyists representing a new group to get changes in that policy. Feminist groups, seeking changes in what they regard as discriminatory legislation in state or local governments, face this handicap, as have all other innovative groups.

The "outsider." What then of the groups that lack legitimacy? Who are they?

We find that they are groups about whose activities citizens feel uneasy—they do not enjoy widespread respect. They are seen as a not quite "legitimate" business. Often the racetracks, the pornographers, or the liquor industry (they prefer the more euphemistic title of "wine and spirits"), and in some states or communities, tobacco groups are so viewed. State legislators do not welcome being tagged as "the racetrack errand boy," while many have no objection to being known as "the legislative friend of the Iowa Farm Bureau Federation."

Not surprisingly, some of the organizations whose legitimacy is questioned do get involved in unethical practices. Duane Lockard reported that forty-four New Hampshire legislators once were employed at the windows of a new Hampshire racetrack.[16] Newspaper reporters discovered that Governor Otto Kerner and some Illinois legislators had, and took the opportunity to turn quick profits on stock in the Arlington racetrack outside Chicago. (They went to prison as a result). Such organizations, perhaps, turn to questionable tactics just to get the sympathetic attention of legislators—attention that more legitimate groups may get without even asking for it.

Officials sometimes regard some groups as not legitimately concerned with policy because of their lack of professional acceptance. The chiropractors and osteopaths at state and community levels have suffered such handicaps largely because of the attitude of the more established medical association toward them. In the past, racial and ethnic groups, such as blacks, Indians, or Chicanos, as well as labor organizations, suffered such treatment in states and communities. In some cases this discriminatory attitude may have encouraged them to use disruptive tactics, including those involving violence. In part this was a

[16]Duane Lockard, *New England State Politics*, Princeton University Press, Princeton, 1959, 75–77.

simple way, and perhaps the only way they had, to gain the attention of officials for what the groups regarded as their legitimate demands.

Other groups now accepted on the surface still are faced with some reservations. A study of lobbying in the state legislatures of Oregon, Utah, Massachusetts, and North Carolina revealed a common pattern in respect to lobbying by labor and education groups.[17] The labor and education representatives were thought by legislators and other lobbyists to "most often exert pressure." Despite this common belief the researchers could find little evidence that this was indeed the case. The opinion was probably based on anticipated behavior. We suggest that these groups still operated under the handicap of being not quite legitimate in the eyes of many state legislators and other lobbyists, at least in some of the states. Where labor organization is weak, we would expect this to be especially the case.

POLITICAL INTEREST GROUPS IN THE STATES AND COMMUNITIES

With this background we can begin to assess the lobbying activities in individual states and communities. We will expect producer groups and those with important resources to have strong influence in most states and many communities. Finally we will want to look for groups whose economic future is uncertain and changing.

The Strategic Position of State-Based Organizations

Each state or community has its own configuration of interest groups active in its politics. As we noted in Chapter 1, James Madison, in *Federalist* Number 10, as early as 1787 figured out that an interest group in a small democracy (a state or community) might be overpowering. As is the case with some corporations and unions, an interest group may have more financial resources and employees than the state or community government itself. In a large democracy, such as the entire nation, any single interest will likely be offset by many other interest groups and so would be less influential.

History has borne Madison out. Some states and communities have been literally dominated by a single interest group—the nation never has been.

State Interest Group Systems. Political scientists have sometimes classified states according to the dominance of major interest groups. In an early study researchers asked political scientists in each state

[17]Harmon Ziegler and Michael Baer, *Lobbying: Interaction and Influence in American State Legislatures*, Wadsworth Publishing Co., Belmont, Calif., 1969, 112–113.

whether the interest groups in their own state were strong, moderately strong, or weak.[18]

Harmon Ziegler and Hendrik van Dalen cross tabulated these data with measures of the political party strength. As measures, they used the level of party competition and party cohesion in roll-call votes in legislatures. They then examined the states to determine whether a variety of interest groups or a few major and many minor groups existed, and what degree of major conflict existed. We report their results in Table 12-1.[19]

Weak party states. In states where the parties are weak the resulting interest group system depends on the economic diversity in the state. Where we find a single interest, such as Anaconda Copper in Montana, or an alliance of major interests (timber, electric power, and manufacturing in Maine), it will dominate. Where we find many interests and none dominate, we get a "triumph of many interests," probably through shifting coalitions.

Strong party states. In states where parties are strong we get one of two patterns. Party dominance (though a far cry from the dominance found in Great Britain) characterizes the interest group system of Connecticut. The interest groups strive to convince party legislative leaders to adopt their position as a party position, rather than by lobbying

---

[18]The technique offers many problems—did all the political scientists define the terms "strong" or "weak" in the same way? Even if they agreed on the definition, were all the political scientists equally perceptive and skillful in making an accurate judgment? Belle Zeller (ed.) *American State Legislatures,* Crowell, New York, 1954, 190–191. The state classifications of interest group influence were as follows:

Strong:	Alabama, Arizona, Arkansas, California, Florida, Georgia, Iowa, Kentucky, Louisiana, Maine, Michigan, Minnesota, Mississippi, Montana, Nebraska, New Mexico, North Carolina, Oklahoma, Oregon, South Carolina, Tennessee, Texas, Washington, and Wisconsin.
Moderately Strong:	Delaware, Illinois, Kansas, Maryland, Massachusetts, Nevada, New York, Ohio, Pennsylvania, South Dakota, Utah, Vermont, Virginia, and West Virgina.
Weak:	Colorado, Connecticut, Indiana, Missouri, New Jersey, Rhode Island, and Wyoming.
Not Classified:	Alaska, Hawaii, Idaho, New Hampshire, and North Dakota.

[19]Harmon Ziegler and Hendrick van Dalen, "Interest Groups in State Politics," in Herbert Jacob and Kenneth N. Vines (eds.), *Politics in the American States,* 3rd. ed., Little Brown and Co., Boston, 1976, 93–138. The other study we refer to was an interesting one by Lewis Froman that relates these data to the length of state constitutions. See Lewis A. Froman, Jr., "Some Effects of Interest Groups in State Politics," *The American Political Science Review* 60, December 1966, 952–962.

TABLE 12-1 Interest Group Systems

	Many Interest Groups with None Being Dominant	One or a Few Interest Group(s) Dominant
Weak Political Parties	*Triumph of the Many Interest Groups* (California)	*One Interest Group Is Dominant* (Montana)
		An Alliance of Major Interest Groups (Maine)
Stronger Political Parties	*The Political Party Dominates the Interest Groups* (Connecticut)	*Conflict Between Major Interests* (Michigan)

SOURCE: Adapted from Harmon Ziegler and Hendrick van Dalen, "Interest Groups in State Politics," in Herbert Jacob and Kenneth N. Vines (eds.), *Politics in the American States*, 3rd ed., Little Brown & Co., Boston, 1976.

individual legislators to vote for interest group goals. In Michigan the pattern was one of conflict among the interests as well as parties. The United Auto Workers union has strong ties to the Democrats. The parties dominate these cooperative efforts.

Changing Interest Group Patterns. Although this classification system is useful as a guide, a word of caution needs to be given. In each of the states used as examples, the influences are still largely as described, but the patterns are beginning to change. California's political parties have been growing stronger because of legislation that eliminated some reforms of the earlier progressive era that so weakened them. At the same time California interest groups may become weaker as the result of the strong lobbying control laws, including Proposition 9—successfully sponsored by Common Cause and passed by initiative in 1974. Anaconda Copper in Montana and the Big Three of Maine no longer dominate their states' economies as they once did. The introduction of an optional primary law for convention nomination has weakened Connecticut's political parties. In Michigan the bitterness of the auto manufacturer–auto union battles has diminished markedly and neither party seems to come very close to fitting the strongly disciplined party model.

What causes pattern changes? We meet two familiar themes again— the nationalization of the federal system and the growing diversity of the country.

At one time states made many of the big decisions for their big industries. They still do for some functions that affect big industry, such as utility rate setting, pollution controls, workers' compensation insurance rules, level of state and local taxation, and incorporation laws. But even in these areas federal regulations and standards often intrude and either preempt or guide state action.

As a result we may even occasionally find little state interest group activity. Robert Salisbury concluded that "there are really no basic economic and social interests in conflict in the Missouri political arena." The politics of the state, he claimed, is bland, and the only active interest group at the time of his study in 1959 were politicians banded together to get patronage jobs.[20]

We can also see the impact on the state interest group system of large-scale industries, and even agriculture, beginning to lose monopolistic status within their state's economy. Because of their own geographical decentralization, large corporations such as General Motors and Ford find Michigan less important to them, just as Anheuser Busch, which now brews beer in Newark, New Jersey as well as St. Louis, Missouri, views Missouri policies as less significant to it. In Hawaii, the Big Five landowners, important since the Great Depression, have been challenged by a growing political force—the Longshoreman's Union and AFSCME.

The Emergence of Second Level Interest Groups. Who, then, fills the interest group vacuum?

Those Regulated By States and Communities. State-based professional and service groups are beginning to dominate the pattern of state lobbying just as many already do community lobbying. These groups are anchored to the state and its governments. Their economic future contains uncertainty. These are the groups who have the largest stakes in state policymaking and regulation today. Organized are the members of state-regulated professions and services, such as doctors, lawyers, ambulance drivers, morticians, electricians, and even garage mechanics. At the community level the most active groups are those especially affected by local planning and zoning practices.

Some of these groups come to a state government requesting "regulation," which may be a thinly veiled way of writing special advantages for themselves into the law. For example, in seventeen states the Milk Producers Association has persuaded the state to set minimum milk prices (to prevent price-cutting competition). The physical therapists, though, want state licensing to differentiate them from the kinds of

[20]Robert H. Salisbury, "Missouri Politics and State Political System," *Missouri Political Science Association Papers*, Bureau of Government Research, Columbia Mo., 1959, p. 17.

AFSCME Maryland members fill the House of Delegates' gallery at the State House in Annapolis to protest a bill that could have reduced their pension benefits. (June 1978).

"professionals" who operate massage parlors. Thus far the national government only touches upon the interests of these trades and professions in minor ways.

Suppliers of Services.   Always present also are subsidiary private groups—for example, those who make a living building state highways or those many vendors who sell supplies to state and community governments. All of these are producer groups who can gain a great deal from government decisions made about their activities.

Community officials as lobbyists.   In every state we also see increased lobbying by community government employees—especially the school teachers, public college and university employees, probate judges, sheriffs, and employees of local government (all of these are becoming actively organized and are among the most important of the lobby organizations at the state capital). Individual cities are also now hiring lobbyists.

The reason, of course, is found in the present uncertainty that faces local governments. In the past ten years the status of local officials has changed markedly and their salaries and numbers have increased. State government decisions, which have affected and sometimes encouraged such change, are crucial to the livelihood of all community officials and employees.

The Cozy Triangle—Interest Group Penetration.

The Pattern of Penetration. The kind of influence pattern that seems to us to be emerging in many states and communities is a blending of three groups of the political elite, each using each other to achieve its own individual goals. The pattern is most clearly found with respect to those professional and service interest groups to whom state regulation is all important.

The interest group. In one point of the triangle, we find the representatives of the political interest groups. Officials accept many of these as having a right to penetrate deeply into decision making at the state level. The physicians, because of their tremendous prestige and legitimacy, are usually intimately involved in making the state rules for their own profession, as well as for programs such as Medicaid. Many see their approval and opinion as essential to the decision process. The increase of government programs, including the proposal for National Health Insurance, has made them especially active in the political arena. Occasionally, we should note, competing groups are involved in the process.[21]

The administrator. The interest group representatives are joined at the second point in the triangle by administrators—in our example, employees in the state health department. Robert Salisbury calls such administrators the "permanent subgovernment." In the health department these are frequently physicians themselves at the top levels, or, at middle and lower levels, people who have had some type of medical training. The administrators thus share many of the goals and assumptions of the private medical profession. They usually see their job as one of cooperation with the physicians, needed to make many of their own programs successful, rather than one of confrontation or conflict. Critics who disapprove of this arrangement point out that the regulators are co-opted by the regulated. They single out instances of administrators who leave their jobs to take jobs in industries they formerly regulated, in this case, perhaps, the pharmaceutical industry or medical laboratories. Nevertheless this kind of cooperation seems to us

[21]The point that some interest groups do not simply want "access" but wish to penetrate into government to achieve long range and comprehensive goals is effectively made by Samuel Eldersveld, "American Interest Groups: A Survey of Research and Some Implications for Theory and Method," in Henry W. Ehrmann (ed), *Interest Groups On Four Continents*, University of Pittsburgh Press, Pittsburgh, 1968, p. 192. For an argument that "Interest Group Liberalism" has encouraged this process, see Theodore J. Lowi, *The End Of Liberalism*, W. W. Norton & Co., New York, 1969.

to be inevitable—given the absence of a competing interest group or the absence of publicity. Its root cause is that administrators, and the private groups they regulate, sometimes inevitably share many of the same interests, values and goals.

The legislative standing committees. The third point of the triangle, we find, is held down by the state legislative committees and their staff members who write or review most legislation—in this example, the public health committees of the House and Senate. These legislators also come to know physicians and their problems very well. Some may even have health related occupations—such as druggists, dentists, or health insurance agents. Retired physician-legislators are almost surely put on this committee.

In some states a tendency exists to "stack committees" with persons from both parties who share the same views or have the same backgrounds. Thus the health committee will be pro–physician, while the labor committee may be heavily pro–union, and at the same time a committee dealing with private business be mainly pro–business. This makes for harmony in deliberations and increases the degree of cooperation with the other participants in the cozy triangle.

The Effectiveness of the Cozy Triangle. The working relationships among the legislative committee members, administrators, and the private organization representatives are much quieter and less flamboyant than the wheeler-dealer, high-pressure lobbying that the sensational journalism describes. They are, we suggest, also much more important and effective. These are the people at the state and community levels who know the most about the problem under consideration. The proposals for legislation that they work out are not always, nor, perhaps, even most of the time, motivated by narrowly selfish goals. Very often, as in the case of health problems, all may work cooperatively to stamp out the incidence of disease, as many states have in recent years to upgrade maternity health services. Still we suspect that the result of the discussions and negotiations within the cozy triangle is seldom displeasing to the political interest group—only so when a number of political interest groups are in competition.

Community Governments and Interest Groups

The same processes are occurring in communities. Less dominance is found by a single interest group than in the old style company town. New interest groups, such as locally based ecology groups, are becoming a part of community politics.

Yet the influence of the traditional interest groups remains great—local industry, local business (including, especially, the Main Street merchants), local contractors, realtors, and developers. The contractors, realtors, and developers are deeply involved in encouraging and guiding community change, and are therefore deeply involved in local politics. You are likely to meet their representatives at any city council meeting you attend, and you will find evidence of cozy triangles in operation.

STATE AND COMMUNITY GOVERNMENTS AS ARENAS FOR LOBBYING

The lobbying organizations are only half of the equation. The other half is the state or community government itself. As we have already noted, these governments are more democratically organized than the national government—certain features make them especially vulnerable to outside influence.

The Visibility of State Government

What effect does a lack of visibility for state activity have on interest group lobbying? It means that influence is less clearly pinpointed. This is especially true of those business and professional organizations whose members are subject to state regulation. Their needs are not as clear to the public as are those of General Motors in Michigan or IBM in New York. And their needs are met by state level action. Who really watches what state government does about writing the laws and administering them in respect to mortuaries, the activities of certified public accountants, or the procedures followed by private adoption agencies? We do not wish to imply that each of these groups has found ways secretly to wring major concessions from state governments. Some, no doubt, have; some have not. But whichever is the case, their interest group lobbying is largely shielded from public view. This, in part, accounts for the findings that sometimes shock public interest groups of the Ralph Nader type when they begin to dig into the activities of state regulatory agencies and look at the legislation that guides them.

The Decentralized Organization of State and Community Governments

Because of their numerous access points, state governments and many community governments are made to order for lobbying by small, tightly organized groups who know what they want. In most states not only the governor is elected, but so, too, is the secretary of state and a host of other executive officers. The same pattern is followed in county government or the weak mayor system. Traditionally the state and local bureaucracies grew up in a hodge-podge fashion. Many units, as we have seen in Chapter 10 on administration, are independent of control by the chief executive or a department head. Some are managed by independent commissions on which interest groups can obtain seats. These commissions sometimes appoint the agency director.

Political parties usually do not bring about a centralization that can resist interest group penetration. The state party systems typically are loosely organized. Most city elections are now nonpartisan. Candidates can run on their own in the primary. In many state legislatures and local councils we find few party line votes. In some legislatures party caucuses are relatively rare. Legislative committee chairpersons may, if they wish, scuttle the program of the governor or their party, and continue to share the same party label with the governor. Typically, mayors face the same situation in city councils. All of these features maximize interest group opportunitites for direct lobbying and penetration.

Access Points and Lobbying. How does this diffusion of power affect lobbying? Previously we noted how different British and American interest groups are organized. These nations also differ in the way their governments are organized. The British government is more tightly centralized in the cabinet and bureaucracy, and the parties are also tightly organized. Party line voting is frequent. To gain concessions interest groups must be large because they face a large centralized government and centralized parties. Lobby activities focus on the political party and the administrator, not the individual legislators. Lobbyists in Britain know that if they gain party support, the party will discipline its own legislators.

In the American states and communities, with a diffused organization of parties and government, lobbying is directed at many points. Especially effective is lobbying that uses the election process. Candidates who run for political office, whether for governor or mayor, state legislature or council, or as a judge, are often pretty much on their own. Each must find a way to finance his or her own campaign. In a few states, such as New York, Ohio, Michigan, or Illinois, the party may channel some funds to its candidates for the general election, but seldom is this enough. And in primaries, the candidates commonly are on their own with no party help. Under such circumstances would you, as a candidate, turn down contributions from political interest groups you did not expect to oppose on most issues or organizations, such as the state's education association, or, perhaps, a labor union or business organization? Would you reject a contribution from someone of wealth who does not seem very much concerned about policies that are your major concern?

Political scientists have found that where there are an unusual number of points of access, "strong" interest groups exist. In such states or communities, interest groups sometimes take over from the political party the job of recruiting candidates and supporting their races.

The choice of access points.   The various segments of the state or community political government are never neutral insofar as any particular interest group is concerned. Structures advantage some interest groups and disadvantage others. Civil rights groups, for example, have gained major victories through state courts, but have found it more difficult to elect majorities to local school boards. Environmentalists have found it easier to get throw-away bottle bans adopted through an initiative vote (as in Oregon and Michigan) than to lobby a bill through the legislature. On the other hand, agricultural and business groups have often found the legislature and community councils and boards easier to convince than the voters. Specialized professional and trade groups have often found a sympathetic ear in the state or local bureaucracy. The choice of government arena depends on the interest group and the policy involved.

Amateurs Run State and Community Governments

Lobbyists especially have been attracted to state legislatures because so many of the legislators are political amateurs. As we noted in Chapter 7, they are political amateurs because the pay is low and they have to make their living in some other way, and because the legislative session is short. Similarly, city councils, county commissions, and school boards are largely composed of amateur officials.

With amateur status we find a number of other characteristics. One is lack of office space or staff. A second is relatively high turnover. A third is a rather haphazard lifestyle for state legislators. While city councillors and members of the U.S. Congress live with their families, state legislators commute back and forth during the session. The rest of the time they roam around a capital city that usually is not a major population center of the state. Evenings may be spent at the movies, in bars or other "watering holes," in hotel lobbies.

All of these conditions are made to order for lobbying. As one newspaper reporter, Frank Trippett, observed, when state legislators are amateurs, it often appears as if the lobbyist is the host in the capital city and the state legislator is the guest. The lobbyists, who have been around for some time, take the legislators in hand. They explain how the system works. They fill in information about the best places to eat. They provide them with entertainment, supply them with information that they have trouble getting elsewhere, and help them draft key amendments. Full-time legislators with professional political careers ahead are less likely to want or need such help.

Another aspect of the amateur status is that the state or community legislator has a main career that is nonpolitical, and it may be affected rather easily by the lobbyist either favorably or unfavorably. Lawyers receive retainers, small businesses get new orders, or a farmer legislator may wish to buy a truck or tractor at the dealer's discount price.

The Amateur Vermont Legislature. An indication of how an amateur in a legislature lacks time to become "savvy" was illustrated by an early study of the part-time legislature of Vermont. During the session the Associated Industries of Vermont (AIV), which had a membership of four hundred fifty manufacturing concerns, and the CIO came to a compromise agreement on a bill. They reached the agreement off the floor and the legislature then passed the bill.

After the session Oliver Garceau and Corinne Silverman interviewed the legislators. One-third had never heard of the AIV and only a few less "had any notion that the labor interests in Vermont were organized." Two-thirds were unable to identify the lobbyists for either group. But the speaker of the House and the president pro tempore of the Senate were directors of AIV, even members of its executive committee. Several chairpersons of standing committees were members. Clearly the AIV lobbyists bypassed many of the amateur members of the legislature.[22]

The Effect of Professionalization on Lobbying. Amateurism encouraged the old style pattern of influence. This was influence sometimes based on outright corruption and bribery, or by imposing on the lack of time and knowledge possessed by the amateur legislator.

As we have noted, the picture is changing at the state level and in some community governments as well. The result makes legislators less dependent on lobbyists. Legislative salaries are rising and being a state legislator or a county commissioner or city councillor in urban centers is becoming, for some, a full-time political career. Legislative reference services write the bills and dig up accurate information for

[22]Oliver Garceau and Corinne Silverman "A Pressure Group and the Pressured: A Case Report" *American Political Science Review*, 42, September 1954, 672–91.

legislators. Leagues of Municipalities aid community councillors. Those legislators with political career ambitions—Congress or the governorship—are becoming more sensitive to possible charges of improper influence.

As a result, lobbying techniques, especially at the state level, have also had to change—a point to which we will return.

Officials Are Sometimes Informal Lobbyists

We need to remind ourselves that state legislators and community councillors, like other human beings, have their own prejudices, likes, and dislikes. At least one study of lobbying discovered that it was the legislators who sometimes attempted to stir up paid lobbyists into action for bills that the legislator favored, rather than the reverse.[23]

If we think about this, it makes sense. A state legislator or city councillor who is or was a labor union member may be as interested in legislation affecting labor as any state AFL-CIO lobbyist. The same may be true of realtors, farmers, small merchants, and college professors and other teachers—in fact, of members of all occupations with respect to their businesses, trades, and professions. They know intimately how a government action will affect their respective areas.

Legislators also do not have to worry about cases of conflict of interest—as, for example, do judges. We expect that legislators will work in cooperation with lobbyists on the same side. As we noted in chapter 7 on legislators, their task is not generally to choose between competing interests (as a judge must do), but to reconcile such interests to a satisfactory middle ground. The idea of conflict of interest is even more rarely raised in community governing.

The ties with interest groups in a legislator's district also encourage identification with certain groups. Legislators with career ambitions—if only the ambition to be reelected—will be concerned about their district's interests. But district ties are stronger than simply the desire to be reelected. Even legislators from extremely safe districts will feel that they have a duty to protect the district's interests.

How then do the prejudices of officials affect the way they treat lobbyists? Knowing that legislators already hold certain positions should make us less prone to accept the notion that every state or community legislator or administrator is up for sale or can be pressured on any issue. We should expect close cooperation with lobbyists where an official already shares the lobbyist's views. We should not expect that un-

[23]Raymond A. Bauer, Ithiel de Sola Pool, and Lewis Anthony Dexter, *American Business and Public Policy, The Politics of Foreign Trade*, Atherton Press, New York, 1964.

ethical influence or pressure tactics will be used when a legislator is already committed to opposing a group. Corruption is more likely when an official is somewhat uninformed about the stakes involved, or where the official is largely indifferent about the outcome of a policy—where it does not appear to affect in any major way the interests with which he or she most clearly identifies.

LOBBYING DOWN AT THE STATE CAPITOL AND IN CITY HALL

The most important of modern lobbyists are professionals. They have a reputation for honesty, and even integrity, to protect. As in many other professions we find an occasional black sheep, but these, we think, are becoming the exception.

The Lobbyists

Around most state capitols, somewhere between one hundred to perhaps three or four hundred lobbyists seek to influence at least some of the goings on. Most of them are part time, and many are amateurs.

In communities we find fewer lobbyists with almost all the lobbyists devoting part time to their job. It is sometimes difficult in communities to determine who, in fact, can be called a lobbyist, since so many of the elected public officials and appointed members of boards are part-time officials with private axes to grind. They and their colleagues tend to see themselves as "citizens involved in government," rather than as representatives of interest group viewpoints.

The Characteristics of Professional Lobbyists. It is difficult to generalize about lobbyists because they come in such assorted types, from amateurs to professionals. As a group the professionals do not make a particularly high income, but this is not true of some of the public relations specialists hired by large corporations to represent their interests in the state legislature or, occasionally, in the community; nor is it true of the most successful of the state-level legislative agents. Still even the most successful are unable to move on to other states or to the nation's capital where the pay might be higher. They would lose one of the main advantages they have—what they know about their own state and its communities, its legislature, and its members.

State-level lobbyists tend to be slightly better educated than state legislators. About one-half to two-thirds of the lobbyists are college graduates. Most are in their late 40s and 50s. Most are men. Most live in the state capital. Fewer than we would expect are ex-legislators, but their number may be growing—in Policy Box No. 24 "A Second Career for Legislators" we discuss some aspects of their professional lobbying. One study reports that a large number of lobbyists drifted into lobbying largely by accident.[24]

The Amateur Lobbyists.　Do not idealize the amateurs. Many of them know little about the legislative process and probably are the greatest users of intimidating tactics. They often have little concern for future issues that may come up, and so they may play hard and fast on the issue that concerns them. They lobby the one bill and leave when it is disposed of. A Michigan estimate placed part-time lobbyists at about 85 percent of those at the state level.[25] Almost all at the community level

[24]For a detailed discussion of the characteristics of lobbyists in four states, see Ziegler and Baer, op. cit., Chapter 3, 38–59. For a particularly appealing autobiography of a Wyoming lobbyist who did go on to Washington, D.C. to lobby, see Olga Moore, *I'll Meet You in the Lobby*, Lippincott, New York, 1950.

[25]Walter DeVries "The Michigan Lobbyist: A Study in the Bases and Perceptions of Effectiveness," Ph.D. dissertation, Michigan State University, East Lansing, 1960.

**POLICY BOX NO. 24　Lobbying:
A Second Career for Ex-legislators.**

Once your career in the state legislature has ended, either because the voters retired you or because you were simply tired of the personal sacrifices involved, what do you do? Where can the skills and contacts of the past few years as a state legislator be put to use?

Lawyer–legislators, upon leaving office, do not face this kind of question. But for others, especially those who have made virtually complete breaks with their pre-legislative occupation, finding the right answer can be difficult. A few ex-legislators can, perhaps, catch on in a job with one of the state agencies, and some others may get a staff job with the legislature itself.

One of the most lucrative possibilities, though, after the career as a legislator is over, is to turn lobbyist. Lobbying is one occupation that builds directly on the legislative experience. Ex-legislators probably know well the legislative ropes. They know legislators as individuals and many, regardless of party, are good friends. Perhaps even more important, they know the personal trials, tribulations, fears, hopes, and concerns of legislators. The ex-legislator turned lobbyist can relate to the legislator in important ways.

What we find, at least in one state, is a growing number of legislators turning to lobbying as a post-legislative career. During the fall of 1977 at least twenty-four former legislators were registered as lobbyists at the Michigan state capitol. A few of them represent a single corporation or interest group, but some of the more successful ones have established firms that represent a rather large number of clients; a few have as many as twenty or more clients to represent on a regular basis.

One news reporter wrote of them, "They are at the top of a growing heap of ex-legislators who roam this town (Lansing) getting things done—or undone—for an array of powerful well-heeled vested interests. Their speciality is legislation. When they want a bill, they usually get it. When they don't, it usually dies."

The fear of the critics of such lobbying firms, especially those that represent a number of high-spending interests, is that the lobbying firms have control of large sums of money to spend on influence-peddling activities—money for lunches, dinners, sophisticated office equipment, advertising programs, and political contributions. In Michigan the amount of money that interests spend for lobbying is not known, but Common Cause, an interest group fighting for lobbying reforms, reported that more than $3 million were spent in New York state in 1976, more than $250,000 in Idaho, and in Maryland, where detailed reporting is required, nearly $1.4 million. Emil Lockwood, a former legislator and one of the more successful lobbyists in Lansing, says that a client should expect to pay about $1500 per month (for a minimum contract of three months) for the lobbying service. James Karoub, another multi-client former legislator turned lobbyist, said that the most he ever received from a single client for one year was $30,000. These data leave little doubt that effective lobbying runs on money and plenty of it.

How do lobbyists spend the money coming into their control? Lockwood estimated that about 20 percent goes for travel and entertainment—tickets for political fund raisers, parties, nights out at the racetrack, big football games in the state, or out-of-state if the state university is playing, and other favors.

Common Cause believes that the wealth of the lobbyists and their clients turns the governmental process away from average citizens who cannot afford to shower legislators with many favors. It seeks to curtail these lobbying practices by requiring disclosure of how much money lobbyists spend, and on whom. In addition, Common Cause suggests that ex-legislators be prohibited from lobbying for at least two years after leaving the legislature. Criminal penalties would apply to all violations.

Common Cause thinks that such restrictions and exposure to public view will clean up lobbying practices at the state capitals.

What do you think? Should ex-legislators be prohibited from lobbying for a two-year period? Should the lobbyist expenditure-reporting rules apply to legislative employees, as well as legislators? Do you think citizens will read the expenditure reports? Will the reports be misused in political campaigns? How do you think legislators will make up for the income loss if lobbyists spend less on them? What tactical changes do you think lobbyists will make to maintain their influence under the new rules?

SOURCE: This policy box is based on Hugh McDiarmid, "If You've Got a Vested Interest, We've Got Just the Man to Protect It," *Detroit Free Press Sunday Supplement*, Jan. 30, 1977, *Common Cause Michigan*, Fall 1977, and Lou Gordon, "Was Karoub's Promise Nothing But a Big Lie?" *Detroit News*, November 17, 1976.

are amateurs—many are realtors, merchants, or persons involved in "cause" groups who seek out councillors on their own.

Professional Lobbyists.   Few professional lobbyists are found in communities. They number between fifty and one hundred in states such as California and New York, and less in more rural states. We find three major types of professional lobbyists.

The executive secretary of an association.   This is the most numerous type of professional lobbyist at the state level. When not lobbying in the legislature, the executive secretary is busy handling details as an officer of the organization. A group such as the state medical association or state AFL-CIO will usually have a number of assistants aiding the executive secretary in lobbying activities. At the other extreme the social workers or the physical therapists may have one person whose duties in the organization require him or her to move in and out of the capital city to lobby as the situation requires. Some, such as labor union representatives, also lobby before city councils, school boards, and county commissions.

The public relations specialists.   They work for large firms, such as Caterpillar Tractor of Peoria, Illinois, or the Ford Motor Co., or Bell Telephone. Because of frequent contact with the state, it is worth a company's while to have an ongoing observer at the legislature, even if only in a watchdog role. Often, though, their lobbyist has other public relations duties with the firm as well, such as publicizing the plant's winning bowling league team, getting stories about the new product line in the mass media, or appearing before city councils, county commissions, or school boards when the need arises.

The legislative agents.   These persons are professional careerists. They handle clients—especially those that only require lobbying from time to time. They work on a contract account basis. The professional agency has a regular string of five or six regular clients whose interests do not compete, or they may take up to a dozen or more clients who have specific short-term goals—either for passing or blocking of a specific piece of legislation. The legislative agents are among the most prestigious and wealthy lobbyists, as their earnings depend on nothing other than their ability to get results in the legislature and, sometimes, administrative agencies. The best agents will at times advise potential clients against lobbying when the agents feel they can accomplish little for them. They will also refuse to handle some clients, if they feel it may damage the firm's image. They seldom lobby at the community level.

Lobbying Techniques

One useful way of looking at lobbyists is to look at what they try to accomplish. We will concentrate in this section on professional lobbyists, most of whose lobbying activities are at the state level. Samuel Patterson, in a study of the Oklahoma legislature, classified such lobbyists as "contactors," "informants," and "watchdogs."[26]

Building Friendly Contacts. The common technique that lobbyists follow is building friendly relationships. The professional lobbyist will begin by working closely with legislators who already are sympathetic to his or her client or organization. Second, the lobbyist will approach those legislators who will generally be undecided or neutral, and hope to make a favorable impression. Thus when an issue arises, the lobbyist hopes to be on a first-name basis so that legislators can more easily be provided with favorable information.

To get the relatively undivided attention of state legislators, lobbyists together sometimes sponsor a weekend cruise on a nearby (and sometimes more distant) lake or river. This may become an annual affair. Some interest groups sponsor annual banquets to which every legislator is invited. Members of the group from across the state also commonly attend.

Pressure tactics may backfire. Almost all observers report that pressure tactics by lobbyists today are not common practice, although on rare occasions pressure may be used. Most lobbyists use pressure; such as "packing the gallery", only under dire emergency conditions, because pressuring a legislator has costs; pressure tactics can backfire and create lingering ill will. In Michigan, Common Cause appears to have used tactics that some legislators regarded as undue pressure. The legislators reacted by publicizing a minor clerical error they found in one of the Common Cause reports on how it financed its own lobbying activities. Most lobbyists prefer to provide information mixed with occasional doses of mild persuasion.

Providing Information. Because a legislator's time is limited, some information may have to be presented in written form or as testimony at legislative hearings. This, of course, puts it in the record. The contact lobbyist will generally line up expert witnesses for such hearings, including officers of the organization, if it is a prestigious one.

[26]Samuel C. Patterson, "The Role of the Lobbyist: The Case of Oklahoma," *Journal of Politics*, 25, 1963 p. 78.

All public officials need information—particularly information that helps them to estimate the effect of a change in a law or administrative policy. Change means uncertainty and unpredictability. Lobbyists have access to accurate information about the interests they represent. How will a proposed change in the regulation of Blue Cross and Blue Shield affect insurance rates? It is a rare legislator or administrator who would not at least want to listen to what the lobbyist representing those organizations has to say and take a look at the figures presented.

But in presenting information most lobbyists, out of necessity, will seek to preserve their own reputations for truthfulness. This means answering a legislator's questions honestly, but not necessarily offering information that may hurt your case unless it is specifically asked for.

The Watchdogs. The watchdog role requires checking all bills for possible harm to a particular organization. Those so employed may seldom enter the capitol building, but can do the work required poring over bills in a nearby office.

Providing "Favors." Perhaps the most difficult problem a legitimate lobbyist faces is dealing adroitly with requests from state legislators for "favors." A lobbyist is expected by many legislators to do minor favors without much question, such as buying drinks and dinners. But the legislator may ask for a "loan" of $25 to buy lunch and such loans may never be repaid. And major lobbyists commonly contribute to "fund raisers" for legislators. The lobbyist has to decide where to draw the line on requests for major services. State universities have been known to offer honorary degrees to state legislators on the advice of the university lobbyist. Another example is the common practice of major universities providing every legislator with several season tickets to its football games. Is that bribery? Or are they just allowing legislators to inspect more closely an activity underwritten by state funds? Is it bribery if the state's racetracks provide each legislator with a free season pass to the tracks? Manufacturers of consumer items, such as air conditioners, automobiles, or power lawn mowers, may offer legislators special discounts. The lobbyist may find a job for a legislator's brother-in-law with the lobbyist's sponsoring firm. Fewer groups invite legislators on a trip to their plants, but the weekend vacation at the group's camp or hunting lodge is common. (Jimmy Carter as governor accepted a few such invitations.) The list of such favors is endless and some of them are often highly questionable. It is at this point and in respect to campaign contributions that full-time lobbyists come closest to using unethical techniques.

The Characteristics of Successful Lobbyists. What characteristics do the most successful state lobbyists have? Walter DeVries, in a study of Michigan lobbyists, concluded that the three top qualities of successful lobbyists were personality and sociability, the power and prestige of the organization represented, and experience with legislative procedures.[27]

Thus lobbyists are always somewhat limited by the strength and prestige of the organization they represent. Casey Stengel once observed that the sports writers somehow found that he was so much more skillful a baseball manager when he managed the powerful New York Yankees, as compared with his skill in managing the basement-dwelling New York Mets. Lobbying is similar—the lobbyist looks more skillful when the interest he represents has powerful resources to back him up.[28]

But as in all games, skill in managing one's advantages sometimes counts. On lazy sunny afternoons in the fall, underdog college football teams occasionally upset the "favorites." So, too, down at the state capitol, a lobbyist with a knowledge of the legislature and a winning personality may occasionally achieve wonders. It pays to have a skilled coach or an experienced lobbyist, but it still pays off more often to go into the game stronger than one's opponents.

CONTROL OF INTEREST GROUP INFLUENCE

Reformers have tried in many ways to control lobbying—even to make legislative lobbying illegal. That, incidentally, was unconstitutional, as the first amendment of the U.S. Constitution guarantees us the right to petition our governments for redress of grievances.

We have divided the reform efforts by the political assumptions that underlie each. From time to time states and communities move from one to another method. Presently most critics of lobbying favor that which emphasizes publicity and regulates practice.

The Interest Groups Can Police Themselves

Few argue that self-regulation can in itself control undesirable practices. Still, such self regulation does little harm and, combined with other methods, may do some positive good.

[27]DeVries, op. cit.

[28]John C. Wahlke, Heinz Eulau, William Buchanan, and LeRoy Ferguson, *The Legislative System*, John Wiley & Sons, New York, 1962, p. 334.

A Code of Ethics.   One form of self-regulation is the adoption of a code of ethics as New York State did for legislators and lobbyists in 1954. (Kentucky, Maryland, Massachusetts, Minnesota, New Mexico, Washington, and Texas also have such codes.) A code spells out proper conduct. The problem is that it depends on voluntary compliance or, at most, mild social pressure. One can hope for self-restraint from other lobbyists, or point the finger of shame at colleagues who seem to stray from the straight and narrow, but that is about all. A code sometimes brings improvement when coupled with other methods. Still, when breaking the code of ethics brings significant advantages and few disadvantages, the code is apt to be bent or broken.

Competing Groups.   A second method of control, borrowed from laissez-faire economics, assumes that organizations will balance off one another as they compete with each other. At one time the economist John Kenneth Galbraith hoped for countervailing power, in an organized form, to most organized groups. Thus unions and industry would check each other, as would railroads and truckers. To some extent the countervailing theory works in practice. Still, many relatively effective interest groups, such as the state association of ambulance firms, have no such countervailing group to oppose them.

Another problem with the countervailing group theory, at least as we see it, is that the groups involved (and legislators as well), begin to view every issue as having concern only to two groups, or at most to the groups immediately involved. We think that you might well agree that the general public often has something at stake as well.

Overlapping and Reaffirming Group Memberships.   The model often used to illustrate the importance of overlapping group memberships is Switzerland, where the population speaks French, German, Italian, and a Swiss language, and are divided between the Catholic and Protestant religions. Any attempt to mobilize any one group fully—say the French—will result in part of the group sharing an important interest with some of the opposition Germans—in this case French Catholics and German Catholics versus French Protestants and German Protestants. Thus no single group can ask for too much since part of its membership is always somewhat in sympathy with part of the opposing group.

Sometimes the theory works, but also, unfortunately, as Robert Salisbury has observed, groups do not always split up that neatly. Sometimes there are reaffirming, rather than overlapping, memberships. The same members of the community who belong to the chamber of commerce are also members of the community church and the country club and the Republican party and those who belong to the labor unions are also members of the Catholic church, an ethnic group organization, and vote Democratic. Every interest group membership sharpens the conflict rather than blurs it. We develop what V.O. Key, Jr. called a "partisan cluster," opposed by another "partisan cluster."

We thus conclude that self-regulation in interest group politics, as in the economy, has some utility, but also it has serious inadequacies.

Regulating What Lobbyists Do

Bribery or intimidation of legislators dates back at least to the Yazoo land scandal in Georgia in 1795. It resulted in a famous Supreme Court challenge to the laws passed by a corrupted legislature.[29]

Corrupt Practices Laws.   The earliest "Corrupt Practices Laws" forbade only the crudest practices—across-the-counter bribery of public officials, the purchase of votes, or the fraudulent rigging of elections.

Conflict of Interest Laws.   A similar type of legislation, still in its infancy at the state and community levels, forbids conflicts of interest. Just as judges sometimes disqualify themselves from cases where they have a personal financial or professional interest, it is hoped that administrators will also do so. Few such laws apply to legislators. The difficulty is that administrators who know their subject matter will often have a conflict where no personal financial interest is involved: beauticians on the state board of cosmetology will rule on a case that their own firm will sooner or later also experience.

Lobbyist Spending Regulations.   A recent type of regulation, adopted nationally, in many states, and in a few communities, sets limits on the money that lobbyists can spend on lobbying any legislator without reporting excess amounts to a state office. A lobbying law written by Common Cause and adopted by initiative in California in 1974 is among the most severe. Lobbyists can only spend $10 per month to influence any one public official. That law is being challenged in the California courts as depriving citizens of guaranteed constitutional rights.

Campaign Finance Regulation.   A related type of law limits what may be spent in political campaigns, either by absolute amounts or by a formula based on the importance of the office and number of voters.

A new type of regulation found in a few states is government financ-

[29]*Fletcher v. Peck*, 6 Cranch 87, 123 (1810).

"He Never Lets Go!"

An interest group portrays itself: Common Cause uses a bulldog symbol in its advertising.

ing of political campaigns as the federal government now does. The purpose of such laws is to reduce a candidate's dependence on lobbyists for campaign contributions. This practice in the states is limited to compaigns for governor.

How can the regulations be enforced? Lobby regulation by publicity works on the principle, that certain practices, if widely known, will be generally condemned. The first laws built on this principle required the registration of lobbyists who appeared at the state legislature. Enforcement was poor and publicity was often nonexistent. In addition some political interest groups refused to register because they called themselves "educational associations," rather than lobbies. Others, especially groups representing state or local officials, did not believe they were required to register.

A different technique is regulation by a commission—a method used in twenty-six states. Such commissions often require extensive reports on the amount of money spent lobbying public officials and the amount contributed to political campaigns. These reports occasionally are printed and even analyzed in the newspapers and sometimes are used in political campaigns. Many students seem to place their hope in control of lobbying with such reporting schemes.

Public Interest Watchdog Organizations

In the late 1960s Ralph Nader began his consumer protection groups. From these have grown a variety of public interest groups designed "to make government and corporations more responsive to the public welfare." Some are inspired by Nader's efforts, others were formed independently.

All of these groups have one thing in common—they all argue for more citizen access into the workings of government. They demand information about decisions—how they were made, and on what basis. More facts, they argue, should be on the public record.

Most of these groups are specialized. Nader's task forces are concerned with consumer matters, from sports to auto safety. Common Cause has placed major emphasis on environmental issues and the regulation of lobbying and campaign finance. (They were responsible for California's lobby regulation law and Colorado's sunset law in respect to six year review of state regulatory agencies.) Some groups have specialized in the legislation involving agriculture and food, others in mental health and child care.

The staffs of these self-designated public interest groups are generally volunteer or are paid somewhat below prevailing wages for their skills. Some recruit lawyers exclusively. A few recruit scientists and other trained specialists. Their activities are investigative reporting, special scientific studies, litigation (CLASP, the Center for Law and Social Policy did the legal work in opposition to the Alaska Pipeline), the publication of books and pamphlets, and testimony to legislative committees at federal, state, and community levels.

The larger groups, such as Common Cause, are financed by individual contributions; the smaller ones depend in large measure on support of the foundations (CLASP received two-thirds of its funds from the Ford Foundation). They also raise some money from speeches, and book and pamphlet sales. But in 1976 the Ford Foundation announced the end of its support of public interest law groups. One way these

---

[30]For a discussion of four such groups see Theodore Jacqueney, "Washington Pressures/Public Interest Groups Challenge Government, Industry," *National Journal Reprints*, 1975–76 edition, "Interest Groups," 20–30.

groups hoped to survive was to get the government, or defendants who have lost in one of their suits, to pay the full legal fees. The U.S. Supreme Court ruled in 1975 that such awards must be specifically authorized by law, and few states or communities have such laws.

Are these private watchdog groups a temporary phenomenon? It is too early to tell. If foundation support disappears, many of the smaller ones will almost surely collapse. Some, such as the Center on Corporate Responsibility that won suits against General Motors already have. Others, such as Tax Analysts and Advocates, have sharply reduced their staffs.

Are such groups effective as a control of lobbying, such as occurs with the creation of a cozy triangle? Effectiveness, of course, varies with the group, but a number have brought issues out in the open to a point where a larger number of citizens can join the conflict and, in the process, some decisions have been reversed or revised.

A Final Comment

Traditionally much of the criticism of lobbying, especially in state legislatures, has been of the associated bribery and corruption. We have not dwelt on such stories although at various points in our discussion we illustrated modern instances. We thought it more important that we emphasize how some groups penetrate deeply into the decision process at the state and community level. Some groups even help prepare the regulations by which they are regulated—so deeply have they penetrated. We are inclined to think that such penetration is inevitable and that the recognition of this fact is necesssary to bring about a more effective regulation of such activities.

HIGHPOINTS OF CHAPTER 12: POLITICAL INTEREST GROUPS IN STATES AND COMMUNITIES

In this chapter we began by (1) reporting general findings about American political interest groups—that the upper middle class were most likely to be organized, that lobbying paid off most for economic producer groups, that groups were most likely to lobby actively when facing economic uncertainty, and that the basic resources for effective lobbying by a group were money and members, ability to work as a unit without divisions of opinion in the membership, and acceptance as being legitimate by the rest of society. We then (2) looked at the pattern of lobbying in the states and communities and suggested that, because of the diversification of business and agriculture and the taking over by the national government of many important economic decisions, the importance of the "big interests" in the state lobbying picture was on the decline. Taking their place were second level groups— service and professional people who are regulated by the state and employees of local government, including, especially, school teachers, whose future is determined by state decisions. We described a pattern of influence that we called penetration of legislative committees, administration, and interest group representation—"the cozy triangle." Next we (3) looked at the state and community governments as arenas that can be penetrated or influenced by lobbying, noting especially the state's lack of visibility, and the decentralization, amateurism, and the potential conflict of interest because officials themselves may be strongly associated with a group. We then (4) looked at who become professional lobbyists and emphasized that the techniques they use tend to emphasize giving information and personal persuasion. Finally (5) we looked at the methods that reformers have recommended for control of interest group influence—self regulation, regulation of what lobbyists do, publicity, and the creation of public interest watchdog organizations.

13

POLITICAL PARTIES IN STATES AND COMMUNITIES

George Washington, in his famous "Farewell Address to his Countrymen," warned darkly that political parties "in different ages and countries . . . [have] perpetuated the most horrid enormities." Yet within a decade, Tammany Hall and similar organizations sprang up. At the same time many Americans up to the present day have agreed with their first president about political parties.

Reforming political parties is an old American tradition. "Good government" reformers from 1800 to the present have never let up in trying to reshape national, state, and community political parties. At times they have even succeeded in stamping out political parties altogether. Two-thirds of American cities as well as other local governments have nonpartisan races. And the noted progressive, George W. Norris, persuaded his fellow Nebraskans in the 1930s to elect their state legislators without party identification.

The reforms adopted, coupled with the organization forced on political parties by the federal system and the separation of powers, have made our political parties a thoroughly American institution—one unique among political parties in democracies.[1] Their key characteristic has been nonhierarchical decentralization. American parties have had an "every person for him-or herself" kind of approach to organizing, the recruiting of candidates, campaigning, and governing.

Party Splintering of Power and Federalism. The splintering of power in America's party organizations has had important implications for its federal system. Because the American parties are not organized into a nationally controlled bureaucratic party structure, state and community politicians can more easily defend their citizens and interest groups from national control. The strength of these one hundred state-based, and the unnumbered community-based parties, Professor David Truman argued, has encouraged and protected the exercise of state policymaking, or if you prefer—party decentralization preserves states rights.[2]

[1]For an excellent review and analysis of the history of such party reform efforts, see Austin Ranney, *Curing the Mischiefs of Faction: Party Reform in America*, University of California Press, Berkeley, Calif., 1975.

[2]David B. Truman, "Federalism and the Party System," in Arthur W. Macmahon (ed.), *Federalism, Mature and Emergent*, Doubleday and Company, Garden City, New York, 1955, 115–136.

Almost every day the newspaper has a story of state officials protesting some action of the national government—the closing of a military base in the state, or trying to get the federal government to give orders to a defense plant within the state, or to change the rules for Medicaid. Such protests are particularly effective when the president is of the same political party as the governor or if a powerful U.S. senator or representative joins in applying the pressure on behalf of the state, one of its communities, or a state-based interest group. What makes such protests possible and significant is the decentralization of American political parties—governors, senators, and mayors are more than cogs in a national organization.

Overview. In this chapter, we will begin by looking at how American parties became as distinctive as they are. We then will look at how American parties in the states and communities function, and consider how they are organized, how parties recruit candidates, how the candidates campaign, and how united party candidates are when elected to office. Finally we consider how much the state and community parties are now coming under the influence of the national party organizations.

THE DEVELOPMENT OF AMERICAN PARTIES

Until the election of Andrew Jackson in 1828, American politics had an aristocratic flavor. Holding government office was regarded as something of an honor for high-status college educated citizens. Party organizations were small cliques that were composed of groups of like-minded notables.

Andrew Jackson rode into office against this system. He immediately threw out of office 2000 government officials and replaced them with his supporters from the frontier. Until then, only seventy-six federal employees had ever been fired. Jackson democratized the bureaucracy. To the victorious party organization went the spoils of office. And more opportunities for spoils were created through Jacksonian reforms that would further democratize government—fill more offices by election, have shorter terms for officeholders, and less stringent voting requirements.

The Early Mass Party Organizations

"Rotation in office," the spoils system, and a wider electorate, set the stage for the birth of mass party organizations based on participation in government by average citizens.

The pre-Civil War party organizations were loose patronage–hungry coalitions held together by the promise of office or favors. The state organizations, revolving around the governor's office, had trustworthy lieutenants in every county to pass out patronage—for votes they traded jobs at both state and local levels. The city jobs and contracts were given out by mayors, with party loyalists in every ward. Among the best known of the early state organizations were those of the Clintons and, later, Martin Van Buren's Albany Regency—both of New York state and, of course, Tammany Hall in New York City.

The Boss Senators and Their Organizations

After the Civil War party leaders in many states set about the task of creating party organizations that functioned more systematically, "perfected" by those the historian Matthew Josephson called "Boss-Senators." The party leaders were northern Republican senators during the period of President Ulysses Grant (1869–1876)—perhaps America's most flourishing era of political corruption.[3] The "Boss-Senators" built state organizations around the distribution of federal as well as state and local patronage. The "plums" were the federal jobs—postmasterships, military commissions, custom house jobs, and positions with the Bureau of Internal Revenue. From 1865 to 1876 Republican senators also controlled the positions in the Reconstruction officialdom, foisted on the defeated states of the South. The most influential senators formed alliances with each other to milk the federal government for a maximum number of patronage jobs.

The officeholders that the senators appointed were not only expected to deliver votes; they also were required to contribute money according to the salary of the office they gained.[4] But the major contribution to development of party machines by the "Boss-Senators" was to perfect the trading of cold cash for political favors to "Gilded Age" capitalists. The whole story is not that the builders of the nation's railroads and industries or its extractors of its mineral wealth corrupted

[3] For a first rate discussion of this process see Matthew Josephson, The Politicos, 1865–1896. Harcourt, Brace and World, New York, 1938. See also Stewart H. Holbrook, The Age of the Moguls, Doubleday and Company, Garden City, New York, 1954. For a perceptive study of the evolution of the Tweed machine of New York City, see Martin Shefter, "The Emergence of the Political Machine: An Alternative View," in Willis Hawley et al. (eds.) Theoretical Perspectives on Urban Politics, Prentice-Hall, Englewood Cliffs, N.J. 1976.

[4] James Bryce, The American Commonwealth, 1888, Book II, p. 110. The leading senators included men such as "Zack" Chandler of Michigan, Morton of Indiana, and Conkling of New York.

its governement. The politicians, from senator to lowly clerk, often were eager to be corrupted. Officeholders sought ingenious ways to extract more monies from the railroad builders and other industrialists. When a few capitalists came into competition with each other, as when Cornelius Vanderbilt, Jay Gould, and Jim Fiske fought over the Erie Railroad of New York state, the rates of legislative bribes and of "staying bought" rose sharply.

The Rise of the State Machines

The "Boss-Senators" system was not as efficient as it might have been. The state organization had to depend on the ups and downs of its leader in the U.S. Senate and on his political skills. When a leading senator retired or died, the process of building an organization had to start all over again.

In the late 1880s "a better system," that is, a more efficient one—what we call a machine—developed in a number of states. A brief description of the Republican "outstate" machine organized by Thomas Platt of New York gives us an insight of how machines worked and why they so infuriated the Progressive reformers of the early 1900's.

The Platt Machine of New York. In the late 1870s Platt was a small town legislator who had worked his way up in the New York state Republican organization to being elected by the New York state legislature to the U.S. Senate. His Republican colleague and political ally, Senator Roscoe Conkling, got into a fight with President James Garfield. In a show of defiance Conkling resigned his Senate seat. He assumed the New York state legislature would promptly reelect him. Platt reluctantly did the same. As Platt waited around Albany for the state legislature to reappoint him to the U.S. Senate, he, a rural politician from Tioga county, described as a "pious churchgoer and *paterfamilias*," was dealt a low political blow. Political enemies put a stepladder up to the transom of his hotel room. They then tiptoed up it in stocking feet to peer in. What they told reporters they saw was "an unspeakable female" in the arms of the former U.S. senator. Platt withdrew from the Senate race an embittered man, without immediate ambition for, or hope of, attaining elective office.[5]

Platt, after a short time, decided to get even with his enemies by using his political talents to reorganize the New York Republican party. He would not hold elective office, however, as the boss senators had.

[5]Josephson, Op. cit., 314–315

Platt found that the old style organization built around U.S. senators was inefficient in many ways. Job holders, who had paid to get their office, often acted as if they owned the office and paid no attention to party leaders thereafter. Their greed in shaking down bankers and railroad magnates led to scandals, bad publicity for the Republican party, and further independence from the party organization. At the same time Platt thought the capitalists wasted a great deal of money because they did not know enough to bribe the "right" people.

The "New" organization. Platt's goal was to make the party both self-supporting and a centralized organization that operated without friction under his direction. He seems to have personally admired the capitalist entrepreneurs, and regarded the job of helping to smooth their way as a useful public service. Platt eliminated or sharply cut back the assessments of officeholders and, instead, turned directly to the capitalists for funds. He sought regular annual payments, made *before* the legislature went into session. He thus acted as a kind of political consultant who was paid a retainer fee to guarantee that everything went well. Capitalists were spared the bother of trying to lobby and bribe every time something came up that affected them. They need only tell their problems to Mr. Platt. The Boss would "fix it."

The funds Platt collected from industrialists went into a war chest handled by Platt, as head of the Republican state central committee. Boss Platt carefully doled out these funds just as he doled out community, state, and federal patronage. In each house of the legislature were a half-dozen or so trusted leaders who received the bulk of the funds allocated to the legislature. They, in turn, would parcel out funds to their fellow legislators as the need arose. With the patronage jobs, Platt carefully controlled the party nominating conventions and the state and local election machinery. He also became adept at "balancing the ticket" among varied racial, religious, ethnic, and regional groupings. And on election day he hired farmers to use their teams of horses to drive voters to the polls. Other votes were bought by renting, at generous rates, local stores for polling places. Newspaper editors also had a share in the rewards—they took money for "advertising," or else Platt appointed editors to state jobs with fine salaries and minimal duties. Platt regularly sent out "boiler plate" news stories about the party organization and its candidates to rural weeklies. Most were printed. Added to all this careful organization was Platt's single-minded interest in New York State politics—he carefully built coalitions with community leaders and promising candidates until few would act without consulting him.

The journalist William Allen White called Platt "The Blind Earthworm in Politics." Platt's family life was over. He had few friends out of politics. For twenty years he spent all his waking hours in hotel lobbies, endlessly discussing with his lieutenants the details of local races, the punishment of party dissidents, the recruiting of prospective candidates, bills in the legislature, and any other political matter, great or small, that mattered to Republicans in the state of New York or their capitalist allies.[6]

The Progressives Reform State and Community Parties

The turn-of-the-century Progressives faced bosses and machines that were both corrupt and efficient, and they set out to smash them. As with many social movements, they succeeded rather quickly and perhaps too thoroughly.

How the Progressive Reforms Changed Political Parties. The three most telling reforms were (1) to take from party officials and active participants the power to organize the party as they wished, (2) also to take from them the power to select the party candidates for office, and (3) to make many local elections non-partisan. All, as we discuss next, further weakened and decentralized American political parties.

HOW AMERICAN PARTIES ARE ORGANIZED

The textbook organization chart of an American political party shows, in boxes at the top, the national chairperson, national committee, and national convention. Lines are drawn down to the state organization with their chairpersons, committees, and conventions. At the bottom are the congressional district, county, city, ward, and precinct boxes. The chart suggests a neat and bureaucratic organization—one in which the political party "generals" at the top make policies and send the orders down to the political party "privates" at the bottom levels. The chart understates the variety among party units as well as the fragmenting of power.

[6]The details of the Platt machine were lovingly described by one of the first "modern" political scientists by Harold F. Gosnell in *Boss Platt and His New York Machine*, University of Chicago Press, Chicago, 1924. See especially 334–349. See also William Allen White, *Masks in a Pageant*, Macmillan, New York; 1928, 30–69.

Variations in Party Structure

The federal system allows the states to write the laws on party organization. Thus we have considerable variation within the same major party.

All states have state chairpersons, state committees, and conventions. Most, but not all, have county organizations of some sort. But from that point on they differ, both in the units that are organized, the names given them, and the number of officers and members of party committees and how they are selected. In North Carolina, for example, the Democratic party is headed by a State Democratic Executive Committee of two hundred and nine members, and the Republican party by a Republican State Central Committee of twenty-four members. In most states the state committee is usually called the state central committee. If it is large, it designates a smaller number of its members as the state executive committee. In 1966 the numbers of state central committees varied from fourteen in Iowa to 972 for California Democrats and 1262 for California Republicans.[7]

State parties differ in how they represent women. The common pattern after women received the vote in 1917 was simply to add an equal number of women at each level, that is, chariman and chairwoman and vice-chairman or vice-chairwoman. In a few states, we find, however, that only one chairperson held office and that that person might be a man or a woman.

Who Runs the Party Organization? We find two theories of who should run a party organization—the professional politicians or those V.O. Key, Jr. called "the party in the electorate."

Control by organization leaders and candidates. E.E. Schattschneider argued that a party should be run by the professional politicians—political scientists call it "the responsible party theory."[8] This group, he argued, should choose the party leaders and candidates and take the major positions on issues and then appeal to the rest of the electorate to support the party. They can thus be held responsible for what the party and its candidates do. Most minor parties are so organized.

---

[7]National Municipal League, *State Party Structures and Procedures, A State-By-State Compendium*, National Municipal League, New York, 1967. No unit publishes an annual or bienniel compilation of state party organizations, such as *The Book of the States* does for government organization of the states. This compilation is the most recent we are aware of.

[8]E.E. Schattschneider, *Party Government*, Rinehart and Co., New York, 1942.

What control by professional politicians meant to progressive reformers was a tight-knit party oligarchy who could do as they pleased —especially in one party states.

Control by the party in the electorate. The Progressive reformers argued, however, that each major party is a public organization which belongs to all of the citizens—Republicans, Democrats, Independents, and so forth. Thus the parties should be open to all who want to put in their two cents, even if they plan to vote for another party nominee for governor in November, or even if they contribute funds to another party's campaign. Such activity should not stop that person from helping select party precinct officials or from voting in party primaries. We recall meeting a distinguished political scientist for the first time when that able person served as an elected delegate to the Republican and Democratic state conventions in the same year. He appeared to have subscribed to the "party in the electorate" theory.

What control by the party in the electorate means is that a political party may have to accept as members and as officers and candidates people who fight the party leaders, refuse to pay any attention to the party platform, and who may on occasion endorse, work, and vote for candidates who are running on the opposition party ticket.

Which theory do American parties follow? Practice varies from state to state. At present our parties are a mixture with the balance perhaps tilted toward the party in the electorate theory of party membership— almost anyone who wishes can participate in party affairs, including helping choose their precinct officials or their candidates. But it appears that the long-term trend may be in the opposite direction, although our parties have a long way to go before they will be controlled by professional politicians. The party leadership of both major parties at state, community, and national levels is struggling to take greater control of their organization, to discipline party officeholders who stray, and to make the organization more consistent on the issues and the candidates it supports. Policy Box No. 25, "New Mexicans Choose Their Party Candidates," is a description of how one state organization is wrestling with this problem.

How party organization leaders are chosen. Legally the key to party leadership begins at the bottom. We find that states vary as to whether the offices and committees at the lower levels are filled in a public meeting (called a *caucus* or, in some states, a *mass meeting*), or by an election that is held at the same time as a regularly scheduled state-

POLICY BOX NO. 25
New Mexicans Choose Their Party Candidates

In New Mexico you must register your party preference in February to vote in primaries held in June. But this rule is complicated by the fact that New Mexico, like most states today, is a state in transition—economically, socially, and politically. Registration is overwhelmingly Democratic—in 1974, 64.5 percent Democratic, 29.3 percent Republican, and 6.2 percent minor party or no preference. Yet some state and federal races are more competitive than these figures suggest. Democrats control most local offices and have substantial majorities in the state legislature. Given the split ticket voting in some major races, the officials and workers of the Democratic party may question whether those who vote in their primaries are really representative of their regular supporters.

Until 1938 the major parties were required by state law to nominate by party convention. Being a state with widely separated cities and having generally high unemployment, patronage jobs with the government were prized and formed the staple for political trades within the dominant Democratic party. The state party convention permitted balancing the ticket between the Spanish speaking and English, and between Bernalillo County (Albuquerque) and the other two-thirds of the state's population.

This system was changed when a Democratic governor and the state party chairperson fought for control of the party—the governor in 1940 pushed a direct primary law through the legislature.

The primary severely handicapped the ticket balancing between areas—40 percent of the state's Republicans, for example, lived in Bernalillo County and were quite influential in its primaries. The primary also made the balance of the ticket between the Spanish- and English-speaking candidates more difficult. The Spanish-Americans are a minority and in statewide races sometimes were completely swept off the ticket. Less ethical politicans might, indeed, attempt to split their primary votes by entering a variety of candidates with Spanish-sounding names. The turnout in primaries varied according to their competitiveness with turnout between 25 percent to 50 percent of the party's general election vote.

Thus in 1949 the state instituted a preprimary nominating convention. Only those who received 25 percent or more of the convention votes could run in the primary. Party leaders would exercise greater control of the choices—indeed, if they could persuade candidates to withdraw or encourage party members to cast a near unanimous ballot at the convention, they chose the nominee. This system lasted through 1954. From 1956 through 1962 the direct primary was tried again; from 1964 to 1966, preprimary conventions; from 1968 through 1974, the direct primary; and in 1976 a different form of preprimary convention—one that only applied to statewide and congressional races. The new rules required a candidate to collect signatures equal to 1 percent of his or her party's last gubernatorial primary vote and file them in advance with the secretary of state. At the party convention only these could be voted on. The convention would vote only once. Every candidate who received 20 percent or more of the convention votes on that ballot would automatically be listed on the primary ballot in order of votes received. But the others who received less than 20 percent could also get in the primary if they could collect signatures equal to 3 percent of the party's last primary vote.

And so New Mexico tries to balance the influence of party workers with that of the party in the electorate and strives to achieve a reasonable system of balance among minority and majority ethnic group candidates. The convention endorsement systems emphasize the influence of party activists and will result in more tickets balanced between important groups and in candidates with a history of party activity. The primary will emphasize citizen input. The newest system attempts to compromise the other two basic methods.

What do you think? Which of the three or four systems described above is preferable as far as you are concerned? Why? Should a party try to balance its ticket with various geographic and ethnic groups, or only represent the wishes of the majority? Is a primary without endorsement likely to seriously weaken a party? Does a convention, even one that only endorses, tend to become a closed corporation that keeps out potentially attractive candidates? Which of the systems do you think is more democratic?

SOURCE: Paul Hain, "Voters, Elections and Political Parties," in F. Chris Garcia and Paul L. Hain (eds.), *New Mexico Government*, University of New Mexico Press, Albuquerque, 1976, 201–218.

wide vote in a primary election. In either case whichever citizens wish to may participate. In practice party caucuses are often poorly attended, and party leader elections attract few voters. But the potential exists for upsets of party leaders, particularly in presidential election years.

The precinct, township, or other small unit leaders who are elected then meet and, in turn, choose delegates to the next level up, and so on in the organization. The state party chairperson is officially elected by the state party convention, but the delegates often ratify the governor's choice when he or she is of their party, or sometimes the choice of a U.S. senator or group of important party leaders.

But one major variation is found in about half the states that reasserts the party in the electorate approach—delegates to national party conventions in all or in part are elected in state presidential primaries. Again, however, the nominees are often persons who have long been active in the party organization. In the other states each congressional district organization selects delegates with some "at large" seats reserved for prominent party officials and organizational leaders.

The Fragmenting of Organizational Power

The party organizational charts are misleading because they suggest a centralized military-type bureaucracy but, as we noted, this is not true. Units at the bottom may, in fact, be more powerful than those at higher levels.

The Importance of Local Party Units.   The basic organizational unit of the national parties is the state and in most state parties it is the county. In some instances, one or more city organizations fulfill this role. In many ways, a state party organization is like a gathering of local chieftains just as the national organization takes on the characteristics of a "pow-wow" of state chieftains.

The federal system encourages this decentralization of party organizations. The special political value of the state and county candidates and party officials makes them the crucial "building blocks" of it. The county unit has important political connections in many directions. State legislators have county ties. Delegations at congressional district and state conventions are frequently seated by county.

The county organization also tends to act as a unit in state affairs just as the state unit does at national conventions. Whenever possible the county leaders bargain support in return for favors. When a state organization has considerable patronage to dispense, a significant share is actually handled by the county leaders. In addition county organizations also may dispense local patronage. This organizational strength of lower level party units leads to disunity within the national political party.

State Parties Defy the National Leadership.   In 1948 the Alabama Democratic party refused to put Harry S. Truman on the Alabama ballot at all, and three other states, South Carolina, Louisiana, and Mississippi listed J. Strom Thurmond, then Democratic governor of South Carolina and the nominee of the State Rights party, as the Democratic party nominee for president. (Thurmond later switched to the Republican Party while a U.S. senator from South Carolina.) By action of the official Democratic party organization of Alabama, the nominee for president chosen by the Democratic National Convention, Harry S. Truman, got exactly zero popular and electoral votes from Alabama in 1948. If a few more state Democratic party organizations in the South had so sabotaged the national party candidate, Harry Truman would have lost the election. That is about as extreme a form of party fragmentation of power as we can imagine.

National Units Sabotage State Efforts.   The process can also work in reverse. A recent study of southern politics describes how Mississippi

Republicans in 1972 recruited an attractive young businessman, Gil Carmichael, to run against Democratic Senator James Eastland. President Richard Nixon, although a Republican, had worked closely with Senator Eastland in Washington and appears to have wanted him reelected, even though Eastland was a Democrat. The White House sent two Republican cabinet members to appear with Eastland on the campaign trail and when Vice President Spiro Agnew, then a hero in Mississippi, spoke in the state, national Republican leaders directed that the Republican candidate for U.S. senator, Gil Carmichael, would not be permitted on the speaker's platform along with other Republicans. In the election Carmichael won 42 percent of the major party vote, and later in 1975 narrowly lost the race for governor, suggesting that he was a viable choice.[9]

When Republican party units can defy the rest of the party and will not support other Republicans, or when Democrats will not support other Democrats, we can accurately describe the party organizations as weak and splintered, despite what the organization chart suggests. We see further splintering in the way our parties carry out nominal party functions—choosing candidates, campaigning, and governing when they win office.

A Local Party Unit Drags Its Feet.   A less extreme form of opposition, but one still effective, is for state or community organizations to do little or nothing for the national nominee. The late Mayor Richard Daley of Chicago, whose local organization was usually described as a machine, "sat on his hands" in the presidential campaign of George McGovern after delegates to the Democratic national convention of 1972 had refused to seat the Daley delegation.

WHO CHOOSES THE PARTY CANDIDATES?

The most important activity for those who work in the parties is the nomination of candidates. When you begin to understand this, all other features of the major parties begin to sort themselves out.

Why Party Nominations Are So Important

The major parties screen out candidates for voters who do not have the time or energy to do it for themselves. Party labels thus cut information costs for average citizens. Research on nonpartisan elections reveals that without the cut the party gives, a good many voters get confused.

[9]Jack Bass and Walter DeVries, *The Transformation of Southern Politics*, Basic Books, New York, 1976, p. 215.

They vote for Republicans under the impression that they are Democrats or vice versa, and some skip voting entirely because they do not know whom to support.

The party label is not, of course, a "foolproof" guide. As V.O. Key observed, "Often the voter who marks a straight party ballot will be voting against himself at least part of the time."[10] Some candidates turn out to be very untypical of the rest of their party on the issues they support. Reformers have pointed out also that straight ticket voters have elected convicted felons and party hacks. Many a fine candidate has seen her or his hopes blighted only because he or she was a nominee of the weaker party. But the fact remains that all of us, even the most "independent voters," use party as a guide some of the time, and a good many average citizens appear to be guided by party a good deal of the time.

The nomination is thus the most valuable political resource the major party organization has. Minor parties, handicapped often by state law and by public indifference, have relatively unimportant nominations. Either the Democratic candidate or his or her Republican opponent is going to fill the state or community office at issue—and all politicians and most of the voters know it.

How Major Candidates Are Nominated

At one time the state political parties, then largely considered private organizations, nominated their candidates at conventions according to their own rules just as presidential nominations are still made. Now, in all but a few states, most major parties nominate their candidates at a regularly scheduled primary election that is provided by state law. The state pays for it, the state elections office supervises it, and the community units of government conduct it.

The Open Primary.   In nine states, located generally along the Canadian border from Michigan to Oregon, selection is made in what is called an open primary.

In an open primary the voters get a primary ballot for all parties, but each voter may vote in only one party. Importantly, though, the voter selects the party ballot in the privacy of the voting booth. Democrats can vote in the Republican primary and vice versa. Following what we have called the party in the electorate theory, voters need not declare their party. Party leaders object that the open primary permits independents and members of the other party to vote to select their party

---

[10]V.O. Key, Jr., *American State Politics, an Introduction,* Knopf, New York, 1956, p. 15.

nominee. In 1972 and 1976 the national Democratic party urged state parties to work for abandonment of open primaries.

The blanket primary.   Washington and Alaska carry the process one step further. Their open primary is called a blanket primary or jungle primary. Voters are given a ballot (jokesters immediately compared it to the size of a blanket) that contains the primary ballots of all parties. They may only vote once *for each office*, but may pick and choose among the parties and their candidates as they go from office to office down the ballot. Thus citizens may vote in the Republican primary to choose a nominee for governor and may be encouraged to do so if only one candidate has filed in the Democratic primary and a hot race is going on in the Republican primary. They may then return to vote in the Democratic primary in say the lieutenant governor race, and so on down the tickets.

The Closed Primary.   The rest of the states have closed primaries. The voters must either register their particular party choice in advance or declare their party membership at the time of voting and risk being challenged by a party worker. Challenges are usually rare but the threat is supposed to discourage crossover raiding. Voters are given only the ballot of their party in the primary.

The Runoff Primary.   A few states with one party dominance hold a runoff election between the top two candidates if the leading candidate does not get a majority of the votes cast in the first primary. The one party South developed the runoff.

Primaries at the Community Level.   Many county and township, and some city, primaries are partisan and the community then selects local nominees by whatever form of primary is used in the state.

In nonpartisan elections, found in many cities and school board elections, candidates are listed on one ballot, sometimes alphabetically but more often rotated so no one candidate is always on top. The voters then screen the potential nominees down to twice the number for each office to be filled—for example, if ten file for mayor, the two receiving the largest number of votes run against each other at the general election.

Alternatives to the Primary.   Only a few states or communities give the party organization more power in selecting nominees. Such rules are vestiges of the older system that have not quite disappeared. Here are some examples. Minor parties generally select candidates in a convention—this is also true of the Republican party in several southern states. Indiana has nominations for all state offices by convention. The party delegates use voting machines provided by the state. Virginia party organizations may themselves decide whether to nominate by primary or state convention. Michigan nominates candidates for top judicial and educational offices and the lieutenant governor at a state convention. New York and Rhode Island allow the state central committee to designate nominees, but these may be challenged in the primary. Party designees for major offices in New York have frequently lost to primary challengers in recent years. Connecticut allows any candidate who loses at the state convention, but who has received more than 20 percent of the delegate votes, to challenge the victor in a primary. Although adopted in 1955, only recently have there been successful challenges. Finally a few states, such as Colorado, New Mexico, and Minnesota, allow state conventions to designate their choices. These are sometimes starred on the primary election ballot and are thus highlighted for loyal party voters.

Extralegal Party Organizations.   Sometimes active party workers have followed the unusual practice of organizing private groups that hold conventions or, through executive committees, endorse candidates in their own party's primaries. This heads off "raiding" by members of the other party, but it is also used when the party organization is divided into two bitterly opposed factions. These organizations seem most likely to appear in one-party states.[11]

The California Republican Assembly, among the first such groups, entered Republican primaries in 1933 and endorsed liberal Republicans. Between 1940 and 1962 the CRA was able to take over the Republican party and, through it, dominate state politics. Conservative Republicans then formed the United Republicans of California (UROC) to back Barry Goldwater for president and conservative Republicans in state and community primaries. Liberal Democrats in 1953 formed the California Democratic Council (CDC), and moderates, the Democratic Volunteers of California (DVC). Such organizations have also flourished for a time in Wisconsin, Illinois, and North Dakota, but have since waned in importance.

We also find such groups at the community level where primaries are nonpartisan. They may take on a special name as "Citizen Action"

---

[11]See James Q. Wilson, *The Amateur Democrat, Club Politics in Three Cities*, University of Chicago Press, Chicago, 1962; Francis Carney, *The Rise of the Democratic Clubs in California*, Henry Holt, New York, 1958; and John Owens, Edmond Costantini, and Louis Wechsler, *California Politics and Parties*, The Macmillan Co., New York, 1970.

or may, as is true in Chicago, be regular party organizations that endorse council candidates in a nonpartisan election.

Party Organization Influence in Choosing Candidates

The major political party organizations can no longer be absolutely certain that they control the nomination of candidates who run under their banner. A bit of Kentucky political history illustrates how a primary may cause an "upset." In 1935 Albert Benjamin "Happy" Chandler served as lieutenant governor under Governor Ruby Laffoon. The governor, through his patronage, controlled the state party convention that would nominate his successor. Governor Laffoon's choice was the director of his highway commission—Thomas S. Rhea. But Governor Laffoon made a mistake; he left the state temporarily to consult with President Franklin Roosevelt on Kentucky problems. As acting governor, "Happy" Chandler at once called the legislature into special session and asked them to pass a primary law and throw out the convention method. To cut a long story short, they did. Chandler, in a tub-thumping campaign, won the primary, then the election. In 1937 he became governor of Kentucky at age 38. Party regulars could only grit their teeth.[12]

Chandler, as his nickname "Happy" suggests, was a dynamic campaigner. As has happened many times in the past, such a candidate can overwhelm the campaign of lackadaisical precinct captains or a less colorful candidate. Modern media techniques, especially radio and television, increase the likelihood of such upsets of the organization-picked candidate.

Why the Organization Usually Controls the Primary. Party leaders have discovered that they are not always helpless in influencing the outcomes of primaries. Sometimes they need not act because all announced candidates are acceptable. But, often, the party leaders quietly build up support for candidates long before the primary by giving them publicity and by acting as if their nomination were self-evident. Incumbent governors or party leaders may then give their public blessing, thus discouraging primary opposition. They may even run "dummy" candidates with similar ethnic names to split the vote of "unknowns."

[12]For a full description of this incident, see Jasper B. Shannon, " 'Happy' Chandler: A Kentucky Epic," in J.T. Salter (ed.), *The American Politician*, University of North Carolina Press, Chapel Hill, 1938.

But the basic strength of the party leaders is that usually less than 30 percent of the electorate vote in primaries—perhaps less than 15 percent in their party. The small turnout maximizes their "bloc" vote. In one way or another the party leaders pass the word on to the organization about who the favored candidates are. Party workers and their families and some of their friends vote *in every primary election* and are seldom confused about the party organization's choice.[13]

Party Factionalism. The ability of the party organization to influence the outcome of primaries depends on an additional factor: how united it is. The most colorful "outsider" had little or no chance against the Daley machine of Chicago in its heyday. Other party organizations have been as weak as the New York state Democratic party, which has lost a series of primaries to candidates who challenged the endorsed candidates.

The clue to this strength or weakness is found in how much party leaders are fighting each other. The factional configuration within each state varies at any given moment, but what infighting exists often determines who will win the primary.

V.O. Key, Jr., described three major kinds of factionalism in his analysis of the one-party states of the South.[14] The same patterns appear in competitive two-party states and in local races.

Chaotic multifactionalism. In Florida primaries Key found that a number of candidates competed with each other and the winner seldom got more than a third of the votes. Candidates had to find their own supporters and there was little continuity between the winning coalition formed in one election and that in the next primary election. Personal ties were important, particularly those Key described as support by "friends and neighbors." A candidate's major base of support was likely to be his or her home county.

Many local races, particularly those with nonpartisan elections, are of this type.

[13]The author of a recent study of Virginia's primary between 1905 and 1970 presents data to demonstrate that, rather than promoting participatory democracy, Virginia's primary, combined with a restrictive suffrage, helped the Democratic organization establish machine control and that the decline of the Democratic primary, as insuring election, coincided with the decline of the machine—a fact, that he argues, is not coincidental. Larry Sabato, *The Democratic Party Primary in Virginia, Tantamount to Election No Longer*, University of Virginia Press, Charlottesville, 1977.

[14]V.O. Key Jr., *Southern Politics in State and Nation*, Knopf, New York, 1949, Chapter 14, "Nature and Consequences of the Party Factionalism," 298–311.

Bifactionalism. In other states, Key found two power blocs of party activists who, over the years, competed with each other for party nominations. Key applied two tests to indicate such bifactional competition. In most of the state primaries over a generation, (1) the two top candidates would divide most of the votes, and (2) neither of them would ever get more than 50 percent of the total vote in a primary election.

The factions might be based on geographic splits. The Platte River split Nebraska Republican party politics into north and south for many years. In Arizona it was urban Maricopa County (Phoenix) against the rest of Arizona. Jack Bass and Walter DeVries detail how, in recent years, a coalition of blacks, union members, and neopopulists have faced off against older style, conservative, and even racist Democrats in such states as Mississippi and South Carolina.[15]

The bifactional split might be built around a dominant candidate, as in the Democratic party in Minnesota where the associates of Hubert Humphrey, especially those living in the University of Minnesota community, were once known as "the Palace Guard" by their less well organized factional opposition. The conflicts may be class or ethnic based or those between business and labor. Michigan Republicans for a time had factions based on Ford Motor Company's strength in Detroit and General Motors' strength in the suburbs. Fittingly, perhaps, George Romney of American Motors united the factions in the early 1960s to make his successful race for governor. The bifactional competition may even be based on national party divisions, such as those in the 1970s in the Republican party between the Goldwater–Reagan faction and the more moderate Ford–Rockefeller faction. Malcolm Jewell and Everett Cunningham found perhaps the most basic division in Kentucky Democratic politics—they argued for many years that the basic difference was between those holding office and those wanting office.[16]

Again some community elections follow similar bifactional patterns based on a mixture of class, geographic area, or local leaders. This is especially true in cities dominated by a single political party.

Dominant unifactionalism. This pattern is relatively rare in American states or communities. It requires that a single group dominate the political party and be able, in effect, to select its nominees in election after election. Under such conditions usually one candidate gets a sub-

[15]Jack Bass and Walter DeVries, *The Transformation of Southern Politics, Social Change and Political Consequence Since 1945,* Basic Books, New York, 1976.

[16]Malcolm Jewell and Everett Cunningham, *Kentucky Politics,* University of Kentucky Press, Lexington, 1968. Chapter 4, "Democratic Factionalism," 131–178.

stantial majority of the primary votes with only token opposition. V.O. Key found such a pattern in Virginia where the organization of Senator Harry Byrd effectively managed the Democratic party from the middle 1920s through the middle 1950s. In that case the party held power by disenfranchising a large number of black and poor white citizens through the poll tax. It also disciplined party actives through a state compensation board that determined the annual salaries and set expense budgets for most county and city officials, including commonwealth attorneys, sheriffs, and tax collectors. As James Reichley dryly observed, such power over local officials did much to "cement the bonds of loyalty."[17]

Such control has also been characteristic of local elections in Chicago and Albany, New York, but is also found in some small towns where a tightly knit political elite still controls the community.

The Impact of Party Factionalism.   From the studies of party battles and factionalism within several states, three generalizations emerge: (1) Factionalism is not the exception within party organizations; it is normal to have intraparty conflict. (2) When two-party competition becomes strong within a state or district, factions within a party tend to unite—generally behind moderate candidates. If they do not a bruising primary may make the nomination worthless because a part of the party organization may sulk and refuse to support the winner, "stay home" on election day, or even worse, may work for the opposition. (3) Factional alignments seldom last for more than a generation or so.

In looking at your own state you can make some assessment of how strong the parties are by how well they control the nominations. Do the primaries have two or many more major candidates? What kind of factionalism exists? Does one faction generally win most races? Are the battles bitter?

RUNNING THE POLITICAL CAMPAIGN

The nomination of a major party is, of course, relatively worthless if that party's nominees seldom or never win any state or local elections, or have little hope of doing so in the future.[18] The state or community

---

[17]James Reichley, *States in Crisis, Politics in Ten American States, 1950–1962*, University of North Carolina Press, Chapel Hill, 1964. Chapter 1, "Virginia: Sense of the Past," 3–23.

[18]We, of course, always find at least a little organizational activity where patronage encourages it, as in minor parties in one party states—in this case, federal patronage used

party may be classed as a "major" party at the national level, but in reality is a "minor" party in the state or in some of its communities. We will begin by noticing how this fact of "having a chance" affects community party organization and campaign activity.

Parties Organize and Campaign Where They Hope To Win

Party leaders sometimes talk as if the party has workers in every county or every city precinct. In fact some communities may have little party organization—the state organization may not even have the address of someone to whom to mail literature. Other communities may be unable to field candidates for the state legislative race or county clerk—few persons enjoy the role of being a "sacrificial lamb" in a hopeless cause.

Organization springs up and flourishes where major party candidates are in a tight race. Look at your own state or community. In districts where major party opposition is weak and the candidate of one major party is a "shoo-in," neither party spends much money campaigning and party workers are few and do very little. The organization is only a skeletal one.

Party Competitiveness.   Political scientists have devised a number of measures to show how competitive states and communities are. The measures usually consist of an average of votes for president, United States senator, and governor over a period of twenty years or so. Comparisons of these averages by party give a rough indication of the chances that the two parties have in any given state, county, or city.

Such measures, we think, present a major difficulty. As Joseph Schlesinger demonstrated, and Table 13-1 confirms, competition is seldom between parties; instead, it varies according to the office at stake. In the South, for example, Republicans have made presidential and some gubernatorial races competitive without being able to capture many state legislative seats. The same is true of Democrats in some western and midwestern states.[19]

to buy support at the national convention. Also we find activity around elected officials who have the power to fill other offices by appointment—for example, the sheriff who appoints deputies or probate judges who appoint the lawyers as administrators of estates. The appointed deputies take no chance of an upset—they work the year-round for their boss.

[19]Joseph A. Schlesinger, "The Structure of Competition For Office in the American States," *Behavioral Science*, 5 July 1960, 197–210.

We adapt for our purposes in Table 13-1, a measure of competition devised by William Flanigan and Nancy Zingale.[20] The measure, based on past results but weighted to favor recent elections, predicts an "expected value" of party strength, combined with a measure of "expected variation" around the predicted party strength value. The variations of results within a state demonstrate how seldom a party organization today can "deliver" for all of its candidates—again, a measure of the weakness of American party organizations.

Methods of Campaigning

The purpose of the campaign is mainly to activate potential supporters and, secondarily, to make converts. Ideally the candidate would campaign by meeting first hand each prospective voter. All other campaign techniques are substitutes for this ideal. Candidates use the other methods because of campaigning costs—they have neither the time nor the energy to meet with every prospective voter or even with their committed supporters. Instead they campaign in two majors ways—using party workers and the mass media to contact voters.

Campaigning Using Party Workers. At one time most campaigning, outside of a few speeches by candidates, was done by the party organization. The precinct captain built up personal relations with the voters *between elections*. He did major and minor favors, passed out jobs, and at election time buttonholed voters on behalf of the whole party ticket. Sometimes the organization also passed out generous globs of what was euphemistically called "election day expenses" for the workers. In less genteel precincts, usually the "river wards" of cities, open buying of votes by the organization was common practice. In rural areas the county courthouse "rings" provided the same types of small favors to local supporters.

This kind of campaigning is less common today. Full-time party workers, who will staff precincts between elections, are difficult to recruit. Patronage jobs to reward them are less plentiful. New laws forbid paying workers to "transport voters to the polls," or other practices that proved very effective in the days of political machines. A few

[20]William H. Flanigan and Nancy H. Zingale, "Measures of Electoral Competition," *Political Methodology*, Fall 1974, 31–60. Flanigan and Zingale rely heavily on the work of two other researchers, David B. Meltz, "An Index of the Measurement of Interparty Competition," *Behavioral Science*, 18:60–63 and Paul J. David, "How Can An Index of Party Competition Best Be Derived," *Journal of Politics*, 34:633–38, and by the same author, *Party Strength in the United States: 1872–1972*, University of Virginia Press, Charlottesville, 1972.

New York City Mayor Ed Koch campaigns one-on-one on Manhattan's East Side.

old style party organizations still exist at the community level, especially in the low-income wards of large cities, but even these seem to be dying out.

Today's campaign workers. The best party organizations can do today is to supply part-time volunteers for the campaign period. The volunteers lack the personal ties to the voters, but they can make telephone calls urging the committed to vote, distribute literature, and do other minor chores. But they fall far short of the efforts of the old style precinct organization.

Interest groups also sometimes supplement party campaign efforts. Businesses may provide highly skilled employees (especially those experienced in public relations work), usually to Republican candidates. Labor unions reward members who work the precincts and advance through the Democratic party organization.

But the most common organizations used today are temporary ones based on the appeal of an attractive candidate (Jim Thompson of Illi-

TABLE 13-1 Competitiveness Scores Using the Flanigan-Zingale Measure

	President	Senator	Governor	State Legislature Senate	State Legislature House
Alabama	Competitive 27	Safe Dem-212	Safe Dem-434	Safe Dem-Infinity	Safe Dem 16667
Alaska	Safe Rep 497	Competitive 44	Competitive 48	Favor Dem 183	Favor Dem 160
Arizona	Safe Rep 298	Competitive 22	Competitive 91	Competitive 60	Safe Dem 254
Arkansas	Competitive 8	Safe Dem 272	Safe Dem 347	Safe Dem-Infinity	Safe Dem 566
California	Favor Rep 104	Favor Dem 69	Competitive 78	Competitive 1	Safe Dem 902
Colorado	Favor Rep 191	Competitive 73	Competitive 8	Favor Rep 179	Competitive 4
Connecticut	Competitive 94	Competitive 1	Competitive 73	Safe Dem 507	Favor Dem 109
Delaware	Competitive 41	Favor Rep 111	Competitive 93	Safe Dem 338	Safe Dem 359
Florida	Competitive 61	Favor Dem 145	Favor Dem 205	Safe Dem 811	Safe Dem 650
Georgia	Competitive 2	Favor Dem 171	Favor Dem 262	Safe Dem 2740	Safe Dem 4948
Hawaii	Competitive 21	Competitive 89	Favor Dem 241	Safe Dem 3200	Safe Dem 719
Idaho	Safe Rep 391	Competitive 71	Favor Dem 136	Safe Rep 436	Safe Rep 392
Illinois	Competitive 94	Competitive 29	Favor Rep 132	Safe Dem 348	Favor Dem 141
Indiana	Favor Rep 142	Competitive 93	Favor Rep 863	Competitive 8	Competitive 38
Iowa	Favor Rep 133	Favor Dem 158	Favor Rep 585	Competitive 50	Safe Dem 220
Kansas	Favor Rep 150	Favor Rep 103	Competitive 88	Favor Rep 200	Competitive 91
Kentucky	Competitive 44	Favor Dem 161	Favor Dem 179	Safe Dem 4703	Safe Dem 7059
Louisiana	Competitive 41	Safe Dem 246	Favor Dem 167	Safe Dem-Infinity	Safe Dem-Infinity
Maine	Competitive 45	Safe Dem 216	Competitive 53	Safe Rep 535	Safe Dem 318
Maryland	Competitive 32	Competitive 28	Safe Dem 252	Safe Dem 3043	Safe Dem 5270
Massachusetts	Safe Dem 276	Competitive 46	Competitive 32	Safe Dem 7700	Safe Dem 4039
Michigan	Competitive 98	Competitive 62	Favor Rep 121	Safe Dem 315	Safe Dem 658
Minnesota	Competitive 73	Safe Dem 286	Favor Dem 174	Safe Dem 301	Safe Dem 720
Mississippi	Competitive 54	Favor Dem 186	Favor Dem 123	Safe Dem-Infinity	Safe Dem 35726
Missouri	Competitive 50	Competitive 1	Competitive 4	Safe Dem 1669	Safe Dem 822
Montana	Favor Rep 196	Favor Dem 174	Favor Dem 275	Competitive 92	Favor Dem 179
Nebraska	Safe Rep 321	Competitive 13	Favor Dem 112	Nonpartisan	Nonpartisan
Nevada	Favor Rep 117	Favor Dem 137	Favor Dem 154	Safe Dem 1300	Safe Dem 514
New Hampshire	Favor Rep 176	Favor Dem 130	Favor Rep 116	Favor Rep 119	Safe Rep 600
New Jersey	Competitive 86	Competitive 17	Competitive 52	Safe Dem-Infinity	Safe Dem 394

(Table 13-1 continued)

	President	Senator	Governor	State Legislature Senate	State Legislature House
New Mexico	Favor Rep 121	Favor Rep 205	Competitive 91	Safe Dem 672	Safe Dem 1218
New York	Competitive 24	Competitive 48	Competitive 23	Safe Rep 506	Safe Dem 299
North Carolina	Competitive 44	Competitive 84	Favor Dem 125	Safe Dem 605	Safe Dem 902
North Dakota	Favor Rep 183	Favor Dem 133	Favor Dem 199	Safe Rep 607	Favor Rep 131
Ohio	Competitive 71	Competitive 76	Competitive 7	Safe Dem 440	Safe Dem 922
Oklahoma	Competitive 91	Favor Rep 176	Favor Dem 107	Safe Dem 8843	Safe Dem 2004
Oregon	Favor Rep 112	Safe Dem 352	Competitive 24	Safe Dem 630	Safe Dem 580
Pennsylvania	Competitive 37	Safe Rep 726	Favor Dem 160	Safe Dem 538	Safe Dem 287
Rhode Island	Competitive 73	Competitive 7	Favor Dem 103	Safe Dem 1036	Safe Dem 1749
South Carolina	Competitive 38	Competitive 49	Competitive 64	Safe Dem 4021	Safe Dem 2057
South Dakota	Favor Rep 176	Favor Dem 363	Favor Dem 198	Competitive 94	Favor Rep 180
Tennessee	Competitive 35	Competitive 45	Competitive 85	Safe Dem 457	Safe Dem 436
Texas	Competitive 52	Competitive 51	Favor Dem 168	Safe Dem-Infinity	Safe Dem 7006
Utah	Safe Rep 404	Competitive 87	Favor Dem 195	Favor Dem 116	Competitive 48
Vermont	Safe Rep 205	Competitive 78	Competitive 14	Safe Rep 322	Favor Rep 140
Virginia	Competitive 91	Competitive 71	Favor Rep 280	Safe Dem 8900	Safe Dem 3339
Washington	Competitive 94	Safe Dem 294	Competitive 1	Safe Dem 3300	Safe Dem 1465
West Virginia	Competitive 2	Safe Dem 270	Competitive 84	Safe Dem 965	Safe Dem 520
Wisconsin	Competitive 63	Safe Dem 420	Favor Dem 199	Favor Dem 191	Safe Dem 1280
Wyoming	Safe Rep 277	Competitive 84	Competitive 27	Favor Rep 137	Favor Rep 176

METHODOLOGICAL NOTE: The figures in this table have been reported as whole numbers rather than decimals—that is, they have been multiplied by 100. State legislative results are in terms of seats won rather than percentage votes for individual races. Our data include three elections weighted as 3-2-1 with the most recent weighted 3. We treated major party votes only rather than attempting to allocate minor party votes between major party candidates. Our choice inflates the competitive index.

The categories presented in the table are our own—the Flanigan-Zingale data were adapted to our categories as follows: 0–100 = competitive; 101–200 = favors one party; and 200 or over = safe for one party.

We wish especially to thank William Boyd of the University of Wisconsin-Milwaukee for his advice and aid in making these calculations as well as William Flanigan of the University of Minnesota and Nancy Zingale of the College of St. Thomas for their advice and aid in applying their measure.

nois in 1976 or the candidates for most community offices), or by appeal to ideology (The John Birch Society or the anti-Vietnam crusaders of the recent past, or the ecologists of today). Such workers are mainly recruited from those who have free time—college students, personal friends, or the often ridiculed "little old ladies in blue tennis shoes." No one else seems to have the time or can be moved by emotional appeals to aid campaign organizations without being paid in cold cash to do so.

The usefulness of campaigning through organizations. Organizational support today is spotty and only partially successful in most states and communities. Candidates can no longer depend, even during the campaign, on the party organization to field a worker in every precinct or even every ward. The candidates thus try to recruit their own workers and, if the race seems exciting and the candidates exciting, they sometimes succeed.

Whatever organized help the party can provide, of course, is welcome, since few candidates can do without some organizational help or can afford to purchase the time of every campaign worker they need.

Campaigning with the Media. Most candidates for major state or community office today are convinced that to win they must spend money on a media campaign—especially, expensive television time. Challengers without this media coverage will remain relatively unknown—incumbents need it to remind the voters of their assets and their work for them. Even in community races for lesser offices, getting known requires some type of media campaign, although newspaper advertisements and lawn signs are more appropriate than television for these races.

The first modern media campaign. During the depression days of 1934 in California the Socialist novelist Upton Sinclair (author of *The Jungle* and the eleven-volume Lanny Budd series) captured the Democratic party nomination for governor. He launched a campaign called EPIC, which stood for "End Poverty in California." To combat his "radicalism," the Republicans hired an advertising agency. The agency sent movie camera operators out to the depression "shanty towns" and "hobo jungles." As the cameras ground away, interviewers asked: "Who are you supporting for governor?" Many of the poorly dressed, unshaven drifters answered, "Upton Sinclair!" Obligingly, some kicked aside old beer, wine, or whiskey bottles or scratched themselves in embarrassing places, as they pledged their efforts to the Democratic candidate.

Another set of responses was collected from the attractive kind of middle-class citizens we almost always see on TV nowadays. Some, when asked who they supported, answered the name of the Republican candidate. The ad agency kept these responses as "takes." The footage then went to editing and cutting and the moviemakers prepared several short feature films. These movies, shown in theaters, displayed a simple message in documentary form without advertising or other comment. The "bums" were for Upton Sinclair, the "straight arrows" for his opponent. Those who saw the films thought them extremely effective, including the losing candidate, Upton Sinclair, and his supporters.

As with so many other things, good and bad, California had introduced the modern media campaign to America. By the 1960s and early 1970s almost every statewide candidate who had a chance of winning, and many in community races as well, hired media firms.

What campaign media firms do. Whitaker and Baxter, a husband and wife team and the first campaign consulting firm, merchandised candidates just as if they were Ivory soap. They argued that the amateurs who staffed the party organization wasted funds and effort. Workers did not show up, money was put into literature that was never distributed, and candidates wasted their time at meetings that were poorly publicized. The campaign media firm, however, knew how to budget funds and the candidate's time for maximum effect. Their advertising agency skills helped them in finding the best media outlets per dollar.

The media firms also pointed out that party regulars often misinterpreted the public mood. Whitaker and Baxter promised to "package" the candidate—that is, create a favorable image to project. Public opinion polling was in its infancy, but they used it to figure out what issues the candidate should stress and what the voters disliked or liked about the candidate. Style was stressed over content—catchy slogans, short "spot" announcements, a television personality that exuded sincerity, a winning smile.

The Michigan campaign of 1970. Walter DeVries described in detail how his firm helped William Milliken win reelection as governor of Michigan in 1970 in what was a generally Democratic year.[21] The firm concentrated on independent, ticket-splitting voters. They isolated the precincts in Michigan that in the past had voted for Democratic party legislators, but had supported such moderate Republican candidates

[21]Walter DeVries and V. Lance Farrace, *The Ticket Splitters, A New Force In American Politics*, Wm. B. Erdmans Publishing Co., Grand Rapids, Michigan, 1972.

for governor as George Romney. They found that 80 percent of these voters were concentrated in nineteen of Michigan's eighty-three counties. They decided to spend most of their campaign funds in these nineteen populous counties.

Next the firm analyzed past opinion data to find out what kinds of people these ticket splitters were. They found that such voters were most likely to be people in suburban areas who were high school graduates with some college education, were more likely to be Catholic than Protestant, were between thirty and fifty years of age, and were viewers of television news, documentaries, and sports programs. Finally the firm pretested a few advertising spots they developed by using follow-up phone calls in the nineteen counties. They found that the split-ticket voters did not want to listen to long political discussions. The viewers also distrusted politicians who made promises.

The firm then developed its final series of campaign TV spots. The format developed was one showing Governor Milliken briefly mentioning a problem, such as poor housing conditions. He showed awareness and concern, but made no promises. To emphasize his competence to handle such problems, he was photographed at the governor's desk with flag, paneled walls, and leather chairs. No solutions were discussed. The TV spots stressed the candidate's knowledge and concern, and implied that he would act in some unspecified way to help solve the problem. The campaign slogan was "a leader you can trust." The spots were run during and after the kinds of TV programs that the split-ticket voters liked to watch—sports events and TV news.

The average vote for Republican candidates in Michigan in 1970 was 40 percent. Governor Milliken received 50.4 percent—he was one of two Republican governors elected in midwestern states that year. The media firm could and did take some credit for the victory.

How Modern Campaigning Methods Weaken Political Parties

The old style year-round precinct worker emphasized voting for the complete party ticket from top to bottom. But candidates today who recruit their own campaign workers or use modern media campaigns further weaken American political party organization.

Attractive unknowns, sometimes young millionaires, are tempted to enter primaries to challenge less photogenic candidates whom party regulars may have groomed for an office. And the challengers can win out. Furthermore, the media campaign and the candidate workers funnel money to the candidate instead of to the party. Finally, and probably most important of all, the media campaign encourages the candidates to disassociate their campaigns from those of other nominees of the political party. If they appear as "independent" today, they create "a better image." When candidates sell personality and style, rather than issues, they downplay party positions.

The Impact of Campaign Spending Laws. In recent years a number of states and the national government have passed and are enforcing stricter campaign spending laws for state and community races. A few states now finance campaigns in part, even in primaries.

Most of the state laws follow the federal law and tie the dispersal of funds to the candidates and committees that operate on their behalf, rather than channeling funds through the party organizations. Campaign financing in primaries encourages challenges by candidates with only minimal backing. Thus both types of laws unintentionally encourage further weakening of the party organization in the campaign process or, at the very least, recognize a condition that already exists as the accepted method of campaigning.

THE PARTY IN OFFICE GOVERNS

What happens when most of a political party's candidates win state or community office?

Let us consider something a little less than a "complete sweep." We assume that control of the executive and a majority of both houses of the legislature or of the city council gives a reasonable opportunity for the party to control policymaking.

How Likely Is Party Control? If we look at the data for a ten-year period beginning in 1968, we find that in only eleven states did the same party control the governor's office and the legislature for the entire period.[22] And seven of these were southern and border states— states that are essentially one-party states and where intraparty factionalism really provides the competition. Party control in most states occurs only for brief periods. Roughly 40 percent of the time we find that the major parties divided control of the governorship and the legislature. Following each election in the ten-year period, the number of "divided control" states ranged from eighteen in 1968 to twenty-three in 1972. Thus we see that most states have had a divided government for at least part of the decade.

[22]Alabama, Georgia, Hawaii, Kentucky, Louisiana, Maryland, Mississippi, New Hampshire, New York, Rhode Island, and Texas. Nebraska has a non-partisan legislature as did Minnesota from 1914 to 1971.

Little data exists for communities with partisan elections, but it is probable that similar patterns hold except that a greater percentage of communities than states are prodominately one–party.

Party Leadership by Governors and Mayors

As we discussed in Chapter 8 on governors, American executives are expected to present a legislative program—even when, as is true in many communities, elections are nonpartisan. They also are viewed as leaders of their party or, in nonpartisan communities, of a factional grouping.

Governors invariably, formally or informally, in fact, select the state party chairperson and thus dominate or guide the party organization. They also frequently head the state delegation at their party's national conventions. They are expected to influence the platform devised at state party conventions and dispense patronage through the party organization. Often they are strong enough to choose other nominees that the party will back in the primary, as well sometimes their own successors.

Mayors sometimes exercise a great deal of influence at the community level, but the spread of nonpartisanship has weakened their organizational leadership position. More frequently than not their influence is based on their media attractiveness, rather than organized support of a party unit or a faction.

The Executive's Program.   The "governor's program" usually does not deal with all of the bills that are offered in a legislative session. Most governors select a small number of the total—perhaps less than one hundred fifty—that are "must bills" or "administration bills." Governor's aides pressure party members in the legislature for support.

What kinds of bills then become the "party program?" Not all the bills that come from executive agencies. Even some the governor may approve are not classed as "must bills." The governor may remain neutral or even recommend passage, but not insist that the members of the party support the governor's position on such bills. Researchers find that the "must bills," or actions, tend to be of three types: (1) bills involving taxes or expenditures, (2) appointments that must be confirmed by the senate or both houses, and (3) bills on major social and economic issues, especially those involving welfare and labor or business regulation. We should also add a fourth to this list: bills the governor has vetoed since a vote override is, in effect, a vote of nonconfidence in the governor's leadership.[23]

[23]Sarah P. McCally, "The Governor and His Legislative Party," *American Political Science Review*, 60, December 1966, 923–942.

Does the Governor's Program Get Adopted?   How often does the governor's definition of the party program get accepted in the legislature? In states where each major party has a third or more of the legislative seats (enough to sustain vetoes), the governor's "must bills" tend to split the legislature along party lines with relatively high frequency. The governor's program defines the issues for his or her party members as well as for the opposition. For example a study of the 1965 session in Iowa found that Democratic Governor Harold E. Hughes had one hundred fifty "must bills." Support in the Senate among Democrats was 92 percent and in the House, 86 percent. Republican support in the Senate was 48 percent and 41 percent in the House. The party division is not perfect, but it is still sharply defined. It is likely that many Democratic legislators on occasion buried their own doubts or preferences so as "to support the party and not embarrass our Governor."

What if the elected governors are not typical of their party—if they veer off in what is regarded by many legislators as in a radical or reactionary direction? Researchers find some lessening of party line support, but also find that a substantial number of legislators will, nevertheless, follow the person they regard as head of their party.

Influence in one party and nonpartisan legislatures. As the governor's party increases its margin above 60 percent, Sarah McCally Morehouse found, his or her influence is less; "rivalries are generated which the governor cannot control."[24] A generally one-party state, such as Tennessee, is characterized by such rivalry between governor and leading legislators. The mood almost becomes nonpartisan. Instead of having a majority leader to work with in the legislature, the governor has an "administration leader." This means that governors in such states expect a good deal of opposition or indifference from legislators of their own party. The support coalition the governor builds is not necessarily based on party, but on favors, ideology, or personal friendship. The same patterns exist for mayors where the council is nonpartisan.

Sometimes a minority party governor in generally one-party states wins a surprising victory and is faced by a legislature almost completely of the opposition. Then bipartisan alignments are likely. Thus a Republican governor of South Carolina bargained for support for his program and gained the needed majority from a coalition of Republicans and dissident Democrats.[25] But such coalitions are tenuous and often do not even last out the governor's term.

[24]Sarah P. McCally Morehouse, Ibid., p. 60.

[25]Cited in Malcolm E. Jewell and Samuel C. Patterson, *The Legislative Process in the United States,* 2nd ed., Random House, New York, 1973, p. 457.

What Weakens A Governor's Influence?   Sarah McCally Morehouse found that those governors were least influential with legislators of their party who received less than 70 percent of the vote in trying to get renominated.[26] Effective opposition in a primary (party factionalism) suggests to legislators that a governor is not fully in control of the party and, thereafter, his or her leadership and program are challenged more vigorously by legislators of his or her own party.

The Party in the Legislature

Previously we noted that the party caucuses in two-party states select legislative leaders, but not much is known about how often such caucuses meet to discuss policy issues. The best estimates are that in about half the two-party states caucuses have regular meetings to discuss party positions on key bills. In only a few states is the caucus vote on policies regarded as absolutely binding. In most states we find caucus votes to be guiding—legislators have had a chance to raise questions and even to delay consideration on bills, and so are more likely to go along with the caucus vote.

Party Line Voting.   Party membership is the best predicter we have of how a legislator will vote on any bill. But in many states it is not a very good predictor. Only on questions of organizing the legislature and on votes in which one party gains an advantage over the other is party voting likely to be almost unanimous. [Note even here we hedge by including an "almost."]

Students find wide variation in party-line voting among the states. In general the urban industralized states of the Midwest and Northeast have more party-line votes. So, too, do states with a history of two-party competition. But in each case we find unexplained exceptions.

As we would expect, party-line votes are more likely when most of the district constituencies held by one party are similar in urbanization, ethnic background, or economic level, whereas those held by the opposing party are all distinctly different. Disharmony within parties and the absence of party-line voting is most likely when both major parties represent similar kinds of districts—when both the Democrats and the Republicans hold some rural seats and both hold some urban seats.

Some of the states with a great deal of party-line voting include Connecticut, Pennsylvania, Rhode Island, Massachusetts, New Jersey, and New York. Some with low party-line voting include states with one-party dominance such as Vermont and Kentucky, but also include

---

[26]Morehouse, Op cit., p. 60.

Idaho, Utah, Montana, Missouri, Colorado, and Oregon. In between in party-line voting are states like Ohio, Illinois, Washington, and New Hampshire and, for comparison's sake, the U.S. Congress.

The Prospects for Party Government in the States

We emphasize again the fact that the separation of powers does not invite or encourage party government. It encourages bickering among officals who have earned office in different ways—and especially so between experienced legislators and a newly elected governor who has no legislative experience.

When a measure of party governing does occur, it seems to depend upon a governor who forcefully proposes a program, and a two-party legislature whose party constituencies are distinguishable and homogenous.

It seems to us that many American party organizations will continue to be characterized by a lack of unity after they win office. Governing will not be the result of party platform promises—that is, policy prepared and pushed by one party and opposed by the other. Rather, such divisions will continue on only a few major issues and, perhaps, rise in intensity at certain periods and then subside. Michigan had intense battles in the 1950s when the Democrats led by Governor G. Mennen Williams proposed a graduated income tax that conservative Republicans fought to the bitter end. Each party seemed to act like a monolithic unit under attack. The state for a period of weeks was unable to meet its payrolls because of the stalemate that resulted. But the crisis was resolved in time. In the late 1970s Michigan again has a divided government, generally characterized by an absence of bitterness. Party divisions are important, but no longer "all important." And that is how, we suspect, most states are being governed.

Connecticut—Once A Party Government. Connecticut, under the guidance of Democratic party chairperson John Bailey from 1946 to 1961, probably came as close to having party government as has any state in the union. Its two parties were closely competitive. The Democrats were especially tightly organized. They nominated candidates by party convention. The voting rules made it difficult for voters to avoid voting a straight party ballot. Bailey rode herd daily on Democrats in the legislature on behalf of the Democratic governor. Patronage was used to reward the loyal and punish dissidents.[27]

[27]See Joseph I. Lieberman, *The Power Brokers*, Houghton Mifflin, Boston, 1968. See also a concise description of Connecticut politics under Bailey, in Joyce Gelb and Marian Lief

The party system of governing provided several benefits. Citizens knew that a vote for Democrats meant one kind of policy and a vote for Republicans meant something different. Campaign platforms and speeches had meaning. But the party system was not altogether cost-less for the average citizen. The access to state legislators was not as easy as in a more disorganized state—lobbying was through the party hierarchy, rather than through individual legislators. Large-scale or-ganizations—labor for the Democrats and industry for the Republi-cans—dominated these party channels. Citizens who did not identify very strongly with either group, rather than having their opportunities broadened, found their choices a good deal more difficult to make.

The Connecticut party system declined, we think, because it was ill-suited to the separation of powers structure of American government and, perhaps, also to the Connecticut electorate. The structural rules of convention nomination were weakened and split-ticket voting on voting machines was made easier. Bailey left Connecticut for Washing-ton. The strong party system of controlling policymaking that Bailey built became less disciplined, and Connecticut parties became more like those of neighboring states—only partially united even when they had the power to govern.

HOW NATIONALIZED ARE THE STATE AND COMMUNITY PARTY UNITS?

Those who wish to tighten up the party organizations to reduce their variety and the splintering of power within them urge strengthening of the national political parties at the expense of state and community party units. The thrust of their reform effort is to centralize the party organizations—to reduce the variety of procedures and insist state parties and their candidates support national party positions. They want the national party to gain more power in selecting party can-didates, in directing campaigns, and in holding winning candidates to platform promises.

As noted a number of political scientists have argued that a major defense of the balance of the federal system is the method in which American political parties presently operate. The best defense of the states, they say, are parties that are weak nationally (allowing state parties to choose nominees and take whatever policy positions suit state citizens), have endless variety (to suit whatever desires state cit-izens have) and are decentralized (leaving a good share of the organi-zational power at the state and community levels).

Palley, *Tradition and Change in American Party Politics*, Thomas Y. Crowell, New York, 1975, 189–192.

Relevant to this debate is knowing the facts about the present state of parties. How different are they? What makes them so. Then we can speculate on what future trends are likely to be.

Democrats and Republicans—Are They Different in States and Communities?

Nationally the parties seem to be distinctly different. But are they as different in the states and communities?

Sectionally Based Parties.   After the Civil War, American parties differed on a sectional basis—the South was "The Solid Democratic South" and those states that provided the soldiers for the Union armies—the Midwest and Northeast—were almost equally, solidly Republican. States with mixtures of northerners and southerners, such as Indiana, Missouri, Ohio, and other "border" states, were likely to be competitive.

Sectionalism still influences elections. One need only look at the composition of state legislatures in states that have recently become competitive at the presidential or even the gubernatorial level. Recently Alabama had no Republicans in its state senate, and North Dakota had eleven Democrats out of fifty-one members.

Yet, the sectional patterns have begun to decline, especially since the presidential race of 1932, and have become less important in state and community races in recent years. South Carolina after one hundred years elected a Republican governor, and Vermont after seventy years of Republicans elected a Democrat. The number of states in which the state legislative divisions are close between the parties is larger than at any time since the Civil War.

Socio-Economic Party Differences.   National party appeals on social and economic issues are becoming more important in distinguishing the parties as sectionalism declines. In most states we find a difference between the interest groups that support each party. Democrats receive a heavier measure of financial contributions and other support from labor organizations and civil rights groups—Republicans receive more interest group support from business and industry. Also we find public opinion polls consistently show on national, state, and community levels that Democratic candidates, as a rule, receive a larger share of the votes of Jews and Catholics, the descendants of the later ethnic immigrations, blacks, the young, lower educational and income citizens, blue collar workers, union members and urban residents. Republicans receive a higher level of support from those groups in the society who to a greater measure enjoy status—whites, Protestants, white collar workers, older people, those with higher education and income, and rural and small town residents.

Party Differences Among States.   However, we are still troubled by differences in policy stands among state parties. The mixture of sectional voting and class voting results in peculiar blends. Wisconsin Democrats and Texas Democrats seem to be of a different breed. So, too, are South Carolina Republicans and those of Connecticut. What seems to us to bring order out of this disarray is the fact that the Democratic party, in whichever state it is found, seems usually to be somewhat more "liberal" than the state's Republican party on the economic and social issues that national candidates stress.

Texas Democrats may seem very "conservative" by Wisconsin Democratic standards, but Texas Republicans are even more so. Connecticut Republicans may seem very "liberal" by Georgia Republican standards, but Connecticut Democrats are even more so.

A "nationalization" of the supporters of each party seems to be occurring. Within each state the interest groups and voters show the same distinctive tendencies—the "have nots" are more often Democrats, the "haves" are more often Republicans. The pattern has many inconsistencies, but the central tendencies are apparent. It is a pattern that encourages party centralization as members of each party are becoming more united in outlook.

Continuing Pressures To Decentralize State Parties

Three legal facts that flow from the federal system make it possible for state parties and their candidates to oppose positions taken by the national party. These facts form barriers to centralization to preserve what one student, C. Frederick Stoerker, has called "the solid political realities of the states."

Nominees Must Meet State Residence Requirements.   Unlike democracies such as England, candidates for office in America must be state residents. This is not only true of mayors, governors, state legislators, and other state or community officeholders, but is also true of such "national officials" as United States senators and representatives. They, too, must have established state residence before they run for office. Custom, but not law, also requires that U.S. representatives be resident and often be born in the district they represent.

Local residence requirements make it difficult for "national" party officials, such as the national chairperson, or officeholders, such as the president, to discipline officeholders of the same party who may do all they can to sabotage the national party program. Almost every president since Franklin Roosevelt has tried to "purge" some of his own party in a few primary races. More frequently than not they have failed or when successful in a primary the opposition party has captured the office in the general election. Added to this, United States senators and representatives know that if they lose a local election they cannot run in some safe district in another state. They are out of office. They must tend local fences and keep on reasonably good terms with the party actives back home.

State and Community Parties Influence Selection of National Nominees. The rules concerning party procedures that are made by state governments assure that state party officials will influence who will be chosen as the presidential nominee. For example what the party regulars in Iowa did in their precinct caucuses in January 1976 was especially important to a potential and little known presidential candidate such as Jimmy Carter. It was an early and very significant gain for him. Aspirants for the presidency will still wend their way to New Hampshire early in presidential years to woo party actives in hopes of winning that state's presidential primary. The state sets up the rules under which presidential candidates compete.

In Policy Box No. 26, "Minnesota Expresses Its Presidential Choices," we describe how one state has changed its methods of choosing national convention delegates to increase the influence of state party organizations on presidential nominations and, hopefully, to obtain maximum leverage to gain special consideration from the winning candidate.

Candidate Jimmy Carter at Iowa precinct caucus in 1976.

POLICY BOX NO. 26   Minnesota
Expresses its Presidential Choices

A state influences national government policy through its influence in the choice of presidential candidates. Before the national party conventions potential candidates go out searching for delegate support. The way a state chooses its delegates influences the kinds of appeal that presidential candidates will make, the kind of exchange they will make for support, and the political bargains that a state organization gets in exchange for support—a place on the national party ticket for a state politician or, more likely, a promise on a specific issue, such as the building of a local dam or closing of a military base in the state, or nothing.

At one time Minnesota had a presidential preference primary. Voters did not need to register with a party in order to participate in Minnesota's open primaries. The votes in the primary selected the delegates to the national party convention. Thus the party in the electorate determined which candidate would get Minnesota's convention support.

This system was used in only two elections—in 1952 and 1956. In each case the party leaders in government and the party organization lost out. The first election was the famous "Minnesota Miracle" of 1952. Supporters of General Dwight Eisenhower wrote in his name on Republican primary ballots in such numbers that he almost beat out Minnesota's former governor, Harold Stassen—an unusual feat since write-in campaigns are difficult, especially with a name any harder to spell than "Smith." In 1956 the Democratic–Farmer Laborite organization leaders, as well as its prominent office holders, ran as delegates on the Adlai Stevenson slate. Estes Kefauver of Tennessee swept the presidential primary and DFL party leaders and officials watched the Democratic national convention at home on television, rather than serving as delegates. After these two elections the system was dropped.

The present system gives the power of choosing which presidential candidate or candidates that the party will support to the members of the party organization. Selection of delegates to the national party nominating convention is made at the state party conventions. Such delegates may be committed to one or several candidates, a favorite son, or be uncommitted. The delegates to the state convention are selected by county conventions who are, in turn, selected at precinct caucuses that are held one night in February every two years and open to anyone who says he will support the party candidates. In recent years the struggle in the precinct caucuses has been between factions supporting different presidential candidates. How representative, then, is this system?

Thomas R. Marshall made a study of the 1972 and 1974 attendance at Minnesota's precinct caucuses. He found that in 1972 the DFL attendance was about 9 percent of the general election vote, but for Republicans it was only 4 percent—usually the figure varies between 5 percent and 10 percent. Men outnumbered women by a small margin; those who attended had more education, held somewhat better jobs, were more likely to be white collar workers who lived in urban areas and were more well-to-do than other party supporters who did not attend. DFL attenders were slightly more liberal, but Republican attenders were similar on policy questions to nonattenders. Those with strong candidate preferences were, of course, more likely to attend. Young people attended at least equal to their proportion of the state population.

Such a system, many Minnesota politicians argue, allows citizen input since the caucuses are open, but also allows the party organizations and its office-holders, who have more familiarity with the political situation, to exercise influence in the final selections of delegates to the national convention.

What do you think? Would it have been more democratic for Minnesota to stay with presidential primaries, perhaps if they had been made closed primaries? Under what system would the state be likely to derive more benefits (assuming that the state or party organization gives support to winning candidates)? Would it be more fair to have county convention delegates chosen by workers who have been active between elections, rather than those who show up at the precinct caucus?

SOURCE: Thomas R. Marshall, "Representation in Minnesota's Presidential Caucuses," in Millard L. Gieske and Edward R. Brandt (eds.), *Perspectives on Minnesota Government and Politics*, Kendall/Hunt Publishing Co., Dubuque, Iowa, 1977, 132–140. See also related articles on Minnesota parties by William L. Hathaway and Millard Gieske, Carolyn and Scott Shrewsbury, Norma C. Noonan, and Charles H. Backstrom.

But neither the national party organization nor the president have the legal power to influence the selection of state or community party nominees including members of the national House of Representatives or U.S. senators. State rules govern the local primaries, precinct caucuses, and county and state conventions. Democratic party presidents at one time may have ground their teeth to see Alabama renominate Governor George Wallace or his wife Lurleen (now deceased), but legally they could do nothing. Governor Wallace, on the other hand, has had considerable influence in the process of selecting the Democratic party nominee for president in every convention since 1968. Presidential candidates need to mend fences with such state party leaders.

The Electoral College Increases State Party Influence. Presidents are elected by electoral, rather than popular, votes. Each state gets electoral votes equal to its number of U.S. senators and representatives. The "winner take all" rule holds in each state.

A state party organization from a large state or a regional bloc of states, such as the South, can thus make a sizeable difference in the number of electoral votes the national candidate captures. Even local party organizations may swing the national outcome. National party conventions reflect to some degree (less so recently) the distribution of votes in the electoral college—this further increases the power of the larger state political organizations.

The basis of decentralization, variety, and national weakness thus rests in legal rules that permit state party regulars and officials to influence the choice of national nominees and discourage the national party officers or officials from influencing the choice of state and local party nominees. That is the political fact that frustrates party reformers who would fashion the parties into a more centralized, hierarchical system.

Pressures to Centralize the Major Parties

But the state and local organizations do not hold all of the political trump cards. As we have already discussed with respect to the federal system itself, the trend to urbanization, industrialization, mass communication, and connecting transportation systems—all of these features of economic development are making states and their citizens more alike. They are watering down state differences and making the American party system more centralized.

The Effect of "National Tides." V.O. Key, Jr., detailed how national tides have appeared in election after election. In a Republican year, Republicans at the national level and in most states and even communities increase their share of the vote—a nationwide trend in voting. If each state race were decided independently of a national influence or of the race in every other state, we would find no national tide, but a random distribution of gains between the parties.[28] To the extent that national tides exist, state and community nominees will find their futures tied to those of the presidential nominee and the national party. We note that some states minimize presidential influence, by holding election for governor in non-presidential years.

Some political scientists, however, argue that Congress in recent years has given congressional incumbents the means to buck national tides: campaign financing, generous travel allowances, expanded mailing privileges, and aides who live and work in the district back home. Such aid, equivalent to the building of district political organizations at public expense, make incumbents much less subject to national tides and, therefore, more independent of both national and state party leaders. Certainly, incumbents have become more difficult to defeat in either primaries or general elections in recent years.

[28]V.O. Key, Jr., *American State Politics: An Introduction*, Alfred A. Knopf, New York, 1956, 28–33.

We think it too early to predict that national tides no longer will influence the outcome of races by congressional incumbents. It appears that as recently as 1974 a national tide resulting from the Watergate disclosures affected Republican incumbents adversely.

Centralization Through the National Party Organization Rules. National party leaders increasingly are taking steps to centralize the Republican and Democratic parties by reducing the power of state and community units—beginning certainly in 1936, when the Democratic party convention abolished the rule that their nominees must receive two-thirds of the delegate votes (a rule that allowed a regional bloc, such as the "solid South," to, in effect, veto a nominee). The "loyalty oaths" for national convention delegates, quota systems of electing delegates who are blacks, women, and young people, national policy committees, the elimination of the "unit rule" which allowed all of a delegation's votes to be cast for the candidate favored by a majority, and midterm policy conferences—all aim at party centralization. The most recent important change was that of 1976 when the Democratic party changed the composition of its national committee in a move away from rough equality among the states to giving greater representation to states with Democratic party strength.

The National Party as Campaign Coordinator. The national party leaders argue that since campaigns require large expenditures for media, the national party should become the campaign coordinator of party-collected funds. Its leaders argue that it can best recruit a trained research staff, is the best source through which funds may be channeled, and is the unit where expertise can be utilized to best advantage. Why, the national party leaders argue, should funds be dissipated in hopeless races when elsewhere competitive elections might be won?

Party leaders also note that the Nixon campaign organization that became notorious during the Watergate investigation for its "laundering" of funds (depositing them in a series of banks, including some in Mexico, so that their source could not easily be traced) was *not* an official party organization. It was a candidate organization—CREEP, the Committee to Re-elect the President. Candidate organizations, they argue, need to be made responsible to the parties, since the parties are permanent and have a reputation to protect.

Disciplining Wayward Members of Congress. In 1974 and 1976, the party caucus in Congress abandoned the seniority system in selecting committee chairpersons and to disciplining leaders who consistently opposed national party positions. The Democratic party caucus has "dumped" several such chairpersons—another step toward party unity on program.

National Laws Affect State and Community Party Units.   In 1944 the United States Supreme Court in *Smith* v. *Allwright* declared that a state political party was not a private club that could exclude members on the basis of race. It thus outlawed the "white primary," a means by which some southern Democratic party organizations had prevented blacks from participating. South Carolina immediately repealed all state laws that regulated the political parties so it could argue that the Democratic party was a private organization. The U.S. Supreme Court did not accept the argument.[29]

Other national policymaking has made it less easy for state parties to write the rules to exclude certain citizens from participation. Rules for voting and for registration have been liberalized by court decisions. The Voting Rights Act of 1965 even provided for federal registrars. Federal courts have set aside rules that kept minor party candidates off the ballot. National campaign finance laws that apply to state U.S. representatives and senators further reduce state influence.

The impact of such national actions has been to chip away at a major bulwark of state party strength—the legal rules. Some reformers want to go further—they argue for a national presidential primary or abolition of the electoral college. Both would lessen the influence of state party politicians on the selection and election of presidential candidates.

A Final Comment

On balance, state and community party influence is still strong, but not quite as strong as it was a generation ago. The ability of local party regulars to defy the national party organization with impunity is less. State governments no longer exclusively write the laws governing all party activities and all election procedures. Both in Congress and at national conventions, independence by state or community party leaders is becoming somewhat more costly to them. More and more the activities of state and community party units are being slowly meshed in with those of the national party organization—state and community organizations have less power and are more like each other in respect to national issues.

[29]321 U.S. 649

Some students doubt that this process of centralization will proceed very much further. We are inclined, rather, to believe that just as the balance within the federal system has been tipped to favor national initiatives, so, too, is the balance within the political party organizations beginning to shift gradually toward national party leaders exercising more power. At this point no one is willing to predict that this outcome is certain and neither will we.

We also suggest that the party organization variety and the weakness of the party organization to select candidates, campaign, and govern in office may also be somewhat modified as party organization becomes more centralized. We doubt, however, that American parties will ever reach the high degree of centralization found in many other democracies because of the influence of the separation of powers and because the states exist in a federal system.

HIGHPOINTS OF CHAPTER 13: POLITICAL PARTIES IN THE STATES AND COMMUNITIES

In this chapter we began (1) by noting how the federal system of government and the Progressive movement's reaction to state bosses decentralized the American party system. We next looked (2) at how parties were organized, stressing their decentralization and variety. We then reviewed party functions and noted that (3) the party, because of the primaries, had lost control of its most important function—the selection of candidates; (4) that parties give up some of their traditional campaign activity to media firms; and (5) that in office, party candidates do not always work together. We ended (6) by considering whether state parties were losing influence to national party organizations and concluded that during the last decade or so, such a trend has developed, although considerable power remains with state and community political parties.

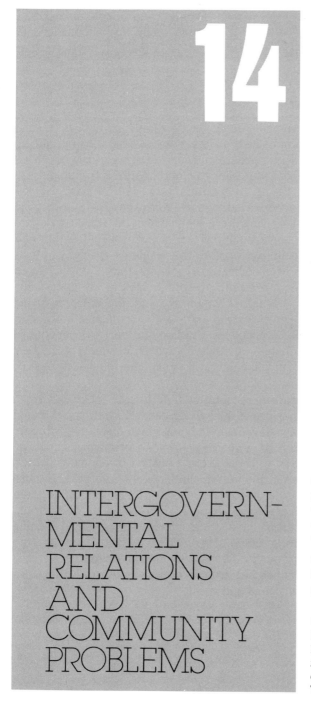

14

INTERGOVERN-
MENTAL
RELATIONS
AND
COMMUNITY
PROBLEMS

Constantinos A. Doxiadis, a flamboyant, world-renowned planner, once argued that the term "city" is obsolete. He suggested that in its place we use the term "human settlement," because "the era when the city was a unit of habitat very defined in space has passed."[1] Doxiadis was acknowledging the change in American settlement patterns—patterns that now "bleed" from urban centers into the countryside without sharp boundaries. Human settlement meets and merges into the extension of nearby urban centers to create one pattern of urbanized settlement. The blending is not as complete as the above would suggest, but an older pattern in which city limits sharply divide the urban from the rural is disappearing.

Within the area of urban settlement, we still find a complicated governmental maze of cities, villages, towns, townships, counties, and special districts that at one time carried out their programs with little regard for or impact on their neighboring communities. Today these neighboring community governments are linked together, not only with ribbons of concrete but with tubes and

[1]Constantinos A. Doxiadis, "How to Build the City of the Future," in Richard Eells and Clarence Walton, (eds.), *Man in the City of the Future, A symposium of Urban Philosophers,* MacMillan Co., Toronto, 1968.

tunnels, and underground wires, signals, and airplane exhaust streams overhead; and, of course, through social and economic linkages. In fact, horizontal relationships are an important part of urban intergovernmental relations.

Why Federal and State Intervention?

Federal and state governments became extensively involved with community problems as an outgrowth of the programs established during the Great Depression. These programs removed many of the concerns of life (safety, shelter, economic security, and health) from the private to the public domain. Like the city political bosses of the past, federal and state officials were motivated by more than simple altruism; they began to see votes in addressing these problems. In the words of Robert C. Wood, "Public programs are authorized for purposes other than the satisfaction of the material wants of all the residents or even of a majority. They are devices whereby political organizations survive. Taxes and public expenditures represent not just 'costs' and 'products,' but 'votes' and 'influence.' "[2] Much of the misery and, therefore, many of the votes were in the large cities and many of the problems thus began to be defined as "urban" problems. And so the vertical aspects of intergovernmental relations—relations between community governments and state and federal levels have become an important part of urban governing.

Finally there is the growing recognition that the less urbanized areas are part of the overall pattern of intergovernmental relations. We tend to think of inadequate housing, decaying downtown districts, pollution, poverty, and poor health care service as urban problems, but these conditions are not limited to large urban centers. In nonmetropolitan America live 37 percent of the nation's elderly, 46.5 percent of those living below the poverty line, and 61 percent of the population identified as having inadequate access to health care services. In addition, these nonmetropolitan areas have twice as many substandard housing units as do the metropolitan areas.[3] More than one-third of us—and the proportion has been increasing—live in nonmetropolitan areas. Thus, the horizontal and vertical pattern of intergovernmental programs touches all communities, urban and rural.

[2]Robert C. Wood, *1400 Governments*, Harvard University Press, Cambridge, Mass. 1961, p. 18.

[3]Neal R. Peirce, "Small Cities, Rural Areas Reflect the Problems Plaguing Major Cities", *Detroit News*, January 22, 1978.

Overview. In this chapter, then, we will examine the intergovernmental relationships of federal, state, and local authorities as they impact on the problems in the places where we live. We begin by looking at the local setting for intergovernmental relationships. We consider the growth of suburbia, decline of the cities, and the problems of rural and metropolitan areas where they all meet. We next review the politics of annexation and consolidation as methods to unify governments at the local level. Next we discuss voluntary approaches to bridging local governmental problems—special districts, interlocal agreements, and councils of governments. We end the chapter by asking whether the states can coordinate.

THE LOCAL SETTING FOR INTERGOVERNMENTAL RELATIONS

As we survey the tasks of government we find that all officials, whether city, suburban, or rural, in cooperation with state and federal officials, must deal with an intricate web of social and economic interactions that we can no longer clearly classify as being either rural or urban. Crime, poverty, traffic, housing, sewage disposal, solid waste, recreation, and unemployment are not just problems for city governments. In this section we look at how the various community governments, rural and urban, are becoming more and more alike in the tasks they face, but we emphasize also how they differ.

The Development of Urban Sprawl

The cities in the late 1800s were centers of commerce whose settlement pattern and boundaries were determined by the available means of transportation—foot, horse, and trolley. They were places of mighty industry powered by steam, immersed in machine technology and the factory system. But as Lewis Mumford notes, they were not places built to please residents. "The city," he wrote "was not treated as a public institution, but a private commercial venture to be carved up in any fashion that might increase the turnover and further the rise of land values. The law of urban growth . . . meant the inexorable wiping out of all the natural features that delight and fortify the human soul in its daily rounds."[4]

[4]Lewis Mumford, *The City In History*, Harcourt, Brace, and World, Inc., New York, 1961, p. 426.

Given such conditions, many city dwellers never lost their yearning for more natural surroundings. When technology and economic conditions permitted, many would seize the opportunity to leave. With that out-migration of people to the edges of the cities, the reality of suburbia began to emerge.

Technological Advances and the Suburbs. Transportation was the key to the development of suburbs. As means of transportation changed, especially with the coming of light rail lines and even bicycles, the wealthier people found that they could afford to live further from their places of work in the city and so escape the smoke, grime, and high densities of city living. Small satellite communities began to develop along the interurban lines. Later on in the 1920s, when American industry began to produce cars in volume—nearly four million were manufactured in 1925—the opportunity for suburban living broadened for the upper classes.

It was not transportation alone, however, that made the difference. Other technological improvements contributed. The extension of the telephone and electricity to outlying areas made many of the amenities associated with cities possible in a more rural setting. Electricity meant, for example, that outlying houses could have inside running water; the hand pump could be discarded. Improvements in septic tanks for sewerage disposal provided one further amenity previously only available in the city.

Suburbanization slowed during the years of the Great Depression and World War II. People seeking available housing during the war years again crowded into the cities. These were not times for constructing new housing. The result was an immense backlog in the demand for housing that was worsened by the returning veterans and the millions of new families they formed. The market for housing outstripped financial and technological capacities, but these did not remain barriers for long.

Suburbia Explodes. The federal government, through the Federal Housing Administration and the Veterans Administration, guaranteed mortgages to "qualified" home buyers, thus solving the financial logjam. Abraham Levitt and his sons led the way in the technological breakthrough. Originally they had planned, on Long Island, a housing project of 2000 single-family homes for "veterans only." They began building in the summer of 1947 and before they finished the project four and a half years later, they had built 17,447 houses—a place that became known as Levittown.[5] Similar developments, but on a smaller scale, had sprung up around every large and middle-sized city in the country.

Central city-suburban competition. Telephone, electric, and natural gas companies happily extended their services to these new markets. Water and sewer services, a city government function in most areas, were different. Many older cities made annexation the price for access to these services. Suburban neighborhoods, caught with failing or polluted water wells and septic fields, needed help in a hurry and some annexed. For others, annexation was too high a price, and mortgaged to the hilt, they voted new taxes for improvements of all kinds, including schools.

By the late 1950s the suburbs had not solved their water, sewer, and school problems, in part, because suburban growth continued unabated. "Metropolitan area studies," often sponsored by downtown merchants, became a fad. Such studies pointed up the growing duplication of facilities and services and usually recommended annexation, consolidation, and even formation of metropolitan area governments. But suburban leaders, especially as they saw businesses and industries moving to the suburbs, for the most part ignored the recommendations.

The freeways that were then being planned and built seemingly offered new hope for the congested traffic of "downtowns" and a brighter future for the waning central city business district. "Shoppers could again get downtown with ease," advocates claimed. Cities built parking ramps and sponsored urban renewal projects to attract new office buildings and department stores. But these, too, were of little help. Both freeway construction and urban renewal reduced the supply of housing, often destroyed neighborhoods, and took property off already shrinking tax rolls.

By the middle of the 1960s the new pattern had become clear. As the middle class, mostly white, left for the suburbs, the central cities became the repositories for the low income, aged, unemployed, and underemployed, plus blacks and other minorities, the victims of racial discrimination. The suburbs incorporated as separate cities, free from annexation and consolidation worries, and concerned only with preserv-

[5]For a favorable analysis of early Levittown, see Harold L. Wattel's "Levittown: A Suburban Community," in William M. Dobriner, (ed.), *The Suburban Community*, G.P. Putnam's Sons, New York, 1958, 287-313.

ing the way of life they established for themselves. What they left behind—poverty, the victims of racial discrimination, and social problems—were for someone else to worry about. Or so the suburbanites thought.

Life in the Suburbs

The suburbs have not been without their problems. They faced the tremendous costs of capital facilities that make urban living possible, and eventually they too had to deal with the problems of crime, traffic congestion, and providing services to the aged and chronically ill. Most of these were manageable, except in older industrialized suburbs, because the percentage of poor, aged, and ill was small. Moreover the percentage with substantial disposable income—income over and above that for necessities—was relatively high.

But some of the suburbs, especially those closest to central cities in the early 1970's, also began to find their populations leaving for "greener pastures" farther out. It became the suburb's turn to deal with problems of "block busting" and "white flight." According to the U.S. Bureau of the Census, the rate of increase for blacks and other races in metropolitan suburbs was three and one-half times that of the increase in the white population from 1970 to 1975. Oak Park, Illinois, an exclusive, largely white suburb of the 1930's on the west end of Chicago, for example, in 1977 proposed a program to assure homeowners staying in integrating neighborhoods that they would have "property value loss" of no more than 20 percent over a five-year period.[6] Other suburban communities near central cities faced similar white flight, as state and federal courts considered involving them in cross-district school busing plans.

Suburban communities are no longer self-contained or self-sufficient. They are no longer exempt from the great changes of technological, social, and economic movements, that we discussed in Chapter 4.

What Has Happened in the Central Cities?

In a paraphrase of the well-worn cliche about the weather, Alan Campbell and Donna Shalala wrote in 1970 about the central cities—"Everybody talks about the urban crisis, deplores it, insists that something be

[6]"Oak Park to Fight White Flight," Nations Cities, National League of Cities, August 1977, p. 26.

done about it, but few define or explain it.''[7] The reason it is not defined, they said, is because the urban crisis affects people in different ways. The meaning of the term "urban crisis" depends on one's vantage point.

What Is the Urban Crisis?   For black or Hispanic ghetto youth the crisis may be the poorly staffed and equipped school that fails to educate them, or the inability to get a job of any kind because of poor education and racial discrimination. For the welfare mother it may be the continuing struggle to get the money for food and housing to last until the end of the month. For the old woman who must walk daily to the grocery store, it may be the fear of having her purse snatched, or even of being raped or murdered. For the commuter to the downtown office building, it may be congested freeways. For the small merchant frustrated by holdups, break-ins, and soaring insurance costs, the urban crisis may come in the form of an offer to "torch" the building for a share of the insurance payoff.

For the police officer on the beat, the urban crisis may be the open dealing in drugs, prostitution, the related crimes of armed robbery and murder, and witnesses afraid and unwilling to testify. For the mayor, it may be a badly unbalanced budget resulting from a shrinking tax base, a growing deficit, rising wages of city personnel, and program failures. For governors and legislatures the urban crisis may be the seemingly insoluble welfare or Medicaid problem, the threat of, or actual, riots, and the cities' insatiable demand for money. The "urban crisis" is all of these, and more. But all resolve themselves to the conditions facing central city residents—poverty, racial discrimination, and the social disorganization that results—crime, drugs, and family breakups.[8]

Can Central Cities Be Governed?   Columnists, politicians, and others increasingly ask whether cities can be governed. Indeed some suggest that they cannot be, and that we should give up on them—especially

[7]Alan K. Campbell and Donna E. Shalala, "Problems Unsolved, Solutions Untried; The Urban Crisis," in Alan K. Campbell, (ed.), *The States and the Urban Crisis*, The American Assembly, Prentice-Hall, Inc., Englewood Cliffs, N. J. 1970.

[8]For a different view of the urban crisis, see Edward C. Banfield, *The Unheavenly City, The Nature and Future of Our Urban Crisis*, Little, Brown and Company, Boston, 1968. Banfield argues that the urban crisis is essentially the result of a large and concentrated culture of poverty for which no cure is known. Other "crises" are exaggerated statements relating to the inconveniences inherent to city living.

very large older ones.[9] William C. Baer suggests that urban death—at least death of urban neighborhoods—is a reality that needs to be recognized. He suggests that urban death may be "hindered by expertise, detoured by cajolery, impeded by charismatic leadership, and delayed by simple faith, but it will come.[10]

The economics of central city housing. Why have some of the nation's central cities reached the point where people are willing to talk about their ultimate demise? Not surprisingly many reasons are offered. At root are the economics of housing in central city neighborhoods, though racism and social disorganization exacerbate the economic down-spiral.

Lewis Mumford, as we have seen, suggests that city-building has been a big commercial venture with speculators considering only short-term economic returns. (He might have said the same about many suburbs.) We see reluctance to invest. Lending institutions through the practice of "redlining," mark off decaying sections of the city as areas where they refuse to accept mortgages, regardless of the ability of the prospective buyer to make the monthly payments. Property owners thus are unable to sell at reasonable prices. They end up selling to slumlords who in turn rent the property to those who can afford little else and then spend little or nothing for upkeep. Ultimately, as the property becomes completely deteriorated, the owners abandon it. Those residents who are able seek housing elsewhere and leave. With the exodus go jobs and with the jobs, personal income and the city tax base. And in this kind of tailspin, the ability of city governments to deal with the needs and demands of an increasingly poorer population declines rapidly and steadily.

Most now agree that such cities cannot lift themselves by their own bootstraps. The question for national, state, and city leaders is how to intervene with the economic system to reverse its central flow. What incentives can be offered? What regulations can be exercised to change the course of the central cities?

The Long Road Back for Central Cities. The urban crisis, of course, did not begin with the riots of the 1960s. But the riots did bring a new and redirected attention and sense of urgency to the condition of the central cities. They became the turning point for serious federal and

[9]See for example, George S. Steinbeck, "Are Big Cities Worth Saving?" in *The Cities in the Seventies*, F.E. Peacock Publishers, Inc., Itasco, Ill., 1971. The article orginally appeared in *U.S. News and World Report*, July 27, 1971.

[10]William C. Baer, "On the Death of Cities" in *Public Interest*, 45, Fall 1976, 3–19.

state involvement in urban affairs. Thereafter the problems of the cities were not merely city problems. They became state problems and federal problems!

Early state and federal efforts have not been particularly successful. Some have argued that neither has put enough money into the effort. Jerry Cavanaugh, mayor of Detroit during the 1967 riot, responded to the suggestion that money would not help by saying, "How do we know? We haven't really tried it."

There is no dispute that the cities have a long way to return. And they may never return to what they once were—a possibility that should not entirely dishearten those who recognize, rather than fantasize about, what some of the cities really were. But we think there are faint signs that cities are beginning the return trip and that they will survive the crisis.

Increase in black's participation.   One important sign, we think, is the greater participation of blacks in city halls and state legislatures and other positions of power and influence. Until recently "accommodation politics"—people getting their share of public outputs on the basis of votes, politics, and political talent—did not work for blacks but this pattern is changing.[11]

Changing state policies.   Another indication is that states, albeit still somewhat reluctantly, are beginning to change policies regarding cities—outlawing redlining, developing more broadly based tax programs, assuming greater shares of welfare, health, and primary education costs, and underwriting the costs of cultural facilities such as universities, zoos, museums, art galleries, and symphonies. Moreover we find states such as Massachusetts, Michigan, and California adopting policies on taxes, roads, parks, and government job locations to redirect the outward flow of jobs and people. Frank Keefe, Massachusetts State Planning Director, says to developers and industrialists, "We'll bust our backsides to help you develop in a city industrial park, to rehabilitate an old mill building, to engage in a downtown recycling project. But it is unproductive for us to spend money extending a sewer line or highway to your development out in the middle of nowhere."[12]

[11]See Nathan Glazer, "A New Look at the Melting Pot," *The Public Interest*, No. 16, Summer 1969, 180–187. Also see Glazer and Daniel P. Moynihan, *Beyond the Melting Pot*, for an application of this theory to New York mayoral politics in the early 1960s.

[12]Neal R. Peirce, "States Take Big Steps to Save Large Cities," *Detroit Free Press*, October 2, 1977.

The long road back in Providence, Rhode Island.

We note too, the restoration of urban neighborhoods, such as German Village in Columbus, Ohio, Queen's Village in Philadelphia, Larimer Square in Denver, and others. In addition, central city buildings, rather than being torn down, are now remodeled. More restoration may occur as costs of commuting and new construction point up the economic advantages of central city locations.

The Changed Rural Countryside

If urban areas are places of human settlement, we think of rural areas as places where people live apart. If we consider the sharp decline in the farm population—from 8.7 percent (15.6 million) in 1960 to 4.2 percent (8.9 million) in 1970 and even fewer (8.3 million) in 1977—we might quickly conclude that people in rural areas are living farther apart than ever before.[13]

What we find in large portions of the nation's countryside today is that much of it is marked by nonagricultural uses. To be sure the old farm homesteads remain, many of them still headquartering enlarged farming operations now heavily dependent on modern machines and technology. But we see many other land uses as well. In the outer reaches of metropolitan areas and towns we see, restaurants, gasoline stations, motels, and other highway service centers clustered around freeway interchanges. Mobile home parks are plunked seemingly in the middle of nowhere, and we find subdivisions that provide peace and

[13]U.S. Department of Commerce, Bureau of the Census, "Farm Population of the United States," 1975 Series Census—ERS p. 27, No. 47, 1976.

quiet and the aroma of the nearby farmer's hog pens. And tucked away off the main roads we see an affluent society's "get-away-from-it-all" facilities—racetracks, professional athletic stadiums, amusement parks, lodges for skiers and hunters, cottages built six and eight rows in from the lake shore, and KAO campgrounds.

We may argue in favor or against these land uses, but, in fact, these facilities have changed the function of government in the countryside and have modified dramatically the rural lifestyle.

Effects on Rural Governments. The intrusions of such land uses have drawn the rural governments into considering policies and programs for which they were not intended. How does the under–staffed county sheriff patrol the traffic on its way to the racetrack or stadium? Or how does the county deal with the polluted wells and inadequate drain-fields of lakefront cottage developments that in some instances are now occupied year around? How does it provide emergency medical care to the senior citizens who have settled in a mobile home park, or operate a landfill. How do they manage a zoning code, subdivision regulations, or a building ordinance?

These rural governments have been affected in other ways as well. They have become involved in the issue of environmental quality—con-

A dump in the "heart" of the famous wheat growing triangle near Joplin, Montana.

trolling agricultural runoff from animal feed lots and soil erosion from nonfarm excavations. Often these rural governments deal with problems of rural poverty, health care, housing, and unemployment that qualify them for federal and state aid. This, in turn, leads the rural officials to data gathering for grant applications and reports; to new accounting and budgeting practices, equal employment opportunity programs, unions and collective bargaining.

Growing dependence on professionals. We find, then, that a transformation has taken place in these rural governments. No longer are they merely a branch office of state government. Citizens find it increasingly difficult to operate these governments on a part-time basis; no longer can the county boards meet only four times or so a year. Instead, they have become governments dependent on technical experts—professionals not unlike those working in the cities—who somehow do not seem to fit the folkways and values of the old county courthouses. The close-knit "family feeling" of the county courthouse is gradually disappearing.

Nor are rural governments isolated from the governments around them. What we find, especially in the metropolitan areas, is a gradual merging of interests—interests, not in the sense that rural citizens want the same things that the urbanites want, though that may also often be the case—but in the sense that each has a stake in the policies of the other.

The Metropolitan Areas: Central City, Suburbia, and Rural Countryside

We use the term metropolitan area (officially, Standard Metropolitan Statistical Area—SMSA) as the U.S. Bureau of the Budget and Bureau of the Census define it. The key elements in the definition are the existence of a central city having a population of at least 50,000, or two adjacent cities with a combined population of 50,000, plus the county in which the city is located. The SMSA may include adjacent counties as well, if certain conditions are met.[14]

We make several observations about SMSAs: (1) They are not necessarily border-to-border concrete, office buildings, factories, and

---

[14]In general the Census Bureau includes adjacent counties if they are "socially and economically integrated" with the central county. The Census Bureau measures the integration by how many people live in one county and work in the other, by cross-county telephone calls, newspaper circulation, and other considerations. Adjacent counties must also be urban—population density must meet certain standards as must nonfarm employment levels. In the New England states the definition differs in that it uses towns, rather than counties.

TABLE 14-1 Estimated Population and Percent of Change, 1970–1974, for Standard Consolidated Statistical Areas

SCSA	Est. Population 1974	Percent Change from 1970	No. of SMSAs Included
New York	17,180,500	-1.8	8
Los Angeles	10,231,100	2.5	4
Chicago	7,615,100	0.1	2
Philadelphia	5,642,300	0.3	3
Detroit	4,684,400	0.3	2
San Francisco	4,585,200	3.7	3
Boston[a]	3,918,400	1.8	a
Cleveland	2,921,200	-2.6	3
Houston	2,401,800	10.7	2
Miami	2,222,700	17.7	2
Seattle	1,794,000	-2.3	2
Cincinnati	1,618,200	0.4	2
Milwaukee	1,588,900	0.9	2

SOURCE: Adapted from Population Estimates and Projections, U.S. Department of Commerce, Bureau of Census, Series p-25, No. 618, January 1976, p. 25.
[a]Includes Boston, Lowell, Brockton, and Lawrence-Haverhill.

houses. In fact, most of them have vast areas of open land, much of it in use for agriculture—20 percent of all farm population in 1975, for instance, lived in metropolitan areas. (2) The boundaries and number of SMSAs may change as population and employment data change. In 1960 there were two hundred and twelve SMSAs. By 1977 the number had increased to 272 (See Figure 14-1). All states, but two, Wyoming and Vermont, had at least one such area. (Puerto Rico had four.) (3) Many of the SMSAs are contiguous and may together include large portions of a state—such is the case in Massachusetts, New York, Florida, California, and other states. Recognizing this fact, the Census Bureau began to report data on what they called Standard Consolidated Statistical Areas—a grouping of contiguous SMSAs. (See Table 14-1).

Even before the Bureau of Census began using the SCSA classification, various scholars were writing about the megalopolis running from Boston to Washington D.C. It covers an area 450 miles long and 150 miles wide and is "home" for fifty million Americans. Experts foresee others developing.

Perspective on Metropolitan Areas. We find four characteristics important to consideration of the SMSAs; (1) changes in population trends, (2) government fragmentation, (3) interdependence of metropolitan units, and (4) specialization among metropolitan units.

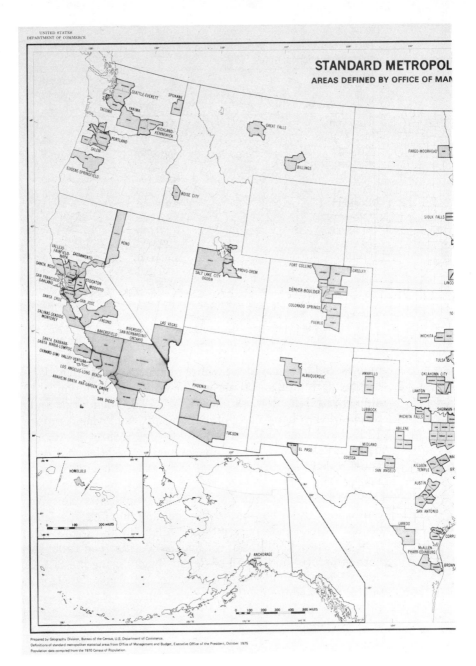

STANDARD METROPOL

AREAS DEFINED BY OFFICE OF MAN

Prepared by Geography Division, Bureau of the Census, U.S. Department of Commerce.

Definitions of standard metropolitan statistical areas from Office of Management and Budget, Executive Office of the President, October 1975

Population data compiled from the 1970 Census of Population.

Figure 14-1

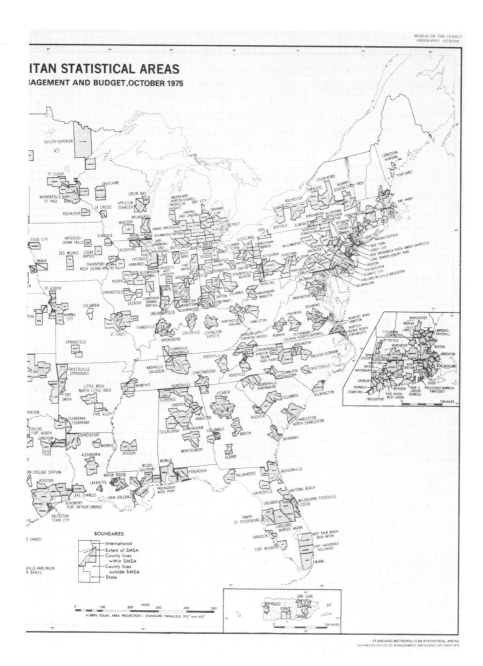

BUREAU OF THE CENSUS
GEOGRAPHY DIVISION

BOUNDARIES

International
Extent of SMSA
County lines within SMSA
County lines outside SMSA
State

MILES
0   100   200   300   400   500
ALBERS EQUAL AREA PROJECTION – STANDARD PARALLELS 29½° and 45½°

STANDARD METROPOLITAN STATISTICAL AREAS
DEFINED BY OFFICE OF MANAGEMENT AND BUDGET, OCTOBER 1975

Population Trends.   What happens in and to the metropolitan areas is of crucial national importance because it is where most of us live— nearly seventy-five percent of us by 1974, compared with fifty-six percent in 1950.

But now we may be seeing a partial reversal of that trend. The Bureau of the Census reported that between 1970 and 1976 the population of nonmetropolitan areas increased by 8 percent while the rate for metropolitan areas was 4 percent. The Bureau estimated that forty-one of the SMSAs had a net decrease in population and the 1970 SMSAs with two million or more population, eight, including the top five, were losing population. Only one, Dallas-Fort Worth, had a rate of growth greater than the national average. To underscore the significance of this change, we note that even during the 1960s when the large cities were losing population, only one SMSA—Pittsburgh—had ever lost population.[15]

We also find population shifts affecting SMSAs differently. Metropolitan areas of the Northeast have lost population, whereas only small increases occurred in the North Central Region. Where are the people moving to? We find that forty-eight SMSAs had population growth rates of 10 percent or more. Twenty-five of these were located in Florida, Texas, and California. Four were in Colorado; only one (St. Cloud, Minnesota) was in a northern state. More than one-half of these rapidly growing SMSAs were the smaller ones, 300,000 population or less, and eight were in the one million and over class.

Government fragmentation.   A second characteristic common to metropolitan areas is government fragmentation. A metropolitan resident may live in the jurisdiction of a good many local government units—for example, a city government, a school district, a county, an intermediate school district, a community college district, and, perhaps, special districts to operate the airport, water, and sewer services, community hospitals, recreation areas, special education, and mental and public health services.

Students of metropolitan areas typically have criticized government fragmentation on the grounds that the governments are too small and weak to meet important urban needs or that they do so only at excessive cost. Some students have also maintained that divided government permits some communities to benefit at the expense of others. Smaller units, they point out, do not equip their fire or police departments ade-

---

[15]U.S. Department of Commerce, Bureau of the Census, "Estimates of the Population of Metropolitan Areas 1973 and 1974, and Components of Change Since 1970," series P-25, No. 618, 1976.

quately, and depend upon the larger ones when specialized and costly equipment is needed. Moreover, the critics have argued that the area-wide problems, the problems that no single unit is responsible for, such as air or water pollution, go untended. The critics often end by recommending that the units consolidate into some form of metropolitan government.

For the most part such students drew their conclusions with little thought about how citizens might gain access to decision makers and bureaucracies; how the costs of coordination for large scale operations might affect overall costs; that there might, indeed, be differing preferences in service levels; or that the bureaucracies might not be able to establish a satisfactory set of priorities. More recently some studies have shown that larger is not necessarily more efficient or economical. In a study of metropolitan policing, for example, Elinor Ostrom and others report that larger departments respond less quickly to calls, are viewed less favorably by residents, and are more likely to have a higher proportion of their personnel in administrative positions than do smaller departments.[16] What advocates of consolidation sometimes overlooked was the cost of coordinating large systems. Those studies that emphasized the uneven matching of resources and problems seemed to have been more reasonable in their recommendations for consolidation.

Growing interdependency. Metropolitan units are increasingly interdependent. Who needs whom is an often debated point, but one seldom settled in the political wars between central cities and suburbs or among the suburbs themselves. Such arguments are often based on the idea that each of these units is independent of the other. Such, of course, is not the case.

The interdependence of people and organizations in metropolitan areas is readily apparent. Business and social organizations in metropolitan areas perhaps illustrate it best. Chambers of commerce now bridge virtually every political boundary in metropolitan areas, as do banks, supermarket chains, and dry cleaning companies. Telephone and power lines form an inseparable network connecting various switchboards and power plants. The community United Way collects its funds and disburses its services with little or no regard for the metropolitan political jurisdictions. And the home to work paths of residents now crisscross the urban areas in ways that only computers can unscramble.

[16]Elinor Ostrom, Roger B. Parks, and Gordon P. Whitaker, *Policing Metropolitan America,* National Science Foundation, Superintendent of Documents, Washington, D.C., 1977.

Specialization of metropolitan units. Within the networks of interdependence we also see a substantial degree of specialization, a specialization often protected and advanced by the political jurisdictions. We find that some suburbs seek to serve only the single family homeowner and are often dominated by specific ethnic groups or income levels, for example, top executives, second echelon executives, or the working class. Other suburbs may specialize in high-rise apartments. Others develop the reputation for having the "proper address" for corporation headquarters or the location for retail shopping centers, far out of proportion to what their own population would support. And a few end up being the place where the industries of the area tend to concentrate. One suburb near Los Angeles, California, was incorporated as a city to keep the land in use for dairying.

What specialization means, perhaps more than anything else, is that the more highly specialized political subdivisions are, the more interdependent they are. Specialists cannot trade exclusively in their own wares.

Few, except the most ardent of the defenders of the central city and suburbs, now deny that each is dependent on the other and that they must interrelate. In the next two sections we consider the intergovernmental relations of local governments as they seek to work out the problems that they face individually and collectively.

INTERGOVERNMENTAL RELATIONS: ANNEXATION AND CONSOLIDATION

Most states have laws that allow for annexation of unincorporated areas as well as for the merger or consolidation of two or more cities. If either of these procedures had been completely effective, the "problem" of governmental fragmentation would not exist.

Annexation

Until the 1920s the larger cities of the country routinely annexed most of the outlying settled areas. Annexation activity slackened off until after World War II when the pace again quickened. Central cities of more than 50,000 nearly doubled their territory between 1950 and 1970. An additional one hundred and thirteen suburban cities of this size increased their land area by 174 percent. Between 1970 and 1975 all cities added another 2,060 to their 17,832 square miles of territory and about 768,000 people.[17]

[17]Richard L. Forstall, "Annexations and Corporate Changes; 1970–75," Municipal Year Book, 1977, International City Mangement Association, Washington D.C., 62–64. In this source, city-county consolidations are treated as annexations.

TABLE 14-2 Land Area and Population Annexed by Cities Over 50,000 Population in 1950–60 and 1960–70[a]

		1950–60		1960–70	
	No.	Area in Sq. Miles	1960 Pop. (000)	Area in Sq. Miles	1970 Pop. (000)
Central Cities					
Over 500,000	29	866	1,484	1,660	1,120
250,000–500,000	26	739	1,271	1,329	868
100,000–249,999	71	660	963	741	795
50,000–99,999 by 1950	62	249	283	198	158
50,000–99,999 by 1960	41	511	886	378	370
50,000–99,999 by 1970	31	94	205	293	435
Sub-total, Central	260	3,119	5,092	4,599	3,746
Suburban Cities					
Over 50,000 by 1950	47	39	84	58	86
Over 50,000 by 1960	33	158	364	119	129
Over 50,000 by 1970	33	210	402	1,037	525
Sub-Total, Suburb	113	407	850	1,214	739
Total-All	373	3,526	5,942	5,773	4,485

SOURCE: Adapted from Richard L. Forstall, "Annexations and Corporate Changes Since the 1970 Census With Historical Data on Annexation for Larger Cities for 1950–1970," *Municipal Year Book, 1975,* International City Management Association, Washington, D.C., 21–29

[a]The data reported here include "annexations" achieved through city-county consolidations. The population data report population in annexed areas at the time of the dicennial censes. Actual population annexed during the 1960s was about 2,886,000. The comparable figure for 1950s is not available.

But we find that between 1950 and 1970 the central cities of the Northeast together annexed only seventy-five square miles; the North Central states annexed about 1200 and the West, about 1300. By contrast the central cities in the South annexed nearly 3600 square miles; 56 percent of this area was in Texas and Oklahoma.

The Importance of State Policies in Annexation Practices. Some states permit areas with populations as low as one hundred to five hundred people to incorporate as cities, if the residents so prefer. Easy incorporation permits small cities to surround the central cities and effectively closes off the option for annexation. This has been true for many cities of the Northeast and Midwest for several decades.

Annexation policies generally revolve around the question of whether residents to be annexed have a vote on the question. If they do, annexation is generally difficult. Where annexation occurs by order of a state boundary commission (California and some other western states), by judicial decree (as in Virginia), or by an ordinance of the central city council (as in Texas in cities over 100,000 population) annexation is much more likely.

Texas law allows any city with a population of over 100,000 to annex any unincorporated territory within five miles of the city limits by city council action alone. During 1977 Houston proposed to annex the settlement of Clear Lake City, the location of the Lyndon B. Johnson Space Center. Clear Lake City, organized only as a water district, wanted to become a city and appealed to the legislature for permission. Fred Hofheinz, then mayor of Houston said, "We get them when they become ripe." David Riley, a Clear Lake City official, responded by saying, "If they could grab everything up to the Canadian border, they'd do it." Houston in 1977 covered 510 square miles, the third largest city in area in the country.[18]

An Assessment of Annexation. Annexation, we think, deserves mixed ratings as a tool for resolving central city problems.

First, it has only limited application in states that permit easy municipal incorporations. If the nonmetropolitan growth trend continues, however, annexation may have broader application for small and outlying cities.

Second, annexation enables cities to recapture middle- and upper-class residents and their incomes, thus requiring their continued attention to the affairs of central city government. In addition annexation can provide cities more industrial and commercial tax base.

But we note, third, that central cities that have had successful annexation policies still continue to experience the ghetto problems of poverty, racism, and social disorganization. Critics have even argued that annexation adds to these problems as central cities spend to bring the newly added areas "up to standards." In addition, of course, continued annexation assures that ethnic minorities will remain political minorities as well.

City County Consolidation

Over the years county government has been involved in various ways in the organization of local governing systems, especially in respect to

[18]"The Octopus," *Newsweek*, June 13, 1977, p.7. Jacksonville, Florida, a consolidated city–county is largest with 827 square miles; Oklahoma City, which has also enjoyed liberal annexation policies is second with 650.

the large cities. In 1854, for example, the city of Philadelphia extended its boundaries to include all of Philadelphia County. They continued to operate as separate governments, however, until 1952 when a new charter consolidated the two governments.

During 1876 the city of St. Louis more than tripled its territory and then was separated from the county in which it was located. This city-county separation eliminated the city subsidy of county operations from which some officials believed the city received little benefit. Later, though, it was also to mean that the city would become "hemmed in" by suburbs in adjacent counties. Annexation then would involve changes in both city and county boundaries.

The present city of New York was formed in 1898 when five counties were consolidated: Queens, New York (Manhattan), Richmond (Staten Island), Kings (Brooklyn), and the Bronx merged to form New York City. The five counties became boroughs of the city.

Contemporary City-County Consolidations.   With the reorganization of Baton Rouge and East Baton Rouge Parish, Louisiana in 1947 into a new government in which both Parishes maintained their identity, interest began to revive in city-county reorganization—some of it involving consolidation and some involving reorganization of functions and relationships.

The next major reorganization involved Miami and Dade County, Florida in 1957. (Here, too, both units maintained their identities and, therefore, strictly speaking a consolidation did not take place; the result was, rather, a two-tier metro government.) Others that followed were Nashville-Davidson County, Tennessee in 1962, Jacksonville-Duval County in 1967, and Indianapolis-Marion County, Indiana in 1970. Other city-county consolidations that received less public notice were Juneau-Greater Juneau Borough, Alaska, Lexington-Fayette County, Kentucky, and Columbus-Muscogee County, Georgia. By 1977 the number of city-county mergers since Baton Rouge and the surrounding parish consolidation, had reached twenty-four.

It does not seem likely that this pattern is one that will sweep the country, in part because, with the exception of Indianapolis and Juneau, the city-county consolidations are a phenomenon limited to the states of the South.

The Politics of City-County Consolidation.   Each of the cases of city-county actions is unique because of local events, politics, and state traditions. But we do find some common threads—most, if not all, of the mergers have similar sponsoring groups, chambers of commerce, business and professional groups, and the League of Women Voters. Efficiency and economy and other reform values appear to be the principal motivations. Mergers also seem to occur in states that do not have a tradition of strong township government.

State legislative involvement. State legislatures are significantly involved in the consolidation deliberations, in fact several have involved state capitals. Consolidations are taking place mostly in those states in which legislatures adopt local acts and where we are less likely to find home rule. (See Chapter 4.) In both the Baton Rouge and Miami cases the local legislative delegation negotiated the law that permitted the areas to adopt local home rule charters. In the Jacksonville case the legislature created the charter commission and named the membership—no public officials were included. Later the legislature adopted an amended version of the charter and submitted it to the electorate. In Indianapolis an act of the legislature at a time when Republican control of state, county, and city government converged, established "Unigov" in Marion County.[19]

Involvement of state legislators from the area in these actions we think provides the opportunity for necessary "deal-cutting" that later weakens or neutralizes opposition when the voters decide the question. Also, of course, the power to adopt local acts permits the necessary custom-made law.

Popular voting. The major city-county consolidation processes have included voter referenda; overall, sixteen came about by referenda and eight by legislative enactment alone. Typically, adoption requires concurrent majorities in both the central city and in the unincorporated parts of the county. Full participation by suburban cities generally has been optional. Not every elected position, of course, is retained, but often the most important ones are. With a referendum requirement, influence of local politicians is pivotal regarding how the final charter compromises are made and how citizens vote. During 1975, for example, the Nevada legislature passed a law to merge the city of Las Vegas and Clark County. City and county officials at first supported, but then later opposed it. They took the legislation to the court and the Nevada Supreme Court ruled it unconstitutional.[20]

Tax policies. How local taxes are to be assessed is another of the political questions to be resolved. Outlying areas that are likely to receive little direct service, no matter what the form of government, will

[19]York Willbern, "Unigov; Local Government Reorganization in Indianapolis," in *Regional Governance: Promise and Performance,* Op. cit., 48–73.

[20]Andrew D. Grosse, "Las Vegas—Clark County Consolidation: A Unique Event in Search of a Theory," *Nevada Public Affairs Report, 14,* May 1976, Bureau Governmental Research, University of Nevada.

oppose a consolidation proposal if they do not receive tax concessions. The usual solution is the establishment of two or more taxing districts—areas that receive few services pay only a general tax, while high service areas pay an additional urban service tax.

Representation. Representation is another issue that the politicians must compromise. Blacks, for example, who may constitute a majority of the central city, must be guaranteed some power in the new government. In the Jacksonville case, for example, blacks represented more than 40 percent of the city population, and their support was essential. Midstream, during the charter campaign, the council districts were changed to avoid pitting two black councilwomen against each other for a seat in the new government.

The Reorganized Governments. From the term "city-county consolidation" we might expect that a single government would be created for the entire county. Although the consolidations usually include the majority of the resident population, the consolidations do not always eliminate all existing local governments.

The problem of small cities. Suburban units within the county typically are given the right to vote separately on whether they will participate in the consolidation. Most often they vote to remain separate.

Under the city-county reorganizations the independent suburban cities relate to the county functions of the government as they had previously and, of course, continue to pay the county or general service district tax rate. But the suburban units also frequently contract with the consolidated government for specific services. In Nashville-Davidson, six cities continued their independent status, but they may not expand their boundaries and no new suburban cities may be organized.

The problem of existing laws. State constitutions may require election of certain officials in all counties. And even when this is not true, the political clout of local elected officials makes constitutional and statutory changes difficult. This was the case in Indianapolis. Marion county continues to exist as a legal entity—the council sits both as a county board and as a city council.

Restrictive constitutional provisions were critical to the design of government for Miami-Dade county in 1957. In contrast to the other city-county consolidations, the Miami- Dade reorganization plan provides a two-tier type of government. The county serves as the areawide government and the municipalities, the local tier. (For the unincorporated county areas, though, it is really a one-layer government, that provided by the county.) Dade County received broad authority to provide area-wide services. Gradually its responsibilities have increased, both as the county adopts ordinances implementing its charter powers and as local units transfer functions to the county as they have been doing.

The Miami-Dade approach, together with one used in the Minneapolis-St. Paul area (an approach we will discuss later), is patterned after in the Toronto plan, one of the best known and perhaps most successful two-tier metropolitan area governments. We digress from our discussion of city-county consolidations momentarily to review the Canadian experiment.

The metropolitan Toronto approach. The Toronto experiment not only represents the first bilevel or two-tier approach to metropolitan government organization in North America, but, perhaps, the most extensive one as well. In 1953 the Ontario legislature established a metropolitan government over thirteen separate municipalities. The area was separated from the county and a metropolitan council assumed the county functions. Membership on the original twenty-five member council was equally divided between the city of Toronto and the surrounding suburban units. The twenty-fifth member, the council chairperson, was appointed by the provincial government. In 1967 council membership was increased to thirty-three with twenty chosen by suburban governments.

The metropolitan council functions as "super government," exercising responsibility for specific programs. The local municipalities carry out those functions not assigned to the metropolitan government. The council is chiefly responsible for water supply and sewer services, main highways and public transportation, judicial administration, welfare, land use planning, and the oversight of local zoning actions. It shares with the localities public housing, redevelopment, and parks and recreation. During the 1967 reorganization some of these functions were shifted more securely to the metropolitan level.

Although the plan is criticized on several points—tight land use control has driven up the cost of housing, and the fact that officials serve both as local municipal officers and metropolitan councillors is somewhat confusing to voters—the Toronto model is also being implemented in the provinces of Manitoba, Quebec, British Columbia and by Ontario in the "Golden Horseshoe" area.

An Assessment of City-County Consolidation. What we see in the recent city-county consolidations and reorganizations, then, is that they are each a product of local political circumstances. Generally they have occurred in middle-sized cities with rapidly growing suburbs—suburbs that rely on the county for urban services. For reasons that are less clear, many have involved state capitals—perhaps because of the politics of the office building location, and because of heavy state involvement for such plans to succeed. Inadequate services in the suburbs, it appears, have encouraged suburban interest in alternative arrangements, especially if suburbanites can obtain some tax concessions until services are provided them. But we also note that other circumstances may play a part in adoptions. The favorable vote in Jacksonville, for example, followed formal charges of grand larceny, bribery, and perjury against eight city officials—a fact that was influential in both city and suburban voting.[21] In Nashville suburbanites had an added incentive to support consolidation when the city required a "green sticker" tax of $10 on all cars that were used on city streets more than thirty days per year. This tax hit city residents as well as suburbanites, but it became a highly emotional item, particularly for the out-of-towners who protested that it was "taxation without representation."[22]

The question of whether the new governments achieve the efficiencies and economies proclaimed by the advocates remains unanswered. Some suggest that savings have been made in consolidated purchasing, but beyond that no one has been able to prove the case. The advocates of reform, perhaps, can rest easy with the thought that taxes would have been higher than they are if there had been no reorganization. And the opponents can point to rising taxes and say, I told you so. But overall, a groundswell of support to reverse the previous decisions to consolidate is not evident.

As we noted with respect to annexation, the city-county consolidations have not eliminated the problems we have associated with central cities. In the early periods of consolidation a great share of the resources typically go into upgrading utilities and services in the outlying areas. But where black leaders have been involved in the deliberations and are able to bargain black votes successfully in the city-county council, inner–city residents may be better off after a few years than they otherwise would have been.

Finally, we note that only for single county SMSAs do the consolidations represent "metropolitan" mergers. City-county consolidations in

[21]John M. DeGrove, "The City of Jacksonville: Consolidation in Action," in *Regional Governance: Promise and Performance*, Op. cit., 17-25.

[22]David A. Booth, Metropolitics; *The Nashville Consolidation*, Institute for Community Development and Services, Michigan State University, East Lansing, Michigan, 1963, 108 pp. Also see Robert E. McArthur, "The Metropolitan Government of Nashville and Davidson County," in *Regional Governance: Promise and Performance*, Op. cit., 26-35.

multicounty SMSAs, such as Miami-Dade where urban development has long since spread beyond Dade County, must continue to grapple with intergovernmental problems that involve adjacent counties. Some reformers, although praising city-county reorganization, maintain that this approach does not go far enough, that the county is not large enough to bring about an integrated metropolitan area government. We are inclined to think that there is merit to the National Association of Counties' rejoinder, as illustrated in Figure 14-2.

INTERGOVERNMENTAL RELATIONS: VOLUNTARY COOPERATION APPROACHES

Voluntary cooperation techniques do not threaten the identity of local units. As we will learn, however, the voluntary approaches can also result in a reallocation of power in an urban area. In this section we examine three of the major voluntary cooperation alternatives—special districts, intergovernmental contracts, and councils of government.

Special Districts

As we discussed in Chapter 4, special districts are the most rapidly growing form of local government. The number between 1952 and 1977 doubled and now total more than 26,000. These units perhaps are the least known by local citizens, largely because they are usually created by other governmental units, because they are financed by service charges and fees or levy only small amounts of local taxes, and because their officials—usually three to five board members—are not directly elected by citizens.

The Popularity of Special Districts.   Robert C. Wood points out, "special districts become the principal means by which the suburban governments meet the new needs which arise in the transition from rural to urban."[23] Moreover because special districts are created by one or more general purpose governments, they present the appearance of not only being an agent of the sponsoring units, but of being under their control as well—the latter because sponsoring units usually appoint the members of the special district board.

Robert Wood notes other more subtle reasons for the popularity of special districts. Creation of special districts enables a government to

[23]Robert C. Wood, Op. cit. p. 74. See Annmarie H. Walsh, The Public's Business M.I.T. Press Cambridge, Mass. 1978.

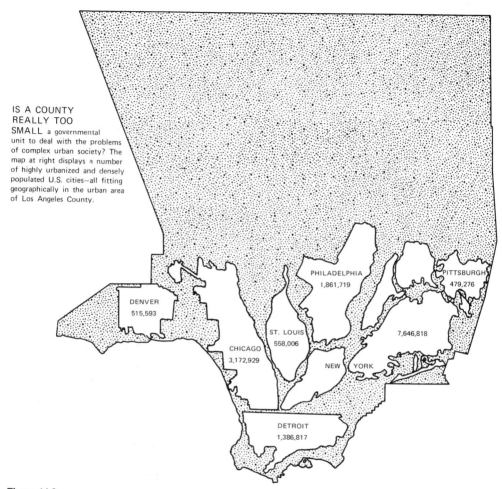

IS A COUNTY REALLY TOO SMALL a governmental unit to deal with the problems of complex urban society? The map at right displays a number of highly urbanized and densely populated U.S. cities—all fitting geographically in the urban area of Los Angeles County.

DENVER
515,593

PHILADELPHIA
1,861,719

PITTSBURGH
479,276

ST. LOUIS
558,006

CHICAGO
3,172,929

7,646,818

NEW YORK

DETROIT
1,386,817

Figure 14-2
(SOURCE: *County News*, March 14, 1977, p. 4, National Association of Counties, Washington, D.C.)

restrict the costs of improvements in growth areas to such places, rather than to fully developed areas as well. Special districts are also a way of making sure that the users of services, such as parking garages, parks, water and sewer systems, and other functions, pay for them directly—especially when such operations are funded by user fees. And, special districts provide ways of circumventing constitutional or statutory limits on local property taxes or indebtedness. To illustrate, two community governments that may have reached their taxing or borrowing limits create a special district that can tax and borrow in its own right. Indiana communities have found this technique especially useful because the state constitution allows local governments to borrow only up to 2 percent of their property tax base.

Finally, we note that for citizens who are seeking a resolution of a particular problem, the special district is inviting because it has authority to deal with only that specific problem—unless it is a multipurpose district, and most are not. Thus if the district is to do anything at all, it will often solve the problem in question, and any tax increase, therefore, will be used for a much-wanted service.

An Assessment of Special Districts. Though special districts continue to grow in number, they also create some special problems. Most serious is their tendency toward independence from the local governments that create them. Financed by their own revenues they may become important power centers determining where important public facilities will be located, who will get the construction contracts, and how many employees will be hired. Moreover, they often set their own service rates—an important consideration when the district has a virtual monopoly in the area and the local unit has no real opportunity to withdraw or disenfranchise the special district. An indication of the kind of problem this creates is presented in Policy Box 27, "Storm Water Runoff in Chicago—A $6.4 Billion Problem?"

Another problem is that special districts tend to focus on only the service they provide. They are not able to balance the importance of their program against other community needs. The most important need in the community, for example, may be local commuter trains, but what it gets is throughway expansions because the road system is managed by a special district that has funds, perhaps collected from bridge or highway tolls as was the case in New York City. We note that special districts operate as a private corporation with but one or two services to sell. The "corporation" and those operating it think they are best off when they sell as much of their services as they can, and it is too bad if their competitors are having problems.

Finally we note that idealists frown upon the special district as a solution to community problems because they only serve to further fragment the local government picture. As such, it is argued, they only add more complexity to an already overly complex set of intergovernmental relationships and forestall the time when "rational" government organization can be developed.

Intergovernmental Contracts

Most states authorize their local governments to contract with each other for services. Most commonly we find these contracts or agreements deal with potential "peak-load" problems, such as in police and fire services. City A, for example, will agree to place some of its fire equipment in City B's fire station as backup when B has a multiple alarm fire. Or they may agree to extend police services to another unit when one unit has a crisis of some kind. Such "mutual assistance pacts" are commonplace in both metropolitan and rural areas and add another dimension to local intergovernmental relations.

But we find contracts extending beyond mutual assistance. One community, usually one of the larger ones—not always the central city—may have developed a water supply system that is large enough to sell water service to adjacent communities. Often such arrangements eliminate the duplication of facilities and provide size and scale efficiencies and economies that none of them could attain on an individual basis. Federal and state granting agencies frequently require, as a condition of the grant, that the recipient community extend services to an adjacent community by interlocal agreement.

But we find there are some difficulties with this approach as well. If the contracts are not skillfully drawn to provide flexibility for cost changes, one community may suffer severe financial losses (or enjoy gains) while the others do not. And we may find citizens of the units purchasing the service wondering if the rates are fair. This is especially the case when customers in the supplying unit have low rates, while purchasers have high and increasing rates. They may even ask for state regulation of service rates.

Virtually all states provide local units with a great deal of flexibility to contract with each other, even to the extent of crossing state or international boundaries.

The Lakewood Plan. Perhaps the most extensive intergovernmental contracting takes place in Los Angeles County, California. Contracting for municipal services between Los Angeles county and municipalities has become so extensive that the contracting cities are sometimes called paper cities. The contracting city may need only a council and a mayor to authorize the contracts and a contract administrator to oversee them. Los Angeles County offers as many as sixty different services to community governments.

The process emerged as "a plan" in 1954 when Lakewood became a city to ward off annexation to Long Beach. Lakewood residents did not really wish to establish a city government, and so they approached the county for municipal services on a contract basis. Lakewood then began to contract for all its services except for parks and recreation.

The idea spread rapidly in the county, and to other California counties as well. In 1970 Los Angeles County had more than 1600 contracts with a total of seventy-seven municipalities, some of them being the

POLICY BOX NO. 27   Storm Water
Runoff In Chicago—A $6.4 Billion Problem?

Back-ups into homes and businesses, flooded underpasses, raw sewage pouring into Lake Michigan, millions of dollars in property damage—these problems occur regularly in the Chicago area. Responsibility for such problems rests with the Metropolitan Sanitary District of Greater Chicago (MSDGC), a special district set up by Chicago and its suburbs.

It is not that Chicago and adjacent communities are without sewers—only that most are "combined" sewers, serving both sanitary and storm water runoff purposes. With each inch of rainfall the system must accomodate an additional four billion gallons of water. Often it can not handle the load.

Federal law makes it illegal after 1982 to pollute any water body and the MSDGC is busy building a system they hope will meet this requirement. (See Figure 14-3.) The MSDGC has already spent more than $400 million. Basically the plan calls for the development of a "river" two hundred feet below the surface consisting of 125 miles of tunnels up to 36 feet in diameter—carved out of solid rock. These tunnels and some surface reservoirs will store the runoff and waste water until treatment plants can process it. MSDGC originally estimated the cost to be $3.3 billion.

Opponents argue that the whole system should be based on a "surface" approach, using natural and created flood plains. The MSDGC says they have spent $20 million studying alternatives and on engineering studies. A surface disposal approach, they maintain, is impossible because the land area is all built upon, and if the 325-square-mile area and fifty communities are to be served in this way, land will have to be cleared. "What areas would be cleared?" they ask. MSDGC says they have held more than twenty public hearings on the project. The U.S. Corps of Engineers and the U.S. Environmental Protection Agency have held other hearings.

Opponents also argue that the project is too costly to construct and operate; that it takes an "unnatural and uneconomical" approach; and that it is environmentally unsound. The construction and interest cost, they say, will be close to $6.4 billion. The EPA will pay 75 percent of the pollution control costs, and Corps of Engineers an unspecified portion of the flood control features. Opponents wonder how local portions and the annual operating cost of $56 million will be paid. Operating costs will be so high, they say, because the system is unnatural. Water will flow into the system by gravity, but it will have to be *pumped* out. In addition if the system is to avoid producing a "big smell," oxygen will have to be pumped into the storage tunnels. This equipment alone will cost $120 million.

But opponents try to make their strongest arguments on the environmental unsoundness of the plan. They fear that cracks in the rock or aquifers will permit fresh water to flow into the system when it is empty—56 million gallons per year they think—and soiled water to flow into underground water supplies when the system is full. Engineers say they can control the aquifer leakage by sealing of such parts, but water now leaks into part of the system already built. The opponents also object because some of the open storage areas are too close to some of the suburban communities.

Figure 14-3
(SOURCE: Chicago Tribune, August 29, 1976.)

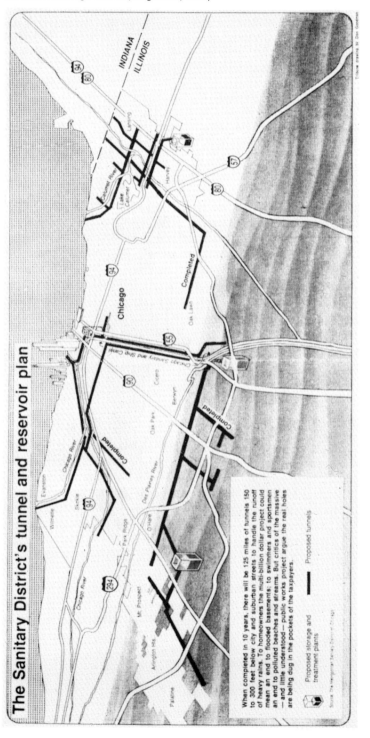

The Sanitary District's tunnel and reservoir plan

When completed in 10 years, there will be 125 miles of tunnels 150 to 300 feet below city and suburban streets to handle the runoff of heavy rains. To homeowners the multi-billion dollar project could mean an end to flooded basements; to swimmers and sportsmen an end to polluted beaches and streams. But critics of the massive — and little understood — public works project argue the real holes are being dug in the pockets of the taxpayers.

Proposed storage and treatment plants

Proposed tunnels

Opponents say that the "super sewer" is being constructed right under peoples' noses and relatively few people are concerned about it.

What do you think? Should the people be concerned? Is this strictly an engineering problem? Do you think the MSDGC should be restructured to be made more responsive to the critics' concerns? What action, if any, would you recommend the residents take? Should the state be involved? Do you think the "super sewer" is a good idea, or should the smaller communities get together in groups of four or five and handle the problem themselves? Or do you think the matter is too complex for the average citizen—that we are better off leaving it to the experts?

SOURCE: This policy box is based on "Deep Tunnel: Is It Really Needed?" in the *Chicago Tribune*, August 29, 1976. The case for the opponents was written by Judith Kiriazis and for the advocates, by Nicolas J. Melas.

older municipalities. The plan has produced a kind of functional consolidation in the Los Angeles area, even though the county employs a large number of special districts to carry on its operations.

Use of the plan has not been without friction, however. The older municipalities object, suspecting that their county taxes are being used to subsidize the suburbs. The new municipalities object to paying an overhead charge on the notion that the county would incur certain of these costs, even if it did not have contracts.

In Policy Box No. 28, "Privatization of Public Services," we discuss another contractual approach—the provision of fire protection services by a profit-making corporation—being pioneered in Scottsdale, Arizona.

Councils of Government

Councils of government (COGs) are a relatively recent invention to provide a forum for conducting intergovernmental relations within a metropolitan area. The idea grew out of a five-county committee formed in Southeast Michigan during the middle 1950s. The intercounty committee first dealt with problems of storm water drainage, water supply, and sewerage treatment. In 1957 the Michigan state legislature gave the committee legal status. Ten years later it was reorganized as the Southeast Michigan Council of Governments (SEMCOG) and was expanded to include a total of seven counties.

The COG is a forum where officials of local governments convene to discuss and iron out area-wide service plans and programs. Participation is voluntary and, therefore, is not viewed as a threat. Each involved unit pays dues to support staff planning and research efforts.

As such, the COG is not a government; it levies no taxes and usually operates no government services. In effect, it is a confederation.

Federal and State Encouragement. By 1965 there were only nine COGs. But federal agencies were looking for more comprehensive ways to deal with urban problems. Federal housing and model city legislation made the COGs eligible for Section 701 grants to conduct studies, gather data, and carry out regional planning. Later the U.S. Office of Management and Budget established the A-95 Review process, that gave COGs the authority to review and comment on grant proposals filed by local governments. This became one of COGs most important tools.

Federal and state governments encouraged the development of COGs in metropolitan areas. And, as we will learn later, most of the states actually required their organization during the 1970s. But it was Minnesota that pioneered some advanced possibilities for regional councils.

The Twin Cities Metropolitan Council. The Minnesota state legislature established the Twin Cities Council for the Minneapolis–St. Paul area in 1967. But the Twin Cities Council is vastly different from COGs established in other states. The Twin Cities Council is a state created agency. The governor appoints the fourteen council members from districts that cut across municipal boundaries. The Council has a modest taxing power—50 cents on $1000 of assessed valuation and exercises policy control over other area-wide agencies.

Twin Cities council powers. The council makes policy on matters of regional concern and recommends plans and programs in a number of public policy areas that range from air pollution and tax assessment to water drainage.[24] These actions are advisory for state agencies like the state highway and health departments. But for local agencies, such as the sewer board, the transportation board, and the counties, council policies are binding. The metropolitan council may veto plans of agencies such as the airports commission but may be overridden by the state legislature.

The council's second major function is to make funding recommendations for the various regional programs in the area. As we have noted, special districts carry out some of the regional programs, but local gov-

[24]Ted Kolderie, "Regionalism in the Twin Cities of Minnesota," in *The Regionalist Papers*, Kent Mathewson, ed., the Metropolitan Fund, Inc., Detroit, Michigan, 1974, 99–121. For a more detailed account of the Twin Cities Council, see John J. Harrigan and Lillian C. Johnson, *Governing The Twin Cities Region; The Metropolitan Council in Perspective*, University of Minnesota Press, 1978.

POLICY BOX NO. 28 Privatization of Public Services

Have local governments tried to do more themselves than they are capable of doing well, simply because they traditionally have had a responsibility? Fire protection services may be an example. We would all probably agree that local governments must assure safety against fires, but are there better alternatives to creating and operating a city fire department?

Apparently most municipalities think not; at least that is the way it appears if we consider how many local governments have their own fire departments. But in Scottsdale, Arizona, a privately owned corporation, not the city government, provides fire protection services. In fact the company also provides fire protection to other suburbs. It services about one-fifth of Arizona's population.

Basically the plan works this way: Scottsdale and other communities in the area contract with Rural/Metro Fire Department, Inc. to put out fires in the city. The company provides all its own equipment with the exception of fire stations. And the company hires and pays all the fire-fighting personnel. Rural/Metro, in 1977, employed some full-time personnel. In addition some city personnel were "on call" as paid reservists. During 1977 the company paid them $50 per month plus $6.38 an hour for training and fighting fires. Reservists carry radio paging units during their "on call" periods. The reservists are required to respond to all structural fire alarms. One pumper truck is kept in the city yard, so that city workers can drive it to the fire if necessary.

How has it worked out? Not badly by most standards. Expenditures for fire protection services in Scottsdale are about 25 percent of the national average for cities of its size. Per capita fire losses in Scottsdale over the last twelve years have been 37 percent of the national average. And, fire insurance ratings organizations give the city a Class 5 rating, which is about optimal for homeowners.

Why does Rural/Metro work? Some suggest that the approach works because private enterprise has to be more efficient than government because it has to make a profit. They point to innovations the company has made. It built "The Snail," a mechanical remote-control track vehicle to fight fire up close where it is too hot for humans. Rural/Metro developed a new truck "from the ground up" at a cost nearly half the usual price. Other innovations on the vehicle permit residential suburbs to double the distance between fire hydrants. Rural/Metro also pioneered use of a four-inch fire hose with "quarter-turn" couplings, a system that they imported from Germany.

Opponents of the plan say that a reason for low costs is that the company provides no fringe benefits and has no retirement plan. The company relies mostly on the younger city employees who aren't so worried about making it to age sixty-five.

Supporters argue that what is important is that the company is privately owned and managed; it can take some chances that bureaucrats and politicians would not risk. Chief Lou Witzeman says, "We have the greatest incentive in the world to innovate, to pioneer, to analyze every little step—sheer survival."

ernments, particularly the seven member counties of the region, also jointly undertake other area-wide projects.

Finally the council, as do the more typical COGs, serves as the principal research and data-gathering agency for the region and the A-95 review agency.

The Twin Cities tax base sharing plan. A second Minnesota innovation is its "tax base sharing" plan. Under this plan, 40 percent of the increase in industrial and commercial property tax receipts since 1972 are received by the Twin Cities Metroplitan Council and are distributed to the local units of the region according to a state formula. The remaining 60 percent of the industrial and commercial tax revenues are retained by the local jurisdiction in which the increase takes place. This device not only reduces intra-area competition for industrial and commercial development, but it enables all the units to share in the region's development regardless of where it occurs.

COGs—an Assessment. Advocates of the COG approach see them as the first step in building a regional type of government and hope that the focus of attention will shift from individual bailiwicks in the metropolis to the metropolis itself.

Others argue that these organizations simply delay the day when a sense of regionalism will develop. They note that COGs give the appearance of progress toward the resolution of area-wide problems, but not the reality. COGs, they argue, actually are an impediment to building pressure for more extensive and powerful area-wide government institutions. As Henry J. Schmandt notes, "Little incentive has existed for politically mobile individuals to invest their efforts and resources in the activities of such bodies or to base their careers on the concept of regional statesmanship."[25] Perhaps in recognition of this fact, the Oregon legislature in 1978 changed the basis of representation for the Portland area council to 12 persons and a regional executive, all elected by citizens of the region.

Schmandt observed that the most valuable contribution of COGs has been in planning—planning for transportation, sewer and water facilities, land use, and conservation of natural resources. But COG planners have often concentrated on the growing and developing areas and focused very little on making central cities more habitable. But we also note that COG planners were probably more welcome in suburban areas where planning staffs were small or nonexistent. Planners employed by central cities may well have seen COG staff as competitors.

Assessing just how effective the COGs have been is another matter. They are faced with several expectations and standards of measurement. The federal government expects a critical and information-based evaluation of grant proposals subject to A-95 review. The record has not been especially good if a person judges by the number of proposals rejected as being inconsistent with regional plans. But as we might expect, officials "logroll"—those from one unit are not eager to criticize the proposals from another unit for fear that the tables will be turned next time. The real impact, however, is probably in work done at the staff level where proposal problems are either worked out or discouraged and withdrawn altogether.

The states have not been sure what they desire from regional bodies. For those states using regions for economic development and planning, the record is probably rather good. But if the states anticipated the regions to produce area-wide development plans and update them in cooperation with state planning agencies, the record is spotty.

At the local level the measure of effectiveness tends to be the size and number of federal grants received. As long as federal aid programs depended heavily upon project grants, COGs could provide helpful assistance in grant applications. As federal grant programs move to revenue sharing and block grants, though, the assistance of the area-wide agencies becomes less essential.

INTERGOVERNMENTAL RELATIONS: CAN THE STATES COORDINATE THE COMMUNITIES?

Up to this point we have focused primarily on interlocal relations. We now turn more pointedly to the vertical relationships that heavily involve federal and state governments.

[25]Henry J. Schmandt, "Intergovernmental Volunteerism, Pro and Con" in *The Regionalist Papers*, Ibid., 149–158.

We found, in our examination of federalism, that the federal, state, and local governments meet over the individual problems of central cities, suburbs, and rural areas: the problems of poverty, racism, and social disorganization in the central cities, of capitalizing the public facilities of the suburbs, and of raising the level of governance in and preserving and protecting the resources of rural areas. The national government has arrived at the point where it is setting its own goals and that is part of the difficulty—we have no national urban policy. But, also, we have a problem in carrying out programs—the problem of not just *what*, but also *how*.

Paul A. Miller, assistant secretary for education in the U.S. Department of Health, Education, and Welfare during the 1960s, said that when you look out from Washington at the thousands of school districts across the land, it is a foreboding sight in terms of program administration. "Somehow, the whole thing looks *a whole lot more manageable* if you can focus your efforts on fifty states." A similar view was made by a local editor "As I look back over ten years it seems to me that many of society's attempts to deal with its problems evoke a state rather than a federal response . . . because the states turn out to be *just about the most manageable unit of government.*"[26] It appears to us that the national government will continue to define national goals and programs, but will depend in large measure upon the states for the coordination of programs among the localities.

Coordination From the State Capitals

We observed in Chapter 4 that the states have been ambivalent about their role as coordinators of local government affairs. We saw that, in part, this attitude resulted from the early state concern with economic development—settling of the hinterlands and harvesting of the national resources. We also saw that for a long period the level of expertise in the large cities was generally higher than that in state government.

Neither of these conditions is as significant today. The states are still very much concerned with economic development, but for most this means they must focus on attracting industry to the urban economic base without ignoring natural resource-based segments of their economies. The effectiveness of community governments relates directly to economic development—a fact that raises the level of state interest in local affairs.

In the late 1940s expertise of bureaucracies began to increase as the states, with respect to one service function after another, decided to

---

[26]Joe H. Stroud, "Power of the States Still Irreplaceable" Detroit *Free Press*, September 17, 1978. Editorial page.

supplement local programs with their own programs. As a result, in such functional areas as police, highways, health, parks and recreation, welfare, tax administration, and many other state services state agency expertise is now probably the equal of that of the cities.

How the States Coordinate

We find that the states are better motivated and equipped to carry out their important "crossroads" function, especially as it applies to coordinating local as well as state policies. It is at the state level where regional issues are sorted out—where governors serve as mayors for the regions and legislatures as regional city councils.

We consider three methods of state coordination.

Direct Participation in Service Functions.   Many state agencies now have the administrative capacity to engage in service programs. State police agencies, for example, have responsibility for patrolling the state freeway systems, systems that now carry a large proportion of a state's automobile traffic. This responsibility has put state police posts in more areas of each state, and the state police are thus readily available to provide "assistance" to local communities, not only for the patrol of busy nonfreeway thoroughfares, but for criminal investigations, crimes in progress, as well as their more customary services to local units such as crime laboratory analysis and communications. The "Matt Dillons" of the counties and cities in most of the states, then, no longer stand alone to face the forces of lawlessness. A state police trooper is generally not far distant.

We can cite many other examples. State highway departments—now gradually becoming state departments of transportation—played an exceedingly important role in locating state expressway systems. They may be equally important in rebuilding urban mass transit facilities. State departments of public health and mental health in many states now develop and oversee detailed program activities for local agencies. Gradually the administration of welfare services is being assumed by states directly, eliminating the localities from any significant role. A number of states are seeking to become directly involved in zoning for "critical state areas" and in the supervision of the development of environmental resources such as rivers and streams and adjoining wetlands. Major public recreation areas are now state operated. Some of the states have developed their own state housing authorities, building and financing low-cost housing in communities around the state.

What we find, then, is that states can deal rather directly with a number of the service functions once considered to be local. This ap-

Can the states save the rails for mass transit?

proach to state coordination often develops first as a response to "emergency" conditions when political turf questions are less of a concern. Its directness circumvents the fights that generally accompany governmental reorganization strategies. These kinds of state actions do not entirely close out involvement by the localities, but the overall developing pattern is one of increased state participation.

State Regulation State coordination also increases through state regulations imposed on the localities. These take various forms. Enactment, for example, of a state law requiring all units to adopt and enforce a uniform state building ordinance gives state government a strong hand in the quality of construction in every community around the state. State laws requiring local tax assessors to pass state tests before being permitted to assess property, or requiring local police officers to have specified training before pinning on their badges are examples of state coordination.

We find many instances of state coordination, such as requiring local units to follow state-enacted open meeting laws, local candidates to disclose personal finance information and campaign receipts and expenditures, local governments to follow uniform budgeting and accounting procedures, state approval for applications to borrow, review of school building plans, of annexation proposals, and land subdivision plats. We discussed in other contexts the state-ordered or state-encouraged consolidation of school districts and the movement of state supreme courts to take greater control of local court systems. Local officials have begun referring to such state requirements as "state-mandated" programs, implying thereby that the state should reimburse local governments for the costs. Communities have had some success in this respect.

Differential Taxation and State Aid. States also coordinate by providing financial assistance in several ways. States may take over selective functions particularly when the specific function, such as welfare, is especially costly to central cities, or when the takeover, such as Detroit expressway patrol by state police, applies only to selected cities. Under these kinds of conditions state services have a redistributive effect.

State shared revenues. The states are also achieving a modest amount of financial redistribution through state taxation, as we discussed in chapter 6. Often the shared revenues give the states added coordinating power. The power of the purse was especially pronounced in California following the adoption of Proposition 13 in 1978. The state specified which community services were to have "high priority" and where layoffs were to be minimal.

Local income or payroll taxes. When the states permit cities to tax incomes earned in the city, it also allows them to tax wage earners who may not be residents—another redistributive tax. When the central cities depended almost exclusively on property taxes, nonresident workers in the city escaped virtually all direct taxation by the central city. However, for many central cities the authority to tax nonresident incomes earned in the city has come too late because many of the jobs have been relocated outside the city.

Special state aid. The states have been able to coordinate through at least two other redistributive state policies. One is through "circuit breakers"—the states assume the costs of property tax breaks to people over sixty-five, veterans, handicapped persons, and those who pay high local property taxes in proportion to their income. Such a policy, while applied statewide, tends to benefit central city residents most— especially if renters can claim a deduction. Previously these benefits were enacted into law with the localities often bearing the costs.

One other emerging policy is that of providing special financial assistance packages to the localities on the basis of the facilities they provide that have a statewide benefit. Typically these are cultural attractions that the great cities were once noted for—art centers, symphonic halls, museums, city universities, libraries, zoological parks, and others that essentially serve a regional, if not statewide, population. As a general rule such special assistance packages tend to benefit most of the largest cities in the state, although not in every instance.

The Politics of Redistributive Assistance. State coordination through redistributive assistance policies, as we might expect, are enacted only after a great deal of bargaining and compromising in the state legislature. More often than not, such bills require firm support by the governor and a formula that assures that most communities share at least some of the assistance. Such bargaining, of course, produces a result where all the local units, not only those in dire straits, become more dependent on state assistance and less dependent on their own resources. At the same time the state aid increases the legitimacy of state coordination dictums.

The Place of Substate Districts As Coordinating Agencies

The idea of localizing power and decision making became popular during the early years of the Nixon presidency. Federal officials suggested that the states should create regional organizations within each state. The councils of government became the model for substate districts that were to become the agencies through which both federal and state officials hoped to plan and coordinate their programs on area-wide bases.

Governors assumed leadership in establishing such organizations in the states. By 1977 all except six—Hawaii, Delaware, Alaska, Rhode Island, Montana, and Wyoming—had "wall to wall" substate districts. Although Montana and Wyoming had some districts, they did not cover the entire state.

Although the authority of these districts rests in some states on executive order and in others on legislative act, most states still consider them to be voluntary organizations. A state-planning agency in each state typically established the boundaries of the substate districts, while the task of organizing them was left to local officials. Substate districts were similar to the COGs, as most governors expected them to conduct planning and data-gathering programs but not to provide direct services. Some saw the main objective as coordinating for economic development. Some also saw these substate districts as the geographical basis for planning and administering all state programs.

From the State Perspective. Governor Tom McCall of Oregon, as well as several other governors, ordered all state agencies to use the district alignments exclusively for their functions. Jimmy Carter, when governor of Georgia, urged state departments to place staff members in each of the districts to carry out state activities and programs.

Most governors were not very successful in securing cooperation from state administrative departments. Some of the departments, of course, already had established different district boundaries, others had buildings and other facilities that did not fit the new districting plans, and some simply preferred not to use the districting approach at all.

Some critical issues had to be negotiated before the states could move further with the districts.

Issues in Substate Regionalism. In our previous discussion we considered the strong legal position Dillon's Rule gave the states over the localities. But we also noted that the states had to exercise this legal power in a political environment that gave the localities a much stronger position than Dillon's Rule would seem to confer. We find that the issues involved cannot be resolved by simple state edicts.[27]

Federal, state, or local agents? One issue is whether substate districts are to be agents for the federal or state governments or agents for the localities. The current status in most states is uncertain. The local governments organize and operate the substate districts and the states set their boundaries and general responsibilities. But substate districts are financed largely from federal funds.

The Advisory Commission on Intergovernmental Relations has suggested that the substate regions' agencies should be state agencies responsible for carrying out state and federal programs. Under this arrangement the local governments would deal with matters that are not regional in scope. The Committee for Economic Development—a national business-sponsored organization—takes virtually the same position.[28]

The public interest groups—National League of Cities, National Association of Counties, and others—argue that the substate districts should be agents of the localities. The concerns of these groups are obvious. They fear that substate districts would be tough competitors for federal and state aid, and regulators of policies that could compromise the identity of the local units.

[27]These issues are summarized in *The Regionalist Papers*, Op. cit.

[28]Committee for Economic Development, *Reshaping Government in Metropolitan Areas*, New York, 1970.

Two other questions are related to the federal-state-local issue. The first has to do with whether substate councils are to be joined in voluntarily. This is the federation versus confederation type of concern. If substate districts were to become federal or state agents, participation would almost certainly be mandatory. As agencies dominated by member communities, participation would likely remain voluntary.

The second related question concerns council membership appointments. As state agencies operating state programs, the governor (or perhaps the legislature) would insist on appointing at least a majority of the council members as is the case with the Twin Cities Council. The community officials would resist turning over such patronage positions to the state capital.

Who will be represented? The question of how to arrange representation on substate councils is not a new issue. It has plagued many of the districts as they sought to organize. Virtually all council members are mayors, city councillors, or county commissioners first, and regional council members second. Units, even those, with small populations usually each have at least one delegate. But to give the largest unit representation proportionate to its population, and still give each small unit one member, would make the council unmanageably large.

The substate councils now manage this problem by giving the larger units several representatives but, nevertheless, leaving them underrepresented. Typically the larger population units are the central cities, where blacks and other minorities predominate. The result is that the suburbs, with largely white populations, are overrepresented. As long as council participation is voluntary, the representation plan is probably constitutional.

Central cities and larger units will, perhaps, go along with the substate council representation problem as long as the duties they perform relate essentially to planning and recommending policy. If the power of councils is to increase, however, the larger units will undoubtedly insist on more equitable arrangements, perhaps like the approach employed by Minneapolis or Portland.

What are the substate councils to do? One alternative is for the regional councils to continue much as they are, using and creating special districts or authorities to carry out service functions. A second alternative is to have the substate districts establish and oversee the policies by which the special districts carry out their activities—a kind of "umbrella agency," such as the Twin Cities Council. This might include such policy actions as approving the budgets of special districts, establishing personnel and purchasing policies, as well as approving service rates or bond issue proposals. A third alternative, of course, is for the regional councils to undertake both functions directly and, in effect, become a general purpose government.

Another dimension of this question has to do with the type of concerns the substate councils will deal with. Are they to continue to focus on public works activities as they have been? Or should they also deal with services that have strong social implications—services such as health, welfare, education, employment, police protection, and others? The more substate districts move into services with strong social implications, the more concerned local units become about such questions as representation and voluntary membership.

The Future of Substate Districts

Substate districts, we think, have not developed a more secure future, in part because of the inability or unwillingness of state agencies to coordinate their programs and plans through them. Legislators receive little encouragement from local officials to strengthen the districts and have taken little or no action to compel state agencies to realign their field programs. Moreover governors began to back away from strong positions on the future role of substate districts because federal support seems to be slipping away.

Federal Failures in Substate Districting. "Substate regionalism today is more complex, more confused, and more competitive . . . than it was when the topic first became the subject of an intensive study." That is how David B. Walker and Bruce D. McDowell of the ACIR assessed the situation in late 1977.[29] They placed part of the blame on interlocal competition—cities versus counties—and the states, which they suggest, have become ambivalent about the substate districts. A major part of the responsibility, though, they maintain, rests with the federal government—its executive agencies and the Congress.

Walker and McDowell point to the uncertain directions set by the federal government. Several newly enacted federal aid programs—revenue sharing, manpower programs, antirecession funds, and the community development block grants—essentially ignore the whole question of substate districts. Not only have these laws specified no planning role for the substate districts, but the flow of money they authorize tends to diminish the consensus of local officials about regional impacts.

A number of federal agencies recently established their own separate planning districts for separate programs and thus delivered a

---

[29]David B. Walker and Bruce D. McDowell, "Substate Regionalism: The Situation in '77," *County News*, The National Association of Counties, January 1978.

frontal attack on the substate districts. Of new federal programs in 1976, eight required use of established substate districts and twenty-one encouraged the formation of new regional systems.

A-95 review weaknesses. By 1978 more than five hundred A-95 clearinghouse agencies had been set up across the country and more than two hundred grant programs were subject to review and comment. In a zero-base review ordered by President Carter—many complaints surfaced. Federal officials complained that the comments were not timely and often were not very useful. Local representatives criticized federal agencies for not giving the A-95 comments serious consideration and said that many federal or state officials do not comply with the stated requirements.

Recent modifications enacted to reinvigorate the review and comment process require federal agencies to notify the district clearinghouses when they make decisions contrary to comments. Meanwhile Congress is considering a proposal to give local elected officials a stronger role in coordinating federal programs in multicommunity areas.

The Proposed Intergovernmental Coordination Act. Senator Warren Magnuson of Washington state has proposed new legislation that is being referred to as the "home rule" bill for federally assisted area planning programs. Although far from being enacted at this writing, the bill may point to some new directions for intergovernmental relations involving federal, state, and community governments. Basically the bill proposes to set uniform guidelines for the federal planning program requirements and to give substate districts, to be headed by locally elected officials, preferential status as the recognized planning agencies and authorities to resolve program conflicts in regional areas. The bill would deal with three principal problems of coordination by:

1. Permitting local elected officials to assume control of any federal planning program unless prohibited by the state law.
2. Providing a uniform set of standards for substate districting.
3. Giving local plans high priority and requiring federal plans to be adjusted to local plans when conflicts arise.

These proposals are intended to strengthen the hand of local elected officials who say that they now spend all their time going from one planning agency meeting to another to keep track of what others are planning for their communities. And, thus, we see the struggle for power to coordinate and control goes on.

A Final Comment

We have come to the point in our national society where a great many aspects of daily living are touched by government at one level or another. It is, therefore, also a society in which one segment depends on many other segments for the necessities, as well as the amenities, of life. These interdependent relationships do not stop at the city limits, the county line, or even the state boundaries. Some extend even beyond the national shorelines. They are complex and interwoven.

If this is true for individuals and groups within society, it is also true for governments that seek to regulate these relationships. The web of intergovernmental relations that has been woven is secured by strands running from our nation's capital, from state capitals, and from our community governments. All of these together hold the web in place. But it is not a web woven for all time.

Our politics are continually reshaping and strengthening (and sometimes, perhaps, weakening) the strands that secure the web of intergovernmental relations. We find that there is a degree of coordination from the states and from our national government. But the decisions are made in a political environment and, therefore, are a product of compromise by the competing interested groups. The product is seldom one that meets the standards of idealists or administrative perfectionists. We find that the future will be negotiated rather than planned. Such is the federal system we have been evolving.

HIGHPOINTS OF CHAPTER 14: INTERGOVERNMENTAL RELATIONS AND COMMUNITY PROBLEMS

We began this chapter by observing (1) that many of the problems we classify as "urban" are not alone the problems central cities face—the problems are evident in suburbs and rural areas as well. Thus, we saw (2) the network of intergovernmental relations as linking both rural and urban governments together with state and federal governments. We next considered (3) annexation and consolidation as methods for unifying local governments and we also reviewed (4) various voluntary approaches for the conduct of intergovernmental relations at the local level. Finally, we discussed (5) whether the states can coordinate the horizontal relationships among their local governments and the vertical relationships between the communities and the national government. We saw that the substate districts that once appeared to be suitable vehicles for the coordination of intergovernmental planning and a forum for the conduct of intergovernmental relations now have an uncertain future.

EPILOGUE

Throughout this book we have emphasized how the states are embedded in a federal system. That system has been changing in response to changing social and economic conditions. We are becoming more one nation than ever we were before as we experience a nationwide industrialization, urbanization, mobility from place to place, and a nationwide mass communications system. And the balance of political decision making power has moved from the states to the nation.

We illustrated throughout the book that the centralizing federalism that is evolving is a response to problems and conditions we face in governing a modern America. What has resulted is a peculiarly American kind of government. The national government is not attempting to go it alone. Rather, the political power of states and communities and our tradition of local control have encouraged the national government to work through the state and community governments instead of around them. American federalism is thus one of the more complex governments operating in the world today— hard to comprehend fully—one often inefficient, but one also especially responsive to the needs and desires of its citizens and of their national, state, and community concerns.

The states have not shrivelled away as some critics predicted they would a generation or so ago. Rather they have flourished. More and more it is apparent that it is to the states we look when we seek to make our government institutions respond to our needs and wants. The national government is too big and too distant and the problems often overwhelm community governments when they stand alone. The state government thus often appears to the citizen as the most manageable unit.

We emphasized that policymaking in our kind of federal system requires considerable politicking. We hope you got some sense of how individuals, including our much maligned politicians, are trying to make our complex system of government work for the benefit of its citizens. We expect you to recognize also that, as in any system, some officeholders sometimes betray their trust, but also that many do not. For example, take this comment of David Pryor, reform governor of Arkansas, elected in 1974. A Little Rock constituent asked him, "What is the one thing you wanted to do when you took office that you have been unable to achieve?" Governor Pryor did not sidestep the question, but answered it honestly—"Hold down state spending and the growth of government. I have had some measured success in this area, but not enough for me or for the people I serve." He is not alone in sometimes wondering why the system cannot be made to improve more rapidly.

Throughout, we have called attention to many problems that the American system is trying to solve and many the nation, states, and communities have yet to solve. In many respects our system has failed some of its citizens, especially the minorities. Yet we think appropriate some words of a typically American novelist, Sinclair Lewis, born and raised in Minnesota. His books of the 1920s and 1930s, *Main Street*, *Babbit*, *Arrowsmith*, and *Elmer Gantry* were among the most bitterly critical of American society and government. In *It Can't Happen Here* he even described how fascism might come to the United States with the enthusiastic help of many prominent politicians, officeholders, and others in our society. Yet this is what he wrote toward the end of his career:

Intellectually I know that America is no better than any other country; emotionally I know she is better than every other country.

The last phrase sounds, perhaps, just a little chauvinistic to today's ears. But it is a sentiment we would like to believe might be true. It rests on faith—a faith that many people, including average citizens like yourself, as those Wyoming students did back on page 1, will take advantage of the privilege of participating in the governing of our nation, states, and communities through the federal system.

INDEX

Virginia, 49, 69n, 89, 138–139, 149, 162, 163n, 213, 219, 250n, 298; 312, 362–363, 512, 516, 560
Virgin Islands, 73, 157
Voting, 426; costs of; policy box on, 440–441
Voting rights, extension of, 165

Waldby, H.O., 370, 372, 373n
Wagenheim, Kal, 72n
Wager, Paul W., 112n
Wahlke, John C., 245, 248, 249n, 252, 266
Walker, Daniel, 295, 396, 417, 443
Walker, David B., 584
Walker, Harvey, 154n
Walker, Jack L., 84n
Wallace, George, 296, 302n, 321, 454, 535
Wallis, Graham, 425
Wallace, Lurleen, 61n, 296, 533
Walsh, Annmarie H., 566n
Walton, Clarence, 541n
Wanat, John, 56n
Warren, Earl, 340
Warren, Robert Penn, 421n
Warren, Roland, 134, 139n
Washington, D.C., 53, 553
Washington State, 56, 61, 297, 381, 490, 511, 529, 585
Waterford, VA, 137, 138–139
Watergate, 10, 537
Waters, Earl G., 171n
Watson, Richard, 347–348
Wattel, Harold L., 545n
Wattenberg, Ben, 57n
Weber, Max, 450
Wechsler, Louis, 512n
West Virginia, 89, 213; policy box on, 45–46

Wetlands, regulation, policy box on, 270–271
Whitaker, Gordon P., 557n
White, William Allen, 503
White, Theodore H., 46n
Whitten, Les, 10
Wildavsky, Aaron, 400, 401n
Willbern, York, 21n, 380, 562n
Williams, G. Mennen, 291, 306, 309, 311, 319, 530
Williams, J. Oliver, 282n, 300n, 302n
Williams, Oliver P., 33n, 136
Williams, T. Harry, 421n
Wilson, James Q., 130n, 374n, 384, 512n
Wilson, Woodrow, 321, 439
Wiltsee, Herbert L., 242n
Winters, Richard F., 43n
Wisconsin, 49, 83, 90, 114n, 116, 166, 168, 204, 268, 270, 312, 357, 400, 404, 442, 512, 532
Wolfinger, Raymond E., 127n, 130n
Women, as governors, 294; policy box on, 296–297
Womens Christian Temperance Union, 14
Wood, Robert C., 542, 566
Woodward, Robert, 10
Wright, Charles R., 460n
Wright, Deil S., 300n, 322n, 387n
Wright, Louis B., 51n
Wurf, Jerry, 395, 398
Wyoming, 36, 59, 61n, 90, 290, 296

Yarger, Susan Rice, 177n

Zeller, Belle, 13
Ziegler, Harmon, 396n, 416n, 463, 465n, 471n, 472, 473n
Zimmerman, Joseph F., 310n, 437n
Zingale, Nancy, 518, 521n